From the Halls of the Montezumas

From the Halls of the Montezumas

Mexican War Dispatches from James L. Freaner, Writing Under the Pen Name "Mustang"

Edited by
Alan D. Gaff and Donald H. Gaff

Number 14 in the War and the Southwest Series

University of North Texas Press
Denton, Texas

Printed in the United States of America.

10 9 8 7 6 5 4 3 2 1

Permissions:
University of North Texas Press
1155 Union Circle #311336
Denton, TX 76203-5017

The paper used in this book meets the minimum requirements of the American National Standard for Permanence of Paper for Printed Library Materials, z39.48.1984. Binding materials have been chosen for durability.

Library of Congress Cataloging-in-Publication Data
Mustang (War correspondent), 1817–1852, author. | Gaff, Alan D., editor. | Gaff, Donald H., 1970– editor.
From the Halls of the Montezumas : Mexican War dispatches from James L. Freaner, writing under the pen name "Mustang" / edited by Alan D. Gaff and Donald H. Gaff.
pages cm.
Includes bibliographical references and index.
ISBN-13 978-1-57441-767-8 (cloth)
ISBN-13 978-1-57441-777-7 (ebook)
1. Freaner, James L., 1817–1852. 2. Chapultepec, Battle of, Mexico City, Mexico, 1847—Personal narratives, American. 3. Mexican War, 1846–1848—Personal narratives, American. 4. Mexican War, 1846–1848—Campaigns–Mexico. 5. Mexican War, 1846–1848—Journalists—Biography. 6. Mexican War, 1846–1848—Journalism, Military.

E406.C47 M87 2019
973.6/2092 [B]–dc23
2019021672

From the Halls of the Montezumas: Mexican War Dispatches from James L. Freaner, Writing Under the Pen Name "Mustang" is Number 14 in the War and the Southwest Series

The electronic edition of this book was made possible by the support of the Vick Family Foundation. Typeset by vPrompt eServices.

To Roger Flood
Semper fidelis

Contents

Editors' Introduction

St. Paul's Cathedral in London contains a bust of Sir William Howard Russell, underneath which is an inscription that reads "The first and greatest of War Correspondents." In recognizing Russsell, Phillip Knightley, author of *The First Casualty*, observed that his "coverage of the Crimean War marked the beginning of an organised effort to report a war to the civilian population at home using the services of a civilian reporter." He went further by calling Russell's reporting "an immense leap in the history of journalism." While there is no denying the accomplishments of William Howard Russell and his successful career, he was actually a latecomer to the role of war correspondent. Years before he began sending dispatches from the Crimea, Russell had been "scooped" as the first recognized war correspondent by numerous American reporters covering their own war with Mexico.[1]

Newspapers gave civilians insight into world affairs and what could be more exciting than to read about your country at war. Most every American town of any significance claimed at least one newspaper and war news boosted circulation. The press had previously relied upon participants to share letters about their

1. Knightley, *First Casualty*, 2.

experiences, but the Mexican War brought a significant change to news reporting. Large newspapers now hired full-time correspondents and began a sometimes bitter competition to become the first to report information. Correspondents were unfettered and roamed wherever necessary to get the best stories. There was no censorship. Within months the best writers became household names as their dispatches were copied by newspapers across the country. Ambitious and probably at least a bit thrill-driven, these first American war correspondents obtained information from personal networks that occasionally saw them drawn into combat themselves. With New Orleans being the closest metropolitan city to the fighting in Mexico, its press had the advantage of geography in the race to publish the latest war news.

Recognized as foremost among this new breed of news reporter was George Wilkins Kendall, an editor of the New Orleans *Times-Picayune*, who attached himself in 1846 as a volunteer to Captain Benjamin McCulloch's company of Texas Mounted Volunteers, commonly known as the Texas Rangers. According to historian John Hohenberg, Kendall thus "began a glamorous career as the most celebrated correspondent of the Mexican War." He sent dispatches, written in a clear narrative form, north to be printed in his newspaper before being disseminated and reproduced across the United States. Kendall's place in history was cemented upon the publication of Lafayette Copeland's biography, *Kendall of the Picayune*, in 1943.[2]

In a review of Copeland's book, Charles L. Sonnichsen began with a brief paragraph: "The first thought which will occur to many readers after going through Mr. Copeland's excellent book is the question, 'Why hasn't this been done before?' If any man's life was ever worth writing, it was George Wilkins Kendall's." We have no dispute with this characterization of George Kendall, but history has not been as kind to one of his contemporaries and rivals. James L. Freaner, a printer with the New Orleans *Daily Delta*, was just as observant as Kendall, arranged a courier system that often proved faster than that employed by the *Times-Picayune*, and was often judged to be a more interesting writer than Kendall. Upon the outbreak of war, Freaner immediately signed up in a Louisiana

2. Hohenberg, *Foreign Correspondence*, 17–19.

infantry unit and enlisted a second time in a company of Texas Rangers when the Louisianians were sent home.[3]

During his service in 1846, James Freaner was a soldier who doubled as a correspondent. When General Winfield Scott received orders to conduct a campaign in the heart of Mexico, Freaner renounced a new enlistment and determined to accompany the army as a fulltime correspondent. Freaner was aboard ship to watch the amphibious assault at Vera Cruz in February of 1847 and remained in Mexico, with only a few interruptions, until he left Mexico City in June of 1848 with the last American troops. His correspondence is as complete a contemporary account, from beginning to end, as exists, filled with action and adventure, in addition to detailed observations of the Mexican people throughout the war. One can only ask the same question that Sonnichsen asked of Copeland's book, "Why hasn't this been done before?" This gripping and insightful narrative of James Freaner's observations of General Scott's successful campaign and the armistice that followed will finally rectify that long unanswered question.

James Logan Freaner, son of William and Margaret Freaner, both native Marylanders of German descent, was christened in the German Reformed Church in Hagerstown, Maryland, on December 29, 1817. William Freaner, a soldier during the War of 1812 in the 6th United States Infantry, parlayed his brief military service into employment as a village constable in his hometown. William had a colorful career for a local lawman and his activities oftentimes spread beyond policing his own village. On one occasion he tracked down a pair of thieves who had surreptitiously removed a traveler's trunk from a westbound stage after they hid out in Winchester, Virginia. Another time he noticed a gang of six men acting strangely near Hancock, Maryland, raised a posse, arrested the men, and found they were wanted in Baltimore in connection with a recent riot. Freaner was still on the job in 1855 when he helped arrest a notorious thief in Chambersburg, Pennsylvania.[4]

3. Sonnichsen, "Kendall of the Picayune," 101.

4. Maryland, Births and Christenings Index, ancestry.com; U.S. Army Register of Enlistments, Record Group 94, NARA; *Frederick Town Herald*, February 11, 1832; *Baltimore Sun*, February 1, 1839; *Chambersburg Valley Spirit*, November 28, 1855.

One of Constable Freaner's important functions was to deal with slaves in western Maryland. In December of 1832 he caught a runaway slave riding a horse stolen from Rockingham County, Virginia. The following year he sold a black woman and her two children when ordered to do so by the local court. Freaner continued this aspect of his job into the 1840s; one public notice regarding two runaway black boys stated that information shared with him "will be promptly attended to." In 1843 Constable Freaner arrested two free blacks who had fled to Pennsylvania after being implicated in "facilitating the escape of fugitive slaves." His father's work, combined with the Freaner family owning its own slave, would color James's political affiliation with the Democratic Party for the remainder of his life.[5]

The Freaner boys were educated at the Hagerstown Academy, which had been established in 1810, and boasted students from as far away as the District of Columbia. Aside from his chores, once each week a teenaged James would saddle his father's mare and long before daylight head east with the U.S. Mail on a round trip from Hagerstown across the mountainous Maryland terrain to Sabillasville, a route just north of the current Camp David. After a few years of mail delivery, Freaner began work as an apprentice typesetter on the Hagerstown *Mail*, followed soon after by a stint at the Hagerstown *Torch Light*. By 1840 James was living near Austin, Texas, having "more brains than dimes" and a bad case of malaria. Partnering with a down-on-his-luck Kentuckian, the pair tried cutting and selling cedar which flourished in the Colorado River bottoms. Finding no one willing to buy what was readily available, Freaner and his comrade decided to kill turkeys and sell them in town. Having shot nine gobblers, the partner immediately set off and left Freaner to follow behind. Much to his consternation, a pack of wolves scented the fresh meat and began to pursue him. When several carcasses failed to satisfy the wolves, Freaner had no choice but to dive into a dense stand of mesquite bushes. He remained there overnight,

5. *Hagerstown Torch Light*, December 20, 1832; December 27, 1832; *Harrisburg Keystone*, February 25, 1843; *Washington Madisonian*, November 2, 1843; 1840 Census, Hagerstown District, Washington County, Maryland, Record Group 29, NARA; *Weekly Mississippian*, January 10, 1851.

just out of reach of the wolves, but in the morning dissolved his partnership and left Austin for better opportunities.[6]

James Freaner first achieved public attention when he began working as a printer for the Tallahassee *Floridian* early in 1844. A cheeky and outspoken Democrat, Freaner naturally joined the Leon County Hickory Club, where an excellent singing voice led to his selection as leader of that political group's choir. He composed a theme song for the presidential campaign of that year, each stanza ending with the refrain,

"Our flag is there, our flag is there—
Behold its glorious stripes and stars!
Our flag is there, our flag is there—
We hail it with three loud huzzas!

On election day, November 6, 1844, joyful Whigs marched to the polls in support of their candidates, Henry Clay, the "Kentucky Coon," for president and Theodore Frelinghuysen of New Jersey for vice-president, chanting,

"Henry Clay and Frelinghuysen,
To James K. Polk will be rank pizin [poison]!"

Rising to the challenge, James Freaner rallied the Democrats for Polk, the so-called "Young Hickory," and led them in singing,

"We'll give our Polk our suffrage poll
To drive the Coon back to his hole,
And Jersey's weasel, and Sunday mail,
We'll ride upon a Hickory rail!
O, Coons, you stand no chance.

The *Floridian* gleefully reported that "the Coons fled, and we skinned them pretty effectually that day, electing our entire Senatorial ticket, and so on." Following the election of James Polk, Freaner left Tallahassee for New Orleans, where he quickly landed a job as a printer for the *Daily Delta* in that city.[7]

The presidential election of 1844 that had James Freaner so aroused was determined by the far-reaching issues of whether the United States could or should annex another sovereign country. Following a six-month rebellion against the Mexican Republic, the Republic of Texas had been established in 1836 with the

6. *Lebanon Daily News*, February 17, 1885; Williams, *History of Washington County, Maryland* 1: 281; *Times-Picayune*, January 17, 1851.

7. *Daily Delta*, November 21, 1847.

United States and various European powers acknowledging its independence. American recognition had been a foregone conclusion since that country had sent troops, munitions, and foodstuffs to aid the revolution. After gaining its independence, Texas had lobbied to be annexed to the United States, but these efforts had been rebuffed by politicians who did not want to add a slave state to the Union and who also thought such an act would result in war with Mexico. In 1844, Henry Clay, the Whig candidate for president, ran on a platform that opposed annexation of Texas. James K. Polk, the Democratic nominee, who advocated adding Texas to the Union and expanding the United States to the Pacific Ocean, won election handily. Just days prior to Polk taking office, in March of 1845, Congress passed a joint resolution annexing Texas that was quickly signed by the outgoing president, John Tyler. The Mexican minister protested what he considered an illegal usurpation of Mexican territory, demanded his credentials, and left Washington.[8]

Although both Texas and the United States claimed the Rio Grande as its southern border, Mexico had never recognized that boundary and retained jurisdiction over several towns such as Laredo and Point Isabel that lay north of the river. Excitement along the border and inflammatory discussions with Mexican officials led President Polk's War Department to order General Zachary Taylor to position troops to assist Texans against a potential foreign invasion under the guise of protecting them against Indian raids. General Taylor established his force of Regulars and base of supplies at Corpus Christi, well north of the disputed border to avoid provoking a military incident with Mexican troops. Under no circumstances was he to assume offensive operations south of the Rio Grande. While rumors of war ebbed and flowed, officers and men spent their off-duty time either hunting in the prairie or fishing in the bay. Even a violent "norther" that swamped campgrounds had a silver lining when the waves stranded fish and turtles enough to last Taylor's small army a week.

While soldiers drilled and enjoyed their sportsman's paradise, the Polk administration sought to normalize relations with the Mexican Republic. John Slidell, a congressman from New Orleans,

8. The following brief summation of the Mexican War is based upon Cadmus Wilcox, *History of the Mexican War*; Richard Winders, *Mr. Polk's Army*; and John S.D. Eisenhower, *So Far from God*.

was appointed minister plenipotentiary and on December 8, 1845, asked to present his credentials to the Mexican president. Differences between what Slidell and Mexican officials were authorized to discuss led to a failure of the mission. Mexican officials did not trust the United States, having never forgotten how thousands of American volunteers had flowed into Texas from the States, a clear violation of international neutrality. President José Herrera had supported Texan independence, rightly concluding that as a sovereign state it would act as a buffer between Mexico and the more confrontational United States. Annexation of Texas and Slidell's failed diplomacy doomed Herrera, who was forced from office at year's end and was succeeded by General Mariano Paredes. A last-ditch attempt to negotiate with the new Paredes government failed.

When the Polk administration learned of Slidell's failure in mid-January of 1846, General Taylor was instructed to begin a movement to the Rio Grande. He was authorized to call for assistance from the militia and prepare for offensive operations should Mexican authorities display an aggressive posture upon his arrival. When Taylor's advance toward Matamoros on the Rio Grande commenced in early March, the general published an order that promised to respect civil and religious liberties of all Mexicans north of the river. After overseeing a shift of his supply base from Corpus Christi to Point Isabel, General Taylor rode to the Rio Grande where his army began to build entrenchments north of the river while the garrison of Matamoros did likewise on the south bank.

General Mariano Arista, the Mexican commander along the Rio Grande, determined to take the initiative and sent a mixed force of cavalry and light infantry north of the river on April 24, 1846. General Taylor sent Captain Seth Thornton with a party of Dragoons upriver to investigate reports of this crossing. On April 25, Thornton's entire party was overwhelmed, Taylor reporting a loss of sixty-three officers and enlisted men either killed or captured, several of the latter being wounded. General Taylor reacted at once. He reported to the War Department: "Hostilities may now be considered as commenced, and I have this day deemed it necessary to call upon the Governor of Texas for four regiments of volunteers, two to be mounted and two to serve on foot." Taylor also requested four regiments from the governor of Louisiana. News of

Major General Zachary Taylor. *Courtesy Library of Congress.*

Thornton's defeat spread throughout the United States, a country that had been at peace for thirty years. When President Polk received Taylor's report, he announced that "American blood has been shed on American soil!" and immediately requested that Congress should pass a declaration of war, an appeal that was honored on May 13, 1846.

Buoyed by his success against Captain Thornton's detachment, General Arista moved the bulk of his army north of the Rio Grande to block the Matamoros-Point Isabel road. Taylor and Arista clashed on May 8 on the coastal prairie at a spot known as Palo Alto. Taylor unleashed his artillery, while his infantry and cavalry remained in defensive positions. Two Mexican cavalry charges on the American flanks were repulsed, leaving Taylor in possession of the battlefield. Next morning the two armies still faced one another. Arista took up a position behind an old riverbed of the Rio Grande where he again intended to defend the Matamoros road. A determined advance in the afternoon drove Arista's troops back south of the Rio Grande after a stiff resistance that often resulted in hand-to-hand fighting at Resaca de la Palma. These victories of May 8 and 9, just days before an official declaration of war, boosted the morale of General Taylor's army and gave the United States undisputed control over the lower Rio Grande.

Arista was relieved of command by General Pedro de Ampudia who brought order to the disorganized Mexican army at the city of Monterrey. Although directed to move farther south to Saltillo by his government, Ampudia decided to make a stand at Monterrey. General Taylor, after building up his supplies and being reinforced by volunteers from Texas and Louisiana, advanced against Ampudia's army. He reached Monterrey on September 19, 1846, and, after making a careful reconnaissance, launched attacks on the east and west sides of the city two days later. By September 23, Taylor's forces had cut the Saltillo road and had penetrated into the city where his men fought from house to house. In return for surrendering the city, Ampudia negotiated an armistice that was to last two months. Using this breathing room, Taylor took care of his many wounded soldiers, built up supplies, and gathered transportation for a future southern advance. Surprised by the armistice, President Polk ordered Taylor to halt further offensive operations, except for a possibility of making Saltillo an outpost, and sent

General-in-Chief Winfield Scott to Mexico to open a second front on the Gulf Coast.

Events farther west coincided with Taylor's victories in northern Mexico. Brevet Captain John C. Fremont had been sent on a surveying expedition and in 1846 his armed party, along with his military authority, helped foment a revolt among American settlers in California. Assisted by sailors and munitions from the Pacific squadron, in July Fremont had taken possession of all towns in northern California. By the following month, Fremont, after a few skirmishes with Mexican troops, also had control of southern California. General Stephen W. Kearny would take a larger force to California, advancing along the Santa Fe Trail from Fort Leavenworth to Santa Fe. By mid-August, Kearny occupied Santa Fe and he reached California in November with only a small detachment that had little impact on the occupation of that territory, although he would claim credit due to his rank. A contingent of Kearny's force, commanded by Colonel Alexander Doniphan, split off to occupy El Paso and Chihuahua. By the end of 1846, nearly all Mexican territory north of Monterrey was controlled by Americans.

Although at first hesitant to send General Scott, an outspoken adherent of the Whig Party, to Mexico, President Polk relented in November of 1846. His instructions gave Scott broad latitude to prosecute the war as he saw fit, the general to rely completely upon his own experience and judgment. Having determined to attack Vera Cruz and its fortifications, Scott wrote to Taylor with the bad news that "I shall be obliged to take from you most of the gallant officers and men (regular and volunteer) whom you have so long and so nobly commanded." Taylor's veterans and newcomers brought from the States by Scott would form a new army, based at Vera Cruz, which would conduct an offensive campaign on a much shorter route to the Mexican capital. General-in-Chief Winfield Scott would enjoy the honor of destroying the enemy forces and ending the war, leaving General Taylor to protect Monterrey and the Rio Grande frontier.

While General Scott assembled his forces along the Gulf Coast for an amphibious assault at Vera Cruz, his plan to reduce Taylor's army became known to the Mexicans. General Antonio López de Santa Anna raised a large army and marched north against Taylor's

Major General Winfield Scott. *Courtesy Library of Congress.*

depleted command. Although instructed to go no farther south of Monterrey than Saltillo, Taylor had selected a formidable defensive position beyond that town and assembled his soldiers just beyond the Hacienda San Juan de la Buena Vista. On February 22, Santa Anna demanded the American surrender, noting that his army vastly outnumbered Taylor's and gave that general one hour to capitulate. General Taylor responded: "In reply to your note of this date, summoning me to surrender my forces at discretion, I beg leave to say that I decline acceding to your request." The bulk of Taylor's army, with the exception of Regular Army artillery batteries, were inexperienced volunteers and, although outnumbered by about three to one, beat back every Mexican attack. General Santa Anna withdrew, leaving General Taylor unmolested in northern Mexico and General Scott free to commence his campaign from Vera Cruz to Mexico City.

In an attempt to keep American readers up to date on this essential war news, newspaper editors sent correspondents to cover the conflict. F. Lauriston Bullard gave a good description of these daring individuals: "The war correspondent is a newspaperman assigned to cover a campaign. He goes into the field with the army, expecting to send his reports from that witching region known as 'the front.' He is a special correspondent commissioned to collect intelligence and transmit it from the camp and the battle ground. A non-combatant, he mingles freely with men whose business it is to fight." This profession of war correspondent, essentially a pioneer in the field, was new to American journalism.[9] Bullard explained what a good correspondent would have to endure, including "the physical capacity to march with the private soldier, to ride a hundred miles at a clip at top speed over rough country, to sleep in the open, to stand the heat of the desert and the cold of the mountain height, to endure hunger and thirst and all the deprivations of a hard campaign." Succumbing to fatigue was not an option: "He must have the tenacity which does not yield to exhaustion until his messages are written and on the way to his paper. When the soldier ceases fighting the correspondent's work is only begun."[10]

Initiative and enterprise were critical in covering the war in Mexico since all correspondence had to be sent overland; there were no railroads, no telegraph wire, and no rivers that could be used to transmit reports. All information had to be sent by courier to Vera Cruz, Tampico, or Point Isabel where it would be placed aboard steamships bound for New Orleans, arriving there after from three to five days at sea. All news from Mexico went through New Orleans where it was dispersed throughout the

9. Bullard, *Famous War Correspondents*, 3.
10. Bullard, *Famous War Correspondents*, 4–5.

country, either up the Mississippi River or across the Gulf of Mexico on the way to Washington and points north. With just one city as the chokepoint for all war news, competition became intense. By 1847, New Orleans boasted nine English-language newspapers, almost as many as London, all priced low enough for most families to afford a daily newspaper. But supporting correspondents and a transmission network was expensive so only the *Picayune*, *Delta*, and *Bee* could bear the cost. Northern papers in New York, Philadelphia, and Baltimore attempted to replicate the success of their New Orleans competitors, but geography was against them and the country depended on the *Picayune* and *Delta* for its war news, the *Bee* a distant third. This was especially true as the American armies moved farther and farther into the interior.[11]

General Scott's 1847 advance from Vera Cruz to Mexico City was covered extensively by George W. Kendall, writing as G.W.K., and James "Mustang" Freaner. Kendall was more of a headquarters reporter, preferring to mix with generals and staff officers, while Freaner was more in the mold of Ernie Pyle or Damon Runyon and would rather chat with company grade officers or enlisted men. At times Kendall would seem to flatter his favorite commanders, but Freaner tended to be more independent, shying away from flattery of individuals. No matter which type of networking they chose, there is no doubt that both correspondents made household names of many individuals. Both men had the luxury of writing about a string of American victories during the years 1846 and 1847, enhancing the military reputations of officers who would otherwise have remained unknown. Perhaps the most important impact of these correspondents was that General Zachary Taylor would ride his war record to the presidency in 1848 as Jefferson Davis would for the Confederacy in 1861. General Winfield Scott would run for president of the United States in 1852, losing to Franklin Pierce, one of his subordinates during the Mexican campaign.[12]

11. Hudson, *Journalism in the United States*, 491–93; Bullard, *Famous War Correspondents*, 370-71; "Gentlemen of the Press," 367.

12. Bullard, *Famous War Correspondents*, 353; Warren, *Encyclopedia of U.S. Campaigns* 1: 869-70.

Freaner at War

By the time Congress declared war on Mexico, New Orleans had already raised troops and sent them into the field. Word of Thornton's defeat reached the Crescent City late on May 1 and the following day was simply pandemonium. Governor Isaac Johnson issued a call to fill four regiments of infantry to be sent immediately to reinforce General Taylor. Placards and posters appeared on walls and fences, directing volunteers to tents in Lafayette Square where men stood in line to add their names to the rolls. Normal business activity was suspended, while national flags floated on nearly every street and intersection. Fifes and drums belted out military tunes to spur enlistments. Editors and printers of the *Delta* hurried to get out three separate editions that day, columns bearing notices such as "Riflemen Wanted," "Texas Volunteers Attention!" and "The Tigers." The *Delta* captured the prevailing spirit, expounding,

> The soil of the United States has been invaded, some of its citizens have been killed, more have been captured. It is a disgrace. It must be wiped off. The country calls for soldiers—for volunteers. Shall the call be made in vain? Gen. Taylor and his army are in danger, shall they

> be massacred without an effort to save them? God and patriotism forbid![1]

Citizens held a huge mass meeting in the ballroom at 198 Tchoupitoulas Street on May 2, followed two nights later by an even larger gathering in the Commercial Exchange on St. Charles Street. One observer said simply, "The most intense excitement prevails, in the city." By May 5, over 1,000 men had signed up for service on the Texas border. The editor of the *Delta* described a constant swirl of activity outside his office,

> We live, move, breathe, and have our being, at the present time, in an atmosphere of enthusiasm, ardor, and excitement. We see nothing but volunteers marching, flags flying, and men mustering for service; and nothing do we hear but the blast of the war-bugle, the roll of the kettle drum, and the shrill note of spirit-stirring fife.

Foremost among those offering to serve were the city's printers. Out of approximately 200 available for service, nearly fifty had traded their composing sticks for muskets, and enthusiasm among those craftsmen ran so high that "the question is not 'Who will go?' but 'Who will remain?'"[2]

Among those printers who enlisted in this first rush to arms was James L. Freaner, who received an appointment as sergeant in Captain Samuel C. Head's Company D, 3rd Louisiana Militia Infantry. In deference to the old hero of the Battle of New Orleans, Colonel Samuel F. Marks named this regiment the Andrew Jackson Guards. Captain Head's company was mustered into service for six months on May 6 by 1st Lieutenant P.G.T. Beauregard, United States Army, and Charles N. Rowley, Louisiana's Inspector General, before being sent into quarters in the city. A week later, five companies of the 3rd Louisiana had been sent off to reinforce General Taylor, including Captain Head's company. That same day, the *Delta* bemoaned its fate, declaring the paper was "in a predicament—in a plight—in a quandry—in a fix," having lost its assistant editor, a valuable reporter, and two "hands."[3]

1. *Daily Delta*, May 3, 1846.
2. *Daily Delta*, May 3, 1846; May 5, 1846.
3. James L. Freaner, Mexican War Service Records, Record Group 94, NARA; *Daily Delta*, May 6, 1846; May 13, 1846.

Captain Head's command encamped at Point Isabel, at the mouth of the Rio Grande, then serving as General Taylor's base of supply. Sergeant Freaner wrote from there on May 15, assuring his friends at the *Delta* that all was well, "The rifle company of Capt. Head is on drill from morning till night, and begin to look more like a company of regulars than volunteers—they will give a good account of themselves; 'the boys' are in fine spirits, and anxious for an opportunity to show what kind of stuff they are made of." But the fun and novelty of playing soldier took an ominous turn when casualties from the battles of Palo Alto and Resaca de la Palma were brought back to hospitals at Point Isabel. Among the wounded officers were Lieutenant Colonel James S. McIntosh, 5th Infantry, who had been "pierced through the mouth with a bayonet, and shot in three places"; Captain John Page, 4th Infantry, whose "lower jaw, part of the tongue and upper teeth [were] entirely shot away"; and Lieutenant Roland Luther, whose lower lip had been shot off. One soldier wandered into a hospital tent containing "seven men with but three legs among them." It was a shocking sight for the naïve volunteers.[4]

Freaner, along with his comrades, quickly began to learn the realities of army life and he confessed, "the truth being told, we find every thing in wretched confusion." Matters got worse later that month when Colonel Marks's troops marched off to a new camp across the Rio Grande from the Mexican city of Matamoros. Sergeant Freaner described the movement: "About one-half of our march between the mouth of the river and this place, was through mud and water half knee deep; about 8 miles through mud about ancle [*sic*] deep, and so stiff that it would frequently draw the men's shoes from their feet, as they trudged through it; while a burning sun shone down upon us the whole time." Some Louisianans reached camp on horseback, while others had to be carried along in ox carts. Freaner, who had absolutely no experience in this area, proclaimed it "one of the severest and most fatiguing marches ever performed by a body of men."

The camp opposite Matamoros seemed even more of a muddle than Point Isabel. Freaner complained, "At present we have not got sufficient ammunition, provisions, or the means of transportation, for one-half the army we have here at present." But this lack

4. *Daily Delta*, May 20, 1846; May 22, 1846; May 29, 1846.

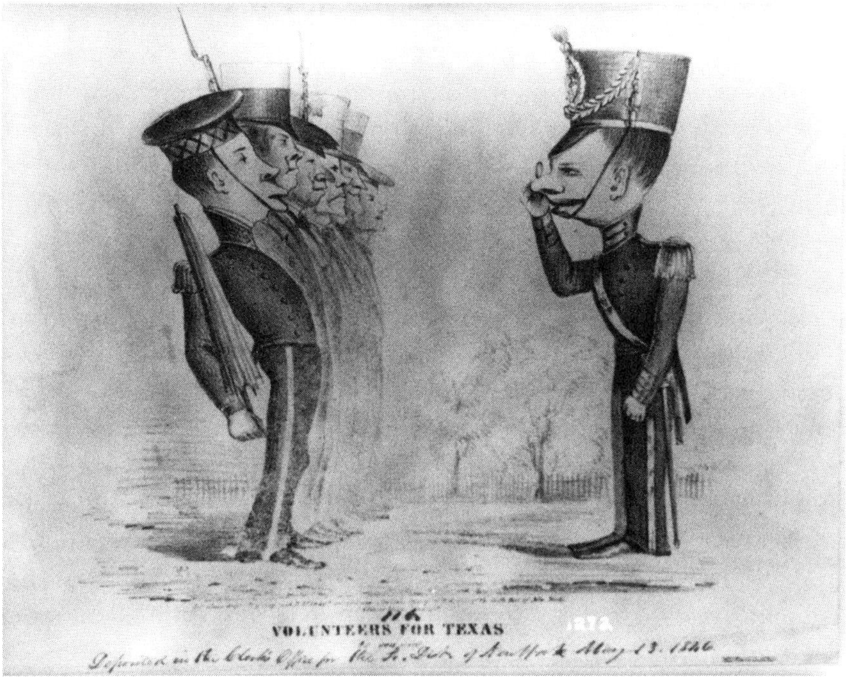

Volunteers for Texas. *Courtesy Library of Congress.*

of supplies and means to move them meant little, since the troops seemed to be stuck in a period of "masterly inactivity." Colonel Marks, a former state senator, spent the long days in perfecting his regiment's training, trying simultaneously to stamp out the vile practice of officers swearing at their men. Isaac Fleeson and Hugh McLeod, publisher and editor of the *Republic of the Rio Grande*, heard that Captain Head's company contained a large number of printers and tried to recruit them to work on their newspaper in Matamoros. The Louisiana soldiers would have none of that, as Freaner explained, "When 'the boys' go a fightin' they go a fightin', and when they go a printin' they go a printin.'" The newspaper project soon failed.[5]

Louisiana boys had enlisted to fight Mexicans and chafed at the inactivity of General Taylor's army. Freaner captured their mood on June 18, "The men are daily becoming more and more impatient and dissatisfied: as very few, perhaps none of them, expected anything else than an active, fighting and laborious

5. *Daily Delta*, June 16, 1846; June 19, 1846.

campaign, when they enlisted." After spending over a month in Texas "awaiting the will of the powers that be," enthusiasm had given way to "loafing and lounging about their quarters." The only Mexicans they had seen so far were scores of peddlers who walked freely through the American camps, selling everything from horses to vegetables, blankets to milk and fresh bread. Likewise, the greatest damage had occurred not on a hotly contested battlefield, but during a storm on the night of June 17, when high winds blew away tents, sheds, and sun shades. After a wet, sleepless night, soldiers spent the next morning "picking up the fragments of the wreck—hunting up hats, coats, &c., and repairing the general destruction."[6]

Independence Day was celebrated in grand fashion among the volunteer camps along the Rio Grande. The "ear-piercing fife and spirit-stirring drum" awakened soldiers in the infantry regiments at 4 A.M., these first notes being echoed by the "shrill noise of the trumpet" from a nearby dragoon encampment. After a patriotic celebration that included a prayer, reading the Declaration of Independence, and a grand oration, the Louisiana troops were reviewed by General Taylor, "Old Rough and Ready," who praised their discipline and promised to personally lead them to victory in the next campaign. Cooks had been engaged in preparing a sumptuous barbecue dinner, Freaner noting that "bottles and canteens, tubs and barrels, pots, kettles and pans, are passing to and fro in every direction," as meat was cooked and special sauces prepared. The former printer explained how a table was made in this desert where building materials were virtually non-existent:

> They selected a level and solid piece of ground in the vicinity of the quarters, dug two ditches about a foot wide, eighteen inches in depth, and four feet apart—the outside serving for seats, and the inside for a table; the centre was covered with blankets, and a thick matting of cane spread over the top as a substitute for a table-cloth.

After a canopy was rigged from tent flies, the food was brought out and "wit, fun and frolic" reigned supreme. General Taylor visited each camp and drank toasts to the health and success of his soldiers.

6. *Daily Delta*, July 7, 1846.

This grand celebration boosted everyone's morale. Sergeant Freaner explained that previous to Taylor's promise to lead them on to victory, there seemed "no other prospect ahead for the whole summer but to loaf, eat and drink within the prescribed limits of the camp." Just two days later, Freaner noticed, "From one end of the camp to the other, instead of growling, dissatisfaction, disease or hiring substitutes, they are busy cleaning up arms and equipments, *washing* clothing, blankets, &c., making every preparation for a march." Even the sick list diminished, "those who feel a little unwell will not complain for fear that they will not be marched with the main body of the army." This euphoria did not last. By July 9, the *Delta* correspondent again complained that army movements were "so tardy, and move with such a snail-like motion, as to tire the most patient." Homesickness set in, inflamed by such trivial events as the movement of steamboats up and down the river. Freaner explained:

> As we hear the noise of their bells, or the steam from their 'scape-pipes, it causes us all to "run and look," not with curiosity, but in hopes that we will be able to recognize an old acquaintance, which seldom occurs, but the sight of the boat makes us feel "more at home."[7]

Just when it seemed that the Louisiana regiments would commence a new campaign under General Taylor, the federal government ordered them to be disbanded. When Old Rough and Ready had asked Governor Johnson for troops, Louisiana promptly raised four regiments to serve six months. After General Winfield Scott, commander-in-chief of the United States Army, heard of this, he pointed out that no law existed authorizing militia troops for a period longer than three months. Since these enlistments were contrary to law, the regiments must be shipped home and mustered out before they exceeded the ninety-day statute. As troops began to reach New Orleans on August 1, the editor of the *Delta* exploded in frustration, "The whole proceeding, on the face of it, betrays gross and reprehensible bungling." Freaner echoed that frustration in late July, writing of his comrades, "They left their homes and their businesses a few months since with spirits light and buoyant; all were eager for the fray, and fondly anticipated winning never-fading

7. *Daily Delta*, July 17, 1846; July 21, 1846.

laurels for themselves and the country." Their places would be taken by twelve-month troops, newly sanctioned by Congress, but the bitterness of returning home with "laureless chaplets" seemed like an insult to the State of Louisiana and her citizens.[8]

Sergeant James L. Freaner had no intention of heading home while there was still a war to be fought, but he had seen enough of garrison duty and longed to join a real fighting unit. That opportunity presented itself on the night of July 31, when Colonel John C. "Jack" Hays and the 1st Regiment, Texas Mounted Rifles (the fabled Texas Rangers) marched into Matamoros. Freaner was impressed with the newcomers, "They are as fine and healthy looking body of men as I have ever seen, and before they leave this post will all be armed with revolving pistols; thus carrying with them fifteen shots, which they discharge in an instant with the most unerring aim." He was so impressed, in fact, that the next day he enlisted as a private in Captain Jerome B. McCown's company.

Anxious to keep the Rangers in line, military authorities in Matamoros attempted to keep the peace by issuing a proclamation "requiring all the rum-mills, gambling houses, with the appurtenances thereto attached, to be closed up and removed from the city forthwith." Freaner noted that "about four-fifths of the Americans" not actually in military service followed "this 'line of business'" and admitted that "numbers of drunken men can be found in the street day and night." Efforts to keep the Rangers in line proved unsuccessful and on August 3 the *Delta* correspondent confessed,

> By the way of pastime, the mixed population occasionally indulge in a street fight, sometimes between the Americans themselves, and occasionally between the Americans and Mexicans; and by way of varying the amusement they frequently murder each other under cover of night.

All the Rangers (including the newly enrolled Freaner) had been given a furlough while supplies were gathered for an advance into Mexico. After a few days' delay caused by heavy rains, the Rangers were "ordered to Camp forthwith" on August 8. Next day, Colonel Hays ordered his men into their saddles and led the regiment southward toward the city of Monterrey.[9]

8. *Daily Delta*, August 2, 1846; August 4, 1846; August 9, 1846.

9. *Daily Delta*, August 15, 1846; August 25, 1846; James L. Freaner, Mexican War Service Records, Record Group 94, NARA.

Freaner found that campaigning with the Rangers was no picnic. Writing from China, a small village about 200 miles from Matamoros and 100 short of Monterrey, he described a "14 days scout, over hills and mountains, swamps and prairies, through under-brush and thickets, every one of which is full of thorns, with no provisions for the last four days but beef." Despite the hardships, Freaner had become ensnared in the Ranger mystique and passed along his observation that "the Mexicans fear the Texan troops more than Gen. Taylor and his whole army." He then related a conversation with a resident of China, who admitted "they were afraid to fight the Texans, as the only way that they could be whipped was to kill them all; for if one was left living or got away, he was sure to do some serious damage." As if to underscore Freaner's transformation into a Texas Ranger, he was promoted to first sergeant on September 12. Despite what would be an ongoing guerrilla war, General Taylor's subsequent victory at Monterrey and ensuing armistice meant there was no longer enough of an organized enemy resistance in that region of Mexico to require such a strong military presence. Therefore, he ordered the Rangers mustered out on October 2, 1846, thanking them for their "efficient service" and wishing them "a happy return to their families and homes."[10]

After the termination of his second enlistment, James Freaner remained in Monterrey, keeping *Delta* readers informed about events in that region of Mexico. By mid-October he could assure folks that the city, although still under American protection, had assumed a more normal appearance. Workers resumed their employment, merchants began to re-open their shops, and farmers started to harvest crops that had been abandoned during the military campaign. An American chaplain began to hold services in the cathedral, with both soldiers and civilians attending in force. Freaner described the building:

> The Cathedral is a very splendid building, of the Corinthian style, occupying a space of ground of about 200 feet front and 300 deep. The exterior bears the marks of age and cannon balls—the interior is most beautifully finished, decorated with a few large scriptural paintings, images and

10. *Daily Delta*, September 6, 1846; James L. Freaner, Mexican War Service Records, Record Group 94, NARA; Orders No. 124, Orders of General Zachary Taylor, 1845–1847, Record Group 94, NARA.

> designs, in signification of the ancients, and a great profusion of finely carved and gilt work—the whole presenting a grand and sublime appearance.

There was even an attempt to start an English-language newspaper, an effort squashed by General William J. Worth, commandant of the troops occupying Monterrey, who claimed it would be "in violation of the wishes of the Government at home." Freaner, who may have been involved in the project, complained, "How a newspaper, chronicling the incidents and news of the American army in a foreign country, would be detrimental to the interests of the nation is a mystery to me."[11]

A group of enthusiastic amateur actors organized a theater troupe to relieve the dull monotony of army occupation, with plans to be in operation by November 1. In the meantime, boredom could be dispelled by attending the "Circus and Menagerie" presented by the firm of Kelly and Bensley, which had been touring the Mexican villages for several years. Their performance included "horsemanship, feats of tumbling, athletic exercises, dogs extraordinary, monkey riding, &c., &c., together with the pranks, capers and gesticulations of a *full grown living and thriving Mexican clown.*" This circus had been traveling from town to town on the road from Chihuahua to Monterrey, but skipped a performance at Saltillo, where a mob had threatened to kill the company. Conditions were extremely unsettled at the latter city, where large bands of robbers terrorized the citizens, killed messengers on the road, and created havoc generally. A good deal of the tension at Saltillo had resulted after Mexican officers had stripped merchants of their goods and used them to pay their soldiers. Now they were selling cigars, tobacco, and other merchandise to buy food, when they could not steal it. Unrest was also reported at Chihuahua, where Freaner said the Americans had fled "from the violence of the mob, composed of the Peons, Greasers, and other portions of the lower class, who take advantage of every excitement of this kind to assassinate the foreigners, and plunder their property." Soldiers also convinced many Mexicans that Americans intended "murdering the citizens—destroying property—violating the persons of the

11. *Daily Delta*, November 3, 1846.

females, and committing other enormities, at every opportunity." When residents fled in fear of the invaders, Freaner reported that "straggling soldiers and deserters, together with the rabble, plunder their houses and ranches of everything they can lay their hands on."[12]

While criminals ruled the countryside, the American army kept occupied areas more orderly. Freaner wrote on October 27,

> The city of Monterey is one of the most peaceable and orderly places in the world—no drinking and rioting—no hallooing through the streets, day nor night; the gambling houses, grog-shops, and all other places calculated to produce disorder, have been closed and their inmates, together with all persons not having special permission to remain here for some specific object, ordered to leave the town in twenty-four hours thereafter, or subject themselves to the honor of a body guard from this place to Camargo.

It was with some relief that Freaner said the crackdown by military authorities had avoided a repetition of those "disorderly scenes enacted at Matamoros" after the arrival of the Texas Rangers. Merchants imported foodstuffs from the interior towns, allowing Americans an opportunity to purchase from a bounty of "fine beef, pork, and mutton, chickens, eggs, vegetables, &c., &c., together with an abundance of apples, oranges, lemons, figs and other fruits." Ignoring objections from the Mexican generals, wealthy landowners agreed to sell meat and grain to the invaders, some of them openly expressing a hope that "the Americans should retain possession of the country, and establish a permanent government" that would assure stability.[13] James Freaner's last letter from Monterrey, dated November 12, appeared in the *Delta* on December 15, 1846. He reported that General Santa Anna, "based upon pretty good authority," had been proclaimed dictator and was then marching toward Mexico City, although the population seemed to be divided over whether to support him against the Americans. Soldiers in the field were unaware that the Polk administration had conducted confidential talks with Santa Anna in hopes of buying California from Mexico. When Santa Anna promised to work for peace between the two

12. *Daily Delta*, November 14, 1846; November 17, 1846.
13. *Daily Delta*, November 17, 1846.

countries, Polk allowed him to return from exile in Cuba, a diplomatic blunder of serious proportions. After lingering about for a few more days, Freaner decided that there were no more important events to report or become involved in, so he started back to New Orleans where he arrived on December 20, 1846.[14]

While still serving with the Texas Rangers, Sergeant Freaner had gotten his hands on a specimen of "hard, heavy and rare species of wood found in Mexico and the West Indies." Upon returning to New Orleans, he shared a piece with friends in the circus world who had it turned into an octagonal cane with a silver ferrule and massive gold ornamented head. This cane bore the inscription, "Cut by James L. Freaner, Company A, of Col. Hays' Texan Rangers, at the Walnut Springs, three miles from Monterey, Sept. 29th, 1846." Freaner's souvenir was presented to John W. Smith, then manager of the Spalding North American Circus, by members of the Great Western Circus Company as a token of their respect.[15]

James L. Freaner had left home a soldier, but returned to New Orleans as a full-fledged war correspondent. His first letter to the *Delta*, dated May 15, 1846, had been signed with his initials, "J.L.F.," but for every subsequent letter he adopted the pen name, "Mustang." Why Freaner chose that particular name is not known, but it was undoubtedly to keep up with other *Delta* correspondents with romantic-sounding names such as "Chaparral" or "Corporal." Claims that he adopted that *nom de plume* after killing a Mexican officer at Monterrey and stealing his horse are simply legend. By the first week in June he was signing his letters "Mustang," the battle at Monterrey not occurring until more than three months later. No matter how he signed his name, Freaner had proven to be a keen observer of the world around him, departing from the typical soldier/writer, who would relate events in his immediate world. When General Scott began gathering troops for an invasion of Mexico, *Delta* editors naturally hired Freaner to go along with the army and report the war news. Unfettered by the obvious military restraints, both to his person and writing, Freaner would seek out the news, whether behind the lines,

14. Greenberg, *A Wicked War*, 148; *Daily Delta*, December 15, 1846; December 20, 1846.

15. *Weekly Delta*, March 15, 1847; *Buffalo Commercial*, June 7, 1847.

at some general's headquarters, or under fire with the troops. A talented writer, Mustang's columns were filled with solid reporting, occasionally augmented by official documents or explanatory material. Whether describing a battle or his passion for liquor, Freaner's letters captured the American army's experience in Mexico and left readers all across the country waiting for the latest installment.[16]

However, Freaner, Editor Alexander Walker, and John Maginnis, business manager of the *Delta*, had found that timely transmission of news from Mexico to New Orleans had been fraught with obstacles in 1846. Despite the "indefatigable" Mustang being "unceasing in his efforts," a simple thing like the late arrival of a steamship could delay publication of his letters for one or two days. While at Monterrey, Mustang had sent off two letters a week, but many never appeared, the *Delta* regarding "their non-arrival as a personal loss." Alexander Walker asked, "What could have become of them? Is a system of espionage carried on in reference to letters leaving the camp?" The paper hinted that some sort of political spy might be intercepting letters "which have not a certain admixture of *soft soap* for certain parties." Sometimes that answer was simply that the correspondence had been carried north in luggage that had been misdirected. Despite their best efforts, Freaner and the *Delta* would never establish a truly reliable network for getting the news from Mexico to New Orleans.[17]

Freaner's arrival in Mexico with General Scott's army meant he could report on exciting events of interest to the entire country. The *Delta* positively gloated at the result: "We perceive that the papers everywhere north and west of us, are copying the account of the bombardment and capitulation of Vera Cruz which was originally furnished to this paper by our intelligent and energetic correspondent, 'Mustang.' We are glad for his sake to observe this

16. The story of Freaner adopting the "Mustang" name was given impetus (and has been repeated by historians ever since) by F. Lauriston Bullard, a Christian minister and eventual Pulitzer Prize winning author, who popularized the legend in his book *Famous War Correspondents*. Bullard wrote, "At the battle of Monterey he killed an officer of Lancers in single combat and seized his charger, whence the name he adopted for newspaper purposes, according to the fashion of the times." Bullard, *Famous War Correspondents*, 361.

17. *Daily Delta*, August 15, 1846; December 1, 1846; *Weekly Delta*, November 9, 1846.

discernment of merit." To bolster its claim, the *Delta* pointed to comments made by the *Richmond Times*:

> We publish below, as the most connected account presented, the diary of "Mustang," the correspondent of the New Orleans *Delta*. We have compared its statements with the official despatches and find no material difference where the same appear in both.

In fact, the *Times* preferred "the newspaper sketches over the despatches" because they contained more interesting material.[18]

Coverage of the army's capture of Vera Cruz was indeed copied throughout the country, but the *Delta* got off to a rocky start. Editor Walker had anticipated important news and arranged for "relays of horses placed at proper points for some sixty miles along the coast, for the purpose of expressing it to the city." But one of the *Delta* couriers had missed his ship connection at the mouth of the Mississippi, the *Delta* apologizing for "one of those unforeseen accidents, or rather, we might say, misfortunes, through which the best laid plans are sometimes frustrated." Forced to copy news of the surrender of Vera Cruz from another city paper, the best the *Delta* could do was publish a Freaner letter dated March 21, eight days prior to the capitulation.[19]

Once Scott's army cut loose from Vera Cruz and started overland toward Mexico City, lengthy lines of communication again threatened Mustang's timely dispatches. Danger lurked everywhere along the route. In late May a coach carrying nine American passengers was found "broken to pieces, and all hands murdered and plundered." When a packet of somewhat out-of-date letters finally arrived in New Orleans from Puebla, the editor wisely printed them anyway "to preserve the connection of this very valuable correspondence." He explained to the readers, "Other letters have been sent, which have fallen into the hands of some rascally Mexicans, who will no doubt be considerably edified by the liberal views of our correspondent in relation to their proper treatment." It was during this period that James Freaner first used the phrase that would become famous, "the Halls of the Montezumas."[20]

18. *Daily Delta*, April 22, 1847.
19. *Daily Delta*, April 4, 1847.
20. *Daily Delta*, June 4, 1847; July 8, 1847.

Another interlude of silence from Freaner was broken with news from Puebla published on August 22, with the following declaration: "The long silence of our principal correspondent in Mexico, has at last been broken; the long-closed communications have been penetrated, and the guerrilleros cheated and deceived, by the following dispatch from our valuable pioneer and correspondent, the far-famed 'Mustang.'" Friends and readers alike were relieved to learn that Mustang was still "alive and kicking, and has made arrangements by which in future the long delays which have tortured us for some weeks past will be avoided and a constant communication kept up between Vera Cruz and Gen. Scott's army." The *Delta* did allude to

> how many of our couriers have been cut off during the last month,—how many have died, fighting bravely with the guerrilleros and staining with their hearts' blood the precious documents consigned to their fidelity,—how many have only got through at incredible expense and by passing through innumerable perils by flood and field, and what small potatoes some of them were when they did get through.

James Freaner would win the fame, but those now-forgotten riders were the ones who faced the dangers of carrying his words to the American public.[21]

Prior to the battles fought within sight of the Mexican capital, Freaner made arrangements to ensure his letters would be the first to reach New Orleans. At the end of July he explained, "I have had always with me four horses for my own use and eight extras, and four Mexicans, faithful and good riders, who accompany me and are always on hand to ride expresses." Despite these plans, five successive letters miscarried and never reached the *Delta* office. Always careful to send duplicates until he saw his messages in print, Freaner must have been relieved to receive the September 10 issue that indicated his diligence had paid off, the *Delta* explaining "our energetic and indefatigable correspondent, 'Mustang,' has sent us a pile of letters, which it would take a dozen numbers of our paper to contain." Despite being "too late to give the incidents which they record much interest or novelty," the most compelling letters appeared in print to continue the thread of Mustang's narrative.[22]

21. *Daily Delta*, August 22, 1847.
22. *Daily Delta*, September 10, 1847; September 11, 1847.

Richard Caton Woodville, *War News from Mexico*, 1848, oil on canvas, 68.6 × 63.5 cm. *Courtesy Crystal Bridges Museum of American Art, Bentonville, Arkansas.*

Following the battles of Contreras, Churubusco, Molino del Rey, and Chapultepec, James Freaner sent the first and most accurate casualty lists to the *Delta*, from whose columns these names were circulated throughout the country. It should be noted that while his contemporary on the *Times-Picayune* sent lists of officers only, Freaner sent long lists that included the enlisted men as well. One of his letters mentioned "a rather funny affair" when he referred to George W. Kendall, correspondent of the *Times-Picayune*, as being shot "right plumb in his horse's ear," while Mustang confessed to having been "struck right in my horse's saddle." While this made for good reading, a later issue of the *Delta* admitted that Kendall, while serving as a volunteer aide, had actually "received a ball in his knee, which gave him some pain, but from which he soon recovered." As for Freaner, he did have a close call with death, confessing to being "knocked head-over-heels by the explosion of a shell" while storming one of the gates into Mexico City. Editor Walker was happy to see both men relatively unscathed, commenting, "The Achilles of the army could not get along very well without the *Homer* of the 'Delta' and the *Hesiod* of the 'Picayune.'"[23]

Columns of the *Delta* continued to promote Mustang's letters, noting he "has never been suspected of flattery, toadyism or favoritism towards any of our officers" and always wrote of "the valor of our men and the good conduct of the Mexicans." This obvious sense of fairness caught the attention of many editors across the United States. The Washington *Union* said of the *Delta* and Mustang's dispatches following the battles of Contreras and Churubusco,

> These letters of its correspondent from the field of action are more circumstantial, more forcible, and they strike us as more correct, even than Mr. Kendall's. We recommend them to our readers' special attention. They not only give the list of killed, wounded, and missing among the officers, but of the rank and file of the whole army. They do more: they present the achievements of all the generals on both days—the gallant generals of the volunteers, as well as the regulars.

Niles' National Register searched the national press for articles it deemed important for future historians. Admitting that letters from Kendall had already come to hand first, its September 25, 1847, edition stated that Mustang was "the no less talented correspondent of the New Orleans *Delta*."[24]

It was during this period that James Freaner became embroiled in an army scandal that became known as the Leonidas Letter. General Gideon Pillow had given him a written account of the battles of Contreras and Churubusco so Freaner could incorporate details into his dispatches. Freaner looked it over, discovered that Pillow claimed too much credit while slighting the efforts of other

23. *Daily Delta*, October 15, 1847.

24. *Daily Delta*, November 26, 1847; November 28, 1847; *Niles' National Register*, September 25, 1847.

officers, and did not use the material. He placed the letter, signed Leonidas, with some other correspondence and it was mistakenly sent to the *Delta* office. Because Pillow's letter came in a package from Freaner, it was assumed to be sanctioned by him. Editor Walker explained how it came to be published:

> I read the letter, and was not pleased with the style or character of it, and therefore laid it aside for consideration. Finding, however, that the letter contained some information relative to the battles, and knowing the great anxiety of the public to catch at every report or statement bearing upon those interesting events; believing that it had been approved by our correspondent, I thought proper to publish it, on the 10th of September, with corrections, omissions, and alterations; the object of which was to improve the style, and to moderate the extravagance of its praise of a particular officer and corps.

Much to the outrage of General Winfield Scott, the Leonidas Letter was used by his political opponents so the entire affair ended with the arrest and trial of General Pillow, followed closely by the recall of General Scott.

General Pillow would be absolved by a court of inquiry into the Leonidas affair, but his reputation had been seriously damaged. Despite his experience as adjutant general of the Tennessee militia, Pillow became a general officer due primarily to his political ties to President Polk. Relations between these two men were so close that many suspected Pillow of being a spy for the Polk administration against generals allied with the Whig Party. His character suffered from feuds with both Zachary Taylor and Winfield Scott, exacerbated by inflated claims of his ability as a field commander. Inept at times on the battlefield and willing to ignore or modify orders at will, Pillow was scorned by Regular officers.

Testimony during the inquiry revealed interesting details of Freaner's activities during the Mexican campaign. He stated, "My social relations with General Pillow, at that time, were as intimate as our different positions would admit of, perhaps more so. I have perhaps half a dozen times taken a drink of whiskey with him at his own request. He has often invited me, and I have generally shunned his invitations to partake of his hospitality, as I have generally done with officers of the army of high rank." Receiving a report of Pillow's actions was certainly within his parameters for obtaining current information, as he explained, "I asked officers for memoranda, in order to see if my own were correct; if we differed, I got others to decide between the two; sometimes the memoranda were verbal, sometimes a few written lines, and sometimes I have seen the reports of officers."

Freaner claimed to have simply a passing acquaintance with General Scott, although the commander did avail himself of the correspondent's connections to New Orleans. Freaner testified:

> When we were at Puebla and the communication entirely or nearly cut off, my couriers brought through communications from commanders below. I loaned him a file of newspapers from the United States, at that time, and I have furnished him with such information as my couriers have brought, concerning the positions of his troops and those of the Mexicans, through his adjutant general or Colonel Hitchcock. Since we have been in the valley I have forwarded his official communications to the War Department and to commanders of posts.

Nicholas Trist, chief representative of the State Department with the army, also used Freaner's couriers to keep in touch with Washington, asserting "it was the safest I could possibly command." Trist explained, "Knowing that a parcel or bundle addressed to the editors of the *Delta* would pass through Mexican hands, even if intercepted, where every thing else would have been opened that fell into the same hands, I got Mr. Freaner to call on me always, during the last moments before the departure of his couriers, and then every thing I had to send by him was put up in his own package." So James Freaner's hard-riding couriers carried not only dispatches to the *Delta*, but also official correspondence back and forth between the army and the Departments of War and State.[25]

Newspapers across the country had come to rely on Mustang's letters, filled with "spirit, humor, and graphic ability" as he informed and entertained readers. Freaner's more accurate casualty lists caught everyone's attention. Editor Walker fumed over actions by

25. Wright, *General Scott*, 267, 277–78; *Message from the President of the United States*, 30th Congress, 1st Session Senate Ex. Doc. 65, 13–19, 250; Reilly, *War with Mexico*, 209–210; Moseley and Clark, *Historical Dictionary*, 147.

the New York *Sun* and New York *Evening Post*, both of which had copied "in full" the lists which Mustang had sent north for publication. Walker griped, "They have shown themselves uncourteous enough not to acknowledge the source from which they obtained them." When the official casualty list was released by the War Department, the Charleston *Courier* chose not to publish it, noting "we observe many inaccuracies, rendering it less reliable than that previously published from correspondents of the New Orleans papers, and we therefore deem it unnecessary to publish it." This was considered a huge compliment to the "accuracy and industry" of both Freaner and the *Delta*.[26]

The New York *Courier and Enquirer* acknowledged the reporting of both the *Delta* and the *Times-Picayune*, saying, "From the commencement of the war to the present time, both these papers have been profuse in their expenditure of money and labor in procuring the earliest and most accurate intelligence. The London *Times* has never evinced more zeal or enterprise than have been shown by these journals." The *Mississippian* wrote of Mustang, "Whatever he touches, he makes interesting; and the descriptions he gives are generally accurate." Although confessing that the paper had published George Kendall's letters, having received them first, the *Mississippian* admitted that Mustang's "are much more satisfactory." After publishing nearly an entire column of praise, the *Delta* said of their premier correspondent that "whilst his letters have been universally admired for their beauty and graphic power, no paper or individual has ever yet impugned their accuracy, authenticity and impartiality."[27]

Mustang soon proved to be more than just a correspondent. James Freaner and Nicholas Trist had both intended to leave with the train that departed Mexico City on December 9, 1847, the former at the height of his fame and the latter recalled by the State Department in disgrace. When Trist had passed along an outrageous proposal from the Mexican commissioners that the international boundary between the two countries should be the Nueces River instead of the Rio Grande, an incensed President James Polk directed James Buchanan, his Secretary of State, to recall Trist. The envoy received notice of his recall on November 16,

26. *Daily Delta*, November 4, 1847; November 12, 1847; November 28, 1847.
27. *Daily Delta*, November 26, 1847.

promptly suspended all negotiations with the Mexican commissioners, and prepared to leave for home with the next military train that departed for Vera Cruz. While he sat with his bags packed awaiting imminent departure, James Freaner dropped by about noon on December 4. In a frank conversation with the diplomat, Freaner finally convinced Trist to ignore the peremptory order to return to Washington and begin a new round of negotiations with the Mexican government, whose newly elected leaders favored peace with the United States.[28]

Trist trusted Freaner completely. Trist explained why in a letter to his wife: "I don't know a man whose friendship is more to be valued, so far as the value of this is to be measured by unswerving uprightness & love of truth, generosity, kindness of heart, courage *á toute épreuve* [unfailing], and a host of other noble qualities." Trist and Freaner delayed their departure in hopes that a peace treaty still could be negotiated. Encouraged by his friend Freaner, Nicholas Trist resumed peace talks that soon successfully concluded the war and added to the United States territory that would eventually become California, Nevada, and Utah, most of Arizona, and sections of Wyoming, Colorado, and New Mexico. The United States paid Mexico $15,000,000 for this territory, plus assuming another $3,000,000 in private American claims against the Mexican government. This acquisition was second in size only to the Louisiana Purchase and was a direct result of James Freaner persuading Nicholas Trist to brazenly ignore the president and conclude a treaty.[29]

Trist employed Freaner on a contingency basis from December 4, 1847, as he waited to carry a signed treaty to Washington. Diplomat Trist explained why he chose a correspondent for this important service:

> For a service of this kind he would be my first choice, by far, of all the men whom I have ever known; as he would be among the first for any service which a man may be qualified for by high integrity of character, strong, manly, good sense, extraordinary sagacity and presence of mind, perfect fearlessness, and many other noble qualities; all united with a frame of steel, and the sinews of a mountain deer.

28. Farnham, "Nicholas Trist & James Freaner," 248–52.
29. Farnham, "Nicholas Trist & James Freaner," 254; Croffut, *Fifty Years*, 315.

Trist concluded this glowing description of his friend by writing, "As generous and disinterested in his disposition as he is brave and upright, he would be perfectly content with the consciousness of having been useful to our country, without any other reward; but I told him that I should insist upon this matter being placed upon the footing just stated." Trist's appointment of Freaner as a quasi-messenger well outside the diplomatic protocols would eventually net him the tidy sum of $263 for his journey to Washington.[30]

Following several weeks of intense negotiations, Trist, literally a minister without portfolio or even authorization, signed "the treaty of peace, friendship, limits and settlement" on February 2, 1848. With ink barely dry on the parchment, Freaner set out the following morning on horseback, accompanied by a company of Mounted Rifles. Finding his escort could not keep up, Freaner galloped on alone. A company of Illinois cavalry provided security for a few hours but soon proved to be too slow as well. Concerned about a region threatened by guerrillas, he happily chanced upon a detachment of Louisiana cavalry under Lieutenant Christopher Lilly, which accompanied him through to Puebla. Freaner safely reached Vera Cruz on February 6. The following day he embarked on a steamer for Mobile, then on around Florida to Charleston and Washington, D.C., reaching the capital on February 19. Although he gave no interviews to the press, editors along his route rightly speculated that Freaner's haste meant he was carrying a treaty of peace with him.[31]

Although drivers along the dock on the Potomac River all eyed him suspiciously, he managed to engage a coach at the wharf and demanded to be taken to the home of Secretary of State Buchanan. Being refused admission by the doorman, Freaner pushed his way in and learned that Buchanan was in bed for the night. Knocking courteously after finding his room, Freaner burst into Buchanan's bed chamber and scared the living hell out of him. After seventeen days by horseback and steamer, Freaner looked like a desperado rather than a messenger bearing diplomatic correspondence; he was dressed in "a blue jacket and pants, one leg of which was strapless, while the want of suspenders displayed a fold of check

30. 30th Congress, 1st Session, House Ex. Doc. 69, *Treaty with Mexico*, 65–66; *Contingent Expenses,* 2nd Session, House Ex. Doc. 5, 17.

31. *Daily Delta*, March 5, 1848.

linen over the waistband, a broad brimmed tarpaulin hat, with a face covered with ranchero looking whiskers." When he learned of Freaner's mission, Buchanan forgave the interruption and eagerly scanned the vital document.[32]

Freaner remained in Washington only long enough to see the treaty sent off to the Senate and to receive important dispatches to General Scott from the War Department. Then he was off again, retracing his route. Freaner arrived in New Orleans on March 4, briefly conferred with Editor Walker and Business Manager Maginnis, and was off by steamer for Vera Cruz the following day. Unknown to Freaner, his friend Maginnis had already written an introduction for Colonel Thomas Standiford, obviously a fan of the correspondent. Maginnis advised Freaner, "He is a fine old cock & particularly friendly towards this office & he told me he would consider it a great favor to have an introduction to 'Mustang.'" To seal the meeting with Standiford, the colonel was bringing along some whiskey that Maginnis advised "will kill a snake sure."[33]

In discussing this accomplishment by what the *Delta* called "the most correct and authentic historian of the war in the Valley of Mexico," the newspaper pointed out that he had travelled, in just over one month, almost 4,000 miles, "much of it alone, through a hostile country, at incredible labor and danger." It was far and away better than any government messenger had ever done. To place Freaner's journey into proper perspective, the *Delta* pointed out that a train of wagons and its escort took the same amount of time to travel only from Vera Cruz to Mexico City.[34]

Even before this near-legendary journey, Freaner was acknowledged to have the best and most reliable system for sending dispatches. One of the *Delta's* own writers, in a tone betraying a mix of envy and complaint, wrote that "I presume your correspondent 'Mustang,' will furnish your columns with news from here, much more efficiently than I possibly can, from his 'knowing the ropes' better, and his much longer residence than mine in the 'Halls of the Montezumas.'" Despite this success, the *Delta* now had even bigger and more expensive plans. In addition to

32. *Philadelphia Inquirer*, March 10, 1848

33. *Daily Delta*, March 5, 1848; Maginnis to Freaner, February 10, 1848, James L. Freaner Letters, Beinecke Library.

34. *Daily Delta*, March 5, 1848.

Mustang's return to Mexico City, other correspondents would be permanently stationed at Vera Cruz, Puebla, Orizaba, and Querétaro. Mustang had been told to spare no expense to organize "a corps of reporters and express riders, throughout the interior of Mexico, so that it will be difficult for anything of importance to occur in that country, which will not be fully and promptly despatched to the *Delta*." This arrangement allowed the *Delta* to boast "that we get the news sometime in advance of the papers in Mexico." Monopolizing the Mexican news had become even easier after George Kendall, Mustang's main competitor, left for home after the fighting was over, reaching New Orleans on November 24, 1847.[35]

In March, Freaner's friend Maginnis, no doubt unable to pass up a dig at his pro-slavery Democratic principles, advised him that "a very high compliment was passed you the other day by a negro!" Maginnis furnished the details:

> The negro though as black as the hinges of hell is a man of intelligence & education & very rich. His name is Clay—he is a builder in this city & owns a vast amount of property. In speaking to a friend of mine he said that he saw a person walk with me whom he immediately knew was "Mustang" & though he tried hard to get a peep at your face, we walked so fast that he failed in the attempt. He told my friend that he buys the Delta every morning, & that he has every line you ever wrote in the Delta carefully made up in a book & there is not money enough in New Orleans to buy it from him. He said that if he had not been afraid of giving you offence he would have madeyou a handsome present while here for he believes you the greatest man inthe United States.

Maginnis wrapped up his story by saying "I'll be dam[d] if in my humble opinion a higher compliment ever was paid you than that by a negro."

While tributes continued to roll in, the army began to pack up and leave Mexico City. On May 26 Freaner received the following cordial invitation from General Patterson: "The Commanding Officer of the 2[d] Infantry has sent me word that he has directed the Band of the Regiment to give me a farewell serenade this

35. *Daily Delta*, February 16, 1848; March 7, 1848; May 9, 1848; May 21, 1848; *Times-Picayune*, November 4, 1847.

Evening—will you do me the favor to come round and hear the Music." Three days later another *Delta* correspondent remarked, "The revels in the Halls of the Montezumas are rapidly drawing to a close." As if to punctuate his statement, he offered a description of a grand fireworks display held the night before at the National Palace. Unfortunately, James Freaner was too sick to enjoy the show. In the absence of Mustang's dispatches, the *Delta* filled his place with another correspondent's letter, apologizing for depriving readers of Freaner's "enterprise, energy and judgment." By June 6 he was able to write out a short letter as the various divisions had started to evacuate Mexico City. His illness would keep him to the end and Mustang would write his last dispatch on June 9, marching off with General William Worth's division and army headquarters on June 12.[36] After the troops had left Mexico, the *Delta* offered an assessment of their most famous correspondent:

> Mr. Freaner has been in the war ever since it broke out, and has witnessed more of its occurrences than any man in the whole country. His letters will constitute the most authentic and unimpeachable history of this war. Mr. Freaner, in addition to the service as a just and impartial historian, placed our government under great obligation by his energy and activity in forwarding despatches from Mexico, at a time when the government was unable to get them through the country, and also by carrying Mr. Trist's treaty with a promptitude and celerity which have no parallel.

The *Delta* completed its appreciative comments with a final tribute to "Mr. James L. Freaner, whose letters, over the *nom de guerre* of 'Mustang,' have given so much interest and value to our columns, and obtained such universal popularity throughout the Union."[37]

36. Patterson to Freaner, May 26, 1848, James L. Freaner Letters, Beinecke Library; *Daily Delta*, June 16, 1848; June 17, 1848; June 22, 1848.

37. *Daily Delta*, August 8, 1848.

Notes on the Text

The editors have searched a complete microfilm run of the New Orleans *Daily Delta* for dispatches written by James L. Freaner under the nom de plume "Mustang." Existing copies of the *Weekly Delta* were compared to the daily editions to verify that they matched completely and exactly. Freaner made frequent use of italics to emphasize certain words and that usage is retained here. Where Freaner's use of italics or other style choices were in conflict with modern style guides, we opted to preserve the formatting of the original source in order to maintain fidelity with the dispatches. We have also carefully inserted first names for important persons upon their initial appearance in the text since they are no longer as well known as in Freaner's day. Brief biographies appear in the notes for military officers with the rank of general, colonel, or lieutenant colonel, as well as important civilians. Freaner would often send documents written by others to amplify his dispatches, so everything not written by Freaner personally is shown in a different size font. Obvious mistakes in 1847 transcriptions or typesetting have been corrected. All images courtesy of Library of Congress, except for Nicholas Trist courtesy of New York Public Library.

Chapter 1

Capture of Vera Cruz

February 22, 1847. Brazos Island.

The magnitude and importance of the expedition against Vera Cruz increases, apparently daily. Within the past week I counted, at one time, twenty-four large ships and barques anchored outside the bar, besides several brigs and schooners—numbering altogether sixty-two sail—independent of those anchored outside. There were at the same time upwards of fifty sail in the bay, off the island, loading or discharging, the greater part of the whole of which have since sailed for Gen. Winfield Scott's head-quarters.[1] The greatest

1. Commissioned captain in 1808, Scott was briefly a prisoner of the British in 1812, but was elevated to colonel following his exchange. A rigid disciplinarian, he was promoted to brigadier general in 1814 and participated in an invasion of Canada, being wounded twice and awarded a brevet to major general. A national hero, Scott used his diplomatic skills during the 1830s, especially with various Indian nations. After Scott was promoted to major general in 1841, President Polk kept him from active command in Mexico until General Taylor's advance had stalled. Outnumbered, operating in a hostile country, and with extended supply lines, General Scott conducted a brilliant campaign from Vera Cruz to Mexico City in 1847. At odds politically with Polk, Scott was superseded as army commander and faced a court of inquiry that would exonerate him from trumped-up charges. A Whig candidate for president in 1852, Scott was soundly defeated. Given a brevet to lieutenant

activity prevails in every department, from the quartermaster to the laborers and sailors, although their movements have been much retarded during the past week by adverse winds. The operations in every quarter indicate that "Uncle Sam" is about to make an immediate effort to crush, with one fell swoop, the defying and self-important Mexican nation, and to so follow up the victories and advantages gained, as to prevent them from indulging even in their gasconade after defeat.

The plan of the campaign is pretended to be kept entirely within the knowledge of the commanding generals, but I do not think it requires any extraordinary wisdom or judgment to tell what the operations will be for the coming two or three months. By the latter part of March, or the first of April, the army will be concentrated on board of vessels in the vicinity of Anton Lizardo, when, with the barge-boats, which have already arrived, they will debark at that place and forthwith move in column on Vera Cruz. They have forty barges, capable of carrying 100 men each. By this means Gen. Scott will be able to land, under cover of the guns of the squadron, 4,000 troops in the course of a few hours, and probably in two or three days, his entire armament, munitions, camp equipage, baggage trains, &c.

Simultaneous with Gen. Scott's movements, Gen. Zachary Taylor will move with his column on San Luis Potosi.[2] In addition to his present force, he will have with him the North Carolina, South Carolina, Virginia, and Massachusetts Regiments. I understand that Gen. Taylor is making all arrangements and taking every precaution to render the march across the desert, from Agua Nueva

---

general in 1855, he retired in 1861, wrote his memoirs, and died on May 28, 1866. Tucker, *Encyclopedia*, 597–99.

2. Commissioned a lieutenant in 1808, Taylor was advanced to captain in 1810 and his successful defense of Fort Harrison in 1812 brought a brevet of major. After reaching the rank of colonel, he led troops in the Black Hawk War of 1832. He campaigned against the Seminoles from 1835 to 1841, but was sent to Texas following its annexation in 1845. While commanding the Army of Occupation, Taylor fought two battles, Palo Alto and Resaca de la Palma, prior to the declaration of war against Mexico. After another victory at Monterrey, President Polk saw Taylor as a political threat and began to shift his troops to the command of General Winfield Scott. When Mexicans attacked his depleted force, Taylor again prevailed at Buena Vista. At odds with both Polk and Scott, Taylor left Mexico late in 1847, became president in the election of 1848, and died in office on July 9, 1850. Tucker, *Encyclopedia*, 634–35.

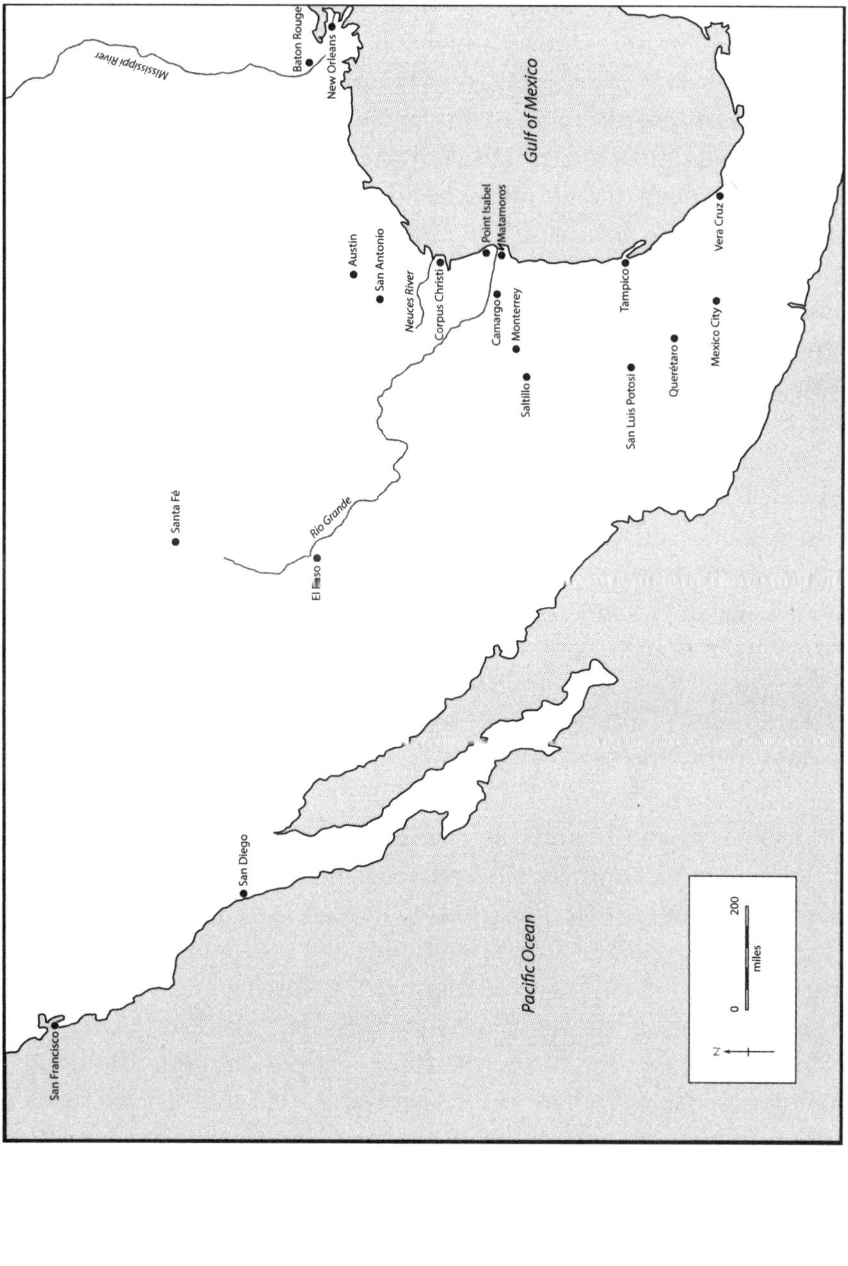

Portions of Mexico and the United States Showing Principal Locations.

to the valley of San Luis Potosi, as little arduous and fatiguing to the troops as possible. His command is composed principally of volunteers, but if they exhibit the same courage and fortitude as those did who were at Monterey, the old hero will achieve a victory that will reflect honor upon the country and himself, and rival in brilliancy any of his former conquests.

Capt. Ben McCullough, of the Texan Rangers, has arrived at Saltillo, and reported to Gen. Taylor. Ben will be a great acquisition to the general's forces. No man has a better knowledge of the Mexican character than himself, besides, he is well acquainted with their mode of warfare, with the country, and with their language. He knows how to avoid their snares, and to thwart their best laid schemes, and at the same time, will acquire a thorough knowledge of the enemy's forces, and their position, in short, he is a "host within himself." There never has been a time since the commencement of the war that the Texan Rangers are so much needed as at the present. The country is full of banditti, commissioned by the Mexican Government, who are murdering and robbing our people at every opportunity. It seems to be the general opinion that we have no force but the Texan Rangers who can keep these fellows quiet. The "boys" are light draught, and move with unequalled alacrity from point to point, not carrying with them any unnecessary baggage, they have nothing to impede their operations, and one thing is very certain, they will never be taken by the enemy sleeping, or drinking at a fandango, let the weather be clear or foggy, raining or shining. There seems to be but one opinion here, both in and out of the army, in reference to bringing them into the service, which is that the Government should enlist them at any expense, and upon their own terms, though it be but six months, or for one or two years. Why should the Government hesitate upon terms, in bringing troops so efficient as they are into the field? If it was known among the Mexicans that Jack Hays, Walker, Chevalie, Ackland, Tom Green, Rhine, Mustang Gray, Gillespie, McCown, Chandler, and Ballow had arrived on the Rio Grande with a force of Rangers, there would not be a Mexican *Commissionaro* this side of the Sierra Madre in two weeks time. I very much doubt if they would stop before they arrive at San Luis Potosi.

To-day being the anniversary of the birth of Washington, the shipping at an early hour was dressed, with colors flying.

It presented a beautiful sight, as they were, with few exceptions, the colors of the United States—bright and new. The exceptions were the Lone Star, which were run up at the mast-head of some vessels, the masters of which prided themselves on hailing from the former Republic, but now State of Texas. The Lone Star, dotted here and there, contrasted beautifully with numerous constellations of the emblem of the Union. The only salute, strange to say, that I heard was from on board the steamboat *Yazoo*, Capt. Reese, who made his small piece of cannon "do its best."

The steamer *Enterprise* was wrecked off the bar at the mouth of the Rio Grande yesterday. Another schooner went ashore, since dark, on the bar at the entrance to the Brazos.

February 23, 1847. Brazos St. Jago. [Brazos de Santiago]

The schooner on the bar last night has since got off, but I could not ascertain her name.

The *Alabama* is to continue down the coast, touching at Tampico, and I will stick to her as long as I can. She is decidedly one of the best boats on the waters, and Capt. Windle is a sailor and a gentleman, every inch of him. We made the run over in fifty-four hours.

Some of the officers of the Virginia Regiment are on shore, six companies of which have arrived outside, and will debark at the mouth of the Rio Grande to-day, and move forthwith up the river in steamboats. The companies arrived are under the command of Col. Thomas B. Randolph, and as follows: Capts. Robert G. Scott, jr., Kenton Harper, Smith P. Bankhead, Montgomery D. Corse, Fletcher H. Archer, and Edward C. Carrington.[3] The remaining six companies are looked for daily.

The volunteers who are stationed between this and Monterey, will not move any farther in that direction. As their term is about to expire, they will be sent back in detachments, in charge of trains, &c.

3. Thomas Randolph graduated from West Point in 1812 and served during the War of 1812, rising to the rank of captain prior to his resignation in 1815. He returned to Virginia where he became a planter and general in the state militia. Randolph served as lieutenant colonel of the 1st Virginia Volunteers from 1847 to 1848, then returned to his former occupation and died November 12, 1867. Cullum, *Biographical Register* 2: 125; Heitman, *Historical Register* 1: 815.

February 25, 1847. Brazos Island.

The steamship *New Orleans* has just arrived off the bar. The ship *Prentice*, with three companies of the 2d Mississippi Regiment, under the command of Major Ezra R. Price, Capts. William J. Daniel, Adam McWillis, and Charles Clark, reported to this post last evening. It appears that their orders from New Orleans destined them to join the expedition rendezvousing off Lobos. They reported at Tampico, and were ordered by Gen. Robert Patterson, and subsequently by Gen. Scott, to this point, and to report to Gen. Taylor.[4] This will throw them into the column to move shortly on to San Luis Potosi.

I regret to learn, from some of the officers, that there is a vast amount of sickness on board of the vessel, and that they have lost nine by death since they left New Orleans. I endeavored to ascertain their names, but could only learn of the following: Messrs. Lucky, Lamb, Scott, Phipps, Ellis, and Lord.

Gen. William J. Worth and staff left this morning in the steamer *Edith*, for Tampico.[5] The whole of the rear of the expedition will sail in the course of two or three days under the command of Lieut. FitzAllen Deas. Contrary winds and bad weather for the last ten days have very much retarded the operations, but through the energy and great exertions of Capts. James M. Hill and Abner R. Hetzel, and their assistants, the troops and munitions will be shipped as soon as could have been expected.

4. A native of Ireland, Robert Patterson became a lieutenant colonel in the Pennsylvania militia during the War of 1812, emerging as a captain in the U.S. Army. He became a successful businessman, prominent Democrat, and militia leader prior to his appointment as major general of Volunteers in 1846. Wounded at Cerro Gordo, Patterson played a role in the first stages of Scott's campaign but did little to distinguish himself later. Re-appointed a major general in 1861, Patterson will be forever linked to the defeat of Union forces at Bull Run. He died August 7, 1881. Tucker, *Encyclopedia*, 496–97.

5. Elevated from private to first lieutenant in the War of 1812, William Worth caught the eye of Winfield Scott who took the young officer onto his staff and became his mentor. Promoted to colonel in 1835, his heavy-handed actions in ending the Second Seminole War brought a brevet of brigadier general. Another brevet to major general followed after his actions at Monterrey. Transferred to Scott's army, Worth helped plan the campaign but soon came into conflict with his former mentor. Worth's division performed well but a bitter feud developed between Worth and Scott that was finally curtailed by a public truce in 1848. After overseeing the withdrawal of American troops from Mexico, General Worth returned to Texas where he died on May 7, 1849. Tucker, *Encyclopedia*, 737–38.

March 1, 1847. Brazos Island.

Great interest is at present felt here in reference to the situation of affairs in Gen. Taylor's column. An express arrived last evening from Col. George W. Morgan, at Cerralvo, together with one from Col. Samuel R. Curtis, at Camargo, to Col. Joseph P. Taylor (brother to Gen. Taylor), who immediately set out post-haste for the country above, intending to go to Matamoros last night.[6] I give you the information just as it has been received, stating what is positive and what is based upon rumor.

By the express of Col. Morgan, we learn that a large Mexican force has made its appearance in the vicinity of Cerralvo, between that town and Monterey, and that a large number of marauding Mexicans are ranging the country between Camargo and the latter place. Gen. Taylor had ordered all the trains of wagons from Camargo going forward, to be stopped—thus you will see there can be but little doubt of there being a considerable body of the enemy in the rear of Gen. Taylor's main body, and I have no doubt their emissaries are in Matamoros, and every post on the river, every night.

There is also a rumor from Cerralvo, from three sources, all corroborating, that Gen. Taylor had fallen back on Monterey with

6. In 1836 George Morgan had enlisted in a company to serve during the struggle for Texan independence. In 1841 he entered West Point but left after two years to pursue a law career. Originally commissioned colonel of the 2nd Ohio Volunteers, Morgan was quickly appointed colonel of the 15th U.S. Infantry. Badly wounded at Churubusco, he received a brevet to brigadier general. General Morgan held several foreign service positions prior to accepting another assignment as brigadier general during the Civil War. Ill health caused his resignation in 1863 and he served several terms in Congress before his death on July 26, 1893. *Philadelphia Times*, July 28, 1893.

A graduate of West Point in 1831, Curtis served one year before resigning to practice law and start an engineering firm. Appointed colonel of the 3d Ohio Volunteers in 1846, he served with General Taylor's command and acted as governor at several points in northern Mexico. Following the war Curtis served four terms in Congress from Iowa but left his seat to serve during the Civil War, eventually reaching the rank of major general. He died, shortly after his muster out, on December 26, 1866. *Daily National Intelligencer*, December 27, 1866.

Joseph was the younger brother of General Zachary Taylor and entered the U.S. Army in 1813. Most of his career was spent in the subsistence department and he received a brevet to colonel for his wartime service in Mexico. Advanced to commissary general in 1861 with the rank of colonel, Taylor was promoted brigadier general in 1863 and died on June 29, 1864. *Daily National Intelligencer*, July 1, 1864.

his main body, and that Gen. Antonio López de Santa Anna was within about thirty leagues of him, and advancing.[7] This rumor is also referred to in a letter from Camargo to a gentleman on the island, the writer of which is a person who has resided in the country for some time, and is intimately acquainted with the Mexican character. In the course of his remarks upon the news received there, he attaches much importance to it, and says: "*There is no mistake this time—we shall be certain to have a brush with the enemy.*"

It was reported at Camargo, and generally believed, that one of the trains had been cut off and captured by the Mexicans, between that place and Monterey. The opinion was sustained by the fact that it had not arrived at its destination after the proper time had elapsed.

The only portion of this news which is questioned here is that in reference to Gen. Taylor falling back on Monterey.

The times are certainly getting exciting, and in case of an engagement with either column of our army, you may depend upon receiving, with the first despatches, a correct and detailed account of it.

Cols. Alexander Mitchell and John B. Weller and Dr. E.K. Chamberlin, of the Ohio Volunteers, arrived in the steamer *New Orleans*, and will leave for the purpose of joining their commands this morning.[8]

7. A political and military figure in Mexican history second to none, Santa Anna led that country's army during the Texan rebellion of 1836 and the Mexican War, as well as serving as the country's president for six terms. A chameleon who changed allegiances almost as often as he changed his pants, Santa Anna portrayed himself as a Mexican patriot to the masses who could generally be called upon to support him, especially since he had lost a leg while opposing the French at Vera Cruz in 1838. A successful campaign in 1836 with victories at the Alamo and Goliad was squandered by his defeat at San Jacinto. Captured at the latter battle, Santa Anna was released in exchange for signing a treaty recognizing the independence of Texas. Undoubtedly a courageous leader, he never lived up to the grandiose plans he formulated for a battle. From Vera Cruz to the gates of Mexico, Santa Anna could never find the key to halting General Scott's relentless advance. Santa Anna resigned as president after the fall of Mexico City and went into exile until he returned for his last term as president in 1852. Driven from power one last time in 1855, he lived aboard until pardoned in 1874 when he returned to Mexico where he died on June 21, 1876. Tucker, *Encyclopedia*, 590–92.

8. Alexander Mitchell graduated from West Point in 1835, but only remained in the service for two years. A civil engineer and lawyer, Mitchell became colonel of the 1st Ohio Volunteers in 1846 and was severely wounded at Monterrey.

A Soldier's Department. *Courtesy Library of Congress.*

He resumed his law practice and was appointed the first U.S. Marshal for Minnesota Territory. His later years were marked by intemperance which left him "the wreck of a man," prior to his death on February 28, 1861. *Milwaukee Sentinel*, March 13, 1861; Cullum, *Biographical Register* 1: 615.

John Weller occupied a seat in Congress from Ohio prior to receiving the appointment as lieutenant colonel of the 1st Ohio Volunteers in 1846 and served

March 4, 1847. Tampico.

All the troops that are intended for the Vera Cruz expedition have left on board transports, with the exception of the Georgia, 3d and 4th Illinois, Alabama, and Tennessee Cavalry. The Louisiana Regiment, Baltimore Battalion, and two companies of artillery will be left to garrison this post. The Louisianians are to commence artillery drill immediately, and will be placed in charge of the principal portion of the ordnance.

Gen. John A. Quitman will leave in the course of two days, and Gen. James Shields to-day or to-morrow, in the steamship *New Orleans*, which lies outside the bar, with Gen. Thomas S. Jesup, Dr. Thomas Lawson, Capt. John B. Grayson, and several other officers of the army and navy on board.[9]

---

in northern Mexico through the following year. Appointed one of the commissioners to establish the boundary line between the United States and Mexico, Weller ended up in California where he became U.S. Senator and governor. He held several minor political appointments following his departure from California before his death on August 17, 1875. *San Francisco Bulletin*, August 20, 1875; *Times-Picayune*, August 18, 1875.

9. Educated in New York, John Quitman moved west, became a lawyer in Ohio, and eventually settled in Mississippi. He joined the state militia and became a major general, also serving as governor for two years and leading a militia force to Texas in 1836. Commissioned brigadier general of Volunteers in 1846, he fought well at Monterrey and was awarded a sword by Congress. Promoted to major general in the Regular Army in 1847, his division played an important role in the attacks on Mexico City. Returning home for muster out in 1848, Quitman boldly suggested to Polk that he annex all of Mexico. A governor and Congressman from Mississippi after the war, he died July 17, 1858. Tucker, *Encyclopedia*, 537–38.

A Democrat from Illinois, James Shields had prior military experience in the Black Hawk War and Second Seminole War. An attorney and commissioner of the General Land Office, Shields resigned to accept an appointment as brigadier general of Volunteers in 1846. He first served under General Taylor, but was transferred to Scott's army in 1847. Thought to be mortally wounded at Cerro Gordo, he returned to duty only to be wounded again at Chapultepec. Brevetted major general, Shields left the army in 1848 as one of General Scott's favorite officers despite being a Democrat. His later career included serving as an ineffective general during the Civil War and being elected to the U.S. Senate from three different states. General Shields died June 1, 1879. Tucker, *Encyclopedia*, 605–6.

Badly wounded during the War of 1812, Thomas Jesup emerged as a brevet lieutenant colonel from that conflict. Appointed quartermaster general in 1818, he would serve in that position until his death forty-two years later. A major general by 1846, Jesup was tasked with supplying the armies of Taylor and Scott far from American sources of supplies. Although often criticized by commanders in the field, his ability to keep both armies provisioned and equipped led to a successful prosecution of the war. General Jesup died June 10, 1860. Tucker, *Encyclopedia*, 327–28.

There is a report here that Santa Anna had sent a large body of cavalry to surprise Gen. Taylor at Agua Nueva, but had been defeated with serious loss. If there has been an engagement between the enemy and Gen. Taylor, you will most likely receive the first news by the way of the Brazos, as I have made arrangements that will ensure it to you.

The greatest anxiety prevails among the troops remaining here, and the Georgia boys in particular, but fear they will not be in time for the "amusements" about to be "got up" at the castle of San Juan de Ulua.

Gen. Scott left Lobos three days since, with all the force that had arrived there, and I am informed that the contemplated attack, if no unforeseen obstacles intervene, will be made in the course of ten days. "Chaparral" is with the advanced troops, and, of course, he will keep you advised by every opportunity of their movements.[10] I go down in the steamship *New Orleans*.

The Shipping Register at the Commercial Exchange has the following report for yesterday: schooner *Phoebe Eliza*, twelve days from New Orleans; schooner *Ellen and Clara*, seventy hours from New Orleans wharf to Tampico City—the quickest trip on record; schooner *Allegheny*, twelve days from New Orleans; schooner *Apius*, eight days from New Orleans; brig *Perfect*, three days from New Orleans. To-day there is no communication with the offing, on account of a Norther last night, which drove all the shipping, anchored outside, to sea.

March 9, 1847. Camp of the Besieging Army, Five Miles Below Vera Cruz.

I arrived at Anton Lizardo to-day about 12 o'clock in the steamship *New Orleans*, which came to at the anchorage among the fleet. Immediately after the steamship's anchoring, the *Massachusetts* sailed by us, when Gen. Scott appeared in the shrouds of the vessel, and inquired for Gen. Quitman. As soon as the General responded to the call, Gen. Scott remarked—"Gen. Quitman, we are to land in the enemy's country. What is your force on board and the condition of your men?" Gen. Quitman replied—"Six hundred and fifty, and in good condition." "Your position, sir, will be in the

10. John N. Peoples.

second line, under the command of Gen. Patterson." Shortly afterwards, Gen. Jesup visited Gen. Patterson and tendered his personal services and those of his staff, which were accepted, and they are now on shore, "all ready," if circumstances require.

Purser Thomas B. Nalle, attached to the frigate *Potomac*, who came passenger in the steamship *New Orleans*, finding it impracticable to join the ship, has volunteered his services to Gen. Shields, has been accepted as his aide, and is now acting in that capacity.

At 11 o'clock the fleet set sail for Sacrificios, the *Princeton* leading, with the *Raritan* in tow. At 1 o'clock, the steamer *Vixen*, with five gun-boats, took a survey of the coast and anchored off the shore opposite the Point, when the troops landed.

The first and second, and part of the third, lines are now safely landed on the beach about five miles below the city of Vera Cruz, contrary to all expectations, without any resistance. The first line, composed of the 2d and 3d Artillery and 4th, 5th, 6th, and 8th Infantry, Capt. Albert G. Blanchard's company Louisiana Volunteers (attached to 5th Infantry), and Capt. John S. Williams' company Kentucky Volunteers (attached to 6th Infantry), under command of Gen. Worth, disembarked on board the barges between Sacrificios and the mainland between 2 and 3 o'clock P.M. and formed in line on the 4th Infantry, preparatory to their departure for the shore. At a signal gun from the *Massachusetts*, at 4 o'clock, the first line "gave way" on their oars and pulled heartily for the landing. This, with the sailing of the fleet from Anton Lizardo, was decidedly the most magnificent view ever presented to the eye of an American citizen. I have a perspective draft of it, which I will send you with the general account of the battle.

The second line, under Gen. Patterson, composed of Gen. Quitman's, Gen. Shields', and Gen. Gideon J. Pillow's brigades, with some artillery, landed directly afterwards, and Gen. David E. Twiggs', the reserve line, made up of the 1st and 4th Artillery, Mounted Rifles, 1st, 2d, 3d, and 7th Infantry, are now landing, and before daylight will probably be on the beach, as also a battery of heavy artillery, under Capt. Francis Taylor.[11] The Mountain Rocket and Howitzer Company

11. Gideon Pillow graduated from the University of Nashville, practiced law, and became friends with James Polk. Commissioned brigadier general of Volunteers by his friend in 1846, he first served under General Taylor but

Landing of the American Army at Vera Cruz. *Courtesy Library of Congress*.

have their battery planted. All the troops that have yet landed are formed in line of battle and will rest on their arms during the night.

Notwithstanding we have now about 6,000 troops on shore, not a single whisper can be heard along the whole extent of the line—all are listening for the first signal of alarm. If the enemy

---

wrote critically of his commander to Polk. Although wounded twice in Scott's campaign, Pillow is best remembered for his self-serving reports and quarrels with his commanding officer. Again, Pillow filled Polk with rumors of Scott's incompetence. When Scott attempted to court martial his unhappy subordinate, the president sided with his friend, recalled Scott from Mexico, and promoted Pillow to major general. He proved to be even a worse officer while serving the Confederacy, living up to his reputation as a quintessential political general. Pillow died October 8, 1878. Tucker, *Encyclopedia*, 508–10.

An attorney from Georgia, David Twiggs served in the U.S. Army as captain and major prior to his muster out in 1815. Re-entering the army soon after, he rose to the rank of colonel in the 2d Regiment of Dragoons. Assigned to General Taylor's army, he received brevets to brigadier general and major general before being transferred to General Scott's army. His division had little impact on the campaign and he acted as governor of Vera Cruz until returning home in 1848. Remaining in the army, he commanded the Department of Texas where in early 1861 Twiggs surrendered his entire force, complete with forts, equipment, and provisions, to secessionists. Commissioned a major general in the Confederate army, Twiggs died July 15, 1862, and is remembered today as the traitor who surrendered Texas. Tucker, *Encyclopedia*, 671–72.

should visit us before daylight, they will find us ready to give them a warm reception.

During the landing of the troops to-day, I was much pleased to see Com. David Conner in his small boat, superintending in person the landing of the troops.

March 10, 1847. Camp of the Besieging Army.

At 2 o'clock this morning, the camp was aroused by a brisk fire from the enemy, and the balls came whistling through "as thick as hail," breaking one man's thigh, and wounding two others. Instead of "beating the long roll," as usual in cases of alarm, a small detachment, under Capt. William H. Gordon, was sent out to reconnoiter. He had not proceeded over 200 or 300 yards, when he found his command in the close vicinity of a body of men. He hailed them, and they answered him in English, but the captain not admiring their accent, withdrew his small force a short distance, and again hailed, when he was answered with a volley of musketry from their whole body, which was returned by the detachment, and had the effect of compelling the Mexicans to retire towards town. Nothing but the sagacity of an experienced and able officer prevented the capture or destruction of the whole of the reconnoitering detachment.

The steamer *Spitfire*, Capt. Josiah Tattnall, at sunrise, took position in front of the castle and town, and commenced a fire, by way of "opening the ball," which she continued for about an hour, and was returned by the castle and city.[12]

Shortly after the *Spitfire* commenced firing, the 1st and 2d Divisions moved in column up the beach towards the city, about a mile, and proceeded to invest the place. A Mexican force of cavalry and infantry, numbering, perhaps, four or five regiments

12. Josiah Tattnall had become a midshipman in 1812, but saw little action afloat in the War of 1812 although he was involved in the battle ashore at Bladensburg in 1814. Following a variety of assignments, he received a promotion to commander in 1838. Assigned to the steamer *Spitfire* in 1846, Tattnall conducted a series of raids along the Gulf coast of Mexico. In March of 1847 Commodore Perry ordered him to take five additional ships and fire upon the Castle of San Juan de Ulua. In a subsequent raid Tattnall was wounded by musketry fire. Promoted to captain in 1850, he commanded the Pacific and East India squadrons before the Civil War. He resigned in 1861 to accept a post as captain in the Confederate navy, but had little to do. Tattnall died on June 14, 1871. Tucker, *Encyclopedia*, 633–34.

in all, showed themselves on the sand heights towards the city at the distance of half-a-mile from our advance, and commenced firing musketry. One of the Mountain Howitzers and Rockets were placed on the hills, and fired a few shots and sent a few rockets whizzing through the air, without any effect. The Mexicans appeared to be a little shy of them at first, but soon re-commenced spreading their line along the hill, and firing their muskets. Capt. Taylor was then ordered to try their mettle with a 6-pounder, which had not been fired but a few times before they withdrew behind the hill, and left for some place secure from danger. In this firing, there was one Mexican killed.

Gen. Worth succeeded in taking his position on the right of the line of investment by 11 o'clock. The line, circumventing the city, when completed, will run along a chain of sand hills about three miles from the city, ranging from 300 to 1,500 feet high, and completely overlooking and commanding the town and fortification, but the heavy guns from the castle can be brought to bear upon the right of the line, when no doubt the quarters will be very hot.

As soon as Gen. Worth had occupied his ground, Gen. Patterson's division took up its march, with Gen. Pillow's brigade in advance, for the purpose of forming on the left of Gen. Worth. The advance, however, did not proceed over a mile before they became engaged with the enemy in a thick cluster of chaparral. A rapid fire immediately ensued, which lasted about twenty minutes. The Mexicans retreated, and no loss on either side that I could ascertain positively, though I have heard it repeatedly this evening that five dead Mexicans had been found.

Gen. Pillow again commenced extending the line, but owing to the great difficulty and labor of cutting a road in the chaparral, through which he had to pass, he had not proceeded more than half a mile up to 4 o'clock P.M., when he again came in contact with the enemy, who were in ambuscade. The firing was so heavy, and appeared so to increase, that Gen. Patterson despatched the New York Regiment, of Gen. Shields' brigade, to the assistance of Gen. Pillow—but only one company of the New Yorkers arrived at the point of attack before Gen. Pillow had routed the enemy by a charge. In the engagement, two of the Pennsylvanians were slightly wounded, viz.: M. Crann, of Company C, and T. Tice, of Company F.

A body of Mexicans was shortly afterwards discovered through a glass, on the left flank of Gen. Pillow's command, at a house known as a magazine, and I expect it has been occupied as such. A 6-pounder was brought to bear on it from one of the heights in our possession, which caused them to leave without ceremony.

Towards sundown, Gen. Pillow's brigade, very unexpectedly, succeeded in reaching one of the highest points in the rear of the city, and planting the "Stars and Stripes," which they greeted—as one of the Tennesseans said—with "*three of the biggest kind of cheers*."

The batteries from town and castle kept throwing 13-inch shells and 24-pound round shot at the entire line until dark. One of them exploded immediately in front of Gen. Worth and staff, and a portion of it passed through Capt. Blanchard's company, but fortunately without injuring anyone.

Gen. Quitman's brigade now moved forward and encamped on the right of Gen. Pillow.

The more I see of the investment of the city of Vera Cruz, the more interesting and exciting it becomes. It is, indeed, a source of pride, and at the same time of pain, to see the gallant little army of ours marching and maneuvering about, over the sand hills and through the chaparral. From morning until night they are exposed to scorching rays of a burning sun, with the thermometer ranging from 90 to 100 in the shade, and while they are wading knee-deep in sand, up and down the hills, with their arms, ammunition and their day's rations on their backs, or chopping and digging out roads, they have been continually exposed to the fire of the heavy guns from the town and castle. But the greatest energy and enthusiasm prevails among them—both officers and men, from the oldest to the youngest—those whose gray hairs would seem to indicate that their race is nearly run appear as anxious to try the temper of their steel as those who are just entering upon the stage of life.

Gen. Scott arrived on shore to-day, and I presume will now take immediate command, and I learn he will refuse any terms of capitulation from the city that may be offered, unless the Castle of San Juan de Ulua is included.

Capt. Blanchard's company will be the only "*legal*" representatives of Louisiana in this highly important battle. Himself and company are all in most excellent health and spirits, and number seventy-four rank and file. If they are called upon, and I have no doubt they will be, I am confident they will add new laurels to those already achieved on the heights of Monterey.

March 11, 1847. Camp of the Besieging Army, Three Miles in Rear of City.

This morning, shortly after daylight, the batteries from the castle and the town opened on our lines, and continued with short intervals throughout the day. I sincerely regret to announce that among our losses to-day is the death of Capt. William Alburtis, of the 2^d^ Infantry. His head was shot off with a 24-pound round shot from the city, while marching with the regiment to join Gen. Twiggs, at the north end. Capt. Alburtis was a printer, and former editor of the *Virginia Republican*, at Martinsburg, Va. There was also killed by the cannonade, Private Cunningham, of Company A, Mounted Rifles, and a drummer boy of Company B, 2^d^ Artillery, had his arm shot off.

About 7 o'clock this morning Gen. Quitman's brigade was ordered to relieve Gen. Pillow from the position he had occupied during the night, in order that his troops might get their breakfast and procure water to last during the day. The Mexicans saw our party leaving the height, but did not see the other coming up with their cavalry, expecting, no doubt, to steal upon their rear, but they were very much mistaken. Gen. Quitman advanced to the top of the hill, and a rapid fire at long shots was kept up for about an hour. Capt. John E. Davis, of the Georgia Regiment, with twenty riflemen, were sent as skirmishers, to incline round under the hill and engage them at close quarters. As soon as they observed Capt. Davis, about 200 advanced on him, but with his small force he held them in check until Col. Henry R. Jackson, with the balance of three companies, and Col. James P. Dickenson, with his regiment, came to his assistance, when the enemy were compelled to retreat under the cover of the guns of the town, with the loss of several dead and some wounded.[13] Our loss in this affair

13. Henry Jackson graduated from Yale with high honors and began a law career in Georgia. He resigned as U.S. district attorney to accept the position of colonel of the 1st Georgia Volunteers, but saw limited service. Following a series of civil and political offices, Jackson became a major general of Georgia troops during the Civil War and in 1864 became a general in the Confederate army,

this morning is seven slightly wounded, viz.: South Carolina Regiment—Lieut. Col. Dickenson, Wm. H. Ballad, Lewis Coka, and J.E. Phillips. Georgia Regiment—B.F. McDonough (son of the ex-Governor), John G. Eubanks, Thos. G. Scott (of Mississippi).

Capt. Davis, who commanded the skirmishing party of riflemen, was very highly complimented for his gallant conduct by Col. Dickenson, Gen. Quitman, and Gen. Patterson.

The column of Gen. Twiggs moved up this morning, with the Mounted Rifles in advance, at 9 o'clock, to take position on the left of the line. The undertaking was a most arduous one, but with Gen. Twiggs there is "no such word as fail." When his cannon could not be hauled by horses they were pulled up and lifted by his men, and they were taken up and over sand ridges that I should think it utterly impossible and beyond the physical strength of men to surmount. The advance of this column arrived at their destination on the sea shore above the town about 2 o'clock, and the rear closed up at sundown.

This entirely, now, circumvents the place, and the entire line investing occupies a space of ground about eight miles in length. As the troops lay stretched along the hills and valleys, with the "Stars and Stripes" dotted here and there, fluttering in the breeze, they present to the view a majestic and sublime appearance. The enemy are now completely within our iron grasp, and whether they can rend asunder the chains that bind them to the confined limits of the walls of the city and castle, remains to be seen. Gen. Worth occupies the right, Gen. Twiggs the left, and Gen. Patterson the centre. If either of these officers can be moved from their positions

---

but was virtually shelved and saw no active service. Ironically, Jackson served as Minister to Mexico from 1885 to 1887. He died May 23, 1898. *Atlanta Constitution*, May 24, 1898.

James Dickenson was a lawyer and had a considerable reputation in the South Carolina courts and legislature. Seriously wounded at Vera Cruz while lieutenant colonel of the South Carolina Volunteers (Palmetto Regiment), he was the first officer in Scott's army to be wounded during the campaign. On August 19, 1847, Colonel Pierce Butler confided to General Worth that Dickenson, now nearly healed, "desires a place near the flashing of the guns." Standing six feet four inches tall, Dickenson was too large a target to miss and the following day at Churubusco, while leading his regiment, was struck in the leg by a ball. Not considered a dangerous wound at first, complications from his previous injury resulted in Colonel Dickenson's death on September 13, 1847. Claiborne, *Life and Correspondence of John A. Quitman* 2: 312, 316, 370.

one foot by any force that can be brought against them, I am very much mistaken. Having our position, by the course of two or three days the mortars and heavy cannon will be planted on the heights, when the enemy will have an opportunity of witnessing the effects of our shot upon their city.

Gen. Pillow has discovered the pipes which convey the supply of water to the city, and intends cutting them off to-night. This will stop their rations of water, and compel them to resort to their wells, which, I am informed, afford but a limited quantity, and that very brackish.

I was informed at a late hour last night that Col. Persifor F. Smith, with his Rifles, has had a very pretty fight with a force of about 800 from the city, and compelled them to retire in quick time, with a loss of about twenty-five killed and several wounded, and sustaining a loss of two or three privates killed and wounded.[14]

I have made diligent inquiry into the health of the army to-day, and the surgeons state that they never knew the army to be in better health and condition, and no evidence of anything like *vomito*.

March 12, 1847. Camp of the Besieging Army.

During the whole of to-day a heavy Norther has been blowing, preventing any communication with the shipping. The air has been completely filled with sand, which drifts off the sand heights behind which the army is encamped. On shore we are waiting for the implements of war, which have not yet been landed. The Mexicans have been perfectly quiet, and fired but two or three shots at our line, at sun-down. We have made no show of troops, and exhibited nothing to the enemy but the picket.

14. A graduate of the College of New Jersey (later Princeton), Persifor Smith moved to Louisiana and served as a colonel of Volunteers in the Second Seminole War. Commissioned colonel of Louisiana Volunteers in 1846, he received a brevet to brigadier general for his actions at Monterrey and another to major general for Contreras. One of the American commissioners during armistice talks, Smith was appointed governor of Mexico City in late 1847. His last command in Mexico was at Vera Cruz where he supervised the departure of the army. Remaining in the service, he was commissioned brigadier general in the Regular Army in 1856 and, after commanding a succession of military departments, died on May 17, 1858. Tucker, *Encyclopedia*, 614–15.

March 13, 1847. 10 O'clock. Camp of the Besieging Army.

The Norther has subsided. No movements on either side of the belligerent forces at the time of writing. This morning at 3 o'clock the picket guard had a few shots with a portion of the enemy's forces. The forts from the city commenced throwing shells at the centre of the line, and it was generally supposed we were about to receive a night attack. The camp was under arms in an instant, but the alarm amounted to nothing. As a great storm usually succeeds a great calm, no doubt in a day or two I will have news of extraordinary interest to communicate to you in relation to our operations.

March 17, 1847. Camp of the Army of Investment.

During the night there was a heavy fire of musketry from the city on our advance, which, however, was not returned. I suppose for the reason that the distance was too far, or the officer did not want to show his position, for fear the artillery from the castle might be brought to bear upon his force, when no good could be accomplished by it.

The Norther having subsided, and the weather being more favorable to-day, the different departments have been laboring with extraordinary exertion to get on shore the ordnance, quartermaster and commissary stores, the former under charge of Capt. Benjamin Huger, the second under Maj. Samuel McRee, and the latter under Capt. Grayson. The duties of these different departments have been so divided and arranged as to move with regularity and despatch, afford every facility to the operations of the army, and conducive to the health and comfort of the troops. It is said that no person is entitled to credit for doing his duty, but in times like these I think the army is very fortunate in having officers who can and will discharge their duties.

The Engineer Department have been going night and day in examining the city and its environs. They have been close under the walls, and, no doubt by this time, have such a knowledge of the location and exterior defences as will enable them to direct the approach of the army with judgment and prudence, and take a position with the batteries so as to bear most effectually on the strongholds of the enemy.

Col. William S. Harney and staff, with Capt. Croghan Ker's company of dragoons, arrived safely on shore to-day, from the ship

Yazoo, which was wrecked on the outer reef a day or two ago.[15] One man attached to the Quartermaster Department was drowned. There was on board at the time of the wreck 110 men and 140 horses—but two or three of the latter were saved. This was truly a serious loss, as the dragoons are needed much at the present time to prevent the straggling parties of Mexicans, who are hovering on our rear, from annoying the line. I did not mention this wreck in my former letter, as I feared creating unnecessary alarm in the minds of their friends, at the time it was generally supposed all on board were lost.

The schooner *Reefer* is on shore about two miles below—it is doubtful whether she will be got off.

Great fears are entertained for the fate of the schooner *Ella*, which has been out twenty days from Tampico. She had on board your correspondent "Chaparral," a large amount of property belonging to officers of the army, Gen. Twiggs' servant, and the horses belonging to the officers of his staff.

The following order, in reference to Gen. Taylor's late victory, was read in camp yesterday:

> Headquarters of the U.S. Army
> Vergara, March 15, 1847
>
> General Orders, No. 54.—The General-in-Chief of the army has received authentic information of a great and glorious victory obtained by the arms of our country under the successful Major Gen. Taylor, at Buena Vista, near Saltillo, Mexico, on the 22ᵈ and 23ᵈ ultimo. The general results were 4,000 of the enemy killed and wounded, against our loss of 700 gallant men. Gen. Santa Anna, sustaining an overwhelming defeat, is known to have retreated upon San Luis de Potosi, and probably will not stop short of the capital. The General-in-Chief imparts this glorious news to the army, that all with him may participate in the joy that is now spreading throughout the breadth of our land.
>
> By order of Major Gen. W. Scott
> (Signed) S.S. Williams, Aide-de-camp

15. William Harney received a direct commission into the army in 1818 and gained experience in the Black Hawk War and Seminole Wars, time in Florida leaving him with a tendency toward consumption. Promoted to colonel of the 2ᵈ Dragoons in 1846, he survived a spat with General Scott and performed admirably at Cerro Gordo, winning a brevet to brigadier general. Harney commanded several military departments after the war, but played no important role in the Civil War due to his extensive Louisiana connections. Retired in 1863, he assumed a life of leisure until his death on May 9, 1889. *Times-Picayune*, May 11, 1889.

A contribution of $100 has been made to the Irish Relief Fund, by Capt. Blanchard's Phoenix Company of Louisiana Volunteers. This act of charity excels anything of the kind that I have noticed throughout the length and breadth of our land. It must be recollected that this little band has been in the service since the first call for volunteers, and this amount contributed out of the small pittance received by a company of soldiers in consideration of their services at a time when they are in active field service, and when they are more in need of their funds in order to procure many necessaries which it is actually impossible to get along without, bespeaks for them the noblest sentiments of soldiers, and entitles them to the highest praise.

A battery of light artillery moved up to Gen. Patterson's division this evening, and took position, but as yet we have not heard anything from it.

A depot of provisions is to be established on the beach above the castle. A steamer starts up in the morning with a supply.

March 18, 1847. 11 O'clock.

To-night the engineers will commence planting their mortar batteries. Nothing new of importance up to time of closing.

March 19, 1847. 11 O'clock. Camp of the Army of Investment.

The weather this morning is clear and excessively warm. If the troops can stand this heat, after the cold and stormy weather we have had for several days past, we have nothing to fear for the health of the army for the season. The city and castle will most likely be in our possession in the course of eight or ten days, and in the course of fifteen days from this time we are all in hopes that the main body of the army will be on their march to Jalapa, which I am told is one of the most beautiful and healthy portions of Mexico.

Col. Harney is this morning straining every nerve to get horses for his dragoons—they having lost 140 by the wreck of the ship *Yazoo*. This officer is very anxious to have an opportunity of meeting a cavalry officer of acknowledged skill and courage who is now hovering on our rear with about 600 men. Every person that I have met seems to desire to see Col. Harney's corps mounted and in pursuit of the foe. His known bravery and his experience as a dragoon officer is a sufficient guarantee to predict for him a brilliant achievement, if he can procure the means to pursue the enemy.

Last night the engineers, with detachments from the infantry and dismounted artillery, were engaged in raising entrenchments and making all the necessary arrangements for planting the mortar batteries. The camp presents quite a different state of things from what it did a few days ago. The beach is now thronged with officers, laborers, mechanics, sutlers, &c., receiving and disposing of goods of various kinds for the use of the army. Large enclosures are being made for the horses and mules, many of which are in a most miserable condition. If we remain encamped here a few days more, this place will present more the appearance of a city than a campground.

The labors of the naval officers and sailors are very severe, as they have the landing of everything from the shipping that is brought to the beach. They apply themselves to the discharge of their respective duties with an assiduity that certainly entitles them to great credit. I understand that, contrary to expectation a few days since, this branch of the service will participate in the bombardment of the city and castle.

March 19, 1847. Sundown. Vera Cruz.

Our fatigue parties, making the entrenchments, have been discovered by the Mexicans from town, and they have opened a heavy and rapid fire on them. A report came into camp, a short time since, that fifteen men had been killed by the explosion of a shell. I inquired at head-quarters, but no report has been made there of it, nor can I trace it to any authentic source, and consequently place no reliance upon it. There are 1,300 men from Gen. Worth's brigade on fatigue, and it will indeed be miraculous if they should all escape the fire of the enemy, which, while I am writing, is reverberating through the air in quick succession.

To-morrow, or the next day, the mortar batteries will be planted, and the fire will be returned upon the town and castle. It seems to be altogether probable that eventually the garrison will be taken by storm, but not until breaches are made with the heavy artillery. There is an opinion prevalent among the officers in camp, that a storm of the citadel would save life, but I presume

Gen. Scott is the best judge of that, and no one pretends to know what his views are.

March 21, 1847. Sundown. Camp of the Army of Investment.

The ship *Catherine* is about to sail for your city, and I will trouble Capt. Herbest with a few lines to you, though we have nothing of much importance to communicate.

The schooner *Pacific*, the *Ellen and Clara*, with government stores, and the brig *Harmonious*, with sutlers' goods for Ogden & Powers, went ashore in the Norther last evening. The latter will be a total loss—the two others may possibly be got off.

The French barque that ran the blockade a few days ago, attempted to get out last night. The steamer *Spitfire* started after her. The former ran ashore on Green Island, and is a total wreck. The latter also grounded on the same island in the chase, and at the present time is in a very precarious situation.

I have been along the whole extent of the line to-day, visited the camp of every regiment, and made strict inquiry of the different surgeons in reference to the health of the army. I find that we have less sick than has ever before been known, and the army bears every indication of continued good health.

The Mexican batteries have been very quiet to-day, comparatively speaking, having fired but a very few shots. The troops are busily employed at the entrenchments.

To-night a small force from the navy will attack the castle on the north side—probably two steamers, two sloops, and the gun-boats. At the same time it is contemplated to plant ten 10-inch mortars, four long 24-pound and two 8-inch howitzers, which is all the heavy artillery we yet have on shore.

The steam frigate *Mississippi* arrived yesterday with Com. Matthew C. Perry, and I am informed will relieve Com. Conner.[16]

16. The younger brother of Oliver Hazard Perry, Matthew Perry became a midshipman in 1809. Promoted to lieutenant in 1813, he spent the remainder of the War of 1812 blockaded in port. After chasing slave ships and pirates for several years, Perry turned his attention to updating an antiquated navy. He pressed for adaption of steam power for naval vessels, then spent 1843–1845 suppressing the slave trade along the African coast. While captain of the *Mississippi*, Perry assumed command of the Gulf Squadron in 1847 and supported General Scott's reduction of Vera Cruz. Perry is best remembered as the officer who

By the next mail you will hear of the effects of our artillery on the city and castle.

March 22, 1847.

The nights are exceedingly cold, and the days exceedingly warm, which has excited the apprehension of some in relation to yellow fever, but I made diligent inquiry along the whole line, in relation to the health of the army, and find that it was never better.

All the government horses in the use of the officers and other persons attached to the army, have been ordered to be turned in for the use of Col. Harney's dragoons, a great number of whom have been left on foot by the wreck of the *Yazoo*.

From the stubbornness of a mule train conveying the mortars to position last night, one of the mortars was dropped before it arrived at its proper place. The Mexicans discovered it, and continued during the night an uninterrupted fire upon it, in hopes, I presume, of killing some of our men if they attempted to remove it.

At 10 o'clock to-day a white flag was sent into the city. The bearer of it conveyed a message from Maj. Gen. Scott, addressed to Gov. Juan Morales, commander of the Mexican forces.[17] The message was a formal summons to surrender the city of Vera Cruz without further defence, as the General-in-Chief of the American forces desired to avoid any further bloodshed. Gov. Morales replied in a very dignified tone and style of language, in substance, that he was sorry to be the cause of unnecessary bloodshed and loss of life, but that he had a high and important duty to perform, involving the honor of his army and the interests of his country, and that he would not surrender until he had exhausted every means of defence.

---

opened relations with Japan in 1853. Commodore Perry died March 4, 1858. Tucker, *Encyclopedia*, 502–3.

17. Juan Morales began his military career in 1821 as a cadet. During the Texas Revolution, he commanded troops at the Alamo and at the defeat of Colonel James Fannin's force in 1836. By 1839 he had become a general of brigade and partipated in several operations against rebel insurgents, becoming a close ally of General Santa Anna. Commander of the Mexican forces at Vera Cruz, Morales slipped out of that city before its capitulation. Santa Anna ordered him tried for treason, but the court never convened and Morales died under unexplained circumstances sometime in 1847. Tucker, *Encyclopedia*, 446.

The Mexicans, during the forenoon, set fire to several buildings, and cleared away the masks to some batteries they had not hitherto exposed, notwithstanding they have kept up a constant firing on our entrenchments during the process of preparation from the castle, Fort Santiago, and a bastion front in the rear of the city.

The conferences between the belligerent forces having concluded at 2 o'clock, at 4 the American battery, consisting of only seven mortars, commenced the bombardment of the city. The shells fell into the place after the first fires, and exploded with as much precision as could have been desired. The city, from one end to the other, soon became enveloped in a cloud of smoke—the vivid and lurid flashes of the artillery, from their city batteries, breaking through it at brief intervals, and report after report followed each in quick succession, until after the dusk of evening had passed, when they comparatively ceased. The round shot and shell fell heavy and fast at the entrenchments behind which our batteries were planted. Louisiana and Kentucky were represented in the first fire upon the city, by a volunteer company from each of those states. The former by Capt. Blanchard's Phoenix Company, acting with 5th Infantry, the latter by Capt. Williams' company, acting with 6th Infantry.

Rumors were passing to and fro in double quick time from headquarters to the man with the spy glass, who duly reported all he could see, which was little else than fire, smoke and dust, but then he had "a right to think," and an official thought in the army is worth the opinions of all the sensible men in it.

Many of the spectators, who were far enough in the rear to be out of danger themselves, expressed strong fears that the gallant little band, who were there as a guard to the mortars, would be compelled to return, but the mass felt confident that no man would leave the spot with his life—that those men went there to perform a duty to their country, and fully understanding and appreciating their position, would prefer leaving their lifeless bodies on the ground to retreating one inch therefrom. The only term that ever can be known in such an army as we have here at present, in the decision of a battle is victory—not a victory made up of "odds and ends"—compromisings and apology—but a victory that will redound to the honor of the country, and one that those who participate in achieving may look back upon from the "sear and yellow leaf" of life, with pride.

As soon as Com. Perry perceived the land forces engaged, he ordered Capt. Tattnall, with what is called the "Mosquito Fleet," consisting of the steamers *Spitfire* and *Vixen*, and five gunboats, viz.: *Reefer*, *Bonita*, *Tampico*, *Falcon*, and *Petrel*, to attack. Capt. Tattnall inquired at what point he should engage. Com. Perry very emphatically replied, "Wherever you can do the most execution, sir." Accordingly the little fleet took position under a point of land known as the "Lime Kiln," about a mile from the city, where they were protected from point blank shot of the castle. As soon as they got their position in line they opened a fire of round shot and shell at a rapid rate, and threw them "handsomely" into the town and Fort Santiago.

The castle soon paid its respects to Capt. Tattnall, and the powerful engines of havoc and destruction were now in full blast from every quarter, hurling their dreadful and deadly missiles into each other's ranks in rapid succession, which they kept up until about dark, when the Mexican batteries comparatively ceased, and the "Mosquito Fleet" also held off for the night.

At 8 o'clock the party that were in the trenches were relieved by another detail. The troops who returned from the entrenchments were literally covered with smoke and dust, and so much disfigured that they could not be recognized except by their voices. Shell after shell exploded in their midst, and shot after shot threw barrels of earth from the embankments over their heads as they lay in the trenches. Their escape seems to have been miraculous, indeed, and every person is surprised that at least one-half of their number was not slain.

But here allow me to relate an incident that occurred during the heaviest of the fire—it is an evidence of the coolness of the American soldier in time of the greatest danger, and at the same time illustrates the ruling passion of a small portion of the army, which amounts to a mania in some instances, brought on, no doubt, by having too much spare time, and no means wherewith to convert it into usefulness. A small party, who had been laying in the trenches all day, becoming tired of doing nothing, as they said, were devising some means of passing away the time. At length one of them proposed a game of cards, and hauled out an old greasy pack, and some half dozen of them sat down in the ditch to play, with nothing but tobacco for stakes. They became much interested, and it was not long before they forgot all about cannon, bomb-shells, Mexican batteries, or anything else, but their tobacco and the cards. It was not long, however, before a 13-inch shell fell on the top of the embankment, the explosion completely covered them with the earth, they all scrambled out as quick as they could, and shaking the sand from their clothing, and cleaning it out from their eyes, one of them very coolly remarked, "Well, boys, I'll be darned if that didn't come mighty near being a 'ten strike.'"

March 23, 1847.

A Norther sprung up this morning, which has been blowing furiously all day, filling the air, and covering everybody with sand. The Mexican batteries have been quiet, with the exception of a few shots about midnight, when they opened a sharp fire for a short time. Our mortars have not ceased during the night, but continued to pour into the city a constant stream of fire. At one time I saw as many as six shells in the air, the whole of which exploded in the city, about the same time, with a terrific and deadly effect.

Just as daylight was approaching, Capt. Tattnall's "Mosquito Fleet" weighed anchor, and under cover of a moon somewhat clouded, approached within 600 yards of the castle. As soon as they had got their respective positions, they opened a broadside from the fleet, which was answered by the castle with spirit, both by round shot and shell. Capt. Tattnall continued the engagement for about half an hour, although the signal from the commodore's ship, calling him off, had been hoisted for some time, but, I suppose, was not seen, on account of a cloud of smoke which hung around the shipping.

This attack of Capt. Tattnall on the castle is considered one of the most daring feats that has been attempted since the commencement of hostilities.

Since writing the foregoing, I have been furnished by a gentleman with the following memoranda:

> Monday Evening, March 22—Hove up anchor and got under way at 5¼, viz.: Steamers, *Spitfire* and *Vixen*; schooners *Reefer*, Lieut. [Isaac S.] Sterrett; *Bonita*, Lieut. [Timothy G.] Benham; *Tampico*, Lieut. [S.P.]

Bombardment of Vera Cruz by the American Navy. *Courtesy Library of Congress*.

> Griffin; *Falcon,* Lieut. John J. Glasson; *Petrel,* Lieut. [Thompson D.] Shaw; came to anchor at 5:30, and opened fire at 5:45; ceased firing at 7:30 by order of Capt. Tattnall.
>
> Tuesday Morning, March 23—At 5:30 hove up anchor and was taken in tow by *Spitfire* and *Vixen* at 5:50 and commenced firing at 6:15; at 6:45 was recalled by the Commodore, but held on about 15 minutes longer; had the fire of the castle and town; they fired grape, round and shell; the shore battery attempted to rake us with grape, but fell short. We had not a man hurt, although the shells burst all around us. The *Petrel* had a hole shot through her starboard quarter from a piece of shell, and her bowsprit shroud cut away. A shell also burst under the quarter of the *Spitfire* and split one of her boats.

During the whole of to-day, Gen. Patterson, in conjunction with the navy, have been making the most extraordinary exertions to finish an entrenchment to plant a marine battery, consisting of three 68s and two long 32s, which have been landed during the course of the day from on board different vessels of war.

The officers and sailors have heretofore borne the brunt of all the labor in landing the arms and munitions of war belonging to the army, and have applied themselves to it with an energy that certainly entitles them to great credit; but now that they had an opportunity of participating in that part of the expedition where honors are to be won and laurels gathered, they exerted themselves with an almost superhuman effort.

About 200 volunteers and sailors were attached to each piece of ordnance, which was by them conveyed over sand hills and hollows half-knee deep in sand, and through a lagoon about two feet deep and seventy-five yards wide, with a soft bottom. They were all placed in position, about three miles from where they landed, during the night. The sailors and volunteers worked admirably together.

During the early part of last evening the town was lighted up by a building on fire, which was ignited by the bomb-shells. It was impossible to tell what building it was, but it was supposed by the engineers to be the barracks. As soon as the fire was discovered from our mortar battery, I was very much gratified to observe the cessation of fire; for, notwithstanding we were endeavoring to destroy their town, or compel them to surrender it, with their other strongholds and fortifications, still humanity would seem to require that a temporary cessation of hostilities should take place under such circumstances. War is terrible in its most modified form, but the besieging of a city like Vera Cruz when we know that we are battering down the houses over some fellow creatures' heads, but cannot tell whether we are destroying the soldiers—our real antagonists—or the women and children. And then to witness the burning houses lighting up the church spires and domes of the prominent buildings, with the families moving about on the tops of the houses in the utmost consternation and apparent despair, cannot do otherwise than excite a feeling of commiseration.

March 24, 1847.

After the fire in town last night, our batteries again opened and continued until morning. During the day, the army guns have worked very slow, on account of a short supply of ammunition, being prevented from landing any yesterday by the Norther.

Early in the day Gen. Patterson let the town hear from him. The entrenchments and guns were entirely undiscovered by the Mexicans, until the "sailor lads" commenced unmasking. They soon commenced pouring into the city a severe and effective fire, until about 4 o'clock—their position being only 500 yards from the walls of the town, and with such a range as to enable them to flank most of the fortifications and works from whence the enemy was firing.

The following is the size and weight of the guns, with their officers, as far as I could learn them:

Potomac—two 32-pounders, 63 cwt, Capt. John H. Aulick and Lieut. Charles H. Baldwin

Raritan—one 32- pounder, 63 cwt, Lieut. Harry Ingersoll

Mississippi—one 8-inch gun, 63 cwt, Lieut. Sidney S. Lee

Albany—one 8-inch gun, 63 cwt, Lieut. Oliver H. Perry

St. Mary's—one 8-inch gun, Lieut. Charles H.A.H. Kennedy

The navy battery set the town on fire again to-day.

The Mexicans did not fail to return Gen. Patterson's fire with great energy and rapidity, and I am sorry to say with some effect—killing four and wounding six—among the latter was Lieut. Baldwin, of the *Potomac*.

At 4 o'clock the officers and crews from the navy were relieved by the following: Capt. J. Isaac Mayo; Lieuts. Raphael Semmes, John DeCamp, James M. Frailey, and Charles Steedman; Passed Midshipmen William Nelson, R.M. Cuyler, and Peter Wager; Midshipmen T.B. Shubrick, Joseph B. Smith, Samuel Magaw, and John H. Upshur.

March 25, 1847.

To-day the combatants appear to be more eager on both sides, and the firing more rapid—the army battery mounts eleven 10-inch mortars, four long 24s, and four Coehorns. During the morning, the Mexicans concentrated their fire as much as possible upon Gen. Patterson and the navy, but the return fire through the day silenced all of their batteries, and the navy breached the wall in different places. Midshipman Shubrick and three sailors were killed, and one mortally wounded. Mr. Shubrick's death was announced at head-quarters in the following laconic note, by the commander at the entrenchments: "Mr. Shubrick has been killed at his gun fighting." On inquiry, I learned the further particulars as follows: He was shooting a gun in one of the batteries in the rear of the city, and was watching the effect of his shot upon that piece of artillery when a ball from the piece he was shooting at struck him—but the last shot he fired dismounted the piece that killed him—thus, in all probability, both artillerists lost their lives in shooting at one another almost simultaneously.

Information was received in camp this morning that a body of the Mexicans were hanging on our rear intending to force the lines if possible and make their way into the city with a number of cattle. Col. Harney, with 120 dragoons, was ordered out in search of them, and report his observations. He discovered them, about 2,000 in number, entrenched at a bridge and supported by two pieces of artillery, three miles from Gen. Patterson's headquarters. Col. Harney started on his return, intending to prepare properly and strike them the next morning. But the gallant old soldier, knowing that delays are dangerous, could not bear the idea of leaving the enemy after having come in sight of them, without a brush. Accordingly, he returned to the place, took a position where he could watch their movements, and keep his men secure from the enemy's fire. The Mexicans commenced firing at him, and threw a perfect shower of balls all around him, but without injury. Col. Harney then despatched a messenger to camp for a small reinforcement, and some artillery to break the breastworks. He was reinforced from Gen. Patterson's division by Lieut. Henry B. Judd, with two pieces of artillery, about sixty dragoons, dismounted, and six companies of the 1st and 2d Tennessee Volunteers, under the command of Col. William T. Haskell, accompanied by Gen. Patterson in person, although he did not take command from Col. Harney, but merely participated as any other individual who was engaged.[18] Col. Harney then formed the Tennesseans on the right, his dragoons on the left, and advanced slowly, to draw the fire of the Mexicans, until Lieut. Judd got his artillery in such position as he desired. The movement succeeded admirably. Lieut. Judd got his ground within 150 yards of the Mexicans, and commenced firing—they attempted to return it, but as soon as a slight breach was made in the parapet, Col. Harney ordered a charge, which was answered by a yell from

18. A veteran of the Seminole Wars, William Haskell was admittedly the most splendid orator ever to come from Tennessee. Having honed his oratory as an attorney, Haskell became colonel of the 2d Tennessee Volunteers and his regiment suffered greatly at Cerro Gordo. Returning home in 1847, he was elected to Congress for a single term. An addiction to strong drink led to his death in a lunatic asylum in Kentucky on March 13, 1859. *Daily Nashville Patriot*, March 17, 1859; Robarts, *Mexican War Veterans*, 72; *Worcester Spy*, March 30, 1859.

the dragoons and Tennesseans. Col. Haskell, Capt. Benjamin F. Cheatham, and Capt. Robert C. Foster were the first men to leap over the breastwork, and, as a naval officer remarked, who witnessed the whole affair, that the balance went over so much like "a thousand of brick" that there was no telling who was first or last. As might have been expected, the Mexicans were unable to stand a charge from "the boys who stood the fire of the Black Fort at Monterey." A few of the incumbrances were soon thrown out of the way, and Col. Harney, with his dragoons, leaped the breastwork and gave chase. He had not proceeded more than a mile before he found the enemy formed in line to receive him. He immediately deployed, and from the head of the line ordered a charge. When he approached within about twenty yards of the enemy's line, they gave him a fire from their side-arms, but overshot. Then came the test of strength and skill—the Dragoon, with sword in hand, met the confiding Lancer, with pointed lance, ready to receive him. The contest was but for a short time. In many instances, lances were twisted from their clenched hold, the Mexicans were unsaddled and driven helter-skelter in every direction, and pursued by the dragoons in detachments. Col. Harney and several of his officers met their men in single combat, but none of them received any injury except Lieut. Lewis Neill, adjutant of the regiment, who was wounded severely in two places from his magnanimity in attempting to capture a Mexican instead of killing him. In full run he overtook the retreating Mexican, and placing his sword in front of him, commanded him to surrender, whereupon the Mexican drove his lance into his magnanimous adversary. As the lieutenant wheeled his horse to despatch him, another Mexican charged up and struck him with a lance. However, severely wounded as he was, in two places, he conquered one of his foes, and a corporal came up in time to "settle accounts" with the other.

In this affair, Col. Harney had four wounded and one killed. Lieut. Judd had one killed, and the Tennesseans had Messrs. Fox, Long, Woodly, and one other of Capt. McCown's company, whose name I could not ascertain, wounded. Mr. Young, a Texan Ranger, who was acting as guide, was also wounded slightly. Nineteen Mexicans were found dead at the bridge behind the breastwork. Col. Harney killed fifty and wounded about the same number. The Mexican force near 2,000; Col. Harney's about 500.

Col. Haskell, Capts. Cheatham, Foster, and John L.T. Sneed, and Lieut. Judd, and all the officers and men in the command, are spoken of in the very highest terms by Col. Harney for their gallant conduct throughout the whole affair.

The naval officers at Gen. Patterson's battery were relieved to-day by Capt. Samuel L. Breese; Lieuts. Samuel R. Knox, Wemford, James Alden, and Alfred Taylor; Purser J. George Harris; Midshipmen John W. Bennett, William K. Mayo, Isaac N. Morris, and some others whose names I could not learn; Drs. Oscar F. Baxter, Robert J. Dodd, and James Hamilton.

To-day a white flag was sent in, asking on behalf of the people, to allow them to leave the city, with their families and persons who were making no resistance. I could not learn what was the precise nature of the reply, but they did not get what they desired—they had waited a little too long. Gen. Scott was not the person to be caught by a ruse of this kind.

March 26, 1847.

Last night Gov. Morales was strongly importuned by the inhabitants, who are said to be suffering severely, to surrender the town—but he was obstinate, and would not listen to their appeals. He declared he would not surrender the garrisoned works until every man was buried underneath the ruins, and not one stone left on top of another. Thereupon a meeting of the National Guard was held, and Gov. Morales was deposed, and Gen. José Landero placed in command.[19]

Our batteries worked last night, and up to 9 o'clock this morning, with apparent increased vigor, when a flag of truce was received by Gen. Scott, with a proffer on the part of the Mexicans to treat for a surrender. Accordingly, a commission on our part was appointed, consisting of Gens. Worth and Pillow, Col. Joseph G. Totten, and Capt. John H. Aulick, of the Navy, who met the Mexican commission

19. Trained as a seminarian, Jóse Landero joined the army and became a local hero while allied with Santa Anna against a French force at Vera Cruz in 1838. Santa Anna promoted him to general of brigade in 1843 and, when he regained power in 1846, sent the general to defend Vera Cruz from an anticipated attack by Amerian troops. He put up a spirited defense against General Scott's forces in 1847, but nevertheless, when that city fell after a twenty-day siege, Santa Anna ordered Landero arrested. Released soon after by Americans, he agreed to refrain from further fighting. He fought against the French under Archduke Maximilian and died in 1869. Tucker, *Encyclopedia*, 349.

at the Lime Kiln, on the right of our mortar battery, about one mile distant, and they continued in session during the day.[20]

Early this morning a Norther sprung up very suddenly, and blew most furiously all day. Rude Boreas piped his shrillest whistle, and old Neptune seemed to do his best, in the general commotion by land and sea; the rifted clouds flew like sable-winged messengers of death through the air; while the furious, lashed ocean piled her created waves far upon the beach. The clouds of sand swept like hail across the strand, from hill-top to the valley's depth, and almost like the famed sirocco of Egypt, with maelstrom-force, or the sweeping blast over Zahara's [Sahara's] desert, filled the air with darkness, and man and beast with feelings of dismay. The mariner was tempest-tossed by the quick surges of the angry deep, and fear might well blanch the cheek of the boldest; the soldier cowered low, to escape the drifting sand that, in almost impalpable particles, penetrated even the smallest apertures; tents were lifted from their positions, and in many instances, torn literally into ribbons, and clothing and camp equipage were strewn in confusion for miles around.

During the prevalence of this violent gale, the steamship *Alabama* went ashore, but was got off with the assistance of the boat's crew of the *Princeton*, under Midshipman Wesley W. Bassett. The brig *Porpoise*, about ten miles at sea, was thrown on her beam-ends, and compelled to throw overboard her lee guns. About thirty vessels were driven ashore opposite Sacrificios, of which the *Eliza S. Lepper* was got off by the boats of the *Princeton*.

The following is, as far as I could learn, the list of vessels:

Vessels ashore, from the gale of the 29th—barque *Mayflower*—foremast and bowsprit gone; barque *Mopang*; brigs *Orion*, *Will*, *Othello*, *Mary Ann*, *Caroline*—masts cut away and bilged; *Apalachicola*, *Peterson*, and *John Potter*; schooners *Mary*, *Peyton*, *Plantagenet*, *Ella*, *Blanche E. Sayre*, *A.J. Horton*, *Corinne*, *Monitor*, *Sea*, *Eleanor*—doubtful; *Phoebe Eliza*, *Louisa*, *Cornelia*, *Orator*, and two top-sail schooners, names unknown.

20. Joseph Totten graduated from West Point in 1805 and was assigned to the Engineers, remaining in that department until becoming Chief of Engineers in 1838. In addition to brevets from the War of 1812, Totten received a brevet to brigadier general for meritorious service at Vera Cruz and another to major general for long and faithful service dated the day prior to his death, which occurred on April 22, 1864. *Washington Evening Star*, April 25, 1864; Heitman, *Historical Register* 1: 966.

Ship *Diadem*—dismasted at anchor, the *Mayflower* ran afoul of her; ship *Shanunga*—dismasted outside, since towed in; brig *E.G. Pierce*, and a brig name unknown—dismasted; a schooner outside—masts and bowsprit gone, doubtful.

During the whole of the day, amidst the prevalence of the storm, the commissioners were endeavoring to settle the terms of the treaty. They adjourned at night, and gave the Mexicans until 6 o'clock on the 27th, to accept or reject. The enemy was evidently in a bad position and trying to get the best terms possible. But Gen. Scott, I think I may safely say, representing the interests of our country, and holding as it were, the honor of our arms in his grasp, will accede to no proposition but such a one in general terms, as he may advance. He would prefer whipping terms out of them, inch by inch, if necessary, than to yield the interests of the nation, or honor of our flag. Our banner must be planted upon the walls of the city and Castle of San Juan de Ulua, in honor and respect by the world at large.

March 27.

This morning the Mexicans did not accede to the terms of the commissioners, and orders were given to fire again at 9 o'clock, however about that hour the enemy solicited another meeting of the commissioners.

While speculation was rife in reference to the result of this meeting, and every person waiting with eager anxiety to hear the finale of the deliberations of the commissioners, I heard a young officer propose a new and somewhat novel mode to induce the Mexicans to come to terms, which was as follows: to despatch a messenger from head-quarters, without being dressed in the pomp, pride and circumstance of glorious war, and announce at the gates of the city that Gen. Taylor had arrived, with a force of Texan Rangers, and intended to sleep in the city to-night. I do not pretend to say what would have been the effect of the young officer's proposition, but it did not appear to meet with much favor among his associates.

Gen. Patterson's battery was relieved to-day, by the following officers of the Navy: Capt. Richard Forrest; Lieuts. Case, Henry Eld, jr., Blunt, Humphrey, John J. Almy, Rogers, and Claiborne; Midshipmen Hunter, William B. Renshaw, Cilley, Smith, Genet, Barbour, Carter, Jones, and Augustus Lodge.

A general impression pervades the camp to-day that the Mexicans are treating only for the purpose of repairing breaches and fixing up their destroyed fortifications, but our engineers and ordnance officers have not been behind them in this respect. During the day, we have been placing our guns to better position, supplying the magazines with ammunition, and providing the army with scaling ladders and their appurtenances, ready to scale the walls, and pass the breaches, if necessary to take the town by storm.

The terms, however, were agreed upon and submitted for ratification.

March 28, 1847.

Com. Perry was preparing to land another battery of ten guns from the *Ohio*, but the necessity was obviated by the ratification by both parties to the stipulations agreed upon by the commissioners.

The Mexicans surrendered the City of Vera Cruz and Castle of San Juan de Ulua, and the armaments and munitions of war, together with their small arms. The officers retained their side arms, and the whole surrendered as prisoners of war, and are allowed to retire into the country on their parole, Gen. Scott furnishing them four days' rations.

The following was issued from head-quarters, which directs the manner and force to take possession of the surrendered works. The brigade designated by Maj. Gen. Patterson, is Gen. Pillow's:

Gen. Orders no. 72 Army Head-quarters

Camp Washington, Before Vera Cruz, March 28.

1. By articles of capitulation signed and exchanged, the City of Vera Cruz and the Castle of San Juan de Ulua, with their dependencies, are to be garrisoned by the forces of the United States to-morrow at 10 o'clock A.M.
2. In the meantime no officer or man of said forces will approach either of those places nearer than our batteries, Nos. 1, 2, 3, 4, 5, respectively, except by special order or permission on some matter of public duty.
3. Pending the ceremony of surrender, the whole army will stand by its arms, each corps near its present ground, ready to advance and attack if necessary.
4. The 1st Brigade of Regulars and a Volunteer Brigade, to be designated by Maj. Gen. Patterson, together with any detachment from the U.S. Squadron, under Com. Perry, that he may be pleased to designate,

will be present at the ceremonies of evacuating and surrendering. These forces will accordingly take positions at the ceremonies as may be assigned by Brig. Gen. Worth, detachments of whose brigade will garrison the surrendered works.

5. Until those garrisons, with their necessary guards, sentinels, and patrols, are duly established, no other person whatsoever will be allowed, except on special duty, to enter either of the surrendered places.
6. The inhabitants of Vera Cruz, and their property, are placed under the safeguard of every American's honor, and any miscreant, who shall do injury to any persons or property, shall be promptly brought before a military commission, under General Orders No. 20.

By Command of Maj. Gen. Scott,
(Signed) H.L. Scott, Act. Adj. Gen.

March 29, 1847.

The camp of the 1st Brigade has been very active in making preparations to receive the compliments of the Mexican army, and their arms, and to occupy the position which they are about to yield to the superiority of our arms and courage of our troops. The following order, No. 16, will show you the disposition of our troops in the garrison, and the order of taking possession:

Orders No. 16 Head-quarters, 1st Brigade
Camp Washington, near Vera Cruz, March 28.

1st. The brigade, except the guard of all descriptions, will be under arms at 8 A.M. to-morrow morning, canteens filled and haversacks supplied as prescribed.

2d. Lt. Col. [James] Duncan's light battery will take the head of the column, and be prepared to fire a salute of twenty-eight guns.

3d. One company of 2d Artillery, and one company of 8th Infantry under Maj. [George] Wright will occupy Fort Conception; one company of 3d Artillery, and one company of infantry under Maj. [John B.] Scott will occupy Fort St. Jago; one company of artillery and one company 4th Infantry, one company 6th Infantry, and one company 8th Infantry, under Lt. Col. [Francis S.] Belton will occupy the Castle of San Juan de Ulua, the remainder of the brigade not on duty, will be marched to the Plaza.

4th. At 2 o'clock P.M., the flag of the U.S. will be hoisted on the several named works, and a salute of twenty-eight guns fired from each, beginning at Fort St. Jago—next Fort Conception—next San Juan de Ulua—and finally from the light battery of the Plaza.

5th. Not an officer or soldier will be allowed to leave their ranks or station until further orders.

6th. During the ceremony of the surrendering of the Mexican troops, not the slightest noise of cheering will be permitted. When our flags are hoisted, in addition to the batteries, they may be saluted with cheers by soldiers not under arms.

By order of Brig. Gen. Worth,
(Signed) W.W. Mackall, A.A.G.

At 9 o'clock, Gen. Worth's and Gen. Pillow's brigades formed about 300 yards apart, opposite each other, and the Mexicans marched out, stacked their arms and marched off. Our troops then moved in column into the city at 2 o'clock, planted the Star Spangled Banner on the walls, where but a short time previous had waved that of a vain and conceited foe. The Stars and Stripes went up first on Fort Santiago, then on Fort Conception, and then on the Castle and other places. Each flag, as it went up, received the national salute, which was answered by the Squadron—the yards of the vessels were manned and our sailors hailed with three cheers.

Com. Perry was present in the "Mosquito Fleet" under Capt. Tattnall at the evacuation and surrender.

The Mexicans variously estimated their loss at from 500 to 1,000 killed and wounded, but all agree that the loss among the soldiery is comparatively small and the destruction among the women and children is very great. Among their killed is Gen. Felix Valdez, an officer of some celebrity. Our loss in the army and navy is about twenty-five killed and about forty wounded, but many of them slightly. Among our killed are two officers of the army and one of the navy. Capts. Alburtis and John R. Vinton of the army, and Midshipman Shubrick of the navy.

Lieut. Col. Dickenson, Lieuts, Neill and Baldwin, I am happy to state, are recovering very fast, and the wounded generally are doing well.

At the time of the surrender, the Mexicans had but two days' ammunition and three days' subsistence, which accounts for their generally withholding their fire during the night.

During the bombardment, our army have thrown the following number and size of shot:

Army Battery

3,000 10-inch shells	96 lbs each
500 round shot	25 lbs each
200 8-inch howitzer shells	68 lbs each

Gen. Patterson's Navy Battery

1,000 Paixhan shot	58 lbs each
800 round shot	32 lbs each

Mosquito Fleet, Capt. Tattnall

1,200 shot and shell, averaging	62 lbs each

Making in all 6,700 shot and shell, weighing 463,000 lbs.

The destruction in the city is most awful—one-half of it is destroyed. Houses are blown to pieces and furniture scattered in every direction—the streets torn up, and the strongest buildings seriously damaged.

Gen. Scott has certainly achieved a great, glorious, and almost bloodless victory over an enemy in a position that was considered impregnable. Throughout the whole affair he has preserved the most perfect equilibrium of temper and the characteristic coolness and courage of a great general and noble soldier, and while, from the necessities of demanding from the enemy his own terms, he has tempered the vigor of the circumstances with humanity—the best evidence of a brave and competent officer.

The Engineer Corps, under Col. Totten, have applied themselves to the discharge of their duties as became them in their position, and endured the privations and exposure to the weather and the fire of the enemy without regard to health or loss of life.

No division or portion of the army has been better conducted than that of the Ordnance throughout the whole of the operations, and no men are entitled to a greater degree of credit than Capt. Huger and Lieut. Peter V. Hagner; their duty has been arduous, and they have labored night and day to discharge it, in fair weather and foul, both at the general depot and in the entrenchments, and I saw these officers up to their knees in water, during the prevalence of the heavy Norther, to rescue their stores from loss.[21]

21. After the surrender, Capt. Huger compiled the following list of captured arms and ammunition: *Taken in the Castle of San Juan de Ulua*—3 10-inch guns, English, 1 mounted; 11 8-inch guns, English, mounted; 12 42-pounders, iron guns, West Point Foundry, mounted; 38 24-pounder guns, West Point Foundry, iron; 23 24-pounder iron guns, old, mounted; 37 24-pounder bronze guns, mounted, old Spanish; 4 12-pounder bronze guns; 2 13-inch iron mortars, very old, on beds, pear-shaped chambers; 2 13-inch stone mortars, bronze; 2,148 13-inch shells; 3,415 10-inch shells; 3,672 8-inch shells; 200 10-inch shells, strapped and loaded; 120 8-inch shells, strapped and loaded; 532 8-inch solid shot; 28 8-inch canisters, filled; 388 8-inch spherical case shot, loaded; 2,130 42-pound shot; 836 42-pound shells; 1,054 32-pound shot; 1,578 24-pound shot; 984 12-pound

Gen. Patterson has acquired for himself a high reputation as a gallant soldier and able officer. His official duties have necessarily been heavy and laborious, in which he has been well sustained by an efficient staff, consisting of Maj. George A. McCall, Capt. George B. McClellan, Lieut. Seth Williams and Lieut. George G. Meade.

Although the veteran Twiggs and that able officer Col. P.F. Smith have not had an opportunity of attacking the city, or figuring conspicuously in the engagement, they have had an important and responsible position assigned them, on the road to Mexico, which they maintained with great vigilance.

The general health of the army is good. The men have been well supplied with provisions since their first landing, but how could it be otherwise, with such an officer as Capt. Grayson at the head of the department, seconded by the quartermasters now in the service.

Capt. Albert G. Blanchard, Lieuts. William Tenbrink and Edward F. Nichols, and the whole Phoenix Company of Louisiana Volunteers, have passed through the battle without injury. By their strict conformity to the discipline of the army, and their noble conduct in the engagement, they have elicited the warm esteem of all who know them. Although they have not the banner of the

---

shot; 2,048 19-pound solid shot, strapped; 413 muskets; 413 musket accoutrements; 28 boxes musket cartridges; 189 sponges and rammers; 282 handspikes; 11 worms; 90 linstocks; 32 pass-boxes. *Taken in the Forts of Vera Cruz*—6 8-inch Sea Coast howitzers, West Point Foundry, mounted on West Point iron carriages; 4 42-pounder iron guns, West Point Foundry, mounted; 4 32- pounder iron guns, West Point Foundry, mounted; 8 24-pounder guns, West Point Foundry, iron; 1 16-pounder iron gun, mounted; 9 24-pounder bronze guns (new), mounted on French barbette carriages; 3 18-pounder Sea Coast and Gav'n and bronze guns, mounted; 20 16-pounder bronze guns; 9 12-pounder bronze guns; 4 9-pounder bronze guns; 6 8-pounder bronze guns; 1 6-pounder bronze gun; 5 4-pounder bronze guns; 6 13-inch Sea Coast mortars, on beds; 2 10-inch Sea Coast mortars, with beds; 1 10-inch Sea Coast mortar, dismounted; 4 stone mortars, bronze; 14 mortars and guns, calibre not ascertained; 135 very old guns, unfit for use; 1 very old 13-inch Sea Coast mortar, a plaque, unfit for use; 30 8-inch shells, strapped and loaded; 1,021 24-pound shot; 2,260 16-pound shot; 304 9-pound shot; 21 boxes musket cartridges; 36 Congreve rockets. *Taken from Troops in the Field*—168 escopets; 3,626 muskets; 3,373 musket accoutrements; 3 standards; 96 carbines; 254 non-commissioned officers' swords; 60 drums; 24 bugles, trumpets or horns; 2 fifes; 21 band instruments; 122 sets escopet accoutrements. Capt. Huger's list did not include large amounts of ammunition, implements, small arms, flags and other military stores located in magazines located throughout the castle and town. *Daily Delta*, April 23, 1847.

State, in the storm of battle they have borne the honor and name of Louisiana, and as Louisianians they have preserved and honored it, both in the investment and siege of Vera Cruz, and in the hard fought battles on the heights of Monterey, and, as a Louisianian, I am proud of them.

Gen. Quitman's brigade is to take up its line of march for Alvarado on the 30th, and Gen. Twiggs will move in column on the National Bridge, three miles from Vera Cruz, where, it is expected, some resistance will be made.

The *Princeton* left on the evening of the 29th, and was saluted by the Castle San Juan de Ulua as she passed out. She made the trip in three days and ten hours.

I learn that Com. Perry has laid in a claim for the captured property as a prize to the navy. The army is not entitled to prize money, and I can see no good reason why the navy should not receive at least one-half of the captured property. They have done all the labor in landing the army and their provisions, armament, and quartermaster's stores—have labored assiduously, in good and bad weather, to perform their part of the service—they have done an ample share of the fighting—their battery has done as much as any other to bring the Mexicans to terms—and from the first landing of the troops to the surrender, have distinguished themselves in the discharge of the duties assigned them. Without their co-operation, in my humble opinion, we would not have been able to operate against Vera Cruz at all.

Chapter 2

Advance of the Army

May 8, 1847. Vera Cruz.[1]

The steamer *Fashion* arrived here on the 7th, making a very quick passage from the Crescent City. We had a very pleasant trip and fine accommodations. The boat is well arranged for the service she is in, and Capt. Ivy, her commander, is just the man to command her, and no person knows better than him how to make everybody on board comfortable, and render a voyage at sea as agreeable as circumstances will admit. We touched at the Brazos and Tampico, and landed the horses we had on board in fine order and good condition at the former place.

The citizens of Tampico are very apprehensive of an attack on that place from a roving banditti, under the command of Capt. Paulino, who has rendered himself as notorious, from his many acts of daring and atrocity, as the great Col. Antonio Canales. However, the troops garrisoning the place appear to look very light upon his threats and demonstrations, and are really anxious he should attempt to carry out his designs. They are confident he will not make a second attempt.

1. Here Freaner resumes his dispatches after a brief visit to New Orleans and therefore missed covering the battle of Cerro Gordo.

The largest train that has ever traversed the soil of Mexico leaves here this evening. It will take with it specie with two paymasters—one of them, I learn, has in charge $400,000, how much the other has I am not aware. Santa Anna, I learn, was seen at a place called Orizaba, about sixty or seventy miles from here, five days ago. He is apprised of the intended departure of the train, and has expressed his intention to attack it, somewhere on the road, with about 3,000 troops, and after he captures it, to make a descent upon this place, with the intention of taking possession of the city, destroying the public stores, and then leaving the Americans to the mercy of the Mexican people. I do not think there is any doubt of Santa Anna having been seen at the place spoken of, and expressing his intentions as I have stated, although a Spanish gentleman stated to me this morning that he was of opinion, from information he had received, that Santa Anna was making his way to Tampico. So convinced are the military that some demonstration will be made upon the train, that an escort of 1,500 men, supported by artillery, will be sent in charge of it. If Santa Anna does really feel disposed to do something valiant with his 3,000 brave men, he had better attack something besides this train. American soldiers do not believe in losing their dimes.

There is a doubt whether Gen. Scott will advance beyond Puebla until he receives further reinforcements. I go up with the train this morning, and you may expect to hear from me at Jalapa, Puebla, and Peroté. I will divide my time between those places.

Gen. Patterson arrived this morning, and is on his way to New Orleans.

There is a large roving banditti between this city and Jalapa, and it seems as if nothing can get them out except a few companies of Rangers. Capt. Samuel H. Walker is looked for daily, and I am in hopes they will let him try his hand on them when he arrives. He, I think, could soon rid the road of them. At present they are murdering and committing the most unprecedented barbarities, even in Indian warfare.

Capt. Grayson, Commissary; Maj. Archibald W. Burns and Maj. Hiram Leonard, Paymasters; Capt. Charles R. Webster, Quartermaster, and many other officers, at present detached, leave here this morning with the train.

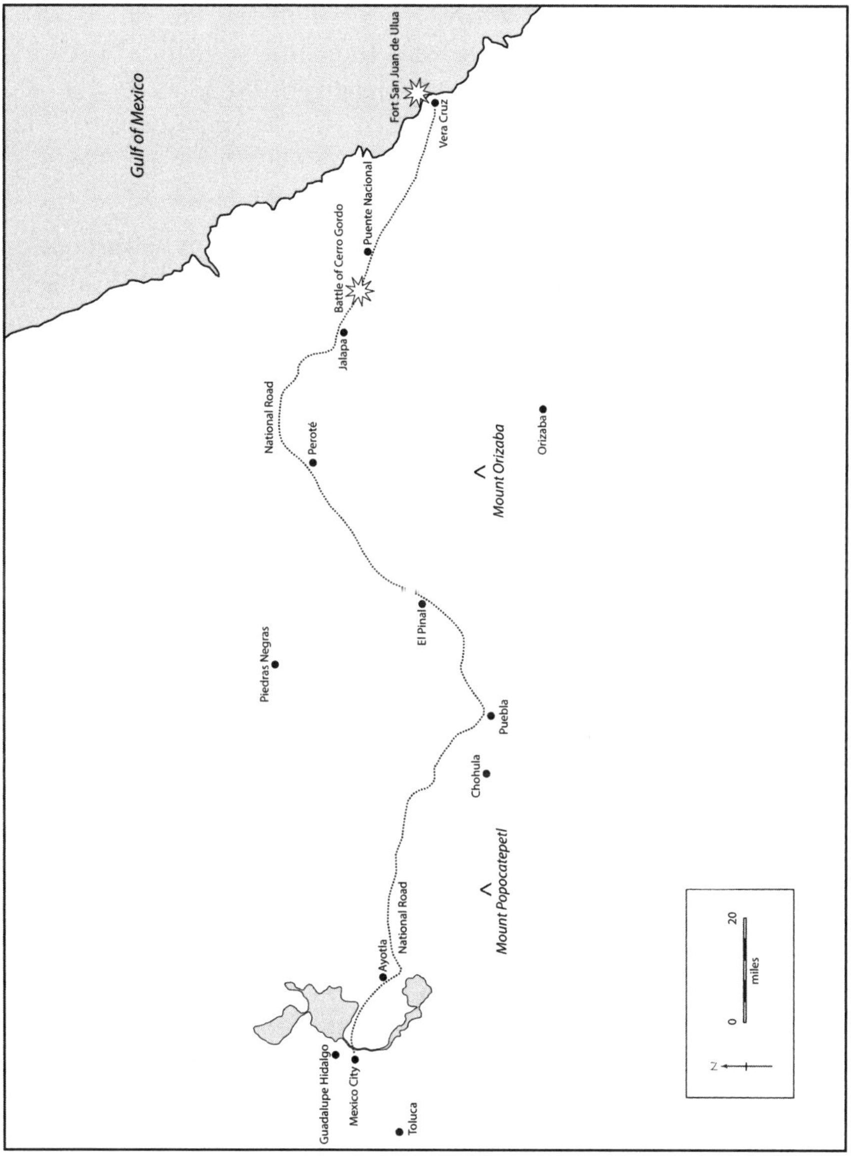

Central Mexico from Vera Cruz to Mexico City.

I learn since writing the above that Gen. Scott will probably make but a short stay at Puebla, and that all communications will be cut off between this place.

The system of police established by the new Council is such as will render this place healthy, I hope, and the fact that over 450 men have been discharged from the general hospital within the past few days, is a proof that the health of the place is not as bad as people want to make out.

May 9, 1847. Mango de Clava.

The large train referred to in my last is now on its way to headquarters. We are at present encamped about one and a half miles from this famous rancho of Señor Don Antonio Lopez de Santa Anna. A small party of us paid a visit to this place this evening, for the purpose of taking a look at one of the country seats of a military chieftain, who is at present attracting so much attention throughout the country. It is a delightful summer residence, and a pleasant retreat from the hot and unpleasant confines of Vera Cruz. It is situated within view of the main road to the City of Mexico, on the side of a prominent hill, and in every manner adapted to defence against odds. At present it is in charge of a servant of Santa Anna's, who is under the protection of a safeguard from Gen. Scott. This servant takes advantage of the magnanimity of Gen. Scott (who has thus given him the means of protecting his master's private property from harm), by organizing and equipping various corps of banditti for the purpose of murdering our men and plundering whatever they can lay their hands on. At this *hacienda* they are regularly supplied and equipped with whatever is necessary to carry out their operations. I am very much mistaken if Gen. Scott does not very soon break up all these arrangements, and effectually put a stop to the many depredations that are now being committed daily.

It is the general impression of all the military men along with us, that the train going up will be attacked between here and Puente Nacional. Many parties of armed Mexicans have been seen at a distance last evening and this morning. At the Puente Nacional we will meet Col. Bennet Riley with a strong escort.[2] So fully confident

2. Bennet Riley joined the army as an ensign in 1813 and gained valuable experience on the Canadian border. Prior to the war, Riley participated in expeditions up the Missouri River to the Yellowstone and down the Santa Fé Trail.

is that officer that an attempt will be made to intercept the train, that he despatched a strong squadron of dragoons to meet us at this place, for the purpose of strengthening our force. From that place we will be under the escort of the old colonel himself, with a strong detachment. As soon as we meet Col. Riley, the Tennessee Cavalry, who are at present with us, will return to Vera Cruz for the purpose of embarking for their homes. The whole of the twelve months' volunteers are now on their return march, and will be despatched as fast as transportation can be procured. The blood they have spilled, and the sufferings they have endured, in the maintenance of their country's rights and honor, will entitle them to, and I am certain they will receive, a hearty welcome with open arms. Many parents, however, will mourn the loss of noble sons, and maidens the loss of their gallant lovers. Large numbers of noble fellows have left comfortable and happy homes, beloved friends and kinsmen, to engage in the strife of arms in which the country is engaged. Most ably and gallantly have they discharged their duty, and maintained their own honor and the high standing and chivalry of their respective states. May they find strong hands and warm hearts to receive them. The graves of those who have died may be leveled over, and no trace left to point to the place of their interment, but their memories will live in grateful remembrance in the bosoms of the people of our country.

Gen. Scott is now at Jalapa, awaiting the arrival of this train. It is likely he will march for Puebla as soon as it arrives.

Santa Anna is at present at Orizaba with about 700 men, which he is at present commissioning as banditti for the purpose of murder and plunder.[3] So strongly has he organized this force, that a man runs a great risk of his life if he drops behind the escort 200 yards. This will be broken up as soon as the dragoons get properly mounted. There appears to be great necessity for an increase of the mounted force.

Most of his career was spent on the frontier until he joined General Scott's army as lieutenant colonel of the 1st U.S. Infantry. Riley received brevets to brigadier general for Cerro Gordo and major general for Contreras. He served briefly in California, received a promotion to colonel, and died a physical wreck on June 9, 1853. *New York Herald*, June 13, 1853; Heitman, *Historical Register* 1: 831.

3. Americans referred to these partisan groups as bandits, but the Mexicans called them *Cuerpo Ligeria* or the Light Corps.

I have heard of a great many patriotic and eloquent speeches to excite troops when going into battle, but I have just heard of one by Capt. Williams, commanding a company of volunteers from Kentucky, which, I think, for effect and brevity, will vie with anything that has ever been uttered. As the troops were advancing up one of the heights of Cerro Gordo, the captain turned round to his company and said, "*Boys, remember old Kentuck!*" The company are at present here on the road home. I heard from one of them relating some of the incidents of the battle to an old acquaintance he met here, and he remarked, "When I heard Capt. Williams say, 'Boys, remember old Kentuck,' I felt as if I could jump headlong into the mouth of every cannon there was in the Mexican battery." I have no doubt, from the manner they fought, that the same feeling pervaded the whole company.

If there is an opportunity to send a letter back, I will write you from every campground on the route, and if there should be a battle, I will send an express to Vera Cruz.

May 11, 1847. Puente Nacional.

To-day we were compelled to encamp after a six mile march, on account of there not being any water on the road for fourteen miles, which distance it is impossible for the large train we have with us to reach in one day's march. Yesterday we traveled from Mango de Clava to Paso del Rio de los Obejas, a distance of twelve miles, and a portion of the train was unable to close up until 12 o'clock at night. It is impossible for any person to conceive the intensity of the heat on the road, or the suffering the men and animals have to endure, unless they have the advantage of experience in such matters.

During the forenoon the train reached this place, and Col. Robert D. Allison, of the Tennessee Cavalry, relinquished his command to Col. Riley, who takes charge of it until it shall have reached headquarters.[4] The former officer returns with his Tennesseans to Vera Cruz, from whence they will soon be on their road home.

4. Robert Allison had a record of public service in Tennessee before receiving the appointment of lieutenant colonel in the 1st Tennessee Mounted Volunteers, no doubt because of his participation as a captain in the Texas rebellion of 1836. Returning to his home state, Allison joined the Confederate army, fought throughout the Civil War, and supposedly had been wounded six times. Moving to Texas

Capt. Philip Kearny, who is in command of the advance guard, with a squadron of dragoons, has scoured the country most completely this far, on both flanks, but has not been able to find an enemy or any trace of them. Last night Capt. Kearny's picket arrested a Mexican under dangerous and suspicious circumstances. He claimed to be an officer of the Mexican army, and said he was released after the bombardment of Vera Cruz on his parole, but the circumstances under which he was arrested—his servant and him telling two stories, and we expecting an attack on the train—induced the commanding officer to detain him, and bring him along with us. I expect he will be delivered up to Gen. Scott as a spy. Col. Riley was asked on our arrival if there was any danger of attack between this place and Jalapa, when the old veteran replied: "We may have a fight, but if they take the train they will have to take the *appurtenances* attached to it." I think the *appurtenances* would make it cost more than the Mexicans can afford to pay for it.

Now, after three days marching, scorching, and thirsting, over an almost barren and deserted country, we have arrived at the famous pass of the Puente Nacional. The road, however, after passing the sand which extends about ten miles this side of Vera Cruz, is comparatively good. The bridge and causeways are of the most substantial order, which renders the crossing of the low grounds and marshes a work of little difficulty. The bridge across the river Antigua at this place is one of the most permanent and magnificent constructions of the kind I have ever met with. It was built in the palmy days of Mexico, when the nation excelled in engineering and science. From the signs on the banks, the river rises at times so as to run entirely over the top of the bridge, but I cannot see any evidence of its ever having made the least impression upon it.

There is a handsome little town here, beautifully located, and taking it all together, it is a delightful place. The towering peaks of the prominent heights overlooking the road and country, adorned by a fortification on the top of each—with a beautiful stream, filled with fine fish, such as trout, perch, bass, &c., gurgling and splashing

---

after this war, he was elected to numerous public offices. When war with Spain threatened in 1898, although nearly eighty Allison tried to join up for another fight. Rebuffed by the government, he died December 16, 1900. *St. Louis Republic*, December 17, 1900; *El Paso Herald Post*, December 20, 1900.

over precipices and rocks, with the largest liberty—the chaparral filled with ripe, wild fruit—the fragrance of the wild flowers—fine bathing, and the cool, fresh air of the Gulf, mingled with the balmy breeze of the mountains—make this quite a romantic and favorable campground. But, notwithstanding all the natural and artificial beauties and attractions, the day's march on either side of the point knocks all the polish off the romance of campaigning, and suddenly transfers us back, with reluctance, to the stern realities of a soldier's life in the field.

May 13, 1847. Jalapa.

I left the train last night twenty-three miles from this place, and came through after dark in company with ten others. We met some Mexicans on the road, two of them armed, who, I suppose, were watching the train, as I learn from some gentlemen who came through to-day, that they were informed there were 300 lancers in the vicinity of us the same night. As our occupation was not fighting, we very willingly let everybody alone who would let us pass without interruption.

Previous to my arrival I had heard so much of the beauty and attractions of this place, that I was prepared to look for something more than I had seen in any part of Mexico. My anticipations have been more than realized. The appearance of the country—its productions—the people—the improvements—far exceeded my expectations.

The papers from the City of Mexico state that large cannon, supplies, and money, have been sent to Santa Anna from that city and other places. If this should prove true, we may find him in a defensive position somewhere between here and the city.

A small detachment came down from Peroté to-day, and report all quiet in that vicinity, and also that our troops are treated very well by the inhabitants. Indeed, the only trouble seems to be between this point and Vera Cruz.

The general health of our army is very good, though I very much fear many of the wounded at Cerro Gordo will not recover. Gen. Shields' wound is doing very well. I went to see him to-day, and found him much better than I expected. His physicians and friends are now confident of his recovery. The preservation of his life is, in a great degree, owing to the attention of Capt. George T.M. Davis, of the Illinois troops, who, I believe, never left him after he fell, and rendered him such assistance as circumstances would admit. Lieut. Sheldon I. Johnson, of the 4th Illinois, died yesterday, from his wounds, and was buried to-day with military honors.

The 1st Pennsylvania, in command of Col. Samuel W. Black, are now at Peroté, but one-half of it will return.[5] This portion, with the 2d Pennsylvania, and a part of the 1st Artillery, under command of Col. Thomas Childs, will compose the garrison of this place, after the departure of Gen. Scott.[6]

May 14, 1847. Jalapa.

Having heard and read so much about the beautiful city of Jalapa, and the adjacent country, I was more anxious than usual, on my arrival, to see what was to be seen—but the more I look and inquire, the more my curiosity is excited. It is really to be regretted that a more industrious and energetic race of men are not in possession of it. The women will do very well—they appear to be suited to the place—they are the most beautiful set of creatures I have ever seen, not only in Mexico, but in any part of the United States. They dress with taste, are well-formed, graceful in their movements, have good countenances, and a fine expression of the eyes, which are generally large and full, and shine like diamonds. They are much pleased with, and express great astonishment at the politeness and courtesy of the Americans. They think it very strange that an American should step off the sidewalk for the purpose of letting a woman, even of inferior grade and rank, pass by.

5. A distinguished graduate of Western University, Samuel Black became a noted attorney and orator in western Pennsylvania. Coming in second during the election for the command of the 1st Pennsylvania Volunteers, he settled for the position of lieutenant colonel. After his regiment mustered out, Black returned to his law practice. Commissioned colonel of the 62d Pennsylvania Volunteers in 1861, Samuel Black was killed in action on June 27, 1862 at the Battle of Gaines Mill. *Pittsburgh Gazette*, June 30, 1862.

6. Thomas Childs graduated from West Point in 1814 and was assigned to the artillery during the War of 1812. Receiving brevets to major and lieutenant colonel for his actions in Florida, Captain Childs commanded General Taylor's artillery and was brevetted to colonel in 1846 although his promotion to major did not occur until early in 1847. Receiving another brevet to brigadier general for his successful defense of Puebla in September of 1847, Childs died on October 8, 1853, while commanding troops in the last effort to rid Florida of the Seminoles. *Charleston Courier*, October 18, 1853; Cullum, *Biographical Register* 1: 115–16.

The Mexican women have always been noted for their kind offices and attention to the American prisoners and other unfortunate persons, but anyone who has ever seen those in this region could not expect other treatment at their hands. They are very apt to call the attention of the Mexican *caballeros* to the respect shown to the ladies by the Americans. The *caballero* generally replies, it is the only virtue we possess; but I should not be surprised if the *señoritas* ascertain some other qualities in our people worthy of consideration, and many gallant fellows be induced to "sign, seal and deliver" in good faith.

The contrast between the face of the country and the men who till the soil is very strong. The former wears the appearance of perpetual bloom and greenness—the latter, with few exceptions, habitual and natural sloth and idleness. How or when they work is a mystery to me. Their fields and gardens are in fine order and well cultivated, but I have not seen a single individual handling a hoe, plough, or other farming utensil. Corn can be seen in every stage of growth, from an inch high to the ear on the stalk. Cotton and sugar produce well. There is nothing within the range of vegetables that is not now daily vending in the market—together with cherries, plums, strawberries, blackberries, currants, pineapples, bananas, lemons, &c; and in riding through a *rancho* last evening, in the vicinity of the town, I saw a large orange grove, and an apple and peach orchard, with fruit on the trees half matured, and I am told they are raised in abundance in the surrounding country. I do not believe there is anything that cannot be produced in this region.

The city is located on a nest of short, sugarloaf-shaped hills, with the Rio Antigua, a blue, transparent stream, taking a circuitous course around it. On this stream are located grist-mills, cotton and woolen factories, and breweries. The streets are all well paved, descending from both sides to the centre. The houses are built of stone, varying in styles of architecture, nearly all have a large court-yard, in the centre of which are large fountains, continually issuing streams of pure, clear water, which make the buildings comfortable, convenient, and healthy. The only objection I can see to them is the iron bars to the windows, resembling our prisons, which produce the impression, for a moment, that the inmates are doomed to perpetual imprisonment, and we cannot help sympathizing with the happy faces and sparkling eyes of the *bonita señoritas*, which peep so bewitchingly through them. The Catholic church is a very large and massive building, occupying some 200 by 300 feet of ground. The interior of it is finished in the most gorgeous and pleasant style. None of the decorations, images, or designs have been removed, on account of Gen. Twiggs' advance arriving in the city before they had time to do so.

The climate is just such a one as could be desired. The nights are cool enough to make a slight covering comfortable, and the days warm enough to make us appreciate good water cooled by the snow and ice brought down from Orizaba's heights—some twenty-five miles distant—which are daily hawked about the streets for sale.

The funeral of a Mexican officer, who died of wounds received at Cerro Gordo, took place yesterday. He was interred with military honors, in accordance with his rank, by an American escort. Gens. Scott and Twiggs, and many of the officers of our army, also accompanied his remains to the grave. It was one of the most solemn and affecting sights I have witnessed, to see the body of a fallen foe borne to the grave by his own countrymen and friends, accompanied by the conquering heroes by whose hands he had fallen. One of the best bands in the army executed the funeral air as the procession passed from the hospital to the church, and thence to the grave. All asperity of feeling, on the part of the Mexicans, appeared to be dissipated by their gratitude for the honor and respect pad by the army to their departed friend.

Like all other cities of the country, this is infested with blind and lame beggars—but they are not allowed to go into the street to solicit alms, except on Saturday. On this day one will be met every hundred yards in the street, and importuned by every age, from the infant in its mother's arms to those whom age has dwindled into a mere nothingness. I am told it is considered quite a God-send to a family of the lower order of the people to have a deformed child born. All those who can talk have abandoned their former mode when appealing to the Americans. They usually stand upon the sidewalks and in the public places, and repeat a prayer to God to assist them, and ask his blessing for those who assist them; but now they go about the streets, the men with their hats in their hands, and the women with something like a scarf drawn loosely over their heads (the Mexican women never wear bonnets), and say, in very good English, "give me picayune," or in Spanish, "*da me un medlo*."

May 14, 1847. Jalapa.

The large train, for which so much anxiety has been manifested, arrived this morning safe and sound, with the exception of a loss of a few horses, and the breaking down of some few wagons. Last night there was a slight demonstration made towards it in the neighborhood of Santa Anna's *hacienda*, ten miles from here, but the robbers could not summon courage enough to make the attack.

Mr. Nicholas B. Trist, who comes in the character of a bearer of despatches from Washington, to Gen. Scott, arrived this morning.[7] I have had an eye on him for several days, and unless I am very much mistaken, his mission is of much importance, and, in a short time, will attract more attention than bearers of despatches generally do. If I am right in my conjectures, I am satisfied from his character as consul at Cuba, and other important positions he has occupied in relation to our country, his knowledge of the people and country, his diplomatic and official acts will be conducted with more ability and dignity than many of those who have preceded him in Mexico.

Capt. Grayson, and his commissary appurtenances, also arrived in company with the train. He has, in a great measure, recovered from a rather serious injury he received a few days since.

Gen. Scott will take up his line of march in a few days for the City of Mexico. In all probability, as soon as the intended increase of the army shall arrive, an expedition will be fitted out at the City of Mexico, consisting of about 4,000 troops, to march on Guadalajara. All idea of peace seems to be banished for the present, and there

7. Appointed to West Point in 1817, Nicholas Trist rebelled against military discipline and left in 1821. He married a granddaughter of Thomas Jefferson and was admitted to the bar in 1826. Offered the position of clerk in the State Department later that year, he accepted, but took leave to act as private secretary to President Andrew Jackson from 1830 to 1831. Trist became consul in Cuba and served from 1833 to 1841. When the Democrats returned to power after the 1844 elections, Trist became chief clerk of the State Department, a post that was actually equal to the Under-Secretary of State. Sent to Mexico as a secret envoy, his mission soon became public. Losing faith in his diplomat, President Polk ordered Trist's recall, but he ignored that order and completed negotiations for what would become the Treaty of Guadalupe-Hidalgo. This treaty was ratified by the Senate, but Polk summarily dismissed Trist after his arrival in the States and refused the pay due him. He took several minor jobs after this public humiliation, finally received reimbursement for monies owed him in 1871, and died February 11, 1874. Tucker, *Encyclopedia*, 665–66.

is no doubt, unless the mission of Col. Trist will change the aspect of affairs, circumstances will compel us to take possession of the country and occupy it permanently. Some of our most able officers, and many of the prominent Mexicans, are of opinion that the shortest way to settle our difficulties with Mexico is to take possession of the country, occupy it, and give them a code and laws adapted to the present condition of the people—the various functions of which to be executed and discharged by such persons as they may see proper to select. I am fully persuaded that, upon the United States adopting such a policy, a part of the Mexicans and foreign residents, of sufficient strength to support and maintain it, would immediately spring up all over the country. There is no question but the people are tired of internal broils and revolutions, the trammels and restraints that are imposed upon their trade and commerce. Whatever course may be adopted, that will ensure permanency and stability in the internal affairs of the country, will meet the hearty sanction and approbation of that portion of the people who can govern and dictate the policy of the country. In fact, the only opposition that we would have to encounter would be from the few who have been in the habit of plundering the mass, through the means of a bad and illy regulated government. This class would soon be overcome and compelled to yield. Whatsoever is well resolved on should be quickly performed.

May 16, 1847. Jalapa.

A few days since the Mexicans, in conjunction with some itinerant Americans, got up a regular bull-fight, of the same character as those in Spanish countries generally. The arena, and all the appurtenances for the exhibition of the science of bull killing and brutality, had been previously prepared. It is an amusement frequently enjoyed by a large body of the Mexican people, with a great deal of delight and satisfaction. The animal had, previous to his entrance into the ring, been provoked, by some means, to madness. As soon as he entered, his antagonist, a Mexican, dexterous in the saddle and the use of the lance, entered with an air of self-importance and confidence that would have been a credit to the *Bombastes Furioso* in his happiest position—indeed, the expression of the fellow's countenance seemed to say—

> "Whoever dare these bonds displace
> Must meet Bombastes face to face."

The bull and the Mexican charged each other in turn, both taking advantage of position as much as possible. The Mexican, not satisfied with the ferocity of the raging animal, continued, at every opportunity, to pierce him with his weapon, until he became so raging that he was provoked with anger almost to blindness. As the fight continued, the anxiety of the spectators increased, until thought of all else was buried in the excitement of the occasion. During the course of the encounters with four different animals, the men and horses were turned over and thrown severely several times, and the whole affair wound up with four dead bulls, one horse badly hurt, one man's arm dislocated, and one other person somewhat bruised. The American curiosity was satisfied, and the exhibitors received the dollars.

In the evening, after the sports in the amphitheatre, there was a grand fancy dress and masquerade *fandango* given at the theatre. A goodly number of ladies, "of some sort or other," were in attendance, and quite a crowd of American and Mexican men. Conviviality took possession of all who participated in the "gay and festive scene," and those who were spectators were as much amused and diverted as those that tripped the "light fantastic toe," with graceful movements, to the airiness of exhilarating music, and exchanged glances with their partners, fair and unfair. Around and across they went, as if all hands were made of gum-elastic—some passing compliments, with a slight discount on flattery, others dealing in repartee and wit (though some "mighty bad Spanish" was called into requisition), while the jocund laugh at intervals added to the hilarity of the occasion. There was, however, a crowd of time-worn old bachelors, who despised laying their rough old hands upon the enticing waists or grasping the hands of the tempting *señoritas*. For their own amusement and especial gratification, they got up an affair in one corner of the room, which they called a "stag dance." They had it all in their own way, as nobody appeared to know or care anything about them. They danced, sang, &c, until they tired themselves out, and then they quietly retired, leaving the balance of the party to "do up the fancy." The amusements wound up at a good hour, and the parties retired with mutual feelings of friendship—some remarking, as the crowd passed out—"If our boys did pay a dollar for it, they were only practicing for the victorious dance in the Halls of the Montezumas."

The church built by Cortez about three centuries ago, with the two-fold view of religious worship and fortification, is about to be applied to nearly the same use. It is at present used by the Mexicans as a convent, and the Americans contemplate placing a battery upon its summit. It commands the whole town, and if occasion should require, the firm old building will tremble with the weight of the destructive engines upon it, which will deal death and destruction in a manner never dreamed of by the original projector of the building. "Time works wonders."

May 18, 1847. Jalapa.

The army now encamped here have been under marching orders for this evening. News was received from Puebla yesterday, to the effect that Santa Anna reached that place in advance of our army, and, on the approach of Gen. Worth's division, retreated, having with him about 10,000 men. There is no doubt expressed in relation to the news, except as to the number of men Santa Anna had with him. However, I do not think the statement overrated, when we come to consider the facility and ability of the Mexicans to bring together an army whenever they can find anything to feed them with. This difficulty Santa Anna has obviated by laying contributions on the inhabitants wherever he goes. The people are compelled to supply his army, or he confiscates their property. Therefore he is able to bring into the field, in an almost incredibly short space of time, any number of men he may require.

Santa Anna, with his entire force, says the information received, has gone towards the City of Mexico. Whether it is for the purpose of giving us battle there, or somewhere on the road, or with the view to throw the weight of his influence in favor of peace, cannot be decided until we hear more of his movements. A contrariety of opinion prevails among the best informed on the subject. If his object is to give us battle, he will receive a more disastrous defeat than he has ever met with before. The larger the force he has with him, the worse it will be for him and his army. They will be newly brought together, undisciplined, untutored in the art of war, and with a lack of proper organization in every department—consequently the more troops he may have, the more unwieldy will they be, and the more subject to rout and discomfiture by the intrepidity of our well organized and superior disciplined army. If Santa Anna should again meet us, the destruction among the Mexicans, I feel convinced, will be very great. It is well known that nearly all of those who were paroled at Vera Cruz and Cerro Gordo have again taken up arms against us. No quarter ought to be shown them, nor do I believe they will be shown mercy, if they are again found in the ranks of the enemy. Our men are tired of taking prisoners for the purpose of letting them off on a parole of honor, and then fighting them twice afterwards in the space of six months. Too much blood has been spilled, and too many valuable lives sacrificed, to allow such a state of things to continue. The Mexicans have violated the most sacred obligations, by taking up arms at Cerro Gordo, after having been permitted to retire into the interior, on their parole, from Vera Cruz. It is forbidden by the laws of all civilized nations, and if they violate the established precepts, I can see no reason why they should not suffer the penalty.

Capt. Stevens T. Mason, of the Mounted Rifles, who was wounded at the battle of Cerro Gordo, died yesterday morning, and was interred in the evening with military honors, in accordance with his rank. Gens. Scott, Twiggs, and Smith, together with the officers of the army, and the regiment of Mounted Rifles, attended the funeral. He was from Virginia, and I am told the last remaining member of his family. A more gallant soldier or estimable gentleman could not be found. He was beloved while living, and mourned by a large number of intimate acquaintances and friends.

Gen. Rómulo La Vega, who refused his liberty on his parole, is now in this place on his route to Peroté, where he will probably remain. He was in bad health in the Castle of San Juan de Ulua, and has permission from Col. Henry Wilson, at Vera Cruz, to report himself at Peroté, where he will remain until discharged or exchanged.[8]

8. Henry Wilson joined the army in 1813 as an ensign and rose through the ranks to become lieutenant colonel of the 1st Infantry in 1842. He received a brevet to colonel for his actions around Monterrey with General Taylor's army in 1846 and became military governor for Vera Cruz. Wilson was colonel of the 7th Infantry when he resigned in 1861 during the Secession crisis. It was said that all of his sons were in the Confederate service. Wilson died February 21, 1872. *Chicago Tribune*, February 29, 1872; Heitman, *Historical Register* 1: 1046.

May 18, 1847. 11 O'clock.

Information has been received, which I think can be relied on, that Maj. John P. Gaines, Capt. Cassius M. Clay, and others, were in the City of Mexico, on the 8th inst., on verbal parole. They had been confined in the prison of the convicts, and were at liberty only a few days. They intended to return again to the prison, although it was a most loathsome and objectionable place of confinement, unless the authorities would give them a written safeguard, that would protect them against the treachery of the people and the government.

May 20, 1847.

Yesterday we had an exhibition of the punishment of four American soldiers on the plaza. Three of them had been convicted of burglary, and one of horse stealing, by a military court. The penalty affixed by the court was, that each should receive thirty-nine lashes on the bare back, forfeit all pay due to the Mexican until he was indemnified, and the balance to revert to the government, to have their heads shaved, and be marched through the town of Jalapa to the tune of the "Rogue's March," with the word "robber," in large letters on their backs, and be imprisoned at hard labor in the Castle of Perоté, during the war with Mexico. The lashing was inflicted yesterday, and the marching through the town to-day. The plaza was crowded with lookers-on, and the men followed through the streets by hundreds of the Mexican rabble, who seemed to take great delight in the suffering of the American soldiers. While the whipping was being inflicted, the different ones writhed under the lash, and water had to be given one to prevent him from fainting. The first sergeant that was called upon to use the lash was imprisoned, because he did not apply strength enough to lacerate the back of the American soldier, in the eyes of hundreds of the gaping Mexican rabble. In the states of the Union, men are confined in prisons, and in some of them they are even whipped, but I doubt if any of our good people at home have ever thought if necessary to whip, shave the head, and drum through the streets, and then confine in a prison like the Castle of Peroté, at hard labor, for an indefinite period. How would it do to adopt the method of killing people and then hanging them? Two Mexicans were arrested for similar offences, but have been turned over to the *alcalde*. They will not doubt be tried—if found guilty, probably receive some slight punishment. Still, we profess to govern the town.

Dogs and watchmen which are to be found in such large numbers in the Mexican cities, and which are about the greatest nuisance encountered, we are comparatively rid of in this place. The barking of the one, and the crying the hour of the other, allows but little time to sleep—especially when we have to take in a small sprinkling of fleas by way of necessity. I do not know how to account for the scarcity of dogs, unless it is as the boy once told his father, that "when sassengers was plenty, dogs was scarce." The watchmen are prohibited from calling the time of night every half hour, which serves no other purpose than to prevent us "paying proper attention to sleeping." In most of the towns, each watchman carries a large lantern in one hand, and a lance in the other—one-third of his time at least is occupied in crying the hour—one-third in resting himself on the curb-stone at the corners of the street—one-sixth in preparing to move—so that he has about one-sixth of the night to walk his beat, with his lantern in his hand, which lights up the street as he moves along, and gives all thieves notice of his approach.

May 21, 1847. Jalapa.

We have positive information of the arrival of Gen. Worth's command at Puebla. On the approach of our army to the city, Gen. Santa Anna, who was there at the time supplying his troops with some necessaries, sent out a detachment to engage Gen. Worth until he could procure his supplies, but the encounter was soon over, and Santa Anna and his army compelled to fly. In the skirmish there were four Mexicans killed—our loss none. He has retreated towards the City of Mexico. One report says he is at Santa Martin, a town about twenty-eight miles from Puebla, but it is generally conceded that his main force, upwards of 12,000 men, have gone to Rio Frio, where he is preparing for another engagement. The latter place is said to be a naturally strong point, and can be made to offer strong resistance, but if Cerro Gordo could not resist the brigade of Gen. Twiggs, what can position avail the Mexican chieftain?

The train looked for the past few days has arrived, together with Capts. Samuel H. Walker and Charles F. Ruff with their commands.

The army here will move four miles on the Perotè road to-morrow evening, and on Sunday take up its line of march. No stop will be made at Perotè. If we should not halt at Puebla, to hear the result of some more propositions of peace from the American Government, you may soon expect to receive my letters dated at the capital of the Republic.

May 21, 1847. 11½ O'clock. Jalapa.

The "Diligence" is about leaving—I will write to give you the latest up to departure. The Mexicans have a report here, which is credited by the Americans generally, that José Herrera is elected President of Mexico, and that he is disposed to treat for peace.[9] The "Diligence" from Puebla is looked for momentarily, which will give us the correct position of affairs at the capital. If it should arrive in time to overtake the line towards Vera Cruz, I will send an express to overhaul it. The reason assigned by the Mexicans for Herrera being willing to make peace with us is that he desires to prevent our taking possession of the capital of the Republic, which he says will be the inevitable result if the Mexicans do not come to terms. Shall we be delayed by soothing promises and friendly professions, or shall we march on, conquering and to conquer? I hope the word will be "Onward!" and not wait until they have placed the capital in a proper state of defence, and then bid us to lose many gallant officers and soldiers. Herrera, no doubt, is favorably disposed, but can he control the factions? Once in possession of the City of Mexico we can treat on what terms we please.

The army is under marching orders for to-morrow evening at 3 o'clock. Gen. Twiggs' column will move at that hour, if no unforeseen circumstances intervene. Nothing further from Gens. Worth and Quitman, except that they are resting, from the fatigue of the march to Puebla.

9. A Spanish officer who fought against Mexican independence, Jóse Herrera switched sides and rose to the rank of general of brigade. For twenty years he held various military and political positions, eventually reaching the office of president late in 1844. Forced out of office a year later, he remained active in politics, sharing the presidency briefly in 1847 and filling that office by himself from 1848 to 1851. An attempt to make the Mexican army more professional during his last administration failed because of lack of funds. Herrera died on February 10, 1854. Tucker, *Encyclopedia*, 299–300.

Gen. Shields had an attack of pleurisy two nights ago, but is recovering from the effects of it, and also his wound. He expects to be able to leave for the United States about the 10th of next month.

Capt. Walker is encamped with his recruits close by the town. It was generally supposed he would be arrested for the course he pursued in reference to a guerrilla party he came in contact with. But I understand his course is approved of. The *Alcade* of Santa Fe, who had been harboring the banditti, and in whose possession the property and clothing of the murdered dragoons were found, had to share the same fate as those who committed the murder. Served him right.

May 21, 1847. 12 O'clock. Jalapa.

The "Diligence" has arrived from Puebla, but nothing official had arrived from the capital previous to its departure. The passengers state that it was current at that place that Herrera had been elected president. I received a letter from Puebla, of which the following is an extract:

> "We entered this place on the 15th inst. The natives, although quiet yet, have stabbed several of the men, and have killed two. We were attacked in Amasoca by Santa Anna, with about 1,500 cavalry—he lost three killed and seven wounded. The old codger took a fit of leaving for Mexico, where he is fortifying the Peñol and Ayotla."

I have seen another letter, from an intelligent source, to a gentleman in this place, which says that Santa Anna retreated from Puebla to San Martin, and subsequently left for the City of Mexico, also that we are to be met on the road, somewhere, with 10,000 men, under one general, whose name I do not recollect, and 4,000 under Gen. José Miñon. So more it be—the more the better. No doubt by the time we meet them, their force will be augmented to double the number. We also learn that murders and robberies are being committed on the road daily, both by horsemen and footmen. The sources of information can be relied on.

May 23, 1847. Jalapa.

The army moved out three miles last evening, and this morning Gen. Twiggs moved with his column for Peroté and Puebla. Gen. Scott did not leave town until this morning, also the commissary and quartermaster departments.

Since my last, we have received positive intelligence that Santa Anna has left San Martin. The spies dogged his steps almost to the City of Mexico, whither he has gone. The Mexicans at Puebla state that the Mexican general has gone to the city with the view of raising men and supplies for the purpose of driving our troops out of Puebla, before Gen. Scott and Gen. Twiggs will arrive with the additional troops. This the Mexicans will find much easier talked of than done.

The news from Puebla states that there is no doubt of the election of Herrera for president, and that there was a very strong expression of public opinion against Santa Anna; that a *pronunciamiento* had been, or was about to be issued, declaring against him. Another revolution in public affairs was daily looked for—guns had been fired, which was considered the signal of an event about to transpire.

The stage was robbed, on the 20th, between Perotė and Puebla—no Americans in it.

An abundance of supplies have been found at Puebla, and the inhabitants are disposed to supply our troops with whatever necessaries they have, but have been prevented by the guerrillas from bringing them in. A large mounted force is highly necessary at this time, to keep these fellows in check, and prevent them from interfering with the inhabitants, who are anxious to sell us their products.

There is a prevailing opinion that we will have another battle before reaching the capital. In case we should meet the enemy after leaving Puebla, it will no doubt be a bloody and sanguinary one. The Mexicans will not meet us without an overwhelming force, while ours will not exceed 5,000 troops, if indeed it reaches that many—the calculations of the Adjutant General to the contrary notwithstanding—the books here will not show more. But three-fourths of the battle is fought before it is begun; our troops do not believe they can be whipped by any number; they go into battle as a regular every-day affair, confident of success, without excitement or doubt of the result. They go into action with energy and pride, every man believing that the honor and glory of the country rests on his own particular shoulders; while, with the Mexicans, it is just the reverse; they are enthusiastic and vociferous until they become pressed by our brave troops, when they cease all their clamor and turn their backs, as if any further resistance were useless.

Mr. Trist continues on with the army. I do not believe he has yet entered upon the discharge of the diplomatic functions with which he is charged by the government. Whether Gen. Scott is to carry the sword, and Mr. Trist the olive branch—or whether Gen. Scott is to carry both—is a subject for further consideration, and a fruitful theme for newspaper editors. "Sands form the mountain, minutes make the year."

The court martial, which has been sitting for several days trying the case of Capt. Ker, of the Dragoons, has honorably acquitted him of all the charges and specifications brought against him, and he has returned to duty.

Gen. P. F. Smith has so far recovered, as to be able to march with the column last evening.

In the course of a few minutes, necessity compels me with regret, to bid adieu to the quiet and peaceable city of Jalapa and its vicinity—to its green and verdant fields—its grand scenery—its blooming flowers and delicious fruits—its transparent and invigorating air and refreshing showers—its good living and handsome women. To-night, I expect, with good luck, to be in Perotć, from whence you will hear from me.

June 1, 1847. Puebla.

In my last I gave you a rather lengthy and detailed sketch of the city of Puebla and our march, but, having reason to suppose it will never reach you, I will give you a brief notice, hoping it may be more fortunate than the last.

After crossing the mountains which separate the valley of Jalapa from that of Perotć, the road to this place is generally level, taking a rather circuitous route through the valley, avoiding on either side the high and almost perpendicular mountains. During the whole of the march, we were never out of sight of the snow-capped peaks. The first night after we left Jalapa we encamped at a little village called Las Vegas, where we found the inhabitants in the enjoyment of *connubial happiness* in a high degree; the men were all drunk, and the women either quarreling and fighting or caressing and admonishing their lords, who seemed to look upon the attentions and interest manifested by their better halves as a matter of course, and therefore paid but little respect to their fighting or friendship. We at first induced them to believe that there were but ten or twelve of us who intended to stop there for the night, when they gathered around us, each fellow examining which was the best horse, equipments, &c., with as much nonchalance as if our nags and ourselves already belonged to them, but as soon as Col. Harney came in sight with his dragoons, they all suddenly vanished like spectres—we know not whither. I never before suffered so much with cold as I did at this place. We built up large fires, burrowed ourselves in straw, and brought all the blankets we could muster into requisition, but to no effect—we were compelled to shiver and shake all night.

As soon as we got down into the plain, the weather again became warm and pleasant, and about 12 o'clock we entered Perotè, the castle of which bears the date of 1711, and which is noted for containing during a long confinement many prisoners of rank and distinction—among others, those from Texas, whose names are written upon the walls. The castle is said by our officers who examined it to be a larger and much stronger work than the Fort

Dragoons in Action. *Courtesy Library of Congress.*

of San Juan de Ulua. It is capable of garrisoning an army of 20,000 men, with a due proportion of cavalry and field artillery.

The town of Peroté is one of the meanest and dirtiest looking places I have ever seen. The people have villainy and degradation stamped upon their countenances, and their conduct does not belie their looks.

Immediately about the town of Peroté the land is rich and well cultivated. I saw some fields that contained at least 1,000 acres, containing either wheat, barley, corn, or Mexican peas. After we left Peroté about five miles, the land became thin and poor for a distance of about fifteen or twenty miles, when the valley again resumed its fertile and cultivated appearance, which it continues up to this place. Numerous villages, containing from 500 to 3,000 inhabitants, and from two to ten churches, are built up along the road and along the base of the mountains. I counted as many as eleven in sight at one time. All the churches, even in the smallest villages, are large, well built, and finely finished—some of them being 250 years old.

On the 29th, Gen. Scott, escorted by Col. Harney's column (mounted men) arrived in this city. On our approach, we looked in vain to see the emblem of the United States—the Stars and Stripes—floating over the surrendered city of Puebla, and its fortifications. Had it not been for due notice, therefore, we would not have known what force was in possession of the city, as Gen. Scott had been apprised by Gen. Worth that the train would likely be attacked that day by about 3,000 cavalry. On the following day, the long roll was again beat at the head-quarters of Gen. Worth. Gen. Twiggs, who was on his march with his division, was notified that there was a force of some 20,000 Mexicans in the vicinity of Puebla, and that the city would likely be attacked during the night. The sturdy veteran and his division, not being accustomed to false alarms and *stampedes*, marched the balance of the road in quick time, in hopes to be able to participate in the desperate conflict they thought was about to take place, but to their surprise found the town, on their arrival, as quiet as it could be under the circumstances—with the streets filled with "greasers" and "greaseresses," and the balconies with the private families, all anxious to behold the entré of the 4,000 troops and the large supply train. The division of Gen. Twiggs did not appear pleased at the false alarm, as they had a vivid recollection of a long, unnecessary march last winter to Saltillo.

It is really remarkable what a vast difference there is between the general officers of our army in acquiring information in reference to the position of the enemy. Gen. Worth, previous to the arrival of Gen. Scott, could receive information almost every day that the enemy was within a short distance, with a very large force, and would probably attack him forthwith; but since Gen. Scott has arrived, he has not been able to learn that the enemy has been near him, or that they ever have been this side of the Piñon since they passed it, after their departure from this place.

On the march up here, I was very much amused at the remark of an officer in reference to the "health of the country," while we were all sitting around and enjoying a very pleasant meal. The gentleman alluded to was "doing his best" on the runner of a regular old Chapman. After pulling and tugging at it for some time, he very unceremoniously laid it down and remarked that he had heard it frequently stated that this was a very healthy country, and he fully believed it—for he had tried beef, mutton, and fowl, and had found that they all lived a very long time.

June 5, 1847. Puebla.

The city of Puebla is located on the plain, and the main position of the place is nearly level—the streets a little wider than those of any Mexican towns I have seen—the style of building is nearly the same throughout the city, and taking it all through, is the best built town or city I have ever seen, and the people are the worst population with which I have ever come in contact. The streets are daily more crowded than either Chartres, Camp, or St. Charles streets, of New Orleans, and depravity, vice, and degradation are depicted in every expression of the great mass, from the infants to the aged and infirm. It seems utterly inconceivable that a population of this kind should inhabit such a beautiful and well built city. The population, I heard before my arrival, was about 30,000; from all the information I can get, I do not think it contains less than 60,000 souls. The people of this place (*los Pueblanos*) are noted throughout the whole of Mexico, for their villainy and the turbulent spirits. I am free to confess that I do not think there is as much religion, and as little morality, in any town on the continent of America, as can be found here. The mass of the people are very poor, while the rich are *very rich*—the poor are always ready to engage in crimes of every shape and hue, and prefer vice to labor for the purpose of procuring the necessary means of support.

There are upwards of 100 churches, 700 priests, and the value of the church property is a little over $148,000,000. The churches are all of a very superior order. It is impossible to convey an idea of the magnificence of the cathedral. I have heard men who have seen every public building in the United States, and many of those in foreign countries, state that they have never seen any building that would, in the least degree, compare with the elegance and gorgeousness of this building and its decorations—the large paintings, solid massive gold and gilded carved work, are all of the finest style, and are so arranged as to present the appearance of sublimity. Although there are a great number of designs and paintings, there does not appear to be too many or too few, but just enough to show well.

Like other places in this country, Puebla has its places of amusement and resort. The *Almeda* (a large public garden), with its wide walks, blooming flowers, flowing fountains, and shading trees, lies all within a permanent and neat enclosure—theatres, amphitheatre for bull-fighting, cockpits, &c., &c., to all of which the men, women, and children flock in great crowds at certain seasons of the year, for the purpose of enjoying such festivities as may "be on hand." Bull-fighting is their great national amusement, which usually takes place on Sundays and feast days, so that it may not interfere with their usual business. Church in the morning, and bull-fighting in the evening, and a *fandango* at night. Men, women, and children, of all ages and conditions, visit the arena as a usual pastime amusement. When the desperate conflict commences, they all, male and female, become excited alike, the men rewarding the victors with roars of applause, and the ladies with the waving of white handkerchiefs. A Spanish company has lately been playing here and at Jalapa, and the Battle of Palo Alto, dramatized, has had a very popular run.

The climate is a most pleasant one, the temperature varying but little between winter and summer, the nights being cool enough to make sleeping under a blanket comfortable, and the days warm enough to be agreeable, the heat not oppressive, and juleps desirable, in which we have the opportunity of indulging. Snow and ice are daily brought down from the mountains, and hawked through the streets for sale.

From the peculiar adaption of the climate and soil to the culture of all kinds of fruit, grain, and vegetables, there is one of the best supplied markets here I have ever seen, there is an abundance of all the fruits and vegetables of the northern parts of the United States, together with those of the south and West Indies. The meats and fowl are very fine, and the supply good, though, unlike our country, it is never offered for sale in the public market places, but usually kept in private store-houses in different parts of the city.

The rainy season has fairly commenced, but I cannot say it is at all unpleasant. The sun shines out fair and brilliant in the morning, and continues until about 2 o'clock, when suddenly a dark heavy cloud makes its appearance on the mountain side, and soon passes over the valley, enveloping it in darkness, and pouring out its floods of water, which completely drench the earth for about four hours, when the rain suddenly ceases. In half an hour after, the streets are as dry as if there had not been a rain for twelve months, all classes and conditions again sally out into the streets, and the city soon becomes the theatre of a motley crowd—those who can lay any claim to decency, are the more gay and lively—while vice and immorality, as if invigorated by a short respite, come out in all the gay and inviting dresses calculated to allure and deceive.

June 12, 1847. Puebla.

The present inactive state of the army at this place allows but little room for excitement, save the speculations on the present and future state of affairs at the capital and the occasional rumors of their advance, and the presence of a small body scouting in our immediate vicinity.

The Mexicans are not behind us in predicting and contemplating the result of their difficulties with the United States. Some of the natives and residents admit it is evident that the consequences of the present war will either be annexation to, or occupation by, the United States. The great majority of the inhabitants are incapable of appreciating their position under any circumstances—they run with the fox and cry with the hounds—and when Reynard falls a prey, they all assist in devouring him. The Church, by its wealth and other influences, holds a great body of the people, as it were, by the ears, and directs and governs their movements; but, notwithstanding, there are a considerable number of the inhabitants, men of education, intelligence, and some influence, who are styled "Liberalists," who have and do still oppose the influence of the Church in relation to state affairs. These men, however, have never, as yet, been able to successfully stem the tide of public favor, although some of them have held offices of much importance under the Central Government. A portion of this class now look forward, with strong hopes, for a favorable opportunity to promulgate and establish their views and principles permanently; for this reason many of them are the most clamorous in favor of continuing the war, with the hope that the army of the "Republic" may be completely destroyed, which has, heretofore, been the great obstacle in their way. However, everything depends upon the treaty the United States may make, and the mutual guarantees upon a cessation of hostilities.

There is one name that will long be remembered in this country. It is that of Mr. Joel Poinsett. All the politicians and public men attribute to him their present dissensions and difficulties. They say it was him who first sowed the seeds of democracy and propagated the principles of a liberal and free government. Since his time, the doctrines that he taught and instilled into many minds have, to a great extent, degenerated, through the blighting and corrupting influences of ambition and a thirst for public plunder; but there are some of the prominent men who have maintained to the present time their consistency and honesty of purpose, and who have taken advantage of every opportunity to carry their object into effect, but as yet unsuccessfully. If the principles taught and urged by Mr. Poinsett will be the means of regenerating, even at a remote period, this beautiful and fertile land, for which nature, it may be truly said, has left nothing undone, it will be the proudest monument that could be erected to his memory, and his name will long be remembered, not only in Mexico, but throughout the world.

The commercial business of the country is principally in the hands of foreigners, so much so that it may be said they completely control it. This portion of the population wield a strong influence indirectly. Not having any natural or native sympathies, they are controlled and actuated by their interests, and always willing to support a course of policy calculated to give prosperity to business and leave commerce untrammeled and free to take its natural course, leaving success to depend upon individual energy and industry. A liberal government is the only one they can expect to leave trade comparatively free; therefore their indirect opposition to the course public affairs have taken in this country for the last few years. The tithes and contributions extracted from the merchants through interior customs, and other imposts, eventually come out of the pockets of the consumer, but the mass of the people have not the perception to comprehend it, and the merchants are left alone to battle against the restrictions and impediments of trade. A portion of the Mexicans are now jealous of the influence of the merchants and the course they will pursue, and I think not without cause; for it is not unlikely, in the closing of our difficulties, they will materially influence the result, and as their interest is identical with the interests of the United States, the disadvantage of their exertions must be on the side of the Mexican government as it at present exists.

Among other evils attending a bad administration of government, is the state of the public domain of Mexico. They have disposed of tracts of land here and there promiscuously, without surveys, to different individuals, until it is extremely doubtful who are the rightful owners, or what portion of it particularly belongs to the government.

Our whole army is on drill every day—the troops on parade look as healthy and strong as it is possible for men to be, although we have a considerable number on the sick report, principally fever and ague, no doubt brought on by a sudden change of climate, and too frequent use of fruit.

When we look coolly at this expedition, and carefully weight our position, at first sight it looks somewhat hazardous. With a force of not over 8,000 men, all told, we are penetrating the heart of a thickly peopled country, occupying their principal coast city, two of the largest forts on the North American continent (San Juan and Peroté), two cities in the interior—one with a population of 30,000, and the other 60,000—and are now within ninety miles of the capital, which contains upwards of 200,000 human beings, within three months have fought two great and important battles, and in the course of five or six weeks will fight another still greater and more important than either of the former. But with the American army "there is no such word as *fail.*" The ability of our officers, and the discipline and bravery of our men, is a sure guarantee of success. With them, to succeed is but to attempt. Wherever the army goes, there is a newspaper published, and may it not be said literally, "we are a great people." After what has passed, the dangers they have braved, and those they know they have shortly to encounter, our army eat, drink, and sleep as though no great event had or was about to take place. Immediately after, or shortly preceding a battle, they go to church, visit the theatre, circus, bull-fights, &c., &c., with as much nonchalance as though they were living in their own quiet and peaceful homes in the United States, and it was a regular every day affair. Ask any man in the army, from the General-in-Chief down to the private, what will be the result of the next battle, and he will answer, "We'll whip them." Tell him there are 50,000 men to fight us in Mexico, and he will reply, "It makes no difference, 5,000 or 50,000, the more cannon they have, the more they have to surrender, and the more men they have, the more we will kill." With such an impression as this in the army, how can we be defeated?

The Tivoli Garden is one of the fashionable resorts for Sunday evening, and it is quite a place of amusement. Ladies and gentlemen flock there in crowds, to see and be seen, and as there is an entrance fee of 12½ cents, it makes it somewhat aristocratic, the rabble not being able to afford that amount for pleasure. Bands of music enliven the scene, and different parties resort to various amusements, according to fancy—coquetting or flirting, promenading or dancing. Billiard-rooms, ball rooms, ten-pin alleys, shooting galleries, flying horses, swings and sailing-chairs, together with fine promenade walks among beds of roses and blooming violets, and a variety of "other amusements too numerous to mention," all have their votaries, and Sunday evening and all holy days, with the Pueblans, glide away happily and joyfully on the tide of time.

The social condition of one class of the people of the place, is not to be judged by what we see of the great majority, and while I am speaking of the degradation of the community generally, I do not mean to include every individual, for there certainly is one class of people here, though few in number, comparatively, that are refined, well-bred, and highly educated. Showing their superiority

Mexican Clerks Seek Safety with Their Prized Possessions. *Courtesy Library of Congress*.

over the mass, they are vain and self-important, and despise the herds of the streets with as much contempt as an American possibly can. The wealth and style of living of this class, at once entitles them to rank and superiority (except, perhaps, when they get into the hands of the robbers), though they very much resemble the little cliques of assumed aristocracy in the towns of the interior of the Middle and Northern States of the Union, and like our people of those places, have a remarkable weakness for a large carriage and fine horses.

June 14, 1847. Puebla.

It is the general talk that we will move towards the capital in a few days, but as straws show which way the wind blows, so do circumstances show that our army cannot march before the 20th, and in all probability, not before, if even on the 1st of July. A large train left here for Jalapa on the 4th, which must return and refit before we move further on. Also, we will have to recruit and rest the troops that are on the march here, about 1,000 of which will arrive to-day.

The Mexican papers report Gen. Scott to have died at Jalapa with the dysentery, but that the Americans have revived him, by announcing his arrival at Puebla. They also state that a large majority of the army had died with this disease, and the balance refused to march any farther.

Capt. Grayson has been confined with severe illness, since his arrival, and I think it altogether probably the state of his health will compel him to return home. I start a courier to the City of Mexico to-night, he will return, if he succeeds in passing the guerrillas and robbers, in about two days, when I will forward the files to the coast by a Mexican. I am endeavoring to make such arrangement as will ensure you a package at Vera Cruz once a week, at least.

The "Dilgence Stage Line" is entirely withdrawn, on account of the road being so frequented by guerrillas and robbers.

June 14, 1847. 12 O'clock. Puebla.

The gubernatorial duties of this place have been transferred to Col. Francis S. Belton.[10]

The prospects of a movement of our troops are not materially changed since I last wrote you. Col. Childs cannot arrive here for eight days yet. After he arrives it will be necessary to stop five days, and probably ten, for the purpose of repairing wagons, shoeing horses, and making other arrangements previous to moving, therefore, it will be about the first of the month before the troops will take up a line of march for the City of Mexico. Perhaps by that time Brig. Gen. George Cadwalader, who is known here to be below with a force of at least 2,000 men, together with 2,000 more who will come at the same time, will arrive.[11] In that case there will probably

10. Francis Belton served during the War of 1812 when he was generally known as "Dashing Frank Belton" while in the Dragoons. Transferred to a different arm of the service, he rose to become lieutenant colonel of the 3[d] Artillery in 1845. Belton received a brevet to colonel for distinguished conduct at Contreras and Churubusco. Promoted to colonel in 1857, he resigned just days before his death on September 10, 1861. Heitman, *Historical Register* 1: 209; *Columbian Register*, September 21, 1861.

11. Admitted to the bar in Philadelphia, George Cadwalader found success in the insurance business and in marriage, taking for a wife the granddaughter of Pierce Butler, one of the nation's founding fathers. He was a colonel

be a strong garrison left here, but if he does not think it altogether likely, this place, like Jalapa, will be evacuated or left with a small garrison. We have troops enough to go to the City of Mexico, and sufficient means of subsistence are in the country, but we want a larger force than we have at present, if for no other purpose than of intimidating a class of wicked and evil disposed persons, who commit depredations alike upon Mexicans and Americans, at every opportunity. Moreover, there is an implied obligation on our part, though no positive agreement or understanding, to protect, against injury, those of the Mexicans who have been trading and dealing with us, and furnishing our army with supplies. Although money is their great object in supplying us, still they believe we will protect them, and it would be morally wrong, if we can avoid it, to leave them to the mercy of their suspicious and revengeful countrymen. It is true, we are paying the highest price for everything, still, I am fully convinced, there are some leeches hanging on to the army as *particular friends*, who are profiting far more than the Mexicans, who allow the Mexican the mill, while they take the dollar. No doubt these same persons will, hereafter, claim fat offices and lucrative employment from our government, in consideration of the important services rendered during the war with Mexico.

We have dates from the City of Mexico to the evening of the 11th. The all- engrossing topic at the capital is the organization of the government and the progress of the war.

The Mexican papers, *El Republicano* and others, speak of the arrival of Mr. Trist in the country, and state that he comes as a commissioner with propositions of peace. Mr. Trist is now here, of which the Mexicans at the capital are also aware, but whether he has been able to overcome the existing difficulties, and open a communication with that government, no person here is at present informed. From my observation of this gentleman, I have no doubt the first information you will receive of his movements will be from Washington City.

---

in the Pennsylvania militia by 1844 and was commissioned brigadier general of Volunteers in 1847. Taking an active though undistinguished part in the final battles of Scott's campaign, Cadwalader did receive a brevet to major general for his participation in the assault on Chapultepec. He returned to his business, served with credit during the Civil War, and died February 3, 1879. Tucker, *Encyclopedia*, 104–5.

The organization of the ministry of the Mexican government was not completed at the last advices. Señor Manuel Rejon has been named as Minister of Foreign Affairs; Señor Domingo Ibarra as Minister of Justice; Señor José Tornel as Minister of War. Two persons have been spoken of as Minister of Finance, Señors Bassedre and Manuel Baranda, the latter, it is said, held his appointment as Minister of Foreign Affairs two days and resigned, for which he has been imprisoned. He is a "liberalist" in his views, and his nomination was looked upon by many as a favorable omen of peace. Ibarra resides near this place, and is also "liberal" in his opinions. He has neither accepted nor rejected his appointment, but his friends are of opinion that he will reject it. Of Señor Rejon very little is known, but the Mexican people say he is "liberal," by which they mean that he is a republican in his opinions and in favor of a liberal government. Those men who are called "liberals" are generally considered as favorable to negotiation. The only answer that they will give in reference to Señor Tornel is, that "he loves money."

By a decree of the Mexican Congress, the present government have power to do anything except negotiate for peace. Santa Anna is left in power until January next, unless a revolution should rout him. If he succeeds in organizing a ministry that will support him, he will be able to do what he pleases—make peace or continue the war. If he does not so succeed, he will be compelled to act according to circumstances. The greatest trouble will arise from there not being in power anyone to act without violating the only legal authority of the land, and we cannot have any guarantee for the fulfillment of any stipulations to which they are willing to agree. We cannot afford to go there and whip them, take their capital, and wait a year for them to organize a government with sufficient powers to negotiate; therefore, on the score of justice to ourselves, and humanity to this benighted race of native inhabitants, we had better pursue the easiest and most practicable course, as I have no idea but that we will have to come to it eventually, which is, to take the country and say it belongs to us, organize a government suited to the condition of the people, and administer it as we conceive to be just. We have plenty of men here who are competent to act as governor, and no doubt a sufficient number could be found, without sending to the United States, who would be willing to act as councilmen.

Of the movements of the Mexican army I have the following information, which can be relied on: Gen. Juan Alvarez, from the south, at the head of 4,000 cavalry, arrived yesterday at Atalisco [Atlisco], a town about twenty miles from here.[12] His son, Col. Alvarez, will also arrive there in the course of two days with the infantry, numbering 3,000. Gen. Julián Juvera has left Mexico with 4,000 troops for Piedras Negras, situated in Llanas de Opan, north of this place about fifty miles, the balance of his command remaining at the fortifications.[13] A party of 200 men are to leave Atalisco to-day for the purpose of reconnoitering in the vicinity of Puebla, committing such depredations as they may be able, and watching the approach of the train. If the force coming to Atalisco has for its object an attack on the train, they will meet with a warm reception, as there will be about 4,000 troops accompanying it. Those gone to Piedras Negras are, no doubt, sent there in order to get them out of the City of Mexico, for the present.

The guerrillas and robbers are almost as violent enemies as the guerrillas and the Americans. A few days ago, a party of guerrillas came in contact with a body of robbers, whom they hung. Now, if the robbers would hang the first set of guerrillas they come to, it would be a sort of "Kilkenny cat business."[14]

June 17, 1847. Puebla.

I did not send my express last night, as I intended, on account of expecting some important news from the capital.

By a foreigner, who arrived last night, we learn that Santa Anna has left the City of Mexico with his force, except a small

12. A veteran of fighting for Mexican independence, Juan Alvarez spent several decades fighting against politicians who sought to consolidate power in Mexico City. A general of division since 1841, General Santa Anna tasked him with operating against General Scott's extended supply lines in 1847, but he lacked the proper troops and ability to perform this assignment. Alvarez disobeyed orders at Molino del Rey, many thinking that he sought to conserve his forces for a civil war that he foresaw. In 1854 he began a successful revolt against Santa Anna, but resigned the presidency after less than three months due to political disillusionment. Alvarez died August 21, 1867 and is now buried in the Rotunda of Illustrious Men in Mexico City. Tucker, *Encyclopedia*, 16.

13. A Spanish officer in the Mexican bid for independence, Julián Juvera, like many other royalist officers, switched sides and became a noted cavalry general of brigade. He performed with credit at Buena Vista, but his cavalry hesitated at Molino del Rey and an opportunity to attack the American flank was lost. Despite his dubious record, Juvera remained in the military, served as civilian governor, and died in 1860. Tucker, *Encyclopedia*, 332–33.

14. "Kilkenny cats" makes reference to folkloric felines, often tails tied together, dueling to death.

portion of the National Guard. This person left at the very moment Santa Anna was marching out, therefore he did not know where he was moving, or what was his object; but, from another source, I learn he is coming to the Piñon and Ayotla, where the fortifications are erected, and await our approach. The movement of Alvarez and Juvera has also somewhat further developed itself. As soon as we move upon the great general and his breastworks, Alvarez and Juvera (the former of whom is now within twenty miles, with 3,500 men, and the latter within fifty miles, with 4,000, together with 3,000 men to be raised in this valley), are to concentrate upon our rear—thus placing Gen. Scott with an enemy in front and an enemy in rear, but when our army gets to work, you may depend there will be a road opened somewhere. All the Americans have left the City of Mexico, by order of the government, also all the "principal families," with their valuable effects.

July 30, 1847. P.M. Puebla.

My cousin has just arrived from the City of Mexico, and brings me the following brief note, which I send you. The courier was four days endeavoring to get out of the city, and at last made a narrow escape.

> City of Mexico, 28th July, 1847—Friend F----- I received the files of the *Delta* and *Washington Union* you had the kindness to send me. Your courier has been endeavoring to get out of the city for four days—although he is a shrewd chap, he has been thwarted in every attempt, the vigilance is so strict—to-day he tries it, dressed as a woman, almost in rags, driving asses, which pack in charcoal, and I only send you a line or two, platted inside his whip lash. The Mexican troops are ranging as far as Venta de Cordova (twelve leagues from the city), and the guerrillas at the Puente. Congress does not meet for want of a quorum. Santa Anna, it is said, has already arranged for Mr. Trist, in reference to peace, and is now about to force Gen. [Gabriel] Valencia to accede to the terms. The population of Mexico is a continued state of alarm, brought on by proclamations, decrees, &c. The number of troops here is 26,000 men, but the general opinion at present here is, that at the first shot of the Americans, they will retire, and never after acknowledge that they wore the dress of a soldier. With the construction of fortifications and breastworks, they are continuing, but it is evident that they are not calculated to be an impediment for the advancing army—at least such a one as the American army—their ditches and obstructions on the road, will perhaps trouble you more than

> anything else, on account of your large train. The object of the Mexicans in continuing their fortifications appears to be to keep the citizens in as great a state of alarm as possible, that this is the best means to make them proclaim for peace. All the large cannon the Mexicans have been casting here, have burst on being tested. The Americans have managed affairs so well as to deceive even the general commanders of the Mexicans, as to the time of your march to this city, therefore, they cast all their cannon hollow, in order to save time, which was the cause of their bursting.
>
> Yours respectfully, -------

Our courier also brought along with him the *Diario* up to the 26th, including the 24th and 25th. He had the 27th and 28th, in which he had some meat wrapped up, but a hungry soldier availed himself of the chance of getting a lunch, and also took the papers in which it was wrapped. Of the three papers he succeeded in getting here, he passed them through the sentinels by stuffing one in each ear of the jackass he was driving, and the other tied round a sore leg. I cannot send them to you by the present course, on account of the bulk—it might be the means of his being arrested. In each number there is an article on the subject of peace. Although it does not advocate it in a decided tone, yet still it argues strongly to favor of a proper consideration of the subject, and lashes the Congress unsparingly for the course they have taken in endeavoring to avoid assuming the responsibility. It also contends that the honor of the Mexican nation, as well as the interests of the people, require that no obstacles should be thrown in the way of an unprejudiced and deliberate consideration of all matters connected with the difficulties now existing between the two countries. When it is considered that this comes from the official organ of the Mexican government and that its articles are either dictated or controlled by the government, we are influenced to think a second time before we concluded that the mission of Mr. Trist will prove entirely fruitless.

Two or three nights since, some Mexicans, who were herding some 125 mules for one of the departments, drove off the whole lot, and they have not since been heard of.

August 4, 1847. Puebla, Mexico.

The city of Puebla, the second in importance in the Republic of Mexico in point of wealth and population, is situated in one of the most interesting parts of this truly interesting country. It is within a few hours' ride of the Chalinche [Malinche], the Popocatepetl, the Iztaccihuatl, Cholula, Tlascala, all of which objects teem with the romantic and classical recollections of Hernando Cortes and the Conquests. Chohula, the most interesting of all these places, is within the short distance of six miles of the city, and is a sort of shrine, to which our officers and soldiers make frequent visits. I was one of a numerous party who visited it, the other day, and I propose to make you a participant in the pleasure I enjoyed on that occasion, by giving you a short description of our Pic-Nic. All the mornings in this elevated region, even in the rainy season, are bright and charming—the sun rises in unclouded splendor, gilding one of the most magnificent landscapes the imagination can conceive, whilst the atmosphere is so pure and elastic, that it is a positive pleasure to breathe it. On such a morning, in company with the 4th Regiment of Artillery, acting as infantry, and a squadron of Horse, we sallied from the city through the *Garita* (City Gate) of Cholula, and soon found ourselves in the extensive plain skirting the base of the volcanoes of Puebla (Popocatepetl and Iztaccihuatl).

Before us glittered in the morning's sun their snow-capped summits; on our right rose the Chalinche—the Storm Mountain—with its craggy crest partially enveloped in a wreath of mist; whilst behind us, in the far distance, rose the indistinct form of the Orizaba—that well known landmark of the seaman, that serves to guide him in calm and in storm, hundreds of miles along the Mexican coast. The nearer landscape was as soft and picturesque as its more distant features were grand and sublime. A green meadow or prairie extended around us for some miles in every direction, dotted with villas and *haciendas*, and relieved by occasional patches of cultivation, and avenues and clusters of the beautiful shade willow. Herds of cattle and horses grazed as quietly on the surrounding estates as though "grim-visaged war" had long since "smoothed his wrinkled front," and our military escort, as it wound its way over the fair landscape, with glittering arms and glancing banners, seemed more like a holy day procession, than a band of stern veterans so recently from the conflict and so soon to enter it again.

A ride of an hour and a quarter, which our horses, as they snuffed the morning breeze and scented the fresh grass of the meadows, seemed to enjoy as much as their riders, brought us to the base of the far-famed pyramid, which, independently of its historical recollection, and the great interest attached to it as a work of art, forms one of the most picturesque features of the landscape. At a short distance, it presents the appearance of a natural mound, covered with a luxuriant growth of trees and shrubbery, and is surmounted by a Gothic chapel, whose belfrey towers some eighty feet above the pyramid. A road winds round the pyramid from the base to summit, up which we passed on horseback. This road is cut into the pyramid, in some places six or eight feet, and here one sees the first evidence of the artificial construction of the latter. It is built of *adobes*, or sun-dried brick, interspersed with small fragments of stone—porphry and limestone. Its dimensions, as stated by Humboldt, are: base, 1,060, elevation, 162 feet, but its altitude is much greater.

On the day of our visit, Lieut. Raphael Semmes, of the Navy, who had provided himself with a pocket sextant and tape-line for the purpose, determined its altitude to be 205 feet. As this measurement differed so widely from that of Humboldt, Lieut. Semmes requested Lieut. Pierre G.T. Beauregard, of the Engineers, who visited the pyramid a few days afterwards, to test his observations, which Lieut. Beauregard, using a longer base, did, making the altitude 203 feet. These two observations, from different points, with different bases, and both with the sextant, show conclusively that Humboldt, who most likely used a barometer, is in error. The mean of the two is 204 feet, which we may henceforth regard as the true height of this extraordinary monument, being nearly half as great as that of the pyramid of Cheops in Egypt. The pyramid of Cholula is quadrangular in form and truncated, the area of the apex being 165 feet square. On this area formerly stood a heathen temple, now supplanted by the Gothic church of Our Lady of Loretto. The temple on this pyramid was, in the days of Cortes, a sort of Mecca, to which all the surrounding tribes, far and near, made an annual pilgrimage, held a fair, and attended the horrible human sacrifices peculiar to their superstition.

Besides this great temple, there were, as we learn from the letters of Cortes to Charles V, and also from the simple diary of his doughty old Captain, Bernal Diaz, some 400 others in the city, built around the base of the larger. The city itself contained 40,000 householders, and the whole plain was studded with populous villages. The plain is now comparatively a desert, and two or three thousand miserable *leperos* build their mud huts and practice their thievish propensities upon the site of the Holy City. It was here the famous massacre of 6,000 of the natives was perpetrated by Cortes on his way to the City of Mexico, an undoubted stain upon his character, although his apologists make a plausible story in his defence, of a contemplated rising and massacre of his forces on the part of the natives. Las Casas, who visited the country soon after the Conquest, and who had ample means of information, condemns Cortes in the most unqualified manner. Whilst on the summit of this vestige, at the same time of the semi-civilization and barbarism of by-gone generations, it was a curious and startling picture to trace, in the imagination, the shifting scenes of its history. Three hundred and twenty-eight years before, Cortes and his 500 armed Spaniards looked forth upon this plain, then a much more glorious prospect than now. Three centuries of Spanish despotism followed. Then came the bloody and turbulent scenes of the Revolution, scenes stained with treachery, murder, and rapine, followed by the short-lived despotism of Iturbide, which was succeeded, in turn, by a series of years of internal faction and discord. And now the Anglo-Saxon race looked forth *from the same spot, upon nearly the same everlasting features of nature*—but how great the moral change! Spain fallen from her high estate, her once rich colony forever lost, and a nation not dreamed of in the time of her glory, following in the footsteps of Cortes, to the Imperial City of the Aztecs!

Undated.

In my last letter, I stated to you that Gen. Smith had gone down the road to ascertain the whereabouts of Gen. Franklin Pierce and to succor him if necessary, and I also stated that if the guerrillas should fall in his road, they would be handled roughly.[15] Since then,

15. A graduate of Bowdoin College, Franklin Pierce became an attorney and prominent figure in the New Hampshire Democratic Party. After several years of service in the state legislature, he was elected to the U.S. House of Representatives and Senate, resigning the latter office to serve as his state's district attorney. Refusing the office of US Attorney General, Pierce instead accepted a commission as brigadier general of Volunteers in 1847. He commanded a brigade but

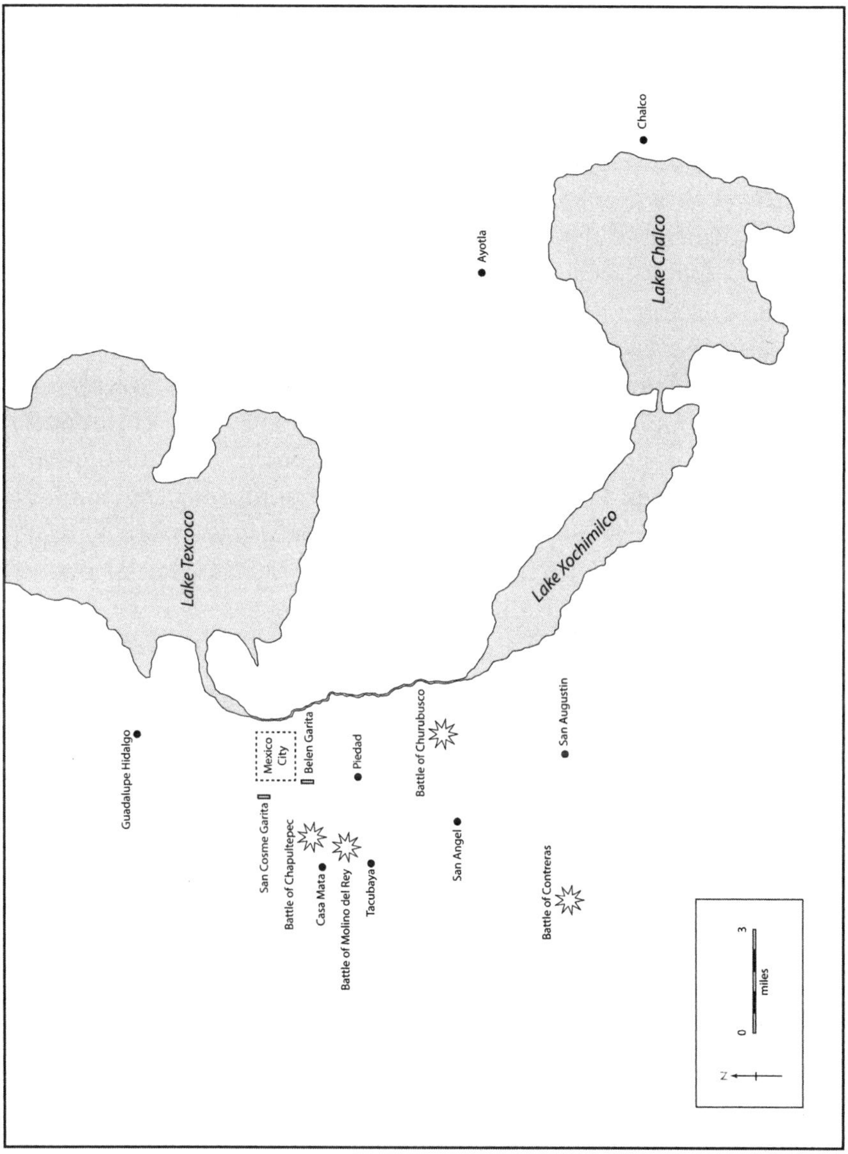

Mexico City and Vicinity.

the command has returned and you will see by the following short account of his operation, that I was not mistaken, and although they did not have any general engagement, I think they taught the guerrillas a lesson which will be remembered some time, and for a small affair, I think it was one of the most brilliant of the season.

On Monday night, July 26, it was reported, on apparently good authority, that a force of several thousand men, with a convoy of 600 mules, loaded with ammunition, was at Piedras Negras, destined to operate against Gen. Pierce, who was reported to be coming by the way of Orizaba. The next morning, Gen. Smith, with his brigade and a squadron of Horse, under Capt. Ruff of the Mounted Riflemen, a battery of four pieces, under Lieut. Henry J. Hunt, and the New York Volunteers, under Col. Ward B. Burnett, marched to meet and sustain Gen. Pierce, carrying with them a supply of provisions for the latter.[16] Finding on the route that it was very probable Gen. Pierce was on the Jalapa road, the command marched to Ojo de Agua. Having intelligence, by intercepted letters, that a large band of *guerrilleros* were at San Juan de los Llanos, fifteen miles off, on the night of the 29th scouts were sent in that direction, who reported that they had heard the regular bugle calls sounded by troops in the town.

Capt. Ruff was immediately despatched with his squadron, composed of one company of the 2d Dragoons, under Lieut. James M. Hawes, and his own company of Mouted Riflemen, in all eighty-six men, to attack the town. He found about fifty cavalry drawn up in front of the town, who retired into it on his approach. Capt. Ruff then divided his command into three parts and entered the town cautiously, finding the stone houses in the centre of the place and the principal churches filled with armed men. Lieut. Hawes was

---

illness and an injury sustained after being thrown from his horse kept him from seeing much action. One of the few general officers to emerge from the war with his reputation enhanced, Pierce was elected president in 1852 and died largely forgotten on October 8, 1869. Tucker, *Encyclopedia*, 507.

16. A graduate of West Point in 1832, Ward Burnett resigned after four years to begin a career as a civil engineer. Commissioned colonel of the 1st New York Volunteers, he led his regiment from Vera Cruz to Churubusco where he was severely wounded in the leg. An attack of lockjaw that lasted three weeks brought the colonel close to death. After being mustered out in 1848, Burnett worked at the Philadelphia and Brooklyn navy yards before resuming his engineering career. He died on June 24, 1884. Heitman, *Historical Register* 1: 264; *New York Herald*, June 25, 1884; *New York Commercial Advertiser*, November 1, 1847.

first fired upon, and dismounting and forming his men on foot and being joined by Lieut. John G. Walker, Mounted Rifles, they returned the fire, and the other party advancing at the same time, they drove the enemy, with great slaughter, from house to house, to the plaza in the centre. The fire of the Riflemen was astonishingly destructive. Here, two of the principal houses, one of them loop-holed, were defended with obstinacy, but carried, and a party was organized to assault the church, from the towers of which a smart fire was kept up. But as the storming party started, a white flag was hung out from the church and the contest ceased. Those of the enemy who were not killed, or badly wounded, escaped through the thick and intricate hedges, as the force of Capt. Ruff was not sufficient to surround the town, which contains 6,000 inhabitants. Forty-three of the enemy were counted dead and many were seen wounded. Only one of ours was hurt, a private of the Mounted Rifle-men, badly wounded in the neck near the ear. The two houses, from which the fire was most obstinate, were burnt. A large quantity of public clothing and many arms were destroyed, after the men had taken of the former what they needed. During the hottest of the contest, the utmost kindness was displayed by our men towards the women and children, exposing themselves to the enemy's fire to place these helpless and frightened creatures in security.

Sometime after Capt. Ruff's departure from Ojo de Agua, the Mounted Rifle Regiment, and a piece of artillery, were sent in the same direction to support him, if necessary, but he met them half way on his return. Capt. Ruff met the highest approbation for his spirit and skill in that affair, and he speaks in great praise of his officers, Lieuts. Walker and Hawes, and gives most special commendation to Sergt. Murphill, orderly sergeant of the company of Mounted Riflemen. The next day the squadron was sent to Peroté, to communicate with Gen. Pierce, the New York Regiment being advanced to Vireges, to cover the road, and a command under Col. Childs directed towards Huamantla, about fifteen miles N.W., to take any party that might be there. But the lesson given them at Los Llanos had been sufficient and in Haumantla the reception of our troops more resembled those we read of as given in the United States to our returned volunteers. In the meantime, a train of wagons had come down to load with forage, at a *hacienda* near Nopalucan, and Capt. Ruff having returned from Peroté, bringing one of Gen. Pierce's staff, the whole command reassembled on the 3[d] of August, at El Pinal, and on to-day returned to Puebla, with its convoy, preceding Gen. Pierce by a day's march, and having seen or heard nothing of the large force said to be marching round by the northward.

August 8, 1847. Puebla.

The long-unanswered question of "when will we march," can now be answered to a certainty. The lofty peaks of the road-side mountains, skirted with Mexican soldiers, which in many instances lift up their towering heads on our path to the capital—the glittering bayonets—the howling of the cannon, as they send their terrible missiles of death hurling through the air—the wading of the ditches against well-lined walls of bristling arms—can all now be seen in the perspective on the road to the goal of our ambition, but it requires no very great stretch of the imagination to carry the vision into the Halls of the Montezumas. For the last two days, all eyes were bright and faces glad with joy at the prospect now before us. The following orders of march have been issued, and all are in a state of preparation to comply with them, and while I am writing, I hear the drums and fifes and see the waving Eagles of the "Cerro Gordo Division," as they are passing out of town on their line of march. The old chief (Gen. Twiggs) looks like a host within himself, his long gray beard and hearty bluff face appear beaming with pride and anxiety for his gallant command, which is no less formidable than it looks, added to the best and hardest set of men I ever saw, are the following, among other able and gallant officers who have already distinguished themselves: Gen. P.F. Smith, Cols. Harney, Riley, &c. What can be expected from such a command? Victory and success in all their undertakings.

To-morrow Gen. Scott leaves with his escort and Gen. Quitman's division follows him the same day, the next day, Gen. Worth, and then Gen. Pillow, which concludes our marching array.

As I leave this morning, I have not time to write you much of a letter, but will say that you will hear from me at the Rio Frio and any other place at which we should become engaged on the road.

I just learn from a gentleman who came up with Gen. Pierce, that some person from your office was captured by the enemy at Jalapa. I could not learn his name, but am told by a person that he succeeded in communicating a letter to a friend, in which he stated that he was in no personal danger.

August 13, 1847. In Camp.

By this you are informed of the long-expected news, the arrival of the American army in front of the capital of Mexico and its defences.

The "Cerro Gordo Division," Gen. Twiggs, with Col. Harney's brigade of cavalry, left Puebla on Saturday, the 7th, and arrived here on Wednesday, the 11th. Gen. Quitman's division left on Sunday, and arrived on the 12th; Gen. Worth's on Monday, and arrived yesterday; and Gen. Pillow's, the last, on Tuesday, and is expected to arrive this evening. Neither of the two former divisions met with any obstacles on the road, further than those incident to a march, but I learn Gen. Worth had a "scare up" at San Martin, but I am not fully apprised of the circumstances, if such was the case. At all events, if there was an alarm, it was like all its predecessors, originating from nothing and terminating in nothing.

The division I came with had a very pleasant and agreeable march, without any rain or bad weather to seriously inconvenience or affect the health of the troops, and that portion of the army, which I have seen arrive, are in as fine health and condition as I have ever seen them.

We are now encamped about five miles from El Peñon, Gen. Quitman in our rear, and Gen. Worth at Chalco, a short distance to the left, where Gen. Pillow will join him as soon as he arrives.

On our arrival at a *hacienda* called "*Buena Vista*," about eight miles in the rear of where we are at present, a body of cavalry, of the guerrilla breed, made their appearance in the road, brandished their lances, and waved hats, apparently challenging a fight. Col. Harney watched their movements for a short time with a spy-glass, in order to ascertain their number and position. They figured, or rather *cyphered* about in the road, as though they were ready to eat up everything alive that might come in their way. Therefore Col. Harney sent Maj. Edwin V. Sumner down the road with three companies, Capts. Ker, William J. Hardee, and George A.H. Blake—as he said, "to teach them a lesson," and soon after followed with the balance of his command present, consisting of Capts. Henry H. Sibley's, Seth B. Thornton's, Ruff's, and C. Roberdeau Wheat's companies. As the Mexicans had chased one or two of our men, who were on fine horses, and found they were unable to catch them, they placed several small parties in ambush along the road, in the hopes of being able to intercept them. In this attempt of the enemy, his wiliness proved unavailing, as some of the amateurs dashed into the corn-fields, and so hurried those who had ambuscaded themselves, as to make them take the trenches on foot and leave their horses behind.

The main force of the enemy formed in the road, and waited until we came within about 600 yards of them, brandishing their lances and yelling as if to intimidate us, but yelling is the last thing they should attempt, for our men can make an Indian ashamed of himself any time when they commence halloing in battle. As soon as Maj. Sumner started at a canter, the cowardly rascals dispersed to every direction, apparently each man flying for his own safety; leaving the dragoons much disappointed. Officers and men confidently expected they would offer a determined resistance, and I never saw a body of troops more anxious or in higher glee. Every man appeared to be inspired with the fiery spirit of their commander.

On the following day, a party again showed themselves, but as soon as a company started after them they dispersed through the mountains. In chasing this party over a broken and rocky piece of ground, the horse of Mr. Robert Hood, of Columbus, Ga., fell with him and instantly killed him.

On the 12th, Capts. Robert E. Lee and James L. Mason, and Lieut. Isaac I. Stevens, of the Engineers, escorted by Capts. Thornton's and Sibley's companies of dragoons, two pieces of Capt. Taylor's battery, and the 4th Artillery, went out to take a look at El Peñon. It is certainly a very formidable looking place, and in the opinion of many, much stronger than the Castle of San Juan de Ulua. I should take it to be about 400 or 500 feet to the highest point, with two or three connecting ridges ranging from 100 to 250 feet from the base; each of these are strongly fortified with heavy batteries. Before reaching the batteries, there is a breastwork all round the hill, and at its base there is a deep ditch about twelve feet wide and about four feet deep, with a soft bottom (all of which is surrounded by the low grounds, which are from 200 yards to a mile wide). The only way in which it can well be approached from this side, is by the causeway, across which there is a fortification with three guns in it, completely raking the road for at least two miles, and the whole commanded by the guns on El Peñon. The fact is, the Mexicans make very good fortifications, and no doubt would whip us very badly if we would walk into the traps they set for us, but unfortunately for them, we always select our own time and our own modes of attack.

To-day the whole Corps of Engineers was out reconnoitering, supported by Gen. Smith's brigade, with Capt. Taylor's battery, and two companies of dragoons. As soon as the reconnoissance is completed, the city and its defences will be attacked, and as the army came here to carry it, they will do so. There are many other items of interest which I would like to communicate to you, but am prevented by the fear that my letter might fall into the hands of the enemy.

August 14, 1847. Saturday. In Camp.

This evening Gen. Quitman's division moved up in the vicinity of Gen. Twiggs' camp, and Gen. Pillow, who arrived at Buena Vista, a short distance in our rear, last night, will occupy the ground Gen. Quitman leaves. Gen. Worth is at Chalco, about a league to the left of the road, where he will probably remain until the reconnoissance is completed, when his position will be assigned him. From present appearances, there will be enough for all our ambitious and aspiring soldiers to do in the capture of the city and the fortifications protecting it.

Yesterday a detachment of dragoons, under the command of Lieut. George J. Adde, were sent to escort Lieut. Schuyler Hamilton, of the General Staff, to a small place called Mileflores, whither Lieut. Hamilton had been despatched by Gen. Scott on matters of business. The command of dragoons consisted of about thirty of Capt. Alphonse M. Duperu's company, and thirteen of Capt. Kearny's company, with Lieut. Lorimer Graham. As the party was returning, they were fired on by a party of guerrillas, about 200 in number, from a corn-field on the road-side. At the first fire, the word "retreat" passed from front to rear, and the 3d Dragoons, who were under the command of Lieut. Adde, commenced a precipitate retreat. Lieut. Graham with his thirteen men were in the rear, and as soon as he saw the situation of Lieut. Hamilton, rushed to his assistance, at the same time endeavoring to rally the 3d Dragoons as they passed him, but without effect. He therefore had to bear the brunt of the engagement at the commencement, or leave Lieut. Hamilton to the mercy of the guerrillas. However, his small command stood their ground, and succeeded in holding the enemy in check until Mr. Garcia, one of Gen. Scott's interpreters, was enabled to rally the 3ᵈ Dragoons and come to his assistance. After those who had been brought back were properly commanded, they fought with as much gallantry as those who never moved an inch, thus proving that good officers are as necessary as good men. The engagement lasted for some time, and the fire from the enemy was very rapid. Lieut. Hamilton was attacked by several lancers, and before assistance could be rendered him, he received a severe wound. The enemy was finally driven from the ground, with a loss of sixteen killed left upon the field. Our loss is, Lieut. Hamilton, of the 1st Dragoons, wounded; two of the 3d Dragoons killed; and two Mexicans, who were with the command as guides, wounded. The 1st Dragoons also had two very fine horses killed. Had the command been properly managed from the start, no serious damage would have been sustained by our troops and the enemy been severely dealt with.

Lieut. Adde is under arrest for cowardice and dishonorable conduct in the face of the enemy. The charge and penalty are very severe and will be properly investigated.[17]

17. The *Delta* was happy to set the record straight about this affair, remarking that "our correspondent only stated the truth in regard to the arrest of Adde" and made no decision regarding his guilt or innocence. Writing under date of September 3, 1847, Captain Alphonse Duperu gave a completely different account of the engagement: "Several days ago I received an order to send a Lieutenant and twenty men to escort Lieut. Hamilton, detached upon a mission, who was accompanied by 2d Lieut. Graham, with twelve men of the 1st Dragoons, to which he belonged. About eight miles from camp, they met some 160 Lancers. Adde retired about twenty paces to a road which led to a corn-field, there to take his position. At that place he gave battle to the Lancers and charged them with his twenty men, and Lieut. Graham did not move. The Mexicans were put to flight with the loss of eight men. I lost two, Deduve and Delsoles, who were killed. I also had five horses killed. Lieut. Hamilton was so severely wounded that he was believed to be dead. Graham, profiting by this for his own advantage, went to Gen. Scott and declared that Adde was a coward, and had fled with his men. After the most diligent search, Lieut. Hamilton was found who, seriously wounded as he was, declared to all the officers of the army, that not only had Graham lied, but that Adde had covered himself with glory, and that he had seen him twice charge the Lancers with success." A careful examination of the facts in this case exonerated Lieut. Adde of the charges of cowardice and unofficerlike conduct that had been lodged against him. *Daily Delta*, October 1, 1847.

Chapter 3

Battles for Mexico City

August 21, 1847. San Angel.

I now have the pleasure of communicating the gratifying intelligence, that during the previous twenty-four hours our army has achieved two of the greatest and most brilliant victories, against large odds and under the most serious disadvantages. "We have met the enemy and they are ours,"—but in acquiring what we have gained, we have yielded up some of the proud spirits of our gallant little army, and those who have survived the clash of arms, are prevented from rejoicing over the glorious achievements of our national arms, by the grief consequent upon the sudden loss of their gallant and highly estimable compatriots. Never since the world began, have there been exhibited in one day so many individual instances of heroic courage, indomitable valor, and determination in overcoming great and apparently insurmountable obstacles. From one end of the army to the other, there prevailed but one feeling and one resolve, and that was victory or death. Our officers set noble examples to their men, which were imitated with as much cool determination as they were set. There was no faltering, no holding back, and there is no corps or command but acquitted itself with honor to themselves and credit to the country.

The Regulars added new laurels to those already acquired, and the Volunteers have given a repetition of the noble bearing of their countrymen on the bloody field of Buena Vista. South Carolina chivalry, and the sons of the Empire State, have inscribed their names on the roll of fame, and will return home bright ornaments to the states from whence they came.

The Mexicans also fought as they never fought before. They strongly resisted us at every point, and contested every inch with the strongest determination and even to desperation. They knew that their capital and their all depended upon the issue, and with this knowledge and thus prompted, they threw themselves into the breach as no person ever expected they would, and one of the best evidences of this is the number of killed and wounded on both sides. Our loss will amount to near 700 killed and wounded, that of the enemy at least 2,000.

Gen. Scott, at the head of our army during the engagement, received a slight wound in the leg, and what is very remarkable, no person whatever except himself was aware of it until after the battle was over. A great deal has been said and written in reference to the ability of Gen. Scott as a military man, but those who have not

Battle of Churubusco. *Courtesy Library of Congress*.

seen him in command and under fire, cannot form any just conception of his abilities. His cool consideration of everything around him—his quick perception—his firm resolves and immediate execution—equal if they do not surpass those of any of the great generals whose deeds have been made so conspicuous in history.

In this engagement with the fortification of Churubusco, Gens. Pillow, Twiggs, Worth, Smith, Shields, Pierce, and Cadwalader, and Cols. Riley, John Garland, and Newman S. Clarke, all bore prominent parts.[1] The charges and insinuations in reference to Gen. Pillow, on a former occasion, are all knocked back into the face of those who perpetrated them, by his gallant and able conduct throughout the whole of this engagement. I am fully convinced that all honorable men, who have been in any way connected with the malicious representations, if they could have seen him wading through mud and mire, corn-fields and swamps, leading and directing his division to the proper point of attack, amidst the storm of bullets, they would willingly retract every word they have said, and withdraw themselves from any connection with the person or persons who were instrumental in originating them.

After the works at Churubusco had been carried by storm, the dragoons, under their valiant leader, Col. Harney, were ordered forward to pursue the retreating foe, and onward they went, like winged messengers of death, their bright sabres glittering in the sunbeams, amidst the huzza of the light troops, flushed with the victory over the fort. The horses seemed to partake of the enthusiasm of their riders, and dashed forward with supernatural strength.

1. John Garland entered the army in 1813 and rose to become lieutenant colonel of the 4th Infantry in 1839. A veteran of the Florida wars, he served under General Taylor at Palo Alto, Resaca de la Palma, and Monterrey. Garland received a brevet to colonel for this campign and another to brigader general for the battles of Contreras and Churubusco while under General Scott. Seriously wounded during the storming of Mexico City, he never fully recovered. Promoted colonel in 1849, Garland died on June 5, 1861. Heitman, *Historical Register* 1: 447; *New York Herald*, June 8, 1861; *Washington Evening Star*, June 8, 1861.

Newman Clarke entered the army as an ensign in the War of 1812 when he received a brevet to captain and had advanced to become colonel of the 6th Infantry by 1846. Awarded a brevet to brigadier general for his services during the siege of Vera Cruz, Clarke would eventually command the Department of California prior to the Civil War. He died while holding this position on October 17, 1860. Heitman, *Historical Register* 1: 307; *Washington Evening Star*, November 5, 1860.

In this spirit and state of feeling, they overtook the retreating army, and continued to cut them down to the very gates of the city, when the enemy, in his fortifications at the city, seeing that the cavalry would inevitably run in behind his breastworks unless something desperate was done, opened his batteries with grape and round-shot, through the masses of his own retreating soldiers. As soon as Col. Harney perceived the exposure of his command, he had the recall sounded and the dragoons ordered back, but they did not hear it in time enough to save the whole command, and some gallant officers were wounded: Capt. Kearny lost an arm, Lieut. Graham, Lieut. Andrew T. McReynolds and a sergeant were killed, and two or three privates wounded.

As soon as the dragoons returned, the whole army went into camp, resting from the labors of two of the hardest and most glorious days work they have ever done, during the greater part of which they were exposed to heavy rains and severe weather, without shelter or blankets.

August 26, 1847. Tacubaya.

The late brilliant achievement of the arms of the United States over the superior numbers of the enemy, and in front of the capital of the country, cannot but excite the admiration and pride of our people, from one end of the land to the other. But those who were not here to witness and participate in the desperation of the conflict—the great and apparently insurmountable obstacles—the privations and hardships endured—never can properly appreciate the brilliancy of the victory, the gallantry and good conduct, and the scientific attainments of our noble little army. Our comparative loss, of those engaged, exceeds that of any battle of which we have any recollection; being about *one out of six*. To attempt to enumerate, in a proper manner, the individual instances of heroism—of determined and deliberate courage—of the perseverance and intrepidity with which great and powerful obstacles were surmounted—would be but commencing an endless task. I trust, when the details of these brilliant affairs are given by the respective commanders, that our country will testify its admiration and respect by some substantial reward—a reward that will live in memory and history when the actors in these stirring scenes shall have mouldered in the dust.

About the 15th inst., it was determined that we should not attack El Peñon, where the enemy had made every preparation to receive us and where, no doubt, we would have been compelled to sacrifice many more lives than we have already done. Accordingly, the engineers having discovered a road by which we could turn it, we took up our march around Lake Chalco. At this movement the enemy were seriously nonplussed, as they were not aware themselves of any practicable route we could take that would so effectually turn their position, and in order to delay our movement, sent out Gen. Alvarez, the general champion of the South, with his *Pintos* (a tribe of Indians spotted by nature), together with a portion of the regular army, amounting in all to about 10,000 men, to attack the rear columns, under the command of Gen. Twiggs, but it turned out to be a feeble attempt. Gen. Twiggs had scarcely formed his line of battle and opened his artillery, under the command of Capt. Taylor, before they fled with great precipitancy. A few well-directed shots from this battery made a forcible impression upon their columns, and they retreated, leaving a portion of their dead and wounded to take care of themselves. The whole affair did not detain Gen. Twiggs more than an hour, and he was again on his march. By this time the enemy had discovered the route by which we were moving, and endeavored to obstruct the road, but the Sappers and Miners, aided by the head of Gen. Worth's column, soon cleared the road at different places. By the 17th the head of Gen. Worth's column arrived at San Augustin—the enemy's skirmishers firing from every hill-top and point which favored them on the route, and their cavalry presenting themselves in force several times during the day, but never daring to attack.

On the 18th, Gen. Worth's column moved down the road in the direction of San Antonio, from which place the enemy fired upon a squadron of dragoons (killing Capt. Thornton and wounding the guide, Jonathan Fitzwater) advanced to protect the engineers in a reconnoissance of the fortifications of San Antonio. Capt. Thornton had been very unwell for some time, and went out in command of his squadron against the advice of his physician and his senior officers, but his energy and gallantry would not allow him to remain inactive when there was the least possibility of meeting the foe. As soon as the dragoons were withdrawn, Col. James Duncan's battery and the Sappers and Miners moved down the road, and took a position that would enable them to operate in any direction, in case of emergency.[2] Col. Charles F. Smith's light battalion was thrown out on the left front, to watch the movements of the enemy, and to hold him in check in case of his advancing his flank.[3] Immediately after, Col. Garland's brigade made a diversion to the right, and took position in line, resting his right at the *hacienda* of San Juan de Dios, about 400 yards to the right of the road. As soon as this movement was completed, the 2[d] Brigade, under Col. Clarke, moved down the road until the head of his column rested on the left wing of Col. Garland. One section of the mountain howitzers was brought forward, and thus they remained until sundown, when the brigade of cavalry withdrew, leaving the infantry and artillery on the ground. About 2 o'clock a heavy rain came on, which completely drenched the troops, and they were also exposed during the night to a slow drizzling rain without tents or blankets. Gen. Worth, with a part of the 1st Brigade, occupied the *hacienda* of San Juan de Dios during the night, and the enemy amused themselves by firing a few random shot at it about sundown from San Antonio, but without any other effect than to riddle the house completely with balls, and to besprinkle the officers with the mortar and dust of the old *hacienda*. During the day Maj. Lawrence P. Graham was sent out from San Augustin (Gen. Scott's headquarters) towards Contreras, to protect the engineers in a reconnoissance of the route in that direction, where, during the forenoon, he engaged a

2. A graduate of West Point in 1834, James Duncan became a distinguished artillery officer. During the Seminole War he was struck in the head by a spent ball, rendering him unconscious and leading his fellow officers to think him dead. Promoted to captain in 1846, Duncan won brevets to major, lieutenant colonel, and colonel for the battles of Palo Alto, Resaca de la Palma, and Monterrey, respectively. Promoted to colonel and inspector general in January of 1849, he died on July 3 of that year. Heitman, *Historical Register* 1: 387; *Daily National Intelligencer*, July 14, 1849.

3. Charles Smith graduated from West Point in 1825 and from 1829 to 1842 acted as instructor, adjutant, and commandant of cadets at that institution. A captain in the 2[d] Artillery, he won brevets to major and lieutenant colonel for conduct during General Taylor's campaign and a brevet to colonel for Contreras and Churubusco. Smith acted as inspector general during the waning days of the American occupation. Promoted to brigadier general in 1861 from his position as lieutenant colonel of the 10th Infantry, he was advanced to major general on March 21, 1862 for his part in the reduction of Fort Donelson. Ill health resulted in him missing the fighting at Shiloh and he died on April 25, 1862. Heitman, *Historical Register* 1: 895; *Boston American Traveller*, May 3, 1862.

force of the enemy's cavalry and infantry, which he drove back, with a loss of eight killed, two wounded, and five prisoners—Maj. Graham's command sustaining no loss.

On the 19th, the enemy fired from the works at San Antonio on the *hacienda* of San Juan de Dios, supposing a part of our forces were still there. About 10 o'clock the Sappers and Miners, under Lieut. Gustavus W. Smith, and the section of mountain howitzers, under Lieut. Franklin D. Callender, returned to San Augustin and joined Gen. Pillow's division, which was then taking up its march in the direction of Contreras. Gen. Pillow continued his march, opening the road as he went, until he reached a high point, from whence he had the enemy and his fortifications in full view. Between 1 and 2 o'clock the division of Gen. Twiggs came up with the advance and moved forward—Gen. Smith's brigade advancing to the left, and Col. Riley's to the right. Gen. Pillow placed at the disposal of Gen. Twiggs, Capt. John B. Magruder's battery and Lieut. Callender's howitzers, both of which belonged to the proper division of Gen. Pillow.

With great difficulty the two batteries moved forward, having to travel half a mile over a broken and confused mass of lava, apparently impassable even for footmen. The enemy opened his heavy batteries from Contreras, and the advancing troops of Gen. Smith's brigade hotly engaged the enemy's infantry, which he had thrown out across a deep ravine and creek in front of his fortifications. He appeared determined to maintain his position in front of his fortifications, using his artillery for a time against the rear brigades of our army as they came up, but he was not able to stand the severity of the conflict, and was compelled to retire with heavy loss. He then concentrated his fire upon the howitzers and Capt. Magruder's battery. These two batteries sustained, for more than an hour, the fire of twenty-two pieces of artillery, mostly of large calibre, when they were ordered by Gen. Smith to retire from so unequal a conflict. Their loss was very severe, and among others, we have to lament the death of Lieut. John P. Johnstone. Lieut. Callender was also severely wounded.

Gen. Pillow had ordered Gen. Pierce's brigade to the support of Gen. Smith, and Gen. Cadwalader's to the support of Col. Riley. At this state of the battle, while it was raging with extreme severity, the enemy appeared on the left of the fort at Contreras, and in rear of the village of Ensaldo, where Col. Riley had arrived, with a force of 12,000 men (which we afterwards learned was under the command of Santa Anna himself) apparently threatening the safety of Col. Riley and Gen. Cadwalader. Gen. Pillow ordered the 15th Infantry, under Col. Morgan, to the support of Gen. Cadwalader. Gen. Scott came upon the ground about this time, bringing with him Gen. Shields' brigade of volunteers (South Carolina and New York), whom he advanced to the support of the forces under Gen. Cadwalader.

Gen. Twiggs finding his command so separated, and that it was utterly impossible, from the nature of the ground, for him to reach the point he intended to occupy, as night approached, fell back with a portion of his staff to the place where Gen. Scott was passing the night, exposed to a severe rain, without shelter, or anything more than his usual uniform, to protect him from the inclemency of the weather.

Magruder's and the howitzer battery being disabled, and it being evident that our left was advancing on a route prepared for us by the enemy—he having cleared away all the brush and other obstacles that obstructed his view—thereby exposing our infantry to a destructive fire as they approached, it being doubtful whether they could cross the ravine after they reached it, Gen. Smith directed Capt. Magruder and the howitzer battery to open, in order to attract the attention of the enemy, while he made a movement to the right, which he had determined on, in order to try one of the enemy's flanks. Leaving three companies of the 3^{d} Infantry to support the battery, and about twenty men from Maj. Justin Dimick's command to reinforce the loss sustained by the battery, Gen. Smith moved off with the Sappers and Miners, Lieut. Smith; 1st Artillery, Maj. Dimick; and 3^{d} Infantry, Capt. Edmund B. Alexander; and as many of the Rifle Regiment as could be got together, they having been detached during the day as skirmishers and to cover the engineers in their reconnoissance. After passing over the broken and irregular surface of land, and crossing the deep ravines, he succeeded in reaching the village of Ensaldo. Gen. Smith being the ranking officer present, Gen. Cadwalader reported to him with four regiments of Gen. Pillow's division. Col. Riley's brigade had crossed the ravine, and gone up towards Contreras, after a strong body of the enemy, which he drove off. The enemy was now drawn up in two lines, above the village, on the right of the fort, the front infantry, and the rear cavalry. The village of Ensaldo is protected on one side by a deep ravine—on the road between it and the stream is a house and garden, surrounded by a high and rather strong stone wall—the village is intersected by narrow lanes, between high dykes, enclosing gardens full of fruit trees and shrubbery, affording protection and concealment for the men. The church, standing in the centre, also afforded protection, if necessary. Gen. Smith now directed Gen. Cadwalader's force to be drawn up on the outer edge of the village, facing the enemy's heavy force on the left of the fort. Gen. Cadwalader formed the 3d Infantry and Rifles in column of company, left in front, on the right flank; placed Lieut. Smith's Sappers and Miners, and Capt. William H. Irwin's company of the 11th Infantry in the church; and Maj. Dimick's regiment in the garden on the road, in order to secure that avenue and his rear.

Gen. Smith now determined to attack the large force on the enemy's right—with Col. Riley on the left—Gen. Cadwalader on the right of the former retired in *echelon*, but before the movement could be completed, night approached and the enemy's line could not be seen, therefore the order was countermanded. Gen. Cadwalader resumed his position on the edge of the village, Col. Riley's brigade was formed in a long lane inside parallel to it, the Rifles on his left and the 3d Infantry in the churchyard. Thus they remained exposed to a severe rain all night without fire or shelter, the officers from generals down sharing the severity of the weather, but perhaps it only whetted their appetites for a more glorious and determined engagement in the morning. But now imagine the position of this portion of the army, numbering 3,500 at the outside, without artillery or cavalry, while the enemy in front and on the left had 19,000, those in the fort said to be the best of Mexico, with twenty-two pieces of artillery, and among his troops about 7,000 cavalry. It was evident that some decisive action had to be taken, that some great effort had to be made, and Gen. Smith and Col. Riley seconded as they then were, were just the men competent to the task. An attack on the main work was determined upon, and the movement to take place at 3 o'clock of the following morning. However, here another obstacle presented itself—the force of Gen. Smith's was not strong enough to attack the main work and hold the village at the same time, and it was of the utmost importance he should do so. For if he drove the enemy from this main work, and in his retreat he secured possession of the village, he could hold it long enough to allow his troops to get away, and in all probability seriously embarrass any further movements of our army until he was safely fixed somewhere else. It is said that fortune favors the brave—and in this instance it most truly did—for while Gen. Smith was preparing for his attack, Gen. Shields reported his near approach with his brigade of South Carolina and New York volunteers, and here was an exhibition of magnanimity on the part of a high-minded soldier to a brother officer. When Gen. Shields arrived, he was the ranking officer and could have assumed the command, but he was not the man to pluck the bright laurels about to be gathered by a brother soldier in carrying one of the strong works of the enemy. Accordingly he moved subject to the command of Gen. Smith, and his brigade was placed in the village of Ensaldo, as circumstances might require, either to cut off the retreat of the troops from Contreras or to take the reserve of the enemy in flank, if it should change its front and attempt to attack our force towards Contreras.

At 3 o'clock, on the morning of the 20th, our troops commenced their movement towards the front of attack. The night was so dark that the men could not go out of reach of one another for fear of losing their way. This caused the movement to be so slow that day-break approached before the head of Gen. Cadwalader's brigade commenced descending into the ravine at the village. As soon as Col. Riley got out of the deep ravine, and at a point where it was thought the rear of the work could be approached, the head of the column halted and closed, at the same time drawing the loads out of the guns supposed to be wet. Col. Riley then formed his brigade in column of divisions, and thus the column stood formed, Col. Riley's brigade on the advance, next Gen. Cadwalader's and Gen. Smith's brigades, together with the Sappers and Miners, under the command of Maj. Dimick, closed up the rear, leaving Gen. Shields at the village. Col. Riley continued up the ravine bearing a little to his left, and as he raised over the bank he stood fronting the rear of the enemy's work, but he was protected from the severity of its fire by the favorable position of the ground.

As soon as Col. Riley ascended the hill and came in full view of the enemy, they immediately opened a warm fire upon him. Col. Riley threw out his two advanced divisions as skirmishers, and said—"Now, boys, give them hell! Close in with them and let the bayonet do its work!"—and his command rushed down the slope with a desperation and enthusiasm enough to strike terror to the heart of the boldest, while the rear of his command moved steadily forward in solid block with the most mechanical precision. The Sappers and Miners and the Rifle Regiment, which had been thrown across a ravine intervening between the one they had passed up and under the brow of the slope which Col. Riley came down, from that position poured in a fire which swept in front of Col. Riley's column, then inclining towards their left, joined in the attack on the troops outside of the left flank of the fort. Gen. Cadwalader followed the route taken by Col. Riley, and as soon as his troops were formed, moved on to his support. The 1st Brigade, which was bringing up the rear, had been ordered to follow the same route, but while it was on the march by the right flank up the ravine and nearly opposite the fort, Gen. Smith ordered the brigade to face to the left and advance in line to attack the enemy's force in flank. This movement was executed in less time than it takes me to write it. They met the enemy outside the fort, just as Col. Riley's brigade rushed into it; the enemy was completely routed and commenced a precipitate retreat. Their cavalry and infantry had been formed to receive the charge, but both were compelled to give way to the bayonet—the rout was most complete and the victory most decided—but while Riley's brigade took possession of the works and planted their colors upon it, the other force continued the pursuit down the road. The retreating force had to pass near where Gen. Shields' brigade was placed to intercept them. They, however, were not aware of it until they received the well-directed fire of the South Carolina Regiment, which mowed them down like grass before the scythe.

The enemy had been completely deceived in reference to the position of Gen. Shields' brigade and the balance of the force, by the sagacity of the general. After Gen. Smith moved off to attack the work, Gen. Shields caused his men to build fires over the ground occupied by the troops during the night, as if the men were preparing their breakfast, which led the enemy to believe our troops were still in force in the village. This also led him to believe we were going to carry into execution the attack we were meditating the night before. Accordingly, the night before he placed batteries along his line, and in the morning moved detachments forward to take in flank the attack he supposed we would make at daylight. How great his surprise must have been when the first thing he saw in the morning was Col. Riley moving down the slope having already turned his strong-hold, but all doubts were soon dispelled by the capture of his works and the dispersion of his army. They were met at every point by the skillful management and energy of Gen. Shields, whose command compelled them to fly in every direction, some taking to the broken and craggy rocks, some to the ravines, while other depended upon their heels and made most excellent time in a race across the fields. One of the most sagacious movements made by a Mexican officer was made at this place. After a large portion of the Mexican army had passed through a very narrow pass and our troops after them, he formed a squadron of lancers in the pass, laid down their arms and surrendered, thus effecting the escape of those who had already passed through, those of our troops who were nearest having to take possession of the prisoners and guard them back, and before another force could go in pursuit, they were out of reach.

In this fort there were captured twenty-two pieces of artillery, mostly large size, a great number of pack-mules, and large quantity of ammunition and munitions of war, and upwards of 1,500 prisoners, among them were several officers of high rank. The enemy left dead upon the field, which we have buried, upwards of 700, but his loss was certainly much heavier, as the Mexicans were still burying their friends when I passed over the battle-ground two days ago. There were many more killed when the Rifles engaged on the 19th than we had any idea, their unerring aim told with perfect effect. The troops in the fort were commanded by Gabriel Valencia, those outside by Santa Anna.[4]

4. A cadet in 1810, Gabriel Valencia rose through the ranks to become general of brigade in 1831. Elevated to army chief of staff in 1838, he spent the next seven years involved in political intrigues that saw him support several governments. In 1847 Valencia was part of the defenses at Churubusco, but his position was overrun by American troops on August 20. Disgraced on the battlefield and with no political allies left, General Valencia surrendered to the Americans in disgrace in 1848 and died later that year. Tucker, *Encyclopedia*, 693.

Among the highest achievements of the morning's engagement was the re-capture of the two Buena Vista 6-pounders, belonging to Capt. John M. Washington's battery by one of the light companies of the same regiment. They now stand before the door of Gen. Twiggs, and I hope when he shall meet his old friend Gen. Taylor, he will present these beautiful trophies to claim the congratulations. All the small arms taken were immediately destroyed.

The arms were secured and a detachment left to protect the ordnance, ammunition, and prisoners. The column formed for the purpose of pursuing the enemy, who had been met by a force from San Angel, when Gen. Twiggs arrived and ordered a speedy and most vigorous pursuit of the enemy, which was immediately done—Gen. Shields' brigade in advance, next Gen. Twiggs' division, and the rear by Gen. Pillow's division—the Rifles and Sappers and Miners in advance as skirmishers. There now ensued a sort of running fight all the way to San Angel, the enemy endeavoring to make a stand at every point on the road, but the unerring fire of the rifle made every place too hot for them, and they were compelled to take refuge in Churubusco.

At San Angel, Gen. Pillow arrived and took the command, when the whole column moved down to Calican, when Gen. Scott came up and immediately took the command of the whole.

As soon as the enemy's forces perceived that Contreras was carried, and that we would be able to turn his position and attack him in reverse, he evacuated the fortification and fell back on Churubusco with his artillery and whole force. This was also reinforced by the troops from Contreras, and some from the city, they apparently determined to make their final stand at this point.

The work and position was exceedingly strong and completely masked by a high growth of corn, and an orchard, which very much precluded our officers getting a proper view of the position and the strength of the work, which proved to be regular fortification, and had been erected in the incredibly short time of thirty-eight hours. The church buildings formed a large square—the lower front, at the north end, was chiefly a wall, scaffolded for infantry—behind it was a higher building, also covered with infantry—and in rear of this, the church itself was also covered with infantry, and a high steeple on its right flank was filled with infantry. In front of the first wall was a curtain connecting two salient angles, which flanked it, and were continued back to the side walls of the church, garrisoned heavily with infantry, and mounting seven pieces of artillery. This was the point at which Gen. Smith's brigade opened the action, soon followed, a little farther to the left, by Col. Riley's brigade, these two composing the "Cerro Gordo Division," Gen. Twiggs. Capt. Taylor's battery of light artillery also took position near this work, on the right of Gen. Smith's brigade. It soon drew upon it a heavy fire from the fort, which he sustained for an hour and a half, losing twenty-three of his company, among whom were Lieuts. James G. Martin, Edward C. Boynton, and Sims, and three sergeants. He also lost during this time fifteen horses. The conduct of Capt. Taylor and his company throughout, was such as to excite the admiration of all who witnessed it, as well as his superior officers.

At the opposite side of the work, the breastwork extended across the road from the church, presenting a similar front, excepting the buildings of the church. The work on the road was also strengthened by a bridge over a creek, behind which was a body of infantry, and the work itself mounting three or four guns. Gen. Pillow, with part of his division, was sent round by Gen. Scott, to assault this part of the work, but as he, with his command, emerged from the mud and mire of the corn-fields (having waded, some of them, waist deep) into the road, he met Gen. Worth coming up from San Antonio, with his division. They had a hearty welcome, and one of them proposed that their commands should go hand in hand in carrying the work, which was readily agreed to.

At the same time that the other commands were despatched, Gen. Scott ordered Gen. Shields to attack the enemy's extreme left, where he was heavily entrenched, at the same time reinforcing his command with the 9th and part of the 12th and 15th Infantry, under Gen. Pierce. This movement was executed as soon as the nature of the ground would admit, the whole command having to pass through corn-fields of high growth, intercepted by ditches running through them in every direction.

The action now became general, and the severity of the conflict never equaled within the recollection of our oldest soldiers. The enemy was more than three times our number, besides his advantage of artillery and position. Added to this, he was stimulated by the fact that it was the last effort of resistance he could make, before we could enter the capital; his troops knew that they were fighting for the last remnant of the Republic, and they stood their ground with as much firmness and resolution as any troops could stand before the army we at present have here. The roar of the musketry was so great that it was almost impossible for the soldiers to hear the orders of their officers. There was no point at which the action did not rage with severity for more than two hours, which is proven by the fact that our loss at this point was nearly 1,000 men.

After the contest had lasted about two hours, our troops had got into such position as to be able to close with them at the point of the bayonet, which decided the affair in our favor—Gen. Pillow and Gen. Worth carrying the work on the road, by an officer of Gen. Pillow's division taking down one flag, and one of Gen. Worth's taking down the other, and the 8th Infantry planting their colors instead. Gen. Twiggs' division carrying the work it attacked at the church, Capt. James M. Smith, of the 3d Infantry, received the surrender of the work, with seven pieces of artillery, two stand of colors, and Gen. Manuel Rincón, together with 104 officers and upwards of 1,100 non-commissioned officers and privates, surrendered as prisoners of war.[5] Gen. Shields had his work more to himself, and he fully sustained that high reputation hitherto acquired on the field of battle. When the contest raged highest, and his men falling around him in every direction, he preserved that even temperament of mind for which he is so characteristic, his countenance wearing that bland and affable appearance throughout the whole engagement. His volunteers stood and moved under the fire with the regularity of veteran troops. South Carolina has sustained a heavy loss. Col. Pierce M. Butler was wounded twice before he received the fatal shot.[6] Two color-bearers were successively shot down,

5. After twelve years fighting for Mexican independence, Maunel Rincón was rewarded with a commission as colonel in 1821. As general of division in 1839, he was stripped of his rank and court-martialed for surrendering the fort at Vera Cruz to the French. In 1847 he battled General Scott's advance, particularly at Churubusco, until forced to become one of the Mexican commissioners selected to negotiate the army's surrender. Rincón left the army in 1848 and wrote poetry until his death in 1849. Tucker, *Encyclopedia*, 560-61.

6. A former governor of South Carolina, Pierce Butler became colonel of the South Carolina Volunteers, the so-called Palmetto Regiment. When his regiment began an advance at Churubusco, Butler, who had been deathly ill for several days, "broke loose from his physicians, abandoned his sick couch, and, weak, ghastly,

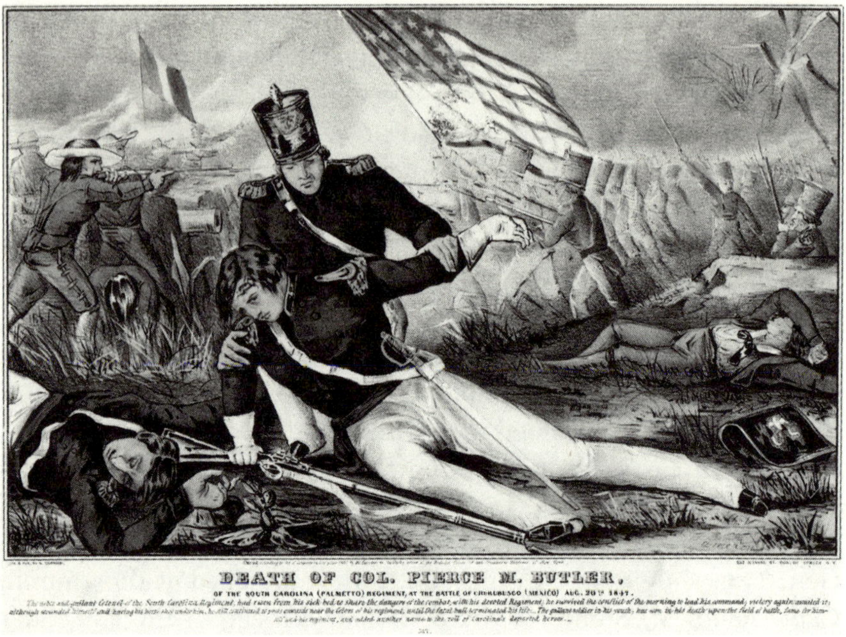

Death of Colonel Pierce Butler at Churubusco. *Courtesy Library of Congress*.

when Lieut. Col. Dickenson took the colors, and was bearing the Palmetto proudly amidst the storm, when he also received a severe wound. About the same time that the three divisions at the forts were enabled to close, Gen. Shields succeeded in driving from their position the large force with which he was contending.

The dragoons were now brought forward, and drove the enemy to the gates of the capital, thus closing, for the present, the most brilliant victory achieved by our arms during the war, and one which will vie with any achievement of our arms in times past.

For more fully detailed particulars, I must refer you to the reports of the several commands. I find that if I were to attempt to record the entire details of the achievements of the 20th, I would not be able to conclude it in time enough to be of any interest to your readers.

---

and almost fainting, mounted his charger, and placed himself at the head of his regiment." His courage proved fatal, one account noting how Butler "had his horse shot under him; continuing the charge on foot, he was wounded in the leg, and finally shot through the head." *Daily National Intelligencer*, September 18, 1847; *Fayetteville Weekly Observer*, September 28, 1847.

Louisiana had two brilliant representatives, who participated largely throughout the whole affair, viz.: Gen. P. F. Smith, of the 1st Brigade, 2d Division, and Lieut. Beauregard, of the Engineers, both of which gentlemen signally distinguished themselves, both by their superior military knowledge and their personal courage. The Engineer Corps throughout has borne a large share of the labors and exposure of the battle.

From intercepted letters which we have in our possession, written on the evening of the battle, we learn the Mexican loss to be 5,000 in killed and wounded, and by them we also learn that out of 30,000 men, they had but between 6,000 and 8,000 men left, and they in confusion, without leaders—the balance killed, wounded, prisoners, or totally dispersed.

I send you a list of the killed and wounded, so near as they can be got at present.

I also send you the muster roll of a company of volunteers, who organized themselves for the occasion, under Capt. Justus McKinstry. They were composed of men who were not attached to any particular command, but mostly belonging to some of the departments; they had five wounded, but I have not been able to get their names. On several occasions they rendered highly important service, and exhibited the mettle all Americans possess.

Muster Roll of the "McKinstry Volunteers"

Wm. Richardson, James Kellogg, C.W. Crow, Geo. H. Murray, N. Van Alstein, C.N. St. Clair, Albert G. Smith, Edward Clarke, Thomas N. Graves, H.N. Clarke, John McKeevers, H. Marks, S. Miller, John Ford, Henry V. Wright, W.D. Hamilton, James Forney, Lewis Bennett, Paul B. Ryan, H.H. Booker, Wm. Cornwell, Edward Rolin, James A. Sawyer, W.J. Maxwell, George Walbridge, A.S. Harris, J. McKinney, Chas. A. Clarke, G.L. Tucker, Geo. Heisner, Robert Embleton, Daniel F. Barry, H. Lumpkin, John Bensley, E.L. Kincaid, Edward Fitzgerald, C.B. Gallagher, Thos. B. Tucker, Wm. Jimmerson, Wm. Forrest, J. Smith McMicken, Wm. A. Evans, Thomas Lynes, John Winner, E.B. Holliday, ------ Barnes, H. Van Loon, John Goodrich, Wm. B. Hood, Manuel Silva.

We also had many persons who bore a conspicuous part in the actions of both days, who were not attached to any particular command, among them I noticed conspicuously Maj. Goode Bryan and Lieut. Lewis Dickenson, formerly of the Alabama Regiment of Volunteers.

After the troops had arrived at this place, all the former Texan prisoners who were present, assembled just below the National Palace, on a fine paved road, made by the labor of their hands, while they remained in this country. On the side of the road stood a beautiful monument, with the following inscription: "Erected to the memory of Gen. Santa Anna, in consideration of his having constructed this road by the labor of the prisoners of Texas." It was not long after the assemblage of the crowd, until down came the monument, and not satisfied with tearing it down, they broke the stone into small pieces, and scattered them to the four winds.

I herewith send you a copy of the armistice agreed upon. On the evening of the 20th, a white flag came out from the city, and on the evening of the 21st, we learned the proposition for an armistice had been made, which were agreed to, and commissioners appointed, who arranged and agreed to the following terms:

> The undersigned, appointed respectively, the first three by Maj. Gen. Winfield Scott, Commander-in-Chief of the Armies of the United States, and the last two by his Excellency D. Antonio Lopez de Santa Anna, President of the Mexican Republic, and Commander-in-Chief of its Armies, met with full powers, which were duly verified in the village of Tucabaya, on the 22d day of August, 1847, to enter into an armistice for the purpose of giving the Mexican government an opportunity of receiving propositions for peace, from the Commissioner appointed by the President of the United States, and now with the American Army, when the following articles were agreed upon:
>
> Art. 1. Hostilities shall instantly and absolutely cease between the Armies of the United States of America and the United Mexican States within thirty leagues of the Capital of the latter States, to allow time to the Commissioner appointed by the United States and the Commissioner to be appointed by the Mexican Republic to negotiate.
>
> Art. 2. This armistice shall continue as long as the Commissioners of the two Governments may be engaged on negotiations, or until the Commander of either of the said Armies shall give formal notice to the other of the cessation of the armistice, and for forty-eight hours after such notice.
>
> Art. 3. In the meantime neither Army shall, within thirty leagues of the City of Mexico, commence any new fortification of military work of offence or defence, or do anything to enlarge or strengthen any existing work or fortification of that character, within the said limits.

Art. 4. Neither Army shall be reinforced within the same. Any reinforcements in troops or munitions of war, other than subsistence, shall be stopped at the distance of twenty-three miles from the City of Mexico.

Art. 5. Neither Army, nor any detachments from them, shall advance beyond the line it at present occupies.

Art. 6. Neither Army, nor any detachment or individual of either, shall pass the neutral limits established by the last article, except under flag of truce bearing the correspondence between the two Armies, or on the business authorized by the next article; and individuals of either Army who may chance to straggle within the neutral limits, shall, by the opposite party, be kindly warned off, or sent back to their own Army under flags of truce.

Art. 7. The American Army shall not by violence obstruct the passage, from the open country into the City of Mexico, of the ordinary supplies of food necessary to the consumption of the inhabitants or the Mexican Army within the city; nor shall the Mexican authorities, civil or military, do any act to obstruct the passage of supplies from the city or the country, needed by the American Army.

Art. 8. All American prisoners of war remaining on the hands of the Mexican Army, and not heretofore exchanged, shall immediately, or as soon as practicable, be restored to the American Army, against a like number, having regard to rank, of Mexican prisoners captured by the American Army.

Art. 9. All American citizens who were established in the City of Mexico prior to the existing war, and who have since been expelled from that city, shall be allowed to return to their respective business or families therein, without delay or molestation.

Art. 10. The better to enable the belligerent Armies to execute these articles, and to favor the great object of peace, it is further agreed between the parties, that any courier with despatches that either Army shall desire to send along the line from the City of Mexico or its vicinity, to and from Vera Cruz, shall receive a safe conduct from the Commander of the opposing Army.

Art. 11. The administration of justice between Mexicans, accordingto the General and State Constitutions and laws, by the local authorities of thetowns and places occupied by the American forces, shall not be obstructed in any manner.

Art. 12. Persons and property shall be respected in the towns and places occupied by the American forces. No person shall be molested in the exercise of his profession; nor shall the services of anyone required without his consent. In all cases where services are voluntarily rendered, a just price shall be paid, and trade remain unmolested.

Art. 13. Those wounded prisoners who may desire to remove to some more convenient place for the purpose of being cured of their wounds, shall be allowed to do so without molestation, they still remaining prisoners.

Art. 14. Those Mexican medical officers who may wish to attend the wounded, shall have the privilege of doing so, if their services be required.

Art. 15. For the more perfect execution of this agreement, two Commissioners shall be appointed, one by each party, who, in case of disagreement, shall appoint a third.

Art. 16. This convention shall have no force or effect unless approved by their Excellencies, the Commanders, respectively, of the two Armies, within twenty-four hours, reckoning from the sixth hour of the twenty-third day of August, 1847.

John A. Quitman, Maj. Gen. U.S.A.
Persifor F. Smith, Bvt. Brig. Gen.
Franklin Pierce, Brig. Gen. U.S.A.
Ignacio de Mora y Villamil
Benito Quijano

A true copy of the original:

G.W. Lay, U.S.A.
Military Secretary to the General-in-Chief

List of the Killed, Wounded and Missing

General Headquarters

Dragoons Attached to Head-Quarters of Gen Scott—Capt Thornton, Co F, 2d Dragoons, killed; Philip Kearny, 1st Dragoons, wounded; Philip McReynolds, 3d Dragoons, wounded; Lieut Graham, wounded; Privs ----- Cowden, 2d Dragoons, wounded; Patrick Hart, Co F, 1st Dragoons, killed; John Ritter, Co F, 1st Dragoons, killed; James McDonald, Co F, 1st Dragoons, killed; Michael Brophy, Co F, 1st Dragoons, killed; Augustus Delsol, 3d Dragoons, killed or missing; Edward Curtis, 3d Dragoons, killed or missing; Geo Duver, 3d Dragoons, killed.

First Division

Return of the Killed, Wounded and Missing in the First Division, commanded by Maj. Gen. Worth.

KILLED—2d Artillery—Sergt C W Cobb, Privs Henry Hear, John Healy, Co I. ***5th Infantry***—John Sheridan, Alex McKenzie, Co H. ***2d Artillery***—Sergt John Farrell, Privs John Daley, Co C; Wm Landolt, Co I; James Wilson, Co G. ***3d Artillery***—Sergt Wm Brown,

Privs Philip Nichols, Chas Ray, John Ruber, Co G; Sergt Wm Mcguire, Privs Nicholas Kenniston, Co I. ***4th Infantry***—Wm Johnston, Co A; Edwd Kirwid, F Pinkerton, Co I. ***5th Infantry***—Corpl T James, Co E; Privs J C McKinney Co A; A Vanaistyne, Samuel Wilson, Co E; B Sirman, Co I; E C Smith, Co K. ***6th Infantry***—Privs Porter Hand, David Noble, Co A; D Harnett, Co C; J McKee, Geo Graham, Co D; A D Harris Co F; Wm Bray, Robert Saddy, John Foss, Co H. ***8th Infantry***—Paul Dutor, Edwd Fleming, Caspar Polk, Co I.

WOUNDED—*2d Artillery*—Priv Jas Reilly, Co A; Sergts Philip Wilson, E Meyn, Privs H Acherman, John Casey, P Dowd, W Gravenhart, John Steward, Andw Casey, Hugh Casey, James David, Co K; Martin Conway, Patrick Kennedy, Wm Lafferty, Joseph Mills, Edward Sullivan, Henry Vuchel, Sergt Joseph Fadding, Corpl Wm Sutherland, Privs Jas Donoho, Michl Lynch, Wm Murray, Co I. ***5th Infantry***—2d Lieut P Farrally, Privs Geo Bishop, Chas Carner, W C Emerson, John Francha, Peter Flynn, Joseph Fry, J A Hooft, Wm Bell, Michl Stezer, John Shimmer, David Wilton, Jacob Mayer, Danl Rodgers, Thomas Sleck, Co H. *8th Infantry*—2d Lieut E B Holloway, Privs Chas Childs, Chas Fitzgerald, Michl Hagan, Jno Sawyer, Co B. ***2d Artillery***—1st Lieut Lewis G Arnold, Co F, Sergt Chas Wilson, Corpl Andrew Bell, Privs Chas Carroll, Geo Heck, Henry Douglass, John Klump, Powell Oullip, Jacob Schriver, Co C; James Gould, Jas Burgen, Rd Birmingham, Co D; Sergt Thos G Allen, Privs G W Church, John Conner, Patk Gallagher, Henry Hatch, Hugh Murphy, Chas Q Putnam, Martin Riordan, Philip Stevens, Lewis Seiter, P Zirngrible, Church Snyder, Co F; David Walsh, E Saunders, Co. E; Sergts Luke Walker, Jas Chappell, James H Starr, Corpl Simon Stanton, Privs H Binart, P Thornton, Lewis Schott, John Harper, J J Moore, Wm Bardo Thos Starr, H Levy, James Hugh, D Hagaman, Co G; Sergts A B Cleveland, John Walters, John Cunningham, Corpl J Ric Redman, Privs F Connors, Chas Birnan, Danl Daly, Henry Frank, James Gourley, John King, Alex Moore, Chas Page. ***3d Artillery***—Bvt Maj Ward, Sergt John Hick, Corpls Wm Young, John Hynes, E Insworth, Joseph Akor, Privs John Coogan, Adam Deflin, Edwd Eagan, E W Gleason, John Hughs F H Lachat, G W Smith, J Thompson, Wm Patton, Co B; Jno Morris, Edwd Porter, Thos Brady, John Maitland, Thos Loftus, Chas Reis, Anthony Sutler, V Kenwater, Co G; Sergt James H Hubbard, Privs C McClyman, Thos McCoy, John Nailor,

John Setser, Co I. ***3d Dragoons***—2d Lieut H Thorn, A D C. ***4th Infantry***—Privs John McLaughlin, Daniel O'Shea, Co A, John Alexander, Co B, J Frob, Jos Shafia, A Hartland, Co I; E Thomson, Co D. ***6th Infantry***—Col N S Clarke. ***5th Infantry***—Adjt P Lugenbeel, Capt W W Chapman, Co G. ***6th Infantry***—Maj B L E Bonneville, Capt W W Hoffman, Co D, 1st Lieut T Hendrickson, Co K, 1st Lieut J D Baron, Co A, 2d Lieut S B Buckner (Reg Q M). ***5th Infantry***—Privs A E Boyer, J Connell, Peter Frazer, M Knott, P Mandy, D Henry, W Weighten, F Moreton, E M Whitford, Co A; O Othman, J Boyle, J Jacobson, Co B; U S Hall, J McAnthony, M O'Brien, G Ritner, S Seal, L Tickelman, W Wheeler, Co E; Sergt Lawrence, Corpl J Harman, Privs F Mather, H Miller, D Reim, J Rodney, P Maloney, J Burgen, J G Wilmer, C Thompson; W G Stansbury, J Rice, J L Clark, Co G; Sergt S Minue, Privs G Smith, P Barine, P Riley, G Rung, Co H; I Mullen, H Riley, L Deray, F Knap, Co K. ***6th Infantry***—Q M Sergt J Mahoney, Corpl W Williams, Privs T Hardy, W Williams, W Loomis, J Hardie, W Bowles, P Connor, W Faley, F Schoup, Co A; Sergts H McKowen, J Kronire, Musician J O'Neil, Privs A Barker, J Connor, D Keefe, W B Manering, H Martineau, J McDonough, W Lerron, J Wilson, Co F; Corpl R O Shril, Privs W Allen, D Dunward, D Carroll, D Hoss, M Hogan, Co B; Sergts W Nevins, F Owens, Corpl H Goodwin, Musician Jesse Brown, Privs G Christy, J Barnes, J Lanoner, J Tuttle, S Madden, E McBreheaty, D Griffin, B Hart, M Smith, J O'Brien, E Laughly, G R Washington, E Jordan, Co C; F Curtis, J Draper, O Austin, R Peples, M Stilwell, F D C Dye, W Biggs, M Sallingo, P Riner, A Stinebaugh, H McCavangh, T Owens, Co E; Sergts W Linderke, J Remington, Privs Geo G Fletcher, C Perkins, S Alcock, J McGuire, H Costolo, O Scofield, R Wogan, G Stigher, H Rudolph, Co H; Sergts J Craig, D M Keefe, Privs G Banghanon, C Burns, J A Eaton, G McCarthy, H Nieham, J Frosk, Co D; J James, J Elwater, A Sorral, W Reynolds, J Misse; W Piercy, Co H. ***8th Infantry***—Sergt J Anderson, Privs N Benerlin, S Taylor, J Curting, J D Knipper, J Englehart, Co A; W Hurst, F Somerhane, Co C; E Cumberbauch, Co D; E Ashworth, B G Barret, J C Kennedy, S Revidon, R Russell, J White, Co E; S Johnson, J Shutz, Co F; Sergt S Stoeffer, Privs C Benner, W Delaney, M O'Brien, Co I; Corpls S Hallinan, Co K; E Capon, Privs J Bennett, J Gordon, C Hopkins, M Wharton, S Donoghaugh, Co H; W Dunn, Co C.

MISSING—***2^{d} Artillery***—Privs Jno Golden, Co D, returned. ***3^{d} Artillery***—Stephen Lamb, Co I. ***4th Infantry***—Michl McGrath, wounded, Pat Green, Andrew McDonald, James Steel, Co F; John Robertson, Co I. ***5th Infantry***—Joseph Spencer, Co D; J R Debaun, Co K. ***6th Infantry***—J Smith, Co B.

RECAPITULATION—Killed, Commissioned Officers, none. Non-Commissioned Officers, 5. Musicians and Privates, 32. Wounded, Commissioned Officers, 13. Non-Commissioned Officers, 41. Musicians and Privates, 235. Missing, Privates, 10. Aggregate, 336.

Second Division—Gen Twiggs

Return of the Killed, Wounded and Missing of the 1st Brigade, 2^{d} Division, in the Actions of the 19th and 20th August, 1847, at Contreras and Churubusco.

First Brigade

KILLED—*1st Artillery*—Capts E A Capron, Co B; N J Burke, Co D; 2^{d} Lieut S Hoffman, Co F; Sergt John Anderson, Co D. ***Mounted Rifles***—Privs M Carr, Co D; J Reed, J O'Brien, Co E; A Troutfetter, Co F. ***1st Artillery***—Joseph Black, Co B; Joseph Banks, Co D; Arthur O'Connor, Charles Taylor, Christopher Wedmayer, Co F; Valentine Way, Co H. ***3^{d} Infantry***—Josh Lutterenger, Co A; John L Martin, Co E; George Fyant, Co F; Alex Meister, Co I; Thomas Crask, Co K.

WOUNDED—*1st Artillery*—Capt J S Hathaway, Co H, slightly. ***3^{d} Infantry***—Capts L S Craig, Co A, severely, D T Chandler, Co I; 1st Lieut and Adjt Don Carlos Buell, Staff, severely. ***Mounted Rifles***—1st Lieut M E VanBuren, Co K, slightly. *3d Infantry*—Sergt G L Read, Co C, slightly. ***1st Artillery***, Corpl Jacob Sammons, Co H, slightly. ***3^{d} Infantry***—Corps Henry Buck, Co A; H G Tucker, J W Kaufman, Co C. ***Mounted Rifles***—Privs F Molumby, Co D, slightly; H Nottage, Co E; J Lyons, G H Hough, Co F, severely; W S Walker, Co F; J James, 1st, J Hooker, Co G, slightly; J McNally, J N Caskey, Co H, severely. ***1st Artillery***—Wm Sheperd, Co B, slightly; Francis Buschman, Co B; Henry Sherman, Oliver Snider, John Swan, Thomas Billing, Co D, severely; James Sheray, Charles Miller, Co D, slightly; Peter McDermott, Co F, severely; Wm B Lambie, Michael McCormick, Julius Johnson, Co H, slightly; Lemuel Horner, Co G, mortally; John Monks, Co G, slightly. ***3^{d} Infantry***—Henry Perry,

Alvin Turner, James Hannan, Co A; David Bartlett, Nicholas Battendorf, John Quinn, John Madden, Co C; Geo W Savory, Diedrick Inergens, Co D; Saml P Perrin, William Leach, Co E; Wm Jones, Co F; Albert Stimpson, Wm Anderson, Jas McNally, Robt Lennox, Co H; Richard Menge, John Halfholden, Charles Rapp, Co I; James Durham, Henry Sagvier, Co K.

MISSING—*Mounted Rifles*—Corpl J O'Connell, Privs W Wood, Co D, both since joined; Josh Newhouse, Co E, since joined. ***1st Artillery***—Geo Karchler, Co B. ***3d Infantry***—Jacob Micar, Co A; Geo Washington, jr, Co B; Geo McDonald, Otis Hopkins, Rudolph Likens, known to be wounded, Co E; Stephen Ferris, Co H; John Curry, Co I; Saml Davis, Co K.

RECAPITULATION—Killed—***Rifles***, 4; ***1st Artillery***, 10; ***3d Infantry***, 5—19. Wounded—***Rifles***, 10; ***1st Artillery***, 16; ***3d Infantry***, 28—54. Missing—***Rifles***, 3; ***1st Artillery***, 1; ***3d Infantry***, 8—12. Total, 85.

Second Brigade

Engineer Company—**WOUNDED**—1st Sergt D D Hastings, slightly; Artificers Wm H Bartlett, J T Smith, severely; Monell, slightly. **MISSING**—Musician Noworing.

4th Artillery—**KILLED**—Sergt Henry D Goodwin, Co G; Privs John B Scuck, Co E; Wm P White, Co F; Timothy Kelley, Co G. **WOUNDED**—2d Lieut Collins, Co C, severely; Sergt G K Donnelly, Co E; Privs Banks Davis, Joseph Athoy, Alex Pierson, Co C, slightly; Enoch Bowles, Wm G Wharton, Co C, severely; John Wymer, Co C, slightly; Wm Wise, Co D, mortally; Benj W Heath, Jno T Williams, Co D, severely; Wm West, Co D, slightly; Christ'r Albock, James Egan, Michael Evans, August Klein, John McLaughlin, Jno McHarney, Wm Robinson, Co E, severely; John Hutchinson, Co E, slightly; Jno B Moore, Co F, severely; William Gaith, Co F, slightly; Jos W Gavin, Co F, severely; Robt Johnson, Co F, mortally; Wm McCaffery, Co G, severely; August Handles, Co G, slightly; Jos S Hackney, Co G, severely; Jas Fletcher, Co H, mortally; Richard W Allen, Co H, slightly; Luther Whitcombe, Co H, severely; Sergt Daniel Wilbro, Co F, severely. **MISSING**—Privs Jer Frisbee, Jas Quinn, John McDermott, Co E.

2d Infantry—**KILLED**—Capt Jas W Anderson, Co H; 2d Lieut Thos Easly, Co K; Privs Saml G Crawford, Co A; Horace Perry, Co C;

Dennis Daily, Jno W Arthur, David Huston, Co D; Henrick Reber, Co E; Abraham Clemens, Co F; John Boyd, Lew P Lamontin, Co H; Danl Striker, Francis Gruber, Michael Leopold, Saml Wilson, Co K. **WOUNDED**—Capts Jos R Smith, Co B, severely, twice; A W Wessels, Co G; 1st Lieuts J Hayden, A D C, slightly; B P Tilden, Co G, slightly, twice; C S Lovell, Co E, slightly, twice; Privs Jas A Taylor, Co A, slightly; Jno Bridgen, Malcom Herrington, Co A, severely; Corpl Jas Turney, Co B; Privs Wm Hawley, Co B, slightly; Wm Stuart, Wm Ears, Co B, severely; John Riley, George Martin, W A Malcolm, Hugh Young, Edward Tierney, Co B; Sergts Jas Stevenson, John Parks, Co C; Corpls Jas Knox, Co C, slightly; Thomas Handley, Co C; Privs Charles Dennin, Admand Tallesson, Co C, severely; John Gallagher, Co C, slightly; Walter Haner, Co C, severely; Wm Hughes, Co C, slightly; Jno D Kelley, Co C, not severely; Percy Page, Th E Thomas, Co C, slightly; Chas Donnelly, Jas Ferby, Co B, severely; Corpl Henry B Knapp, Co D, slightly; Privs Mont'y Barkholm, Frantz Ratman, Co D, severely; Wm Donnoghy, Patrick Dirgen, Wm H Bobles, Co D; Jno Kelley, Co E, slightly; Levi Fisher, Co E, severely; H Ward Sharpless, John Quinn, Jacob Fry, Co E, slightly; Michael Gormily, Co E, severely; Sergt James Mann, Co F, Privs E M Bascom, G A Hornett, Patrick Linn, Co F, slightly; Jno Hannington, Co F; D M Fullen, J G McNelly, M Sheridan, S R Thornington, Co G, severely; Corpl P A Taylor, Co G; Privs Wm Mills, Wm Walsh, Co G; Sergt G S Bradley, Co H, slightly; Corpl John Conroy, Co H; Privs John Bombard, Roger McDonough, Tim Mahon, Co H, severely; Sergt Wm Merrick, Co I; Corpls H Snow, Jno Farley, Co I, slightly; Privs Thom Blake, Danl Clarke, Co I; Thos Dodd, Co K, severely; Frs Gruber, Wm Ruket, Ed Gilligan, Co K, slightly; Thos Crawford, Jno Peoples, Geo A Pay, Corpls Michael Jaranski, Co K, severely; Jos Lathrop, Priv Frs Meyer, Co K, slightly.

7th Infantry—**KILLED**—Capt Charles Hanson, Co E; Sergt Jas Truman; Privs R Stewart, Co G; Wm Webb, Co H. **WOUNDED**—Capt R H Ross, Co D, severely; 1st Lieut C H Humber, Co B; Privs Jno Sires, Co A; Francis Brown, Co C, slightly; Dennis Cardy, Co C, severely; Saml Benton, W Parmentier, Co D, slightly; Corpl J Crangle, Co E; Privs P Mony, J Walker, O Sullivan, Co E, severely; L Clarke, Co E; Musician J Mabin, Co E; Corpl J A Roberts, Co G; Priv Geo Bull, Co H, slightly; Corpl H Doleman, Co I, severely;

Privs Albert Hart, Co I; Peter Maloney, Saml Ratcliffe, Co K, slightly; Benj Veny, Co K, severely. **MISSING**—Priv Rice.

Total in Second Brigade—Killed, 23; Wounded, 126; Missing, 4. Engineer Company—Wounded, 4; Missing, 1. Total, 158.

***Company K, 1st Artillery—Light Battery, 2d Division*—** **KILLED**—Privs Francis Melvin, Harvey Tyng. **SEVERELY WOUNDED**—1st Lieut J Martin, 2d Lieut Edward C Boynton, Sergts Patrick Martin, Joseph McGee, Privs David Adams, Alex Bruce, Michael Circhlaw, G W Fish, Alex McCabe, John Jones, Adophus Shaffer, Patrick Walker, Henry Williams. **SLIGHTLY WOUNDED**—Corpl John Jones, Privs John Krahuler, Henry Parrow, John T Prath, Christopher Phillips, Louis Loup, Louis Christian, John Gow, Artificer Ebin F Shedd.

Total—Killed, 2; Wounded, 23; 15 horses killed or totally disabled; 3 severely and 5 slightly wounded.

Third Division—Gen Pillow

Return of Killed, Wounded and Missing in the Actions of the 19th and 20th August, 1847, near the City of Mexico, of the 1st Brigade, 3d Division, Commanded by Brig Gen Pierce.

First Brigade

9th Infantry, Col T B Ransom—**KILLED**—1st Sergt L B West, Privs W Thompson, B McCluskey. **WOUNDED SEVERELY**—Lieut W N Newman, Lieut A F Palmer, Lieut Cranum, 2d Corpl W E Hoss, Privs S S Sweet, J B Hale. **WOUNDED SLIGHTLY**—Capt Johnson, 1st Corpl N W Grout, 3d Corpl W W Page, 4th Sergt J C Stowell, Privs T A Pratt, W R Haskins, Jas Webber, Geo G Goodman, T Beedle, C Gettins, J Moore, S P Hall, W Soule, M Wight, C F Blood, W Traub, H Dixon, J W Bondel, Jas Henderson, G Melville, D K Richmond, A W Brown, D Hogan, B Bean, J Flinn, W Gould, A T Pike, G W Woods, G Barnes, S F Davis, D Canfield, J Hosse, D Brown, J F Charterton, W Rhodes, J Scales, R Higgins, J Linsey, J T Fry.

12th Infantry, Lieut Col M L Bonham—**KILLED**—1st Sergt Wm C Oliver, 2d Sergt Peyton Randolph. **WOUNDED MORTALLY**—Priv Henry L Dermitt. **WOUNDED SEVERELY**—1st Corpl Jno L Tubbs, Privs Wm J Enos, Chauncey Howard, Martin Earls, Pinkney Anderson, Levitt Severs. **WOUNDED SLIGHTLY**—Capt N B Holden, 2d Lieut Jno C Limpkins, 2d Sergt Thos Smithers, 3d Musician Sam Church,

Jno A G Warneck, Wm M Davis, Fran M Bradly, Beverly Faughn, Warren D Blanton, Jas Calvin, Isaac Baker, John T Bowers, Adam Peyton, Geo Tatnon, W Morgan, Elijah Bowlin, Joseph Smith. **MISSING**—Privs Leander Crutcher, L Sherman.

15th Infantry, Col G W Morgan—**KILLED**—Lieut John D Goodman, Musician Chester G Andrews, Privs William Roberts, Samuel Carney, Jno Sleath, Peter Hill, Michael Spencer. **WOUNDED MORTALLY**—Capt. Augustus Quarels, Lieut Wm H H Goodloe, Privs Jno Glaze, Geo Gouph, Dan P Hanks, Fitch Cornall, Geo White. **WOUNDED SEVERELY**—Col Geo W Morgan, Sergts Jno Cunningham, J M Camm, Wm Mabee, Dan Rodes, Corpls Isaac W Griffith, Wm B Hopkinson, Jas Healy, Musician Jo Clark, Privs Jno W Cook, Wm Reed, Henry Widner, Alex Davis, Dorr H Fuller, Hiram Brown, Wm Rogers, Wm G Adams, Francis Fahrin, Jos Francis, Geo Steinman, Jacob Salinger, Jacob Hocer, Cornelius Westfield, Richard Northrap, Jacob J Bartim, Wm Barnett, Lewis Voight, Rupert Whitney, Clark Munson, Napoleon B Perkins, Wm H Miller, Thos Shortall, Peterson Lowry, Robt Linsey, John H Early, Michael Fratenger, Bidwell Cilley. **WOUNDED SLIGHTLY**—Lieuts Charles Peternell, J R Bennett, Sergt Major Thos McKeen, Sergts Fabian Bydol, Thos French, Fdk W Schooner, Corpl Horace Hancock, Privs Westley Gordam, Jas G Corbus, Geo Cooper, Isaac A Smith, Jas Soule, Alva Taylor, Jno McCamm, Jas Hill, Wallace W Wood, Jeremiah Griffith, Mather H Chance, Sam Trask, Edw B Calklin, Martin Klien, John Witson. **MISSING**—Maj Fredk Mills, Sergts Fredk Lawbenheimer, John Smith, Privs John Hochstetler, Wm Schimer, Joel Shively, Jasper Matley, John Stall, Balthaser Happle.

Recapitulation—Commissioned Officers: Killed, 1; Wounded, 11; Missing, 1. Non-Commissioned Officers and Privates: Killed, 11; Wounded 124; Missing, 10. Total, 158.

Second Brigade

Voltigeur Regiment, Col S B Andrews—**KILLED**—Sergt Rich'd S Pullinger, Corpl Rob't Enlow. **WOUNDED**—Sergt Robt B Taylor, Privs Miles K Bell, Rich'd Brooks, Jno Fitzsimmons.

14th Infantry, Col Trousdale—**KILLED**—Corpl John P Miller. **WOUNDED**—Privs Jas G Taliaferro, John J Jones, Theo Martins. **MISSING**—Privs Timothy A Wooden, John DeBarnes.

Rocket and Howitzer Battery, Lieut F D Callender—**KILLED**—Privs Jno Humphries, Robt Dougless, Jno Ungerer. **WOUNDED**—1st Lieut F D Callender, Corpls Lybanus Rabb, Albert J Borie, Jno Naglee, Privs Peter Strassner, Christian Schwartzweiler, Ezra Craven, Henry D Perry, Michael Fitzgerald, Michael Farrel, Thos K Polk, Geo Sweekard.

Fourth Division—Gen Quitman

Shields' Brigade

South Carolina Regiment, Col P M Butler—**Field and Staff**—**KILLED**—Col P M Butler. **WOUNDED SEVERELY**—Lieut Col Dickenson. **WOUNDED SLIGHTLY**—Capt Jas D Blanding, Adjt Jas Cantey. ***Company A***—**KILLED**—Capt C Wilder. **WOUNDED MORTALLY**—Priv Thos Black. **WOUNDED SEVERELY**—2d Lieut S Sumter, Corpl W T Norton, Privs R Caughman, J M Smith. **WOUNDED SLIGHTLY**—C H Moody, E Hunt, Jas Dunn. ***Company B***—**KILLED**—Priv W R Davis. **WOUNDED SEVERELY**—Corpl E C Postell, Privs Thos Charles, D McHenry, Jas Young, Jas Faucett. **WOUNDED SLIGHTLY**—Sergt G W Curtis, Corpl A J Hood, Privs T Cahill, J Connor, T E Dallas, T O Estes, J M D Hood, T Robbins, S Terrell. ***Company C***—**KILLED**—Priv Hitton. **WOUNDED SEVERELY**—2d Lieut R S Billings, Sergts Gay, George Waters, Corpls Gaston, Horton, Privs Bradley, Hunter, Meggs, Stratton, Sidwell, Villipigue. **WOUNDED SLIGHTLY**—Capt R S Moffatt, Privs Ballard, Wooten, Humphreys. ***Company D***—**KILLED**—2d Lieut David Adams, Priv Thos F Tillman. **WOUNDED SEVERELY**—2d Lieut Joseph Abner, Corpl W B Brooks, Privs Jas Joff, J Whitaker, J Addison, F Posey, R J Key, W F Uuthank. **WOUNDED SLIGHTLY**—Privs J Lark, E Linkins, S Stoman. ***Company F***—**WOUNDED SEVERELY**—Sergts J D Walker, J N Hicks, Corpl J McCollum, Privs Campson, Hartman, Murken, Valentine, Gilbert, Mackey, Pratt, Weatherby, Vauney, Wagner. **WOUNDED SLIGHTLY**—Corpl J F Quinn, Privs Miott, Wright. ***Company G***—**WOUNDED SEVERELY**—1st Lieut J R Clark, Sergt Row, Corpl McCreight, Privs M Harper, T H Reynolds, J McNeil, J Cain, W B McCreight, M B Travis, M B Stanley, R J Barber, R J Gladney, S Alexander, Wm Nelson. **WOUNDED SLIGHTLY**—2d Lieuts J W Steen, J R Davis, Corpl I Myers, Privs S F Bone, S Camak, S Newman, W J Sanders, W M Goodlet, J Romedy. ***Company H***—**KILLED**—Privs Timothy Kelly, Shedrick Wiggins.

WOUNDED SEVERELY—J Kennedy, Wm Mooney, R H Corly, W S Johnson, W F Purse, W Doolin, T Price, E Price, J B Cantwell, R Waddell, J F Watts, W Barkelow. **WOUNDED SLIGHTLY**—Capt W D Desaussure, Sergt H Beard, J L Percival, J M Miller, T Beggs, Privs M Brown, H J Caughman, J Campbell, J T Lune, E G Randolph, J D Stanford, D Pollock. ***Company K*—KILLED**—2[d] Lieut W R Williams, Priv John Slattery. **WOUNDED MORTALLY**—Privs Bernard Cregan, J Baughman. **WOUNDED SLIGHTLY**—Corpl W B Eaves. ***Company L*—KILLED**—Sergt Jas Denson. **WOUNDED SEVERELY**—Corpl J A Speers, Privs W Shephard, C Wood, M R O'Neale, G H Abney, M Clopton. **WOUNDED SLIGHTLY**—Privs B H Mattis, J Warner. Total, 137.

New York Regiment—Col Ward B Burnett, severely wounded; Sergt Major Jeremiah Rielly, killed. ***Company A*—KILLED**—Priv Benj Bennett. **WOUNDED**—2[d] Lieut T W Sweeny, severely; 2[d] Lieut C S Cooper, severely; Corpl Louis Albourgh, severely; Privs James M Boyle, severely; John S Drew, severely; James Stacum, slightly. ***Company B*—KILLED**—Sergt H Von Romain, Color-bearer; Sergt Louis Bovet, Privs David Rathbone, Peter Wilsse. **WOUNDED**—Sergt Carl Becher, severely; Corpl H Dardonville, slightly; Privs John E Tweedy, dangerously; L Muir, slightly; C Pingoll, slightly; P Sheen, slightly; Geo Daub, slightly. ***Company D*—WOUNDED**—Priv G Spaulding, slightly. ***Company E*—KILLED**—Lieut F Chandler, Priv Jacob Tuers. **WOUNDED**—1st Sergt G Fitzgerald, severely; Privs James Grady, severely; Chas Thompson, severely; John H Leech, severely; Francis Conroy, slightly; Munson, slightly, Armstrong, slightly, Hoe, slightly; Searle, slightly; Slowly, slightly. ***Company F*—WOUNDED**—Privs John Boyle, severely; D Costello, severely; P McCaun, severely; Thos Supple, slightly; Wm Tompkins, slightly; John Meyer, slightly. ***Company G*—KILLED**—Privs Robt Devoe, Bernard Crummy. **WOUNDED**—1st Lieut Chas H Innis, slightly; 1st Sergt John Wilson, slightly; Privs Andrew Kline, severely; Wm Hart, severely; Chas Crapp, severely, Alex E Fisk, severely; Peter Farley, severely; James Smith, severely; Jas McGill, severely; Alex Rodney, severely; Edward Carr, severely; Adam Saun, severely; Martin Finney, severely; Nelson Barnes, slightly; Albert E Dennis, slightly; Bernard DeYoung, slightly; John Shaw, slightly; J Smith, slightly; Lott Swift, slightly; Musician Patt Berry, slightly.

***Company H*—KILLED—**Priv Wm Allison. **WOUNDED—**2d Lieut Jacob Griffin, jr, slightly; Corpls H Moorehead, slightly; T W Gray, slightly; Privs Jas Brady, severely; Wm Brumagem, severely; Robt Dyss, severely; John Gower, severely; Wm Boyd, slightly; Alfred Doherty, slightly; Edward Fisher, slightly; Cornelius Winter, slightly. ***Company I*—KILLED—**Corpl Smith Harris, Priv James Murphy. **WOUNDED—**Capt Morton Fairchild, slightly; 2d Lieut Jas D Potter, severely; Sergt Edward Cook, severely; Privs Robt Dooley, slightly; Samuel Gardner, slightly; Harry Lake, slightly; Stephen Streeter, slightly; John Gardner, slightly; Jos Duffin, slightly; Richard Orden, slightly; Danl Robertson; Joseph Franklin, slightly; Henry Phillips, slightly; Jacob Rielly, slightly. ***Company K*—KILLED—**Privs Pat Fagan, Henry Maxlam, Charles Foley. **WOUNDED—**Capt G Dyckman, severely; 1st Lieut Jas S McCabe, slightly; 2d Lieut Malowhousky, slightly; Corpl Alex Moran, severely; Privs Wm Jones, severely; Jas Brown, severely; Jas Tomkins, severely; Henry S Woods, severely; A Van Allen, severely; Randolph Tuttle, severely. **MISSING—**Priv John Cook.

Killed—Commissioned Officers, 1; Non-Commissioned, 4; Privates, 11. Wounded—Commissioned Officers, 9; Non-Commissioned, 9; Privates, 68. Missing—Private, 1. Total, 103.

August 28, 1847. Tacubaya.

Thus rested matters until the 26th, when a small train of our wagons started for the city to procure supplies, according to one of the provisions of the armistice. They were stopped on the road by the enemy's guard, owing to some misunderstanding. On the next day, after an explanation, they again started, and after entering the city, notwithstanding the Mexican escort, the rabble and lepers of the streets fell upon the teamsters and persons accompanying the train with missiles and stones, and severely injured several of them. I believe they have again apologized and explained; what will be the course of our authorities remains to be seen.

August 29, 1847. 9 O'clock.

We still remain *statu quo*. Mr. Trist has been in session two days with Gens. Herrera and Mora, the Commissioners appointed by the Mexican Government to negotiate peace. Matters, I am informed, are going on smoothly between the Mexican Government and its agents and our authorities, but with the rabble of the city, there's no telling, they have neither sense nor reason, and are governed entirely by their passions.

It would really be unfortunate if anything should occur at present to prevent concluding the negotiations. Our authorities will remain passive until "forbearance ceases to be a virtue."[7]

Undated.

The Dragoons

The services of the Dragoons being of a distinct nature from the other corps of the army, I have deemed it preferable to embody them in a separate article, especially devoted to that purpose. This course, while it will enable me to do greater justice to all parties, will also permit me to enlarge on certain points, in relation to this arm of the service, which it would not be proper to introduce into the details of an engagement.

It is a well-known fact that, since the commencement of the present war, the cavalry force has been entirely inadequate to the exigencies of the service. This want has been severely felt in every engagement with the enemy. It has prevented us from following up and reaping the full fruits of our victories; and while it has imposed an unusual amount of labor on the mounted force, the officers complain that, from the same cause, they have not been admitted to a full participation in the glory of our achievements. Detachments are so frequently and necessarily called for, by the different divisions of the army, for picket-guards, escorts, and other purposes, that, at the decisive moment, the amount of force at a given point has not been found sufficient to act with vigor and success. This fact is deeply to be regretted, not only for the considerations which I have already assigned, but on account of the officers themselves, who, always in the van of the army and constantly exposed to be cut off while reconnoitring, have gallantly confronted danger wherever it was to be met.

When the cavalry force was embodied into a brigade at Puebla and placed under the command of the gallant Harney, it was hoped that a sufficient force would be kept together to act with efficiency.

7. Edmund Burke.

This hope was also strengthened by the removal of Maj. Sumner from the Rifle Regiment, which he led so nobly at Cerro Gordo, to the command of the 2[d] Regiment of Dragoons. But these expectations, I regret to say, have not been realized. Immediately after the action had commenced at Churubusco, Col. Harney and Maj. Sumner joined the General-in-Chief with three companies only, and these companies being withdrawn, one after another, to strengthen different points, they soon found themselves without commands. But the Dragoons, though detached, were not idle, being constantly and actively employed, as will be shown, in different quarters since the 7th of August, performing the most arduous and indispensible duties.

On the 10th, as the army descended the grand slope of the Sierra which divides the beautiful and productive valleys of Puebla and Mexico, and the Dragoons, who were in advance, were about to take position at the Hacienda of Buena Vista, the enemy appeared in front with a large force of cavalry. It was confidently expected that a fight would ensue, and preparations were instantly made to commence the attack. Col. Harney directed Maj. Sumner to charge this force with a squadron, comprising the companies of Capts. Blake and Hardee, while he supported him with the remainder, but the enemy fled precipitately on the approach of our troops and, although pursued, could not be overtaken. On the 17th, Capt. Blake, commanding the advanced guard, entered the town of San Augustin, after a slight skirmish with the enemy. On the 18th, Capt. Thornton was killed instantly by a cannon-shot, fired from San Antonio, while he was reconnoitring that position with his company. This gallant officer met death with the same heroic resolution which he had uniformly displayed in all the events of his checkered career. The first to encounter the enemy in the present war, at Caracita, where he narrowly escaped with his life, he was also the first of the many victims in this engagement, who have sealed their devotion to their country with their lives, and whose memories will be enshrined in the hearts of a grateful people.

At the battle of Contreras, on the 19th, the entire cavalry force was held in reserve for hours, within the range of the enemy's shells. On the 20th, this force was so cut up into detachments that not more than three companies were enabled to act together at any time or place. Capts. Hardee and Ruff were ordered, on this day, to hold important points near San Augustin and the former, while in the performance of this duty, was attacked by a large band of guerrillas, but they were promptly and handsomely repulsed by Capt. Hardee and his subaltern, Lieut. Richard H. Anderson, and about thirty of the enemy's horses, with their arms and accoutrements, captured. Capt. Blake and his squadron were engaged in securing and bringing in the prisoners taken at Contreras. Col. Harney, finding himself without a command on the field of battle, was actively and usefully employed with his staff, consisting of Capt. George W.F. Wood, A.Q.M.; Lieut. William Steele, A.A.A.G.; and Lieut. Julian May, A.D.C., in rallying troops that had broken under the enemy fire. Towards the close of the engagement, Maj. Sumner was placed, by the Commanding General, in charge of the last reserve, consisting of the Rifle Regiment and one troop of Horse, and was gallantly leading it to the attack, when the enemy broke and fled. The burst of enthusiasm with which the Rifle Regiment received its old commander, gave earnest of what might have been expected had this favorite corps encountered the enemy.

Perceiving the enemy retreating in disorder, the intrepid Harney collected all the cavalry within his reach, consisting of parts of Capt. Ker's company, 2^d^ Dragoons, Capt. Kearny's company, 1st Dragoons, and Capts. McReynolds' and Duperu's companies, 3^d^ Dragoons, and pursued them vigorously to the gates of the city. Many of the enemy were overtaken in the pursuit and killed. The impetuous and gallant manner in which this charge was executed is a theme of universal admiration. Officers and men seemed to vie with each other which should be foremost in the pursuit. Capt. Kearny and Lieut. Steele led the advance and charged with a few men into the very entrenchments of the enemy. Had this movement been supported, or the Dragoons embodied, the city would have been entered the same evening and our flag would now be flying from the highest point of the Palace of the Montezumas!

In this charge, Capt. Kearny lost an arm and Capt. McReynolds and Lieut. Graham were wounded. Lieut. Ewell had two horses shot under him.

September 15, 1847. National Palace, City of Mexico.

At last after seven bloody and obstinate battles, the American army has possessed itself of this famous city, after having routed its defenders from point to point, at each one of which a most vigorous resistance was made, encountering obstacles and impediments which only the intrepid valor of our soldiers, and our superior knowledge of the art of war could have enabled us to overcome. The discipline of our soldiers, in the various contests around the city, even more apparent than it had been before, and the advantages of our military science became in every successive engagement more visible to the eyes of the spectators. Our small and valiant army has performed the most heroic acts, and history does not present a parallel to the achievements of the American army within the last two years.

We have invaded a country of 7,000,000 inhabitants, capturing its capital, containing 200,000 souls, and defended by 30,000 troops of the line, well-paid and equipped. This has been effected by an army of not exceeding 15,000 men, including all those stationed between Vera Cruz and this place, and the number with which we arrived before the capital, including the train, was a little less than 9,000 men. The battles of Contreras and Churubusco cost us in killed and wounded over 1,000 men, so that at the termination of the armistice we had a force of less than 8,000 men, with which we attacked the enemy in his positions, he having had an opportunity during the truce to reorganize and reinforce his army, which had been defeated on the 19th and 20th ult. It is said that on the 10th of the present month, the Mexican army consisted of 18,000 men.

The Mexicans, when they had attained their object, having violated the armistice and not accepting the conditions offered them, were, on the 6th inst., notified by Gen. Scott, that if satisfaction was not given, the armistice would be considered at an end, on the following day at 12 o'clock. The Mexicans did not comply with the requirement, and the general commenced preparations for the attack of the city and its fortifications, ordering the forces to the neighborhood of Molino del Rey.

To the west of the Castle of Chapultepec there are three or four buildings which had formerly been used as a foundry, and Gen. Scott having been informed that they were still used for casting cannon, he determined immediately to destroy them. Gen. Worth, with his

Castle of Chapultepec. *Courtesy Library of Congress*.

division, and Gen. Pierce, with his brigade, were charged with the execution of the order on the morning of the 8th. The ground over which our troops marched towards these buildings was an open plain, descending towards them, and from this point our men could perceive a deep ravine which inclined gradually around the hill towards our right flank, at a distance of 200 yards from the buildings.

The line of battle was formed on the summit of the hill; two 24-pounders of Capt. Huger's battery were placed in an elevated position where they could command and batter down the fortifications of the enemy. It was thought that a short time would suffice to attain the object, but as our infantry was far in advance of the artillery it could not operate without injury to our own troops. Consequently, as our line advanced to the summit of the hill, our infantry was exposed to a most terrible fire of musketry from the Mexicans, stationed behind the houses, walls, and fortifications, which mowed down our men like grass before the scythe. A small body of Mexican lancers, who were stationed on the opposite hill about 800 yards distant, seeing this, and supposing that it was the time for them to complete a victory, put spurs to their horses, charging like a legion of devils. But as quickly as this was noticed, a section of Col. Duncan's battery—the two recaptured Buena Vista pieces—was stationed upon the left wing and opened a fire upon the enemy, while Maj. Sumner, with his command of mounted riflemen, which had been held in reserve, charged from the north of our line, passing under the fire from the houses (by which he lost six killed, thirty-two wounded, and 103 horses, only two officers not having their horses shot under them) and compelled the lancers to re-pass the ravine in great disorder and confusion. A short time afterwards, Maj. Sumner was joined by Capt. Kearny's company of the 1st Dragoons, under the command of Lieut. Richard S. Ewell, who went in pursuit of the Mexicans, but after repeated efforts they found that their force was too small to dislodge them. During this time the infantry took the buildings and surrounding works, and the artillery, which consisted of one 24-pounder, commanded by Lieut. Charles P. Stone, and the Buena Vista battery of Capt. Simon H. Drum, opened a fire on the retiring forces of the enemy, scattering destruction among them. Col. Harney arrived on the field towards the end of the action, and participated in the charge of the dragoons, which did not take full effect on account of being impeded by the walls in the rear of the enemy's works.

But you can imagine our astonishment when we discovered that these buildings, which had cost us so much, contained not the slightest appearance of a foundry, we having watered the field with the blood of our best troops, giving in exchange for the place the lives of our veteran soldiers. As the occupation of the place was of no interest to us, we retired, after having collected the dead and wounded, which amounted to about 600.

The name of Molino del Rey will never be forgotten by us, nor the veterans who there fell, and whose names will be engraven upon our memory as long as life endures. Among them I find Col. Martin Scott, a veteran of the War of 1812, Col. William M. Graham, Capt. George W. Ayers, Capt. Moses E. Merrill, and Lieuts. Joseph F. Farry and Erastus B. Strong, killed; mortally wounded, Capts. Ryley and Ephraim K. Smith, and less seriously, Col. James S. McIntosh, Capt. Albermarle Cady, Capt. William H. T. Walker (of the 6th Infantry), and Capt. Robert Anderson, and Lieuts. Sidney Smith, Charles B. Daniels, Henry Prince, Muscoe L. Shackleford, &c.; in all, thirty-two officers killed and wounded.[8]

8. Martin Scott served in General Taylor's army in 1846 as captain in the 5th Infantry, but received a promotion to major that same year. He won

Battle of Molino Del Rey. *Courtesy Library of Congress*.

---

brevets for Palo Alto, Resaca de la Palma, and Monterrey, the last to lieutenant colonel. An acknowledged sharpshooter in the Green Mountains of Vermont, Scott could hammer a nail part way into a board and then drive it home with a bullet. Scott was killed in the attack at Molino del Rey on September 8, 1847. Cullum, *Historical Register* 1: 869; *Times-Picayune*, November 4, 1847.

A West Point graduate in 1817, three of William Graham's brothers—Campbell, James, and Lawrence—also served in the army. William and Campbell were both seriously wounded on the same day in 1835 during the Second Seminole War, the former winning a brevet to major. Promoted to major of the 2^{d} Infantry and lieutenant colonel of the 11th Infantry while in Mexico, William Graham was killed on September 8, 1847 during the attack on Molino del Rey. Heitman, *Historical Register* 1: 468; *Washington Daily Union*, October 23, 1847; *Boston Evening Transcript*, October 26, 1847; *New York Herald*, October 24, 1847.

A veteran of the War of 1812, James McIntosh had been seriously wounded in the neck resulting in a distinct tilt of his head. While lieutenant colonel of the 5th Infantry, at the battle of Palo Alto McIntosh was dismounted by Mexican soldiers; "one of them thrust a bayonet into his mouth, cutting out a row of teeth, the point passing out near the ear; another cut him upon the side of the neck with a lance or sword, severing the cords." Strangely, this latter wound was on the opposite side of his original injury and, upon the latter healing, his head straightened out. Returning to Mexico after a period of convalescence, McIntosh was struck by two balls during the fight at Molino del Rey and died of his wounds on September 26, 1847. Heitman, *Historical Register* 1: 669; *Nashville Tennesseean*, November 1, 1847; *Newport Mercury*, November 6, 1847.

The 8th, 9th, and 10th were occupied upon our side principally in reconnoissances of the different approaches to the city, bringing up the rear, removing the wounded to a place of safety, and making preparations for the attack. During this time Gens. Pillow, Quitman, and Twiggs reconnoitred the suburbs without being disturbed by the enemy. The cavalry and artillery had some encounters with the Mexicans, who continued to make demonstrations on different points. On the 11th a large body of cavalry attacked Capt. Hardee, of the Dragoons, who was despatched with a small party to reconnoitre, but they were repulsed with the loss of six killed and some wounded, leaving Capt. Hardee in possession of the field. It was a portion of the force which Santa Anna had employed in the charge upon Maj. Sumner, and fearful of being severely reprimanded for their conduct, they wished to distinguish themselves individually. Accordingly, a soldier came to the front, brandishing his lance as a challenge to single combat. As quickly as it was understood, the challenge was accepted, and a sergeant advanced to him and despatched him in less time than is spent in referring to it. An officer and soldier then approached, brandishing their arms, when Capt. Hardee advanced to them at full speed, but they, thinking discretion the better part of valor, retired to the rear of the line, apparently well satisfied with their experience of the dragoons.

After the middle of the day, a column of about 1,000 men sallied out of the fortifications of La Piedad, in front of the encampment of Gen. Pillow, moving as if they were in quest of a favorable place to attack our forces. When they approached, Capt. Magruder opened upon them with his battery, firing until they retired to their entrenchments, the cavalry retiring in disorder in all directions.

In the evening, Gen. Twiggs, with the 1st Brigade of his division, moved from San Angel, to Le Piedad, where Col. Riley's brigade had been before, and took possession of the advanced works of the enemy, Gen. Pillow at the same time moving from Tacubaya. The position of the army being completed, on the 11th, Gens. Pillow, Quitman, and Worth being at Tacubaya, and Gen. Twiggs at Piedad, they commenced arranging their batteries preparatory to the cannonade of the 12th, the first three in front of the Castle of Chapultepec, and the last 500 yards from the enemy's fortification on the Piedad road. Battery No. 1 was under command of Capt. Drum; No. 2, of Lieut. Hagner; and all under the supervision of Capt. Huger; and that at La Piedad under the orders of Capt. Edward J. Steptoe.

On the morning of the 12th, all the batteries which had been arranged in the night, opened their fire, the enemy answering it with much rapidity and precision. The attack of Gen. Twiggs, intended solely as a feint, was believed to be a real assault by the Mexicans. They supposed in the city that that was the point assailed, and they commenced to march reinforcements to the place, which on account of the nature of the road and position of Capt. Steptoe, were compelled to pass within range of his guns, and he repeatedly and effectively discharged them among their forces, the Mexicans answering with firmness. But our position was so well chosen, and their fortifications so well made, that neither received any injury, and when the troops of the enemy had arrived at the castle, our battery was again turned in that direction, the cannonading being continued, which resulted in dismounting the artillery and killing the artillerymen. If that opportunity had been improved by Gen. Twiggs with his division, the works of the *garita* would have been taken with very little loss.

During the whole day the heavy batteries continued their fire upon the Castle of Chapultepec, destroying the edifice, and completing the destruction of the parapets, by this means the greater portion of the troops who defended them becoming exposed.

On the morning of the 13th, the heavy pieces were opened with frightful effect upon the forces which had arrived in the night, and at 7 o'clock Gen. Smith's brigade marched to Tacubaya to reinforce the division of Gen. Quitman. In order to make the assault, parties of volunteers were chosen from the different divisions, they being placed in the direction of the points they were destined to occupy. Some interesting incidents then occurred at the head-quarters of the "Cerro Gordo Division." When the volunteers arrived opposite Gen. Quitman, he approached them with a small stand of the national colors in his hand, saying to his companions in arms: "This is the national flag. It was given to me many years since, and I promised that it should triumph.

Since that time, it has conquered the Seminoles, it has seen Black Hawk defeated, and has been victorious in the battles of Palo Alto, Resaca, Monterey, Vera Cruz, Cerro Gordo, and in those which have taken place around the City of Mexico. I put it into your hands, confident that you will complete its glories by planting it upon the highest part of the Castle of Chapultepec." Lieut. Gaud, as commander, received the flag, and the soldiers raised a shout of enthusiasm. Those colors were the first that waved over the Castle of Chapultepec.

In making the assault, Gen. Pillow was ordered to ascend to the breach at the highest part towards the west; Gen. Worth, on the northward; and Gen. Quitman was to approach at the southwest with the volunteers, sustained by Gen. Smith's brigade, to cover the works of the *garita*, and take possession of them. The signal gun being given, Capt. Drum and Lieut. Hagner continued their fire upon the castle from their respective positions, in order to dismount the enemy's cannon, and to protect our infantry. But the Mexicans ceased their fire in that direction and concentrated it upon those who were supporting Gen. Worth's movement, and upon the dragoons, against whom they appeared to cherish a personal animosity. A thousand heroic deeds were acted at all points, to refer to which I have no space, nor could words have power to describe them. Suffice it to say that the New York Regiment planted its banner upon the first tower, the Riflemen placed theirs upon the bastions which surrounded the castle, and the flag of the "Cerro Gordo Division" waved upon the highest part of the edifice. This division with Gen. Quitman captured the fortifications constructed for the defence of the road.

In the attack, we lost, among others, Col. Trueman B. Ransom and Maj. Levi Twiggs.[9] Gen. Pillow and Col. Charles Baxter were

9. Levi Twiggs was a younger brother of General David Twiggs, both sons of General John Twiggs, the "Saviour of Georgia" during the Revolution. Levi left college for a commission as lieutenant in the U.S. Marines in 1813 and commanded the detachment aboard the frigate *President* when it surrendererd to the British frigate *Endymion* in 1815. Promoted to major in 1840, his career had included desk jobs and chasing Seminoles in Florida. Major Twiggs commanded the Philadelphia Naval Yard until sent off to Mexico in 1847. He "fell at the head of his command, leading them to the assault at the storming of Chapultepec, pierced by a bullet through the heart." Major Twiggs

Voltigeurs and Infantrymen Assault Chapultepec. *Courtesy Library of Congress*.

---

was fifty-four years of age. A son, George D. Twiggs, acting as an aide to Major F.T. Lally, 9th U.S. Infantry, had been killed on August 12, 1847 in an encounter with guerrillas while en route to Jalapa. *Augusta Chronicle*, December 9, 1847; *Brooklyn Daily Eagle*, October 11, 1847.

seriously, and Gen. Shields slightly wounded.[10] The latter, notwithstanding his wound, placed himself at the head of his brigade and conducted it into the hottest of the combat.

An incident occurred in taking the breastworks on the road, which is worthy of recording. Lieut. Robert M. Morris, of the Rifles, was ordered with his company to assault the point before which Maj. Twiggs had been killed, but not believing his force sufficient, he ordered some sailors to join him, but they refused because he was not their commander. Morris said that he was an officer, but the sailors replied that he did not belong to their branch of the service. "Well, then," said the lieutenant, "I am the son of Commodore Morris, of the Navy, and if you venerate his name, advance with me." A shout was the answer of the sailors, and they captured the place at the point of the bayonet, and routing the Mexicans from it.

Chapultepec and the surrounding works being taken, and Gen. Pillow being wounded, Gen. Scott decided that Gen. Quitman, with his division, and Smith and Pierce with their brigades, should advance to the city along the aqueduct, while he himself should proceed to San Cosme by the main road, with Gens. Worth and Cadwalader. It would be impossible for you without a map to comprehend perfectly the various maneuvres, as I shall content myself with describing the last events of the day.

At about 600 yards distance from the gates, Gen. Quitman encountered a fortified house, from which the Mexicans, when they discovered us, opened a terrible and incessant fire of musketry. A regiment of Riflemen, protected by the aqueduct, drew their attention by their fire, while another force attacking sword in hand, dislodged the enemy, and Lieut. James Stuart planted our flag on the building, and the division continued its march towards the *garita*. The Mexicans then took shelter in the

10. Charles Baxter held positions in the New York legislature, custom house, and state militia prior to receiving his appointment as lieutenant colonel of the 1st New York Volunteers in 1846. While leading his regiment in the attack on Chapultepec, Baxter was struck in the groin by two musket balls. Taken to a hospital in Mexico City, he died of his wounds on September 18, 1847. Baxter's last words sent to his father by a surgeon were that "the New York regiment was there, and that I fell where I should have fallen, at the head of it." *New York Commercial Advertiser*, January 12, 1847; *Annual Reunion and Dinner of the Old Guard Association, 1894*, 104–5.

gardens and fortified enclosures, but they were quickly dislodged when Capt. Drum brought his artillery to bear upon them. The enemy then commenced a tremendous fire of musketry and shells, which rendered it necessary to take the fortifications of the *garita*. Lieut. Beauregard advanced to reconnoitre, and while he was making his report to Gens. Quitman, Shields, and Smith, Maj. Benjamin L.E. Bonneville, and others, a large shell burst precisely over our heads, bringing us all to the ground, but no one received any injury except by the fall, among them is included your humble servant.

In accordance with the information obtained through Lieut. Beauregard's reconnoissance, the South Carolina Regiment advanced to storm the works of the *garita*, supported by the rest of Smith's brigade. Gen. Quitman charged in person, and with his own hands placed our standard upon the walls of the fort, at half-past 1 o'clock. Lieut. Stuart, of the Rifles, leaping the ditch, was the first who entered the City of Mexico. The Riflemen captured two pieces of artillery, which Capt. Drum turned upon the enemy, causing them great loss. But this valiant soldier and accomplished gentleman, who had always lived an irreproachable life, after many brilliant military actions, fell mortally wounded. Every eye was turned towards him with admiration and compassion. It was he who recaptured the Buena Vista pieces, and used them with such effect at Molino del Rey; it was he who commanded Battery No. 1 during the cannonade of the two preceding days upon the Castle of Chapultepec; it was he, in short, who advanced his battery over the causeway in the face of a most terrible fire, acquiring eternal honor and fame, and dying in compliance with his vows. I believe that he has left a numerous family to mourn his loss, whom the nation as well as the army should support.

Gen. Quitman commanded during the action and when night arrived was in possession of a strong building in the city, where he established a battery of heavy pieces, in order to command the citadel on the following morning.

During the period of these operations, Gen. Worth arrived at the *Garita of San Cosme*, of which he immediately took possession, Capt. Huger having prepared to salute it with a 24-pounder.

The enemy, discovering that they would be totally destroyed the next morning, evacuated their position during the night. The next day, we commenced our march towards the Grand Plaza, under a fire directed upon us from the tops of the houses.

Gens. Quitman and Smith, at the head of the troops, were the first two American officers who entered the National Plaza of the ancient city of the Aztecs, and, by order of Gen. Quitman, Capt. Andrew Porter, of the Rifles, at 7 in the morning, unfolded the national flag of the "Division of Cerro Gordo" over the Palace of the Montezumas.

Chapter 4

Establishment of Martial Law

September 17, 1847. City of Mexico.

Now that we have conquered the capital and placed our victorious standard on the grand National Palace, we naturally look around us and inquire what are the circumstances in which we are placed, what is likely to follow on the heels of our late victories, and what measures and policy can be adopted most likely they ensure us the fruits of our labors and permanently secure the interest of our country with the least trouble and expence. I presume no one will doubt that the United States, in the present aspect of affairs, is at perfect liberty to pursue whatever policy the judgment of its proper authorities may consider her interests require, and the laws of nations justify.

Our victorious march from the coast, and the brilliant successes of our arms have placed us in possession of the Capital of the Republic, which we find at present without a government, legislative, executive, or judicial, with an army about, if not completely, dispersed or destroyed, without anyone with whom we can treat or talk to. Even if we desired to surrender all that we have acquired, there is no one with whom the formal ceremonies could be performed. What probability then is there that we will be able to find a body or even a single person with sufficient authority to sign, seal and, deliver us a valid bond for that which we require and will have? The whole country is in a state of anarchy, confusion, and dismay, with scarcely two persons agreeing upon any one point, and the commerce and trade of every department literally at a stand, and without any prospect of reviving under the present state of affairs.

The attitude of affairs, by which we are surrounded leave us but one of two alternatives, to-wit: military occupation and government of the country, or to fall back upon the base of our operations, take up one boundary line, and hold the harbors of the country until Mexico, tired of her oppressed condition, sues for peace, to relieve her from the chains which bind her upon the Gulf and the Pacific.

Annexation of the States of Mexico, Puebla, Vera Cruz, San Luis, Guanajuato, Guadalahara, or any other of those populous states included in the line drawn from Vera Cruz to the Pacific being totally out of the question, and makes it one of the greatest fallacies ever propagated. If we did annex them, the North never would consent to the existence of slavery in any of them. To allow them all the rights and immunities which we as free citizens enjoy, would bring about a state of affairs, which would endanger the existence of our own free institutions, and so disturb the equilibrium of the movements of our government as to make us rue the day we ever put foot upon the soil of Mexico. The people are totally and wholly unprepared by habits, education, and nature for exercising those high and important duties required by civilization and a free and liberal government. I have mixed and mingled with them to a great extent, and find that all their actions and course of living are prompted and based upon superstition, fraud, and villainy of the deepest dye—the great mass of natives ignorant beyond conception—totally without the least education, and entertaining the strongest prejudices, most generally based upon religious superstition, easily exasperated, and subject to be excited to the disorder and anarchy to which they have so long been accustomed.

Their pride and vanity induces everyone to consider himself a hero, and competent to overthrow any measure which his ignorance and prejudice will not enable him to fathom. Moreover, is there any American, of any religion whatever, willing to admit, in case of annexation, the right of a privileged and special church government, or a thraldom of monks and friars? The system of church government at present exercised here would have to be admitted and continued, or we would have to encounter a foe more formidable in its resources, more powerful in its combats, than all the bristling bayonets, glittering swords, and death-dealing artillery over which we have already triumphed. A war of religion is one of those wars which is never ended until one or the other of the parties is exterminated or so enfeebled as to be unable to offer resistance, and in a country as thickly populated as this it would inevitably be the result. Therefore, in view of things as they actually exist, I take it for granted that annexation of this section of the country is totally impracticable. Those who have been its advocates in the United States, myself, to some extent, among others, are ignorant of the difficulties our Government would have to encounter and the endless trouble and exasperations it would lead to.

Military occupation and government of all the country we have conquered, in my mind, offers no fewer obstacles than annexation. According to the opinions of the persons in this army whose views, by their acknowledged ability are entitled to the most weight, it would take an army of at least 100,000 men to occupy and garrison the different states and military posts. How long would it take us to get this force equipped and in the field? The President last winter called for ten additional regiments (10,000 men), and although it was during the short session of Congress, a portion of the troops have not yet arrived, and those which have come did not arrive at the seat of operations until the month of August. They were enlisted for the war under the excitement of active operations and a spirited campaign. Now that the excitement of the campaign has ended—that the next session of Congress is a long one—how long will it take us to throw into this country 100,000 troops, when they know their life is to be the dull monotony of the garrison? But admitting, for the sake of argument, that they could be sent here by the expiration of one year, is a standing army of 100,000 men in consonance with the spirit of our republican and free institutions? Would it move with the same simplicity and regularity our old army has? Would the military profession retain its present ability, its scientific attainments, its dignity, and its high character, by being so suddenly enlarged to 100,000? I think I may safely answer, no! Again, how would this large army have to be supported? Will the people of the United States consent to supply a revenue for its support? Will they consent to any further and permanent enlargement of the public expenditures for the sake of holding a territory from which they would derive very little benefit for years to come?

If we may judge of the aversion of the people of the United States to high taxation, high duties, and unproductive expenditures of the public treasure, I think I may be safe in concluding that they never will consent to the support of a standing army sufficient to garrison and occupy that portion we have already, and what of necessity we would have to conquer. Then the only alternative for the support of this army would be contributions drawn from the people of the states we occupy, by different means of direct and indirect taxation. This would have to be done by military authority and by officers of the army, which would lead to the existence of a state of affairs incompatible with the spirit of our institutions and the dignity of the army. Large amounts of money would have to be drawn from the country by means of contribution through the hands of the officers. Gradually, opportunities for speculation and traffic would offer itself, which is very difficult to resist. By degrees, means to avoid the law would be discovered. Men would seek the military profession prompted by the sole desire of accumulating money, not possessing a single one of those high, ennobling, and dignified traits of character which have heretofore characterized the conduct of the officers, and not having for their object the worthy and honorable ambition of serving their country and distinguishing themselves upon the red field of Mars. They would gradually become corrupt, profligate, and dishonest, and our own country would have to suffer the mortification of seeing our gallant little army stripped of the laurels they have so nobly won, and which they are so justly entitled to retain, and then be compelled to abandon the system they had adopted, perhaps at an irreparable loss.

Therefore, let us examine the other alternative, and see if our interests do not require that we should fall back upon the base of our operations, and if nothing more, await the dispositions of the American Congress.

We are here, and for the present, isolated from the government and the balance of the army. From the time the army set foot on the Rio Grande, we have had nothing but a succession of brilliant victories. We have penetrated the very heart of Mexico with four different columns, and from each point there has been a triumphal march, the Stars and Stripes have never as yet suffered a defeat. During the last campaign, within six months, we have lowered the Mexican colors from the strong Castle of San Juan de Ulua, and placed thereon our own. Then, after a hard march through the burning sands of the low country, we ascended the heights of Cerro Gordo and after encountering an army of more than double our force, we there unfurled our banner. Thus we continued our march to the valley of Mexico, with an army of 9,000, and before the capital of the Republic we met their army numbering 32,000, strongly fortified, and in the best position they have ever occupied, at Contreras, Churubusco, Molino del Rey, Chapultepec, and the gates of the city. At each place our arms have proved victorious, and we concluded by unfurling our national colors on the National Palace of Mexico, and they are not planted there for a day or a week, but just as long as we say they shall flutter in the breeze they will remain. This has completely settled the question of national honor; the valor and superiority of our own arms have been established beyond question or doubt. Mexico has been humbled and degraded in the eyes of the world, while our own brilliant achievements stand up prominently as a precedent in the annals of the world, to be admired and boasted of when the actors themselves shall lie mouldering in the dust. National and personal ambition has been satisfied. The nation will be proud of the trophies and those who won them. But with our successes we have arrived at the end of our rope, the capital has fallen, and there is nothing to offer us any further resistance. The president, Santa Anna, has abdicated the presidency and the commander of the army left, with a small body-guard, for parts unknown, and is now in fact a flying fugitive. The army of 32,000, which they had when we arrived before the city, does not now number over 2,000, without means of support, and deserting every day.

Can our army do anything more, could it be expected to have done anything more? Now there is no new enterprise which offers itself, and there is no government with which we can arrange our difficulties. Therefore, I would ask, if we had not better pack up our wagons as soon as the sick are able to be moved, and fall back upon the base of operations, and await the actions of our government. Then our wounded and sick men could be better provided for, and our army better and cheaper supplied and placed in good quarters, the volunteers sent home, the Regulars drilled, and the regiments filled up and prepared to occupy the boundary we may determine. This course of policy, in my opinion, considering the existing circumstances, is preferable on more accounts than one. It leaves the government at home in a position to carry out its views with facility and without delay. It would leave the army in a position as convenient in point of transportation, to the occupation of our boundary, as though it were in barrack in the United States.

If the government determined upon military occupation and government of the country, the army would have no more difficulty to encounter with 100,000 men than we have already met with 12,000, and after the conquests of the 12,000 already accomplished, I can scarcely believe any resistance whatever would be offered to 100,000.

The Mexican Congress, previous to our attack upon Chapultepec, by a secret vote agreed, in case the Americans should enter and occupy the capital, to meet on the 5th of October, at Querétaro, some twenty-one leagues from here. They are now endeavoring to effect a meeting at the appointed time, but it is extremely doubtful whether they will be able to do so, and if they should meet it is still more doubtful whether they will be able to come to any understanding among themselves. But if they should, or even if there was a present probability of their doing so, our determining to fall back upon the coast would in no wise affect their conduct or inconvenience ourselves. We would only be the better prepared to immediately take up the retrograde movement according to the condition of any treaty that might be made, and moreover, we would be in a position not likely to be affected by their humbugging and prevarications. Any delay or detention on our part would depend upon the prospects of an amicable adjustment.

But, in case they do not accomplish a meeting or agree upon terms, let us for a moment consider what would be the advantages derived from withdrawing the army immediately from its present position and occupying the boundary we have already claimed, with the Regular Army we at present have in the field.

By the beginning of the next summer the regiments as they at present exist could be placed upon the line of the boundary, and by fall can have their houses and necessary buildings for their protection from the inclemency of the weather completed. Also, by the time supplies can be placed at the various depots on the route, from whence the army can be well supplied, without delay and the trouble incident to slow and tardy movements. In twelve months from this time we would be peaceably and quietly occupying our boundary line, settlers would begin to pour into the new territory, which is the best protection a frontier can possibly possess, thereby enabling us in a very few years to reduce our army to nearly the former peace establishment, which by a judicious reduction would be more effectual than any 50,000 men we would be able to throw suddenly into the field. The amount of indemnity we have offered to pay the Mexicans on their yielding to us the territory we ask would transport our army, supply and maintain it in its position for at least three years, the revenue derived from the duties on imports would maintain the garrison occupying the harbors on the coast.

Is the United States not fully justified and sustained in pursuing such a course? Our armies have met those of Mexico upon every portion of her soil where she has been able to offer any resistance. We have conquered them and driven them from wherever they have met us. Upon the result of each battle we have tendered them the olive branch of peace. At each and every time they have either stubbornly refused or evaded a meeting of authorized agents, except upon terms that would debase us in our own estimation and lower us in the standard of nations before the civilized world. Thus has she persisted without rhyme or reason, until the elements of even a semblance of government have been scattered to the four winds, leaving us "monarchs of all we survey from the centre all round to the seas."[1] I sincerely hope that the United States will now determine with promptness and decision to pursue such a policy in her future contests with Mexico as her own interests may dictate and the laws of nations authorize, that she will determine her boundary, move immediately upon it, erect her forts and depots, invite settlers, and afford them such facilities as will soon

1. Paraphrase of a William Cowper poem.

people the frontier, and then defend and protect them until they are able to maintain themselves. If Mexico or any other power feels aggrieved at the course we have taken, let them drive us from our position if they can.

September 18, 1847.

During the operations of the army before the city, we have had cause to notice with especial pride the conduct of the rank and file of the army. Innumerable have been the instances of gallant bearing and lofty valor, of patriotic impulses and noble deeds. Not that style of patriotism usually so abundant about election times and Fourth of July celebrations, but patriotism and devotion worthy the soldiers of the American army, worthy the sons of the land of the free and home of the brave. It was at a time when their hearty co-operation with the officers was needed, at a time when death was being dealt in their midst unsparingly, and at a time when it tried the hearts of the bravest of the brave. These noble soldiers are worthy of some reward from the country, and I sincerely hope those designated by their officers will receive, as they are justly entitled, commissions in the army in accordance with the late act of Congress. The heavy loss we have sustained will require that many appointments will have to be made, either from the ranks or from civil life, and those who have acquitted themselves so handsomely in the ranks, will make far better officers than those taken from civil life. Gen. Scott refers to the conduct of the soldiery with as much pride as he does to any other department of the army, and I am confident he will give his hearty consent and influence to the appointments from the ranks as you will see by his published order, which I send you.

September 21, 1847. National Palace, Mexico.

An orderly and peaceful disposition seems to have taken possession of the people of this city. The citizens tell us that the city has not been as tranquil for two years as it is at the present time. This has been brought about by the well-regulated disposition of the troops by Gen. Scott, together with the other regulations adopted by the government of the city. Yesterday being Sunday, the clergy kept all the churches and places of religious worship closed, which had a tendency to excite the minds of the populace and impress them

General Scott's Triumphant Entry into Mexico City. *Courtesy Library of Congress.*

with the belief that something serious was going on unseen. Gen. Scott had previously informed the clergy that he desired they would continue as heretofore the exercise of their religious ceremonies, informing them at the same time that they should be protected in their person and property, and, as you will see by a clause in the General Order which I send you, placing all churches, monasteries, and public edifices under the protection and safeguard of every American. Gen. Scott again sent to the clergy and desired them to open their churches for regular worship, but they heeded him not. He then informed them, in substance, that their course was calculated to inflame the prejudices of the people and excite them to disorder, and if they thus continued their course of conduct, he should forthwith withdraw all protection from their property, let the consequences be what it might. This had the effect of bringing these gentlemen to their senses, their buildings were opened at once, and their religious ceremonies continued.

You will see by a General Order that the General-in-Chief has imposed upon the city a contribution of $150,000, of which $20,000 is to be appropriated to the purchase of necessaries and conveniences for the sick and wounded, $90,000 for the purchase of shoes, blankets, &c., for a gratuitous gift to the rank and file of the army, and $40,000 to be appropriated to other military purposes. The levying of contributions is a new movement in the prosecution of this war. The manner in which it has been appropriated reflects the highest credit to the head and heart of the General-in-Chief, and shows that he has not forgotten the gallant army who have followed him through fire and flood, and erected a lofty temple of fame on which he will stand admired by all the world. To the army it is but an act of justice to compensate them for the pecuniary loss they have sustained by the various movements incident to so many battles as have been fought before the capital. It is but fair and just that the inhabitants of the city should pay it, as I do not believe there is an instance on record when an army has captured a city by assault, that the people have been protected in their persons and property as they have been in this instance. Our army entered the city by storm after the most determined and stubborn resistance, in doing so they lost many of its proudest ornaments, and our whole loss amounts to one-third of the number we brought here. Our victories, one after the other, were the most decided, finally driving the defenders of the city from their very firesides. Even after we had entered the city, our men were shot from the tops of the houses. Their whole line of conduct was calculated to provoke pillage and plunder, yet still the property of this rich and beautiful city was left untouched and unharmed. These facts reflect high and honorable credit upon the discipline of the army, and are the brightest trophies of our victory.

September 23, 1847.

Gen. Scott, with Mr. Trist and his staff, have removed from the Palace to a residence in a more retired and quiet part of the city, where he is, no doubt, free from the incessant annoyances to which he was subjected in the Palace, and it is only now, by a strict guard at the door, that the populace are prevented from harassing him during the whole day. Every *Greaser*, *Greaseress*, and *Greaserita* that has lost a horse, an ass, an ox or a cow, a hog or a chicken, is daily seeking an opportunity to see the Commander-in-Chief, to know if they will not be remunerated for them. Some state that the Mexican army destroyed their property, but, as the Americans drove the Mexicans away, they think we ought to assume all the responsibilities. They have heard so much of the liberality of the Americans that they think they have nothing to do but to make out and present their accounts. One fellow had the impudence, a day or two since, to apply for indemnity for losses sustained during the street fight, under the following circumstances. When the Americans entered the town, some ten or twelve men were posted on the top of his house, and were firing indiscriminately into our ranks. A small detachment was sent to dislodge them, which could only be done by forcing the doors of the house and ascending through the interior. As soon as the detachment accomplished their task, and cleared all the buildings in the vicinity, they returned to the command, leaving the doors of all the buildings from whence the firing had proceeded to be closed and re-locked by the proprietors, or whoever might take the trouble to do it. But it appeared that as soon as our troops left the neighborhood, the *leperos* entered the building and robbed it of its contents and for this the fellow wanted to be indemnified. As he stated, if the Americans had not entered the building in order to drive the people away who were firing from the top, it would not have been plundered. The fellow was informed that he might consider himself very fortunate that his head had not already looked through a halter, and if the authorities took any further notice of the case, it would be to give him that consideration which his conduct merited. So it is every day, persons applying for redress who, if they had their dues, would already have received three feet of rope.

Gen. Scott being removed, Gen. Quitman occupies the Palace, and it has been placed under the superintendence of Capt. Charles Naylor, according to the following regulations:

1. Officers quartered in the Palace, or having troops quartered in it, will report immediately to the Superintendent, the number and locality of the apartment occupied by them, or their troops, respectively.
2. No apartment, in the Palace, can be taken possession of or occupied, as quarters for either officers or men, or for any other purpose, without having been first previously assigned by the Superintendent, upon proper application made to him.
3. No book, record, paper, article of furniture, or piece of property of any kind whatever, found in the Palace, will be permitted to be removed from the Palace, or from one apartment to the other, without the written permission of the Superintendent, first had, for that purpose.
4. No burial will be allowed within the Palace, or any of its grounds or enclosures.

5. Troops quartered in the apartments, containing any of the public records, or national archives, will immediately vacate them and find quarters elsewhere.
6. Any interference with, or mutilation of the books, papers, or records contained within the Palace, is strictly forbidden; and all persons are most earnestly requested to observe and enforce a compliance with this regulation and to preserve, as far as possible, the Palace itself, and all its furniture and contents, from injury or spoilation.

By order of Maj. Gen. Quitman, Military and Civil Governor,
Capt. Charles Naylor,
Superintendent of the National Palace and
Custodian of the National Archives, &c.

National Palace, Mexico, Sept. 21, 1847.

The grand reception room of the late President is now occupied by Gen. Quitman as an office, as also a portion of his suite of private rooms are occupied in the same manner as heretofore, except that they are protected by close and heavy guards. The suite of rooms which her ladyship, Doña Señora, had the honor of filling are now occupied by the general's staff, which, no doubt, contributes to render their duties more agreeable than for some weeks previous. Several other rooms are occupied by different officers of the general's staff, but all the troops have been removed. The only change which has been made in the building, was one of a strictly National character—the portrait of Agustin de Iturbide hung up over the reception chair of Santa Anna, which was all very well a month ago, but Lieut. Richard P. Hammond finding a full length portrait of Gen. George Washington in one of the rear rooms, and thinking that as the changes had been so general in the Palace, the portraits might as well change places also. Now the portrait of the Father of *our* country faces the principal entrance to the chamber, whilst his much loved "Stars and Stripes," enveloped in a halo of glory, wave over the halls of the National Palace.

September 25, 1847. City of Mexico.

Having sent you by two couriers a detailed account of the operations of our army since the conclusion of the armistice, but fearing that my first accounts have not reached you, I send you a short synopsis, together with a list of the killed and wounded. I also enclose to you the propositions of Mr. Trist to the Mexican government, and the counter proposition presented by them, together with the correspondence connected therewith.

The Mexicans having repeatedly violated the armistice agreed upon between our army and themselves, Gen. Scott, on the 6th, notified the Mexican authorities that unless they made explanation, satisfaction, and reparation for the injuries we had sustained, they should consider the armistice at an end on the 7th, at 1 o'clock. They not complying with the demands of Gen. Scott, we commenced preparations for the attack.

The General-in-Chief received information that at Molino del Rey, where stood several buildings, the Mexicans were at work casting cannon, shells, shot, &c. Desiring to stop their military operation, he directed Gen. Worth, with his division, supported by Gen. Cadwalader's brigade, to attack and destroy the place, on the morning of the 8th, and then retire. The buildings, which the Mexicans call *Casa Mata*, is situated on the west side of Chapultepec, and within 6-pound range of the guns of the fort. On the west side of the buildings, and the breastworks around them, is a large open plain, gradually descending to the position occupied by the Mexicans, a deep ravine inclines round this plain, or open space, until it arrives within about 200 yards of the building upon which rested the enemy's right flank. Two 24-pounders, belonging to Capt. Huger's siege train, were placed in position to batter down the breastworks and buildings, if they were found to be occupied by a heavy force, but they did not fire but a very few shots before Gen. Worth advanced his infantry down the plain, and attacked the enemy's works in the front and centre. The Mexicans opened upon them a most murderous fire from the point attacked, and both their flanks, which mowed down our troops like grass before the scythe. Many of the best officers of the division were cut down, and the heavy loss in the ranks caused the advance to waver for a moment, until the supporting force came up, which also sustained a severe loss. A column of lancers, numbering 4,000 to 5,000, which were stationed on the enemy's right, perceiving the effect of this deadly fire on our infantry, came charging down, in the hope of being able to take advantage of the circumstances, and put our troops to rout, but they were soon checked in their onward career. Col. Duncan brought two pieces of his battery to bear upon them, and Capt. Drum, with the two captured Buena

Vista pieces, also opened his fire on them. At the same moment, Maj. Sumner, with two squadrons of dragoons, and Capt. Ruff's company of Mounted Rifles, which, until then, had been held in reserve, passed down under the fire from the enemy's works, and charged the head of their column, which they could not stand for a moment, and commenced a confused and precipitous retreat. After that, they rallied twice, and attempted to return, but at each time our little handful of dragoons made them leave without exchanging cards.

The cavalry and infantry, rallying, succeeded in carrying the buildings and breastworks which the enemy held, and compelled them to retreat, capturing seven pieces of artillery, a large quantity of ammunition, small arms, &c, and about 600 prisoners. As soon as they were driven from the buildings, Capt. Drum and Col. Duncan advanced their light batteries, and Lieut. Stone brought forward one of the 24-pounders, the whole of which opened a most destructive fire upon them, as they retreated across a low plain to the rear of the position they at first occupied. Our loss was very heavy, and I regret to say, that some of the very best officers of our army fell killed and wounded, while the Mexican loss was very slight, until they commenced their retreat. While the cavalry were passing in front of the enemy, in order to charge the column of lancers, they were not under the fire more than ten seconds, and during that time they sustained a loss of six officers wounded, thirty-two privates killed and wounded, and a loss of 105 horses. There were but two officers that did not have their horses shot under them, but there is one thing very remarkable, that the horses from which the riders had been shot, wheeled and moved with the same regularity as though they had been mounted, until they came to halt from the charge, when they all kept on in a body in direction of the enemy.

We were deceived in reference to the character of the buildings, as there was no foundry, or even a semblance of one, and, after blowing up some of the buildings, and bringing off our killed and wounded, we evacuated the place, as the occupation of it would give us no advantage. Our loss was 800 killed, wounded, and missing.

The result of this engagement taught us one lesson, which was, that the Mexicans use their arms well, and fight well, when they are in position. Although the superiority of our arms, and the valor of the troops, will eventually triumph, yet still we must call into requisition all our military science and skill, or we purchase our victories at too dear a price. A list of the killed and wounded you will find in the general recapitulation which I send you. Many a tear will be shed on its perusal, and many a heart will bleed for the noble souls, and the old and firm veterans which fell in the assault.

Col. Riley was now advanced from San Angel (his former camp) to El Piedad, in order to make a diversion, and hold the entrance to the Piedad and San Antonio road. Gen. Pillow's division moved up to within supporting distance, and thus rested our army until the 11th, without anything of moment occurring. The Engineer Corps were busily employed night and day in their reconnoissance, ascertaining and examining the positions of the enemy, and the different entrances to the city. The Engineers, throughout all our operations, have performed a most dangerous and laborious duty. They have proved themselves to be men of sterling worth, of masterly ability, and bright ornaments of their profession. There was a little incident which occurred to Capt. Mason in one of his reconnoissances, which is worthy of record. It became necessary on one occasion for him to go very close to the enemy's breastwork, in order to ascertain its true position. As he approached, a Mexican officer rode out with two of his escort, and came up within a very short distance, when Capt. Mason drew his revolver. The Mexican then, in Spanish, saluted, "Good morning." The Capt. responded. The Mexican then said, "You seem to be very curious, suppose you come a little closer." "No, I thank you, sir. I can see very well from where I am." "Walk inside, sir. We will endeavor to treat you as well as the accommodations of the camp will enable us." "I am much obliged to you, sir, for your kindness, but prefer partaking of your hospitality on some future occasion." And, holding his spy glass to his eye, he continued, "I only want at the present to see how you are situated. I can see two guns in embrasure, one in barbette, and I think you have one in embrasure a little farther to the left. That gun I see your men loading I do not think you will be able to bring to bear on me, as I will keep you between it and myself." Moving round a little to the right, he continued his observations. One of the escort then spoke in English and said, "You damned rascal, you know better than to come in here. If I was to get hold of you, I'd cut your damned throat." Capt. Mason then said to the officer, "That fellow of yours speaks very good English, but he makes very bad use of it, and his scurrility is in striking contrast with your own respectful language. If we had him in our camp, we would teach him to be more respectful." The Mexican officer then rode off to one side. Capt. Mason, who had been making his observations during the whole time of the conversation, said to the officer, "I have no desire at present to be brought within the range of your guns, and having learned all I want to know about your position, I will bid you good morning, sir." He then returned to where he had left his escort, which until then had been unseen by the Mexican, who rode back to the fort, apparently much mortified and disappointed that he had not been able to decoy the captain into the trap that had been set for him.

On the 11th, a column of cavalry sallied out from the fort on the San Antonio road, either for the purpose of threatening our position or taking Capt. Magruder's battery, which was stationed with the picket within about 300 yards of their fort, though in a great measure covered from the range of their guns. As soon as they got their column moved out into a place free from all obstructions, Capt. Magruder opened two pieces upon them with shot and shell, which passed through them with great destruction, and they took to their heels, and got back to the fort as quick as possible. The fort opened two guns on the battery, but without further effect than killing one man of the 15th Infantry. An officer shortly after rode up and inquired of Capt. Magruder if the foe had fired on him. Holding a 12-pound shot, he replied that he had the gentleman's card, and he expected the cavalry would carry back his compliments to the fort.

About sundown, Gen. Twiggs, with the balance of his division, arrived at Piedad and Gen. Pillow moved with his division to the south of Tacubaya, and took a position on the west side of Chapultepec, and Gen. Quitman, with his division, occupied the road from Tacubaya to the City of Mexico, Gen. Worth's division remaining at Tacubaya.

In the course of the night, three heavy batteries were planted in front of the Castle of Chapultepec: No. 1, commanded by Capt. Drum; No. 2, by Lieut. Hagner; No. 3, by Lieut. Stone, all under the general command of Capt. Benjamin Huger, Chief of Ordnance.

Also during the night, Gen. Twiggs' division planted Capt. Steptoe's in front of the fortifications on the San Antonio road, it being intended that Gen. Twiggs should make a feint for the purpose of drawing out the enemy in that direction.

At daylight on the morning of the 12th, all the batteries opened, the first made by Gen. Twiggs' division succeeded admirably. As soon as Capt. Steptoe opened his guns, the enemy marched out several heavy columns and, in reaching the fort, passed within range of Steptoe's guns, when he turned a heavy and destructive fire upon them. As soon as they reached the work, he turned his attention to the fort, and in the course of an hour's cannonading drove them out of it, and silenced all the guns. Capt. Steptoe's fire throughout was one of the most effective and well-directed that has been witnessed during the war, while his position was such that the enemy's shot had little or no effect upon him.

The siege batteries continued an uninterrupted fire upon the Castle of Chapultepec throughout the day, which was answered by eleven guns in the work. Our guns proved to be very destructive, as we found after the work was taken, the dead men unburied, but thrown in ditches. The building also was completely riddled.

It was determined on the morning of the 13th to storm the Castle of Chapultepec and the works connected with it. The General-in-Chief, knowing the strength of the fortifications and the strong force with which it was garrisoned, concluded to assault it with old and well tried troops, not that he did not possess confidence in the divisions of Gens. Pillow and Quitman, but in carrying a point which was the key to all our future operations, it would not do to make a mistake or omit to take every advantage. Therefore, the storming parties from the divisions of Gens. Worth and Twiggs, which had so frequently been under severe fire, were selected. The heavy batteries continued their fire upon the fort, and about 7 o'clock, when the brigade of Gen. Smith arrived as a supporting force to the division of Gen. Quitman, the division of Gen. Pillow passed Molino del Rey and ascended the hill on the west side, the Voltigeur Regiment, which had been advanced into the timber to clear it of the enemy's skirmishers, became the assaulting force, supported by the balance of the division. Gen. Worth was situated to the north and on the left of Gen. Pillow. A part of Gen. Quitman's force ascended the hill on the south and to the right of Gen. Pillow. As the division of Gen. Pillow, and a portion of Gen. Quitman's, ascended and carried the castle in most gallant style, the balance of Gen. Quitman's force and the brigade of Gen. Smith swept the works on the road, the whole of the command moving harmoniously and simultaneously together, much to the honor and credit of their respective commanders, struck the enemy in their different positions at one and the same time a fatal blow. The hill, where Gen. Pillow's command ascended, had been mined for the purpose of blowing up our troops when they arrived at this point, but the rapid movements of the Voltigeur Regiment, and the deadly effect of their rifles, as they followed up the enemy from the first position, prevented their carrying out their views and intentions. Just as the command of Gen. Pillow rose the hill, and while in the act of assaulting the work, he fell wounded, and Col. Ransom was killed, but so lucidly had Gen. Pillow explained his objects and intentions of carrying the work, and aided by an active and efficient staff, that his command moved on and carried the work without even being brought to a stand. As Gen. Quitman's division was charging on the work in the road, Brig. Gen. Shields received a severe wound in the arm, and as soon as the works were carried, he returned and had it dressed, and again mounted his horse, which was shortly afterwards killed under him, but he continued to command his brigade, which was actively engaged throughout the day, and the name of Shields will long be remembered in connection with the laurels won by the Palmetto of the South and the Empire of the North.

Gen. Pillow being disabled by his wound, Gen. Worth took the command of both his own division and that of Gen. Pillow, and advanced along the aqueduct leading to the gates of San Cosme. Gen. Quitman, with his own command and Gen. Smith's brigade, also advanced towards the city by the aqueduct leading into the city at the gate of Piedad, which is commanded by the Citadel. On each of the routes the two columns met with a decided and stubborn resistance, and after the advance of Gen. Worth's command had reached the gate of San Cosme the fire was so hot that they were compelled temporarily to abandon it. They did not make a permanent lodgment until towards evening, when a portion of the siege train battery was brought into action, as also a piece or two of the mountain howitzers, which hurled the shot and shell about the ears of the enemy a little hotter than they desired. Gen. Quitman's column, with the Rifles at their head, continued steadily and cautiously on, taking position and breastwork as they came in contact with them, until they arrived near the gate of the city. Here the firing was so heavy, both from small arms and artillery, that it was deemed prudent to carefully reconnoitre it before attacking it. Accordingly, Lieuts. Beauregard, of the Engineers; Mansfield Lovell, of Gen. Quitman's staff; and Earl Van Dorn, of Gen. Smith's staff, went forward to ascertain the position of affairs. They returned and upon their report the Rifles, supported by a small force of infantry, was advanced forward for the purpose of picking off the artillerists, which they did, being partially covered by the aqueduct, with the same success and accuracy as one of our Southern or Western men would shoot squirrels. This rendered the situation of the Mexican artillerists so uncomfortable that they were unable to stand to their guns long enough to load them, and they commenced moving their guns, which was perceived by Gen. Quitman, and he ordered a charge, which was carried into execution as soon as commanded, Lieut. Stuart, of the Rifles, leading the way. It captured the main work, with two pieces of artillery, which Capt. Drum turned on the retreating enemy. Gen. Quitman was himself among the first to mount the breastworks and plant the standard thereon, at 1 o'clock. The enemy then formed and three times attempted to charge us and retake the position, but the unerring and deadly fire of the Rifles, together with a volley of grape from Capt. Drum, so cut them to pieces that they would not approach nearer than rifle shot. The third time they tried to advance under the cover of the arches of the aqueduct, but if ever a Mexican poked his head out for the purpose of slipping from one arch to the other, some rifleman would be sure to put a ball through it.

During the whole of the afternoon, the Citadel and a fort on our right continued a concentrated fire upon the gate, where our troops were, in the hopes of driving them out, but in this they were much mistaken, although we had but little cover. Here it was that the lamented Capt. Drum fell mortally wounded. The death of no man in our army has been more sincerely regretted than his; throughout the bombardment of Chapultepec he stood by his guns and when the works of the enemy were stormed, he continued

Garita Belen during the American Attack. *Courtesy Library of Congress*.

to advance his battery under the heaviest fire, himself possessing and infusing into his men a cool and deliberate bravery and self-possession surpassed by none. You will recollect it was him who recaptured the Buena Vista guns, still covered with the blood of those who fell over them at the time they were lost, and afterwards used them with such decisive effect at the battle of Molino del Rey on the 8th inst. Under cover of the night, Gen. Quitman's column erected a breastwork, and put into position a battery of two 18s, one 68-pound howitzer, and one 24-pound howitzer, intending to warm up the Citadel in the morning. Gen. Worth's column got his guns in a position to rake everything in his vicinity, and after night Lieut. Hagner threw a few shot and shell into the city, which no doubt intimidated the enemy very much, as they had a taste of this at Vera Cruz.

After the results and successes of the day, Gen. Scott intended, on the morning of the 14th, to make a lodgment on the "New Paseo" (entering by the San Cosme gate) and bombard the city, and for this purpose the balance of Gen. Twiggs' division was ordered from El Piedad to the support of Gen. Worth.

On the night of the 13th, Santa Anna evacuated all of his positions, and retreated from the city, having had more than one-half of his army killed and wounded or taken prisoners, among the latter, Gen. Nicolás Bravo, with his staff, at Chapultepec.[2] Santa Anna found that if he fought us on the 14th, he would hardly have a body-guard left to cover his retreat.

Early in the morning, the two columns took up their march. Gens. Quitman and Smith, at the head of their commands, entered the Grand National Plaza at 7 o'clock. The column was formed in the Plaza, and, by order of Gen. Quitman, the National Standard of the "Cerro Gordo Division," while the command came to a present, was flung to the breeze over the National Palace, and it now triumphantly waves over the Halls of the Montezumas, and, with one of our national poets, we may say:

"Our flag is there, our flag is there—
Behold its glorious stripes and stars!
Our flag is there, our flag is there—
We hail it with three loud huzzas!"

Gen. Worth's command halted four or five squares from the Plaza, where Col. Garland was wounded.

About 3 o'clock, Gen. Scott and staff, in full feather, escorted by the cavalry, entered the city, amidst the huzzas of the soldiers on all sides. As he entered, the band of the 2d Dragoons, mounted, interested the staring crowds with "Hail Columbia." As the escort entered the Grand Plaza, the band moved the patriotism of the whole of us to a little higher pitch, by the good, old-fashioned national air of "Yankee Doodle."

One of the first acts of Gen. Scott was to appoint Gen. Quitman Civil and Military Governor of Mexico and Col. F.S. Belton Lieutenant Governor. Gen. Quitman's department embraces the following officers: Capt. Francis N. Page, Ass't Adj. General; Lieuts. M. Lovell,

2. After Mexico won her independence, Nicolás Bravo was honored with the title of "national hero" for his dedication to the cause. A man who mixed his military positions with political ambitions, by 1847 Bravo twice had been vice president and interim president three times. Assigned to repulse General Scott's advance in 1847, his force proved woefully inadequate. Given the command of Chapultepec, Bravo held out until overwhelmed by American artillery and determined infantry. Santa Anna, in his usual reaction to bad news, ordered Bravo's arrest on trumped-up charges. He served as a governor and national representative until his death on April 22, 1854, just one day after his arch-foe Santa Anna had visited his hometown. Rumors abounded. Tucker, *Encyclopedia*, 87.

Cadmus M. Wilcox, and Richard P. Hammond, Aide-de-Camps; Capt. George T. M. Davis, Secretary; and Mr. Levi, Interpreter.

Throughout the 14th, and on the evening of the 15th, the Mexicans continued to fire from the corners and tops of the houses, killing some and wounded many. The artillery was at first tried on them, but owing to their concealed position it was not effective. The Rifle Regiment, and some of the infantry, were then sent in pursuit, which forces silenced them wherever they went. The Mexicans are very much mistaken when they came to engage the Rifles on the house-tops. During their revolutions they would fight in this way for several days, without doing each other much injury, but the deadly fire of the Rifles picked them out from their hiding-places when they least expected it, and made them very willing to cease so unequal a combat.

The officers of our army have suffered severely; they were foremost in the fight, and of course the first to fall. Louisiana and Mississippi, twin sisters of the South, have been most ably and nobly represented. Gens. Quitman and Smith, who bore conspicuous parts in the battle of Monterey, have been no less prominent in the operations which resulted in the surrender of this city. Mississippi, which has sent heroes to this war by regiments, may well be proud of her representative, and she has the honor of having one of her citizens the first American Governor in the Halls of the Montezumas.

What will Lousiania say, when she hears of the successes and masterly ability displayed by her own son, Gen. Persifor F. Smith? If it were possible for any one man to wear more laurels than he acquired at the battles of Contreras and Churubusco, we might speak of his conduct in the movements on the city. He has proven himself to be not only a good general, but one of the best of the army or of the age. Lieut. Beauregard, of the Engineers, also one of Louisiana's sons, has highly distinguished himself. I saw him complete his reconnoissance of the *garita* (gate of the city) after he had received two severe contusions.

One fact has been clearly demonstrated, both before and since the entrance of the army into the Valley of Mexico—that our cavalry force is entirely too small. The service of this corps has been so severe, owing to the smallness of its numbers, that after the battle nearly all the men and horses were, in a manner, unfit for service. This was calculated to destroy the efficiency of even those we have here, and even at the present time, one-half of the command is on extra duty every day. Mr. G.W. Barnes, of Georgia, and Mr. Lewis Dickenson, of Alabama, at the cessation of the armistice, organized, mounted, equipped, and supported a company of about twenty men, at their own expence, to serve during the fight, and by order of Col. Harney, were attached to the squadron of Capt. Hardee. They had several skirmishes with the enemy, both before and after entering the city. Mr. Harlow, of the company, was killed, and Mr. Dickenson and Mr. J. Pierce were badly wounded.

The following memoranda will show you the number of shot and shell fired by the siege batteries. The small number fired at Chapultepec, and the manner in which the castle and fort were completely torn to pieces, is one of the very best evidences of the power of that arm of our service, and the superior abilities of the officers commanding it.

> Battery No. 1. On the Tacubaya Road. Served by Capt. Drum, Co. G, 4th Artillery. Two 16-pounders* and one 3-inch howitzer.* Fired: 300 round shot, 100 shells, and 50 rounds of canister.
>
> Battery No. 2. On the ridge south of Molino del Rey. Served by Lieut. Hagner and Company of Ordnance. One 24-pounder and one 3-inch howitzer. Fired: 146 round shot and 74 shells.
>
> Battery No. 3. On same ridge, nearer the Molino del Rey. Served at first by Capt. Horace Brooks, 2d Artillery, and afterwards by Lieut. Samuel S. Anderson, 2d Artillery. One 16-pounder* and one 3-inch howitzer. (The carriage of the 16-pounder broke, and on the 13th September was replaced by a 24-pounder gun.) Fired: 70 rounds 16-pound shot, 37 24-pound shot, and 30 shells.
>
> Battery No. 4. 10-inch mortar. Served by Lieut. Stone and Company of Ordnance. Fired: 84 shells.
>
> From the Garita San Cosme, a few 24-pound shot and five 10-inch mortar shells were thrown into the city after dark on the 13th, and a few 8-inch shells into houses from which the firing came on the 14th.

Since our army arrived in the valley, we have lost about 3,000 men, in killed and wounded. We have destroyed the Mexican army, of over 30,000 men, upwards of 6,000 of which have been taken prisoners. We have captured seventy pieces of artillery—twenty-seven at the battle of Contreras, ten in the fort at Churubusco, and thirty-three on the 12th, 13th, and 14th.

---

*captured guns

List of the Killed, Wounded, and Missing

First Division—Maj. Gen. Worth

Names of the Killed, Wounded and Missing in the action of Molino del Rey, September 8.

KILLED—*Ordnance*—Priv Hugh Donahue. ***2^d^ Dragoons***—Privs Jacobus, Co A; Ullenbrook, Brown, Co B; Lane, Co C; Fansen, Co F; Lansing, Co I. ***4th Artillery***—Privs John Gracie, Samuel Grove. ***2^d^ Artillery***—Privs Timothy Sullivan, August L Gremer, Co K. ***5th Infantry***—Priv John Conner, Co H. ***8th Infantry***—Privs William Hanson, Jacob Frank, David Campbell, Co B. ***2^d^ Artillery***—Priv Jacob Dyas, Co I; 1st Lieut Wm Armstrong, Sergt Austin B Howe, Co F; Privs William J Barnhard, John C Elloes, Co C; Herman Levy, Co G. ***3^d^ Artillery***—Bvt Capt G W Ayres, Privs J F Farry, John Walsh, Simon Margarum, Co B; Benj M Harris, Co F. ***4th Infantry***—Sergt B Henry, Co E Corpl John Cameron, Co D; Privs Stillman Coburn, Patrick Ronnan, Co E; John McLoskey; Co F, Fred'k Workman, Co C. ***5th Infantry***—2d Lieut W S Burwell, Bvt Lieut Col Martin Scott, Capt M E Merrill, 2d Lieut E B Strong, Sergts John Gottenger, Co A; Augustus Ohitman, Co B; Stanislas Minal, Co I; Corpl Samuel Carr, Co E; Privs Timothy Howby, Thos Weidman, Frederick Hobber, Co A; Hy Mamark, Francis McKay, Thos S Pole, John P Ronner, Chas Steward, Co B; Sam'l Calhoun, Rob't Crawford, Griffith Owens, David Sharpe, Thos Gooding, Peter Henz, Owen Marray, Co E; John B Hoffer, Co F; John Kourstoupfads, Co G; Peter G Moore, Co I; Wm McCloskey, Co K. ***6th Infantry***—Sergt Jas McGlynn, Co F; Privs Bernard Althor, Martin Munneman, Michael Sheehan, Co B; Matthew Murphy, Victor Durand, Co C; John B Hond, Co D; Nicholas Ramsey, John Smith, Co E; Wm Agol, Wm Fahee, John H Plant, Christian Schuman, Wm Loeey, Michael Murphy, Co H; John Broderick, Peter Kolte, Isham Canalizo, Co F. ***8th Infantry***—Sergts Edw Bertram, Co F; Nicholas Ford, Co H; Corpls Jas Crogan, Co E; John Hughes, Co F; Wm Shadys, Co I; John Clark, Co E; Sergt Reuben Brown, Co F; Musician Patrick McGrath, Co D; Privs Thos Lanson, Co C; Geo McGrad, Gabriel Wilson, Co D; Patrick Green, Alex Prentice, Co E; Peter Cafferty, Bernard McFarlin, Jacob Neish, Chas. Shwarykoryl, Co F; Wm Irwin, John A Jackson, Geo M Lightfell, Barthel Mahon, Henry Passor, Co H; Lewis Henme, Co I; Thos Flea, Sam'l Clark, Rob't Simpson, Co K; Sidney W Gunroyer, Co F. ***14th Infantry***—Corpl

Henry W Erwin, Co E. ***11th Infantry***—Lieut Col Wm M Graham, 1st Lieut R H L Johnson, Sergt Geo Johnson, Corpls Chas Fenner, Co E; John McMahon, Co F; Privs John Sigler, John Buchanan, Co E; John Manning, Jas. Simpson, Co F; Daniel Kippy, Co H.

WOUNDED—*Engineers*—Capt J L Mason, severely; 2^{d} Lieut J B Foster, severely. ***Ordnance***—Priv John Dougherty, slightly. ***2^{d} Dragoons***—Capt C Ker, 2^{d} Lieut Smith, 2^{d} Lieut Tree, severely. ***Rifles*—**2^{d} Lieut Walker, severely; Sergt McGuire, Corpl Slade, Co C; Sergt Young, Co F, slightly; Corpls Buxton, Buckley, Co I, dangerously; Sergts Murphy, Brooks, Co I, slightly. ***Dragoons*—** Privs Usher, Co B, dangerously; Boling, Co A, slightly; Klaws, Co A, severely; Zink, Co A, dangerously; Sweeney, Co A, slightly; Russell, Co A, severely; Kerr, Co B, slightly; Wallers, Co B, Thos. Murphy, Co C, severely; Porthouse, Co C, slightly; Zahkiwick, Co C, severely; White, Co C, slightly; Fielding, Co F, severely; Freeman, Co F, slightly; Kolde, Mundeig, Westerdelot, Co F, severely; Bugler Drawn, Privs Wyatt, Co I, slightly; Gardener, Fritshe, Co K, slightly. ***Rifles*—** Hamilton, Paul, Cottrell, Carter, Harris, Co I, slightly. ***4th Artillery***— Sergt Jacob Price, severely; Privs Richard Boone, J M Quick, slightly. ***2^{d} Artillery***—1st Lieut H J Hunt, 1st Lieut W Hayes, 2^{d} Lieut H F Clark, slightly; Corpl Hugh McCoy, severely; Privs Richard Gilmore, James Witter, George Wagner, Abram Hart, Wm Smith, Lawrence Dunivan, John Forgy, Saml Stanley, David Wheeler, John Murphy, slightly; Richard Harper, Joshua H Corwin, Jas Devine, Christopher Yeager, severely. ***5th Infantry***—Capt E K Smith, Co H, mortally, since dead; 2^{d} Lieut F S Dent Co H, Sergt Jos Updigraff, Co H, severely; Sergt Thos Johnson, Co H, slightly. ***2^{d} Artillery***— Sergt Saml Meeker, Co K, slightly; Corpl Gilbert G Fancher, Co K, severely. ***5th Infantry***—Corpls Jacob Nichols, Edw Green, Co H, severely; Corpl Darius Ballard, Co H, slightly. ***8th Infantry***—Corpls Thos Low, Co B, severely; Patrick Reilly, Co B, slightly. ***5th Infantry***— Musician Jas Alexander, Co H, slightly. ***2^{d} Artillery***—Privs George Barr, Wm Cordes, Herman Knickerbocker, Anthony Rounder, Thos Sullivan, Andrew Casey, Co K, severely; Alphonse Schaiffer, Co K, severely, died on 13th. ***5th Infantry***—Privs Daniel Rodgers, Chas Linder, Jas H Brooke, Geo Kraffenbaner, Augustus Beaver, Co H, severely; Wm Bell, Jos McGarlin, Patrick O'Rourke, Thos L Sleek, Geo W E Sherman, Co H, slightly. ***8th Infantry***—Edw Kinneford, Elijah J Cain, Levi Miles, Co B, severely; John Kavanagh, Tim Collins,

Ezra Higgins, Michael Leonard, W Lewis, Thos Parson, Thos Joyce, Co B, slightly. ***2d Artillery***—Nicholas Seminoff, Wm Wright, John Flemming, Co K, slightly. ***3d Dragoons***—2d Lieut and Aide-de-Camp H Thorn, slightly. ***2d Artillery***—1st Lieut M L Shackleford, Co G; 1st Lieut C B Daniels, Co C, severely; Sergts Geo Gordon, Co D; Jas McCormick, Co H, slightly; Corpls Henry Balleman, Co G, mortally, since dead; Hugh McDonald, Co H, severely; Musician Thos Clark, Co D, slightly; Privs William Shoppe, Co C; Christi Bower, Co. F, mortally, since dead; Jas Rochford, Chas Hoover, Hy Durlin, Martin Sharbuck, Wm Moore, Co C, severely; Patrick Kean, John Conway, John Garrey, Co C; John Hill, Co D, slightly; Fred Blunt, Thos Furian, Francis Webb, Co F, severely; William Crook, Saml H Dickman, Co F, slightly; Arch'd McFayden, Co F, severely, died on 11th; Rob't Alexander, Jas Montgomery, Thos O'Brien, Thos Starr, Rob't Michan, Co G, severely; John Wiley, Co G, slightly; J D Reynolds, Co G, slightly, died 19th; William Sharp, Co G, severely; Edw Ellsworth, Jas Bohannon, Jas Heany, John McNeil, John R Smith, Co H, severely; William Cook, Co F, severely. ***3d Artillery***—Capt R Anderson, severely; 2d Lieut G P Andrews, slightly; Sergt Anton Achenback, Co I, severely, since dead; Corpls John Mathews, Co B, severely, since dead; John Hynes, Co B, slightly; Privs Jas Walsh, Geo Willcox, Wm F Taylor, Philip Rouse, Co B, slightly; Julius Martial, Co B, severely; John Coogan, Co B, mortally, since dead; Thos Juit, Chas Beistrenger, Thos Brady, Co G, slightly; Wm Bloom, Saml Brown, John Conner, Peter Derit, Rob't McGee, Dedrick Derr, Co G, severely; William Parker, ----- Watchman, Co G, severely, since dead; Jos Finch, John Turnis, Co I, severely; Marshal Kimball, Co I, mortally, since dead; Philip Bucher, Wm W Walker, Co I; Michael Ley, Co K, slightly; John Sullivan, Co K, severely. ***4th Infantry***—Asst Surg J Simons, slightly; Adj H Prince, 2d Lieut A B Lincoln, Co A, severely; 1st Lieut S Smyth, Co I, slightly; Sergts. Geo W Anderson, Wm Quin, Co A, severely; Jos Holybee, Co F, severely, since dead; John B Weedon, Chas Metz, Co I, severely; Corpls Wm Castigan, Co C, slightly; Ephraim Cain, Co I, severely; Privs Jas Carrol, Oswald Drury, Wm Ehrenbaim, Co A, severely; Jas Keenan, Christian Smallbark, Co A, slightly; David Coleman, John P Smith, Hy Stoneham, John Clancey, John Montgomery, Martin Rush, Wm Allen, Co B, severely; John Gallagher, Lewis Merans, Jos L Moody, Co B, slightly; Philip Hady,

Co B, severely, since dead; Richard Abercrombie, Sam'l Collier, Robert Kuntz, Michael Bonet, Edw McKeon, Peter W Syms, Co C, severely; Wm C Goddard, Daniel F McKee, Meredith Quails, Levi Leitz, Co C, slightly; John Coyle, John Hill, Justin O'Brien, Wm Lawrence, Martin Meyers, Edw McCready, Co D, severely; Gilbert Goodrich, Co D, mortally, since dead; Lile Barton, Alex Miller, John T DeHart, Co D, slightly; Jules Gasse, Co D, severely, since dead; John Housiner, Lawrence Kenny, Adam Brecker, Theo Cranz, Co E, slightly; Wm Wiernest, Co E, severely; Michael McGuire, Co F, slightly; Jas Steel, Co F, mortally, since dead; John P Wirrick, severely; Chas Skolinski, Edward. Kirevin, Co I, slightly; Philip Felby, Co I, severely, since dead; Martin Loughest, Co I, severely. ***5th Infantry***—Bvt Col J S McIntosh, Commanding Brigade, severely, since dead; Asst Surg Wm Roberts, severely; 2d Lieut C S Hamilton, badly; Sergts Alfred Landrage, Co A, severely; Elisha Buel, Co A; Henry Farmer, Co B; James O'Brien, Co E, slightly; Alex McClellan, Co G, severely; David Thompson, Co I, slightly; Jas. Eversteine, Co K, severely, since dead; Corpls Wm Godfrey, Co A, slightly; H J Haskell, Co B, severely; Francis Smith, Co E, slightly; John Doyle, Co F, severely; Geo Emerick, Geo. Morely, Co I; Nicholas Reid, John Clarit, Co K, slightly; Musician Wm Babb, Co A, slightly; Dediah Meir, Band, severely; Privs Morris Sayers, Co A, mortally, since dead; Wm Wetherspoon, Wm Goodwin, Hugh Frazer, Jeremiah Delong, Co A, severely; S Tiflans, J Weight, Co A, slightly; Geo Kingsman, Co A, severely, since dead; Isaac Christman, John Lyons, Co B, slightly; Adam Eichstein, John Irwing, Jas Lollen, Co B, severely; John S Beach, Wm A Place, Co E, severely, since dead; Abner Dixon, Co E, slightly; John Clark, Wm Wheeler, Henry Wilkie, Moses Papiner, Thos McDermott, Co E; Edw Annison, John Coglin, Josiah Ettinger, Wm Cain, Bernard Riley, Jas Shepherd, Patrick McElroy, Wm O Mocht, Co F, severely; Thos Hogg, Josiah Cartwright, Co F, severely, since dead; Edw H Brown, John Eisdar, Patrick McCue, Patrick Scanlan, Peter Yorick, Leonard Johnson, Co G, severely; Chas Butterling, James Burns, Charles Evans, John Hunter, John Wrick, Co G, slightly; John Helm, Matthew Switzer, Wm H Morris, Wm Schaeffer, Michael Coll, J M Montgomery, Chas Sanders, Co I, severely; Edw B Conner, Peter Bragine, Geo McElrie, Jos W. Brush, Jos Wolf, Co I, slightly; Thos Foster, Co I, mortally, since dead; Wm Chapman, Wm Curtis, John Gorlan,

John McCameron, Cornelius O'Neil, Sam'l Tucker, Chester R. Tully, Thomas H Wood, Jacob Watson, Co K, severely; Benj Slater, Thos Gloveen, Co K, slightly; Augustus De Lonza, Owen Melvin, Co E, slightly. ***6th Infantry***—Capt A Cady, Co H, slightly; Capt W H T Walker, 2d Lieut R F Ernst, Co F, severely; Sergts Rob't F Jackson, Co A, slightly; Geo Williams, John McIntyre, Co A, severely; James E Dresser, Co C, slightly; John Cummings, Co E, severely; John Webb, Co K, severely, since dead; Corpls John Ferguson, Co B, severely; Sylvester Jones, Co C, slightly; Chas Rafferty, Co F, mortally, since dead; Michael Eannes, Co F, severely; Privs Francis Kline, Band, mortally, since dead; Sam'l Morgan, Band; Bennet Keere, John Finnerghty, Jacob Kennard, Richard Wilkinson, James Bradley, J B Johnson, Co A, slightly; William Spears, Co A, severely; Calvin Wells, Henry Cropp, John Martin, Co B, slightly; John King, Co B, severely; D Loundensborough, Co C, slightly; Michael McAulley, Co C, severely, since dead; E W Dexter, Loreny Flood, John McGuire, Co D, slightly; Jas Victory, Wm P Moore, Jefferson Wells, Co D; Abraham Riber, Henry Bertoled, Geo Smith, Co E, severely; Joseph Roland, Co E, severely, since dead; David Bruney, Daniel Emerson, Daniel Boughanan, Co E, slightly; Richard Cherry, Co F, severely; Brian Curry, Thos Down, Wm C Howe, Co F, slightly; Deobald Snyder, Alfred Carlisle, John A Reading, Jeremiah Ryan, Ebenezer Gill, Gregory Kepler, Co H; Henry S P Armtz, Co K, severely; John Meon, Co K, slightly; Matthew Kols, Co K, severely; Wm Jones, Co K, severely, since dead. ***8th Infantry***—Maj C A Waite, Bvt Maj Geo Wright, Bvt Maj A Montgomery, slightly; Capt L Smith, Co A, severely; 1st Lieut J Barbank, Co G, mortally, since dead; 1st Lieut J Beardsley, Co E, severely; 1st Lieut C Morris, Co K, mortally, since dead; 1st Lieut J D Clark, Co C, severely; 2d Lieut G Wainwright, Co C, badly; 2d Lieut J G Snelling Co F, severely; Sergts John Fink, Co E, severely; Thos Moir, Co E; David Pink, Co C, slightly; Thos Sewell, Co D; John Robinson, Co. E; James H Kearny, Co F; John Smith, Co H; Fred'k Backhaus, Co I, severely; Corpls Arch' T Osbourne, Co A; A C Edson, Co. D, slightly; Wm Fairchilds, Co D, severely; David Lawler, Co E; Jos Scanson, Co F; Caleb Smith, Co H, slightly; David Springham, Co K, mortally, since dead; Privs Wm Sheppard, L B Hanley, Abraham Fitzpatrick, P R Maloey, J A Burtyman, Co A, severely; Solomon Viedenberg, Meion Miller, Lyman H Royce, Jos Schwager, Hy Stevens, Co A, slightly; Hy Jordan,

Co C, severely, since dead; E Hamer, Anthony Brooks, Rob't Hawkings, Jas Wilson, L Kinney, John Graves, Jas Edmonds, Co C, severely; Chas Evanson, Co C, slightly; Wm Angel, W T Bishop, Geo Coffee, Chas Hess, Michael McEwen, Michael Pickett, Wm Smith, Thos A Wilson, Co D, severely; Lawrence Fagin, Wm Gippard, Jas Hannigan, Co D, slightly; Jas B Hill, Jas B Kelly, Co D, mortally, since dead; Chas Brown, Patrick Cassin, David Doace, Chester C Kennedy, Peter King, Patrick McCarty, Hy L Sneilers, Nathaniel Ross, Jos Arnold, Patrick Keany, Co E, severely; Benj Burritt, Jas Carroll, James Gamble, Oliver W H Kellogg, Co E, slightly; Patrick Green, Co E, Aug Bliss, Co F, mortally, since dead; Henry Buckland, Wm Collan, John Chari, Co F, severely; John K Knock, Theo Shinard, Co F, slightly; Jacob Missil, Co F, severely, since dead; Luther Schouts, Sidney W Pumroyer, Co F, mortally, since dead; Wm Shad, William Looney, Co F, severely; Michael Walsh, Co F, mortally, since dead; John Young, Co F; Thos Brennan, Thos Burke, John Cosgrove, Phineas Cook, Co H, severely; Hez Eubank, John Gordon, Co H, slightly; Nicholas Hoyt, Wm McDonald, Dewitt McDaniel, John McCarthy, Bernard Malone, Jas Mooney, John Paul, Co H, severely; John M Rentor, Henry Rumears, Co H, mortally, since dead; Oscar F Sweet, Co H, severely; Sam Pooler, Co H, mortally, since dead; Pat'k McMillan, Co I, slightly; Job H McGuire, Co I, severely; John Bermingham, Co I, mortally, since dead; Stephan T Templeman, John Weith, Co I, severely; Smith A Weller, Co I, slightly; Wm Wilson, Co I, mortally, since dead; John T Blair, Co I, slightly; Wm Sourley, James Raby, Co K, mortally, since dead; Chas Daniels, Co K, slightly; Mark Chapple, Co K, severely; Michael Conrey, Wm C Morris, Hy Morinar, Wm Thomas, James A Terril, Co K, slightly; Henry Bohan, Co K, since dead. ***Voltigeurs***—Maj Geo H Talcott, 2[d] Lieuts G L Kintzing, R Swan, Wm J Martin, Washington Terrett, slightly; Sergts W B Vertrees, C D Weymouth, Co A; F W Jennings, Co B, severely; J C Malbon, Co B; R Harding, Co C; W J Herbert, Co E; C R Edwards, Co G; L S Elliott, Co H; J F Gardiner, Co I, slightly; Corpls W S McCorell, Co A; E D Denson, Co B; B Ogle, Co E; Jas H Walker, Co G; Sergt R H Turner, Co G, slightly; Privs D Graybeer, A R Shacklett, Co A, severely; J Hall, J Brown, D Wymp, Co A, slightly; A Wamsall, J Potter, Co A, severely; G W Seaton, Co A, slightly; R Simpson, Co A, severely; J Thompson, J Metcalf, A Adamson, Co A, slightly; T Davis, J Howell, J Pugh, J Bunger, Co A, severely; A Funday, T Farish, T Pugh, J L Knott, S A Evans, M Conway, V Collins, ----- Holandorf, Co B, slightly; T Clark, R Sylvester, H Wells, H Kilgrove, W A Ward, Co C, slightly; J Bean, M G Good, J L Silverhorn, Co E, severely; J Mahony, W Allison, D Deraughn, Co E, slightly; J Rowinski, Co E, severely; J Spencer, T C Parish, J Donly, J J Nickerson, M Benton, Co E, slightly;G W Bungeant, Co E, severely; John Sloan, J L Hisse, T Evans, H Kidwell, A W Millwright, J McCaslin, Co E, slightly; J Cromley, D Davis, Co F, severely; J V Franklin, Co F, slightly; S Field, T Higginson, Co F, severely; A Idler, G Kriner, H Keenan, R Lemon, W S Mendenhall, J Massey, P Morrel, B McCabe, J V Perry, J Picken, J Pierce, B J Ross, Co F, slightly; W Jackson, O Morton, G Spencer, J Kock, G Eckhart, Co G, slightly; G Beckenschitz, F Korse, J Rutter, Co G, severely; T Grooves, J Sigmac, Co H, slightly; J F Dentlinger, J A Yates, G W Jones, Co G, severely; W H Fitzhue, H White, W Baldhurst, Co I, slightly. ***14th Infantry***—Maj John H Savage, Capt Thos Glenn, Lieuts James C C Hays, Thos Shields, Samuel B Davis, Co F, slightly; Corpls L Warren, Co C, dangerously; Monroe Fleming, Co A, slightly; Privs Chris Papst, Co A, severely; Thos Pierson, Jas M Cox, Co A; Robert Brenton, Co B, slightly; Fielding Young, Co E., severely; Jackson W Lowry, Co E, slightly; Asa Sawyer, Co F, severely; Kayrans Lynch, William Farrell, Co F; Louis H Mallerby, David Hall, Co H, slightly; Jas Gillespie, Co I; Hardy Johnson, Co K, severely; Jas R Austin, Thos M Hayter, Henry Dannigan, Co K, slightly. ***11th Infantry***—Capts Wm H Irwin, P M Guthrie, severely; Adjt D S Lee, slightly; Sergts John P Weldon, Co E, severely; ----- Freeze, Co E, slightly; Lennox Rea, Co H, severely; J C Handy, Co H; Corpls Chas Barturkey, Michael Freeney Co H; Rob't Raasch, Co I, slightly; Privs Isaac Mahon, Uriah Kitchen, Co D, severely; John Hayes, Co D, mortally; James Rager Co D, McCluny Radcliff, Co D; Rob't D Brown, Co F, slightly; Foster R Carson, Jas Dilks, Wm S Sathall, Co D, severely; Jas Hight, ----- Schmidt, Co D, slightly; Wm R Call, Jesse Flowers, Wm Dorman, Co H, severely; Isaac Pierce, Jas Nesbitt, Co H, slightly; Herman Bickerstine, Fred Babe, Co I, severely; Benjamin Dickie, Simon Pickett, Co I, slightly; John Rovering, Co I, mortally; Albert McGill, Co I, severely. ***4th Infantry***—Oscar Wood, John Wilson, Co D, severely, since dead.

MISSING—Privs Rob't McKee, Co K, ***2^d^ Artillery***; Joseph Scott, Co B, ***8th Infantry***, since discovered to have been blown up at Casa del Mata; Francis Beer, Co G, ***2^d^ Artillery***; Artificer Israel Barton, Co B, ***3^d^ Artillery***, killed; Priv Jno Jacob Divine, Co G, ***3^d^ Artillery***; Sergt John Coyle, Co C, ***4th Infantry***; Privs John Gillespie, Thos Hardy, Wm. Reynolds, Co E, ***5th Infantry***; Jas Smith, Jas G Smith, Co I, ***5th Infantry***; Conrad Young, Henry Moillier, Co K, ***5th Infantry***; Jackson Adams, Co F, ***6th Infantry***; Jas Leary, Co A, ***8th Infantry***; H A Wood, Co C, S Vandergriff, Co F, J L Hass, Co H, ***Voltigeurs***; David Ayres, Co H, ***11th Infantry***.

Names of the Killed, Wounded and Missing of the First Division in the Actions of 13th and 14th Sept., 1847.

KILLED—*2^d^ Artillery*—Priv Richard Gilmore, Co A; Sergt John Scarr, Co I; Musician Joseph Cool, Co D; Privs Chas Carrol, Co C; John Kennedy, Co F; Wm O'Neil, Co G. ***4th Infantry***—2^d^ Lieut A J Rodgers, Co D; Sergt Wm Donagan, Co D; Sergt George Blast, Co B; Corpl Jas Hagan, Co A; Privs Conrad Graf, Isaac I Johnson, Co A; Alex McCoy, Karl Sigmond, Co B; Michael Kelly, Co D; Wm Billington, Joel Barrom, Co E. ***5th Infantry***—2^d^ Lieut J P Smith; Privs V E Reed, Co I; James McLoy, Co K. ***6th Infantry***—Privs Pat Hines, Co C; Wm Mooney, David Trush, And Leet, Henry Jones, Co F.

WOUNDED—A A Gen'l W W Markall; Volunteer A D C George W Kendall, slightly. ***Engineers***—1st Lieut I I Stevens; Sergt D Hastings, severely. ***Ordnance***—Sergt P Maguire; Priv Davis, slightly. ***2^d^ Artillery***—Artificer Edmund Ring, Co A, slightly; Privs Thomas Murphy, Co A, severely; Jos Bateman, Wm Smith, John Wolf, Francis Desmond, Co A; Sergt James McCormick, Co H; Corpl Henry Beigie, Co D, slightly; Musician Anthony Baker, Co H, mortally; Privs John Sweeny, Herman Von Steen, Co C, severely; Carl Chapparcan, George Chiveton, Frederick Brugh, Co D; Jeremiah Cavangh, Wm Garlick, Co G; David Rikin, Co H, slightly; Patrick Born, John Young, Michael Halloran, Co H, severely; John Klinz, Co H, slightly. ***3^d^ Artillery***—Privs Nathan Randall, Co G, slightly; John Zear, Co G; Godfrey Piermont, Co I, severely; Marcus Bain, John Haggerty, Co K, slightly. ***4th Infantry***—Lieut Col John Garland, Commanding 1st Brigade, severely; 1st Lieut S Smith, Co I, mortally, since dead; 2^d^ Lieut Maurice

Maloney, Co B, condition not stated; Sergts Wm Blaidsdell, Co A, severely; David Toobwiller, Co E, slightly; Corpls Theodore Gregg, Co A, severely; Daniel Bennet, Co B, mortally, since dead; Jos F Cooper, Co D, slightly; Hamilton Sparks, Co E, severely; John Witnell, Co E, slightly; Wm Grant, Co E, severely; Privs Patrick Toole, Co A, severely; Lonesee, Co A, slightly; Wm Burton, James Lawless, Stephan Mann, Adolphus Schuyar, Jacob Shores, Co B, severely; John Mallindar, Co B, slightly; William Verrel, William Wilson, Mark Spaulding, Co C, severely; Vernon B West, Co C; Geo Henry, Co D, slightly; Wm Lawrence, Duwilda Myers, Co D, severely; Thos Collis, Wm Cross, Co D, slightly; Joseph Peck, Co D; John C Christie, Martonier Crofot, Co E, severely; William Thompson, Henry Byrnes, James Fisher, James Parker, Co I, slightly; Gropincamp, Co I, severely; Aganus Dowis, Co I, mortally. ***5th Infantry***—Capt D H McPhail, slightly; Sergt Henry Farmer, Co B; Corpl Darius Ballard, Co H; Privs Joseph McGartlin, William O'Shaughnessy, Co H; John A Schuber, Co B, severely; Wm Montgomery, Co B, slightly; John Dillon, Co B, severely; Jas Harny, Co F, slightly; Thos Oats, Co G; Geo Gill, Co K, severely. ***6th Infantry***—1st Lieut L A Armistead, Sergt Major Edward Thompson, slightly; Privs Geo Ernst, Co D; Alex Maddox, Co F; Wm Dowley, Co H, severely; Sergt Francis Fox, Co K; Privs Bernard Lynch, Co K, slightly; And Piper, Co D, severely. ***8th Infantry***—2d Lieut Jas Longhurst, 1st Lieut Jos Sheldon, Sergts John A Noon, Co B; J L Fisk, Co K; Corpls Rob't Shaw, Co I, Thos Smith, Co K, severely; Privs Wm Shaw, Co I; John Hisner, Co D; John Flummery, Co E, slightly; M Monaghan, Jas C McIntyre, Stephen McConnel, Co H; John McAulay, Wm Palmoter, John Kibler, Co I, severely; Wm Fox, Co K, slightly; Alex Reinhart, Co K, Nath'l Clegg, Chas McLosky, Hanson Palmer, Co B, severely.

MISSING—Privs Chas Quick, Co D, ***2d Artillery***; Valentine Impoff, Co G, ***3d Artillery***; Jos Farramier, Co C, ***4th Infantry***; Ed Blackman, Victor Whipple, Co H, ***5th Infantry***; Jas Leise, Co C, ***6th Infantry***; John Briolon, Chas Whiitty, Co F, ***8th Infantry***.

Second Division—Brig. Gen. Twiggs

List of the Killed, Wounded, and Missing of the Second Division, in the actions at Chapultepec and the Garita de Belen on the 13th, and in the City of Mexico on the 14th and 15th September, 1847.

First Brigade

KILLED—*Mounted Rifles*—Corpls Dennis Byrne, Co A; C C Arms, Co H; Privs Thos D Wheeler, Geo Town, Wm Donovan, Elijah O Pointer, Co A; Jas L Reed, Co D; Jesse James, Co G; Myron Bell, Co H. ***1st Artillery*—**Hiram Dengh, Co D; Wm Hagan, Co F; Wm Finney, Jas Harrigan, Thos McGlone, Co G. ***3d Infantry*—**Sergt Jno Bald, Co I; Lance Corpl Jas Huntley, Co C; Privs Wm Portiton, John J O'Donnell, Co B; Jas Welsh, Co C; John Alexander, Co E; Walter Scott, Co F; Henry Boyle, Co H; Michael O'Loghlin, Co I; Florence McCarty, Co K.

WOUNDED—*General Staff*—1st Lieut Earl VanDorn, 7th Infantry, slightly. ***Mounted Rifles*—**Maj W W Loring, severely, arm lost; Capts J S Simonson, Co G; J B Backenstos, Co H; S S Tucker, Co K; 2d Lieut T S K Russell, Co G; Bvt 2d Lieut J A Palmer, Co A, slightly. ***1st Artillery*—**Capt Geo Nauman, Co F, slightly; 1st Lieut and Adjt J M Brannan, Co F; 1st Lieut J A Haskin, Co H, severely. ***Mounted Rifles*—**Sergt Major Alonzo Stanton, slightly; Sergts Sam'l Harp, Co A, severely; Z M P Hand, Co D; 1st Sergt James Manly, Co F; Sergts Wm P Sanders, Co G; Hiram Dwyer, D N Frame, Co H, slightly; Corpls Wm M Winter, Co D, severely; L L Worcester, Geo Taylor, Co D; J M L Addison, Co F; Rufus Peck, Co G; Jer'h O'Connell, Co H, slightly; J Freeman, Co K, severely; J Millard, Co K, slightly; Lance Corpls Thos Davis, Wm P Cook, Co F, slightly; Privs Jas Farrel, Co A, severely; Edw'd Allen, Chris Linden, Fred Pilgrim, Co A, slightly; Jas M Cannon, Co D, severely; Anthony Stickler, Co D, slightly; Geo W Raymond, Stanislaus Moraski, Co E, severely; Jos Newhouse, Co E, slightly; John Barber, John Richardson, Jos Habau, Co F, severely; W F Herrington, J C Morton, Geo B Moshers, J W Robinson, Jos Watson, Co F, slightly; Levi Grunsby, Co F; Benj Tabler, Jno Dillon, Jno C Myers, Lyndsey Hooker, Dan'l Williams, Lewis Copsey, Thos Brasheno, Co G, severely; John Fickle, Lawrence J Filsome, Barth W Wilson, Josh P Santmynie, Clinton Frazier, Wm W Wilson, Wm Spear, M Hamilton, Co G, slightly; M Batsner, Francis Whitebread, J Hok, J Murry, S Young, J C Roberts, J C Christian, Joseph Patterson, Co H, severely; E A B Phelps, Co H; Robert Williams, Josh Garrison, Josh Debecque, Allen Overly, Co K, slightly; Daniel Wills, Co K, severely. ***1st Artillery*—**1st Sergt Thos Williams, Co H, severely; Corpls Henry D Silner,

Co F; Wm Perry, Co G; Dan'l B Baker, Co H; Artificer John Weins, Co B; Privs Rich'd J Shepherd, Co B, slightly; Thos S Perkins, Co. D, severely; Amos Kingsley, Co F, slightly; Bradly Laud, Co F; John McFarne, John Thompson, Co G, severely; Robert Kugan, Henry Watts, Co G; Harvey Gamperd, John Miller, Lewis Russell, Francis Fletcher, Co H, slightly; Fred'k Wissall, Co H, severely. ***3^d^ Infantry***—Sergts Stewart Dougherty, Co D; Dixon Ashworth, Co F; Lance Sergt Orlando B Miles, Co C; Corpls Nelson Chamberlain, Co B, slightly; John Storm, Co E, severely; Wm Adams, Co I, slightly; Privs Jas McNulty, Henry Varner, Moses Gleason, Co B; Bavna Upton, Edgar Watson, Francis J Shlaihan, Co C, severely; Francis Oestrich, Co C; Henry Haldman, John O'Brien, Co D, slightly; Henry Aberlee, Co D; Amos Barnheart, Co F, severely; Wm Campbell, John Childers, Cornelius Crowley, John Hamilton, Wm Myers, Philip Ryan, Timothy Sullivan, Co F; Wm Kenny, Chas E E Kyer, Edw'd Zimmerman, Patrick Morran, Co H. slightly; Henry McCamphill, Thos Pritchard, Leonard Elias, David Jermon, Co H, severely; Eli Gable, Chas McKinne, Jacob Varnes, Co G, slightly; Jos Butterfield, Co G, severely; Geo Frank, Thomas McFarland, Co K, slightly; Terry Dale, Charles J Truman, Co K, severely; Frederick A Collins, Elliott Ellmer, Daniel Smith, David Wise, Co B, slightly.

MISSING—Privs Edmund Quin, Co H, ***1st Artillery***; Isaac Tracy, John Witty, Jno Venator, Co B, ***3d Infantry***, storming party; John Montgomery, Co F, ***3d Infantry***; Theodore Woodbury, Co H, ***3d Infantry***.

Second Brigade

KILLED—*7th Infantry*—1st Lieut Levi Gantt, Co C. ***2d Infantry***—Sergt Wm A Morrison, Co F; Corpl Jas Tierney, Co B; Musician Michael Elwood, Co A; Privs John M Nash, Co A; Patrick Sheridan, Co B; Lewis Rinhart, Co E; Wm Steinson, Co I. ***7th Infantry***—Jos N Garnett, Keyran Temple, Co E; Richard Shore, Co F; Neill Donnelly, Co I.

WOUNDED—*2nd Infantry*—Capt Silas Casey, Co C; 1st Lieut N Lyon, Co D; Corpls Robert Bailey, Wm Bond, Wm M Evans, Co B, slightly; Privs F McNally, Co A; John Keely, Geo Martin, Jno Wallace, Co B, slightly; Corp Elias Ellis, Privs Stevenson, Wm Feather, Titus S Gillow, Wm Hughes, Ervin Levin, Nicholas C James,

Patrick McKenna, Jacob Miller, Ab'm Sammons, Corp Thos Handley, Co C, severely; Privs Chas Clarke, Co D, slightly; Benj Little, Co D; Sergt Asahel H Wells, Musician Thos Rose, Privs John Brown, Daniel Carr, Peter Kerr, Co E; Alex Beebe, Patrick Gallagher, Co F; John Daly, Hiram Shippey, Co G, severely; Rich'd G Martin, Wm T Ray, Co H; Thos Graham, Lewis Hastings, Jno Kavenaugh, Patrick Kelly, John Semple, Co I, slightly; Daniel Lanahan, John Lynch, James Sullivan, Co I, severely. ***4th Artillery***—John Steevier, Samuel Noble, Augustus Walker, Co C; Corpl William Anderson, Co E, slightly; Privs Francis H Fox, Co E, severely; Jno McLaughlin, Thomas Navy, Co E, slightly; Sergt Rt W Howard, Co E, severely. ***7th Infantry***—Sergt Rd S Cross, Privs James Lilly, Co C; Jos Gillhuly, Patrick Murphy, Co E; Charles Howard, Co F; John Barnes, Co I, slightly; Geo F Flagg, Co I, severely; John Hughes, Patrick Murphy, Co I, mortally.

MISSING—Stephen L Rouse, Co C; John Pierce, Co F; Michael Gilmore, David Mayer, Co I, 7th Infantry.

TOTAL—Killed, 36; Wounded, 194; Missing, 10.

Third Division—Maj. Gen. Pillow

Return of the Killed, Wounded, and Missing of the Third Division, commanded by Major General Pillow, during the attack on Chapultepec and the City of Mexico, on the 13th and 14th Sept. 1847.

General Staff—Maj Gen Gideon J Pillow, wounded severely; Lieut G T Beauregard, wounded twice slightly.

Co. I, 1st Artillery—**WOUNDED**—Capt J B Magruder, twice; Privs Paul Dalym, Edmund Lonergan, severely; James Donelly, Anthony Kreiss, Wm Merrick, slightly.

9th Infantry—**KILLED**—Col T B Ransom; Sergt Geo C Spencer; Corpls John Bailenan, Geo E Barnes; Privs Foster Edson, John Dorset, George Ball. **WOUNDED**—Musician Geo W King, slightly; Privs E T Pike, Charles B Horsewell, Clark H Green, Wm March, Jas Mohan, Pat'k Connars, Wm Welch, Rob't M Brown. N W King, Benj Osgood, N G Shett, severely; Wm H White, H B Stone, Chas Twist, John Welston, John S Lock, Isaac Ware, Alfred Noyce, Wm A Brown, John Moody, John Bridges, slightly.

14th Infantry—**KILLED**—Privs Benjamin Hall, Rob't Arnold, H R Manning, Jas M Monypenny. **WOUNDED**—Col Wm Trousdale, severely; Capts J M Scantland, severely; Rob't G Beale, very slightly;

2d Lieuts Richard Steel, Rob't W Bedford, slightly; Sergt Wm M Bledsoe, mortally; Corpl H Montgomery, slightly; Privs Wm D Pharris, S Sutzenhizer, W F Beatty, James Kennedy, Stewart White, John Philand, Bolivar Vincent, Calvin C Forola, severely; A D Aujon, A Chadwick, John Wilkinson, F Faobali, J Donnelly, slightly. **MISSING**—Privs John Crawford, Wm Dearing, Jas McDermott, John Blair, W R Watson.

15th Infantry—**KILLED**—Privs Joseph Grant, John Haviland, John Herrick, Henry W Stoy, James D Kensil. **WOUNDED**—Capt E A King, slightly; Sergt Jonathan Jones, severely; Corpls Wm Koch, James McGill, mortally; Harvey Lyon, severely; Privs Thos McClaren, Jacob Ebeham, Seth Millington, Jonas Auglemyer, Geo Momeney, Caleb B Sly, Marvin Ward, severely; Lewis Anderson, Christian Hammel, Duncomb McKinsey, Frank L Hartinaw, Henry Hess, slightly. **MISSING**—Priv. ----- Harkin.

Voltigeurs—**KILLED**—Privs H Frick, E Miller, S Richardson, N Salisbury. **WOUNDED**—Lieut Col Jos E Johnston, slightly; Capt Moses J Barnard, twice slightly; 1st Lieuts James Tilton, H.C Gongenecker, Adjt, slightly; 2d Lieuts J L Reno (Rocket and Howitzer Battery), severely; W J Martin, slightly; Sergts W Peat, severely; J C Malbon, T S Gardner, H P Long, slightly; Corpls H E Reed, M Finley, mortally; M Conway, severely; J Muldoon, R Cooper, J McGowan, slightly; Musician A Fair, severely; Privs M Bancroft, E Brass, mortally; S McCall, W H Fitzhugh, W Wood, Z Cox, J Dwyer, T Evans, W E Fletcher, J Amey, J Smith, C Redding, M Rain, G Spencer, C Miller, J Young, P Henry, D Haughney, J Deitz, severely; T Wallace, O Russell, E T Gooden, J H Malbon, J M Floyd, T H Gill, T Trumble, slightly. **MISSING**—Privs James Hall, J Medcalf, J A Maples, G Weygand.

TOTAL—Killed, 21; Wounded, 111; Missing, 10—142. Horses—Killed, 9; Wounded, 3—12.

Fourth Division—Maj. Gen. Quitman

List of the Killed, Wounded, and Missing of the Second Division, in the Several Actions Near the City of Mexico, on the 14th and 15th of September, 1847.

KILLED—***Marine Corps***—Maj L Twiggs. ***New York Volunteers***—Capt A Van O'Linda. ***South Carolina Volunteers***, 1st Lieut J M Morgan, 2d Lieut J Wellis Cantey. ***2d Pennsylvania Volunteers***—Privs

Wm Carlin, Co B; Wm C Bolton, Co G; Isaiah Wondus, Co H; Chas Stewart, Co I; John Street, Co K; Jno Tarn, Co L; Jno McClanahan, Co M. ***Marine Corps***—Corpl Hugh Graham, Co B; Privs Anthony E Egbert, Co D; Andrew McLoughlin, John Herbert, Co E; Matthew Banks, Co B; Thos Kelley, Co E. ***South Carolina Volunteers***—1st Sergts Wm Blocker, Co D; B F Mattison, Co E; Priv T McHenry, Co B; Corpl L Good, Co B; Privs W B Devlin, J Morwood, Co E; C Meyer, Co F; D H Tresevant, Co H; H Calahan, T Cooper, T Lyles, M Martin, Co D; John Patrick, Co E; J C Tunison, Co H. ***New York Volunteers***—T Golden, Andrew Jelard, Co C; Jno Wright, Jno Seaman, Co D; Theds Zimmerman, John Homer, Co E; Corpl James Williams, Co E; Privs Joseph A Dennis, John Shaw, Co G; John L Young, Co K.

WOUNDED—*2d Pennsylvania Volunteers*—Lieut Col J M Geary; Corpls Wm Herbert, Peter Hogan, Privs John Freymon, John Miller, Jacob Armprister, Henry Boyer, Thos McGhee, Jacob Rapp, Co A, slightly; John Arthur, George Henry, Daniel Saul, Co A, severely; Nathan Martz, Co A, dangerously; Peter Moyer Co. A, mortally, since dead; John Worthington, Wm Humphreys, Sgt John Brookbank, Privs Abraham Rhodes, W J Stone, John Campbell, Hugh Storm, John McLoughlin, Tho Holland, Co B, slightly; Orderly Sergt. Francis McKee, Priv Andrew Dripps, Co B; Privs Wm H Dietrich, Jno Snyder, Co C; Corpls A Patterson, E A Downey, Privs F C McDermot, Co D, severely; B F Davis, G W Neff, Co D; Sergt David Meckling, Privs R McCleland, George Decker, Henry Fiskil, Co E, slightly; Chanay F Sergeant, Co E; Lieut A S Towrison, Co F, severely; Corpl Wm H Sogur, Co F; Privs Thomas Humphreys, Co B. slightly; John Vanson, Jas T Sample, John Betchtel, John Copehart, Co F, severely; Wm Rice, Samuel E Major, Co F; Capt E C Williams, Ensign Christ'phr Sieb, Co G; Privs Joseph Palmer, M Fraxter, P Ward, Co G, slightly; Corpl Jacob Meyer, Co G, mortally; Privs R Rodgers, J Cosgrove, E Moyer, Co G, severely; Sergt A Cummins, Privs Henry Rist, Co H, slightly; Saml Morgan, Co H, mortally; Wm Mendenhall, Co H, severely; Arch Graham, Isaac N Hoops, Fred'k Myers, Co I, slightly; Capt Jas Miller, Privs Wm Clements, John Horn, James Bustard, John Solomon, Emor M Davis, Co K, severely; Wm Snyder, W Smyth, Michl Hasson, H Thomas, Edw'd Blain, Co K, slightly; Lieut John Keefe, Corpl A J Jones, Privs Wm Smyth, Co L, severely; Joseph Lutz, Thos Davis, Christ Malone,

Jas Stewart, Wm Bishop, Wm Crabb, Co L, slightly; Capt James Caldwell, Privs Joshua Hamilton, John Keever, David Shine, Chas Epler, Co M, severely; Benj Shine, Lewis Bonnetts, Saxfere Heasbly, Co M, slightly. ***Marine Corps***—1st Lieut and Adjt D D Baker; 1st Lieut and A Q M J S Devlin, Co M; 2d Lieut Chas A Henderson, Co F; Sergt Major Jas Montgomery, slightly; Commissary Sergt Jas Orr; Sergts John Roach, Co B, severely; John Curran, Co D, slightly; W J Wilson, Co D, severely; Grandisen L Tansill, Co D, slightly; Privs Seebeck, Co A; Martin Fogg, Hugh Roney, Co B, severely; John McGuigan, Philip Phoenix, Saml Williamson, Co B, slightly; Biggs, Co C, severely; Connor, Co C, slightly; Francis Quinn, Co D; Thomas B Smith, Elhanan Stevens, Co E, severely; Edward Cooper, Co F, slightly; James Linns, Co F, severely; Musician McDonald, Co F, slightly; Milburn, Co A, severely. ***South Carolina Volunteers***—Maj A H Gladden, Acting Adjt M Clarke, severely; Sergt Major O T Gibbs, slightly; Priv Thomas Gafney, Co A; Sergts R Payan, J Dunnovant, W Triplett, Privs M M Adams, J Thomas, M Ward, Y Muller, Y Evans, J Onley, Co B, severely; Corpl. J Hood, Privs Y Cahill, N R Evans, J Ferguson, Y Robins, C Ingram, H Lafferty, Bennett, Co B; Sergt L B Weaver, Privs Y Anderson, C H Kenny, Co D, slightly; Delany, Co D; 2d Lieut F Sellock, Priv R Watson, Co E, severely; Corpl W L Rodgers, Privs J H Saxton, J Calvert, J Davis, R Jenkin, C L McCowen, Co E; 2d Lieut Bell, Sergt J N Easterby, Corpl Bold, Privs R Hitchfelt, J Martin, P S Graham, C Rankin, C Anderson, W L Beadon, Co F, slightly; 2d Lieut J W Steen, Privs H Scott, D Noland, James Walsh, Co G, severely; 2d Lieut J B Davis, Sergt J W Shedd, Privs S Camak, E Duke, W S Tidwell, R J Barber, W Claxton, J Woodward, Jas M Craig, C J Gladney, J W Brittenham, J E Odum, Co G, slightly; Privs A Tunison, J B Glass, R S Morrison, H J Caughman, D Polock, J D Stanford, Manning Brown, J Fitzsimmons, B Hutchinson, J Kelly, Co H, severely; 1st Lieut A B O'Bannon, 2d Lieut. C J Kirkland, Privs J G Atkinson, Co K, slightly; J K Parker, Co K, mortally; Capt J H Williams, Sergt J Caldbeeth, Corpl J J Feague, Privs T Chapman, J Graham, J C Higgins, D Brown, H Suber, Co L, slightly; A Little, R B Lyles, A Feagle, Co L, severely. ***New York Volunteers***—Lieut Col Chas. Baxter, mortally, since dead; Privs McGennis, Rowalt, Co A, severely; Corpl McGwen, Privs Fife, Duncan, Waggoner, Co A, slightly; 2d Lieut Mayne Reed, Privs John Eber, John Hunt, James Kelly, Co B, severely; Corpl John Hal,

Privs John Keeber, Chas Newman, Co B; Capt J Barclay, Sergt Wm Peel, Privs J White, John Russell, Corpl Jas Saxon, Co C, slightly; Privs C Reymansnyder, B Vandief, Co C, severely; Corpl John Whaley, Privs R Anderson, John Cassedy, James Smith, James Kenneda, D Standerwick, L Strobill, Co D, slightly; Capt C H Pearson, Privs Wm Connell, Y Donovan, Co E, severely; John T Olneys, Co E, slightly; James Burke, G Barry, M Cohlin, H Hardenbrook, W Tomkins, Co F, severely; Capt D E Hungerford, 1st Lieut Chas H Junes, Sergt D Montgomery, Corpl Chas Thompson, Privs Owen Elwood, Thos Healy, Co G, slightly; John McKinney, John Snyder, V VanSlyke, Jas Hart, Co G, severely; Sergt John Duffy, Privs Pat Roney, O Hanzel, Co H, slightly; Michl Butler, Co H, mortally, since dead; Capt M Fairchild, Lieut J W Green, 1st Sergt Barker, Privs Thos L Decker, James Franklin, Geo Pemberton, John L Gardner, R Hendrick, Wm Daly, Co I, slightly; D Robertson, Geo Thistleton, Co I, severely; Sergt John M Kane, Corpl Clipolett Everett, Co K, slightly; Priv Alex Cook, Co K, severely. ***General Staff***—Brig Gen James Shields, severely; F N Page, A A G; M Lovell, A A A G, slightly, Capt Danly, Volunteer Aide, severely. Total—Killed, 41; Wounded, 267–308.

General Total

	Killed	Wounded	Missing
1. Gen. Worth's Division	140	766	27
2. Gen. Twiggs' Division	36	194	10
3. Gen. Pillow's Division	21	111	10
4. Gen. Quitman's Division	41	267	—
Total	238	1,338	47

Killed, wounded and missing in the four divisions of Gens. Worth, Twiggs, Pillow and Quitman, 1,623.

September 28, 1847.

I send you the three first numbers of the *American Star*, published by Messrs. John Peoples & J. R. Barnard. You will find in them the orders of Gen. Scott, since our entrance into the city, as also the list of the names of the captured deserters, executed in pursuance of a sentence of a general court martial.

Our prisoners, who were sent to Toluca on the approach of our army, have arrived safely in this city. I understand that they are still prisoners of war, and will probably soon be exchanged, and that they have been sent here by the Governor of Mexico, on his own responsibility, he not having received the proposition for their exchange. I think it altogether more likely that they are indebted to the increasing and untiring exertions of Maj. Gaines, for their release from confinement. Those who arrived yesterday, are Capts. Clay, William J. Heady, and Green C. Smith; Lieuts. Thomas J. Churchill, George R. Davidson, and William T. Barbour; and sixteen privates.

Although the city up to the moment of writing, is as quiet as it could possibly be under any circumstances, we have daily reports of the rising of the populace, and the assassination of our army. No doubt some such movement has been contemplated, but whether they will be able to bring themselves up to the "sticking point," is a matter of extreme doubt. I can hardly believe an enemy who could not stand against us in the field, will now attempt to overpower us by such means.

The Mexican Congress does not meet until the 5th of October, at Querétaro. We can form no idea of what they will be able to do. The seven Northern states, which some time since formed a coalition, pledging themselves to the support of each other, in opposition to negotiations for peace, have held a meeting of delegates, who have denounced Santa Anna in strong terms, have declared him an outlaw and a traitor, and at the same time have passed a resolution requiring each state to furnish 3,000 men, armed and equipped, for the further prosecution of the war. Gens. Mariano Paredes y Arrillaga and Anastasio Bustamente have been appointed to the command.[3]

3. A career army officer with many entanglements in Mexican politics, Mariano Paredes was a foe of any person who seemed willing to give up claims to the territory of Texas. He finally led his own coup and become president early in 1846. As General Taylor stood ready to attack Monterrey, he headed north but was himself deposed by a coup headed by Santa Anna. Sent to France in exile, Paredes came back and and after the fall of Mexico City urged his countrymen to keep up the fight. Opposed to the peace treaty, Paredes led another short-lived uprising, was sent again into exile, and returned only to die in 1849. Tucker, *Encyclopedia*, 491–92.

After rejecting Spanish rule in 1821, Anastasio Bustamante began a tumultuous military and political career that saw him repeatedly rise to the top (two terms as president) and bottom (two exiles after being deposed as president). Serving as an influential general, Bustamante helped to prop up several Mexican administrations by subduing provincial rebellions. He remained in the

President and General Antonio López de Santa Anna. *Courtesy Library of Congress*.

The last reliable information we have had of the whereabouts of Santa Anna is that he was a few days since at or in the vicinity of Puebla. What his object is in going there, I cannot imagine. I can hardly think he would undertake to attack Col. Childs in position, when he has not been able to sustain himself behind the best

---

army and crushed several revolts after the war before his death on February 8, 1853. Tucker, *Encyclopedia*, 99.

fortifications, and further, as soon as the reinforcements arrive, he will have to take his lodgings somewhere else.

Since I last wrote you, Cols. Dickenson and Baxter have died. Gens. Pillow's and Shields' wounds are doing well, and I think it probable Gen. Shields will start for the United States in the course of a few weeks. Maj. William W. Loring has lost his arm, but will be able to be out in a few days. Col. McIntosh died last night.

The new Rifle Regiment has had a fair opportunity of testing their ability, and although much was expected from them, they have exceeded the expectations of every person. They led the way from the time the attack was made on the 13th, until they crossed the Gate of the City, led by Lieut. Stuart, who unfurled their banner on every breastwork. Although the infantry shoot three times to their one, still their fire is more destructive to the enemy. Never, at any one point, or under any circumstances, have the Mexicans been able to stand the severity of their fire. When they arrived at the Gate of the City, they picked off the artillerists with such accuracy, that they were unable to load their guns, or even show their heads above the breastworks. This regiment has never, as yet, been furnished by the government with a stand of colors. At Puebla, the officers had a stand made at their own expence. This flag has been the first on every breastwork, until Gen. Quitman's column entered the city. Now, I would ask, has not this regiment handsomely won one from the hands of some city of the United States, and then let me ask, who are more ready to reward gallantry, than the fair ladies of the Crescent City.

Headquarters of the Army,
Mexico, September 14, 1847.

General Orders, No. 234.

1. Under the favor of God, the valor of this army, after many glorious victories, has hoisted the colors of our country in the capital of Mexico and on the palace of its government.
2. But the war is not ended. The Mexican army and government have fled only to watch an opportunity to return upon us in vengeance. We must, then, be upon our guard.
3. Companies and Regiments will be kept together, and all stand on the alert. Our safety is in military discipline.
4. Let there be no drunkenness, no disorder, and no straggling. Stragglers will be in great danger of assassination, and marauders shall be punished by courts martial.

5. All rules so honorably observed by this glorious army in Puebla, must be observed here. The honor of the army, and the honor of our country call for the best behavior on the part of all. The valiant must, to win the approbation of God and our country, be sober, orderly, and merciful. His noble brethren in arms will not be deaf to this hasty appeal from their commander and friend.

6. Major-General Quitman is appointed Civil and Military Governor of Mexico.

By command of Maj. Gen. Scott,
H.L. Scott, A.A.A.G.

Headquarters of the Army,
National Palace of Mexico, Sept. 17, 1847.
General Orders—No. 287.

The General-in-Chief re-publishes his order No. 2, of 19th February, 1847, declaring Martial Law, with important additions.

1. It is to be feared that many grave offences may be committed by or against the persons composing the armies engaged in the present war between the two Republics, which are not provided for in the act of Congress "establishing rules and regulations for the government of the armies of the United States," approved the 10th of April, 1806. Those offences are here alluded to, which, if committed in the United States, or in their organized territories, would be tried and severely punished by the ordinary civil tribunals of the country.
2. The following offences are meant: Assassination, murder, poisoning, rape, or the attempt to commit either of these crimes; violent assaults, theft or robbery; the profanation of temples, cemeteries or other sacred places; the interruption of religious ceremonies or the destruction of public or private property without the express order of a superior officer.
3. For the welfare of the military service, for the interest of humanity, and for the honor of the United States, it is absolutely essential that all the crimes above mentioned should be severely punished.
4. But the code commonly called the "rules and articles of war" does not provide any punishment for the said crimes, not even in case they are perpetrated by individuals in the army against the persons and property of the same, except in the very restricted case in Art. 9; and they are only partially referred to in Arts. 51, 52 and 55, when committed by individuals of the army against the persons and property of a hostile people; and the said code does not refer to the injuries which may be committed by individuals of a hostile country in violation of the laws of war upon the persons and property composing the army.
5. It is evident that Art. 99, independent of any reference to the restriction in Art. 87, is entirely negatory and does not reach these capital crimes.
6. Therefore, a supplementary code, covering the crimes mentioned in the second paragraph of this order, whether committed in, by, or against the army, is absolutely necessary.

7. This unwritten code is simply *martial law*, and is an addition to the military code prescribed by Congress in the "rules and articles of war," and all armies in a hostile country should adopt the martial law, not only for their own security, but for the protection of the peaceful inhabitants and their property from detriment on the part of the army in violation of the laws of war.
8. In consequence of this overpowering necessity, martial law is declared as a supplemental code, and it will be observed in and about all posts, cities, villages, camps, hospitals, and other places which may be occupied by portions of the army of the United States in Mexico; and it will be equally observed in the columns, escorts, convoys, guards and detachments of said army, during the present war with that Republic, and while it shall remain in the same.
9. Consequently all the crimes mentioned in the second paragraph, whether perpetrated, 1st. By a Mexican citizen, inhabitant of or a sojourner in this Republic, against the persons or property of those belonging to or following the army of the United States of America; or, 2d. By any individual belonging to or following said army, against the persons or property of the citizens or inhabitants of, or sojourners in this country; or, 3d. By any individual belonging to or following said army, against the persons or property of any persons appertaining to the same, shall be judged and punished under the supplemental code.
10. For this purpose it is ordered, that every delinquent in the above-mentioned cases shall be promptly arrested, and notice thereof given, that he may be tried before a military commission, which shall be convoked in conformity with what follows.
11. Every military commission under this order shall be named, governed, and conducted as far as practicable in accordance with Arts. 65, 66 and 67 of the rules and articles of war; and the proceedings of the said commission shall be duly recorded in writing, revised and corrected, approved or disapproved, and the sentences executed, so far as practicable, in conformity with the proceedings and sentences of a court martial, under the following limitations: No military commission shall have a jurisdiction in any case that may be properly tried by a court martial, and no sentence of any military commission shall be executed against any person belonging to the American army, unless the nature and grade of his offence be established by evidence, and then he shall be punished in the same manner that similar cases are punished in any State of the United States.
12. The sale, waste and loss of warlike stores, horses, arms, clothing and provisions of soldiers, shall be punished by law under the Nos. 37 and 38 of the articles of war, and whatever Mexican, whether a resident or a transient person, who shall buy from any soldier, arms, ammunition, provisions or clothing, horses or their trappings, shall be tried and severely chastised by a military commission.
13. The administration of justice, both civil and criminal, shall be meted out in all the established courts throughout the country, without the slightest

interruption or hindrance from the officers or soldiers of the American army, excepting the following cases: 1st. In case the person be an officer, soldier, agent, servant, or other person following the North American army. 2d. *In political cases*, that is to say, suits against other individuals, in which it is alleged that friendly information, protection, or kind reception, has been given to the American army.

14. For the convenience and protection of both parties, in all cities and towns occupied by the American army, a body of Mexican police shall be established and organized to act in concert with the military police of the said army.
15. This beautiful Capital, its churches and its religion, its convents and monasteries, its inhabitants and their property, are placed under the especial safeguard of the good faith and honor of the American army.
16. As a consideration of the aforesaid protection a contribution of $150,000 is levied on the Capital, payable in four payments, at the rate of $37,500 per week, commencing on Monday next, the 20th inst., and terminating on Monday, the 11th of October.
17. The ayuntamiento, or municipal council, of this city is especially charged witht the collection and payment of these sums.
18. From the entire contribution which is to be paid to this army, $20,000 shall be appropriated for the purchase of some very necessary supplies for the wounded and sick in the hospital; $90,000 to purchase blankets and shoes, which shall be distributed gratuitously amongst the soldiers of the army; and $40,000 shall be retained for other military wants.
19. This order shall be read to and circulated amongst all the companies of the American army now in service in Mexico, and shall be translated into Spanish for the information of the Mexicans.

By order of the Commander-in-Chief,
H.L. Scott, A.A.A. General

Office of the Civil and Military Governor
National Palace, Sept. 22, 1847

To enable the city authorities to raise the contribution levied upon them, the following orders are made with the approbation of the General-in-Chief:

I. The municipal authorities of the city and district will retain all their usual sources of revenue. In addition thereto, the internal customs or duties which have heretofore been collected at the Customhouse, City Gates and elsewheree, are for the present surrendered to the Ayuntamiento to be collected and disposed of by them, subject to such modifications and orders as may from time to time be received from this office, or from the General-in-Chief.

II. The management and revenues of the Postoffice are likewise for the present yielded up to the Ayuntamiento.

III. After setting aside a supply of the public segars and tobacco, sufficient for two months' consumption, to be distributed in kind to the army, the residue will be disposed of to the municipal authorities at the rate of --- per arroba, with leave to dispose of it in the manner and at the prices heretofore usual with the Mexican Government. The price and terms of the sale to the Ayuntamiento, to be determined on between them and the principal Quartermaster of the Army.

IV. Tobacco not belonging to the Mexican Government, and which may hereafter be brought into market, may be disposed of by the city authorities as heretofore.

V. All supplies for the army shall be introduced free of any duty or charge whatever.

VI. Semi-weekly reports of the receipts into the City Treasury, and of the expenditures, will be made to the Civil and Military Governor.

J.A. Quitman,
Maj. Gen. U.S.A. and Civil and Military Governor

September 28, 1847.

We have quite a number of rumors flying about from Puebla. One says that Santa Anna has defeated Col. Childs, another is that Col. Childs has taken Santa Anna prisoner. But as far as I have been able to trace them to a reliable source, I find our latest dates from Col. Childs are to the 23[d] inst., at which date he was as comfortably situated as could be expected, but by the same conveyance you will likely learn what is the exact state of affairs there.

Among others of the unfortunate wounded who are doing remarkably well, is Mr. George W. Kendall, of the *Picayune*, volunteer aide-de-camp to Gen. Worth, and your modest but humble servant. Mr. Kendall you will find in the list of wounded slightly. I do not think his wound was considered dangerous from the first, as the ball struck "him right plumb in his *horse's ear*," and at present time he looks to be in as fine health and spirits as I have ever seen him, and as well as a "war-worn soldier" might expect to be. I was so "unfortunate" myself as to be struck right in my horse's saddle, but the ball was spent and did not go through the saddle-skirt, therefore as yet, "*I* have not suffered any inconvenience from it." I also happened to be caught in bad company at the *garita*, and, with several others, was knocked head-over-heels by the explosion of a shell, but being in a hurry to pick myself up, I trod upon an officer, who pettishly said I had "no business there, anyhow!" I don't count that as anything, as I hurt somebody else worse than I was hurt myself. Now, having "taken a bath, brushed off the smoke and dust of battle," and between good liquor, good segars, and a moderate share of the balance of the good things of this world, "am as comfortable as might be expected under the circumstances." Having neglected to have my name put down on the list of wounded until after it had been made out, that all the world, and "my numerous friends in particular," might know that "I, too, was hurt," will excuse this paragraph from your *modest* correspondent.

His Excellency, Don Lopez de Santa Anna that was, but is no more, the President and Commander-in-Chief of the Army of the Republic of Mexico, having determined to locate himself somewhere out of the reach of the horrible Yankees, has requested his better half to join him in his pilgrimage. She therefore applied to Gen. Scott for permission and protection out of the city. Accordingly, the general, no doubt properly appreciating her object, and for the purpose of enabling here to join her disconsolate lord in his misfortunes, directed that she should have the proper escort. Capt. Hamilton W. Merrill, of the dragoons, as celebrated for his affability and courtesy, as he is for his bravery in battle, was selected to do up the amiable, and place her ladyship, Doña Señora Santa Anna, out of the reach of the "loathed barbarians of the North," and particularly "that animal called the volunteer." The officer was peculiarly fortunate in discharging his task to the entire satisfaction of the lady, from whom he received many "thanks and salutations," and assurances that, if chance should ever cause them to meet under different circumstances, he should be entitled to the "distinguished consideration and respect" of herself and unfortunate lord. I expect by this time, she is soothing him in his misfortunes, and endeavoring to assuage his reverses by that kindness and devoted attachment for which the women of this country are justly notorious. No doubt, in the course of one or two months from this time, His Excellency will be diverting himself by his favorite pastime and amusement—cock-fighting—in which combats he has, heretofore, been more successful and fortunate, than he has in his combats with *los Americanos del Norte*.

The following incident evidences the enthusiasm and state of feeling pervading the ranks of the army. On the evening previous to the storming of the Castle of Chapultepec, an order was given from head-quarters that the 1st and 2d Divisions should furnish storming parties to assault the work. Its formidable appearance, the nature of the ground, and the strength of the force with which it was occupied, in the opinion of the General-in-Chief, required that is should be assailed by tried and veteran troops. Accordingly, instead of drawing them by detail, it was stated, that if there was enough of volunteers, they would be taken. When this was announced, so great was the anxiety that in many instances it had to be decided by drawing lots. In the 2d Infantry, which is attached to the 2d Division, there was a private who was employed by a lieutenant as a cook, and from the nature of his occupation he did not have an opportunity of drawing lots. As soon as he learned of the result, he sought the lieutenant's quarters, and apparently deeply mortified, bitterly complained at his misfortune, as he called it, and implored the lieutenant to let him go with the detachment in the morning, as he had never yet had "a chance." The lieutenant sympathized with him, but told him he had no authority to let him go. The private left the officer's quarters, and nothing more was heard of him until next morning, when the officer was called to his breakfast at a much earlier hour than usual, and has since told me that it was the best cup of coffee and the best breakfast he has enjoyed since he left Puebla. Shortly after the soldier was missing, and nothing more was heard of him until Col. Riley's brigade entered the Plaza on the 14th, which was some time after the 1st Brigade, Col. Riley having entered with Gen. Worth, and Gen. Smith with Gen. Quitman. As soon as the 2d Infantry took its position, the first thing the officer observed was his cook approaching him with a tin cup of hot coffee, one piece of fresh bread, a boiled egg, &c., remarking at the same time: "I thought, sir, after the lieutenant had been lying out all night without even a blanket to cover him, maybe he'd like a bite of breakfast, and a little hot coffee, so I just fixed up a little something for you this morning, sir. It's not much, but the best I could hunt up, sir."

"But where have you been all this time, sir?"

"Why, sir, the lieutenant will recollect that I wanted to go with the storming party to that bloody strong-hold of a castle, and when I heard the old Gen. Twiggs say to them, 'Now, boys, do your duty,' I couldn't keep back, sir, particularly as I was cheated out of my chance in drawing the lots. So I determined, live or die, I'd go with the boys, and I did get hurt, nothing but a little scratch on the shoulder, but I wouldn't say I was wounded. I was determined to stick by the flag of our division until I'd see it go up on the big flag-staff of the castle, and as soon as I saw it up there I went back and a doctor tied a bit of a rag round my shoulder. But I couldn't find the lieutenant, sir, so I kept on with Gen. Smith's brigade until now, sir, and I am glad to find the lieutenant on his feet, without being killed or wounded." Inquiry was made, and all he stated found to be true.

Now, does not this soldier's conduct, although he had violated his orders, exhibit the very highest degree of patriotic bravery, and a devotion to the standard of his division, a glorious standard, worthy of a devotion of which the above is but one of a thousand examples?

Passing over the battle-field of Molino del Rey, immediately after our victorious standard had been planted on the enemy's works, where lay the dead and wounded mingled together, my attention was attracted to different places, by the scenes of grief and sorrow, scenes which pained my feelings and shocked my sight. There I found many acquaintances, dead and wounded, whom I had seen but a short time previous full of health, and with buoyant spirits, marching at the head of their commands, in the strong hope that they would soon, by their noble deeds and heroic valor, achieve fame for themselves and glory for their country. But, alas! how uncertain are the ways of life. There I found the strong youth and the aged veteran, who fell side by side, to rise no more. Many of the most noble souls of the army, and the pride of the country's chivalry, there performed their last gallant acts on the stage of life. After going over a portion of the ground, and finding here and there a valued acquaintance, my attention was attracted to a gray-headed veteran, who was standing by the side of one who had fallen. He leisurely took his blanket from his back, and spread it over the corpse with great care. I rode up to him, and asked him whether that was an officer. He looked up, and every lineament of his face betokening the greatest grief, replied, "You never asked a question, sir, more easily answered. It is an officer." I then asked him who it was. He again replied, "The best soldier of the 5th Infantry, sir." I then alighted from my horse, and uncovering the face, found it was Col. Martin Scott. As I again covered the face, the soldier continued, without apparently addressing himself to any person in particular, "They have killed him. They will be paid for this. If it only had been me.

Burying the Dead. *Courtesy Library of Congress*.

I have served with him almost four enlistments, but what will his poor family say?" And as he concluded this, the tears coursed down his furrowed cheeks, and the swelling of his bosom showed how deeply he was affected by the death of his veteran and gallant commander. Could there have been anything more affecting than the grief of this soldier on the battle-field? How truly sublime and eloquent was his reply to me, that it was "*the best soldier of the 5th Infantry*." If the greatest orator of the age had dwelt upon the memory of our departed friend until he had exhausted his eulogy and eloquence, he could not have said anything which would make a greater impression on our feelings, than did the reply of this soldier. Col. Martin Scott was among "the bravest of the brave." He fought his way into the army in our last war with Great Britain, and since that time he has been one of the brightest ornaments, and has signally distinguished himself in the war with Mexico, for which he has been promoted and breveted.

The following notice of Capt. George W. Ayers was handed to me by one of his surviving brother officers, which I cheerfully forward to you:

"Was killed, on the 8th of September, 1847, during the assault upon the Mexican fortified lines near Chapultepec, Brevet Captain George W. Ayers, 3d Regiment, U.S. Artillery. A graduate of West Point in 1841, and promoted to a 1st Lieutenancy in December, 1846, he at the same time had received the brevet rank of captain, 'for gallant and meritorious conduct in the several conflicts at Monterey, Mexico, on the 21st, 22d, and 23d of September, 1846.' It was there that, being of the storming party against the Bishop's Palace, he was the first to enter the work and seize the Mexican colors. After passing unscathed through the several battles of the past year, he fell pierced with numerous wounds, while in the act of forcing the barricaded gateway of the Molino del Rey, maintaining to the last his reputation for unflinching courage and gallant daring. His many excellent qualities as a soldier, cause him to be admired and esteemed by his brother officers, and respected and beloved by the men of his command. The deep grief of those who have shared with him the dangers and hardships of the campaign in Mexico, is the best tribute to his qualities as a friend. 'His ambition was to gain a soldier's fame, his fate to fill a soldier's grave.'"

Chapter 5

Occupation Duty

October 5, 1847. City of Mexico.

Last night, about 12 o'clock, we were again visited by an earthquake. Although the vibrations of the earth were not so severe as the former one, it was sufficient to produce a very strong impression upon our people, who really have a greater dread of them than they have all the engines of death that the Mexicans have ever possessed. Occurring as it did, when half the world were wrapt in slumbers sound, it was calculated to produce more fright than if it had happened in daylight.

Col. William B. Roberts, of the 2d Pennsylvania Regiment, died on Sunday last, and was interred with the military honors due his rank, and followed to the grave lamented by his friends and acquaintances.[1]

1. The owner of a grocery and furniture warehouse in Uniontown, William Roberts was elected colonel of the 2d Pennsylvania Volunteers in January of 1847, although there seems to have been some questions regarding his qualifications for that office. His performance under fire at Cerro Gordo removed all doubt of his ability. Stricken by fever and a hemorrhage of the lungs in August, his health steadily declined until his death in Mexico City on October 3, 1847. *Times-Picayune*, January 16, 1847; *Pittsburgh Daily Post*, May 25, 1847; Hadden, *History of Uniontown*, 145, 543.

Newspapers Boasted Headlines Confirming the Peace Treaty. *Courtesy Library of Congress.*

Yesterday a report reached this place that Gen. Taylor was on his road to San Luis Potosi. The source of information is considered reliable, that you will probably know the correctness of it in New Orleans better than we will at this point.

I enclose to you the address of Gen. Santa Anna to his fellow citizens of the Republic of Mexico. You will see that he sets out by stating, with "profound and bitter regret," that he was obliged to abandon the capital after continued and extraordinary efforts during an engagement which lasted fifteen hours. He goes on to say what he has done, and what he intends to do, not forgetting to place himself before his deluded and ignorant countrymen as a man of "many sacrifices," all for the sake of his "unfortunate" country. You will also see that he tried to throw himself in the way of good luck, but it was of no use against the "Barbarians of the North."

The Mexican Congress was to meet to-day at Querétaro, but whether they had a quorum present is doubtful. Some of the states have failed to elect their secondary electors. At Querétaro, Herrera has been nominated for the presidency, and *Señors* Manuel Pedraza and José Guadalupe Covanubias for the senate.

El Monitor, a Spanish paper published here, has commenced to deal out its abuse unsparingly on our authorities. The *Star* and *North American* have drawn their pens, and a very spirited controversy has ensued. The man of *The Monitor* has threatened something personal, which is right into the hands of the American editors, and the affair promises something decidedly rich. *The Monitor* has been celebrated in times past, when the Mexicans reigned supreme, for fault-finding and scurrility, but if he gets the Americans fairly started, I think they will teach him a lesson that will force him to be more respectful to others, if he has no respect for himself.

The man of the *Star* has also got himself into a controversy with the fair *señoritas*, if so they may be called, of this famous city. He being a verdant youth, and full of life, took the liberty of expressing, through his paper, his admiration for the "softer sex," in terms highly complimentary, whereupon a communication, signed "*Varias Mexicanos*," is published in a little paper called *The Eagle*, soliciting the man of the *Star* "not to flatter them, for,"—as they say—"flattery from an enemy is an insult to their dear patriotism." But the *Star* is not to be driven off in that way, and seems determined to admire and flatter them, despite of their effusions through the columns of *The Eagle*. It is the first time I have known flattery to offend a lady, friend or foe, and the editor of the *Star* being rather good-looking, and moderately amiable, I should not be surprised if, by energy and a liberal share of good luck, he succeeds in inducing these indignant creatures to listen with an attentive ear to his sentences of admiration, particularly, as he says, since they have got his "*dander up*." He will step boldly forward, and say, that he does not only admire them, but that he *dotes* upon all the pretty women of the country, and is determined to worship at the shrine of beauty.

October 7, 1847.

An order has been issued by Gen. Quitman, Governor of the City, requiring all the newspapers to present their sheets for revision before publication. The rebellious and incendiary spirit manifested by some of them, calculated to produce serious trouble between our army and the Mexicans, required the adoption of such a course.

Between the drills of the day and the nightly performances of the theatre and circus, together with the *other* amusements and curiosities of the city, our army is enabled to pass off the dullness following our late exciting scenes very pleasantly and agreeably. The drills on Sunday are suspended, and our people "have the privilege of doing as they please, so that they don't get drunk." Some of them promenade the streets and public walks, some attend the ceremonies at church, while others pay some attention to the Mexican national amusement of bull-fighting!

October 8, 1847.

Last night we had an exciting scene at the theatre. Between the pieces the orchestra, which is really a very fine one, gave us two or three beautiful airs, and concluded with a Mexican national air. As soon as they finished, the audience, being mostly American, called for "Yankee Doodle," but the orchestra paid no attention. They stamped and rapped, as if they would bring the house down over our heads, but still the orchestra heeded not. At length the bell rang, and up went the curtain. The audience seemed for an instant as if they were willing to give it up, but at this moment a tall slab-sided-looking genius, who bore the appearance of being a real, thorough-bred patriotic volunteer of the first water, raised himself about "half straight," and said,

> I otten heard that "Yankee Doodle" was the Americans' fightin' tune, but as the darned eternal Greasers kept us so busy while we were fightin', that we couldn't have time even to whistle a little, I think we might have a little touch of Uncle Sam's favorite, if it's only to make a feller think of the white settlements.

This acted like an electric shock upon the audience, and they re-commenced their calls for "Yankee Doodle." The actors appeared upon the stage, but still they continued to stamp and halloo. Señora Cañete bowed gracefully, and smiled bewitchingly, but it was no use; they had determined upon hearing our national air, and nothing could persuade them from it. The actors withdrew, the curtain fell, the orchestra complied with their demands, and the balance of the evening's entertainment passed off in excellent order. A Mexican gentleman, sitting in front of me, remarked to his friend, that it was the best illustration of the American character he had ever witnessed, that when they once determined upon anything, neither the firmness of man, nor the solicitation of woman, could induce them to cease in their exertions until they had accomplished their object, and that in ten minutes after or before any efforts, you would think, from their appearance, that they were as docile as lambs and as harmless as infants.

October 8, 1847. City of Mexico.

The Mexican force, which in one of my late letters I stated to you as being under the command of Vincente Filisola, and intended to infest the roads leading into this city, have turned out to be about 1,500 men, parts of the late dispersed army. They are now to the north of the lake—what they have for their object we have not been able to ascertain—but the most probable conclusion is, that they are intended to parade around Querétaro during the sitting of the Mexican Congress, where they are now collecting the remnants of their army, I presume for the purpose of making a show of carrying on the war, if such a manifestation should be found necessary to facilitate the views of the ruling aspirants.

The following article from *El Porvenir*, published at Toluca, I send you more as a matter of curiosity than anything else. You will perceive that he handles the officers of the Mexican army with a good deal of severity. The Mexicans themselves are ever ready to abuse their military whenever an occasion offers, but they claim the especial privilege of doing so. If any foreigner insinuates that they are not as valiant as any other nation, they will commence blustering in a manner that would make Bombastes ashamed of himself. *El Povenir*, it is generally supposed, speaks the sentiments of Manuel de la Peña y Peña, the present Chief Magistrate, which position he acquires by holding the office of Chief Justice. You will observe that the pith of the article is concentrated in the last two paragraphs. A large portion of the Mexicans have been endeavoring for a long time, to get rid of the army, which is a great drain on the public funds, and holds a powerful political influence. Now that an opportunity offers they want to avail themselves of it, they are also apprehensive that if the former officers of the army, who all have political connections, should again acquire an influence, they may thwart the views and intentions of the new dynasty.

Still continue arriving in this capital the generals, colonels, and officers who failed to defend that of the Republic, because they lacked the valor to present their front to the enemy. They have sufficient courage, however, to come here and quarrel about the chief command, seniority of rank, and other points—where, free from risk, they continue eating up the property of the unhappy people, who have already made sufficient sacrifices in maintaining them, without obtaining any other return than to see themselves on the eve of losing their nationality, on account of the cowardice of those whose duty it was to defend it.

It is anything but pleasant to repeat these remarks, which are in the mouth of every inhabitant of this unfortunate country; but, we are constrained to it at witnessing the effrontery of these gentlemen of the epaulette; and, we add, who pretend not to hear the just and well-deserved clamors of their fellow-citizens against their imbecile, thievish and cowardly conduct. The time of being undeceived has arrived. The people now know that these laced-covered gentry, who have ever been so ready to oppress their fellow-citizens—to create political revolts, in order that they might find occasions of being enriched or promoted—they have not the coolness to stand up in the presence of a contemptible horde of North American volunteers, but when they saw these latter approach them, have run off with the velocity of lightning, leaving in their power our artillery, our army, our ammunition, our unfortunate soldiers; and, in fact, all those elements of war which we had collected at great sacrifices, and which our nation had entrusted to them to preserve its independence and its honor.

The United Mexican States are decided to prosecute the war, they will create new elements, at whatever sacrifice; but these military gentlemen need not expect that the new elements will be placed in their hands. No! the States are resolved never again to trust such gentry: they will call in the assistance of their true sons, who, adorned with patriotism, valor, and good faith, will bring about a more happy termination of the war, notwithstanding that they are not covered with spangles, usurping the title of skilled in the art of war.

These generals, colonels and officers, had better find some retired corner in which to hide their shame, or make a guerrilla war against the enemy at their own expence. By doing deeds of valor they may one day meet the approbation and pardon of their country, now highly offended at their conduct.

October 13, 1847. Mexico.

The military and political affairs of this country are in a state of commotion, and it is impossible to predict with any degree of certainty what will be the result of the different movements now on hand, and the effect of those which have been previously brought forward by different parties. The country has heretofore been divided into two parties—one called the *Polkos*, and the other the *Puros*. The former is composed of the former Centralists, and a large portion of the *hacendados* or landholders, and, by the great mass, are looked upon as the "upper ten thousand," so much so that when their revolutions were in a state of fermentation, a gentleman walking in the street with a black coat on, would be the signal for his assassination by the mob. The *Puros* are made up of the old Federalists and the thorough "Republicans" or "Liberalists," and have generally been supported in their revolutionary movements by the rabble, and the great mass of *Rancheros*, and the majority of the highway robbers. There has also been a small Conservative party, who availed themselves of the advantages of circumstances to further their political views or their personal interests. These, with the Monarchical party, which has heretofore been merely nominal, make up the parties and factions, as near as I can fathom them, for the present. What turn they may take, and how divide off, hereafter, remains to be seen.

Santa Anna, few will doubt, has maintained himself in power against an opposition which scarcely another man in the Republic could have resisted. This he has done through the means of his large army, supported by the Centralists, and some others, who were anxious to share his successes and profit by his position. Added to this, he is possessed of great genius and sagacity, and never fails to avail himself of his treachery and deceitfulness, which are always ready as occasion may require. The manner in which he has maintained himself against a strong and violent opposition, has kept the people, who are naturally inclined to be turbulent, in a state of turmoil, and while this opposition has not been powerful enough to overthrow him, they have availed themselves, through tact and good management, of means sufficient to defeat any of his projects that would tend to perpetuate his power of conduce to his personal interests. To effect this object, they have left nothing undone, and hesitated not to make any sacrifices both personal and national.

The result of our late negotiations with Mexico, and the present political movements, clearly show the motives by which the different parties were actuated, and the failure of Mr. Trist in making a treaty is mainly to be attributed to the occupation of the presidential chair by Santa Anna, he thereby having the command of the army, and the control of the resources of the nation.

Santa Anna desired to make a peace, for the purpose of getting clear of our army, which he saw would eventually overwhelm him, and rout him from the place and power he held; and also that he might then, after concluding a treaty, fix himself more permanently in the position of Chief of the Nation, and assume an attitude by which he could, at will, sweep from existence any opposition to him that might arise. The country desired peace, that they might put an end to the deadly strife, that commerce and trade might resume their former routine, that they might not be subjected to the humiliation and mortification of having their capital fall into the hands of their enemies, and their apprehension of the destruction of life and property that might unavoidably ensue. At the same time, the *Puros* clearly saw that if they allowed Santa Anna to conclude a treaty, he would immediately proclaim himself Dictator, call around him a large army, and, by means of the twenty or thirty millions of money he would receive from us, together with our protection, sustain himself until he could fasten his fangs upon the country in a manner that would perpetuate his power to the end of his life. Therefore, between the two alternatives of having Santa Anna as a perpetual ruler, and the loss of the capital and, in a manner, their nationality, they preferred the latter, for the reason that there was a probability that they might recover from it, while, from the former, it was a matter of great doubt.

Therefore, the opposition, in carrying out their designs of overthrowing Santa Anna, opposed a peace and urged a prosecution of the war. Their first aim was at the destruction of the army, and to this end they organized it as large as possible, and lent their aid without reserve to arming and equipping it in the best possible manner, that it might have no excuse for its reverses, but, at the same time, confident that whenever it came in contact with the American forces its rout and destruction would be inevitable. Thus far they have succeeded as well as they could desire, and following up the advantages they have gained, every opposition press in the country has attacked the "lace covered gentry" (the officers of which number 22,000, according to their army register) in every assailable point, calling them cowards, robbers, and every other epithet which they can attach to them. The Government, *ad interim*, has officially withdrawn the nominal command of the army from Santa Anna, placed Gen. Manuel Rincón at its head, and ordered a court-martial to try Santa Anna for the defeat sustained by the army in defence of the city. Whether this party, who are endeavoring to profit by the advantage of circumstances, will be able to make peace is a matter of uncertainty, some of them evidently and ingeniously endeavoring to bring about such a result while others are lying apparently still watching the progress of events.

At this crisis of the affairs, another Richmond has entered the field, who requires *our* particular attention. The visit of Paredes has developed itself. We have heretofore been led to believe that the idea advanced, that one of the European powers was desirous of planting a sprig of its dynasty in this country, was one of those political speculations frequently emanating from fertile imaginations. We could not be induced to believe that Louis Phillippe, in his declining days, would for a moment entertain the project of sending here the Duke de Montpensier (for I cannot think who else it could be) for the purpose of extending his sovereign power over this benighted country, which would inevitably terminate in the assassination of his son, and the usurpation of his authority by some military aspirant; and that too, at the hazard of involving France in a war with the United States, but, to our surprise, such is the fact.

A proposition has been agreed to on the part of France, by which, if Mexico will produce the signatures of 3,000 landholders, pledging themselves to support and maintain the measure, then France will place a prince of its throne here to govern and rule. A paper to that effect is now in circulation, and every effort being made on the part of its friends to accomplish the object. Nearly the whole of the Church are giving it their warm support, and using every means in their power to carry it successfully through, looking upon it as the only means of perpetuating the interests and influence of the ecclesiastical body. A great many of the Centralists, of wealth and strength, who have heretofore opposed the measure with decision and energy, conceiving their power and place to be among the things that were, and hoping by this movement to be able to regain a portion of what they have lost, are not only coinciding with it, but are lending it their undivided aid and influence. Also, some of the Conservatives and those of a neutral temperament in politics have yielded to the project.

The main body of the opposition to Santa Anna are busy combining all the elements of their forces to avert the threatened blow, and retain the advantages gained over their political adversaries. They are very seriously alarmed with reference to the new movements, and we are led to believe that they are doubtful of success against their new competitors.

However, the time has now arrived that requires our government to act instead of talk, and to assume a position in reference to the political movements upon this continent that will enable it to be clearly and distinctly understood, and whereby it will be able to speak in a decided and emphatic tone—that its intentions cannot be mistaken—that the Powers of Europe may be able to judge of what they will have to encounter when they attempt to place their feet upon this continent.

I herewith forward you an able article from *El Razonador*, which paper is about to be reestablished.

PEACE OR WAR. This question of life or death to the Mexican republic, which involves the social existence of the present generation, and the fate of those yet unborn, is agitated and debated by the pens of different citizens of the two contending nations, is observed with uneasiness by the European continent, and is generally denaturalized and merged in the diverse passions excited by so serious an affair. We might well wish to excuse ourselves from taking part in so delicate an affair—to which science should contribute its treasures, and patriotism its purest virtue—especially as it does not pertain exclusively to any of our most prominent factions. But what subject concerning out internal organization can be touched upon which does not presuppose an opinion based upon that question which absorbs the universal attention? In the midst of the uneasiness and anguish of torment, who can preserve the calmness necessary to the complicated and tranquil consideration of domestic economy? Is it not the result of stoicism, or perhaps, even of criminal indifference, to withdraw attention from the common danger, and fix it upon local interests, when even the extent of the enemy's intentions is unknown, and he preserves a mysterious taciturnity while taking advantage of the favors extended to him by the hand of prosperous fortune? What is the foundation of such flattering hopes, when we are ignorant of the aid which can be extended to us, or the resistance which can be offered to any political organization?

To avoid these accusations, which candor or malice might make against us, to cause to be discontinued the accustomed and sad motto of Mexico, dictated by indolence acquired through our vicious education—"it is not yet time, we are not prepared for such excellent things"—has been the principal stimulus which has determined us to grapple with the greatest difficulty, which, in our transient journey through this world, may, perhaps, be presented to us.

It is possible that all our readers may not be men of education, for them we more especially write, asking the more learned to grant us their indulgence. These latter, know very well that war between nations is not exactly the expression of the anger and vengeance of two nations, prosecuted without mercy even to extermination. Some political opinion, some alarm, well or ill-founded, which the operations of one cabinet originate in another; the desire of territorial extension, or of cherishing some branch of industry; and lastly, the desire upon the part of one people of achieving some object, in the execution of which, another may consider itself offended, is the origin of war.

When diplomatic science was unknown in the world, nations had no other method of salvation than a resort to physical force. Should they then succumb, they were irremediably subject to the conqueror. Thus did the empire of Assyria fall before the army of Cyrus; thus did Persia disappear before the power of Alexander; so was extinguished the empire of this conqueror, the kingdoms created by his captains, and the republic of Carthage in the conquests of Roman republic; and thus was dismembered at last the great empire of the Caesars, by the irruptions of the barbarians of the East and of the North.

In the same manner, was formed and dissolved the empire of Charlemagne; and in this confusion the feudal ages passed, without any other title to the acquisition of power than that of brute force.

The different nations that came forth from this chaos, had limits more definitely marked, a safer policy and government, and reasons of State commerce to interfere in the disputes of nations. Their mercantile interests, and all their relations with one another were computed, so that even the most distant took an interest in the contests which were excited. In proportion with the progression of arts, of the sciences, of commerce and of industry, arms in connections with diplomacy, which is the science regulative of the common interest, decided the fate of nations.

From the time of Charles V, emperor of Germany, we have a series of diplomatic treaties; of peace, of truce, of commerce and alliance, which have influenced the creation or extinction of dynasties, the diminution of augmentation of territory, or the greater or less influence of nations. The history of the last three centuries, during which diplomatic negotiations commenced to take that character which we now notice, presents us with a catalogue of events, corroborative of this truth. The Prince of Orange would have lost all his dominions, if the treaty of Vervins concluded in 1598 had not restored to him all the provinces which the power of arms had wrested from him; and from that time to the present, from the treaty of Mineguen in 1678 to the Congress of Vienna in 1814 and 1815, all the civilized nations of Europe have been comprehended and listened to. Those of the first order, such as England, Austria, Prussia, Russia, &c., have acceded to the propositions of France, on account of having become unable to prosecute war, from the immense losses they had suffered. The treaty of Luneville in 1803 deprived the Germanic confederation of all its territories situated on the left bank of the Rhine, and produced in the interior of Germany great territorial novelties, and substantial variations in the constitution of the Empire, such as were the secularizations. The treaty of Presburg ratified in December 1805, transferred the kingdom of Naples to the domination of France. Prussia ceded to France the Duchy of Anspach, of Neufchatel and Valengin, part of the Duchy of Cleves, and of the Electorate of Hanover. The King of Bavaria ceded the Duchy of Berg and received in indemnification that of Anspach. By the treaty of Tilsit, concluded on the 7th of June 1807, Prussia, after having lost in twenty-eight days its army and its monarchy, recovered, notwithstanding, its possessions on the other side of the Elbe, which were Silesia, Brandenburg, Pomerania, and the part of Poland lying on both sides of the Vistula, and totally lost its provinces between the Elbe and the Rhine, renounced all its rights over other States, and recognized Naples, Holland, and the confederation of the Rhine. In the year 1809 Austria, by the treaty of Vienna, lost more than three million and a half of inhabitants. Sajonia increased its territory by the Duchy of Warsaw. Russia acquired Gallicia, and there remained at the disposition of France, Salsburg, the districts of the Inn, half of Carinthia, and the whole of Carniola, all of which were distributed among its allies. France itself, in 1814 and 1815, saw itself compelled to receive the peace of the allies, losing all its conquests and glories, and admitting a dynasty which it detested, and whose blood had flowed, mingled with that of thousands of victims; and this peace it accepted after having seen its capital occupied by the allied armies. The congress of Vienna, composed of the diplomatists of Austria, Spain, England, Portugal, Prussia, Switzerland, Russia, and France itself, made this definitive arrangement.

And now, in order to apply these historical examples with precision, let us see what is the present condition of Mexico. It is that of the most profound stupor after the most mournful undeceivings. Homogeneous armies, organized according to all the rules of tactics, and in the midst of their homes, went to combat against undisciplined masses, collected by force, heterogeneous in origin, language and interest, and in a foreign country; so that whatever might have been the personal courage of the soldiers, or the ability of the General of the invaders, the means of action were so unequal that the probabilities ought to have been the same way. Six combats took place; and what was the result of all. What does the country find in its "men of war," who had cost it so many burdens and so many sacrifices? We cannot answer without finding ourselves overwhelmed with opprobrium and shame. What a picture does the country now present? That of a victim, who, in his desperation tears out his own entrails. Those men who retrocede, those who are voluntarily blind, ask with shouts the suicidal measure of the introduction of monarchy. The men of violent passions, and of limited intelligence, clamor for an insurrectionary war; those interested in the old system of anarchy, who see their interest in its continuance, and who have their plans traced for the prosecution of their system of usurpation, and depredation, invoke peace at whatever cost; they are insensible to any feeling of honor, and neither the good name of the country nor its future interest entering into their plan, they would cut our Gordian knot at a single stroke. But the reflecting men, those who have material interests to preserve, and families to support, who have noble sentiments, which identify them with the country in which they were born, and which they have afterwards adopted as their own, are horrified at the appearance of the obscure future of which they obtain a glimpse, if the war should have no other result than the misfortunes inherent to this calamity of society—in the loss of some provinces, the humiliation of being conquered, and as a conclusion, the restoration of the same vices and the same disorders. These men are the chosen of the country, they sigh for an honorable way of extricating themselves from this conflict of uncertainty and violence; and at the same time they ardently desire a political theory, which shall insure peace and prosperity for the future. We believe that diplomatic science, profiting by events, can provide for the two exigencies, which, without doubt, constitute the true state of the question.

Of the four methods recognised to terminate war between nations, the first, which is an adjustment, has proved unavailing, and perhaps powerful obstacles would prevent its consummation. The second—mediation—should be rejected as impossible, because there is not upon the continent among the other republics, one which is sufficiently powerful, and has enough influence with the two belligerents, and to invoke Europe, would be the greatest rashness. The third—which is arbitration—is subject to the same objection as the previous ones. There remains then, the fourth, which consists in a conference of the most eminent persons of both nations at a certain designated place. As the formation of a protocol demands serious and prolonged discussions and consultations, which consume much time, a preliminary truce could be concluded, which would give rest to this poor nation, and would permit it to organize itself in such a manner that it should exist in prosperity, and live in peace with its neighbor. In this manner, we believe we can connect the subject upon which we have touched, with the programme of interior organization which we are going to present.

October 16, 1847. Mexico.

We yesterday had the melancholy and painful duty to perform, of following to the grave three of the gallant officers of our army who entered the Valley of Mexico full of hope and vigor, in the bloom and strength of manhood, with the bright prospect before them of being able, at some day, to return to their countrymen and friends, with their companions in arms, full of glory and honors. But, alas, Lieut. John D. Bacon, of the 6th Infantry; Lieut. M. L. Shackleford, of the Artillery; and Dr. William Roberts, of the Medical Staff, now "sleep the sleep of death," and although "they shall not wake to glory again," their distant friends and relatives will cherish their memories as having been of the number of those who yielded up their lives in defence of their country's honor. The former fell in the battle of Churubusco, severely wounded, from which he died, and the two latter in the battle of Molino del Rey. Their remains were followed to the grave by one escort, accompanied by a long line of weeping friends, who had known them in war and in peace, and seen them each signally distinguish himself upon the bloody and sanguinary battle-fields in the Valley of Mexico. Peace to their ashes, all honor to their memories.

Since writing the above, I have just heard of the death of Capt. Creed T. Huddleston, of the 14th Infantry, who died of diarrhoea. Capt. Huddleston had been in bad health since he left Vera Cruz, but persevered, in the hope of recovery, although unable to do duty.

The whole of Mexico is in a state of the most unprecedented anarchy and confusion. While their capital is in the possession of their enemies, their government and army dispersed, instead of combining their energies and resources against their common enemy, they are wrangling among themselves with the severest bitterness of feeling who shall govern their own discord and factions, and with each the motto seems to be, "rule or ruin." The military and the civil authorities at Querétaro are arrayed against one another, each trying to acquire the ascendancy, while at the same time a portion of the Congress, or rather the Deputies, who are there, are planning and scheming against Peña y Peña, a portion of the latter having gotten up a protest against his holding the presidential power. Juan Almonte, we learned, has arrived at Querétaro, was well received by the army, and was concocting a plan to overthrow Peña y Peña, and establish a military president in power, but whether at his instance or for the purpose of thwarting both him and the president in their views, Gen. Joaquin Rangel has placed himself at the head of a party and pronounced against Peña y Peña and in favor of Santa Anna.[2] In the face of the protests and pronunciamientos, there is an order from the government for the trial of Santa Anna by court martial for the loss of the actions wherein he has commanded, and particularly the loss of the capital.

We have intelligence to-day from Guadalajara, which if it be true, will shake this country in a manner that it has never been shaken before, and while eventually, if persisted in, must tend materially to advance the prosperity and dignity of the people as a nation (if such a thing be possible), it will be fraught with inconceivable events. Private letters received by Mexicans state that the State Congress of Guadalajara have issued a decree, announcing that there shall be freedom of thought and opinion in matters of religion. If the torch of dissension is lighted between the Church and the State government, one or the other, or probably both parties, will be consumed by the conflagration. If they should both be destroyed, then in the embers there may be found a coal that will kindle the fire of intelligence, which will lead them to the paths of virtue and honesty, and enable them to shun the corrupt and blighting influences which have controlled all their actions and sunk them so low in the scale of nations. Some such movement is the only hope for the salvation of the country.

I have seen a letter from San Luis Potosi, within a few days, which states that the only feeling prevailing there for the loss of the capital, is that of indifference. The liberalists, or moderate party, have carried the election in San Luis Potosi.

We have advices from Puebla to-day, to the 10th. They state that the American reinforcements were at Acajete, ten miles distant, but do not inform us what their numbers are, or who is in command of

2. Joining the Mexican army in 1823, Joaquin Rangel became devoted to General Santa Anna who named him chief of artillery. Court-martialed and sentenced to prison for involvement in a failed coup, he was resurrected in 1847 by Santa Anna and tasked with opposing General Scott's army. His best hope of stalling Scott was at Molino del Rey, but the Americans prevailed and soon were at the gates of Mexico City. Badly wounded while defending one of the gates into the city, Rangel remained in the army and filled several military and political posts before his death in 1874. Tucker, *Encyclopedia*, 545–46.

them. We also learn by our letters, that the Mexican forces continued to retire and disperse. The courier, who left the day after, says that they entered Puebla on the 12th, and that on Gen. Joaquin Rea taking up his line of march, Col. Childs went out of the forts and gave him battle.[3] He does not inform us what was the result, further than that Gen. Rea was compelled to retreat a little further than was convenient.

We also learn from different sources (one of them a letter from a Mexican officer to a friend in this city), that our troops coming up, instead of taking the national road took the road to the north of it, for the purpose of turning El Pinal, and that on the 9th they unexpectedly met Santa Anna, at Huamantla, where they engaged him, and routed him, capturing all his cavalry horses and four pieces of artillery, Santa Anna, himself, barely making his escape. We have had so many rumors of late that many are disposed to doubt it as we have not yet received any official confirmation of it.

The health of the army continues good, and the wounded generally continue to improve.

I enclose you a literary gem, emanating from the army, the "Sidewalk Musings" of "John of York," published in the *North American* of this morning. Mr. William C. Tobey has long been favorably known to the literary world, and more latterly as the army correspondent of the *Philadelphia North American*. To properly appreciate his muse, you must see the little beggar boy at the massive church gates, inside of which is wealth and store—you must see him heedlessly passed by those who were intended by Heaven to be the ministering angels to the poor and unfortunate—you must see gaiety, wealth, and affluence, disregarding his humble petitions—you must hear his soft and melodious supplications of "*Limosna por amor de Jesus*"—and then you must see the war-worn soldier, with his trophied scars, who never stopped to listen to the thunder of cannon, or the clash of arms, turn a listening ear

3. Joaquin Rea was a successful businessman who had offered his services to the military of Mexico in the 1830s. A general of brigade with a large force of guerrillas under his command, Rea operated against General Scott's supply line in the region of Puebla. Rea, supported later by Santa Anna, laid siege to the city of Puebla from September 14 to October 12 in 1847, but a stout defense by Colonel Childs and reinforcements led by General Lane drove off the Mexican force. Rea's guerrilla command slowly evaporated and the general was killed in 1850 during another internal rebellion. Tucker, *Encyclopedia*, 546.

to the little boy's pathetic appeals, and then putting his hand in his pocket and giving him perhaps his last dime.

Sidewalk Musings—The Beggar Boy

A little blind boy daily waits
Beside a convent's many gates,
To ask of every passer-by
Some little gift of charity;
And as the gay and happy throng
Heartless and thoughtless pass along,
The little beggar pleads his cause,
And many strangers listening, pause—
"*Limosna por amor de Jesus*."
Hundreds passing hourly by
Saw not the sightless, upturned eye—
Hundreds saw, yet heeded not,
Or heeding, very soon forgot
That little voice and trembling tone—
Between a prayer and a moan—
That all the livelong day was heard,
Like notes of an animated bird—
"*Limosna por amor de Jesus*."
A soldier, who 'mid fire and smoke
Through iron ranks had often broke,
With shattered arm and face of scars,
Trophies of sanguinary wars,
Passed as he careless went that way,
And listened to the beggar's lay,
And dropped a *rial* in his hat,
The boy said, weeping, as he sat—
"*Limnosa por amor de Jesus*."

Mexico, 1847 John of York

P.S. Since writing, I am assured that the Cathedral of Guadalajara had been sacked, by the party opposing the Church. I can hardly believe it, although I am positively assured it is correct.

One of the most striking things that has been observed during our operations is the extraordinary effect produced upon the rank and file of the army by the presence of the general officers. Two instances of this kind came under my notice, and I have no doubt there are a great many more. On the evening of the 19th August, when the first demonstration was made on the command of Valencia, at Contreras, the commands of Col. Riley and Gen. Cadwalader had crossed the *pedregal* and arrived on the left flank of the enemy about 4 o'clock P.M. As soon as the Mexicans ascertained their position, they brought round their cavalry and made a strong demonstration towards them, while at the same time, they opened two or three pieces of artillery upon them. At this juncture a heavy reinforcement from the city made its appearance, under the immediate command of Santa Anna himself. Thus the two brigades became situated, with Santa Anna's heavy column, with artillery, on their right; the fort, with twenty-two pieces of artillery, on the left; and a column of about 5,000 lancers on the hill immediately in front. The nature of the ground, being covered with irregular and unbroken rocks of lava, prevented their retiring, even under cover of the night. Nothing could be seen of our force advancing, at first intended to bear upon the other flank of the enemy, and, truly, matters looked gloomy enough in the isolated command.

As soon as Col. Riley's brigade emerged from the little village on the banks of the deep ravine, the lancers in front charged down upon him, and I give you his own version and language: "They charged me and I formed square, and then they run away. They charged me again, and I again formed square, but they would not come closer than thirty or forty yards, when they wheeled and run away the second time. I found they were afraid to try my square. They charged me the third time. I waited until they came close enough, and then charged them and opened fire, and before they could get out of the reach of my men there were a great number of their horses running about without riders." This last movement so completely surprised the lancers that they withdrew to their first position, on the ridge of the hill in front, and we fell back to the village, to where Gen. Cadwalader was.

The whole command now began to look around and view their position. Here was a force more than quadruple their own upon each flank, and one of more than double theirs, in front. If the whole of the enemy bore down upon them they must be overpowered and crushed by overwhelming numbers, and so confident was Santa Anna that such would be the result that he sent an express to the city announcing that he had got one column of the Americans into such a position that they must either surrender or be cut to pieces, as it was impossible for them to get away. Affairs looked gloomy; the brigade of Col. Riley now became particularly disheartened.

They were in a tight place, supported by a brigade of new troops of which they knew nothing, they were under the command of Gen. Cadwalader, who was a new man in the field, and as they said, "might be a very good officer," but they did not know him, and if he made one misstep in so important a crisis they were utterly lost beyond redemption, and old troops have a great aversion to new commanders. How were they to be extricated, and where was the giant mind to plan and direct it?

At this important stage of the affair, Gen. Smith, who had found it impossible to approach the enemy on the other flank without great loss, now crossed the deep ravine and joined the force with his brigade. While his command was crossing, he sent his aide-de-camp, Lieut. Van Dorn, forward to ascertain the situation of the forces and the nature of the ground. As soon as he was seen by the old Regulars, they exclaimed, "Here's the Little Lieutenant!" "Here's the Little Lieutenant!" "Gen. Smith is about somewhere!" "We're all right now!" "No, there's no such good luck. I am sure he went with his brigade to the other flank, it's him they've been firing on so heavy." "But, if he is over there, what's the little one doing here?" While they were thus remarking and conjecturing, Gen. Smith, with his brigade, turned the corner of the lane and came into view of the whole line. As soon as their anxious eyes fell upon him, a hundred voices joyously exclaimed, "Here he is!" "Here he is!" "Here's Gen. Smith!" "Now we'll have them!" "Now we'll give it to them!" A cheerful bustling hum was heard among them where all was a dead dispiriting silence before, their dullness became a lively gayety, confidence and enthusiasm took possession where distrust and lethargy had just now prevailed. While this was the very highest compliment that could or can possibly be paid to the eminent ability of the gallant general, it also showed that the rank and file never lose confidence in themselves—they feel competent to surmount any difficulties and overcome any obstacles—they only want to feel that they will be properly commanded, that they will be skillfully handled, and that their commanding officer possesses the ability to dispose of them to the best advantage that the circumstances will admit. They fear not to die, but they want to be satisfied that they will not be unnecessarily sacrificed.

Gen. Smith took command, and by different movements diverted the attention of the enemy until the Engineers reconnoitred their positions and the nature of the ground. At night the plan of attack was formed. Gen. Shields joined with his brigade about 2 o'clock. At dawn of the morning, the enemy, who but a few hours previous felt so confident of success, found the brigade of Col. Riley, supported by Gen. Cadwalader, in their rear, bearing down upon them like an avalanche, their commander infusing into them, by his language and his looks, his own unconquerable enthusiasm and determination, the unerring Riflemen riddling their flanks, and as they commenced their retreat, the brigade of Shields dealing them death and destruction. Victory perched upon our banner, our arms triumphed, our loss was very small, the enemy suffered severely, and were routed from a position they deemed impregnable. One of the first things I heard was a soldier exclaiming, "Didn't I tell you, boys, when Gen. Smith joined us last night, we'd give them hell before they knew what they were about?" "But," says another, "you didn't think we were going to come this way." "Hell, who says I did? But I knew there were 'foxes about,' and that we were as certain to whip them as my name is John!"

Again, there was another instance, equally strong, showing the affection of the men for their commander. Gen. Shields was wounded in the attack upon the works under Chapultepec. As soon as he saw the fortifications carried, he returned to the rear for the purpose of having his wound dressed. As he passed along the line of his brigade, the men seemed to sympathize with him as though he had been a brother to them all. But the feeling showed itself stronger when they came to advance upon the city along the aqueduct, and as they were compelled to halt at different points, I heard them frequently asking, "I wonder who will command our brigade now?" "I don't know," says another, "but live or die, I'll stick by the Palmetto as long as there's anyone to carry it." "That is not the thing, exactly. We will all stand by our colors. We want some chief that we all know, who will look out and see that our colors don't get where we will all get our heads knocked off standing by it. We want someone who will not get us all killed off without doing anything." At this moment, Gen. Shields came riding up, with his arm in a sling. His appearance at the rear was announced by the cheering salutations of his command, which extended along the whole line. His men, officers and privates, are devotedly attached to him, and would follow him anywhere he would lead them, with pride and confidence, and his appearance among them was equal to an addition of a force equal to their own numbers.

Many instances of this kind occurred, and it is impossible to describe the difference in the appearance of a command when they feel confident in their commanders, and when there are doubts flashing across their minds.

October 28, 1847. City of Mexico.

To-day or to-morrow a train and escort leaves here for Vera Cruz. It is under the command of Col. Harney, and will be escorted by details from the different branches of the service—seven companies of infantry under Col. Joseph E. Johnston, six companies of dragoons under Capt. Hardee, and a battery of artillery (the re-captured Buena Vista guns) under Lieut. Lovell.[4] It will be accompanied by Gen. Quitman and Gen. Shields, who are on their road to the United States, as also Col. Harney, Dr. Lawson, and Dr. Benjamin F. Harney, and the following list of officers who were wounded in the battles in the Valley of Mexico and are disabled for service in the field.

Bvt. Col. John Garland, 4th Infantry; Cols. George W. Morgan, 15th Infantry; Ward B. Burnett, New York Volunteers; Timothy P. Andrews, Voltigeurs; Lieut. Col. Samuel E. Watson, Marine Corps; Bvt. Maj. Richard D.A. Wade, 3d Artillery; Maj. William W. Loring, Mounted Rifles; Capts. Robert Anderson, 3d Artillery; Philip Kearny, 1st Dragoons; Andrew T. McReynolds, 3d Dragoons; James W. Denver, 12th Infantry; Pierce B. Anderson, 14th Infantry; Julien P. Breedlove, 14th Infantry; Garret Dyckman, New York Volunteers; Edward A. Kind, 15th Infantry; Robert Porter, 2d Pennsylvania Volunteers; William H. Irwin, 11th Infantry; Eugene

4. A graduate of West Point in 1829, Joseph Johnston resigned from service after eight years. Re-appointed in the topographical engineers, he was a captain when elevated to lieutenant colonel of the Regiment of Voltigeurs. Brevetted to major and colonel for Cerro Gordo, where he was seriously wounded while reconnoitering the Mexican lines, Johnston was later given a brevet to lieutenant colonel for Chapultepec. Promoted to lieutenant colonel of the 1st Cavalry in 1855 and quartermaster general in 1860, Johnston resigned in 1861 to serve the Confederacy. One of the Civil War's most famous, if not one of its more successful, commanders, General Johnston died on March 21, 1891. Heitman, *Historical Register* 1: 578.

Vandeventer, 15th Infantry; James Miller, 2d Pennsylvania Volunteers; James Murray, 2d Pennsylvania Volunteers; Alexander P. Churchill, Voltigeurs; Lieuts. Henry Prince, 4th Infantry; William Moralles, Louisiana Mounted Volunteers; David Hopkins, 2d Pennsylvania Volunteers; James D. Potter, New York Volunteers; Charles S Cooper, New York Volunteers; Thornton F. Brodhead, Adjutant, 15th Infantry; John T. Brown, 3d Dragoons; Franklin D. Callender, Ordnance Corps; Thomas W. Sweeney, New York Volunteers; Lorimer Graham, 10th Infantry; William A. Newman, 9th Infantry; William H.H. Goodloe, 15th Infantry; John M. Hathaway, 9th Infantry; Henry De Wolf, 9th Infantry; Mortimer Rosecrants, 5th Infantry; Alphonse F. Palmer, 9th Infantry; Edward Johnson, 4th Infantry; Edward C. Boynton, 1st Artillery; Charles H. Jones, New York Volunteers; William Brown, New York Volunteers; Llewellyn Jones, Mounted Rifles; Michael E. Van Buren, Mounted Rifles; Henry A.M. Fillmore, 2d Pennsylvania Volunteers; D.D. Baker, Marine Corps; John W. Stewart, South Carolina Volunteers; W.C. Comorsyne, South Carolina Volunteers; Gustavus S. Kintzing, Voltigeurs; George R. Kiger, Voltigeurs; Robert H. Archer, Voltigeurs; Frank H. Larned, Voltigeurs; William Merrihew, 3d Dragoons; Alpheus T. Palmer 9th Infantry.[5]

Here is a list of men who, since the war commenced, passed through your city in the strength of health, with bright hopes,

5. Appointed a paymaster with the rank of major in 1822, Timothy Andrews served as such until commissioned colonel of the Regiment of Voltigeurs in 1847. Distinguished at Molino del Rey and Chapultepec, Andrews won a brevet to brigadier general for the latter battle. Returning to the paymaster department, he was promoted to lieutenant colonel in 1851 and colonel, as paymaster general, in 1862. Retired in 1864, Andrews died on March 11, 1868. Heitman, *Historical Register* 1: 167; *Washington Evening Star*, March 12, 1868.

Samuel Watson commenced his career in the U.S. Marines in 1812 and eventually rose to command the Portsmouth and Charlestown naval yards. In spring of 1847 six companies of Marines under Major Twiggs, followed by another eight companies under Watson, sailed for Mexico where they would be joined by all "disposable" Marines attached to the Gulf Squadron. The plan was to organize two regiments, one under Watson and the other under Twiggs. Following the occupation of Mexico City, Watson was assigned to protect the National Palace from robbers and thieves. Suffering from extreme debility, Colonel Watson died at Vera Cruz on November 16, 1847, his body being buried in the same grave alongside Major Twiggs until the pair could be shipped home. *Daily National Intelligencer*, December 9, 1847; *Washington National Whig*, May 17, 1847; *Washington Daily Union*, November 15, 1847; December 7, 1847.

anticipating for themselves the honors to be won in warring for their country's cause. They came here to defend the nation's honor and to bare their breasts to the storm of battle to secure the nation's rights. The question is not to be asked how did they conduct themselves in the trying times just passed, their loss of limbs and the tracks of the enemy's balls yet fresh through their bodies is evidence of where they were when the missiles of death flew thick and fast. They are now returning to their homes because they are unfit for service in the field. They will plant their feet upon the shores of Louisiana about the 15th of November, literally a band of cripples. They are war-worn and battle-battered veterans, fresh from the bloody scenes and hard-fought battle-fields in the Valley of Mexico, some of them passed safely through the different actions until they fell in the ditches at the gates of the city. How will New Orleans appreciate their noble and patriotic conduct? Let them be received as becomes the "Emporium of the South" and the character of its people. Let them be honored as their conduct here deserves, and let New Orleans manifest that degree of magnanimity which has ever characterized her. Meet them with firm grips of the hands and warm embraces. Light up the city in a halo of glory, and let the deep-toned notes of your artillery echo from the old Cathedral and reverberate along the banks of the Mississippi. Pay to them that tribute which is due to the bravest of the brave and the sons of our country who have woven around our flag fresh and never-fading laurels, at which we can all point with exulting pride.

The return of Gen. Quitman for the purpose of joining his proper division in the column of Gen. Taylor, required a new appointment to the office of Civil and Military Governor of the City of Mexico. The high honor has been conferred on Gen. P.F. Smith, who, from his high judicial qualifications as well as his military abilities, is one of the most fitting persons that could have been selected to discharge the important duties. Gen. Quitman has filled the office he has just left with honor to the American arms and credit to himself. The gallant old Southron will soon be among you—recollect his services on the hard-fought fields of Monterey—recollect how he led his command in the Valley of Mexico—recollect he was the first soldier to hoist the American colors with his own hands on the breastworks at the gates of the City of Mexico—and recollect that

A Caricature of Disabled Veterans Returning from Mexico. *Courtesy Library of Congress.*

he, with Gen. Smith, was the first officer of the American army to enter the Grand Plaza of the city of the Aztecs.

In addition to the officers going home under orders, the following persons will accompany the detachment. Many of them have "seen the elephant" in all its phases and different dresses, they have suffered a severe confinement in the Mexican dungeons, and have participated in the achievements before the capital. May they meet with a warm reception from their friends in the "white settlements." From Kentucky: Maj. John P. Gaines, Capt. C.M. Clay, Capt. Wm. J. Heady, A.Q.M. George P. Smith; Lieuts. Wm. T. Barbour, Thomas G. Churchill, George R. Davidson, appointed to the 11th Infantry. From Arkansas:

Maj. Solon Borland, Capt. Christopher C. Danly, wounded at *Garita Belen*. Of the Navy: Lieut. Robert Clay Rogers.

October 29, 1847. Mexico.

Yesterday a party of guerrillas came into the edge of town and run away from our Quartermaster's Department about 500 mules. The animals were under charge of some Mexicans, and I expect they were the fellows who committed the act. The dragoons started in pursuit, but I doubt if they will be able to come up with them.

By the time I write again I will endeavor to send you a list of the persons who have died since the battles of Mexico.

Among other melancholy events of the campaign is the death of Capt. Samuel Walker, formerly of the Texan Rangers, but latterly of the Mounted Rifles. He has served his country faithfully, and his own daring bravery at last cost him his life. He was killed in charging Santa Anna's large body at Huamantla, with about 200 cavalry; the charge succeeded, but he fell. Many of his old friends, the Texan Rangers, are here, and the only expression I heard them make on learning of his death was, with a sigh, "Poor Sam, he was a brave man, but I never expected he would die anywhere but in a charge."

October 29, 1847. City of Mexico.

Since my last, a great change has come over the politics of this country. Indeed, these people are so fickle that it is impossible, with any degree of certainty, to calculate by their actions to-day, what will be their determination and their policy to-morrow. When I wrote about twelve days since, the monarchical party seemed to be progressing most successfully in carrying out their designs of placing a prince upon the administrative chair of this Republic. Then many persons of wealth and influence, who had formerly opposed it, and a great portion of the Church, were warmly and boldly advocating the measure as the only means of perpetuating their power and their influence over the government and the people. But somewhat fearing their success, and believing that if they were thwarted in their views, they would also receive a severe shock by the defeat, endeavoring to take advantage of circumstances so as to turn whatever may transpire to the best advantage.

However, a different feeling appears to be prevailing the whole country since our entry into the capital. Señor Peña y Peña has taken a firm hold of the reins of government, and has called around him as advisors and counsellors a much better and more intelligent class of men than has honored the Cabinet of Mexico for some time. He has scattered and dispersed the factions which were breeding disturbances at Querétaro a short time since. The new elections of Deputies have resulted in the choice of a more liberal and better class of men than heretofore, and nearly all have signified their anxiety for a speedy peace. However, a majority of the old Deputies are also known to be in favor of peace, but the great obstacle in the way is that all parties are anxious to be left in power, or acquire some advantage over their opponents, before the consummation of such an event. Thus, whenever one party makes an advancement, the other opposes it because they think it would give the one concluding such a measure some advantage, upon the consummation of their design. The Democratic party are willing and anxious to make a peace, if they can overthrow and break down the privileged Church Establishment, and see some means by which they can prevent the recurrence of the state of affairs which has always kept them under the weather. If not, they oppose it, and thereby force us, if possible, to occupy the country until they recuperate their forces sufficient to enable them to carry out their views. *El Razonador*, which is the organ of this party, has several articles on this subject, which I send. All parties, as well as the government, agree in abolishing the military establishment, and attribute to it all the anarchy to which this country has been subjected. For myself, I have no confidence in the honor, honesty, or the acts of any portion of either party, as I have always found that there is no reliance to be placed in anything they say or do. There are always some under-currents running which are liable to change their determination from day to day. Furthermore, they are wanting in stability of character and talent, although they write and talk well and fluently, when we come to fathom them, the very best of them are not superior to the mediocrity of talent of our own country. In judgment they are woefully deficient, however some of our most enlightened men, who, by their position, should be enabled to judge, make no hesitation in saying that they are fully persuaded that the prospects of arranging a peace are more flattering, at the present, than they have been since the commencement of the war. There certainly has been a great change produced upon the minds of the Mexicans, whether it is the fear of having to support our large army now entering the field, I am not able to say, but think it has had some effect.

Since writing the foregoing, I learn that the Democratic party, having ascertained that there will be a quorum of Deputies present this week, and that the Aristocracy, as they are designated, have a majority in the old as well as the new Deputies, have gone to Querétaro, for the purpose of endeavoring to create dissensions and anarchy, and thereby prevent the present government from entering into any arrangements that will bring about a peace, they fearing, in such an event, being left in a worse state of corruption and confusion than they were when we entered the capital. It is somewhat remarkable, that the people of this country who entertain the best feeling for us, and are desirous to establish a government fashioned after our own, are the persons who are straining every nerve to prevent the consummation of a treaty of peace. Their object is to break down the Church and Military establishments, and in order to accomplish this they are trying to create a state of affairs which will force us to occupy the country.

October 29, 1847. City of Mexico.

Day before yesterday I witnessed the presentation of a handsome pair of spurs to Capt. G.T.M. Davis, formerly of the Illinois Volunteers, by the New York Volunteers. They are of solid silver, ornamented with gold. On each side is carved in inlaid gold the flag of our country, and our national bird holds in its beak the scroll. On the inner side is inserted: "To Capt. G.T.M. Davis. '*Benemerito de su patria*.' From the Officers of the New York Regiment." Capt. Davis entered the war at an early stage of it, and continued in that capacity until the arrival of the army at San Augustin. He became a volunteer aide of Gen. Quitman and Secretary to the Governor after the capture of the city by our troops. His attention and devotion to Gen. Shields, after he fell at the battle of Cerro Gordo, will long be remembered by those who witnessed it.

We see by letters published in *El Monitor* of yesterday, that Santa Anna has complied with the requisitions of Peña y Peña, the present president, and fixed his residence at Tehuacan, where he awaits orders.

The requisitions were that he should take up his residence at some place he might select, and await his trial by court-martial for the failure of his battles before the city, and the loss of the capital.

Señor Don Luis de la Rosa has been nominated as Minister of Relations, Mora y Villamil has been nominated Minister of War, and Bustamente, it is expected, is about to be appointed Commander-in-Chief of the Army. The other appointments to the Cabinet have not yet been filled up.

I enclose to you the sermon of the Rev. Mr. John McCarty, chaplain in the U.S. Army, delivered by him in the National Palace, on Sunday, the 3d last, on the occasion of a "Public Thanksgiving for the Victories achieved by the Army of the United States, under the command of Maj. Gen. Winfield Scott, in the Basin of Mexico, consummated by the capture of this Capital." I commend the sermon to the attentive perusal of your readers. It is full of exciting interest, and will amply pay for the reading. It was delivered by a man to whom the whole army feels peculiarly indebted for his kind attention and Christian bearing during the times of peril and danger. Where the battle raged hottest, and the balls fell thickest, our Christian friend was upon the ground, administering the departing spirits the last earthly consolation. His presence under such circumstances, with a countenance mild and serene, assisted many a gallant soldier in meeting grim-visaged death with Christian fortitude. Aye, more, the wounded were also objects of his especial attention, supplying and aiding them in whatever might alleviate their sufferings. I sincerely hope that our reverend friend, so much reverenced by the whole army, and to whom we all owe a debt of gratitude, will receive some substantial token of regard at the hands of the country.

The following extract from General Orders No. 31 may interest some of your readers who are engaged in bringing goods to this country:

> Returning from Vera Cruz, the train will bring back, besides a mail, essential supplies for the army generally. Extra baggage or stores, for individual officers or others, will be rigorously excluded, and not an

> ounce of sutler's goods be admitted into any public wagon. Any violation or neglect of these prohibitions shall be punished by the forfeiture of the goods, stores, or other baggage, for the benefit of the hospitals, and the individuals concerned placed for punishment before the proper military tribunals.
>
> The foregoing prohibitions will be considered as *standing* and *general* for all trains. Quartermasters will take care that they are not violated by escorts, wagon-masters, or teamsters; and if violated by any officer superior in rank to the particular quartermaster of the train, the latter, besides remonstrance, at the time, will not fail to report names and circumstances.
>
> All reasonable protection, not to the prejudice or hindrance of the public service, will be given without toll, per centage, or reward, to the goods of sutlers and other merchants, by the military posts and escorts of this army—the objects being to increase the comforts of all as well as the receipts of the custom-houses.
>
> By command of Maj. Gen. Scott:
>
> H.L. Scott, A.A.A.G.

We had a very nice little excitement a few days since, produced by the following article from *El Monitor*, which paper has been using every exertion to prevent the families of the city from associating or mingling with the officers of the army, thereby keeping the prejudices of the parties from being obliterated as long as possible:

> "A certain young lady, of a frolicsome disposition and romantic inclinations, a good singer, and who, since the arrival of the Americans at San Angel, had become *familiar* with an officer of the army, will be annexed and passed over to American dominion, like Texas, but on whom the censure of the fair sex of Mexico has fallen."

The young lady referred to, as well as her parents and family, feeling themselves under obligations to some officers for their kindness during the armistice, made no hesitation in treating the persons to whom they were indebted with respect after our entry into the city, which brought out the abusive article in *El Monitor*. As soon as it appeared, it was like throwing a fire-brand into a keg of powder. Cow-hides and other dangerous edge-tools were procured, and several young gentlemen started in pursuit of the editor. He got wind of their intentions, and eluded their grasp for several days, and it reminded me very much of a deer-drive, each fellow posted, anxious to get first sight of the animal. At length the editor, Señor Vicente Torres, thinking the whole affair had blown over and that time enough had elapsed to allow the wrath of the young gentlemen to cool down, made his appearance on the street, but never was man more mistaken. Before he reached the Plaza he encountered one of the young gentlemen, who gave him as severe a cow-hiding as ever a man received. He made some resistance, but finding it was no use, concluded that it was best to try a run, by which he succeeded in escaping. He then appealed to our military authorities for redress, and made a great ado about the liberty of the press, and the extent to which it was tolerated in the United States. But I believe the only satisfaction he received was the reply, that editors in the United States had the right to publish what they pleased, but if they violated the laws or insulted the feelings of private individuals, they must take the consequences. This did not seem to suit the appetite of the gentleman, particularly taking the consequences, and I think he will be more careful in future.

The following incident occurred on the 13th of September, previous to the storming of the Castle of Chapultepec, and I think it exhibited as much courtesy as anything I have ever heard. Maj. John F. Hunter, of the 11th Infantry, at the head of his regiment, was marching up to take his position in line, preparatory to the storming of the castle. Maj. Sumner, with the 2d Dragoons, came round in a run from the opposite side of the hill, expecting to have to charge a field battery or the retreating forces of the enemy. The head of the two regiments met at a point where both were compelled to halt for a moment. Maj. Hunter rode up to Maj. Sumner, extending his hand, saluting him with, "How do you do, Maj. Sumner?" who replied, "Really, sir, I do not recollect you." "Do not recollect me?" "No, sir," replied Maj. Sumner. When Maj. Hunter, as it were, straightening himself up in his saddle, remarked, "I was one of your sergeants at Carlisle, sir." At this, Maj. Sumner recognized his former sergeant and, extending his hand, remarked, "Well, really, sir, I am exceedingly happy to meet you, and more particularly at the present time, going into battle with the same rank as myself, and both of us in command of regiments. I wish that good fortune may attend you, and that we may meet hereafter, when we will be able more fully to renew our former acquaintance." At this time it became necessary for both commands to move to their different positions, and the two majors separated, wishing each other success and good fortune.

Since the occupation of our army, a portion of the officers have formed themselves into an association called "The Aztec Club," having for its object the more intimate and social intercourse of its members, its organization is similar to that of the military clubs of England. It will, at the same time it produces a more social and immediate intimate intercourse of the officers, enable them to live in the best style and avoid the imposition of the hotel-keepers. Every general officer, except one, is a member. The following are officers, according to its present organization: President, Gen. John A. Quitman; 1st Vice President, Col. William S. Harney; 2d Vice President, Capt. John B. Magruder; Treasurer, Samuel S. Anderson; Secretary, Richard P. Hammond, Esq.; Committee of Arrangements, Capt. John B. Grayson, Maj. Abraham Van Buren, Lieut. Henry D. Grafton.

A Thanksgiving Sermon

"Only fear the Lord, and serve Him with all your heart; for consider how great things He hath done for you." *1st Samuel*, 24th Chapter, 12th Verse.

My Brethren of the Army—Our General-in-Chief, having, in an order, prompted by Christian duty and feeling, and highly proper and becoming in an official point of view, called upon his "brethren in arms, to return both in public and private worship, thanks and gratitude to God, for the signal triumphs, which they have recently achieved for their country"—and assembled as we now are thus publicly to acknowledge the favoring Providence of the "Lord of Hosts," and to render to His holy name, our praise and thanksgiving for the same—which is our reasonable and bounden duty—let us, my brethren of the army, consider with some attention the nature and greatness of the blessings for which our gratitude is called forth.

Although it has been questioned, still it can be shown to be the duty of a Christian people, and more so of the army of a Christian land, to offer thanksgiving to the Great Ruler of nations, for the victories by which He has crowned their arms, as well as for all other blessings of His Providence, and if so, who will measure the amount of gratitude due Him from our country and its army, for the uniform and great successes which have attended our arms at large, from the first battle to the last, and more especially of this portion of our forces, from our landing at Vera Cruz to the termination of the campaign by our victorious entry into this capital of the nation?

War, though a great calamity, attended with much that is to be deplored, and involving a terrible responsibility on the government who are parties in it, is still in the actual condition of mankind necessary and right, at least on one side, as the means of national defence and preservation, of preventing the repetition of national wrongs by their punishment, or redressing injuries inflicted and obtaining rights withheld. When, therefore, a people succeed in a war waged by the government for these ends, they have cause of thanksgiving to the Great Disposer of events from whom that success has proceeded—for victory in war is not only amongst the greatest of national deliverances and blessings, considered in itself, but it is the only means of gaining the object contended for and procuring an honorable and advantageous peace, the true end of victory.

It should, however, be borne in mind, that the responsibility of the war, as before observed—that is to say, the determination of its necessity and righteousness, rest not on those who serve in the army, but on the constituted authorities of the country, whose orders it is the soldier's duty to obey and execute. He should, to be sure, in his private capacity, desire and pray that he may never be called to do battle but in a righteous cause—righteous on the part of his government. Still, as a general rule, it is his duty to submit to the official determination of the authority of the country over him, and with courage and might to prosecute in his station the war it has declared or sanctioned. And without reference to the origin of this war, it is unquestionably our duty as officers and soldiers, vigorously to wage it, in order to obtain the ends for which it exists, and to conquer a just and honorable peace as its happy conclusion. In the prosecution of this war, waged as it has been, with the most scrupulous regard on our part to the laws of warfare recognized by the civilized and Christian nations, valor on the part of the soldier, whether in command or in the ranks, is due to his country; and on the other hand, his achievements should be celebrated and his services rewarded by appropriate distinctions, for he not only renders the most important service to his country, but in doing so, braves the greatest dangers and perils his dearest possession—life itself.

My brethren—we have cause of gratitude to God, in the reflection that we belong through his providential appointments, to a brave as well as a free race—and that He has inspired our commanders with wisdom and military skill to combine these elements of individual power in the achievement of exploits, which, as they are the proper subject of our own wonder, we may modestly deem, will be that of our country's admiration. But that we may be truly influenced by gratitude, we must believe, what we acknowledge in the thanksgiving of the Church, that "as the Sovereign Commander of all the world," He is indeed "the only Giver of all Victory," and that not unto us—not unto us—but to the Lord, belongs the praise. And assuredly, if the hand of the Almighty Disposer is ever to be recognized in the affairs of the world, it would seem that it must be in such signal and important events as those we are now called upon to consider and be thankful for. And all but the utterly irreligious will own His favoring Providence, manifestly displayed in our behalf; not, indeed, that we infer from success, his approval of the cause of our country, or that he has taken our side because we are better or more deserving than our opponent; no, for often does He, in his inscrutable wisdom, permit the apparent wrong to succeed, and the right to be defeated. Such an inference is not involved in our thanksgivings, which have a distinct and all-sufficient object in our individual deliverance from great and imminent danger from "the arrow that flieth by day,"—from "the pestilence that walketh in darknkess," and from "the destruction that wasteth at noon-day;" that while "a thousand have fallen at our side, and ten thousand at our right hand," He, in his mercy, hath not permitted this sudden death to "come nigh us." We find a further object in the benefits conferred by these repeated victories on our army and country, and the more unmerited are our blessings, the warmer should be our gratitude.

In considering how great things the "Good Lord hath done for us," we must regard the *uniformity* of our success. What is true of the whole war is especially so of this entire campaign, from the landing of our army at Vera Cruz up to the capture of this city. We have succeeded in all we have undertaken; never engaged in fight but to conquer; never attacked but to defeat our enemy. All difficulties, however great, have been overcome; all opposition, however formidable, borne down. No place of defence so strong by nature or by the art of fortification, has been able to resist our assault. And more remarkable still, the peculiarities of the climate and seasons have not presented their anticipated obstacles; and the very elements have been made to minister to our aid; the "fortune of war" (so called) has been uninterruptedly with us, crowning with eminent success all our plans and battles, and consummating the campaign in our possession of this Capital of Mexico. Say, then, ye oppugners of Providence—ye advocates of blind chance, can aught but the admission of a purpose in the mind of the great Disposer of Events, who holds the very winds in his fist, account for such marvellous uniformity?

Then, further, to see the hand of God in all this, let us consider that in all our principal battles we have been greatly outnumbered by the enemy, who, nevertheless, instead of making attack, has awaited it from us, and that, too, in positions selected and fortified, so as greatly to increase his power of resistance, yet all in vain. Well might our foe be astonished at our daring, with such diminutive forces, to penetrate so far into the interior of a country, inhabited by at least seven millions of people—at our venturing to march so far from the sea-board, thereby encountering the great difficulty of keeping open our communications with the places whence our reinforcements and supplies were to be drawn; and how greatly must that astonishment have been increased, when they saw us, with forces so apparently inadequate to the object, abandon that very communication, those reinforcements and supplies, and with a hardihood which can only find a parallel in the army of Cortez, trust to our stout hearts and strong arms in forcing our subsistence from themselves. It only remained that their emotions should amount to the wonder which now possesses them, when in despite of all these disadvantages, added to our deficiency in heavy artillery—(since supplied from their own superabundance at Contreras and Churubusco,) we forced our way into the very heart of a country so capable of defence by passes and defiles, that it seemed to bid defiance to all skill and numbers! Yet such is the fact; and, "when," in the words of the order before referred to, "the very limited numbers who have performed those brilliant deeds, shall have become known, the world will be astonished, and our own countrymen filled with joy and admiration."

Again, we have cause to thank the Lord that our operations have been conducted under a commander who has felt and avowed his responsibility to God, for the lives of the men committed to his charge; who not seduced by the vulgar reputation of fighting bloody battles, has sought and gained victory by the application of his own generalship—baffling the councils of the enemy by superior talent, availing himself of every advantage which keen military sagacity could discover, and saving as far as possible the lives of his soldiery, while winning the numerous victories, in which they have been periled. Accordingly, it is cause for grateful joy, that, with but one exception, our loss has been small in comparison with that of the enemy, and with the advantages gained.

But while we award praise, high and merited, to the generalship and heroic courage displayed in the achievements of our army, let us not forget that it was God who not only bestowed these abilities, but by his assisting hand, crowned the employment of them with success. The history of war, in which so much is ascribed to the "fortune of war," verifies the saying of the wise man, that "the race is not to the swift nor the battle to the strong, but time and chance happen to all;" teaching us it is not in human wisdom or might to ensure victory, but "time and chance," by which is meant the unseen hand of the Almighty, by interposing circumstances, prosperous or adverse, gives success, where often it could not have been expected, and produces defeat where frequently it could not have been looked for. And this is wisely so ordered that men in the enterprises of war, as in other things, may feel their dependence on God for success, and so be led to iimplore His aid, and render Him grateful thanks, as we would now do, for the victories they ascribe to His goodness. To feel this more, by a reference to particulars, let us but suppose the weather, in the rainy season, when we entered into this basin of Mexico, had been as wet as it proved unusually dry; that the rain had fallen in torrents and flooded this low country, as is the common case, how could we have traversed this valley at all, much less with our artillery and baggage? What but disaster in every form could have resulted? Had our army, indeed, through one of the many mischances that might have happened, in our circumstances, sustained a single defeat, or even met a reverse, we might have feared it would so have encouraged the Mexicans, so have roused and united their efforts, that the result of the campaign would have been far different—aye even as disastrous as it has been successful. And the few of us who might have survived, would now have been deploring our failures and defeats, instead of rejoicing in our victories. But God be praised, who has seen fit to order it otherwise, who has permitted no adversity to come nigh us, who has favored us greatly, crowning us with complete success.

We should also consider the results of our battles and victories, that the numerous army we have contended with has not only been defeated, but captured or dispersed; and the enemy's government almost without organization, deprived of the means of equipping and furnishing another army. Our foe, then, as a consequence, is at this time, to say the least, incapable of a further prosecution of the war with any vigor or effect; and now that we are safe, in the heart of the country, and in the capital of the nation, we may thank God, in the hope that there is well nigh an end to fighting and the horrors of war; and in the anticipation that a campaign so entirely successful will probably result in what is so much to be desired for us and this people, in a just and honorable peace, we may hope to change our notes of praise into thanksgiving for the latter.

Furthermore, we have cause to thank God, with grateful hearts, when we consider that never was there war, carried into an enemy's country, with so little of suffering and injury inflicted on the unarmed people. Never have the peaceful inhabitants of a theatre of hostilities had so little cause to complain of the treatment received from invaders and conquerors. Yes, we may boast—thanking the Lord—that we have sacked no cities, robbed no towns, violated no women; that we have never authorized any plunder of the people, and that very few outrages of any sort have been committed by our soldiery; and that, instead of subsisting on the country as we might have done under the laws of war, we have paid for all we have consumed, and that at the highest price. They have been better treated by us than by their own armies; indeed, we have been rather protectors than destroyers of the Mexican people. Although we have contended with enemies often cruel, treacherous, and regardless of the usages of civilized warfare, yet we have never retaliated the wrongs and cruelty we have received from them. The hearts of our soldiers, that never failed them through fear, did not fail them through humanity and pity, when, under other influences, they might have cut down the defeated and unresisting. We have heard of no instance in which quarters have been refused, and that to an enemy, too, who has often robbed and murdered our wounded. Yes, we may thank God, with heartfelt satisfaction, that we were too American; have had too much respect for the rights of humanity; too much regard for our character, to come down to the low level of a Mexican soldier's notions of humanity, honor, and civilization. And, though *here*, we must not glory in our courage and prowess, nor on this occasion exult in our achievements; yet we may glory and exult (so that we be humble before God) in our having most scrupulously observed and upheld the laws which mitigate the horrors of war, and prevent the soldier's valor from degenerating into personal hatred and destructive ferocity. Estimating things in the light of Divine truth, the glory of our superior generalship and courage of our splendid victories and wonderful success, is a small thing when compared with the glory resulting from the humanity, justice, and generosity, displayed in our warfare with this people.

Such, however, is the character of the war, that our song of triumph and thanksgiving must be mingled with notes of woe at the recollection of the brave men who have fallen or suffered in achieving our success. While mourning for the dead we sympathize with the wounded; yet our pity and their sufferings are relieved by the consciousness that their wounds are honorable testimonials of their valor, and will be regarded by their country as marks of distinction and praise. When we recount our battles or rejoice in our triumphs, none but have to lament the loss of some dear companion or esteemed friend, who fought their last fight, and to whom our victory was their death. Still whilst we give the sigh of regret and the tear of affection to their cherished memories, we feel relieved and reconciled by the reflection that they fell in the discharge of their duty, on the field of their glory, and have met the most appropriate and honored end of the soldier. Their deeds and names will ever be associated with the history of our exploits, in this memorable campaign, and honored by our nation's tribute of grief and praise; and it will be said, in all time to come, wherever their remains may repose—

"That honor comes, a pilgrim gray,
To deck the sod that holds their clay."[6]

When we thank God for our victories, let us consider what is due to the private soldiers by whose courage, and in so many cases, by whose lives and wounds, our success has been achieved. And recollecting, how little they individually share in the distinction and advantages of victory, let their officers not only sympathize with them in their privations and sufferings, but be led to pay a scrupulous regard to their rights and feelings—to treat them in word and deed with justice and kindness, giving them every privilege and indulgence consistent with subordination and the maintenance of discipline; taking a lively interest in their welfare, exercising their power over them and treating them, as under a change of circumstances, they would have their superiors to do themselves.

When our saddened thoughts turn to the sorrowing relatives of the lamented dead, who, when the nation at large rejoice and triumph in the victories gained, must mourn their sad bereavement; let us realize it as our duty not only to sympathize in their affliction, and to aid them to the utmost of our ability, from our own means, but employ whatever influence we may possess to direct our country's gratitude to make a far more adequate provision for the families of those who, by the sacrifice of their lives, have conferred such benefits on our country; and thus to rescue our republic from the charge of ingratitude and injustice, in neglecting to provide for those, by whose husbands' and fathers' deaths in their country's cause, they have been made sorrowing widows and orphans.

Furthermore, in offering our thanksgiving, each of us should consider the goodness of his Heavenly Father, in his own preservation, not only from the violence of the enemy, but from the hand of disease. When we reflect that so many during this campaign have languished on beds of sickness—to how many their last—those who have been preserved, especially those who have been blessed with health, should thank God with an unfeigned heart, for this the greatest of temporal blessings, so indispensable to enjoyment and usefulness; gratefully owning the preserving care of the Lord, "in whose hands are the issues of life and death." And such as have escaped the imminent perils of our battlefields, should seriously consider their own wonderful preservation, while the instruments of destruction flew thick about them, and their companions and fellow soldiers were falling on every side. They should deeply consider and gratefully acknowledge, not their good luck and fortunate escape, which is but the religion of the atheist, but the sparing goodness of their Great Preserver, owning, in the words of Holy Writ, "God is the Lord, by whom we escape death." Yes, my brethren, it seems, that escape from the great dangers to which our officers and soldiers have been generally exposed, would constrain the most irreligious gratefully to unite with the warrior Psalmist in the acknowledgement, "The Lord hast covered our heads, and made us stand in the day of battle," and with him to call upon their souls "praise His Holy Nature, who saveth our life from destruction, and crowneth us with mercy and loving kindness."

6. Paraphrase of a William Collins poem.

In the next place, let us regard the end for which we should now "consider the great things the Lord hath done for us," in these deliverances and victories. It is not to foster national pride and vain glory, for these need rather to be restrained, but that we may be led, according to our text, "to fear the Lord and serve him with all our heart." We recount the victories which by the help of the God of Battles, we have achieved, not that we may sacrifice to our own valor and might, but be led "to fear the Lord and depart from evil"—"to fear Him and keep his commandments;" that a sense of his goodness manifested in preserving our lives and crowning our arms with success, may constrain us to serve our Great Benefactor "with all our hearts." As in the thanksgiving for victory we pray Him "to give us grace to improve the great mercy to His glory, the advancement of His gospel, the honor of our country, and as much as lieth in us, the good of all mankind;" whilst we ascribe to Him all the glory, as our preserver and the giver of victory, let us see that we "glorify Him in our bodies and spirits, which are His"—let us realize that He has not preserved and brought us here to "revel in the Halls of the Montezumas," but to serve Him and do our duty; especially by turning our success and our consequent influence over this people into the means of enlightening their religious ignorance and raising them from the degradation to which they are reduced. And this by extending the light and the blessings of our purer faith, so that by our Christian influence and example and by the intercourse between us, they may imbibe something of our free spirit and throw off the shackles of military and spiritual despotism. Believing that the Mexicans most need for their improvement a purer exhibition of the Gospel of Christ (which toleration and the light of the scriptures would eventually give them,) may it be ours to secure by all proper means the toleration of Protestants, so clearly their right and which we know from experience in other countries would exert an enlightening and purifying influence on the church of this country. May we as Protestants keep in mind that we have to recommend our profession of Christianity to them by our example, and that we are accountable as far as we have any influence, for the impression they receive of our religion. Let neither the neglect of our religious worship nor our vices strengthen the belief, sought to be impressed on them, that we are not only heretics, but are not Christians, and have no religion at all. Let them have no reason to infer that what we regard as superstitious and idolatrous in them is at least as good, if not better, than our Protestant irreligion. But let us show by our piety, humanity and benevolence, and by our exemption from vice, the blessed fruits of our more scriptural faith; our purer and more edifying religious services. That witnessing our superiority not only as soldiers, but as Christian men, they may honor our land, not only as free, enlightened and prosperous, but as blessed by superior means of Christian knowledge and piety, which are the foundations of all.

Devotion to God, and good will to this people, who are equally with ourselves His children, are enforced by a grateful sense of our personal deliverances from sickness and the perils of battle, and it becomes us, in acknowledging His preserving goodness, "to show forth His praise, not only with our lips, but in our lives, by giving up ourselves to His service, and by walking before Him in holiness and righteousness all our days." Let us dedicate the lives He spared us, to His service, improving our lengthened day of grace by being better prepared for death, to which we are always exposed. When we render thanksgiving to God, let us recollect that this is a vain oblation in those who continue to abuse His blessings, disregard His authority and neglect His reasonable service. Offering our thanks as members of the army, may we be reminded of the duty of abstaining from the vices to which military men are most tempted and addicted; imitating the Centurions, whose piety is recorded in the New Testament, one of whom, Cornelius, was the first fruits of the Gospel among the Gentiles; and thus keeping in mind what their good examples were designed to teach us, that the soldier's life, so far from excusing allowed wickedness or irreligion, is perfectly compatible with Christian piety. Let us remember, and act under the conviction, that religion is also binding on us in every station and in every place; and that nowhere and under no circumstances, can we be absolved from its obligation to lead a godly, righteous and sober life. To none is Christian piety more indispensable than to those who serve in the army, and nowhere are restraints, motives and ordinances more needed than in this country, where we are exposed to many temptations to vice and irreligion. Standing before God, this day, as those who have been mercifully spared and greatly blessed, let each and every one resolve here after to guard against yielding to passion or pride, to violence or hatred; and to cultivate the mild, humble and benevolent virtue which becomes us as gentlemen, as well as Christians. Putting away the vices of profanity, licentiousness and intemperance, let us be men of chastity, sobriety and reverence for sacred things. Remembering that it is as true of an army as of a country, that "righteousness exalteth a nation, but sin is a reproach to any people," may gratitude to God, for all His benefits, restrain us from profane swearing and execrations in our conversations, which not only tend to destroy all reverernce for the Deity and holy things, but are expressly forbidden in His commandments, and are in express violation of the laws of the army. These vices, therefore, are as contrary to our duty as soldiers, as they are inconsistent with our religion.

Then let us conclude by praying God that as soon as we shall have finished our tour of duty in this land, and a just, and as we may hope, a lasting peace shall have been made between our United States and those of Mexico, we may leave it and its influences so unfavorable to our piety and virtue; but leave it in good will towards its people, wishing them toleration, a purer form of religion, better and more stable Government. And returning to our own country, let us be more thankful to God from what we have here seen, for having cast our lot in a land of civil and religious freedom, and for having given us so goodly a heritage. Here let us to determine that when again restored to our dear homes, and to those we love, we will show forth our gratitude to the "Giver of every good and perfect gift," by being as entirely devoted to His service and zealous for good works, as becometh those "to whom much hath been given, and of whom much will be required;" and employ our lives and influence to make our people as eminent for Christian holiness and virtue, as they have been "highly favored of the Lord."

Undated.

Views of the War

Situated as we are at present, at the theatre of war and the centre of all attraction, we find ourselves indulging in thoughts and endeavoring to digest subjects, which we had thought many years ago we had probed as far as our limited education and our natural gifts would enable us, but we now find that we had merely scanned the surface and gathered the phantoms flying in the air. Upon points which we had long thought we had exhausted our national pride and given it its fullest scope, we find we were but only indulging in chimerical fancies, and at the present we are lost in wonder, love, and pride. We wonder at our own majestic greatness as a nation—our love for our laws, our institutions, our habits, and our customs swell our bosoms with emotions of patriotic devotion—and our pride in our resources and the success of our national arms has taken the largest liberty and exultingly prompts us to challenge the world for a parallel.

Two years since found us in the pursuit of our peaceful and quiet occupations, enjoying the blessings of being a free people, and prospering in our avocations under the auspices of a liberal and just government—the planter, the mechanic, the merchant, the professional character, and the man of science, were all alike reaping the rewards of their industry and energy, and thinking of little else than the usual routine of every-day life. As a nation we are a peace-loving and law-abiding people, confident in our abilities to repel invasion and defend ourselves with success against the attacks of a foreign foe, by land or sea. But when our little army was about to take its position on our territory acquired by the annexation of Texas, the question was asked, in case of a war with Mexico who would command our army and from whence would we derive our force if a war of invasion ensued. It was at once conceded that the Regular Army in the field was insufficient and doubts were expressed by many whether our citizens would leave their comfortable and happy homes to endure the perils and exposure of a campaign in a foreign land. Whilst this was being thought and talked of, the tocsin sounded to arms! The citizens were called upon to rally around their country's flag and stand by the nation's honor. They were called upon to go forth to battle in a land when it was known that disease and death were dealt out unsparingly, and where more would probably perish by disease and pestilence than would fall amidst the roar of cannon and the clash of arms, but did they falter? did they hesitate for a moment? Let anyone who witnessed the scenes that occurred in Louisiana answer the question.

On the 2d of May, 1846, a proclamation calling for volunteers was promulgated. It was scarcely posted against the walls before the drum and fife was heard in the streets, crowds were seen hurrying towards the place of rendezvous, companies were filled up in an hour, and regiments formed in a day. The news spread with electric speed throughout the land, and every city, town, village, and hamlet responded with excitement. The country was alive with anxiety—the legislature only met to afford money—the farmer laid by his plow—the mechanic his tools—the merchant his wares—the professional man his books—and each taking up his musket, threw off his former habiliments and put on the rough garb of a soldier. All business was in a manner suspended in order to prepare the troops for the field, and thus in less than two weeks a brigade of four full regiments was organized, armed and equipped, and ready to sail. On the 14th of May, this brigade sailed from New Orleans and arrived at the scene of active operations on the 18th, outnumbering the army with which Gen. Taylor fought the battles of Palo Alto and Resaca de la Palma. Shortly after, two more regiments arrived, making six in all. This activity in preparing an army for the field existed not only in Louisiana, but every state responded with promptness and alacrity, and thus from the peaceful days of '45 we might, with the poet, say:

> The sky is changed!—and such a change! Oh night,
> And storm, and darkness, ye are wondrous strong,
> Yet lovely in your strength, as is the light
> Of a dark eye in woman! Far along,
> From peak to peak, the rattling crags among
> Leaps the live thunder! Not from one lone cloud,
> But every mountain now hath found a tongue,
> And Jura answers, through her misty shroud,
> Back to the joyous Alps, who call to her aloud![7]

7. "The poet" being George Gordon, Lord Byron.

And what has been the result of our operations since that time? Encountering frosts and snows of the north, one column has traversed New Mexico and reached the Pacific, where they have planted our standard. Another has gone from our Western States, and after arriving at Santa Fe, has taken its course through the rich and populous State of Chihuahua, and reached their homes in the United States, having driven the enemy from wherever they came in contact with them. A third, amidst the disease and vermin of the Rio Grande, after four hard-fought battles, are now occupying the Valley of Monterey, and the country between there and the coast. A fourth has marched through the burning sands of the southern coast, and the frosts of the mountains, after encountering that fell destroyer, *vomito*, and met the enemy at every point which the natural and artificial advantages of the country would enable them to offer resistance, from the mountain-top to the plain, from the well-constructed fort and the deep *barranca*. Each time has our victory been decisive and glorious, and the great drama has been concluded by unfurling the national standard over the Capital of the Republic!

When we look back at our successes and conquests, it seems difficult to realize them; it looks more like a romance than a reality. Were it possible to collect all the instances of individual and collective gallantry and noble conduct, truly we might claim the present days as the "days of chivalry." To see our columns marching up and pressing steadily forward, with whole platoons, officers and all, mowed down at a single fire—with officers and men falling over one another, killed and wounded—their colors riddled to pieces, and the bearers cut down—was really a scene to make the boldest heart quiver. But would they falter? No, never! On one occasion three successive color-sergeants were shot down, when the lieutenant colonel picked up the colors, and was gallantly bearing them aloft, when he, too, received a mortal wound, but still his forces wavered not, and continued their onward course until they triumphed.

Although our victories have cost us much of the best blood, and many of the noblest spirits of our nation, they have been of such a character that we may well be proud of them, and they will be remembered in song and in story when the actors themselves will be mouldering in the dust. The grief of those who have lost their friends and their relatives will be great, and we can truly sympathize with them, but their sorrows will be alleviated by the brilliancy of the achievements of their friends. If we could but penetrate the recesses of the private chamber, we would, no doubt, find the aged parent imploring the Great Creator for his divine mercy on their fallen son, but it will be but very few years before the strong-armed youth will rise up and with enthusiastic pride exclaim, "*My father was there!*"

A free people have stretched forth their giant arm and Mexico has fallen, our Eagle has spread his wings from the shores of the Gulf to the shores of the Pacific, and now holds in his talons a population of over four millions. The army has maintained the nation's honor and the nation's pride, and has brought to the altar of liberty, new and fresh laurels. Now the high and important duty devolves upon the government for preserving them unstained, and of preventing, by her future policy, any measure which may affect, directly or indirectly, the harmonious workings of our republican institutions. The nature of our successes, and the aspect of political affairs in this country, require our government to take a firm and decided step. If that step be misplaced, it may involve us in interminable and disastrous difficulties, and instead of being a peaceful and domestic people, loving our homes and firesides, we may become a turbulent and dissatisfied nation, with a military institution engrafted upon us, which it will be impossible to shake off.

The government is now left to decide whether it will withdraw its army from its present position, take up a boundary line, and for a few years retain the Regular Army now in service, and then gradually reduce it, or hold the country we now occupy, and increase the present army to four times its number. By withdrawing our army we lose nothing, and get all that we have asked for by treaty, at a better price than we have offered to pay for it. We fall back into our former habits and vocations as citizens, and the government retains its republican simplicity without the incumbrances and difficulties incident to a war. If we continue to occupy the country we now hold, we must adopt an entirely new and different policy. Hereafter it will be a war of detail, and to meet this new aspect of the war we will have to occupy the country by a large standing army. We will be compelled to create under our republican government a military despotism, the evils of which, the most sagacious eye is not able to discern.

From the manner (which, of necessity, must be adopted) of supporting this increased army, evils and corruptions will grow up which the strongest checks will not be able to prevent. By degrees it will acquire an influence in our government, which, by its very nature, is detrimental to the interests of the people at large, and may endanger our existence as a nation. Therefore, how careful should we be in marking out for ourselves, as a nation, any line of conduct that *may* bring with it never-ending troubles. With a smooth sea we may have plain sailing, but if there be breakers ahead we may wreck the vessel.

Beyond doubt, the destiny of this country is fixed. It commenced with the revolution of Texas, and has been steadily progressing ever since. The people who now hold it are incapable of governing themselves, the nation is filled with ignorance and superstition, prompted by a bare-faced villainy and deceitfulness unequalled. They have heretofore been governed by fraud and vice, and the governors have been paid for their trouble in the same coin. The few honest men who have been ardent in their desires to see matters take a different course, have been powerless and unable to contend against the tide that has overrun the country. Beyond all doubt or question the Anglo-Saxon race will eventually possess and govern her, and, administering good and wholesome laws, by degrees sweep from existence the degenerate race which now cumbers the land. We have seen the fertile lands, the blooming fields, the rich mines, and enjoyed the salubriousness of the climate. This fact is enough to seal the fate of Mexico.[8] But this cannot be the work of a day or a year, the actions of our government may hurry or retard it, but in hurrying it she may strike a blow which will be more fatal to herself than to Mexico. It should be left to the steady laws of Progress, so that in the end all will be accomplished that is desired, and ourselves left uninjured. Let the people of the United States think and reflect seriously before they put around their necks the collar of a military despotism, never intended to be worn by free men.

November 1, 1847. City of Mexico.

To-day the train left. It has been detained several days on account of some repairs to be made on the causeway between this and El Peñon, before the road that far could be rendered passable for

8. Here Freaner is expressing a sentiment common to both Southerners and Democrats at the time that would later bear the term Manifest Destiny.

the wagons. It consisted of about 400 government wagons, 100 on private account, and a mule train of about 500 head, also on private account, many merchants availing themselves of the opportunity to bring up a small stock of goods for the Christmas holy days. I understand it is the intention of the General-in-Chief to establish a semi-monthly communication with the coast, as soon as the reinforcements shall arrive. This will give a great stimulus to the business of the country, and materially increase the receipts of the customhouse.

With the train went the sick and wounded of the army, and some others who were ordered out of the country on recruiting and other service. Their separation from those remaining, recalled vividly to mind some reminiscences of the past, and their parting "good-bye" was one of no ordinary character, and not likely to be forgotten by either. It was a parting of soldiers! of soldiers who, side by side, had endured the fatigues and exposures of a long and laborious march—who, side by side, had crossed the rough "*pedregal*" and the deep "*barranca*"—who, side by side, had waded the deep marshes and climbed the craggy heights—who, shoulder to shoulder, had met the enemy's massive hosts, in the proud array of glittering steel—who, shoulder to shoulder, had bared their breasts to the deadly fire of the enemy's deep-toned artillery—and who, shoulder to shoulder, had scaled the enemy's well-constructed forts, and planted the Stars and Stripes on their ramparts in glorious triumph, maintaining the nation's honor, and exulting the nation's pride.

> These are deeds which should not pass away,
> And names that must not wither, though the earth
> Forgets her empires with a just decay.[9]

On the separation, we heard not the empty words, "Farewell," "Adieu," but the good, old-fashioned ones, full of meaning, "Good-bye—God bless you!" and so affected were many on the occasion, that had we not known it, we could hardly believe that these were the men who, but a short time since, had "bearded the foe" in his own castles. The departing ones have gone to "the land of the free and the home of the brave," where peace, happiness, and prosperity reign supreme; where they will be

9. George Gordon, Lord Byron.

met by the approving smiles and congratulations of a grateful people, capable of appreciating their valor and their patriotism; where they will be met by warm-hearted acquaintances and kind friends, ready to bestow upon them the high honors they have won upon the "red field of Mars."

Although a gallant band has left us, many of whom will never again be able to enter the "tented field," there are "a few more left," with the great general of the age at their head, upon whom devolves the important duty of closing the brilliant scene already opened to enchanting view, and of bearing back our Eagles from whence they came, unsullied in their flight, and unstained in their resting-place. If the past is any guarantee for the future, the country can well confide in the hands to which they have committed this sacred charge, and believe that whatever foe they meet, or whatever difficulties may present themselves, they will all be surmounted.

November 2, 1847. City of Mexico.

Yesterday was "All Saints Day," the great annual festival of all countries where the Catholic religion predominates. For the preservation of good order, Gen. Smith directed that all the liquor-shops should be closed, except for two or three hours, in the day, which was complied with. I regret that the time-honored custom of communing with the dead, was not celebrated with as much spirit as usual, but the church-yards, in the early part of the day, were tolerably well crowded with people of every age, sex, and condition, the tombs were lighted up with tapers, and flowers, a beautiful token of remembrance, were scattered over the sepulchres of those who now sleep the sleep of death. It was really a novel and interesting scene to many of the Americans, who had never before witnessed anything of the kind. In several instances we beheld the aged widow, in deep mourning, paying homage at the grave of her husband, the young maiden to that of a brother, the parents to that of their son, who had fallen in battle in the late strife between the combatting armies in front of this city. As we looked upon them, our imagination wandered, and we fancied to ourself the scene where the remains of our own slain soldiers shall be borne to their friends, with the mournful dirge of melancholy music—when our countrymen and fair countrywomen, with bleeding hearts and sorrow-stricken souls, shall pay the last sad funereal rites to their deceased friends—when orators, over their inanimate bodies, shall portray their manly bravery, and their devotion to their country's standard—when poets shall sing of their lofty patriotism and their willing sacrifice. We left the church-yard with the feeling of sadness, recalling to mind the high-toned character and happy faces of our best friends, whom we had known in life but to love and admire.

Every person in the City of Mexico endeavors to make the most out of the festival days, and the pauper population are not behind the rest, those resident in the city turn out in full force, augmented in numbers by an increase from the little towns and churches adjacent. While we gaze upon the extravagantly dressed ladies and gentlemen, who parade themselves upon the balconies overhanging the side-walks, to see and be seen, almost every step is interrupted by the beggars soliciting alms, some of whom make a regular business of it, and others are prompted to it by the pinchings of poverty. Previous to the Americans coming to this country, they were licensed by the Church. Whenever they failed to comply with the requisitions of the ecclesiastics, they were sent to the alms-house, from which they would fly as a thief would from prison, faring better from the scanty pittance they would gather in the streets and highways, than they did in the institution for which the Church annually collects large sums from the people. The diseases inherited and those brought on by their corrupt morals, intemperate and debased mode of living, render it impossible for a large number of the inhabitants to exist unless upon theft or public charity, thus we are enabled to account for the numbers with which the streets are daily infested. They are of all ages, and of every conceivable deformity, and some of them travel over the country, stopping at the towns longest where they are the most successful.

Almost daily we find ourselves accosted in the street, at every corner, the first that we generally meet is a little child that one would suppose had but a short time left the cradle. She is possessed of one of the most angelic countenances we have ever seen, with a pair of dark eyes that shine like diamonds, and what is most remarkable, a face as clean as water can make it. In her solicitations, however, she is perfectly drilled, putting the tips of her fingers together across her breast, turning her head a little to the side, casting her eyes upward, with an apparent smile upon her face, saying in a voice like that of an unmated bird, whose companion has fallen prey to some rambling sportsman, "*Señor, Amo, tiene usta* [usted] *una flaco por la pobre niña que tengo una mama en fierma* [*enferma*]?" (Sir, have you a cent for a poor child that has a sick mother?) There are few, indeed, who can resist her appeals and we should think her daily collections would well support a moderate sized family. A little further on and we come in contact with several blind or deformed creatures, either moving along or sitting by the sidewalk, repeating prayers in Spanish or Latin, however, our people pay but little attention to them. Then at the next corner is posted the regular church beggar, with his long, brown tasselled robe, endeavoring to wear as sanctified countenance as possible, but it requires no very severe scrutiny to see the devil lurking beneath. He holds in his hand a tin box, with a hole cut in the top large enough to admit the money, and so arranged as not to allow the money to come out of the same place it went in; on the back it is fastened by a little lock, and encased in a glass front is the "Patron Saint." This fellow, in the name of the "Spirit of Guadalupe" asks for money for the repairs of some church, convent, or monastery—which at the same time is never intended to be made—or for some hospital, where the sick are dependent principally on the gratuitous charity of the public, bestowed by private hands—or for some alms-house, where the poor are starved and punished, and, as we said before, from whence they desert. He, however, taxes the poor Indian heavier than any other, never allowing one to pass without presenting it to him, when the poor credulous being kneels and kissing the glass covering of the Saint, gives him something, if it is the last "*flaco*" he possesses. (The "*flaco*" is a copper coin of one and a quarter cent.)

Next is a little blind boy kneeling by the sidewalk, who continues to repeat a prayer for the charitable from morning to night. I have noticed he is very fortunate in attracting the attention of our soldiers, and many a war-worn veteran divided his last change with him. Then we come to a blind Indian, who sits in front of the Cathedral, as fair a specimen, I expect, in every respect, of the noblest of the original Aztec race, with the exception of the loss of his eyes, as can be found at the present day. He modulates his appeal in between talking and singing, sometimes in Spanish and then in his native tongue, and scarcely a stranger passes by but is attracted by the peculiarity of the tone of his voice, which usually results in his receiving some charity at their hands. The only thing to which we have been able to assimilate his peculiar voice, is to that of a soft-toned flute, played by some skillful artist, in a country village, at an hour of night when all nature is wrapped in slumbers sound, and its melodious warblings wafted by a gentle breeze through the surrounding shrubbery. Again, we find as very prominent of the beggar-class, a singular trio. It consists in all of a dog and two blind men, one a cripple; one of the blind men carries the other upon his back, who is deformed beyond description, and is led by the dog with a strap around his neck. This specimen of the canine race is so poor that he can scarcely stagger along the street, and has one grey eye and one black one, so that he, too, has the appearance of being blind. So well drilled is this dog, that whenever he meets a genteelly dressed man in the street he halts, then the walking man commences his petition in a kind of prayer, while the one who is borne upon his back turns up the palm of his hand and puts on the most ghastly grin ever witnessed. This body of beggars is so offensive to the sight as even to endanger an appetite for a good dinner. And thus, as we passed the streets, we meet them at every turn.

Determining to see all we could on this festival day, in the evening we sallied for a ride on the fashionable public grounds, the *Alameda* and the *Paseo Nueva*. Here we saw the gaiety and fashion of the city, gentlemen upon prancing steeds, pedestrians promenading the walks, and carriages, filled with lively and extravagantly dressed ladies, some of the latter, through ogling glasses, examining the faces and figures of the "lords of creation," some peeping through the rich-colored curtains, and others, the prettiest by far, showing as much of their faces and delicate little feet as the custom allows. Many of the Americans here are disposed to compare favorably the ladies of Mexico with the fair ones of our land, and we often hear them descanting at length upon the attractions and charms of the "sedate and stately Spanish beauty, with her clear olive, Castilian complexion, and the sweet and lovely Mexican." For ourselves, we are willing to admit that they have bewitching eyes, little feet, and, in some instances, are tolerably well formed, sing delightfully, and are

The Fashionable *Alameda* in Mexico City. *Courtesy Library of Congress*.

well versed in music, but we could never admit that they will compare either with the dark-eyed Creole of our own Louisiana, or the fair, rosy-cheeked lass of the more Northern and Eastern states of the Union. If they have small feet and pleasant faces, they lack that grace and dignity of character of our ladies, and what is more than all, they are wanting in that staple education and maternal tuition, necessary to make them good wives and mothers. We have followed the meanderings of the army through Mexico up to this point, and we are free to confess, that if we desired to end our bachelor days, we would cast our lot among the fair daughters of our own native land.

Chapter 6

A War in Name Only

November 8, 1847. City of Mexico.

We are all at a perfect stand and anxiously awaiting the disposition of our government. The city is much more quiet than it has been for many years, indeed, it is as well regulated as any city in any country. The only difficulties occurring are caused by an occasional drunken soldier falling in with the *leperos* at night, which usually results in the assassination of the soldier. Many of the families who left during the siege are now returning to their homes. The wounded are recovering and the general health of the army is good. Day before yesterday the Archbishop paid a visit to Gen. Scott. His Holiness was received with marked distinction by the General-in-Chief, and I should not be surprised if the general's affability and easy style of conversation somewhat pleased him, at least for the moment.

It is absolutely impossible to conjecture what course the politics of this country will take. The discordant factions are jarring, each jealous lest the other should conclude a peace and be left in power. The democrats (*Puros*) have been endeavoring for many years to break down the privileged establishments of the church and military, and are now striving to accomplish their object through us. For that reason they are striving to prolong the war and prevent, by sowing the seeds of discord and anarchy, the present party in power from taking any measures that may lead to a peace. Señor Don Luis de la Rosa, Minister of Foreign Relations, has called a meeting of the governors of the several states, for the purpose of saying whether they are in favor of prolonging the war, and if they are, that they shall pledge themselves to furnish the necessary men and supplies to prosecute it. The meeting was intended to have taken place some time this month, but in anticipation of it, some of the governors of different states have visited the government at Querétaro, and returned to their homes, taking active measures in support of the present government, who are evidently desirous of concluding a peace. *El Progresso*, the state paper of Guanajuato, of October 31, says, "it has been assured that the Governor intends making a peregrination to the different towns of the State, for the purpose of making speeches to the people, in order to excite a spirit of peace, which, his Excellency says, has already commenced to revive." The Bishop of Guadalajara also recognizes the Government of Peña y Peña, and avows his determination to give it his earnest support. The States of Vera Cruz and Oajaca have also made a similar determination. With this additional support, one would be led to believe that the present party in power would be enabled to pursue whatever policy they might please, but there is so little confidence to be placed in anything the Mexicans say, that there is always room for doubt. At last they have been enabled to get a meeting of Congress at Querétaro, which assembled on the 2^d^ of this month, and are already beginning to make demonstrations towards a revolution, which seems to be the universal means taken by the weaker party to overthrow the stronger. The Peña y Peña government, it appears, will have to contend with the friends of Santa Anna and the *Puros*. The former is endeavoring to rally the old army in his favor, and the latter exerting themselves to prevent the government from doing anything at all.

The election for president has been postponed. When it comes on, Camplido will likely be the candidate of the *Puros* and of the Moderates, I think it will lay between Peña y Peña, Godoy, and Hernandez. Almonte, who stood prominent a short time since, being, for the present, apparently dropped.

Santa Anna has written another address to the Mexicans from Tehuacan, and although he has been stripped of every vestige of power by the Constitutional Government, still he ranks himself as President *ad interim* and Commander-in-Chief of the Army. I send you the *precious* document.

I also enclose you a letter from Querétaro, published last evening in *El Monitor Republicano* of this city. You will by it be able to form some idea of the movements at the present seat of government.

Antonio Lopez de Santa Anna, General of Division, well-deserving of his country, and President ad interim of the Republic, to his fellow-citizens:

MEXICANS! Since my return to my country I have, upon various occasions, given you an account of my actions as commander-in-chief of the army, as first magistrate, exercising power. But, separated as I now am from those offices, with the most profound grief, I find myself compelled to complain to you of the cruel ingratitude of some, and of the perfidy of others, who, not content with their criminal and indifferent conduct during the time of the great conflict, endeavor to throw upon me alone the blame of those public evils to which they have contributed so much.

Such a proceeding does not surprise me, as it is a year since I began to observe in the press of the capital that I was the mark for the factions who so unfortunately have convulsed our country. Their audacity has even branded me with the character of TRAITOR before a society witness of my repeated efforts for its independence and liberty, and of the sacrifices which I have made to free it from the yoke which menaces it.

But that which was not possible to expect, was my violent separation from the theatre of war, in the manner in which it was effected by him to whom I had intrusted the supreme power, while I was combatting against our unjust invaders. As this inconceivable conduct wounds my heart still more deeply, I am compelled to present to the world a historical view of my conduct during the fourteen months which have elapsed since my return to the republic, in order that my labors may be seen, and also the arts made us of to weaken my efforts, and the injustice with which I have been attacked by those who should have aided me, and the origin of this invention of traitor, which perversity has put upon me, to lower me in public estimation, when, in reality, I have served my country the best of all. I have wished to respond faithfully to the call made upon me to save the country from the most barbarous and unjust invasion which it could suffer. But, as that work requires time, and as I could not present it as quickly as could have been wished, while malevolence would not lose an instant in clinching its venomous teeth in my reputation, I supplicate all impartial men, who were not immediate witnesses of my efforts, to suspend their judgment for a time, with the certainty that events will prove what has been my true course, and what that of my unjust detractors.

As for the atrocious injury so perversely done me, I repel it with all the energy of my character, and with the courage of outraged innocence.

I convoke and challenge all my accusers to present their proofs, now that I am without power and influence, and if they fail to do it, I denounce them as vile calumniators and enemies of the nation.

I conjure Gen's Taylor and Scott, and every individual in their armies, to declare upon their honors, whether the Mexican general, who has combatted against them in the north, and in the east, and even in the centre of the republic, until the 10th of the present month, has not fulfilled all his duties to his country.

Fellow-citizens, calamity has deprived us of the incomparable satisfaction of giving you a splendid victory, but misfortune was never treason. They insult you who endeavor to persuade you that so much infamy can rest upon an old veteran of the war of independence, covered with honorable wounds acquired in defence of your rights, and who has grown gray in serving his country with loyalty. Recollect that they themselves are the ones who, upon other occasions, have abused your sincerity and misled your reason, in order to put on the pages of our history the blot which now defaces them. In them are found the assassins of Padilla, and of Cuilapan; for them were sacrificed the two chiefs who, in Iguala, traced the plan of our independence. They also were the authors of the attempt to disinter the foot which one of your fellow-citizens lost while fighting against the foreign enemy, that they might publicly insult it, on pretence of its having belonged to him who, in that moment of dizziness, was called TYRANT.

If my conduct during the stated period merits reproach; if it must be submitted to an examination, because it has not resulted felicitously, I am willing to answer any charges which may impartially and in a legal manner be preferred against me; but, above all, I believe that I merit the consideration which the fundamental compact concedes, which my services demand and justice requires.

If, as I wish, you await events, in order to judge with certainty, you will see that those who from their clubs have diffused malignant sentiments and distrust of my authority, will, taking advantage of our mischances, hasten to treat with the enemy, and conceded him what I denied. They, themselves, whose voice cried loudest for "war without truce," and called by the name of treason the armistice which necessity compelled me to enter into in the capital, when it was the duty of our government to hear that of the United States, have hypocritically endeavored to persuade, that no elements of war remain, that the nation is fatigued, and that its penury and sufferings demand peace at any price. Time, I repeat, will make you acquainted with the evil deeds of those factious authors of our disasters.

You well know that I am not the only captain whom victory has shunned. Let Palo Alto, La Resaca, Matamoros, Monterey, New Mexico, Chihuahua, California, Vera Cruz, Tabasco and Padurna, answer for me. The Mexican soldiers have been unfortunate, but not traitors. There have also been some cowards; but this could never be said of him, who has sought the enemy everywhere; who has been foremost in danger, and who is the only one who during this war has presented the nation with trophies wrested from the battalions of the enemy.

The most appropriate post in which to serve the invader is the government, and I refused it many times, preferring the hardships of the campaign to the comforts of the palace.

The ardent solicitude with which the representatives of the people bore me from the field of Angostura to the capital, to put an end to the civil war which consumed it, made me assume power for a few days, which I left as soon as I had restored public tranquility, to proceed to encounter the army of the enemy, which had taken the city of Vera Cruz and the Castle of Ulua; having unexpectedly to march an army, which, although small and inexpert, disputed with the enemy as well as it could the pass of Cerro Gordo. My duty and my purpose have been to fight, and neither obstacles nor the superiority of the invaders has deterred me. If, after these events, I again assumed power, it was only to defend the capital, which was about to surrender to the enemy. In a few days I raised strong fortifications, collected resources and a sufficient materiel of war; important actions took place before the enemy arrived at the capital, because the ground was disputed with him hand to hand, and his losses gave the lie to those who wished to spread the report that it was abandoned by the army without a contest. The accounts of these remarkable events will appear in the historical review with which I am about to occupy myself.

In the city of Guadalupe de Hidalgo I resigned power to the President of the Supreme Court of Justice, in accordance with my decree of the 16th of September, with the object which I explained in my manifesto of the same date; and in this I had no other motive, as malignity pretends. It was an error, it only consisted in not having foreseen that the man to whom I had entrusted power would employ it in rendering my services useless. This event will be fully explained in my review, the responsibility being his, for the prejudice which the nation may be caused by a measure impolitic in any point of view, and, in my opinion, of fatal consequences.

And the citizen who has acted as I have! should *he* be called traitor? Can he be a traitor who repelled the propositions of peace with the prejudice and humiliation which they involved? What more opportune occasion to extort the admiration of the invaders of Mexico? Let those who pretend to defame me, be covered with eternal opprobrium and shame, for a thousand acts can be placed in evidence against them.

Mexicans—I am a man, and I have faults, but I have never sinned against my country, because I could never nourish in my bosom anti-national sentiments. A good name hereafter, has been as much as I have coveted. I have done everything for the grandeur and glory of Mexico, and I have not spared my blood in achieving that purpose. You know it, and you will do me justice.

Antonio Lopez de Santa Anna
Tehuacan, October 22, 1847.

Your wishes are at last accomplished and Congress, whose meetings all so anxiously desired, has resumed its labors. How little did our people know what they expected when they hoped that the presence of Scott in Mexico would inspire these men of limited views and violent passions with a single generous sentiment. We have seen some men in office to whom *Puros*, Moderates, and Federalists were all the same so long as they had a country whose name their children would bear.

On the first day nothing of importance was done; on the second, a proposition was approved, by which Gen. Santa Anna was to be called to give an account of all the military events which occurred in the defence and loss of the capital of the Republic. There was also taken into consideration a project, of Deputy Benito, for suppressing the General Commands, which is very ill received by the military, who speak of nothing else.

To-day there was a great scene; the Satanic League commenced its opposition to the Government because it does not make war. And whom do you think was its antagonist? The illustrious Minister, D. Antonio. The scene was truly comical. D. Vicente Romero wrote a severe philippic, which his son, D. Eligio, adopted and read. The substance of it was, that all the States are for war, and it is necessary to continue it without any truce, for which purpose troops, money, and *generals* abound. Imagine that according to the "wise man," when he was deprived of power by Peña y Peña, we were upon the eve of a splendid victory. The illustrious Hero of San Jacinto and Cerro Gordo went to Puebla; Reyes went from San Luis to that place, and promised to command 1,000 men. But, oh horror! the universal Minister has the absurdity to believe that the general who loses a place, with triple the force of the beseigers, ought to ask for his conduct. Should the command be taken from the illustrious man who, from San Jacinto to La Ciudadela, has led our hosts to glory—adieu, victory! There is no remedy, it is the fault of the Government that the Americans are in Mexico! And to place immediately in the Cabinet, Mora, one of the commissioners of peace (says the Minister who wished peace), is this not a crime? Was it not better, sir, to make a peace, and afterwards, as counselled by some, to conquer one, by one of those rascally States which dared to doubt the courage of our soldiers?

All this is interspersed with references to Greeks and Romans, is read with a pompous and sonorous voice, and concludes with recommending that the Ministry should give information as to what measures had been taken in regard to the war, or whether we are to remain in the condition between peace and war of which Señor Peña y Peña speaks. You see how advanced we are, and what lessons in dignity and good education our people receive from the representatives. The proposition was lost by fifty-odd votes, against twenty-five, including the two Romeros, Pacheco, Rejon, Farias, Alcalde, &c.

The ejection is deferred in expectation of some *Puros*, who it is supposed will decide the election *cumplido*. Every moment there are heard menaces of a *pronunciamiento* in favor of declaring Santa Anna dictator, and of the convocation of a new constituent Congress, as recommended by the *North American*, which you may have read. Last night they endeavored to seduce the guard of Peña y Peña. That you may know the state of affairs, I will tell you that these people see with the greatest indifference the state of Mexico. One of them has rejoiced in the punishment of the prostrate city. What is the blood of Penunuri, of Leon, of Balderas, of Martinez, to them; they were not *Puros*; they might have been Monarchists, and were fools to let themselves be killed in order to gain liberty and happiness for their country.

A few days since we had the news of the death of Gen. Herrera, but have since learned that his health is improving.

The remains of the Mexican army are scattered about in small bodies, where they can be most easily supported, not more than 500 at any one point.

The French population are making a good deal of disturbance, but to no effect, on account of Col. Harney having flogged one of their countrymen. It appears the fellow had been flogging his wife and "kicking up a row" in general. After he was arrested, he continued to be uproarious, and the colonel cooled the fire of his enthusiasm by administering a little of the oil of raw hide, which "served him right," because, in the first place, "he had no business to get drunk;" in the second place, "he had no business to whip his wife;" in the third place, "if he had no respect for himself or anybody else, he ought to be taught it." And I don't know if the method adopted is not the best, because he will be sure to recollect it.

November 20, 1847. City of Mexico.

I learn, by your letters received to-day, that my letters have not reached you in due season. I am totally at a loss to account for the delay. I received acknowledgements in Puebla, previous of the march of Gen. Scott from that place, of a portion having arrived in Vera Cruz which you did not receive until the 8th of September, and I cannot imagine how it was that they were so long going from Vera Cruz to New Orleans. I start from here on the 28th or 29th for your city, and on my route I think I will be able to discover where they were detained.

A movement is at present making in the army to promulgate the principles of Temperance, and to prevent the use of intoxicating liquors. It is certainly calculated to enable many of the "rank and file" of the army to enjoy many comforts which the use of ardent spirits prevents. It will also be the means of ameliorating many of the rigors of military discipline at present necessary on account of a want of firmness of a portion of the soldiery to resist the temptation to dissipation. This effort at a reform is highly creditable to the originators and to the army as a body, and I send you their address, as follows:

> *Gentlemen*—In placing before you the Constitution [adopted by the Grand Division for the government of subordinate Divisions] and the By-Laws of the "Walter Chiles Division of the Brothers of Temperance,"

we deem it necessary to add a few remarks relative to its organization, object, and benefits.

On the first day of November, 1847, some four or five men of the Rifle Regiment accidentally met in one of the Company mess-rooms, when their conversation turned on the subject of Intemperance and its effects; after a mutual exchange of thought, opinion, &c., one of their number proposed signing a total abstinence pledge; it was immediately written and signed. Seeing that they were in earnest, and believing that if a beneficial society was connected with the pledge, it would be a greater inducement to some, and be a shield of protection to others, to unite and remain steadfast in the cause—one of the Sons of Temperance (who was present) proposed getting other signatures and organizing an Order, based upon principles similar to those advocated by the Sons of Temperance. Consequently, on the evening of that day [Nov. 1st], having procured the signatures, and obtained the consent of the commanding officer of the Regiment, we held our first meeting. The frightful extent to which the practice of intemperance was carried by the "rank and file" of our army (rendered still more frightful by frequent assassinations) demanded that an effort be made to stay its onward progress; it was unanimously determined to open the "Walter Chiles Division of the Brothers of Temperance," and the determination was immediately carried into effect.

By reference to the first Article of our Constitution it will be seen that our object is the dissemination of the principles of FAITH, LOVE, and UNITY, and we trust that by the gentle influence of our example we may ultimately *crush the hydra-headed Monster—Intemperance! the bane of society, the foundation of wrong, the progenitor of crime, dissentions, and vices!*

But this is not all; should one of our brothers be visited with affliction, it not only becomes our duty, but we deem it a privilege, to tender whatever assistance he may require; and should our Supreme Ruler see fit to remove him from this to another world, our Institution vouchsafes a decent burial, after the manner adopted by the Grand Division of the Brothers of Temperance.

Thus, we have launched our little bark upon the Ocean of Uncertainty; but whether it will reach the anchorage for which it is destined, or be wrecked on some of the shoals that surround it, or be engulphed in the Gulf Stream of Disappointment, remains to be seen. But with the banner of "Faith, Love, and Unity," floating from the mast-head, and Temperance and Benevolence at the helm—under the guidance of an allwise God—we think there can be but little doubt of our ultimate success.

[By order of the Walter Chiles Division of the Brothers of Temperance]

C.E. Irvine, W.P.

J.P. Santmyer, S.

"A mail! A mail!" passed through our streets yesterday, with as much earnestness as a fellow would halloo "Fire!" on seeing his own dwelling suddenly enveloped in flames, and as soon as the office opened for the delivery of letters, an immense crowd assembled around the window, each trying to be first, inquiring, "Have you got a letter for me, sir?" As fast as they were delivered, seals were broken and sheets opened, and their contents read with as much avidity as a starving man would devour a fine roast. As they passed from the place of delivery, head down and reading, every few steps a fellow would come butt-up against this one and that one, very much to the amusement of those who had been fortunate enough to hear from home. But taking it altogether, it was a happy day for the army. Many heard from their wives and little ones the first time for several months, others from their betrothed lovers, who were waiting patiently at home for the "end of the war," when they expect to be bound in the silver chains of wedlock, but there were many, very many, letters received, addressed to persons who have passed from the theatre of earthly existence. Really, the greatest pleasure that a soldier in Mexico can receive, is a letter from home, and I sincerely hope that as soon as all the reinforcements arrive, that an effort will be made to establish a weekly communication with the coast.

Mr. Wilson Manning, attached to the Circus Company of Mr. Bensley, died a few days since, after a long and severe illness. He was a son of Col. John Manning, of Brooklyn, New York. During his sickness, he received the kindest attention from his numerous friends.

We have received advices from San Luis Potosi to the 18th inst., and by them we have the report, received and believed there, that 1,500 American troops were on their march from Santa Fe for Chihuahua. However, here we give but little credit to it, as we are not informed of any disposable force of that number in Santa Fe. We also learn, by the way of Durango, that two ships of the American Squadron had arrived off Guaymas, and demanded the surrender of that place. We have no doubt, from the information we have here, that all the harbors and principal ports of entry on the Pacific are blockaded by our squadron.

Mr. Trist has received instructions from the government at home to repair to Washington, therefore, all negotiations and talks must cease. The Mexicans, in the language of Gen. Sam Houston, have been coquetting with our government, under the hope that the next Congress would give them more favorable terms than those proposed by Mr. Trist.

November 25, 1847. City of Mexico.

Two or three days since, Gen. Pillow was placed under arrest. I am not aware what the charges are, but the general supposition is, that "the Leonidas Letter" will come in for a share of the investigation.

Since the last instructions received from the Home Government, it appears that quite a different policy is to be pursued in reference to conducting the war. Heretofore our occupation of their towns and cities has been of advantage to the Mexicans. We have paid high rents for the houses we occupied, paid high prices for all we eat, drank, and wore, and at the same time allowed them to collect and retain all the taxes, state and city, which they had previously received. It is now fixed and determined that Mexico shall bear "the burthen of the further continuance of the war," and the first step towards the consummation of the design, was taken by the Civil and Military Governor of the city, in the following letter to the *Alcalde* (first civil magistrate of the city):

> Office of the Civil and Military Governor,
> National Palace, Mexico, Nov. 19, 1847.
>
> Sir—I am directed by the Civil and Military Governor of this Capital, to make to you, for the information and guidance of the Mexican civil authorities, the following communication:
>
> When the American army entered the City of Mexico, the principles upon which the occupation would be conducted temporarily, were announced by the General-in-Chief in his order, No. 227.
>
> Circumstances have determined the Government of the United States to throw on Mexico the burthen of the further continuance of the war. In consequence of which, it is now necessary to advise the authorities of the city as follows:
>
> 1st. That all the revenue collected, or to be collected, from whatever source, or for whatever purpose, must be considered as collected for the United States, and only to be expended under their authority, and with their consent; all payments not made in conformity with the rule, will accordingly be disproved, and the amount thereof required to be refunded by those who made them.
>
> 2d. All the troops of the United States are to be quartered without expence to them, and if it be necessary to occupy private property, in order to insure this, it will be done.
>
> Nevertheless, not to cause more inconvenience than is necessary to obtain the end, viz.: the comfort and health of the troops, public buildings pointed out by the city authorities will be preferred, where they are suitable, but no rent will be paid in any case.

It is therefore desired that such buildings as can, with the least inconvenience, be occupied with troops, be designated by the First *Alcalde*, to Capt. [James R.] Irwin, the Chief Quartermaster, that they may be examined.

I am sir, very respectfully,

Your obedient servant,
R.P. Hammond, Secretary

To Señor M.R. Veramendi, *Alcalde*

The next movement will be towards the Mining District in the States of Zacatecas, San Luis Potosi, &c. This will be done as soon as the reinforcements arrive, a portion of which are already on the road. A division of some 4,000 men will be sent out then, and extended out over the country to as far as the General-in-Chief will have disposable force to go. Also the Federal Government, now exercising its functions at Querétaro, will be put upon wheels, and some enterprising officer, with a sufficient force for any emergency that may arise, will keep stirring it up with "a sharp stick," whenever it attempts to locate itself anywhere within our reach. Several other movements of magnitude and importance are in contemplation, but, in my humble judgment, the Government will find that they will not be able to carry out the plan successfully, and make it move smoothly and harmoniously, with the number of troops they have counted upon. It is true, we will be able to occupy and garrison any place we march to, but will we be able to keep open the communication between the different points? put down the robbing parties that infest the road, plundering our wagons and murdering small bodies? keep down the turbulent populace, and prevent the assassinations of the officers and soldiers? All these are important to themselves. The productions of the mines are of but little value if there is not safe and undelayed communication between them and the coast. If the contemplated movement is carried into effect, we will then have extended our line of operations from the base, in one direction, some 700 miles, then, added to that, there is a branch from here to Querétaro, of not less than 100 miles more, making at least 800 miles of communication to be guarded, and the depots of supplies and ammunition to be protected. Furthermore, if we expect to make the mines productive, in order that they may be able to pay their taxes, we will necessarily have to establish and protect the communication from San Luis Potosi to Tampico, which is an additional 300 miles.

If the Government has determined upon the occupation of Mexico, let her do it with a giant strength, send into the field forces adequate to accomplish the object. We have had enough of that kind of occupation where we can sit down, in the cities we are holding, quiet and safely, and if we put our heads outside of the gates of the city, we get our throats cut. We have had enough of the soothing system. It is certainly true, it was the best policy we could have adopted, during the campaign of the past summer. Then, we were situated, with a very small army, in the heart of a populous country, having an army in our front of three times our number, with all communication entirely cut off in our rear, without money, and with very little credit. Therefore, it was the best policy to conciliate as many of the inhabitants as we could, in order that we might lessen the number of our foes in the field, and also that we might acquire our supply as easily and as peaceably as possible. However, in the course of a few weeks, if we do not overreach ourselves, we will be strong enough to adopt and put into execution any policy our interests may require. If it becomes necessary, in carrying out the design of the Government, for us to extend our arms over more country, let us have the troops to do it with, and do not expect 20,000 troops to accomplish an object which it requires 75,000 to do. Although I am sorry to see any further movements on this line of operations, for the reason that I believe they will be attended with results injurious to the interest of my country, still, whatever is done, let it be executed with promptness and vigor, as we have all seen the evils following in the track of delays, and feeble and protracted movements.

Since the election of Gen. Pedro Anaya as President, there has been a meeting of the Governors of the different States, in pursuance to call by the administration of Peña y Peña, for the purpose of expressing their opinions on the subject of negotiating with the United States for peace.[1] With the exception of the Governor of

1. An experienced general officer with participation in Mexican political entanglements, Pedro Anaya was appointed "interim president" in 1847 while Santa Anna went off to fight General Taylor's army. Upon Santa Anna's return, Anaya was assigned to the defenses of Mexico City, specifically the Convent of San Mateo at Churubusco. After running out of ammunition while defending the convent, General Anaya, who had been badly burned in the face and hands and wounded by an iron splinter from an explosion, surrendered to General Twiggs. After the fall of Mexico City, Anaya served two brief terms as president and

San Luis Potosi, they were all in favor of the measure, and I believe the present government is authorized to negotiate a treaty, but if President Anaya should determine to do so he will have to send a deputation to Washington City. We learn by the last mail from Querétaro that all the members of the *Puros* party in Congress have withdrawn (thereby preventing a quorum), having failed in carrying out any of their measures, the most prominent of which was to establish a new modelled government upon republican principles, as understood in our country, in the State of Mexico while the American troops occupied the capital, the object being to make this a nucleus around which they could, by degrees, rally the different States. Had they succeeded in this, they would then have effected their object of destroying the establishments of the Church and the Military.

One of the curiosities of Mexico, is the manner of selling milk. Instead of the great white wooden vessel, or the long-spouted tin can, with the different measures hung upon it, and the rattling bell-cart to convey it from place to place with despatch, or an old home-spun looking negro packing it about on his hard-crowned head, we have the live animals themselves driven from door to door of the different regular customers, where they are milked, and a regular stand where the transient patrons are supplied by milking it into the vessel in which they take it home. Besides a drove of cows, with the calves all muzzled, running and bleating after them, there is also a gang of goats and asses driven along, that people may suit themselves as to quality and price, as also their different tastes, for which there is no accounting. It is impossible to devise the reason or origin of this mode of vending milk, unless it arose from the natural villainy of the people and their distrust of each other, it being a preventive against adulteration and of their disposing of a quality of milk inferior to that represented.

November 26, 1847. Mexico.

We have just begun as it were to crowd the Mexicans and make the country feel the war in reality. The Church comes in for its share. You will see by the following official documents how our

---

appointed the commission that would negotiate a treaty of peace. A hero for his defense of the convent, Anaya held several ministerial positions prior to his death on March 21, 1854. Tucker, *Encyclopedia*, 19.

authorities are progressing, and it may give you a faint outline of the change of policy.

The following decree is published in the *Monitor Republicano* of the 8th July, 1847:

> BY AUTHORITY—Department of Justice and Ecclesiastical Affairs . . . . CIRCULAR—His Excellency, the President *ad interim*, having ascertained from persons of respectability and who are besides interested in the preservation of ecclesiastical property, that abuses of a serious character are being perpetrated by certain agents not to the advantage and increase of the aforesaid property, but to the benefit of the agents and to the prejudice of their principals; and there appearing from these manoeuvres a new method of clandestinely alienating the property of churches sufficient for the payment of their stipulated contracts with the Supreme Government, His Excellency has deemed it proper to enact that rural and urban mortgages can neither be sold nor encumbered belonging to the clergy, secular and regular, convents of nuns, confraternities, or any congregation or corporation established for pious purposes, without previous notice to the government, setting forth in the petition the property to be sold, the price, the motive for the sale, and the person or persons who purchase. It is further more enacted, that in order to impose mortgages, previous notice should be given of the object for which they are imposed, explaining the motives for the expedient, and the application or destination which it is proposed to give to the mortgages imposed, or those voluntarily redeemed.
>
> It is prohibited to every clerk, notary and judge executing acts requiring witnesses to complete documents of any class without previously ascertaining the approbation of the government sanctioning the petition already notified thereto, and inserting the same in the document, whatever it may be; and whoever contravenes this enactment shall incur the punishment of suspension from office, for the period which the government may designate, in proportion to the offence, without prejudice to other penalties to which he may render himself liable, conformably to the sentence which may be passed upon him; and every proceeding shall be null and void which contravenes the enactments of this circular.
>
> The foregoing is communicated to you by order of His Excellency, the President *ad interim*, for your information and guidance.
>
> God and Liberty! . . . . Mexico, July 6, 1847.
> [Signed] Romero
> A true copy. [Signed] Jose Maria Duran

> Office of the Civil and Military Governor,
> National Palace, Mexico, Nov. 23, 1847.
>
> The Army of the United States, having become possessed of the City of Mexico, and its neighborhood, on the 14th of September last, all the rights and authority of the Mexican Government, in and over the district so

occupied, vested in the United States; consequently, no sale of ecclesiastical property, described in the above decree, is valid; unless made with the consent of the authorities of the United States, and in the form and under the conditions above expressed.

For any infraction of these rules, not only will the penalties, prescribed in the decree, be inflicted, but any attempt to sell ecclesiastical property, without the consent of the United States authorities, will cause the confiscation of such property for the benefit of the United States. By the Governor:

R.P. Hammond, Sec'y
Headquarters of the Army,
Mexico, Nov. 25, 1847

General Orders, No. 358—Under instructions from the Government at home, requiring that this army shall, as soon as practicable, begin to raise within the country it occupies, the means, in whole or in great part, of maintaining the expenses of the occupation, until the Federal Government of Mexico shall submit terms of peace which the United States may honorably accept—it is *ordered* that no uncoined bullion, bars or ingots, either of gold or silver, shall be shipped from any port of Mexico, until the further orders of the Government at home shall be made known on the subject, so as to give time for said Government to fix the rate of export duty on such bullion, and, perhaps, a smaller duty on gold and silver coins.

As the beginning of the change of system intimated above, all rents for houses or quarters occupied by officers or troops of the army, in any city or village in Mexico, will cease as soon as contracts may permit, and absolutely from and after the end of this month, wherever this order shall be received in time; and, in future, necessary quarters, both for officers and troops, where the public buildings are insufficient, will first be demanded, as required, of the civil authorities of the several places occupied by the troops, so as to equalize the inconvenience imposed upon the inhabitants and diminish the same as much as possible.

If the authorities fail to put the troops promptly in possession of such quarters, then the commanding officer, in every such case, following out the same principle of giving the least distress practicable to the unoffending inhabitants, will cause the necessary buildings to be occupied.

Subsistence, forage and other necessaries for the army, will be purchased and paid for as heretofore; and the injunctions and penalties of the *Martial Law* order, dated Feb. 19, 1847, originally published at Tampico, and republished several times since, with additions, will, as from the first, be strictly enforced, as also, in general, all the obligations of good morals and the most exact discipline.

By command of Maj. Gen. Scott,
H.L. Scott, A.A.A.G.

November 27, 1847. City of Mexico.

I expect you are all anxiously waiting the receipt of intelligence from the army, in relation to its future movements, and impatient to know what will be done hereafter. I can assure you we are no less desirous to hear from home what the army has already done—although we were here on the ground, observing as closely as we could, and watching attentively night and day, to see and know what was going on, it would appear, from the accounts already received from the United States, that our labors were in vain and our exertions entirely fruitless. We find by accounts published, the brilliant achievements of men portrayed in vivid colors, who were quietly enjoying a sound nap at the time of the operations for which they are endeavoring to be made heroes in the war and candidates before the people for important and honorable offices. Others, with a vaulting ambition and haughty association, arrogating themselves and their friends the full credit of important military movements which they were specially ordered to make, and because their exceeding vanity, amounting almost to idiocrasy, would be allowed its fullest scope, to the prejudice of honorable and worthy men, means are sought to overthrow and break down the checks to the course they have pursued, which is as discreditable to them as individuals as it is to them as officers of the American army. It would really seem that the men who enter the army with the object of making it their profession, that they may be able to defend their country's honor and interest whenever called upon, have nothing else to do than shed their blood and offer up their lives, that they may appear prominently before the people of our country to be very small men with great pretensions for having important offices. Let me ask if our soldiers enter the field with this intention? If our military academy, the off-spring of which, by their gallantry and their requirements in their profession, have won high and lasting honors, was established with this object? I think I may safely answer, "No!" However, there are politicians in this army, and there are men who are gambling for office and honors to which they are not entitled. Out of this has arisen disputes, and hard feeling, which should never have taken place, at least in the heart of an enemy's country, and which has resulted in the arrest of three officers: Maj. Gen. Pillow, Maj. Gen. Worth, and Lieut. Col. Duncan. These internal wranglings are disreputable to the army, and calculated to tear the hard-won laurels from the brows of those who are best entitled to wear them, viz.: the subalterns and the rank and file. And this dispute as to who shall be considered the hero of this war, is ridiculous and nonsensical. The heroes of the war are THE ARMY, and if anyone is entitled to the appellation of *the hero*, I should think it is the person who orders and directs its general movements, and devises the various plans of operation, in short, the General-in-Chief.

These disputes will no doubt be a fruitful theme for some of the political papers at home, whose interest lies in making the breach wider between their friends and their antagonists. The whole matter, as soon as the President sees proper to order a court martial, will become the subject of judicial investigation, and the affair sifted to its very bottom. The result, from what I have heard intimated from the charges, will develop a state of affairs our people little expect to exist here, and, I have no doubt, cool their ardor for elevating to prominent offices, "Military Chieftains."

November 28, 1847. City of Mexico.

On the 26th inst., the officers of the 2d Division gave a dinner to their commander, Brig. Gen. Twiggs, who was then about to leave in order to take command of the post at Vera Cruz. The affair went off in fine style, and it was truly "a feast of reason and a flow of soul." Gen. Twiggs has commanded his division from the plains of Palo Alto and Resaca, until it arrived in the "Halls of the Montezumas," and it has won high distinction during that period, and all, from the commander down to the privates, at different periods, have met the enemy in his strongest holds, the results of which you are well aware. The plains of Palo Alto and Resaca, the forts of Monterey, the city of Vera Cruz, the heights of Cerro Gordo, and the entrenchments and fortifications in this valley all bear evidence of its gallantry and discipline.

Yesterday the order for the departure of Gen. Twiggs was countermanded, and therefore he will remain here in the command of his division. Also the departure of the escort of Mr. Trist, which was to have left to-morrow, is indefinitely postponed, but I think it will leave with Mr. Trist, about the 5th of next month, and arrive in Vera Cruz about the 17th. The cause of Mr. Trist's detention for the present, has not been made public.

Brevet Major General David Twiggs. *Courtesy Library of Congress*.

We have no positive news of interest from Querétaro since the withdrawal of a portion of the *Puros* party from the Congress. We learn now, indirectly, that the government of Anaya is making a movement towards re-opening negotiations with our government at home. This government is authorized to negotiate a peace, but I think it is extremely doubtful whether it will act previous to the election of the new president in January. However, it is now ascertained that they would have made an immediate movement, had not Mr. Trist been recalled. The Governors, who were assembled by Señor Don Luis de la Rosa, Minister of Relations under the government of Peña y Peña, were all, with the exception of the one from San Luis Potosi, in favor of concluding an immediate peace. It is now also positively ascertained that the Commission which met Mr. Trist during the armistice, with the exception of Herrera, who expressed no opinion, were in favor of concluding a peace upon the terms proposed by us, but as Santa Anna could not command force enough to sustain him, it failed, and then, to cover their retreat, as it were, they made a counter-proposition, which you have published.

The last advices we have from Querétaro, are to the 23^d^. At that time the Governors were in session, and in conference with the Ministers. The Minister of Relations stated that he had received a note from Mr. Trist, "which was answered in the same manner that the Minister of Santa Anna replied to the note of the American Commissioner previous to the late armistice." The *Puros* party are endeavoring to retard the operations of the present government, and are charging it with having entered into a secret armistice with Gen. Scott. If they cannot effect their object in any other way, I think it is likely they will endeavor to get up a revolution, originating it in Oajaca. However, notwithstanding the report of an armistice between the two authorities, they were daily looking for a detachment of American troops at Querétaro, which detachment will be sent as soon as reinforcements arrive.

Herrera continues very ill, and is not expected to survive the present attack.

The last that we hear from Santa Anna, is through a letter from Oajaca of the 17th inst., which states that he has gone to Tuxtepec with a small escort.

On the 31st ult., forty Americans entered the village of Paso, with the design of taking Manuel Armijo prisoner, but it is said they gave up their purpose, and a treaty was entered into between the government and the Americans, by which the latter remain neutral until the decision of the Mexican government was known.

The papers from the interior bring us the news of the death of President James K. Polk, and state that Gen. Taylor has issued orders for the celebration of his funeral.[2]

We have what is considered positive intelligence of the occupation of Mazatlan, Guaymas, and other ports on the Pacific coast, by our squadron. The *Congress* and *Portsmouth* bombarded Guaymas an hour before they took possession. So say the advices. The terms granted to the different places are similar to those established in other places occupied by our forces. W.A. Robinson was appointed Collector, and the rates of duties were as follows: the duties of importation, until otherwise ordered, will be five per cent per ton, and ten per cent, *ad valorem*, the value in port to be determined by persons appointed for that purpose. Until quarters shall be provided for the troops who were to garrison the place, the United States flag would be hoisted on some point in the bay from the U.S. frigate *Congress*.

We have advices from Lower California to October 3[d], which state that some small portions of our troops have had severe engagements with the enemy, and were defeated. The idea of defeat destroys the probability of truth in the whole affair, and therefore we attach no importance whatever to the intelligence.

For the last three Mondays, several thousand *leperos* have collected in the Plaza for the purpose of witnessing the execution of a sentence, on one of their clan, of thirty-nine lashes on the back, well laid on, for four successive Mondays. At the first flogging, they threw stones and exhibited other signs of disorder. Three of them were caught, upon whom the same sentence is in course of infliction, and profiting by the example set them, they have not since that time been guilty of riotous conduct. Our city government is bringing them to their senses, if such a thing be possible.

2. A rumor began to circulate in fall of 1847 that President Polk had died of a severe illness. This rumor spread like wildfire through the press. One local paper from Illinois dressed its front page with suitable mourning symbols and announced in a bold headline, "DEATH OF THE PRESIDENT." As if to make the story even more convincing, this editor added that Polk had died of apoplexy. One Demoratic journal, in debunking this idle speculation, wrote, "The President is happily still alive, and better in health than he was." "Gossip of the Month," *United States Magazine and Democratic Review* (December, 1847), 563.

Last night we had an exhibition of the gallantry of the American army, towards Señora Cañete, a star actress on the theatrical boards here of Mexico. It appears that, on the entrance of our army, the actresses and actors held a meeting, with a view to determine whether they would play for an American audience. Those, with the exception of this lady, who were in circumstances to live without it, determined that they would not. Cañete agreed to comply with their resolution, if they would agree to support the performers of their former company, who were without the means of support, until they derived it from their profession. This they refused to do, and then Cañete stated that she would play for any people who would pay her for it, particularly under the circumstances then existing, and if the Mexicans would not patronize her after the Americans left her, she then would remove to the United States. Accordingly, she has nightly contributed to the amusement. She is a fine actress, and worthy of patronage in any country, and the officers of the army determined to give her a complimentary benefit in the "*Gran Teatro Nacional*." It is the finest finished theatre I have ever seen, and I doubt if any similar building in the world will surpass it in grandeur and magnificence. It was decorated with evergreens and beautiful flowers, and the house crowded—the first and second tiers of boxes with the "fairest of the fair" of Mexico, and the balance of the house principally with military. The trappings of the officers and the clean cross-belts of the soldiers, contrasted beautifully with the fine finish of the building. Several bands of music were in attendance, and, after a very interesting performance, the affair closed in good order.

At the conclusion, the lady advanced to the lights, and in tolerable English, thus addressed the audience: "My dear friends, even in my own language, I could not express to you my gratification for your kind reception. I will only say, in the language of your native land, Cañete thanks you from her heart." During the performance there was a fancy dance, which tried the credulities of all present. Such a mixing up of legs, arms, &c., was never before seen, and it was really impossible at different times to tell to which bodies the different legs belonged, and to myself, I was apprehensive that someone might get hold of the wrong leg when they came to separate, and by that means break up the dance before finished.

The city is now more quiet that it has been since we entered. Assassinations are less frequent, and both the Mexicans and our soldiers in a better state of discipline. Police arrangements now in preparation will ensure the peace and order of every hole and corner, of even the suburbs.

December 1, 1847. City of Mexico.

It has often been a subject of remark that the true-hearted brave man wants no other incentive to great and giant efforts, than a consciousness of being right, of being engaged where he feels that it is a duty incumbent upon him to sacrifice his life, his social relations, the comforts of home, and the blessings of a plentiful and prosperous land. When this is the case, there is no difficulty, no danger, and no suffering, that he will not meet with a cheerful countenance, and a cool, deliberate self-possession, that will arm him against intimidation or fear in any shape that it may appear, and by these means frequently rallying and cheering onward to glory and to victory his comrades and fellow soldiers. A single look will sometimes re-animate a whole army in despair, a single word turn the fate of an important battle, by infusing into troops a spirit of enthusiasm and confidence.

Many instances of this kind occurred in the desperate battles of this valley, and I have frequently heard one of the Rev. Mr. McCarty, Chaplain to the army, who, in a highly commendable manner, has been assiduous in his attention to the sick, wounded, and dying, both upon the field and in the hospital. While one of the commands was passing to a position in order to turn the enemy's works at Churubusco, they encountered a murderous fire, which swept off nearly one-third of the command, and was calculated to produce momentary confusion even among the most veteran troops. The reverend gentleman was among those left standing, and turning to them with a calm and placid countenance, raising his hat from his head, called out, "Never fear, my brave fellows! The Lord is on our side. Do your duty, and we are certain of victory." As the troops proceeded on, they encountered an almost impassable ditch, where they suffered severely from the guns of the foe before they could reach the point of assault, when he was again foremost in the van, remarking, "My friends, war is a very bad trade, but this is not the time to discuss it. Just hand me your guns, and I will hold them until you hurry over the ditch." His language and action produced a most happy effect upon the men, and as they were led on by their gallant chiefs they raised a shout, charged the enemy in fine spirits and confidence, and most signally routed and defeated them. As soon as the contest between the two armies was decided, we found our reverend friend among the wounded, and the dying, endeavoring to alleviate the sufferings of the former, and administering the last of all earthly consolation to the latter.

On another occasion, when our brave soldiers were falling fast in every direction, and no one knew but it would be his misfortune to fall next, we saw our reverend friend in the midst of the fray, assisting the wounded men from the field to the hospital, and rendering such other kindness to them as was in his power. Someone remarked to him, "You had better be more cautious, Mr. McCarty. You will be certainly shot down, sir, if you continue thus to expose yourself." "I cannot help it, sir," he replied, "I am doing the Lord's work."

How truly sublime was the sight, to witness a sincere follower of the Lord and Saviour in the midst of death and destruction, rescuing his fallen fellow men from the jaws of death, and endeavoring to ameliorate their sufferings and pains, and how strongly does his conduct contrast with that of the fanatics of some of the states of the Union, who have refused to do honor even to the lamented dead, whom they had known in childhood, and in whose companionship and social friendship they had together ripened into manhood.

"Time works wonders," someone has said, and if any evidence of its verification were wanting, we might cite the present appearance and the situation of affairs in the famed City of the Aztecs. How very different do matters and things present themselves from what they did a few months ago. Instead of the anarchy and corruption which then reigned supreme, the terror of all who were not the favored recipients of the products of the then despotic tyranny and the iron rule of military authority, there is peace of mind and security of person and property, the height of human happiness. It is true the ears are saluted with the sounds of martial music, but it comes not from the armed hosts of vainglorious army, marching forth to meet in deadly strife a foe that knows no other motto than "death or victory." It emanates from a band of heroes, the magnanimous conquerors whose waving banners and proud emblems are the existing evidences of the might and valor of a free people, of the power originating from a free exercise of thought and the right of speech. Instead of the anxiety of mind for father or brother, closed doors and windows, and the streets deserted of everything bearing a respectable appearance, there is life and gaiety—fashionably dressed ladies and gentlemen riding and walking, and showing themselves off to the best advantage from balconies, in every part of the city, sweet-toned music finding its way into the streets through rich-colored curtains, behind which "may or may not be" some dark-eyed *señorita*, coquetting with a gay Lothario. Instead of guards and sentinels, as they then were, posted in the streets to keep the people in subjection and force from them contributions and taxes for the support of a set of worthless and indolent hangers-on in the government, there are guards to protect the people in the pursuits of life, and in the enjoyment of their pleasures. Instead of Mexican castles, building in the air, we have pyramids of American fame, glittering in the sunshine of glory.

We have the principles of Christianity expounded every Sunday, in the Grand Palace, by an American chaplain, in the tongue of our native land. Besides these, there are other changes, the *Diario* has given place to the *American Star*; the *North American* is now issued from where a Mexican journal formerly emanated; and the *Yankee Doodle*, full of mirth and humor, pokes his comical face from behind a corner, weekly. Nor do the changes cease with these—a band of Negro minstrels have crowded out the Spanish operatic company, gymnastic geniuses sport their heels in the air, and an American theatrical company revel in the halls of the *Gran Teatro Nacional*. The "tigers," too, are showed off by clever gentlemen, dressed in black, for the amusement of innocent young men who have cash to spare. The "*Café de Independencia*" has swapped off its title for that of the "Old Kentucky House." Other houses, in a like manner, have changed their cognomens, and we now have the "Eagle House," the "Lone Star House," the "St. Louis," the "Alhambra," the "Verandah," the "Merchants," the "St. Charles," the "New York Restaurant," the "American Eating Establishment," the "Shakespeare Dining Saloon," the "Indian Queen," &c., &c., where everything to eat and to drink, from "pigs' feet and buttermilk" to the very best "bald-face and Jamaica," are sold, all done up in the very best manner. But I must not forget to tell you that in these "diggins" people abhor the idea of drinking such common things as "Cobblers," "Juleps," "Rose Punches," "Cocktails," &c., &c., nothing short of "a Churubusco," "an Old Chapultepec," "a Contreras," "a Belen," or "a San Cosme," will satisfy the lofty ambition of our aspiring tipplers. Verily, we are a great people—"progressive democracy" is the spirit of the age—and who cares? What will you take?

To-day there was a review of the 2^d Division, commanded by Gen. Twiggs, in the Plaza. After the review they marched through a portion of the city, and what surprised many persons who looked upon them, was to see many of the companies commanded by non-commissioned officers. The battles in this valley have made dreadful havoc among the officers of the old regiments, many a good soldier has forfeited his life, and the loss is severely felt, but if ever an occasion should again offer, the fine appearance of the division of "OLD ORIZABA," and their movements and discipline, warrant the assertion that they will not be found wanting.

December 4, 1847. City of Mexico.

It is with the most pained feelings that I have to announce to you the death of Dr. James B. Slade, of New Orleans, surgeon in the army. He died on the 29th ult., of typhoid fever, after a short illness, and was buried on the following day with military honors, lamented by all who knew him, and especially by his regiment, the 15th Infantry.

Mr. Daniel Murphy, a native of Ireland, but for some years a citizen of Texas, is also dead. "Dan," as he was familiarly called, was for a long time closely identified with the successes and misfortunes of the frontier inhabitants of Texas. He participated in the capture of the Alamo, afterwards he composed one of James W. Fannin's command, and was one of the few who made their escape at the time of the massacre of that body of men. He continued in the Texan army until the battle of San Jacinto, and then joined the Rangers on the frontier. When the Santa Fé expedition was organized, he was one of the number, and was then again taken prisoner and confined for a long time in the prisons of this country, from which he made his escape. When the war broke out between Mexico and the United States, "Dan" joined the Texan Rangers, and was again upon the field of fight in the battles of Palo Alto,

Resaca de la Palma, Monterey, Vera Cruz, Cerro Gordo, and in this valley. Here he amused himself entirely on his own account. Ever and anon could we see "Dan," on his war-horse "San Antonio," as he named his old bay, rifle in hand, in the midst of the hottest part of the engagement, taking a shot wherever an opportunity offered. He possessed a most violent hatred for the Mexicans, and they dreaded him as much as any Ranger they have ever known. He was devoid of fear, and thirsted to revenge his imprisonment. He at last had the proud satisfaction of seeing the flag of the Union unfurled in the capital of his enemies, and here yielded up his life.

We have advices from San Luis to the 27th ult., and corresponding dates from the other interior towns, but they bring us no news other than the change of military commanders and some of the civil functionaries, which are of little interest to you.

I have been puzzled for the last ten days to fathom the object of the detention of the train, with which Mr. Trist is going to Vera Cruz on his road home. Everything has, apparently, been ready for that time, but it has been detained from day to day without any perceptible cause, and Mr. Trist is so cautious in reference to "matters of State," that even his most intimate acquaintances cannot "talk enough out of him," as we say here, to base an opinion upon. However, I think my letters from Querétaro, the present seat of the Mexican Government, which are to the 2d inst., throw some light upon it. The information I have received is undoubtedly correct, and I have no hesitation in unequivocally vouching for its accuracy. At the time Mr. Trist received his communication from our government, he had already entered into the preliminaries of negotiating a peace with the Mexican Government, and the Mexican Commissioners are now in this city, clothed with the power to conclude such negotiations. The Mexican Government, in conjunction with the Convention of the Governors of the different states, just adjourned, have determined that they will make an "honorable peace," and that "it is not dishonorable in them to sell their territory." My letters further inform me that Mr. Trist will continue and conclude his negotiations, if possible, before he leaves here, that although he was directed to by his government to return home at the earliest possible period, yet still they had not abrogated his powers while he remained in the country. Of this my informant may be mistaken.

It has been currently circulated that Mr. Trist received peremptory orders to cease his official capacity on the receipt of Mr. James Buchanan's communication. However, be this true or not, if Mr. Trist is the man I have taken him to be, he will conclude a peace, if the Mexicans are willing to make it upon the terms we have offered. Considering the character of these people as a nation, and the circumstances existing, the interests of the United States require it at his hands. If he should delay or refuse, the opportunity will not probably again offer shortly, and in the course of the delay ensuing, we will be compelled, in accordance with the policy at present adopted by our government, to reorganize our army, increase it to at least 75,000 men, as the idea of occupying the country properly with the army at present in the field is farcical, and not based upon a correct knowledge of the affairs existing, to say nothing of the train of evils and difficulties that will follow. Therefore, I contend, let the instructions be what they may, if any opportunity offers to Mr. Trist of negotiating peace, he should assume the responsibility at all hazards, and the country will sustain him. There is no doubt but that the Mexican Congress, which sits in January, will confirm any treaty the government may make, as a large majority of them have been elected with the special pledge to support the present government. This, together with the pledge of the governors to sustain the movement, I think, warrants the belief that the treaty, if made, will be confirmed by the Mexicans. I think that the delay of the train, as it is only Mr. Trist's escort, is significant of his intentions, and I hope that he will at least hear what the Mexicans have to say.

December 5, 1847. City of Mexico.

By the laws of our country, the widows of the deceased officers of the army are allowed one-half of their pay proper, for five years, which is indeed a very meagre pittance for the support of the wives and children who have been left widows and orphans by the casualties in the war with Mexico. In many instances families were entirely dependent upon a portion of the pay received, from time to time, from those who were here in Mexico, encountering the severities of a laborious campaign and the dangers of battle. And now that they have passed to that "bourne from whence no traveller returns," this source for the support of their families ceases, and in its stead they receive in many instances $20, $25, or $30 per month for five years, which falls far short of furnishing the necessaries of life, to say nothing of the education of their children. It is no more than just that the government should in some way provide for the maintenance of the families of the gallant soldiers who have fallen in battle, defending the rights and honor of our country. These men would have been honored and worshipped from one end of the Union to the other, if they had survived the shock of battle. They would have been pointed at as heroes, and rewarded by a grateful people for their sacrifices and exertions in filling the measure of the country's glory, and is it not justice in the clearest sense, that their families should inherit, as far as possible, the rewards of their labors, at least that they be kept from the pinchings of poverty? I take it for granted, that there is not one American that would throw an obstacle in the way of any measure on the part of the government that would have this for its object.

Therefore, if there is nothing more done, I hope that the government will brevet every officer who has fallen in battle, and allow his family his brevet pay. On the day they received their fatal wounds they established their claims to promotion, and would have received it, had they survived. Many fell after they had signally distinguished themselves. Many fell at the very gates of the city, after they had won honors and rank in every battle from Palo Alto and Resaca to the Valley of Mexico. All the glory they have won is the property of the nation at large, and I hope that the people and the press of the country will require at the hands of their public agents that something be done for the relief of the families of those who have fallen, either upon the field, in face of the enemy, or who have fallen victims to disease. Let us prove for once that Republics are not ungrateful.

I have seen some sport in the way of duck shooting, and have heard of a great many exploits in that way, but I think that the way they do it up on the lakes around Mexico is more successful than anything I have ever seen or heard of in the "white settlements," and well worthy the consideration, at least, of our most scientific and expert sportsmen. Instead of the double-barrelled fowling piece, or the boat, sand bag, and swivel gun, the Mexicans erect a battery on shore, at the edge of the lakes, where the water is of the depth of from one to two feet. This battery is constructed of gun barrels, with a stock about six inches in length from the breech pin, six barrels put upon one stock, and an iron pin one inch in diameter fastened to the stock and fitting into a log underneath, to prevent it from rebounding, and at the same time thus enabling the owner to easily remove them for the purpose of loading them with ease and facility. The heavy pieces of timber are properly placed, in order to give the proper direction to the guns, five or six tier high, and of a length in proportion to the number of guns the person may have. Into these timbers the guns are placed, and held by the pin running from the stock into the hole made to receive it, and fastened still further by an iron elevating screw at the end of the breech. Thus they are directed so as to bear upon the water from twenty to one hundred yards from the battery, and others at different distances from the surface of the water, in order to take the ducks on the wing as they rise from the water. Food is placed in the water which they are very fond of, and morning and evening they come to feed in great numbers. The guns are discharged by a trail of powder running along the whole length of the tiers. Thus prepared, as soon as the game gathers, they touch the barrels bearing on the water, and then as they raise they fire the balance, and by this mode they not infrequently kill over 1,000 birds at a time, which are brought to the city and sold, however, they are often disposed of at a "mere song." How would it do to try this method around New Orleans, Mobile, Charleston, Savannah, the mouth of the Potomac, &c., &c.? If it would succeed as well there as it does here, it would enable many to feast on ducks who now only enjoy them occasionally. There is no doubt but that ducks can be induced to congregate at any place where they are properly baited for.

December 13, 1847. City of Mexico.

We have advices from Querétaro to the 9th inst. The Mexican Government is in a most deplorable condition. Although there are signs of a *pronunciamiento*, with the object of overthrowing the government now in existence, it is doubtful whether there is any chieftain, in the present distracted state of the country and the prostration of all business, able to command the elements necessary to succeed in such a movement, the principal requisite being money. Any man who heads a revolution must satisfactorily show the persons he enlists in his cause, that he will be able to pay them better than they were paid previously, and that he has means sufficient to carry out all his projects. If, thereafter, he fails to comply with his pledges, his downfall will be more speedy than his rise to power and authority. Therefore I conclude that it is extremely doubtful whether any party will be able to succeed in overthrowing the present government, as it is with great difficulty that the party now in power can furnish the amount daily required for the ordinary routine of the affairs of government, both their internal and coast-wise revenues being almost entirely cut off, and every new party coming into power would have to depend upon their individual resources for the money necessary to support the government proper, the army, and "hangers-on," without which they could not exist a day. From such a state of affairs, the "private stealings" would be small, and therefore offer but little inducement to speculators. The only advantage a new party could gain by coming into power, would be to make a peace, with themselves in power, but in case they would succeed in negotiating, the Congress to meet in January of the coming year would not confirm it, as a large majority have been elected from the present party in power, and are pledged to support the present government. With such a state of affairs existing, what can the revolutionary spirits accomplish.

I informed you, in my letter of the 4th inst., that the government at Querétaro were anxious and willing to make a peace, that if the despatches to Mr. Trist had been three days longer reaching him, a treaty would have been concluded, of this there is no doubt. My informant is a gentleman at Querétaro who is well conversant with the movements and measures of the Mexican Government. He also informed me, as I then wrote you, that the Convention of Governors, which adjourned about the 1st inst., were unanimous in their views, that the only way for the Mexicans to preserve their nationality and retain any portion of their territory, was immediately to conclude a peace—an "honorable peace"—and that it was "not dishonorable in them to sell their territory," and, furthermore, that the governors there assembled and the National Government had mutually pledged themselves to the support of each other, if they succeeded in concluding with Mr. Trist a treaty of peace. The Commissioners on the part of Mexico have been in this city, and, I am informed, have been endeavoring to arrange with Mr. Trist. Whether they have succeeded, no person as yet is apprised, but I hope, for the interests of our country, that he will, if he is so enabled, go home with the treaty in his pocket. Not only the interests of the country, but the interests of the world and the preservation of the honor of our gallant little army, who labored so hard and accomplished so much, requires it at his hands.

One thing is certain: Mr. Trist did not go home with the last train which left here on the 9th inst. From this we might conclude, that he intends having some understanding with the Mexicans before he leaves. I think it altogether probable he will either make a treaty or take home with him the propositions of the Mexicans. If he makes a treaty, there is but little doubt of its being confirmed immediately after the organization of the Mexican Congress in January. If he does so, it will prevent the necessity of our extending our military line of operations, at a great trouble and expense, some five hundred miles further. In the course of the next ten days I will be fully informed what is the correct state of affairs at Querétaro, and if there is any amicable arrangement entered into, you may depend upon being correctly informed thereof at an early date.

The army is now about being thoroughly reorganized—the new and the old regiments so disposed of as to give the whole a better tone, and I have no doubt add to its general efficiency—and if the present peace movement does not result in something definite, in the course of the next two weeks, a division of 4,000 effective men will be despatched to the mining districts situated in Zacatecas, and the states thereto adjoining. It is more than probable that it will be under the command of Brig. Gen. P.F. Smith. The object of this detachment will be to enable us to avail ourselves of the national resources of the mines.

On the 7th Inst. Gen. Patterson, with his command, arrived at this point. It was composed of the following troops, after leaving garrisons at the different points on the road: 1st Lieut. William F. Barry, A.A.A. Gen.; Lieut. Col. John J. Abercrombie, 1st Lieut. Seth Williams, Aides-de-Camp; Lieut. Oliver H. Perry, U.S.N., Act. A.D.C.; Brig. Gen. Caleb Cushing; 1st Lieut. Christopher C. Augur, A.D.C.; Lieut. William W.H. Davis, Massachusetts Regiment, Act. A.D.C.; 1st Pennsylvania Regiment, Col. Francis M. Wynkoop—450 men; 1st Massachusetts Regiment, Maj. Edward Webster—450 men; Battalion of Maj. Folliot T. Lally, 11 Companies—700 men; Battalion of Capt. Benjamin Alvord, 6 Companies—550 men; Battalion of Capt.

Seneca G. Simmons, 3 Companies—250 men; 1st Regiment Texas Cavalry, Col. John C. Hays—500 men; Company K, 1st Dragoons, Lieut. Bezaleel W. Armstrong—75 men; 2,975 men.[3]

Generally speaking, they are a good body of troops, and after they have been taught the necessary duties, drill, and discipline, will be good soldiers. However, there came along with them the greatest American curiosities that, as yet, have entered the city of the Aztecs. They were the observed of all observers, and excited as

3. A graduate of West Point in 1822, John Abercrombie was commissioned into the 1st Infantry, rose to the rank of captain by 1846, and had won a brevet to major for fighting in Florida. Wounded at Monterrey while commanding his regiment, Abercrombie gained a brevet to lieutenant colonel and was sent home to recuperate. Promoted to major and assigned to the staff of General Robert Patterson in 1847, the ship carrying them and some Florida Volunteers from Pensacola to Vera Cruz almost foundered in a storm, causing Abercrombie to miss the end of General Scott's campaign. A colonel in 1861, Abercrombie became a brigadier general of Volunteers and served three years during the Civil War. He resigned in 1864 and died January 3, 1877. Heitman, *Historical Register* 1: 150; *New York Evening Post*, November 27, 1846; *Philadelphia Inquirer*, August 20, 1847; *New York Herald*, October 1, 1847.

A graduate of Harvard, Caleb Cushing began a law career but became interested in politics. Elected congressman from Massachusetts for four terms, he was one of the few Whigs who supported President Polk's war policy. When Cushing's bill to raise money for a Massachusetts regiment failed in the state legislature, he responded by raising the regiment with private donations and led it off to Mexico as colonel. His regiment saw no important action, although Polk did reward his chutzpah by promoting him to brigadier general. He filled a series of political offices until his death on January 2, 1879. Tucker, *Encyclopedia*, 185.

Prominent in the Know Nothing Party, when the war broke out Francis Wynkoop volunteered as a private but was almost unanimously elected colonel of the 1st Pennsylvania Volunteers. Wynkoop performed well at Vera Cruz and Cerro Gordo, eventually acting as governor of Perotė. Returning home in 1848, he joined the Democrat Party and was appointed a U.S. Marshal by President Franklin Pierce. Thrown out of office by the incoming Republican administration, Wynkoop died December 13, 1857, when accidentally shot in the leg by his servant while hunting pheasants. *Philadelphia Public Ledger*, December 15, 1857; *New York Tribune*, December 15, 1857.

John Hays struck out for Texas where he served under General Sam Houston during its bid for independence from Mexico. When Texas entered the Union, various Ranger organizations were gathered into a small army under the command of Hays. He and his Rangers performed important work during the war, especially at Monterrey, and Hays was tasked with protecting General Santa Anna after his surrender. Always a prominent Democrat, Hays headed to California in 1849 where he was elected sheriff of San Francisco. After laying out the city of Oakland, Hays retired to his farm where he died on April 21, 1883. *Sacramento Daily Union*, April 23, 1883.

much lively interest as if President Polk and the American Congress had suddenly set themselves down in front of the Palace to organize and regulate a government and laws for the people of this benighted land. Crowds of men flocked to see them (however always keeping a respectful distance), and women, affrighted, rushed from the balconies into the houses. Perhaps you would like to know who these terrible beings are. Well, they are nothing more nor less than Jack Hays and his Texan Rangers, with their old-fashioned maple-stocked rifles lying across their saddles, the butts of two large pistols sticking out of the holsters, and a pair of Colt's six-shooters belted around their waists, making only fifteen shots to the man.[4] Do you think this was anything to be scared at? There are only 500 men in the regiment, and summing them all up they have only got 7,500 shots, which it will take them at least from eight to ten minutes to fire into the ranks of an enemy, when they are at a charge. But then they have got a name, and I am beginning to believe there is something in a name. The Mexicans believe them to be a sort of semi-civilized, half-man, half-devil, with a slight mixture of the lion and snapping-turtle, and have a more holy horror of them than they have of the evil saint himself. And do not be surprised when I tell you that I have several times been asked by some of the inhabitants, if the Texans will be allowed to go out into the streets without a guard over them. It is really surprising that men with such a reputation should be among the very best disciplined troops in our army, and not disposed to commit outrages, or create disturbance in any way. But the greasers must not interfere with them, as was illustrated this evening. About an hour ago some of them were quietly passing through one of the streets, when a crowd of *leperos* gathered around them and commenced throwing stones, the result of which was, that in a very few minutes there were ten dead Mexicans lying in the street, and two men, badly wounded, taken to the guard-house.[5]

4. During an investigation into the efficiency of Colt's pistols, Freaner, who was unaccountably listed as a major on General Scott's staff, considered these revolvers "the best arms in use." He testified that "he was informed by Colonel Hays, if his men had not been armed with them, when Padre Jarauta attacked him at Teotoleucan, that he would have lost his command of 70 men; and that it was by the aid of this weapon that he was enabled to repulse the guerrilla chief without the loss of a man." 30th Congress, 1st Session, Senate Committee Report 136, 3, 7.

5. Lieut. Col. Ebenezer Dumont, 4th Indiana Infantry, described the arrival of the famous Rangers, "Texan tatterdemalions" as he called them, in Mexico City:

A train left here for Vera Cruz on the 9th, accompanied by many officers going home, a greater portion of whom have been wounded in the battles before this. Gens. Twiggs and Pierce also went down, the former to take command of the post at Vera Cruz and the latter to report at Washington. Gen. Twiggs will be a great acquisition to the post at Vera Cruz, but he is as great a loss to the army here, and I regret that he should be parted from the gallant division he has commanded in every engagement in the war in Mexico, except Buena Vista, at which time he was at Vera Cruz, engaged in the investment and bombardment of that city. Gen. Pierce has only been in the army during the present campaign, but in the course of that time has deservedly become one of the most popular men in Mexico, his master mind and manly conduct have endeared him to all who know him, his gallantry and coolness upon the field of battle will live with the honors won by his brethren of the East. New England may well be proud of her sons, when they combine the rare qualities possessed by Gen. Pierce.

Gen. William O. Butler, with his command, is expected to arrive to-morrow or the next day.[6] The old general will be heartily welcomed back to the army.

"They rode—some side-ways, some standing upright, some by the reverse flank, some faced to the rear, some on horses, some on asses, some on mustangs, and some on mules. Here they came, rag-tag and bobtail, pell-mell, helter-skelter. The head of one covered with a slouched hat, that of another with a towering cocked hat, and a third bare-headed, whilst twenty others had caps made of the skins of every variety of wild and tame beasts." Dumont then told how a Mexican standing on the sidewalk threw a stone at one of the Rangers: "As usual with the Mexicans, he overshot the mark, and took off the cap instead of the head of his intended victim. Never was a guilty act more instantly punished. It was the last stone he ever threw—for, quicker than thought, a flash was seen, a report was heard, and the offender fell dead. A flash of lightning from the Eternal Throne could not have been more speedily called him to account. The Ranger quickly replaced the pistol in his belt, reclaimed his cap, and rode on. Ere long, another stone was thrown, and another greaser launched into eternity." *Washington Daily Union*, March 6, 1848.

6. William Butler gave up his Kentucky law career to serve in the War of 1812, where he was wounded and captured. Returning to serve under General Andrew Jackson, he received a brevet to major for fighting at New Orleans in 1815. After two terms in Congress and an unsuccessful run for Kentucky governor on the Democratic ticket, Butler was commissioned by Polk as a major general of Volunteers in 1846. Badly wounded at Monterrey, Butler was invalided home where he was voted a sword by Congress. In 1848 Polk chose Butler to replace General Scott and he supervised the evacuation of Mexico by the American army.

Capt. Hiram Fairchild, with about thirty of his company, arrived yesterday, having escorted Mr. Percy W. Doyle, the English Chargé d' Affaires, from Vera Cruz.

I was very happy to meet, a few days ago, our old friend, Adjt. (now Capt.) Christopher M. Haile, formerly of the *Picayune*. They say the captain don't speak to common folks, now-a-days, such as correspondents, reporters, and editors of newspapers, but I am inclined to think this is a mistake, for, although the straps sit very well on his shoulders, and he looks about as well as captains generally do, there is a sort of unnatural appearance about him, which I do not think can be corrected until they take the soldier's clothes off of him and put the quill in his hand. The cunning leer in his eye was not put there for soldiering, that knowing look was not implanted on his phiz [face] to stare a colonel in the face, and that playing, laughing mouth was not made for the purpose of bellowing out, to a company of raw recruits, "Right dress!" Nor do I think, although he is a *captain*, that the *adjutant* will ever be himself again, until there was all the soldier out of him, dress him up in citizen's dress, give him a quill, and the use of the columns of a widely circulated newspaper. At all events, I think the President ought to be severely punished for depriving the press gang of one of its most useful members, particularly at a time when soldiers are plenty and good editors are scarce.

December 14, 1847.

The all-absorbing topic, in and out of doors this morning, is the expected arrival of Gen. Butler, with a mail and news from home. If our friends in the "white settlements" could appreciate the pleasure we experience in receiving a "letter from home," they would write more frequently than they do, and longer letters.

Up to the hour of despatch, we have nothing new or funny. So, *adios*, as we say in Mexico.

P.S. *Important*. If a "*safe chance*" offers, I wish you would send us out here a little of the creetur'—a little Old Monongahela, if nothing else—it makes us feel so much like "we used to was"—a civilized being.[7]

Unsuccessful in politics after the war, his law career flourished until his death on August 6, 1880. Tucker, *Encyclopedia*, 101.

7. Monongahela was a specific type of rye whiskey, originating in Maryland and Pennsylvania. Old Monongahela refers to the barrel-aged version.

December 17, 1847. City of Mexico.

In my last I announced to you the death of the lamented Dr. Slade, one of Louisiana's highly gifted sons. I now have the unpleasant duty of again recording the death of another highly distinguished medical gentleman from Louisiana, Dr. Alexander Suter, attached to the Rifle Regiment. He was highly distinguished for his scientific attainments in his profession, and his dignified and gentlemanly deportment in the social relations of life. He was kind and assiduous in his attention to those who were placed under his charge, and no doubt the disease (typhoid fever) which terminated his existence was brought on by his untiring exertions in behalf of the unfortunate sick and wounded soldier, who can never fully appreciate the loss of so kind and attentive a friend as he was, but it is impossible for me to convey to you the expression of grief that pervaded the whole army at the announcement of his death.

I have my letters from Querétaro to the 13th inst.; they contain little news of interest to you. The members of the Congress, with few exceptions, having received news that our army had made a movement for the interior in that direction, packed up bag and baggage, and left the place without much ceremony. The running away of the members can have no effect on any intentions or policy of the Mexican Government, as their term of service expires with the present year, and during that time they are merely a nominal body, and were not occupied in anything else, while they remained in Querétaro, than plotting mischief and rascality. Thus, the quicker they are dispersed, the better it is for the Mexican Government.

The Mexican Government still continues to be very much pressed in her financial affairs, and it is with great difficulty that the different departments are enabled to supply the daily demands upon them.

I learn that it is expected a decree will shortly be issued by the government, requiring the different states to furnish their quota for the organization and support of an army of 20,000 men. There are no fears or hopes of their succeeding in such a movement, unless it is for the purpose of supporting the existing government in consummating a peace. The old army has been almost entirely shaken off—what the Americans have not killed off, the Mexicans themselves have driven off—and if there is a new one raised, it will be entirely new material, and so composed as to be at the disposal of the government. The old one will be powerless, for the want of arms, if nothing else.

The advancing column of Gen. Butler's command will come into town to-day.

Capt. Wm. H. Walker, of the 6th Infantry, who was so severely wounded in the battles in this valley, I am happy to say, is recovering very fast of late, although at the time he received his wound, there was no hope of his recovery, being shot directly through the body.

List of Deaths in the Military Hospital in the City of Mexico, For the Month of October, 1847

Royce, Hall, Delahy, Bernard, Harmon—*3^{d} Dragoons*. Buchanan, Putnam, Heinman, Ross, Watson, 1st Lieut. Shackelford, Sergt. Douglass, Capt. S. McKenzie, Connors, Page, Sergt. Beard, Ormas, 1st Lieut. C.B. Daniels—*2^{d} Artillery*. McCorgan, McGava, Bird, Vegel, Delacey—*Voltigeurs*. Sergt. Peath—*Ordnance*. Salisbury, Brooks—*2^{d} Infantry*. Irons, Lesenfalt—*1st Artillery*. Raymond—*Rifles*. Myers—*1st Artillery*. Dale—*3^{d} Infantry*. Thompson—*1st Artillery*. Scofield—*3^{d} Infantry*. Lenze—*2^{d} Dragoons*. Leigh—*1st Artillery*. Anderson—*3^{d} Infantry*. Sergt. Brooks—*Rifles*. Hill—*2^{d} Dragoons*. Upton—*3^{d} Infantry*. Barber—*Rifles*. Rainer—*3^{d} Infantry*. Lewis—*1st Artillery*. Spenser—*2^{d} Dragoons*. Meade, Dingle—*1st Artillery*. Door—*3^{d} Infantry*. Debaugh—*Rifles*. Sergt. Williams, Sergt. Allen, Trowbridge, Bayles, Davis, Stanton, Smith, Parhall, Ruth—*3^{d} Infantry*. 1st Lieut. Bacon, Rupert, Fernando, Edwards, Mathias, Francis, Smith, Tibbets, Schyder—*6th Infantry*. Lauless, Heskinson, Wilson, Crofoot, Smallbeck, Dehart, Carmichael, Oliver, Loomis, Barton, Sparks—*4th Infantry*. Sergt. McClelland, Camon, Coglan, McElroy, Corpl. Green, Clarke, King, McCary, O'Neil, Lindon—*5th Infantry*. Silver, Chappel, Cain, Hess, Wilson, 2^{d}, Smith, 3^{d}, Sergt. Simmons, McCormack, Holt, Smith, 2^{d}, Palmer, Pickett, Brenan, McKoun, Kubanks, Keniford, Hatfield, Fitzpatrick, Corpl. Hood, Carl, Force, Knepper—*8th Infantry*. Buell, Wiernett, Woods—*4th Infantry*. Everson, Buckland, Leaban, Hopkins, Landis, Henneer—*8th Infantry*. Hoover, Tiernan, McWade—*2^{d} Artillery*. Disbrow—*11th Infantry*. Butler, Byrnes, Janpear—*7th Infantry*. Elkins—*4th Artillery*. Morrison, Cooke—*6th Infantry*. Gooban, Pearson, Stuart—*2^{d} Infantry*. Shadd, Collins, Wilson—*1st Artillery*. Corpl. Ballard, Powers, Yolly, Carlin—*5th Infantry*. Short—*1st Artillery*. Corpl. Patterson, Varnes,

Eldred, Haberstein, Durham, Cain, Waldron, Leggett, Miller, Frederick, Spear, Cohen, Forbes, Reyno, Corpl. Dougherty—*3^{d} Infantry*. Horton, Williams, Baker, Adams, Fassett, Cornice—*3^{d} Dragoons*. Dugan, Zink, Ginters—*2^{d} Dragoons*. Haughrey, Corpl. Bryan, Dinas, Herchy, Corpl. Mager, Pryer, Braugnard, Miller, Wimp, Barnheart—*Voltigeurs*. Hallstead, Tillman, Loupeau, Rodgers—*South Carolina Regiment*. Setzer, Finch, Walsh, Devitte, Watson, Whitaker, Clement, Artif. Kingsbury—*3^{d} Artillery*. Johnson, Tracy—*4th Artillery*.

I have not been able to get the deaths in the South Carolina and New York Regiments, but will endeavor to do so, and send them to you by the next courier I despatch, which will be in the course of ten days, or sooner if anything occurs, either political or military, to warrant it. For the month of September they were included in the reports forwarded by Gen. Scott with his official despatches, which will be published before you receive this. Since the 1st December up to the present time it is impossible to get them accurately, but I will forward them to you at the end of the present month.

December 23, 1847. City of Mexico.

I can only write you a line by this conveyance, both for the want of space and time, before the courier leaves.

All the new troops under Gen. Butler have arrived, in good health generally.

I wrote to you in my last that there could not be any movement to San Luis, Querétaro, &c., for some weeks, which turns out to be true. If the expedition does move, of which there is some doubt, it will be under the command of Maj. Gen. Butler, and consist of about 4,000 troops. Col. Riley's brigade is now at Tacubaya, three miles from the city, Gen. Cushing's at San Angel, seven miles from the city, and is formed out of the South Carolina, New York, and Pennsylvania Volunteers.

War stock is down, and peace stock is up, but I must admit that the market, among the outsiders, is rather fluctuating, and speculation has taken a wide range. On the 1st of January next is the day fixed for the meeting of the Mexican Congress, with Herrera as President. Their proceedings will be of a highly important character, and full of interest to the people of the United States. I have sent a correspondent there, who is thoroughly conversant with the people and politics of the country, in order that I may be able to keep your readers correctly advised of anything that may occur in reference to peace or war movements. I have also made arrangements for a semi-weekly courier from there, and as I receive news of importance to the people of the United States, I will forward it by special courier to the coast, but I hope you will take the necessary precaution not to have my letters detained after they arrive at Vera Cruz. We are all anxiously awaiting the arrival of the President's Message, which is expected one of these days.

December 24, 1847. City of Mexico.

Somewhere about a week ago, the rear column from Vera Cruz, under the command of Col. Johnson, arrived in the city, and I cannot say that I am thoroughly acquainted with the details of occurrences since that time. However, of one thing I cannot be mistaken, as it has made an impression on me that I doubt if I cease thinking about it until after Christmas, viz.: that a great many very suspicious looking barrels, demijohns, &c., suddenly made their appearance in the city, about the time of the arrival of the train, and bearing marks of the "white settlements." Accordingly they all had to be examined with the severest scrutiny, and I, among others, have been engaged assiduously in these examinations for the aforesaid week. My attentive and unceasing efforts in ascertaining the contents of these barrels, produced much fatigue, and at night I usually found myself completely prostrated with symptoms of "bricks in my hat." However, I have not ceased in my exertions to procure the necessary information, until I succeeded beyond my fondest expectations, and am now able to inform you that it was nothing more nor less than the very best Monongahela and Bourbon, at least twenty or twenty-five days old, and branded, "Rectified." But it was American, something from home, and served to remind us of the days of peace, of happiness, and of prosperity, of our own native land, and the friends we have left behind us, of the happy times and happy faces we were accustomed to meet in our perambulations through the Crescent City, in days gone by, and which we hope soon to meet again. Aye, more, it reminded us of the bright-eyed lass who once gave us the go-by for indulging beyond her ideas of prudence, and to-day we find ourself philosophizing on the evils of intemperance. To-morrow is *Christmas*—a happy and a merry one to you all! We expect to spend it in high glee, with a host of clever friends and boon companions, in the best spirit circumstances will admit, and after we put it fairly through, Mustang will endeavor to be himself again.

I told you in one of my former letters that we had a band of Negro Minstrels here, and I now take the liberty of giving you two of their conundrums—they at least have the semblance of originality:

"Why is the American Army like a *sheaf of wheat*?"

Do you give it up?

Answer: "Because it never has been *thrashed*!"

"What *keys* did Uncle Sam use in opening the Halls of the Montezumas?"

Do you give it up?

Answer: "The Yan*kees*!"

Chapter 7

No End to the Occupation

December 26, 1847. City of Mexico.

Christmas has come and gone, and we have had the pleasure of spending it in the Halls of the Montezumas. With the Mexican part of the population, it was celebrated according to their time-honored customs, and in accordance with the spirit and usages of the Catholic religion. I spent at least two hours in examining the toys and curiosities of the Indians, prepared for the occasion, and offered for sale in the Plaza. I do not, really, think I ever looked upon anything with more lively interest, than I did upon their various designs and imitations. There is nothing that they do not caricature—the rich and the poor, the high and the low, all come in for a share of their criticism and ridicule—all their figures are true to life and exhibit their natural talent in a very strong light. The Americans were quiet in the enjoyment of the various festivities that were presented for their benefit, but, notwithstanding, participated liberally in everything that was going on, and seem as much delighted by the annual return of the great holy-day, as though they had had the pleasure of passing it by their own happy firesides, surrounded by family and friends. We can get up as fine dinners here, I presume, as almost anywhere in the United States, the markets being well supplied with fine meats, fish, fowl, and vegetables, but no one's ambition seemed to reach above a fine roast turkey, with the fixtures and appurtenances properly belonging to it. I had the pleasure of dining off of a superb gobbler, stuffed with oysters, and a haunch of venison with applesauce. What do you think of oysters and applesauce, in this benighted land of the Aztecs? Is it not an evidence of the progress of civilization? While we were paying our attention to the substantials, we did not forget the "fixins,"—egg-nogg, apple-toddys, milk punches, &c., commanded a proportionate degree of respect and consideration, and I must confess that myself and some of my acquaintances towards the close of the day, seemed to care little about the cares and perplexities of life, or whether corn was worth five cents or five dollars a bushel. Taking it altogether, I shall never forget or regret the Christmas I passed in the City of the Aztecs.

Yesterday we received the President's Message, and as far as my acquaintance extends, it is, generally speaking, considered rather a tame affair and rather inferior to the former messages emanating from Mr. Polk. His ideas of occupation, withdrawal, &c., have at least the credit of being original, and although they *may* show that he is a very good president, still they prove that he is not as good a general as he might be.

On the 24th inst., we had a genteel excitement in the city, caused by a flare-up between our governor, Gen. Smith, and the *Ayuntamiento* (City Council). The difficulty originated in the Mexicans having acted in bad faith towards our authorities, in the election of its members and the furnishing of our troops with quarters. A short time ago, there was a decree issued by the Mexican Government, at Querétaro, directing that there should not be any elections held in any of the towns or cities occupied by the Americans, and that the officers then in office should continue in the discharge of their various functions. The people desired a new election, and our authorities, determining that the government should not exercise any authority in the Capital while we hold it, directed a new election to be held, in accordance with the wishes of the people. Accordingly an election for a new Council was held about a week ago, which resulted in the choice of another set of persons, to take their place on the first of next month. The old Council then set themselves to work to prevent the new Council from taking their places. To the Governor

(Gen. Smith), they stated that they were not acting in accordance with the decree of the Government at Querétaro, while at the same time they arraigned one of the new electors before a criminal judge, for a violation of the decree. This was a subterfuge that Gen. Smith would not submit to, but one well worthy of a Mexican legislator or lawyer. Gen. Smith immediately put a stop to all such proceedings. The Council then addressed Gen. Smith an exceedingly insolent and impertinent note, in reference to the occupation of quarters by the American troops, and accusing Gen. Scott of a violation of pledges. However, before they sent it to the governor, they gave it to the editor of *El Monitor Republicano* for publication, with the object of exciting the populace and breeding disturbance, as only one side of the question could be presented, unless the governor was allowed time to answer it before it was published. Such conduct as this could not be tolerated by Gen. Smith, and the Mexicans have been made to feel that they were dealing with a man of decision and firmness. Immediately on the appearance of this note, Gen. Smith demanded that the Council should withdraw the publication and apologize for it. They refused and persisted. Gen. Smith then directed his secretary, Lieut. R.P. Hammond, to depose the old Council and install the new. Accordingly at the same time they received the note, informing them of the cessation of their functions, they were saluted with a file of blue jackets to enforce the order, and the gentlemen were compelled to leave the council room without fingering what cash was left. At the same moment of the removal of the Council, an officer with a file of men presented themselves at every part of the city where there are any revenues collected, and took possession of the cash on hand.

To-day the new Council was installed with as much form, solemnity, and swearing on the Holy Books, as if the people of this country were in the habit of testifying to the truth.

I send you the correspondence of the governor, and you will find the objectionable note in *El Monitor*, a file of which I also send you.

Office of Civil and Military Governor,
National Palace, Mexico, Dec. 23, 1847.

Sir—I am directed to say to you that the communication addressed through yourself, by the President of the *Ayuntamiento* to the Civil and Military Governor of this city, upon the subject of the occupation of quarters by American troops, although exceedingly offensive and objectionable in its tone and language, would nevertheless have been made the subject of a special reply, at the Governor's earliest convenience, had time for such reply been permitted him by the *Ayuntamiento*. The communication referred to was received at this office on the 19th of the present month, and on the same day was transmitted to the editor of *El Monitor Republicano*, by the Secretary of the *Ayuntamiento*, and published in that paper on the 20th, thus improperly and indecently publishing their communication to the public when it had scarcely been received at this office, and when no time had been permitted for the action of the Governor.

The Governor now directs that the *Ayuntamiento* be immediately assembled, and that this communication be laid before that body, with his positive and peremptory order that they forthwith withdraw the publication of the letter in question, and make a public apology for having addressed it to the Governor, the withdrawal and apology to be published in *El Monitor Republicano* to-morrow morning. I am, sir, very respectfully, your obedient servant. [Signed] R.P. Hammond, Sec'y &c.

Al Señ. Dn. M.R. Veramendi, *Alcalde primero*, Mexico.

Office of Civil and Military Governor,
National Palace, Mexico, Dec. 24, 1847.

The bad faith and improper conduct of the present *Ayuntamiento* having rendered them unfit agents to administer the affairs of their fellow citizens, in the City of Mexico, their functions are hereby declared to be at an end from this moment; but the members, individually, will be held responsible for any appropriation of funds not made with the consent and approbation of the American authorities.

All treasurers, collectors and depositaries of public revenues or funds are hereby directed not to pay over any part of the sums in their hands, without the order of the Civil and Military Governor.

[Signed] Persifor F. Smith
Bvt. Brig. General and Civil and Military Governor

Office of Civil and Military Governor,
Mexico, December 24, 1847.

Gentlemen—The functions of the members of the present municipality having ceased to-day, and you having been elected to succeed them, to avoid the inconvenience to the inhabitants of remaining a week without a municipal government, I request that you will to-morrow, at 10 A.M., each assume the authorities and duties to which you have been named in the late municipal elections.

Respectfully, your obedient servant,
[Signed] Persifor F. Smith
Bvt. Brig. General and Civil and Military Governor

Alcalde Lic. Francisco S. Iriart, Antonio Garay, Tiburcio Canas, Anselmo Zuratuza, Miguel Lerdo, *Lic*. Agustin Jauregui, Ramon Aguilera, *Lic*. Justo P. Macedo, Regidor Jose Maria Arteaga, Adolfo Hegewish, *Lic*. Manuel Garcia Rejon, Frederico Hube, Juan Palacios, Teodoro Eucoing, Cayetano Salazar, Henrique

Griffon, Joaquin Ruiz, Pedro Vanderlinden, Jacinto Perez, Marcos Torices, *Simdicos Lic*. Miguel Buencostro, *Lic*. Ignacio Nieva.

Office of the Civil and Military Governor,
National Palace, Mexico, Dec. 24, 1847.

The laws of the country direct that the Municipal Elections of the city of Mexico shall take place on the first and third Sundays of December. A decree of the Government at Querétaro forbid these elections, and the *Ayuntamiento* ordered them not to be held, assuring the Civil and Military Governor, after it was done, that it was not in obedience to the decree of Querétaro, but to prevent disorders. Nevertheless, they accused the Electors, chosen on the proper days, before a criminal tribunal, of an infringement of this decree, thus showing the falsehood of the assurance given to the Governor.

The latter declared said decree null, and ordered the elections to proceed. Under this order the *Ayuntamiento* directed elections on days different from those fixed by law, and were required by the Governor to present their motives and reasons for the validity of the elections thus to be held, and the nullity of the others.

On the 22d inst., they presented to the governor an article published in the *Monitor Republicano*, of the 19th inst., as containing the arguments on their side of the question. The very argument shows that the elections can only be held on the first and third Sundays of December; and it also appears that any want of the formality prescribed, is not the fault of the electors or voters of those days, but of the *Ayuntamiento* itself, who forbid and opposed, in all possible ways, the legal elections.

The criminal judge before whom the electors were accused of acting illegally, has decided that their acts were lawful, consequently they are valid, and the persons shown by them are the legal members of the *Ayuntamiento*.

Founding their action upon the legal decision of a Mexican tribunal, construing the laws of its own country, the American authorities will recognize as the *Ayuntamiento* of the city of Mexico, the following persons chosen according to law, viz.: 1st *Alcalde*, *Lic*. Francisco S. Iriarte; 2d do, Antonio Garay; 3d do, Tiburcio Canas; 4th do, Anselmo Zuratuza; 5th do, Miguel Lerdo; 6th do, *Lic*. Agustin Jauregui; 7th do, Ramon Aguilera; 8th do, *Lic*. Justo P. Macedo.

1st *Regidor*, Jose Maria Arteaga; 2d do, Adolfo Hegewish; 3d do, *Lic*. Manuel Garcia Rejon; 4th do, Frederico Hube; 5th do, Juan Palacios; 6th do, Teodoro Eucoing; 7th do, Cayetano Salazar; 8th do, Henrique Griffon; 9th do, Joaquin Ruiz; 10th do, Pedro Vanderlinden; 11th do, Jacinto Perez; 12th do, Marco Torices.

Sindicos, *Lic*. Miguel Buencostro, *Lic*. Ignacio Nieva.

And all persons are forbidden to proceed further with the elections ordered by the late *Ayuntamiento*, under the penalty of being considered as the disturbers of the public peace.

By the Governor,
R.P. Hammond, Sec'y, &c.

The *Star* announces the death, from the effects of a wound received at Chapultepec, of Samuel W. Brady, of Winchester, Va. Mr. Brady was one of the three that escaped the massacre of Maj. Francis L. Dade and his company, in Florida, December, 1835.

December 27, 1847. City of Mexico.

Yesterday morning, a detachment, under the command of Col. Jones M. Withers, consisting of the 9th Infantry, a section of artillery under Lieut. -----, and a company of dragoons under Capt. Edgar B. Gaither, started for Pachuca, a town situated near the mines of Real del Monte.[1] The object of the expedition I understand to be to protect the proprietors in working the mines, and at the same time to collect the revenues arising therefrom.

The prospects for negotiating a peace immediately increase daily, and, in fact, we have every reason to believe the Mexicans will conclude it during the next month, if our government will accede to the terms they offered during the armistice. An entirely different opinion exists in the councils of the Mexican Government, and with a large majority of the people. My correspondent at Querétaro writes me, under date of the 20th inst., that about thirty of the new deputies had already arrived, and that by the 5th or 10th of January, there would not only be a quorum, but nearly, if not the whole of the Congress present, that there is no opposition to the negotiation of a peace, except among the deputies from the States of San Luis Potosi and Jalisco. The new President, Herrera, is known to be in favor of immediate negotiations. The present government has succeeded in destroying the old army, and has organized a new one, composed of the National Guard, the organization of which I send you. This new army will enable the government

1. A graduate of West Point in 1835, Jones Withers served in the Dragoons until his resignation late in 1835. He acted as a volunteer on the staff of General Robert Patterson during the Creek trouble of 1836. An attorney and cotton merchant, Withers became lieutenant colonel of the 13th Infantry and colonel of the 9th Infantry in 1847. After his resignation in 1848, he became a member of the Alabama legislature and mayor of Mobile. During the Civil War he served as colonel of the 3d Alabama Volunteers and a brigadier general in the Confederate army. After holding political positions and heading a newspaper, Withers died March 13, 1890. Heitman, *Historical Register* 1: 1058; *Montgomery Advertiser*, March 15, 1890; *Huntsville Gazette*, March 22, 1890.

to keep down the old one, and also will be its support in any measures it determines upon.

I informed you in a former letter, that there would be no movement from this place upon San Luis and Zacatecas or Querétaro before the middle of January, and I now repeat it, although the city is full of rumors every day about the march of a large column upon those places.

The *Puros*, or democratic party, of this country, are at present completely powerless. They have been defeated in their opposition to the present government under their former colors, and they are now attempting to rally under the flag of annexation, hoping by these tactics to tickle the ambition of the Americans, and thereby prevent any negotiations being entered into, until they can have time to recover their strength sufficient to overthrow the government, and then make a peace with themselves in power. I think our authorities are a little too shrewd to listen to their humbugging to our own disadvantage, and with the exception of some *very smart people*, with very little *good sense*, the tactics and politics of the different parties are well understood.

The speeches of Mr. Henry Clay and Mr. Daniel Webster have been received here.[2] If these gentlemen want to aid and assist the enemy, why do they not go into their ranks at once? If they had Mexican muskets on their shoulders, they could not assist the Mexicans as much, or do us as much harm, as they have done by their speeches. In the name of God, will the politicians of our country never cease gambling for the Presidency upon the blood of our countrymen? Our army dreads not danger, nor do they fear to die *in defence of their country*, but they do dislike to be sacrificed to the unholy ambition of aspiring politicians and political knaves. Is there no way by which our friends at home can put a stop to the unpatriotic conduct of politicians, who would sacrifice the whole army in order to give tone to the next Presidential election? The army will defend and fight the battles of the country, then let their friends at home defend them from the injuries arising from such speeches as these, or the conduct of such men.

2. Freaner, as both a Southerner and supporter of the army, is objecting to speeches delivered by Clay and Webster in opposition to President Polk and the expansion of slavery into what would be annexed Mexican lands.

January 2, 1848. City of Mexico.

During the past week the greater portion of us have been engaged in paying our respects to the holy days. Christmas and New Year days come but once a year, and if we do not take advantage of their presence, of course we lose our chance for a holy day frolic, which is of no ordinary importance in these blustering times of war and excitement. We have celebrated the annual return of "Christmas Times" with as much good humor, mirth, social intercourse, and hilarity, as circumstances would admit of, and we hope that you at home have done likewise. During the time, we have all had an opportunity of enjoying ourselves according to our tastes and fancies, either at the church or at the dance, at the play or at the bull-fight, &c., and it was no very hard matter to "chase up" a smile of "something to take." Egg-noggs, apple-toddies, hot punches, &c., &c., have stared us in the face until, indeed, they made our head swim in admiring them. Although the festive boards in and about the City of the Aztecs have not been enlivened by the merry laugh and happy faces of our fair country-women, which seemed to be the only thing wanting to complete our festivity, still we have endeavored to supply the vacuum by thinking and talking of them, and drinking their health with "three times three." Therefore we hope that all the maidens and maids, who have husbands or sweethearts that are "reveling in the Halls of the Montezumas," will consider themselves saluted, with "all the honors," and, before another Christmas or New Year day returns, if our lives are spared, we will pay our compliments, courtesies, and amiable attentions in person.

We have received the news of the safe arrival of Col. Withers' command at Pachuca, a town about two leagues from the mines of Real del Monte, where they are to be stationed for the purpose of collecting the revenues arising from the working of the mines. The colonel represents having found the inhabitants in a state of alarm at the approach of the American soldiers, but, as soon as they found that they would not be interfered with in their usual pursuits and occupations, and that they would be protected in their persons and property, they were rather rejoiced than otherwise at the presence of an American force, as they then felt confident in being protected from the depredations of the robbers and strolling bands of guerrillas.

A Party of Mexican Guerrillas. *Courtesy Library of Congress*.

Last evening a small party of Texan Rangers, and Col. Wynkoop, of the 1st Pennsylvania Volunteers, went out in pursuit of Padre Celedonio Jarauta, the "Guerrilla Priest," who, it was ascertained, was lurking in this region.[3] In "beating the bush" for a buck, they caught a rabbit. The Rev. Guerrilla had left the place a few hours previous for Toluca. However, acting upon the proverb that "half a loaf is better than no bread," they paid a visit to the *hacienda* of Gen. Valencia. They searched the house from top to bottom, but without being able to find him or anyone else, except Col. Silea, a wounded officer on parole, and an old woman, who appeared to be very ill, and who uttered, in the language of the Texans, "many a groan."

3. A parish priest in Vera Cruz in 1844, Jarauta became a chaplain in a Mexican infantry regiment after General Scott's invasion. When the government called for the formation of partisan bands to fight the Americans, he organized one of the most effective. Jarauta's skill in attacking convoys and lone riders led to the establishment of a command just to stop him. General Lane never caught the famous padre, who refused to accept the validity of the peace treaty. On February 25, 1848, Lane did finally locate Jarauta's band and killed several hundred guerrillas, although their leader escaped. Captured by Mexican forces later that year, Jarauta was found guilty of excesses against his own people and executed by firing squad on July 19, 1848. Tucker, *Encyclopedia*, 326.

Feeling confident that the general was somewhere about the premises, a guard was posted so as to prevent his escape. Finding himself in a rather critical position, he stepped out of the house, and, in a tone savoring very strongly of Mexican dignity, said, "*I am Gen. Valencia!*" and protested in very strong language against being made a prisoner upon his own *hacienda*, while in the peaceful pursuits of life. This was of no avail, and to-day, about 12 o'clock, he was brought into the city and turned over to Gen. Scott, to whom he was also very severe in his remarks, and talked about the laws of nations and the rules of civilized warfare, until the general cut him short by telling Valencia that he thought he also knew something about the laws of nations, and a little about the rules of war, and, further, that he did not regard Mexican notions or sophistry in reference to those points, that Gen. Valencia and Col. Arrieta should report themselves to Col. Ethan A. Hitchcock, the Inspector General, and give their parole, or they would be placed in close confinement.[4] Now the valiant Valencia can have an opportunity of returning Gen. Smith's visit, made on the morning of the 20th of August at Contreras. It is a little remarkable that after Valencia had given himself up, there was no sick woman to be found in the house. While the guard was posted around Valencia's house, someone attempted to escape therefrom, but he was stopped short by a Texan "six-shooter," which is one of the very best things we know of to prevent the escape of either a dying enemy or a prisoner.

January 4, 1848. City of Mexico.

Died, yesterday morning, of the typhoid fever, Lieut. Perrin Watson, of the 14th Infantry, a native of Monroe County, Tennessee. In his death the army has lost a gallant officer, and his acquaintances

4. A grandson of Ethan Allen of Revolutionary War fame, Ethan Hitchcock graduated from West Point in 1817. His career was spent on garrison duty, as a professor at West Point, and in the Seminole Wars. Elevated to lieutenant colonel of the 3d Infantry in 1842, Hitchcock served as inspector general on General Scott's staff and received brevets to colonel for Contreras and Churubusco and brigadier general for Molino del Rey. Promoted to colonel in 1851, he resigned in 1855 to devote himself to philosophy and mysticism. Appointed a major general during the Civil War, he served as a Washington bureaucrat and was a confidant of President Lincoln and Secretary Stanton. Mustered out in 1867, Hitchcock died August 5, 1870. Heitman, *Historical Register* 1: 532; *Washington Evening Post*, August 18, 1870; *Philadelphia Public Ledger*, August 20, 1870.

an esteemed friend. He was not yet twenty-one years of age, and but a few days ago we saw him in the fullness of health and manly vigor. His zeal and bravery in action, and his notable social qualities, had particularly endeared him to the officers and men of his regiment. In the memorable battles in the Valley of Mexico he had highly distinguished himself, but particularly in the severe contest between the 14th and the Mexican batteries under the Castle of Chapultepec, on the 13th September.

For some time past we have had a spell of exceedingly cold weather, the winter of Mexico. Although it was no comparison to the cold in many parts of our country, yet we felt it sensibly, and it affected me more while it lasted than the severest winters of New York, Iowa, or Wisconsin, and you will, perhaps, be surprised when I tell you that the coldest morning did not make ice more than the sixteenth of an inch thick, yet still, it is a fact. Within the past few days, however, Nature has changed countenance, the weather gauger has moved his pegs, and we now have smiling, balmy Spring with its invigorating freshness in the morning, and its genial, warming sun during the day—not too cool or too warm to be disagreeable. So beautifully and so pleasantly does the sun rise and traverse the unclouded sky, and then so gracefully and majestically recline behind the high, dark mountains encompassing the Valley of Mexico, reflecting the brightness of its rays upon the eternal snow-capped peaks of Popocateptl and Iztaccihuatl, that even the most vocal grumbler among us cannot find fault, but like the great mass, must smile too, and say, "A pleasant day—fine weather." Everything, animate and inanimate, appears to be affected by the inspiring and stimulating influence of happy and merry-making Spring. The trees are filling their buds, the flowers are bursting their pods, and the fields are assuming their Spring robes of green verdure. Lads in their best and lassies in their finest, daily throng the streets, courtesying and bowing to each other, and exchanging salutations in the most captivating manner. Speculators, traders, and shavers are moving about with all the powers of locomotion they possess, endeavoring to "make hay while the sun shines." The lazy, filthy *lepero*, wrapped in his *serape* [long blanket]—which contains more life than his own degenerate body—strolls carelessly and slothfully along, looking out for somebody who has the corner of a handkerchief sticking out of his pocket.

But, hark! While we are thus writing we hear the stentorian voice of the soldier in the Grand Plaza, commanding, at guard mounting, "Inspection arms!" and immediately the bugles of the Rifle Regiment send forth the notes of martial music, which are echoed and re-echoed through the Halls of the Montezumas, and as soon as the rattling of bayonets ceases, some forty drummers and as many fifers strike up "Washington's March." As the guards pass in review, we are again reminded that "grim visaged War," with all its horrors and corruptions still prevails, and continues to desolate this land of sunshine and flowers, of cloudless skies and productive fields. And we have but to let ourselves wander off two blocks and there we find our own gallant countrymen, who have left their happy homes, their parents, their wives, and their own dear little ones, to bear aloft on the points of the swords and bayonets our victorious eagles, amidst the storm of battle and the shower of bullets, now borne down by disease, without the soothing hand of an affectionate wife or sister, or a devoted mother, to cool their parched and fevered foreheads, without the kindness and consolation of relatives and friends while his noble spirit is departing to worlds unknown. How gratefully would we all hail a cessation of hostilities with Mexico. How will we all rejoice when peace, happy peace, shall spread its welcome wings over our proud and conquering army, and enable us to return to the land from whence we came, full of honors and of glory, and amidst the welcome and greetings of friends and acquaintances, receive the consolation of having done our duty to ourselves and our country, and by the pleasant fireside portray the beauties of the country we have seen, recount the dangers and fatigues we have encountered, and tell of the glories we have won, and of the laurels we have woven around our much loved Stars and Stripes.

January 6, 1848. City of Mexico.

This morning, the brigade of Gen. Cadwalader marched for Toluca, a town situated to the southwest, about forty-five or fifty miles of this city, for the purpose of permanently occupying it and collecting the revenue. The following is the organization of the brigade, and you will see that it has not only a large proportion of the military talent, but also a full share of unflinching and indomitable courage and perseverance. They will have no foe to meet, or no more honors to win, farther than they will acquire by a high state of discipline, soldierly and gentlemanly-like conduct in the discharge of their duties in the occupation of Toluca. They have already filled the measure of glory full to the brim, and we hope that they will have a pleasant and healthful time at their new garrison.

Brig. Gen. George Cadwalader, Commanding
Capt. George Deas, A.A.G.
Lieut. S.S. Anderson, A.D.C.
4th Regiment Artillery, Maj. John L. Gardner
6th Regiment Infantry, Capt. William Hoffman
8th Regiment Infantry, Maj. George Wright
11th Regiment Infantry, Maj. John F. Hunter
Field Battery, 12-pounders, Capt. Edward J. Steptoe
One Squadron, 1st Dragoons, Capt. Philip R. Thompson
Medical Director, Dr. John M. Cuyler
Quartermaster, Capt. Samuel McGowan
Commissary, B.C. Caldwell
Paymaster Hiram Leonard, to follow in a few days.

The brigade formed in the Grand Plaza, this morning, at an early hour, when there was an old-fashioned bidding "Good-bye." I always love to see soldiers bid one another "Good-bye"—it is so warm, so enthusiastic, and so full of the sincerity of true friendship, and invariably accompanied with the emphatic and expressive sentiment, "God bless you!" How strongly does it contrast with the cold, unfeeling, hackneyed phrase of civilians at home, "Adieu, my dear friend." As the column emerged from the Plaza, and marched by the quarters of Gen. Scott, who, hat in hand, exchanged salutations, as they passed, the air was filled with the spirit-stirring notes of "Yankee Doodle." The rank and file entertain the most remarkable degree of enthusiastic feeling for the Chief who has directed them through so many trying and perilous positions, and who has conducted them to the topmost peak of the altar of fame. When they stand before him or pass by him, they appear to look better, and assume the more correct character of the soldier than at any other time. This, however, is one of the great secrets of the success which has attended our arms in the war with Mexico. If the rank and file had ever doubted, or ever entertained the least want of confidence in the officers who led them, there is no judging what would have been the result.

As the command took the direct road leading to Toluca, every band in the brigade, as if prompted by the same feeling, and entertaining the same sentiment, struck up the tune of "The Girls We Left Behind Us," and, although they went off happily and cheerily, it came upon them like an electric shock, like a voice from their far-distant homes. How many recollections of the past does this little incident bring to our mind? It recalls vividly to our view the bright and happy days of our childhood—our sports upon the green lawn in the springtime of life—our frolics when we attended the primary school—our progress and growth to the age of maturity—the dear sister we have left behind—the weeping mother, offering up ardent petitions to kind Providence for our safety—the bright-eyed girls we promised never to forget—our youthful associations and the realities of manhood—the friends who started with us on the journey of life, and who have fallen by the wayside, and of those who, with manly fortitude, are still climbing up the steep and rugged cliffs of time, striving to reach the topmost tower of fame—and as we first survey the field of our past operations and then endeavor to scan futurity, we cannot help thinking how many there are of us here who will never again return to the "Girls We Left Behind Us."

The following, from the *North American* of this morning, is so extremely characteristic of some of the oddities we have here, that I send it:

Not too good to be looked at.—A few days since, one of the cleverest members of the medical staff was in conversation with a friend in the Grand Plaza, when he was interrupted by the approach of one of the newly arrived volunteers, who stopped short and looked him straight in the face, apparently as though (and this was probably the case) he thought he recognized him. As the man continued his fixed stare, without speaking, the doctor turned to him and asked:

"Do you want anything?"

The man looked steadily for a moment and answered, "No."

The doctor continued the conversation with his friend, but in a little time noticed that the man had passed round him, and was taking another look, probably still unsatisfied as to whether he knew him or not.

"Do you *want* anything?" he inquired again with emphasis.

"No," was the response from the imperturbable volunteer.

"Well, do you know me?"

"No."

"Well, why the devil don't you pass on?"

The volunteer, without relinquishing his stare, answered, after a moment, "Why, you aint too good to be *looked at*, are ye?" and sauntered on without moving a muscle of his face.

January 8, 1848. City of Mexico.

Two days ago some ten or twelve of the 1st Tennessee Volunteers went out from San Angel (their present camp) some few miles, in search of one of their men who had been missing several days. They were without arms, except a small revolver, and while in their search they were attacked by about a hundred Mexicans with stones, clubs, and knives. They succeeded in keeping the Mexicans at bay until all the shots were fired from the revolver, when they were compelled to make an effort to reach camp. While the row was going on in the fields, Col. James C. Burnham, of the New York Regiment, happening to pass on a road in the vicinity, and observing that there was something serious afloat, immediately went to see what it was, when he found one of the men belonging to Company H, of the 1st Pennsylvania Volunteers, dying from wounds inflicted with a knife, and one or two others slightly hurt.[5] He then sent to camp for assistance. Upon the arrival of the messenger, some of the Texan Rangers, who were already mounted, immediately set out at full run for the scene of the disturbance, and arrived before the main body of the assassins had time to escape. The revolvers of the Rangers soon settled the difficulty. It is useless to say that no formal ceremonies were gone through with in chastising the Mexicans for their unprovoked assault. Gen. Cushing reports four Mexicans killed. One of the Rangers told me he saw between thirty and forty "dead creaters."

Yesterday, a small party of Col. C.F. Smith's Police Guard of the city was fired on by a band of robbers or guerrillas occupying

5. A major in the 2d New York Volunteers, James Burnham commanded the regiment after the colonel had been wounded and the lieutenant colonel killed. Promoted to lieutenant colonel shortly after Chapultepec, he had distinguished himself during the final attack on Mexico City. Appointed marshal of New York City after his return home, Burnham died September 2, 1866. *New York Herald*, September 4, 1866.

a house in the suburbs of the city. Not deeming their force sufficient to assault the house, they took a position that would prevent their escape and sent for a reinforcement. The doors were then forced, and all its inmates captured except one, who jumped out of a window, mounted a horse, and dashed off at full speed. As he started off, he drew a pistol and fired it back into the crowd, without, however, injuring anyone. There was one of Jack Hays' Rangers standing close by, apparently a silent spectator to the whole affair, but as soon as the Mexican fired his pistol, he leisurely drew his revolver, remarking, "Ah, ha, my larkey, that's a game that two can play at!" and at the crack of the pistol, down came the Mexican. The Texan then mounted his own horse, and after running four or five hundred yards, *lassoed* the horse and returned with him, saying to the officer present, "Well, Captain, as I knocked the centre out of that fellow, I s'pose I'm entitled to his pony." The officer replied in the affirmative, and the Texan rode off as cool as though it was an every-day business with him. The Mexicans who were taken in the house were sent to the guard-house, and will be tried by a military commission.

Padre Jarauta, the Guerrilla Priest, paid a visit to a *hacienda* about twelve miles from the city night before last, and took a number of horses therefrom. After he had taken possession of all the horses he could find, he directed the overseer of the *hacienda* to inform the proprietor that the horses were very inferior, and that he must keep better ones, that he (the priest) was in the habit of riding horses worth more. Jack Hays has his attention directed towards this guerrilla captain, and "if he does not keep his eyes open, the first thing he knows, he won't know anything." I'm told a rope would fit his neck remarkably well.

The *North American* of this morning has a letter from a gentleman in Col. Withers' command, now at Pachuca. It gives the incidents of the march thence, and an amusing anecdote arising from the humble ideas the people of the interior at first entertain towards the "barbarians of the North," as they are wont to call us.

Pachuca, January 4, 1848.

Ed. North American—As a small party return to Mexico to-morrow, I shall attempt to fill my engagement to write to you, though I have no battle to rehearse.

Our command did not move till late on the day of starting, consequently we did not proceed farther than Guadalupe—the famous shrine where Our Lady appeared to the Indian. Next day we moved early, and after winding between the two lakes (it is a lovely road, but a dense fog hid most sights from us) until near noon; we passed between the villages of Santa de Maria and St. Thomas. Farther on we came to the town of Tiajoca, where the alcalde and other principal men came out to meet us with a white flag, and formally tendered the surrender of the place, offering to furnish everything in their power for our comfort. The churches and principal buildings were covered with white flags.

In this and all other towns we found but few people, all had fled to the hills and stood gazing after us until we were lost to the sight. They had heard terrible accounts of the Yankees, and expected to be harshly treated. That night we stopped at the *hacienda* of Don Pedro de Terrieras, Conde del Jaral, the queerest character I have met in Mexico. Let me give you a description: Don Pedro is about five feet five, so fat that it is impossible for him to ride, I should think, but with all his grossness he is said to be a commander of *guerrilieros*, which I doubt. However, he sent out a man to meet us, invited us to his *hacienda*, and offered us everything he had. On arriving at his splendid mansion, the doors were thrown open to us, and all we desired, quarters, provisions, forage, wood, &c., were freely given out and without charge, though the colonel offered to pay him. He declared that Col. Withers was the most gentlemanly man he ever met and that Lt. Col. Jeremiah Clemens was the next cleverest. In fact he covered us all with compliments, and gave us a fine supper.

After we reached Pachuca we heard that our hospitable friend had gathered about *forty* men, and declared he would whip us; however this was, he did just the reverse, as you see. He got over this in Pachuca by telling the people that, instead of being the barbarians we were called, "we were the greatest gentlemen he had ever met." "Praise the bridge that carries you safe over." He was the most hospitable man that I have ever met in Mexico, and we can well forget his braggadocio, if he was actually guilty of it.

On the third day we started, after Don Pedro had given us a magnificent breakfast, he going an hour ahead to pacify the people and tell them that the stories they had heard about us were false—and he certainly had allayed their fears very much. We reached this place early in the day. It is a small village, with one principal street, and looked very lonely at first, as nearly all the people had left. It seems they went away partly to get rid of paying taxes, but Col. Withers issued an order stating that he would tax the property whether the people were there or not, and this brought them back again, so that now a majority have returned. There are a number of English families here, but more at Mineral del Monte, about four miles distant. Col. Withers occupies the treasury, and the other officers the house of Don Pedro. We are all in good health.

I must tell you an anecdote that occurred the first day we arrived. The people had been told that the Americans eat children, and all those pledges of love have been removed. Lieut. M., of the dragoons, having heard this story, accosted a man, and asked him if he knew where he could get "a *nice fat boy* for supper"—adding that he was "very hungry."

The astonished Mexican answered, with a doleful shake of the head, "*hay no*."

"Well," said M., "as I'm hungry, I ain't particular—let us have a little girl, then."

The poor man, still more horrified, declared that there "were none of these in the village."

M. then turned to him and inquired, "Well, show me a market where I can get a nice piece of a full-grown man."

This was too much for the Indian, and he took to his heels and was off in the twinkling of a jack-knife.

Can't you send your paper here? A stage runs now and then, I believe. I will write by next conveyance, if there is anything to write about. Yours, Dick

January 10, 1848. City of Mexico.

To-day, a universal gloom was spread over the army by the death of Capt. James R. Irwin, Acting Quartermaster General, after a few days' illness, from pneumonia. Capt. Irwin was a graduate of the Military Academy, and a native of Franklin County, Pennsylvania. His position as a Quartermaster General, has been one of the most laborious and attended with endless trouble, but his military talent and business capacity enabled him to discharge the duties devolving upon him with surpassing facility. His loss at this time will be most seriously felt throughout the army. But there is one place his loss will be more strongly manifested—it is in the bosom of his relatives and acquaintances. His high-toned, gentlemanly and dignified character was equalled by few and surpassed by none—honest in all his transactions with mankind, and liberal in his charity—warm-hearted towards his friends, and enemies he had none, but was warmly beloved by all who knew him—brave, chivalrous and enthusiastic upon the field of battle, he narrowly escaped in many of the desperate and hard-contested actions in this valley. He was the very personification of the noble soldier and magnanimous gentleman. "Peace to his ashes—eternal honor to his memory."

January 12, 1848. City of Mexico.

The train which was to have left here for Vera Cruz to-morrow, will not start until the next day or the day after. It was intended to have been escorted by the 2d Dragoons, but I understand that an addition of four companies and a light battery will be added to it. By the following order you will see a list of officers accompanying it returning to the United States. Nearly all of them have done their country good service, and have highly distinguished themselves in the battles of the Valley of Mexico. May they meet a warm reception from their friends in the United States.

Headquarters of the Army,
Mexico, January 11, 1848.

General Orders No, 14. The following named officers, sick, wounded, or reported supernumerary in compliance with General Orders No. 382, of the last year, will proceed to their respective homes, and on arriving at New Orleans, report, by letter, to the Adjutant General's Office, Washington, for (if able) the recruiting service:

1. Maj. Edwin V. Sumner, 2^d^ Dragoons
2. Maj. Carlos A. Waite, 8th Infantry
3. Capt. William J. Hardee, 2^d^ Dragoons
4. 1st Lieut. Lewis G. Arnold, 2^d^ Artillery
5. 1st Lieut. Arnold Elzey, 2^d^ Artillery
6. 1st Lieut. Caleb H. Emery, Massachusetts Regiment
7. 1st Lieut. J. Ward Henry, New York Volunteers
8. 2^d^ Lieut. Henry F. Clarke, 2^d^ Artillery
9. 2^d^ Lieut. William C. Wagley, 3^d^ Dragoons
10. 2^d^ Lieut. Patrick A. Farrelly, 5th Infantry
11. 2^d^ Lieut. Henry B. Clitz, 3^d^ Infantry
12. 2^d^ Lieut. George Wainwright, 8th Infantry
13. 2^d^ Lieut. James G. Fitzgerald, 14th Infantry
14. 2^d^ Lieut. Lewis W. Templeton, 15th Infantry
15. 2^d^ Lieut. James E. Slaughter, Voltigeurs
16. Capt. Joseph R. Smith, 2^d^ Infantry

By command of Major General Scott,
H.L. Scott, A.A.A.G.

To-day the funeral of Capt. Irwin took place. He was followed to the grave by a long line of mourning friends. The Rifle Regiment paid the military honors to his remains, but it was no one corps that grieved at his death. When he died, the army wept.

By the following order, Maj. J.L. Gardner has been appointed "Superintendent of the direct and indirect taxes to be levied for the support of the army, on that portion of Mexico called the Federal District."

Headquarters of the Army,
Mexico, Jan. 11, 1848.

General Orders No. 15. Maj. J.L. Gardner, of the U.S. 4th Artillery, is appointed Superintendent of direct and indirect assessments to be levied for the support of this army for the part of the Republic of Mexico called the Federal District. He will accordingly open an office in the National Palace and enter upon the duties assigned him.

He will ascertain the amount of assessments as they may, from time to time, fall due; make demands for their regular payment, and when ready, report the same to General Headquarters in order that disbursing officers may be named to receive and give acquittances for the same. Acquittances will be attested and registered by the Superintendent, who will also transmit to the proper accountant at Washington, documents charging the disbursing officers with the amounts received by them respectively.

By command of Major General Scott,
H.L. Scott, A.A.A.G.

A Mexican officer has been detected in endeavoring to induce the soldiers to desert. A military commission of which Gen. Smith is President and R.P. Hammond, Judge Advocate, is now in session trying him for the offence. If he is found guilty, as I expect he will be, he will be either shot or hung.

By the order of Gen. Scott, Capt. Abraham C. Myers has been assigned to the Chief of the Quartermaster's Department. From what we know of his capacity, we have no doubt but that he will discharge the duties to the interest of the Government and with credit to himself.

The improper conduct of some of the officers of the late Mexican army, has rendered the following order from Gen. Smith necessary. If these gentlemen do not walk up to the "*chalk mark*" very suddenly, we will soon have something to interest the attention of newspaper correspondents. *Quien sabe* [Who knows].

Office Civil and Military Governor
National Palace, Mexico, January 11, 1848.

It is ordered that all officers of the Mexican Army, all retired officers, as also those of the corps of National Guards, including certain regiments known as those of the Independence, Bravo, Victoria, Hidalgo, Galeana, Mina, and the corps of Zapadores, who may now be in the city of Mexico, not on parade, shall present themselves at the office of the Inspector General of the American Army, between the hours of 10 A.M. and 3 P.M., on the 12th, 13th, or 14th inst.

It is also ordered that all officers of the Mexican Army and of the above-named corps, who may hereafter arrive in the city, shall report themselves at the aforesaid office within twenty-four hours after reaching the city.

This order is rendered necessary by the highly improper conduct of certain officers of the Mexican Army, known to be in the city, and any failure to comply with it will subject the offender to the most rigorous punishment known to the laws of war.

By the Governor. R.P. Hammond, Sec'y

Since the organization of the new Military Police, an important and creditable change is visible in the order and peace of the city.

Gen. Cadwalader has arrived at Toluca. The following letter from a friend will give you an account of the march, and their arrival at their place of destination:

Toluca, January, 1848.

My Dear Mustang—I promised to tell you what kind of country we traversed in reaching this place. Hearing that the "Diligence" is robbed every day, I have waited some other opportunity of writing, and now hear that the Dragoons leave for Mexico in a few moments, which gives me little time.

After quitting Tacubaya, our road began to ascend, the country continuing sterile and volcanic, like that around Contreras. Towards sunset we reached a *hacienda*, or inn, and encamped, the night closing upon us bitterly cold. The infantry encamped mostly around the brow of a hill adjacent, and few pleasant dreams, I ween, did the cold wind permit them. Early on the 7th, we started again, the earth white with frost, and icicles hanging from the rocks, the road, if possible, harder and more finished than yesterday, and ascending always. Arriving at the highest point of the mountain ridge, we saw a number of crosses together, and were told that they commemorated a desperate conflict that came off here some thirty years ago between the Spaniards and Mexicans. The first were attacked in position by the latter, and gained the day. One cross fastened into the solid rock marks the grave of the Mexican general.

At this point opened upon us one of the finest views I ever saw—the Valley of Toluca. Stretched out in front and on either side it lay, studded with villages and *haciendas*, and just enough watered to give variety, while far away rose the snowy summit of Nevado de Toluca, with its wide crater. I thought to myself, had Tom Moore seen this, he had certainly written the "Sweet Vale of" Toluca, instead of that other.

The road now descended regularly, and we came upon Lerma, a small dirty village, every house filled with children, gaping women, and surmounted by a white flag, the only clean thing about the premises, and that prepared, no doubt, just for this occasion only.

Before getting to Lerma, however, we passed a small bridged stream, the passage of which was defended by a sandbag fort, and the hills adjacent were also crowned by works, all made while we lay at Puebla and abandoned on the fall of the capital. It is said that the fort at the bridge was carried by "*Dutch Mary*," certainly she was first there.

Capt. Thompson took his squadron on to Toluca this afternoon, in company with the *alcalde*, who has come out to meet the general.

At sunrise on the next day, 8th, we started for Toluca, some ten miles distant, marching for some short distance on the edge of a marsh, where we perceived abundance of waterfowl, and promised ourselves some good sport anon. The country on either side became more and more fertile, a superior cultivation to any we had seen in Mexico: fine *haciendas*, with American-looking farm-yards and granaries, abundance of cattle, &c., &c., all proclaiming a decidedly improved state of society.

We reached Toluca after a few hours' march, and, as usual, were surrounded by a dense mass of wondering beings, and took our quarters, the soldiers in convents, &c., and many of the officers by billet. I have never seen a more pacific-looking people in all our progress, notwithstanding the preaching of Father Jarauta, who was lately here. Some thousand troops, it is said, left here on our approach, with the government, for Morelia.

This town is capable of holding from 10,000 to 12,000 people, but at present has not so many. It is prettily built, is very clean, and is supplied with good water by an aqueduct. Nor have we felt the degree of cold for which it has a reputation.

Yesterday the 11th Infantry were ordered to retrace their steps as far as Lerma, and occupy that place. Rumor says that the convent in which they were quartered suffered a *few* in the way of gold vessels, and the general thought it prudent to quarter the regiment where gold and silver are *apparently* unknown.

There are no pretty women here!!! Whether the good friars are looking after their morals, I cannot tell.

Farewell. I have not time to write more at present.

Col. Manuel Dominguez, of the Native Spy Company, or Contra-Guerrillas, arrived yesterday, with a letter mail from Vera Cruz.[6] On his way up, he made a haul among the guerrillas infesting the road. The following account of it, from the *Star* of this morning, is the correct report. Dr. Alfred W. Kennedy also comes up with the escort, as bearer of despatches from Washington to Gen. Scott.

A little towards the left of Santa Fe, Col. Dominguez ascertained that there were some fifty or sixty guerrillas, under Col. Manuel Zenobia, hovering in the vicinity. He charged upon them, and they dispersed without firing a gun. On the 6th, on the plains of Salao, between Ojo de Agua and Nopalucan, the proprietors of the *haciendas* of St. Gertrude, Santa Clara, &c., requested aid of Col. Dominguez in their efforts to liberate themselves from the robberies of Anastasio Torrejón and his party, composed of 150 cavalry and

6. An infamous Mexican bandit, Manuel Dominguez had been captured by Americans early in 1847 but agreed to raise a company of Mexican spies and serve the United States in exchange for his release. A dozen of his fellow bandits liberated with him soon swelled to a command of almost 2,000, leading to his appointment as colonel although none of the spies ever mustered into Federal service. Dominguez and his spies proved adept at espionage, scouting, interpreting, and providing a liaison with the civilian population. Following the war, Dominguez lived in Louisiana and died at Brownsville, Texas, on June 30, 1868. Tucker, *Encyclopedia*, 402–3; *Times-Picayune*, July 10, 1868.

two American deserters.[7] The colonel, with his escort of seventy men, charged upon them, and, after a slight brush, put them completely to rout, taking Gen. Torrejón, Gen. Miñon, Gen. Guana and five other officers, prisoners, fifty Mexican cavalry and the two American deserters.[8] They were all placed at the disposal of Col. Childs at Puebla. It appears that Torrejón, when captured, was about proceeding to San Andres, to join the forces in that place, and march thence to Orizaba. Pursuing his course towards the city, the colonel, upon entering the Pinal, perceived a party of guerrillas on both sides of the road, but was not attacked. On the 10th—that is the day before yesterday—near the Venta de Chalco, Padre Jarauta was seen with some 200 guerrillas.

A few days since, Gen. Joseph Lane went out some six or eight miles from the city, when a guerrilla party endeavored to pay their respects to him, but they "couldn't come it, quite."[9] Several other parties have been seen in this vicinity lately, and Padre Jarauta is known to be about. Col. Jack Hays and his command have been out two days, and have not yet returned. His attention

7. An officer since about 1816, Anastasio Torrejón commanded a cavalry brigade on the United States border in 1846. On April 25 his force encountered a reconnaissance under Captain Seth Thornton of General Taylor's army on what was claimed as United States territory. Heavily outnumbered, Thornton was forced to surrender, news of which propelled the United States to a declaration of war. Torrejón would perform with dubious ability at Palo Alto, Monterrey, and Buena Vista. Joining the army arrayed against General Scott, his troops fought better at Contreras and at the gates of Mexico City. Torrejón remained in the Mexican army, rose to become a prominent general, and died about 1861. Tucker, *Encyclopedia*, 657–58.

8. After Mexico gained its independence, José Miñon rose to become a general of brigade, but failed to carry out Santa Anna's battle plan at Buena Vista. Arrested for his supposed incompetence, Miñon fought back in the press and blamed his commander for the defeat. He remained in the army, supported Archduke Maximilian during the French occupation, and died shortly after his retirement in 1878. Tucker, *Encyclopedia*, 431.

9. Joseph Lane resigned from the Indiana legislature to act as colonel of the 2d Indiana, but, as an outspoken Democrat, he quickly received a promotion to brigadier general of Volunteers. He commanded a brigade at Buena Vista, but his unit's behavior reflecfted badly on his leadership. Missing the fighting under General Scott, Lane was relegated to countering guerrillas on the army's supply line between Vera Cruz and Mexico City, his service resulting in a brevet to major general. Lane later served in the Senate and House of Representatives, but his pro-slavery stance doomed further political success and he died quietly on April 19, 1881. Tucker, *Encyclopedia*, 350–52.

is especially directed to the venerable priest. Woe be to him if Jack strolls across him.

A conspiracy has been set on foot, in Puebla, to assassinate the Mexican Governor of the State of Puebla, Don Raphael Izunsa, by Gen. Rea and some of his worthy associates. Their letters were intercepted by Col. Childs, from which it appears that their first object was to get Gov. Izunsa out of the way, by assassination, and then murder some of the peaceably disposed inhabitants of Puebla, seize the reins of government, and proclaim Rea dictator. Gov. Izunsa is known to be a strong advocate of peace. The project, nipped in the bud, has caused the following proclamation to be issued by Col. Childs, the American Civil Governor and Military Commandant of that department:

Headquarters, Dep't of Puebla,
Puebla, Jan. 5, 1848.

Proclamation—Whereas, a diabolical and bloody correspondence has been detected between Don Manuel Perez, and other (as yet unknown) citizens of Puebla, with a person called Gen. Rea, a guerrilla chief, in which the said Perez and his confederates recommend the assassination of the person who styles himself the governor of the State of Puebla, as well as many of the peaceably disposed citizens, in order to "strike terror in to the whole community," and then for the said Rea to pronounce against the State and General Government, and declare himself Dictator: this is to give notice to the inhabitants of the city of Puebla, that so long as the troops of the United States of North America shall hold military possession of the city, and Mexican, or other person, not owing allegiance to the United States, corresponding with known *guerrilieros*, or with any organized military body, in arms against the forces of the United States, will be considered in the light of spies, and any attempt to furnish such armed bodies with supplies of any kind, will be deemed as a violation of good faith, and persons thus detected, will be regarded as in open hostility against the forces of the United States, and treated accordingly. Citizens remaining in the city of Puebla during its military occupation by the United States troops, enjoying protection of person and property, tacitly acknowledge such military authority, and any aid of theirs compromising their neutrality is, by the laws of war, severely punished.

Thomas Childs, Col., U.S.A.
Civil and Military Governor

January 13, 1848. City of Mexico.

The City of Mexico is rife with rumors in reference to peace; some have it that peace is made, others have it that commissioners have gone on to Washington, &c., &c., and thus we have it up and down every day—peace and war alternately. Believe nothing you hear from this city at the present time on this subject, for I assure you no one, unless it is Gen. Scott or Mr. Trist, knows anything more about it than "the man in the moon." And these gentlemen are exceedingly cautious in everything relating to the movements in the army, and everything connected with it. The nearest that I can come to the present state of affairs, is from my correspondent at Querétaro, who informs me that there has been no treaty concluded, but he adds: "The whole subject rests with the United States—the Government of Mexico is willing to make a treaty, and are prepared, and are strong enough to sustain it." Many of the most influential men in the Republic, who have heretofore been violently opposed to making a treaty, are now advocating it vigorously. Those persons, who formerly belonged to the army and have been discarded by the government, are perfectly prostrate, their influence is nothing on either side of the scale. The Congress had not yet met at Querétaro at the latest dates, but it was expected there would be a new meeting by the 15th or 20th inst.

The brigade of Col. Riley is still at Tacubaya, and the brigade of Gen. Cushing at San Angel. No movement of troops for San Luis can take place before the 1st of February, even if Gen. Scott most ardently desired it. The command, before it starts from here, must be fully appointed for five or six months, as it will take that time at least before they would be able to make a road from San Luis to Tampico, by which they would be enabled to bring supplies from the latter place. At present they are without one of the most necessary articles, clothing, for such an expedition. Gen. Scott has sent twice to Vera Cruz for it, and both times has received a very meagre supply, therefore he has had to resort to one of the poorest means of procuring it—having it made here. Capt. McKinstry, of the Quartermaster's Department, has now about 1,000 men and women engaged in making clothing for the soldiers, and I understand they will be at least until the 1st of February before a sufficient quantity will be ready. It is a very easy matter to move armies on paper, but more difficult in the field.

P.S.—11 O'clock—Col. Jack Hays has returned. He routed Padre Jarauta from one of his dens, killing some ten or twelve of his men and wounding about fifteen others. One of the men shot at the Padre, whether they killed him I am not informed, but they

Diplomat Nicholas Trist. *Courtesy New York Public Library*.

brought in his horse, saddle and bridle, and cloak and other trinkets belonging to the Reverend Father.

We have received the intelligence of the attack on Col. Dixon S. Miles' train, and are sorry to learn that the fine company of Mounted Rifles has been cut up.[10] We suppose it to be Capt. Ruff,

10. A graduate of West Point in 1824, Dixon Miles had become a captain in 1836 and won a brevet to major for his defense of Fort Brown during the first days of the Mexican War and a brevet to lieutenant colonel for Monterrey. Promoted to major of the 5th Infantry in 1847, he reached the rank of colonel of the 2d Infantry in 1859 after service on the western frontier. Ordered to cover the retreat after

as we do not know of any company of Mounted Rifles down there except his. The gallantry of Capt. Ruff and his company in several of the most important battles in this country has been severely tested, and always highly distinguished themselves. If the Mexicans did, as we are informed, "cut him up," you may rest assured they had a dear bargain of it. No men in the service use all their arms better than this company.

Yesterday the Police Guard discovered about a wagon load of muskets concealed in a convent in this city.

Mr. Trist does not go home with the train going down to-morrow.

The gallant Capt. Walker, of the 6th Infantry, so severely wounded at El Molino del Rey, will be sent down; he goes in a litter, still being too weak to travel otherwise.

January 13, 1848. City of Mexico.

The following is the proceedings of a meeting of the "Aztec Club," in reference to the demise of Capt. Irwin:

> The members of this Club have received with deep regret the intelligence of the death of Captain James R. Irwin, whose loss as a friend, comrade, and Vice President, they sincerely mourn. Associated with them in the late interesting operations of this army, they have witnessed with admiration his energy as an officer, his benevolence as a man, and his bravery as a soldier. Filling the high post of Chief of the Quartermaster's Department, he has neither shrunk from responsibility or labor in the discharge of his duties, and has looked with equal care to the claims of the individual as to the interests of the Government. Having escaped the perils of battle, his sudden and unexpected death gives poignancy to our grief, while it forever extinguishes the pleasing anticipations of a long intercourse in future years, and better times with one whom we regarded as an honor to his comrades and a delight to his friends. Be it therefore
>
> *Resolved*, 1st. That we deeply deplore the death of Capt. James R. Irwin, 2d Vice President of the Aztec Club, who, cut off in the prime of life, and in a sphere of usefulness, has rendered his loss a public calamity.
>
> 2d. That we sincerely appreciate the manly and noble qualities, the high toned character (public and private), the good sense, the uncompromising integrity and honor, which ever adorned the deceased.

---

the Union army was defeated at Bull Run, Miles was charged with drunkenness and sent off to garrison Harpers Ferry. At the capture of that post by Confederates on September 16, 1862, he was mortally wounded and died that same day. *Brooklyn Daily Eagle*, September 17, 1862.

3[d]. That the Aztec Club will attend the funeral of the late Capt. Irwin as a body.

4th. That as a mark of the high regard for him while living, and their deep felt regret at his death, the Aztec Club will wear crape on their sword hilts for the period of 30 days.

5th. That the Secretary of the Aztec Club write a letter of condolence to the relatives of Capt. Irwin, and enclose a copy of the foregoing resolutions, tendering them all the sympathy and kind feeling of this Club, in this, their melancholy bereavement.

6th. That the Aztec Club now adjourn.

By order, Henry Coppee, Sec'y A.C.

Undated.

[The following continuation of the deaths in the General Hospital in the City of Mexico was accidentally mislaid. *Eds. Delta*]

Priv. Farrel	Priv. Richardson
Priv. Johnson	Sergt. Maxwell
Priv. Duncan	Priv. Steele
Priv. Lewis	Priv. David Nillock
Capt. Pearson	Priv. Moses D. Day
Priv. Nelly	Priv. D.W.Craig
Priv. Heland	Priv. T. Halsey
Priv. McKenne	Priv. Boerum
Priv. Elwood	Priv. Horton
Priv. Horton	Priv. William Cornell
Priv. Haskvil	Priv. Mullins

Some of these names may have been reported before, as I have sent you once an incomplete list. This includes all who have died of disease and wounds since the 1st of October.

I have not as yet been able to get the list of deaths for the balance of the army for the month of December, but will endeavor to do so by the next time I send. The army is so scattered at present, that it is a difficult job to gather the whole before the middle of next month.

I have been endeavoring to collect some data in reference to different corps of the army and their operations in Mexico, not that it will be very interesting to the general reader, but it will be a good reference in times hereafter, and may, in some degree, assist those persons whose shall be the glorious task of writing a history of the war with Mexico. I will, from time to time, as I am able to collect them, forward them to you.

Second Dragoons

Col. Wm. S. Harney—Left Puebla in command of the Cavalry Brigade on the 7th August—present with his brigade at the field of Contreras on the 19th; on the 20th, pursued the retreating enemy, from Churubusco, on the causeway leading to the gate of San Antonio—came on the field of battle near the close of the engagement of Molino del Rey, but did not command—in command of the depot at Miscoac from the 10 to the 15th September.

Maj. E.V. Sumner—Left Puebla August 7, 1847, in command of the 2d Regiment of Dragoons—held in reserve at Contreras, August 19th—placed in command of the Regiment of Rifles, and ordered to support the left of our line at Churubusco, on the 20th of August—commanded the cavalry in the battle of Molino del Rey on the 8th of September; on the 12th, covered the left of Gen. Pillow's division during the bombardment of Chapultepec; on the 13th, ordered to report to Gen. Quitman with his command—subsequently ordered to report to Gen. Worth, and by him ordered to cover our left until Chapultepec was carried, then ordered to join him in his advance upon the city, and afterwards ordered by the General-in-Chief to return and protect the depot at Tacubaya; on the 14th, escorted the General-in-Chief into the City of Mexico with three squadrons—horse shot under him at Molino del Rey.

Capt. G.A.H. Blake—Left Puebla on the 7th August—held in reserve on the 19th August at Contreras, engaged in escorting the prisoners from Contreras, on the 20th; on the same day came promptly to the assistance of Capt. Hardee, when attacked on the San Augustin road—engaged with the enemy at Molino del Rey on the 8th September—present with his regiment on the 12th, 13th, and 14th September—horse shot under him on the 8th September. [Whenever it is remarked that an officer was present with his regiment on the 12th, 13th, and 14th September, reference is required to the remarks under the name of Maj. Sumner for information.]

Capt. Croghan Ker—Left Puebla on the 7th August—held in reserve on the 19th at Contreras; on the 20th August, was present at the rout from Contreras—pursued the enemy to Churubusco and afterwards towards the gate of San Antonio—engaged with the enemy at Molino del Rey on the 8th September; severely wounded and horse shot under him, both on the same day.

Capt. S.B. Thornton—Left Puebla on the 7th August—shot dead while reconnoitring the enemy's works at San Antonio on the 18th August.

Capt. W.J. Hardee—Left Puebla on the 7th August—held in reserve at Contreras on the 19th; on the 20th, posted on the San Augustin road to watch the enemy; while in this position was attacked by a band of guerrillas—promptly repulsed them before the arrival of succor and captured thirty or forty of the enemy's horses with arms and accoutrements—engaged with the enemy at Molino del Rey—present with his regiment on the 12th, 13th, and 14th September.

Capt. H.W. Merrill—Left Puebla on the 7th August—held in reserve on the 19th August at Contreras; on the 20th engaged escorting prisoners from Contreras—came promptly to the assistance of Capt. Hardee when attacked on the San

Augustin road on the same day—engaged with the enemy at Molino del Rey on the 8th September—present with his regiment on the 12th, 13th, and 14th September—horse shot under him on the 8th September—struck with a fragment from a shell on the 13th September—clothes pierced by three balls on the 14th September in the streets of Mexico.

Capt. H.H. Sibley—Left Puebla on the 7th August—held in reserve on the 19th August at Contreras; on the 20th pursued the enemy from Contreras—held in reserve near the General-in-Chief at Churubusco—sent afterwards to reinforce our left flank—engaged with the enemy at Molino del Rey—present with his regiment on the 12th, 13th, and 14th September—horse shot under him on the 8th September.

1st Lieut. Wm. Steele—Left Puebla on the 7th August as A.A.A.G. to the Cavalry Brigade—present at Contreras on the 19th August– pursued the enemy down the causeway leading to the gate of San Antonio on the 20th—came on the field of Molino del Rey towards the close of the engagement on the 8th September—with his chief at Miscoac from the 10th to the 16th September.

2d Lieut. R.H. Anderson—Left Puebla on the 7th August—present with his regiment at Contreras on the 19th August—posted with Capt. Hardee on the San Augustin road on the 20th; materially aided in repelling an attack of guerrillas on that occasion—engaged with the enemy at Molino del Rey on the 8th September—present with his regiment on the 12th, 13th, and 14th September.

2d Lieut. J.Y. Bicknell—Left Puebla on the 7th August—present with his regiment at Contreras on the 19th August—pursued the enemy from Contreras to Churubusco—detached to the General-in-Chief to ask for reinforcements; returned too late to join in the pursuit at the San Antonio gate—engaged with the enemy at Molino del Rey on the 8th September—present with his regiment on the 12th, 13th, and 14th September—engaged with the enemy in the streets of the city on the latter day—horse shot under him on the 8th September at Molino del Rey.

2d Lieut. J.M. Hawes—Left Puebla on the 7th August—with his regiment at Contreras on the 19th August—held in reserve at San Augustin on the 20th of the same month—engaged with the enemy at Molino del Rey on the 8th September—present with his regiment on the 12th, 13th, and 14th September—horse shot under him on the 8th September.

2d Lieut. T.F. Castor—Left Puebla on the 7th August—present with his company on the 19th August at Contreras—engaged in guarding prisoners on the 20th—came promptly to the assistance of Capt. Hardee on the same day—engaged with the enemy at Molino del Rey on the 8th September—present with his regiment on the 12th, 13th, and 14th September.

2d Lieut. A.D. Tree—Left Puebla on the 7th August as Regimental Quartermaster—present with his regiment at Contreras on the 19th August—remained at San Augustin on the 20th—engaged with the enemy at Molino del Rey on the 8th September—wounded same day, and horse shot under him.

2d Lieut. J. Oakes—Left Puebla on the 7th August as Acting Adjutant—was present with his regiment at Contreras on the 19th August—was at Churubusco on the 20th—engaged with the enemy at Molino del Rey on the 8th September—present with his regiment on the 12th, 13th, and 14th September—horse shot under him on the 8th.

2d Lieut. W.D. Smith—Left Puebla on the 7th August—present with his regiment at Contreras on the 19th—at Churubusco on the 20th—engaged with the enemy at Molino del Rey on the 8th September—present with his regiment on the 12th, 13th, and 14th September—horse shot under him on the 8th.

Signed, W.J. Hardee, Capt. 2d Dragoons, Commanding.

List of Casualties in the 4th U.S. Infantry, Including Those Officers Who Belonged To It On Their First Entry Into Service, Commencing In July, 1845, When The Regiment Was Ordered Into Texas

Josiah H. Vose, Col., died at New Orleans Barracks, July 15, 1845, en route to Texas.

John Garland, Bvt. Col., severely wounded at the City of Mexico, September 14, 1847.

William M. Graham, Lieut. Col., killed at Molino del Rey, September 8, 1847 (promoted to 11th Infantry).

William W. Lear, Maj., mortally wounded at Monterey, September 21, 1846 (promoted to 3d Infantry).

John Page, Capt., mortally wounded at Palo Alto, May 8, 1846.

Collinson R. Gates, Capt., severely wounded at Resaca de la Palma, May 9, 1846 (transferred to 8th Infantry).

George Lincoln, Capt., killed at Buena Vista, February 23, 1847 (transferred to 8th Infantry).

Henry Prince, 1st Lieut., severely wounded at Molino del Rey, September 8, 1847.

Charles Hoskins, 1st Lieut, killed at Monterey, September 21, 1846.

Richard H. Graham, 2d Lieut., mortally wounded at Monterey, September 21, 1846.

Richard E. Cochrane, 2d Lieut., killed at Resaca de la Palma, May 9, 1846.

Theodoric H. Porter, 2d Lieut., killed on the Rio Grande (sixteen miles from Matamoros, while on a scouting expedition), April 19, 1846.

Sidney Smith, 1st Lieut., mortally wounded at the City of Mexico, September 14, 1847 (slightly wounded at Molino del Rey).

Thaddeus Higgins, 2d Lieut., killed on steamer *Dayton* (by explosion of boiler, while on board on duty), September 12, 1845.

Henderson Ridgely, 1st Lieut., killed near Matamoros [November 24, 1847].

Benjamin A. Berry, 2d Lieut., killed on steamer *Dayton* (by explosion of boiler, while on board on duty), September 12, 1845.

Allen H. Norton, 1st Lieut., drowned [November 27, 1846].

John D. Clark, 1st Lieut., severely wounded at Molino del Rey, September 8, 1847 (promoted to 8th Infantry).

James Longstreet, 1st Lieut., severely wounded at Chapultepec, September 13, 1847 (promoted to 8th Infantry).

Edmunds B. Holloway, 2d Lieut., severely wounded at Churubusco, August 20, 1847 (promoted to 8th Infantry).

Robert Hazlitt, 2d Lieut., killed at Monterey, September 21, 1846 (promoted to 3d Infantry).

James S. Woods, 2d Lieut., killed at Monterey, September 21, 1846 (breveted 1st Lieut.in 4th Infantry for gallant conduct, promoted to 2d Infantry).

John A. Richey, 2[d] Lieut., murdered at Villa Grande [January 13, 1847] (promoted to 5th Infantry).

Patrick A. Farrelly, 2[d] Lieut., severely wounded at Churubusco, August 20, 1847 (promoted to 5th Infantry).

Abram B. Lincoln, 2[d] Lieut., severely wounded at Molino del Rey, September 8, 1847. Alexander P. Rodgers, 2[d] Lieut., killed at Chapultepec, September 13, 1847 (while leading a storming party of the 4th Infantry).

Archibald B. Botts, Bvt. 2[d] Lieut., died at Camargo [January 1, 1847] (en route for Monterey).

Maurice Maloney, 2[d] Lieut., slightly wounded at San Cosme, September 13, 1847.

James Simons, Asst. Surg., slightly wounded at Molino del Rey, September 8, 1847 (while engaged in professional duties)

Recapitulation

WOUNDED—*Mortally*		KILLED—*Accidentally*	
Field Officers	1	Subalterns	3
Captains	1	*In Action*	
Subalterns	2	Field Officers	1
Severely		Captains 1	
Field Officers	1	Subalterns	7
Captains	1	*Murdered*	
Subalterns	6	Subalterns	1
Slightly		Aggregate	13
Assistant Surgeon	1	DIED—Field Officer	1
Subalterns	2	Subaltern	1
Aggregate	15		
Grand aggregate	30		

Recapitulation, Exhibiting The Casualties
In The 4th Infantry Alone

KILLED—*Accidentally*		WOUNDED—*Severely*	
Subalterns	3	Field Officers	1
In Action		Subalterns	2
Subalterns	5	*Slightly*	
Wounded—*Mortally*		Subalterns & Doctors	3
Captains	1	DIED—Field Officers	1
Subalterns	2	Subalterns	1
Aggregate	19		

NOTES. On leaving the Rio Grande, and until after the taking of the City of Mexico, there has not been a single captain of the regiment serving with his company.

Although only six companies in the field during the whole of the operations in Mexico, there have been but two officers for each company, not infrequently one to each for duty.

The 4th Infantry were at Vera Cruz and Cerro Gordo, hence, they were in every battle in Mexico or had their regiment represented by some one of their officers, as, for example, Maj. William W.S. Bliss, Capt. 4th Infantry, A.A.G., in Buena Vista; and Capt. Lincoln, Lieut. Ridgely, with Gen. Lane; and Capt. Alvord, with Maj. Lally. In nearly every obstinate engagement with the Mexicans, their officers have carried off the evidence of having been in the action, by either the dead or wounded.

Including those officers who have been promoted or transferred to other regiments, the list is really appalling—the regiment might, indeed, be styled, "The Bloody 4th."

The colors of the 4th have nineteen ball-holes through them. They have been shot down six times in the battles in the valley. A color-bearer and six color-guards are the number assigned to each stand of colors, and, during the engagements in the valley, eleven men, discharging this duty, have been killed.

January 20, 1848. City of Mexico.

We have been delighted for some time with the carollings of one of your poetic correspondents, over the signature of "Lella," and have often thought that if she looks as beautiful as she sings, she must indeed be a lovely lass. Often and again have we endeavored to conjecture who she was, but until lately have been unable to fix the person, and when, by one of her own stanzas, we made the important discovery, we said to ourself, "well done, Lella," and thought her lines still more beautiful as we placed her handsome figure in our mind's eye. Each production appeared to be an improvement on the former, and we looked for them eagerly as the *Delta* arrived, when, to our utter astonishment, in the file we received this morning, we came across the following sentence published on Christmas day:

> A merry Christmas to the *Delta*, too!
> Long live the eyes that read its columns through;
> Long may you prosper, merriest of papers,
> With Lella's humble rhymes, and Mustang's capers,
> Cut up far down in distant Mexico,
> Where bloom Señoras, and Reporters "*blow*."

Here we find that "Lella," not only like the sweet-toned songsters of the forest, singing for their own pastime and amusement, and charming all nature with their carollings, but while in the same sentence she carries out a finished and delicate compliment to the *Delta*, and modestly yields her "humble rhymes" for the prosperity of the "merriest of papers," she "cuts up" "Mustang's capers" most unmercifully, and this is the "unkindest *cut* of all." Why, "Lella!" who can help it, if "far down in distant Mexico" there "bloom Señoras"—if they smile bewitchingly—if they dazzle our eyes enticingly—if they sing delightfully, and yield to courting easily! Nature so intended it, besides, "what's the use in being proud because one's a little bit handsome?" And do not the fair daughters of our own happy land bud, bloom, and ripen into stately and fascinating womanhood, with sparkling eyes, and pretty faces, and still prettier and more graceful figures? And as for *blowing*, why "Lella" should have known that it is our special business; we not only have to *blow* for ourself, but we have to *blow* for the whole gallant army, who are gathering flowers and evergreens to entwine in beautiful wreaths around the brows of their loving wives and sweethearts, on their return from "the wars." We have to *blow* for the chivalric chiefs who have led them on from victory to victory with honor and glory, and last, though not least, God bless the fair damsel, we *will blow* for "Lella" herself, if she will but give us half a chance. But stop—if we said anything more, we might run the risk of disturbing the equilibrium of the lady's temper, which we would not do for the world. However, if, perchance, an unwilling frown should steal over her fair forehead, and a little temper affect those dancing blue eyes, and prompt her to give us another "back-handed *blow*," then you may set down your correspondent as a miserable "Mustang."

I have been intending for some time, to relate to you an incident of the battle of Contreras, which more truly illustrates the character of Col. Riley, who commanded the assault, than anything that has occurred during the war. You will recollect that the difficult and almost impassable nature of the ground over which the troops had to pass in order to get at the rear of the enemy's work, delayed them much longer than was anticipated. The object was to get into position from whence they were to assault unperceived, so that they might surprise the enemy. By the time the advanced troops were formed, "grey day" peeped over the mountains, and fears were entertained by some that the movement on the fort perceived was hazardous. Accordingly, a young officer stepped up to the "Old Sinner," as we familiarly call him, and said, "Colonel, I am afraid we are too late. It is perfectly light. The enemy have discovered us. They will annihilate the whole command if we approach down this smooth gradual descent." "I don't care a damn," replied the old soldier. "I have Gen. Smith's order in my pocket," and suiting the action to the word, taking his sword in his left hand, commanded,

"Quick time—*charge!*"—and remarked to his men, "Now, my brave fellows, give them hell! Let the bayonet do its work!" It acted like a charm upon the men, who, promptly supported by Gen. Cadwalader with his command, swept the enemy's works like a hurricane. As soon as the fortification was carried, he very coolly remarked to the young officer, "Sir, the first duty of a soldier is to obey orders." This strict observance of the first military principle, carried out the beautifully conceived plan of Gen. Smith, and secured the most brilliant victory of the war.

A few days since, we had a touch of an earthquake again, but this last one was no *great shakes*.

Chapter 8

Waiting for Peace

March 17, 1848. City of Mexico[1]

I arrived here yesterday. I found, on my arrival, that the Court of Inquiry had been in session two days. I enclose to you a sketch of the proceedings from the *Star* and *American*, and also the report of your correspondent. To-day the court has adjourned over to Monday next. I will endeavor to be present then and prepare for you a succinct account of the proceedings, as they progress. I have some remarks to make upon the course of the Government in this affair. It is the opinion of many persons that the course adopted by the Government at Washington, in reference to the difficulties in the army, has not been solely with the view of dealing out justice to all the parties concerned. Time and an examination of the documents will develop the true state of the case, and I shall not be surprised if the sequel proves that our "wise men at Washington" are gifted with a little more cunning than good sense. As yet, there are more things to be brought forward that are "decidedly rich,"

1. Freaner resumes his dispatches here after after taking time off from reporting to carry the peace treaty to Washington DC. For more details consult the first chapter.

and those who are facetiously gifted will have a fine opportunity for the exercise of their talents.

The health of the army has somewhat improved during the last two weeks.

There are fifty members of Congress, at present, at Querétaro, there are fifteen at this place who will leave on Monday for the seat of government. There has been an order issued by the Mexican Government for the holding the elections in the States from which no delegates have been elected. I hear not a doubt expressed among the Mexicans in reference to the ratification of the treaty—I have heard several of the *Puros* party say that they would vote for the ratification, and if possible, put an end to the war. I am of opinion that the vote in favor of ratifying the treaty will be a very strong one. If the treaty should come back from the United States amended, there will, probably, be a good deal of debate and delay.

I wrote to you some time ago that a delegation from a party of brokers, shavers, and broken-down politicians, had gone from here to Washington, for the purpose of preventing, if possible, our Government acceding to any terms, and bring about a military occupation of the whole country. These persons have in view their own interest without regard to what may be the interest of the United States, they want to better their own political and pecuniary fortunes without caring who suffers.

March 19, 1848. City of Mexico.

It is generally believed to-day the Court of Inquiry will adjourn to-morrow without trying the case of Gen. Pillow upon its merits, Gen. Scott having refused to prosecute, before the present tribunal, unless required to do so.

Gen. Scott and Mr. Trist will start for the United States about the 25th inst., with an escort of cavalry for Vera Cruz.

Yesterday, all business was suspended in the army, in conformity to the order of the President of the United States, on account of the death of Mr. John Quincy Adams. At the dawn of day, the colors were hoisted at half mast, the light battery of Capt. Taylor fired a salute, in the Grand Plaza, and continued to fire half-hour guns during the day, and at sundown another salute. At 9 o'clock, the army was paraded, and the orders of the President read.

From present appearances, I have no doubt but that the Mexican Congress will ratify the treaty, as soon as they hear that it will meet the approbation of the United States Senate.

Chihuahua—An express reached Querétaro, on the 13th, bringing the news that the Americans were within three days march with the object of occupying that capital.

Santa Anna will not leave by this packet. A party of Americans have advanced from Real del Monte upon Marapil to collect contributions.

You will be able to hear from me three times a week, in a few days since, as the "Dilgences" will soon commence running to Vera Cruz.

March 22, 1848. City of Mexico.

We have the melancholy duty to perform of recording the death of Capt. John Squires, Company B, 4th Kentucky Volunteers, of typhoid fever. His remains were followed to the grave by his regiment, many officers of the army, together with the General-in-Chief and his staff. His death is regretted by a large list of warm personal friends, and he was known in life to be one of the first officers of his rank in the Volunteer Corps, as well as a high-toned gentleman, kind and generous in his intercourse with mankind.

To-day the Court of Inquiry has taken a different course from what was expected a few days since, therefore Gen. Scott will not return home as soon as was expected.

Mr. Trist has been arrested by Gen. Butler, and required to leave the Headquarters of the Army, in accordance, I presume, with orders from the President through his Secretary. He will not, however, probably leave immediately, as he is a witness before the Court of Inquiry, now sitting here. This is a singular state of affairs. The President says he recalled Mr. Trist, after this, Mr. Trist makes a treaty, which the President accepts, and lays before the Senate, and recommends its adoption, with a slight modification, then has his Commissioner arrested and sent out of the country with an armed force. When will the wonders cease? How will the historian be guided in his record?

We are all anxiously awaiting the action of the United States Senate on the treaty. If it should come back ratified by the United States, it will be immediately ratified by the Mexicans. If it is amended, no doubt there will be some delay and debate in the Mexican Congress, which is ready to convene as soon as they hear the action of the United States Senate. Some of the most radical *Puros*, or democrats, in the Republic have come to the support of the Mexican Government in the course they have pursued in concluding a treaty, and their efforts to restore peace and tranquility. God send that our gallant army will be able to leave the country before the *vomito* assumes the character of an epidemic on the coast.

An escort and mail will leave this city for Vera Cruz on the 23[d] inst., when you will receive duplicates of the proceedings of the Court of Inquiry.

The health of the army has somewhat improved, although I saw six corpses pass along the street to-day, followed by an escort.

The police of this city is good, no disorders or improper conduct occurring.

March 28, 1848. City of Mexico.

Having been particularly engaged during the past week, I have not given you the news and prospects, in relation to Mexican affairs, as full as I desired. It is impossible to form a precise opinion as to what will be the action of the Mexican Congress on the treaty, until we hear what has been its fate in the Senate of the United States. If, in the latter body, it should meet with no other modification than the section in reference to the *Empresario grants*, I am convinced, from all I can learn, and my sources of information are good, that that modification will be acceded to by the Congress, although possibly it may cause a delay, which will prevent our troops from reaching the coast before the *vomito* becomes an epidemic. However, a great deal depends upon the person whom our Government may send here as Commissioner, or agent, to conclude the negotiations already entered into, for I take it for granted, that no further powers will be vested in Mr. Trist, since his arrest by order of the Government at home. If our government should see proper to vest this authority in some of the ablest officers of our army, already here, or some such gentleman as Gen. Pierce, of New Hampshire, or Gen. Shields, who is well acquainted with the Mexican character, and their manner of doing business, and at the same time a person of practicable talent and masterly ability, then there may be a probability of our army passing the range of the *vomito*, before it becomes very dangerous.

During the past week, this city has been rife with reports of a revolution in San Luis Potosi, Guanajuato, Guadalajara, and Zacatecas. No opportunities have been lost by the speculators, shavers, and persons who are pecuniarily profiting by our army remaining in Mexico, to give currency and credence to the reports set afloat. It was positively stated, that last night we would receive news affirming their assertions, and while we were all anxiously looking for the news confirming, or disavowing their statements, we learn that Señor Ramone Adame, the Governor of San Luis Potosi, has positively been arrested by the Mexican Government, and brought to Querétaro, a prisoner. From three different sources, since confirmed, we hear that they have also arrested Paredes, and placed him in close confinement, together with his few followers, who have been endeavoring to create a remonstrance against the actions of the Mexican General Government, in the northern and distant provinces, and also that the *Comandante General*, has fixed a day during the early part of next month, when Santa Anna must leave the country, or he will be made a prisoner and placed in close confinement. In accordance with this notice, Santa Anna has requested his banker in this city to place funds, subject to his order, in the West Indies. However, his friends say, it is his intention to go to Venezuela. It is also asserted at home, on information received from here, that the army is opposed to the treaty, and that they would sooner stay here forever, than to go home on such terms. This is not the fact. Since my return here, I have not seen half a dozen officers, who are not warmly in favor of, and hope that the treaty may be, adopted by our Government.

The present Government is certainly acting with more energy and determination than has ever been known in this country since the conquest by the Spaniards. Every revolutionary spirit that has thus far, either by his own designs, or the promptings of others, stood up, exciting rebellion against the powers that be, has been taken by the collar and placed in safe keeping.

All the official newspapers coming from the interior for the past week, manifest a decided determination to support the present Government, and all agree that the only salvation of Mexico depends upon an immediate peace. Some of them are lashing the revolutionists in good round terms, and contending that their only object in producing new dissensions is either for personal aggrandizement, or for the object of selling the country to a foreign power. Jalisco, which has been slow to express the sentiments of the State Government, uses the following language through the State journal, *El Republicano*: "Will a new revolution restore the public confidence—awake public enthusiasm? Will it inflame anew the fire of patriotism or change, by enchantment, the sad aspect of a society almost in complete dissolution, by the beautiful prospective of a people waking from their lethargy, and rushing with new hope and vigor to the strife, conscious of their own strength and confident of victory?" And then goes on to state, that it will certainly not, that a new revolution will be fraught with new evils, and that one evil will succeed another until the Republic will be left entirely to the mercy of the invader. Other journals from different sections are calling upon all good citizens to support the present Government, and aid it in putting an end to the evil of war, and recommending the imprisonment and severe punishment of all the deputies to Congress who shall refuse to attend the called session of Congress. *El Ingenio* from Morelia says it is "at a loss to say whether the conduct of the army in the defence of the Republic is more shameful and discreditable than that of the National Representatives at the same epoch of danger and trial." The tone of every paper which I have seen from the interior, breathes a decided tone in favor of peace, except a temporary sheet at Querétaro, got up by some of the officers of the old line of the army, who have been dismissed by the Government. Their object is to keep themselves in place in order that they may get their daily bread easier than by honest labor.

The people of San Luis Potosi, together with the subordinate officers of the Government, express the greatest satisfaction at the arrest of Paredes and his coadjutors, who have been laboring to excite remonstrance, and stating at the same time that they hoped the General Government will continue their stringent measures to restore tranquility to the country at large.

A great many slurs and base insinuations have been thrown out through the press at home and from persons here, about English stocks and English influences in the negotiation of a treaty, all wholly untrue and without any foundation whatever. The opponents of the treaty, or a peace on any terms, and the mouth-pieces of a set of factionists and shavers, who would sell their country or their souls either to the almighty dollar, still continue to cry out British influences and British interests. Has not Mr. Trist negotiated this treaty on a basis acceptable to our Government? or else why would the President recommend its adoption? The section of the treaty referring land claims in the acquired territory, was not adopted with a view to the claims of any persons, except the bona-fide citizens of Mexico. No English subject has any claim whatever in any of those territories, unless he is in the actual and peaceable possession of it, and which we would respect under any circumstances. Indeed there is a doubt, and I do not believe that there is any claim, Mexican or otherwise, which had not been forfeited previous to the time spoken of in the treaty. Is there any American who will believe that the patriotic Scott, at the head of his conquering legions, was guided in his course or controlled in his movements by British influences? or is there any American who will believe that the valiant Butler, who has before shed British blood, would be governed in carrying out the provisions of the treaty, in negotiating an armistice, if he thought there was British influence used in the negotiation, and that he was yielding the interests of *his* country for the benefit of *another*? And let me again ask if these persons who were here on the ground, and acquainted with all the circumstances of the past and the present, are not likely to know the motives and promptings of the negotiator, and the object he had in view? When Mr. Trist is thus assailed, Gens. Scott and Butler are assailed, the American army is assailed, and the honor and fame of our nation comes in for a large share of the disgrace, if any there be. But more of this anon. I intend hereafter to refer to this subject, and I pledge myself to show, clearly, and distinctly, at the *proper time*, that these slanders and libels have been originated by aspiring demagogues and pecuniary interested individuals, and that instead of their promulgation of them being governed by a patriotic impulse, they have given currency and circulation to them with a sordid interest, or governed by a most inveterate personal hatred and unjustifiable ambition.

March 29, 1848. City of Mexico.

On Saturday next, the 1st of next month, will commence the first regular meeting of the Peñon Jockey Club. Three days fine sport is anticipated, as many good 'uns are being fixed up for the occasion—several fine stables of American stock will be "all right," together with a few cracking ones belonging to foreigners and Mexicans, expected to be "wide awake and full of fleas." I will be there of course, and although not much of a sportsman, will endeavor to furnish you an account of the progress and results. Don't you think the Mexicans are advancing in civilization?

We have accounts from our different posts at Toluca, Real del Monte, and Cuernavaca. There is nothing very instructing or important from them, except that the health of our troops is improving. No doubt the prospect of peace and the idea of going home has some effect on the sick.

Mr. Trist is still here, being detained on account of being a witness on the Court of Inquiry, there is no telling now when he will be able to go, perhaps next fall—he may get away from here previous to the rage of the *vomito* on the coast. The Court, however, is "in for the balance of the season."

April 5, 1848. City of Mexico.

As I informed you in my last, the news of the ratification arrived here on Saturday last, and Maj. Graham with the despatches arrived on Sunday night. Our Government at home, have some very singular ways of doing business. Every day that we delay, in case the treaty shall be ratified by both countries, may lose us the lives of hundreds of our veteran troops. What was the use of the President sending the treaty here as ratified, without authorizing someone to lay it before the Mexican Government. Still such is the fact I understand. I suppose there are to be several caucuses held in Washington before a Commissioner will be appointed, and then Mr. Ambrose H. Sevier will come here with powers for new negotiation, and prepared to conclude and exchange the ratifications.[2] If he should arrive here within a reasonable time, and then lay the treaty, as ratified by our Senate, before the Mexican

2. Ambrose Sevier became a territorial representative to Congress from Arkansas and served from 1828 to 1836. Elected to the U.S. Senate that same year, he served until 1848, becoming an outspoken expansionist and strong supporter of President Polk. In mid-summer of 1848 Sevier resigned his Senate seat to go to Mexico and iron out details of the peace treaty. Becoming seriously ill, Sevier came home, lost a race to regain his Senate seat, and died on December 31, 1848. Tucker, *Encyclopedia*, 604.

Government, it will probably be ratified by the Mexican Congress. Such is the opinion of the friends of peace among the Mexicans, as well as the well informed of our own people, although I must confess I am not sanguine myself, that such will be the result, and if we pretend to open further negotiations for the arrangement of the article stricken out by the Senate, and those altered, I have but slight hopes that any good will result, or that we will eventually succeed in consummating the treaty. In reference to the ratification of the treaty, by the Mexican Congress, no difficulty will arise about the section in reference to claims of land in Texas or the acquired territory, if unconnected with any other point. But taking this in connection with the alteration of the mode of payment, they may hesitate.

I do not think the Senate has acted for the interest of our own country, by the manner of adopting the mode of paying the $15,000,000—and for this reason—Mexico, at present, lies prostrate, by the natural course of war, which could not have been averted. We have, to a great extent, destroyed her commerce, devastated her fields, broken up the trade of her interior towns and cities, and impoverished her people. When we leave, her authorities or Government, will have to come back to this city, and assume the reins of power, without any sources of revenue, or means of support, except what we leave them, while at the same time their current expenses will not be reduced from what they formerly were, but rather, if anything, increased. They will not only have to re-organize their army on a new and different basis for the support of Government, against any internal dissensions which may be brought about by any of the disappointed aspirants, but the whole system of government must be set in motion, all of which will be an extraordinary expense, and must be met by cash in hand. Therefore I am fearful the mode of payment by us adopted, will present a new obstacle, as the Government would sooner fall before, than after concluding the treaty, as they could then place the failure on some reasonable ground, whereas, after, they would have no excuse whatever. If we had agreed to pay them $6,000,000, and the balance in annual installments, it would have been more to our interest, but as I said above, I am fearful the $3,000,000, with the revenue they will receive, will not be sufficient to see them through the first year's expenses, with a stable government.

We have advices from our correspondent at Querétaro to the 3[d] inst. By them I learn that there was a quorum of Congress then, and that there will be a meeting in the course of this week. Added to this number, there were nine left this city on Sunday last. I also learn that the Government was in high spirits at the prospect of peace. They had not then received the ratification of the treaty, but supposed it would be ratified by the United States Senate, with the exception of the section in reference to land claims. At that date there was no opposition to the treaty in the Mexican Senate, and very little in the House of Deputies.

We have dates from Chihuahua to the 20th ult., Durango to the 23[d], San Luis to the 29th, and Zacatecas to the 26th. The news is unimportant unless the approach of our army from the North, and their engagements with the Mexicans, be true. From all directions, the people, as well as the State Governments, breathe a spirit of peace, and all express a determination to support the present Government.

April 7, 1848. City of Mexico.

One of the most daring outrages ever attempted or committed in this city, was perpetrated on the morning of the 6th, between 3 and 4 o'clock, in which one of the parties defending his household was killed by a pistol shot. A gang of thieves made an effort to rob the house of Messrs. Murrill Brothers. It is well known that the proprietors of this building have large amounts of money on hand, and I understand they are in the habit of receiving large sums on deposit. The burglars descended from an adjoining house (a hotel known as the "Bella Union"), by means of a rope ladder. In forcing a door they alarmed the inmates of the building, who repaired to the spot from whence the alarm proceeded, and at once discovered that an effort was being made to rob the house, whereupon they fired at the burglars, wounding one of them. The fire was returned, and Señor Manuel Zorillo, a clerk of the house, was killed. A great confusion and excitement ensued, and further assistance was soon procured. One of the parties not being able to make his escape in time was arrested in the house. Yesterday, five others were arrested, on the information of the first one arrested, and there are yet some others who have made their escape. The following are the names of those arrested, and you will be surprised to learn that there were two officers connected with the nefarious and disgraceful transaction:

Jesse Armstrong (arrested in the building), discharged teamster

John Hollister (wounded by the fall), an American in search of employment

Lieut. Isaac P. Hare (wounded by pistol shot), of the 2[d] Pennsylvania Volunteers

John Laverty, gambler

Sergt. B.F. Wragg, 7th Infantry

Priv. John Wall, 7th Infantry

Lieut. Benjamin F. Dutton, Adj. of the 2[d] Pennsylvania Volunteers ever since its organization

There are some others implicated who have not yet been arrested. There are some fifteen witnesses, I understand, for the prosecution. The whole of them will be tried before a Military Commission, in the course of a few days, and if found guilty will be immediately executed on the gallows.

Several officers arrived here yesterday evening from Cuernavaca, as witnesses before the Court of Inquiry. Among them are Col. Milledge Bonham, Maj. Samuel Woods, Lieuts. Wilcox and Bryant P. Tilden.[3] From some of them I learn that a number of deaths had occurred from sore throats and influenza. This disease has prevailed and is prevailing to considerable extent at nearly all our posts in the valley, and there is a good deal of other sickness also. The Georgia Battalion of Mounted Men are represented as very sickly.

As I informed you in my last, in anticipation of the consummation of a peace, a train will start from here the latter part of next week, with all the sick and disabled of our army, which, together with those from all the posts on this line, will rendezvous at Jalapa, Encero, or in that neighborhood. In case the treaty shall be ratified,

3. After graduating from South Carolina College in 1834, Milledge Bonham acted as captain of South Carolina Volunteers in Florida. Beginning a law practice in 1837, he later served four years in the state legislature. Appointed lieutenant colonel of the 12th Infantry in 1847, Bonham was promoted to colonel the same year. Mustered out in 1848, he entered politics and served as congressman from 1857 to 1860. During the Civil War Bonham served as general of South Carolina and Confederate troops, representative in the Confederate congress, and governor of his state. He died August 27, 1890. Heitman, *Historical Register* 1: 229; *New York Herald*, August 28, 1890.

this will facilitate our movement several weeks. I understand Dr. Presley H. Craig goes down as Medical Director.

A mounted escort will also leave this place on Saturday (to-morrow) for the coast, but I do not think Don Nicholas P. Trist will go with it, as he is a witness before the Court of Inquiry, and therefore cannot leave before he tells what he knows about the questions at issue.

It is the general impression that the Court of Inquiry will get through examining all the witnesses here in the course of ten days or two weeks, and will then adjourn to the United States. I wish they were gone. You have no doubt read the proceedings with a great degree of interest; if you have not, I hope you will. The proceedings of the Court are well worth the study and attention of all military and civil lawyers. The decisions of the Court remind me of the story of a raw recruit, whom the drill sergeant could not make recollect his right hand from his left. In order to strengthen the memory of the recruit, the sergeant blacked one hand and told him that was his right hand. Then taking hold of both hands, and turning them one over another in quick succession, asked the recruit which was his right hand. "Why," replied the fellow, "you have mixed them up so, that I cannot tell t'other from which." So it is with the Court—they have got the decisions so mixed up, that I do not believe they or anyone else can tell what has been the rule carried out any two days in succession, unless it is that Gen. Scott is always wrong, and the defence always right, let the question be what it may. If precedent were law, the decisions of this Court would support an attorney in argument on any side of any question whatever.

One day Gen. Scott complains of the course of proceeding of one of his antagonists, and the Court says, "It is a matter over which they have no control." In the course of a few days, a complaint is made that Gen. Scott has done what the Court had said they could not control, and then the Court decides that it is "*indelicate and highly improper*." Put a peg there, and save the mark! Gen. Pillow asks a witness for his opinions, or the reasons for belief in a certain matter. The Court at once decides he must state it. In five minutes after, Gen. Scott asks the witness what were his opinions in reference to another matter. Objections are made, the Court is cleared, and, after some forty minutes' *wise, knowing, and very honest (?)* consultation, decide that the witness *may state the facts* which led him to *conclusions* or *opinions*, but he must not state what those opinions were. And so it has been from first to last. I have endeavored to find out what system or rule has governed this Court in their decisions, but without effect, and I am sorry to say that I look upon it as an anomaly in military jurisprudence.

However, the evidence and documents brought out in the course of the trial, show, most conclusively, the determined and deliberate effort, on the part of the Administration, to overthrow and break down Gen. Scott, to consign to infamy and disgrace the warrior chief who has accomplished the most wonderful achievement recorded on the pages of American history, and who has done all this, with the prejudices and influences of the Government at home against him, and the political aspirants in his own camp playing second fiddle to them. The private bureaus, and the confidential correspondence of the departments at Washington, have been ransacked, and every paper that could be brought to bear, directly or indirectly, on the questions at issue, have been copied and sent to the defence, in hopes to influence the decisions. Private correspondence to the military bureaus, written at a time when it was impossible to forward regular official communications from here, have been published in the *Union*, and the letters, with the names of the officers, sent to the defence, in hopes that it would prove that persons belonging to Gen. Scott's general or personal staff had written letters for publication, or that it was the practice of officers to write letters, in order that they would find their way into the public prints.

But the Administration have made a great mistake. When they aimed at the object of their destruction, they selected a gun with too small a calibre.

April 8, 1848. City of Mexico.

To-day an escort leaves for Vera Cruz, as also the mail. With the escort, Mr. Trist takes his departure from the Halls of the Montezumas. Yesterday, the prosecution and defence before the Court of Inquiry got through their examination of him. Col. William H. Emory also returns, to join his regiment at Jalapa.[4] I am exceedingly sorry

4. William Emory graduated from West Point in 1831, resigned from the army in 1836, and was reappointed in 1837. He served as adjutant general of General Kearny's column in 1846 and won two brevets fighting in California. Joining the army at Mexico City, he became lieutenant colonel of the Maryland regiment of

to see among the officers returning to the United States, Brig. Gen. Cadwalader, more particularly as he has tendered his resignation. No officer in the army has been more laborious and energetic in discharging the sanctions of his office, than Gen. Cadwalader. But at the present time, his division is scattered all over the country, until he is left with the immediate command of one squadron of dragoons, which is used to communicate with the different ports, one regiment being at Jalapa, with the remainder of the division divided between Cuernavaca, Pachuca, Lerma, and Toluca. In this state of his affairs, and having important private business to attend to at home, and also there not being a probability of any immediate active operations, Gen. Cadwalader applied for a leave of absence, which Gen. Butler could not grant under the rigid system he has adopted, whereupon, Gen. Cadwalader sent in his resignation, which Gen. Butler did not see proper to accept, but left the option of acceptance with the War Department. Therefore, Gen. Cadwalader will go to the United States, where he will meet many warm friends to greet his arrival and safe return to the "Old Keystone," after having passed through many of the hardest-fought battles in Mexico. The honors he has won belong to his state and the Union, and they may well be proud of them.

Since writing the above, I learn authentically, that Col. Withers, of the 9th Infantry, has resigned, and also some other officers of the Volunteers.

Last night, about twenty soldiers and teamsters deserted, taking with them the best horses they could lay their hands on, together with their full arms and equipments. It is supposed, with good reason, that their object is to form a *banditti* for the purpose of plundering the highway, the *haciendas*, and the churches of the small towns. We learn that there is already a band of American deserters and followers of the army, to the number of about 100, now organized and operating in this way. They may have Mexicans connected with them, for all we know. Active measures have been taken to ferret them out, but as their places of rendezvous are

---

Volunteers until mustered out. In 1849 Emory was named chief astronomer of the Boundary Commission. During the Civil War, he became a steady commander, rising to command the 19th Corps and ending the war as a major general. He retired in 1876, having authored several military works, and died on December 1, 1887. *New York Herald*, December 3, 1887.

Brevet Major General George Cadwalader. *Courtesy Library of Congress*.

in the mountains, they will be hard to break up, as a party large enough to destroy them could not move as fast as they can, and a small party they would be able to defeat, for there are some very desperate men among them.

Last evening, as the Rev. Mr. McCarty, Chaplain to the Army, was riding through one of the streets in the city, two *leperos* placed a pistol at his head and made him dismount, and then very quietly robbed him of his watch, all the money he had in his pockets, and his horse. Shortly after, Lieut. William H. French came along the same place, and they attempted the same thing with him, but with not so much success—he drew his sabre and soon extricated himself. All the persons in the neighborhood were arrested, as they must have been some of the parties or accessories or know who the persons are that committed the theft. They will be kept in prison, I expect, until further examinations are made. Verily, we are getting into a nice state of affairs, and if we are to remain much longer in this country, quietly occupying it, I should not be surprised if we will have to keep a larger army to prevent robberies and murders than it did to whip the Mexicans.

The primary elections, which took place in this State and Pachuca on Sunday last, for President, Senate, and Deputies, resulted, as they have all over the country where new elections have been held, in favor of the "Peace Party."

Our latest dates from Querétaro are to the 4th inst. The advices of that date state that there would be a meeting of Congress during the past week. We shall look for their first proceedings about the 12th inst., but their meeting will not result in anything further than an organization, until after the arrival of Mr. Sevier at this place. It will be unnecessary for them to act upon the treaty, after their having learned that it had been altered by our Senate, before they are officially informed what those alterations are. This cannot be done until after the arrival of Mr. Sevier. All parties seem to agree in the opinion that it will be ratified, and the impression continues to grow day after day. Although I have heard it from high Mexican authority, that there will not be any difficulty in its ratification, I must see some of the obstacles removed before I come to the full conclusion that such will be the result of the action of the Mexican Government, but, as I said previously, the chances are decidedly in favor of ratification.

April 13, 1848. City of Mexico.

Day before yesterday, we had the pleasure of witnessing the most brilliant military display it has ever been our fortune to look upon. Every beholder viewed it with pride and admiration, and it must have been particularly gratifying to the recipient of the distinguished honors, the Hon. Mr. Nathan Clifford, our Peace Commissioner, who arrived about 11 o'clock, having been escorted from Vera Cruz, by Capts. Fairchild's and George Ker's companies of Louisiana Horse.[5]

The troops were formed on the road outside the *garita*, and were composed of the "Cerro Gordo Division," Gen. Smith; the brigade of cavalry, Col. Thomas T. Fauntleroy; two batteries of light artillery, one under the command of Capt. F. Taylor, and the other under Lieut. French; the 3d and 4th Kentucky Volunteers, Cols. Manlius V. Thomson and John S. Williams—all under the command of Maj. Gen. Patterson, and numbering about 5,000.[6]

5. An attorney, Nathan Clifford held a series of state offices in Maine before assuming his seat as congressman in 1839. In 1846 President Polk appointed Clifford attorney general, a post he held until March of 1848 when he became a minister to Mexico. He and Senator Ambrose Sevier traveled to Mexico to work out details of the peace treaty. Sevier soon left, but Clifford remained and attempted to smooth relations between the two countries. He returned to his Maine law practice in 1849 until appointed to the Supreme Court in 1858. Clifford became head of the Electoral Commission established to determine the winner of the presidential election of 1876, Rutherford Hayes being elected along a party line vote. Justice Clifford died on July 25, 1881. Tucker, *Encyclopedia*, 150–51.

6. An attorney and newspaper editor who had been a firm supporter of Andrew Jackson, Thomas Fauntleroy received the appointment of major of the 2d Dragoons in 1836 and went off to fight Seminoles. Having been sick for many months, he became embroiled in a dispute when promoted to lieutenant of his regiment in 1847. Some thought Charles May deserved the position, but Fauntleroy was rightly May's superior and was given the job. Promoted to colonel of the 1st Dragoons in 1850, Fauntleroy resigned in 1861 to join the Confederacy. Receiving a commission as brigadier general, he was too old for field service and remained on duty in Richmond. After the war he retired to a country estate and died there on September 12, 1883. Heitman, *Historical Register* 1: 415; *Staunton Spectator*, September 4, 1883; *Richmond Enquirer*, July 5, 1847; *Baltimore Sun*, September 13, 1883.

A graduate of Transylvania University, Manlius Thomson was an attorney who has been elected lieutenant governor of Kentucky on the Whig ticket. Appointed colonel of the 3d Kentucky Volunteers, he sold his residence to the Western Military Institute prior to leaving for Mexico. Never able to regain his health after his military service, Manlius Thomson died July 22, 1850. *Lexington Leader*, May 6, 1970; *Louisville Daily Courier*, August 3, 1847; July 24, 1850.

After graduating from Oxford College, John Williams began a law practice in Kentucky. He raised a company of riflemen attached to a regiment of Regulars that performed admirably at Cerro Gordo. When his company's enlistment expired, the governor gave him a commission as colonel of the 4th Kentucky Volunteers. After a term in the state legislature, Williams was appointed to a commission to observe the Crimean War, one of his associates being George B. McClellan. After serving as a brigadier general in the Confederate army, he became a U.S. senator

Gens. Patterson and Thomas Marshall, with a squadron of cavalry, met Mr. Clifford some distance in advance on the road.[7] As they reached the right of the column, drawn up in line, a salute was fired from the battery of Lieut. French, and the cavalry band (mounted) saluted him with their flourishes, and playing "Hail Columbia," as he passed them. Next the Rifles, with their shrill, vibrating trumpets, followed likewise, and so on each regiment, until the Hon. Commissioner passed the entire line. The column then formed, and escorted him to his quarters in the city. This was an honor, of which any man or functionary in our country might well have been proud. The old "Cerro Gordo Division" never looked better, never moved with more precision, or never showed to more advantage. This, too, is the glorious division that never yet, as a body, or a regiment, company, or detachment, has been checked a single instant, by the enemy, at any point whatever, and has made the Mexicans feel the effects of its discipline and indomitable courage, throughout the whole campaign. The cavalry brigade were as clean as new pins, and as gay as peacocks in full feather. The light batteries presented, in their order and discipline, a faithful portrait of "grim visaged war," announcing in reverberating tones the arrival of a messenger of peace. The Kentuckians were "Old Kentuck" all over, and as one of their officers presented his sword in salute, I could not help thinking of his conduct at Cerro Gordo, while under a most destructive fire, rallying his command, calling out to them, "Men, do your duty! Remember 'Old Kentuck'!" They really deserve great credit for the superior state of discipline to which they have already arrived in the short time they have been in the service. Mr. Clifford, after arriving at his quarters, and the military being dismissed, went with Gen. Butler to his quarters, accompanied

---

for one term before retiring to his farm where he died on July 17, 1898. *Louisville Courier-Journal*, July 18, 1898.

7. A nephew of Supreme Court Justice John Marshall, Thomas Marshall served in the War of 1812 from Kentucky. His prominence as a Democratic politician led to his appointment as brigadier general of Volunteers in 1846. While serving in General Taylor's army, he allowed top secret orders, concerning the consolidation of Taylor's Regular troops into the army of General Scott, to be captured. After his late arrival at Buena Vista, Marshall was not given another important command. Following the war, he was murdered on his Kentucky farm on March 28, 1853. Tucker, *Encyclopedia*, 384.

by a large number of officers, apparently much gratified at the brilliant reception he received on his *entre* to the "Halls of the Montezumas," but at the same time preserving that equanimity of feeling and expression of countenance indicative of high-toned gentlemen, and one knowing and properly estimating his own abilities and position.

The Military Commission for the trial of the persons engaged in the late burglary and murder in this city, in which two officers of the 2d Pennsylvania Volunteers, Lieuts. Hare and Benjamin F. Dutton, are implicated, commenced its investigation yesterday. They had a meeting day before yesterday, and the day before, but did not proceed on account of the officer being absent, who was detailed as Judge Advocate. The following are the officers composing the Court, as at present fully organized:

Col. Manlius V. Thomson, 3d Reg't Kentucky Vol.
Col. John W. Geary,[8] 2d Pennsylvania Vol.
Lieut. Col. John W. Whitfield,[9] 3d Tennessee Vol.
Lieut. Col. Adley H. Gladden,[10] South Carolina Vol.

8. Educated at Jefferson College, John Geary received a commission as captain in the 2d Pennsylvania Volunteers, being promoted to lieutenant colonel in January of 1847 and colonel in November of that year. Disabled briefly when struck by a spent ball at Chapultepec, he led his regiment in the occupation of Mexico City. After being mustered out, Geary went west and became the first mayor of San Francisco. He was also the governor of Kansas for a year. From 1861 to 1865 Geary served in the Union army, first as colonel of the 28th Pennsylvania Volunters and then as a brigadier general in some of the most notable battles of the Civil War. After being mustered out in 1866, Geary became governor of Pennsylvania for two terms before his death on February 8, 1873. Heitman, *Historical Register* 1: 450; *Weekly National Intelligencer*, November 27, 1847; *New York Herald*, February 9, 1873.

9. John Whitfield raised a company and served with distinction as captain in the 1st Tennessee Volunteers at Monterrey and Vera Cruz. When his enlistment expired, Whitfield received the appointment of lieutenant colonel of the 3d Tennessee Volunteers in 1847. Elected to the state senate in 1849, he served four years before accepting positions out west. After being elected to three terms as congressional representative from the Kansas Territory, Whitfield moved to Texas where he raised troops for the Confederacy. Appointed brigadier general in 1863, he was wounded three times prior to his removal from field command in 1864. After the war he remained active in politics until his death on October 27, 1879. *Galveston Weekly News*, November 13, 1879.

10. Adley Gladden had gained military experience in the Second Seminole War prior to his appointment as major of the South Carolina Volunteers (Palmetto Regiment) in 1846. Promoted to lieutenant colonel, Gladden was seriously wounded during the attack on Mexico City after the fall of Chapultepec. Moving

Lieut. Col. James C. Burnham, New York Vol.
Maj. Francis L. Bowman, 1st Reg't Pennsylvania Vol.
Maj. William T. Ward, 4th Reg't Kentucky Vol.

The case is one of a very aggravated nature, and you will see that the Court organized for this special investigation, is not only composed of rank, but persons of sound discretion, judgment, and intelligence. I will report the proceedings in detail, and you will be regularly furnished with them. Whatever may be the result of the trial, justice will be religiously and strictly dealt out, and if the accused should be found guilty, they will have to undergo the sentence without regard to rank or position; if they, or any portion of them, should be found innocent, as a matter of course they will be restored to their former rank and position. There is a great deal of indignation in the army, but every person is anxious to see a fair, impartial investigation.

Tuesday morning we had a current report of the assassination of three officers by some robbers, outside the gates of the city, but a thorough investigation proved it to be a humbug.

On Sunday night there was a great alarm created in the city by a heavy fire of musketry in the suburbs of the city. It appears that a party of Mexican robbers occasionally enter the suburbs of that part of the city for the purpose of plunder, and on this evening they came in in force of 150. Meeting a patrole of the Police Guard they fired on them, the sergeant in command of the patrole (six men) was driven back some three squares, until he got good cover in a house and sent to his officer for reinforcements. The officer finding the robbers in too great force for him, asked assistance from one of the Kentucky regiments, close by, who turned out four companies. As the guard and the Kentuckians approached, the robbers fired on them, two balls taking effect on the Marines, but the distance was so great that they only produced a slight contusion. As soon as the officer of the guard got near enough, he directed six men to fire. The Kentuckians misapprehending the order, fired three or four volleys,

to New Orleans, he raised a regiment of Louisiana Volunteers and moved them to Pensacola. Promoted to brigadier general in the Confederate army, Gladden was mortally wounded at the battle of Shiloh on April 6, 1862, dying six days later. [Columbia, South Carolina] *The State*, March 22, 1914; *Washington Daily Union*, November 15, 1847.

which produced the alarm in the city. The robbers fled, leaving two of their party dead in the road.

We have received letters from Querétaro to the 9th inst. There had not yet been a quorum of the Congress, three Senators and six Deputies being absent. I am fully satisfied, from my letters, that the real cause of there not having been a quorum previous to this, is on account of their not having any official information of the action of the United States Senate on the treaty. However, I learn by my advices this evening from the interior, that the Deputies and Senators from the State of Puebla will be in Querétaro on Monday next, and those just elected from this State will set out on Monday next. This will make a quorum and some to spare, and therefore we have every reason to believe that the next week will find the Mexican Congress acting on the treaty. So far as regards its fate and the final result upon the Mexican Government, my letters inform me that but six Deputies and two Senators are opposed to its ratification, but as I stated in my former letters, much depends upon the course Mr. Clifford pursues. He has now arrived, and I am in hopes he will immediately lay his documents before the Mexican Government without talk or negotiation. I am exceedingly sorry Mr. Trist did not remain here longer. He could have exercised a stronger influence in the ratification than any person of the Government could send here, and our Government certainly made a great mistake in sending him home a prisoner, at this particular juncture.

The news received a few days since will no doubt have some effect on the action of the Mexican Congress. It will destroy all hopes of the Paredes or monarchical party.

I have established a daily communication with Querétaro and a special correspondent, well versed in Mexican affairs, at that place. I will endeavor to supply you with the latest intelligence from there, and the action of the Mexican Congress on the treaty. I shall send it through by extraordinary express, or go with it myself as far as Vera Cruz.

There is no news of importance or interest to you from the States of Chihuahua, Zacatecas, San Luis Potosi, Guanajuato, or Guadalajara. Everything appears to be quiet, except the announcement of an engagement with a small American force on the frontier. This, however, wants confirmation.

April 18, 1848. Tuesday night. City of Mexico.

Since my last there is nothing of importance in the military or political world. The Court of Inquiry is progressing steadily, and there is a prospect of its adjourning in the course of a very few days. Gen. Pillow expects to get through with his evidence to-morrow, then Gen. Scott will have a few witnesses to call, which will exhaust all the evidence then in Mexico. Then, in accordance with the former announcement, the Court will adjourn to the United States, and examine what witnesses there are there. So, if the Court and the parties are not fearful of encountering "Yellow Jack" upon the coast, you may expect to have the dignitaries with you in a short time. What a sight it will be for our citizens to look upon! Instead of our gallant old chief, who has led our arms to victory and glory, returning to his native land, honored and respected by the Government he has saved from destruction, he returns goaded and persecuted by Executive power, because he would not allow the "pet-familiars" of the President to rob the whole army of its rights, and by these means become the successor of the present occupant of the Presidential chair. Executive power may assail Gen. Scott, but they can never crush him. The country will have a voice in doing honor to those who deserve it, and they will undoubtedly honor those who merit it.

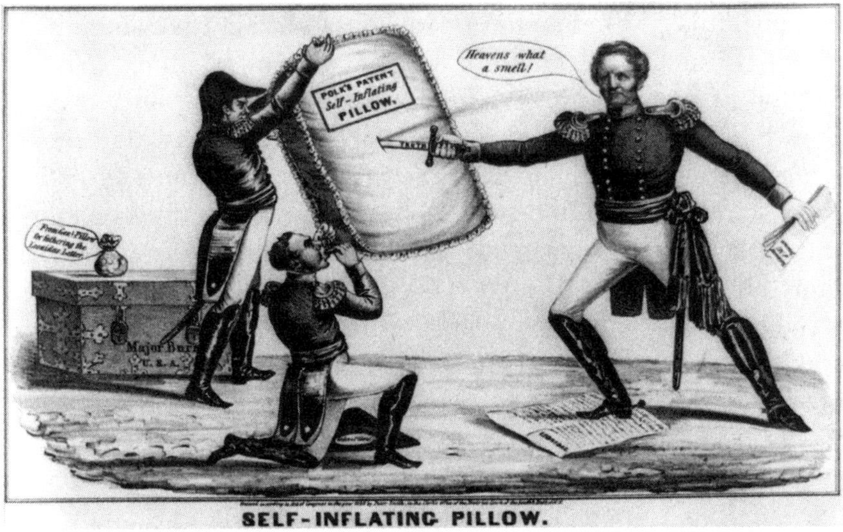

A Cartoon Ridiculing General Pillow during the Leonidas Affair. *Courtesy Library of Congress*.

The Court for the trial of Lieut. Hare is still progressing, but have not yet got through with the evidence for the prosecution.

The army is still unhealthy at some of the inferior posts, and I learn that in Cuernavaca there have been a great many deaths.

Scarcely a day passes without some daring attempt at robbery, assassination, and murder. There are now three commissions sitting for the trial of these offences, and the Lieut. Gov., Maj. Patrick H. Galt, is engaged from morning until night, examining cases of petit larceny. These revolutions of law have become so common of late that they scarcely excite curiosity enough to make people inquire who are the authors of the crime.

Politics are at a dead stand. Mr. Sevier and Mr. Clifford are here. At every corner of the town we hear they are to act with exceeding promptness and despatch, and not allow the Mexicans a chance to take second breath. But, notwithstanding Mr. Clifford was here a week and Mr. Sevier two or three days, before they thought proper to inform the Mexicans of the object of their visit. To be sure they have had several talks with a member of the Mexican Government, but Mr. Clifford was too delicate towards Mr. Sevier to open an official communication with the Mexican Government. Thus you will see that "delicacy" has more influence with our extraordinary commission than the lives of several hundreds of our brave soldiers. Is this right? But, perhaps, this gentleman has taken a lesson from the valiant hero of San Jacinto, who wanted the President to allow him "the gratification of hanging Mr. Trist on a dog-wood tree," and striking Gen. Scott's name from the muster roll of the army, and therefore was only coquetting with the Mexican Government for the purpose of feeling them. If so the Mexicans stand it very quietly and look very calmly on the scene—if there is any advantage gained by it I do not think it is on our side—the friends of peace are getting less confident every day, but eight or ten days more may change the aspect of affairs very much. I think, myself, that the chances in favor of peace have not increased in the last eight or ten days, and if we continue to talk, they will continue to decrease. The impression has been made at Querétaro, that if the Mexican Congress refuses to receive this treaty, they can negotiate on better terms, and then base their opinions on the course of our two Commissioners.

Some few days ago I thought it altogether likely there would be a meeting of the Mexican Congress on the 25th inst., but now I hardly think it probable that it will assemble before the 5th of next month, then I do not think there is much doubt of its meeting. One reason of their not assembling on the 25th is, that the present is a week of idleness, feasting, and church going with them, and it is utterly impossible to get Mexicans to do anything but enjoy themselves as best they can, on their holy days. They will sacrifice all interests, and all duty to themselves or their country, for the purpose of idling and feasting, on the days established by the Church for this purpose. Enough members have already gone from this State and Puebla, to fill the vacancies in the quorum of Congress, but, as I said before, I do not think they will meet.

During the day this city has been rife with the rumor that a courier extraordinary had arrived, from the interior, with the news that Bustamente had pronounced, in one of the Northern states, against the Government at Querétaro, and that Bustamente with 7,000 and Paredes with 8,000 men were on their march to overthrow the Government. I have endeavored to trace it to some reliable source, but have not been able to do so. I find that a courier has arrived, but he brought despatches of a different character, and I think it not unlikely that they are the instructions from the Mexican Government to their functionaries in this city, and that they had reference to the Treaty of Peace. From all that I can learn I do not think there is any reliance to be placed in the rumor set afloat, but am more inclined to the belief that the reported *pronunciamiento* has had more effect on the stock market than on the Mexican Government. However, I will receive my letters from Querétaro before I close this, and if there is any truth in it, or reason to believe that any disturbance has occurred in the north, I will have advice of it and you will be informed of it.

April 21, 1848. City of Mexico.

He is gone! and the blessings of the whole army go with him. Yesterday the Court of Inquiry adjourned to the United States, and this morning Gen. Scott set out for Vera Cruz, whence he will sail directly for New York. I have never yet seen such a sensation produced in the army, as his departure from this city caused. It really seemed like the breaking up of the "Old Homestead," and the departure of the parental head to a foreign land, leaving the unprotected household to take care of itself. Almost every man in the army so felt it. Last night, at a late hour, it became partially known that Gen. Scott would leave this morning. About 100 officers, Regular and Volunteer, gathered together for the purpose of paying him a formal visit, but his engagements prevented his seeing them. A short time afterwards, the 2[d] Infantry band appeared in front of his quarters, and serenaded him with "Hail to the Chief," "Home, Sweet Home," and "Hail, Columbia." By the time they had concluded, the street was jammed in front of his quarters, with officers and citizens, and they saluted him with nine deafening cheers, such as were never before heard in the Capital of the Montezumas.

At an early hour this morning the general left the city in a carriage, escorted by Capt. Blake's company of the 2[d] Dragoons. As he got into the coach, the street was filled by warm and sincere friends, each anxious to bid him good-bye. The old chieftain, who never yet quailed before the most formidable enemy, was so much overcome by the manifestations of warm regard, that he could but turn to the crowd and bid them, one and all, adieu. As he left his quarters, there seemed to be a simultaneous expression of "God bless you!" When he passed the guard of the Rifle Regiment, they could not restrain their tears as they came to present arms. When the feelings of soldiers, such as these, who have looked upon death, and stared it in the face with firmness and determination, who have made the heavens ring with their shouts of victory, as they made their deadly charge, are overcome by their grief, to such a degree as to cause them to shed tears, you may imagine the feeling that pervades the army in parting with their leader and noble commander. Nor did this sympathy exist only with the Rifles, but I have been told by several officers of different regiments, this evening, that many of their men had come to them with language approaching insubordination, which, if it had been countenanced for a single moment, would have so inflamed as to produce serious results. However, it was promptly dispelled by the conduct of the officers. Many officers, who were not aware of the general's departure until he had gone, mounted their horses, and followed him outside the city, to bid him good-bye. He was overtaken outside the *Peñon Garita*, and for miles along the road, crowd after crowd continued to overtake the carriage, and exchange the heart-felt words, "God bless you!"

He is gone, and he left the army as no man ever left it before, not with the formal parade and military display, with the thunder-toned artillery announcing his departure, and the long array of bright muskets saluting him as he passed, but with the unrestrained sympathy and warm regards of brave and honest men, wishing him long life and happiness, praying most fervently that the remainder of his life may be as calm and cloudless as the past has been bright, chequered, and glorious. Let us look back to the time he first entered this country, and follow him through the trying and exciting scenes. The strong Castle of San Juan de Ulua, supported by the well fortified city of Vera Cruz, fell at his command, after a desperate resistance—the heights of Cerro Gordo yielded to his science, supported by the bravery and confidence of his troops—then follow him to this valley, and view him descending the mountain from Rio Frio, at the head of his invincible legions, with all eyes and ears turned towards him with the most implicit confidence and firm reliance, each and all believing that as long as Winfield Scott lived there was "no such word as fail"—and then look back and recall to your recollection the sanguine reliance with which his gallant army followed him through the perilous times and bloody battles, until he entered the Grand Plaza of the ancient Aztecs, amidst the victorious shouts of the most noble army the world has ever known. But all this time, while he has been overthrowing the enemies of his country in front, exalting our national character, redressing our national injuries, and adorning our national history, his enemies "in the rear" have been working to tarnish his fair fame and destroy his just claims to the gratitude and admiration of his countrymen. In the very face of the enemy he had routed and defeated, and in the capital he has conquered, he has been placed in the humiliating attitude of one scrambling for justice with his inferiors, inferiors in rank, in talent, and in the high traits of character and education which make the great and successful warrior, the statesman, and the logician. And now, this day he leaves the capital of his enemies of his country, not with his victorious divisions following him to his native land, exulting in his unparalleled triumphs, but escorted by a single company of dragoons, disarmed but not dishonored.

"Truth, crushed to earth, will rise again—
The eternal years of God are hers,
But error, wounded, writhes in pain,
And dies amid her worshippers."[11]

Undated.

Good Friday in Mexico

"Black Spirits and White,
Red Spirits and Grey,
Mingle, mingle, mingle,
You that mingle may."[12]

This day (Viernes Santo), ushered in by the commencement of the last three days of Lent, and standing in sacred observance by the faithful adherents to Catholicism, has been replete with interest to the curious of the Protestant world. The sun rose, bright and beautiful, and as he cast his warms beams upon the City of the Aztecs, her dusky sons and daughters, rich and poor, old and young, arose to the religious observance of this time-honored custom, the commemoration of the Crucifixion. Sacred indeed must be that recollection of this day to the Christian world, a day that stamped with the prestige of eternal Deity the mission of Him whose blood, pure fountain, cleansed the world from sin.

The remarkable features of the day cannot pass unnoticed by the looker on. From the thousands of habitations, of the millionaire and the beggar, as the day advanced, gradually emerged, in costume strange and various, the devotees of Catholicism, the colossal faith of Rome. Never have I seen an illustration stronger pictured, with such bold relief, of the Papal sway over the minds of the entire people, than was this day presented in the unique *tout ensemble* of the celebration of *Viernes Santo*.

In various parts of the city were erected booths, after the fashion of the Toltec and Aztec *jacali*, in which assemble the Indians of unmixed blood and whose proud boast is that "not one drop of Spanish blood courses through their veins." These stalwart representatives of their ancestors, in all but their independence and religion, have travelled many miles to bear witness to their faith taught there 300 years ago by the good Las Casas.

11. William Cullen Bryant.
12. William Shakespeare.

Amid all the solemnities of the day, mirth had its place, and strange services with stranger superstitions, mingled in the crowd. There was scarcely an individual, old or young, but was provided with some illustration of what they deemed of service to the advancement of their faith and the total demolition of heresy. In the early part of the day you could hear from remote alleys and avenues an occasional rattle. One was loud—died away in the distance—when its almost inaudible r-r-r-re-re-re-e was taken up by another. As the day advanced, rattles increased, and concentered in the direction of the Grand Plaza. There was another instrument of music not unlike the croaking of a frog, mingled with the rattle. Hour after hour, from sunrise, did this strange species of music increase and become more and more distinct in character. The first may be likened to a juvenile tree toad in its maiden effort at song, another like the hoarse croaking of the bull-frog who has long reigned major general of his pond, and when he croaked other small frogs must hide under a rotten chunk. Presently something like the hooting of an owl was heard, then a chirping cricket, then the scream of the night-hawk, and the raven's croak; these served only to arouse all the frogs of intermediate grade, from Major General Bull Frog, down to Corporal Tree Toad. Towards sun-down all their forces were assembled in the Grand Plaza, which seemed but one universal frog pond, where

> Frog answer'd frog, with high and boastful croak,
> Piercing the night's shrill ear.[13]

Beauty was there; they whose dark eyes, windows of the soul, reflected love moved like spirits of some fairy world, plain to the eye, but elusive to the grasp. One, the most unfortunate, was engaged in the purchase of a monkey, a most vicious, devilish monkey, who could neither be appeased by caresses nor subdued by punishment. Thrice had he been put to bed, and as many times had he refused to remain; the fair one's patience was at length exhausted; she struck the monkey, and the monkey returned the blow, and demolished much of her finery. The main injury was the loss of her starched rumple, which fell before the destructive bombardment of this furious animal, materially changing the lady's beautiful aspect.

13. Freaner's playful rewriting of Shakespeare.

I am told that the meaning of all the rattles is this: the laymen of the church are taught to believe that they are grinding the bones of the heretics, and sure I am, that from the universal grinding power of the magnanimous Mexican people, not a whole bone is left in a single heretic, from the days of Pontius Pilate down. Heretics in miniature were appended to the rattles of the juveniles, and most incessantly did they grind their bones. There seemed to be a strange unison between heretics and jackasses, many having a heretic on one end of the rattle and a jackass on the other, by which, I suppose, they mean that heretics are no better than jackasses. The beggars begged from the people, and the priests begged from the beggars. Angels were mounted on rattles, and so was the devil. Ladies were mounted on rattles, and so were their looking-glasses. Gentlemen were mounted on rattles, and rattled after the ladies. Angels, devils, heretics, jackasses, gentlemen, and ladies rattled after each other until they were all rattled off in one highly concentrated "*rattle-ation!*"

The day closed with a grand illumination of the cathedrals. The golden images, which had been veiled during Lent from the gaze of sinners, were now divested of their sombre covering; the thousand glittering candelabras poured their bright volumes of light upon the sumptuously gilded altars; their high-arched domes, gem'd with bright angel-forms, plumed for heavenly flight, cast back their golden rays; and priests robed in jewelled surplices, chanted sweet requiems of the dead. The Catholic world was around the altar, from

> "The infant muling and puking in its mother's arms to him
> "In the lean and slippered pantaloon" he,
> "The lover, sighing like furnace with woeful ballad to a mistress' eye-brows," and she,
> "Whose beauty hangs upon the cheek of night, like a rich jewel in an Ethiop's ear."
> Amen—glory![14]

April 25, 1848. City of Mexico.

Yesterday and to-day there has been no business done before the Military Commission for the trial of the murder and burglary. Yesterday Lieut. John J.C. Bibb was unwell, and to-day Capt.

14. A mix of Shakespeare's *As You Like It* (first three lines) and *Romeo and Juliet* (fourth line).

John G. Lair, 4th Kentucky, was detailed but was taken unwell on entering the Court, and the Court adjourned. Lieut. Dutton, Pennsylvania Volunteers, is now on trial. A few days ago I stated that *Lieut. Tilden* was arrested and charged as being implicated in the affair. There are two Lieut. Tildens in the army, which I did not think of at the time. The one arrested is *Lieut. B.P. Tilden*. The case of Hare is closed, as you will see by the proceedings I send you—the verdict will not be rendered until all the cases, some eight in number, are disposed of.

To-day an attempt was made to rob the stage on the road from here to Puebla. There were two American soldiers in the stage as an escort. The robbers, fifteen in number, sallied out from the thick wood by the roadside, the guard fired on them, killing one and wounding another badly, when the whole party retreated.

The Court of Inquiry left this city for the United States yesterday, escorted by Capt. Sibley's dragoons.

My arrangements for procuring the proceedings of the Mexican Congress are complete, as soon as they meet I will have a daily communication with Querétaro and you will have an express to the coast whenever anything occurs to justify the expence.

Gen. Butler has received official announcement of Gen. Sterling Price's engagement with the Mexicans on the northern frontier. Gen. Price does not give any of the particulars, he writes that he doubts if his letter will reach head-quarters, and therefore does not send any of the details. The *Star* of this morning has a compiled statement of the account furnished by Angel Trias Alvarez, the late Governor of Chihuahua, to the Minister of War, and I send that for what it is worth. There is no mistake but that a fight of some kind took place, but I cannot credit the sanguinary spirit with which it was fought. You may recollect of a "murderous fire and bloody battle" in that neighborhood once before, in which there were some half dozen and a mule or two killed and wounded.

The Battle of Rosales

We have before us the official account of the battle of Rosales, on the 16th of March, addressed to the Minister of War, by Trias, the late Governor of Chihuahua. It occupies some four columns of the papers, and we can of course give only an abstract of it. We have already given the newspaper accounts of the affair. He commences by saying that being unable to maintain his position, on the 16th, on the Plaza of Chihuahua, on account of the American troops marching so rapidly and in so much greater numbers, he took all his stores, artillery and men—about four hundred—and marched to Rosales, twenty-two leagues distant. He was soon reinforced by over 100 men, twenty deserters among them, and a few of the National Guard, under command of Lieut. Col. Sanchez. At ten o'clock at night he entered Rosales, and planted his artillery at the principal avenues to the Grand Plaza, consisting of 10 eight and 2 four-pounders, two seven inch howitzers, and ten swivels. The roofs of the principal houses in the centre of the town were occupied, and the wagons, containing stores, ammunition, &c., were packed in the Plaza. At 6 o'clock on the morning of the 9th, the Americans, to the number of 400 mounted men, came in sight. After having reconnoitred the position of the Mexicans, they formed into two columns of attack, and immediately demanded the surrender of Trias. This he peremptorily refused, urging that a treaty of peace had been signed by the Commissioners of the two Governments, and that the receipt of the armistice was momentarily expected; on this account he was opposed to hostilities, and to avoid them had evacuated Chihuahua, standing on the defensive only, but that neither from this nor any other reason should he fail to sustain the honor of the national arms. Gen. Price replied that he desired a conference with the Governor. This was agreed to, and it was had in the outskirts of the town. The American general stated that having received no official notice of the treaty or of an armistice, he could not suspend military operations. The surrender of the Mexican troops was again insisted upon—the Governor being assured that all his train was at the disposition of the Americans. Still Trias refused, and the parties separated without coming to any arrangement. A second parley was had, but no terms were agreed upon. The Americans shortly after withdrew to a wood beyond the fire of the Mexican artillery, and there established their camp. Trias continued to occupy his position, throwing up some entrenchments, etc., and taking other precautionary measures against a surprise. On the 10th the Americans received a reinforcement of 100 men and ten pieces of artillery, and Trias was informed that the place was besieged. In the meantime, he had received a reinforcement of 200 of the National Guard.

The place was held in siege by the Americans from the 10th till the night of the 15th, when they received a further reinforcement of 300 men, and six pieces of heavy artillery. At 7 in the morning of the 16th, Gen. Price asked for a conference, and demanded the surrender at discretion of the Mexican forces in half an hour. The response was that it could not be thought of, but that he (Trias) would consent to the appointment of commissioners to agree upon honorable terms. But the half hour had expired, and the parties prepared for the conflict. At 8 the Americans opened with their batteries, and the fire was returned by the enemy. The engagement became general, and was conducted with vigor on both sides till half past 12. The Americans then withdrew beyond the reach of the enemy's guns. At 1 o'clock the Americans concentrated their forces upon another point, and soon after received further reinforcements. At about three they commenced another attack, stationing their forces in the rear and to the right of the Mexicans, guarding them with the houses which prevented the play of the enemy's cannon. The infantry, also, made their way from one house to another, gaining a footing, while the artillery beat down the Mexican defences. The battle lasted till half past 6 in the afternoon. The enemy abandoned one position after another, and at last asked for a parley. This was refused—the battle was resumed by the Americans, and continued until dark, when the place was taken by assault. It seems that the sound of the bugle for a parley, in the din of the conflict, was not heard by the Americans. The place having come into their possession, the Mexicans dispersed, and Trias was taken prisoner, together with most of his officers.

The Governor concludes by hoping the President will not look upon his conduct as rash, as he looked only to the honor of the Mexican arms, but that if through ignorance he has committed any fault, he is willing to abide by the decision of a council of war. He states the Mexican loss at 2 officers, 30 privates, 11 citizens killed, and 25 or 30 wounded. He thinks the American loss triple this. Trias was sent to Chihuahua by Gen. Price, who, he says, "treated me with the most distinguished consideration." The other officers received a passport, under their word of honor, for any part of the Republic. The Governor concludes his narration by stating that Gen. Price, with more than 1,500 men, and twenty pieces of artillery, including six pieces taken at Rosales, holds military occupation of the State of Chihuahua, in the name of the Government of the United States.

On Sunday last there was a splendid military performance on the plains of Molino del Rey. The division of Gen. Worth, and the division of Gen. Marshall, was reviewed by Gen. Butler, in the presence of our peace commissioners, Mr. Clifford and Mr. Sevier, who have been lionizing here for some few days among the military. The plains of Molino del Rey afford a beautiful opportunity for a brilliant military show, being some three miles long, gradually rising from the Molino to the north. The city lays off in the distance, a beautiful prospect, and the valley opens to the enchanted view, surrounded by a ridge of dark towering mountains, with the snow-capped peaks of Popocateptl and Iztaccihuatl ascending heavenwards, high among the highest. The associations of this place is fresh in the memory of us all. It was here we witnessed the indomitable courage of the 1st Division. It was here 800 brave American troops fell in one hour's fighting, and among them some of the very pride and chivalry of our army. The day was beautiful; the sun shone out in grandeur, reflecting the dazzling brightness of the arms, and giving as it were, a still deeper hue to the true blue jackets. The 1st Division of Regulars never looked better or made a more soldier-like appearance. Long life and success to the

Brevet Brigadier General William Worth. *Courtesy Library of Congress*.

1st Division! They here fought their way to distinction, and may they long enjoy their laurels.

The pride of the west, Kentucky and Tennessee, composing the division of Gen. Marshall, vied with each other in their stalwart sons. These patriotic States have sent many gallant troops into the field, but never did they offer up to the God of War a nobler specimen than are now here. Their appearance and discipline showed to a remarkable advantage, and no man ever looked upon a finer body of citizen-soldiers. Good citizens at home and soldiers in the field, are synonymous, and whenever I see a good soldier I set him down as a good citizen, morally and physically strong. If we are to have no more fighting, these men then will not, as a body, have an opportunity of measuring their steel with the foe, but there were many there who showed the stuff they were made of, in front of the battlements of Monterey, the cliffs of Buena Vista, the sands of Vera Cruz, and the heights of Cerro Gordo. And if they are to have no more fighting, they will go home with the proud consolation of having done their duty to their State and to their country.

On Monday, the old "Cerro Gordo Division," Gen. Smith, were reviewed and drilled in front of the city on their parade ground in the direction of the Peñon. Mr. Clifford and Mr. Sevier were present, together with a large number of officers of the army and citizens. The movements and evolutions of this division, will excite the pride and admiration of every man who has "Uncle Sam" branded in his countenance. The old veteran, war-beaten countenances, with the neat, clean uniforms and their glittering armor, was peculiarly pleasing to look upon. They exercised on the same ground on which the Mexican army was disciplined, whom they met so often afterwards when bayonet crossed bayonet and foes fell together. The weather was magnificently fine, and the heavens seemed to be striving to add grandeur to the scene. The tall cupolas of the churches of the city standing prominently in the rear, with our Stars and Stripes, the brightest of them all waving among them, while across a level plain in the foreground stood the towering height of the old Peñon, whose iron-bound crest challenged us to combat on our entrance into the valley. There then stood the formidable peak, originally thrown up by one of nature's freaks, the guardian of the far-famed Halls; behind it was the finely equipped and well disciplined Mexican army anxiously awaiting our approach. Where are they now? The very men who are parading and moving in the majesty of conquerors have scattered them to the four winds, and forced them to yield respectable consideration to the olive branch in the hands of two gentlemen who are spectators in the review. I cannot tell you of any accidents that occurred in the two days' review, because our people know how to do things up a little browner than you have any idea of, and as it is not customary to have accidents, I will not offer an apology or excuse for not having any.

The health of the army is much better in the city and vicinity than it has been for some time, though I learn there is some sickness at the outposts.

Here is an advertisement which caps anything you have heard of lately. It was published in *El Monitor* of yesterday. You will see that the good citizens of Mexico are ever ready to preserve and protect the fair reputation of their daughters, and although the ladies are, generally speaking, accommodating in their ways, this lady is not willing to satisfy the curious, but is willing to be made a public show for the purpose of satisfying the gazing community that she is not what they take her to be. Here is the advertisement, judge for yourselves:

> "A young lady who has attended the public balls, bears a strong resemblance to a daughter of mine—and being anxious that the reputation of my family should not suffer for any cause, I entreat those persons who were present at the ball, to call at my house, at No. 1 *Calle de Belefonso*, and (though resembling each other) they will observe the difference between the two."

April 26, 1848. City of Mexico.

We received letters last night from Querétaro, and learn that they have not yet got a quorum. They will probably succeed in procuring the number this week. There are now members enough in this city on their way to make the requisite number, but they are not able to procure seats in the stage, and will, therefore, be delayed here until the latter part of the week. We learn that the Mexican Government contemplate having a quorum by the first of next week under any circumstance. According to the present number necessary to form a quorum, they count in the delegations from Texas, Yucatan, and New Mexico; by throwing them out they have enough present to form the constitutional quorum. There has been a meeting of the Ministers and General Council. They have determined upon this course if it becomes necessary, and, further, if they are driven to the alternative, that they will declare all the seats of the members vacant, and fill them up by persons who will attend. This last resort, however, they will not be driven to, nor do I think of even throwing out Yucatan, Texas, and New Mexico, but they will do so if it becomes necessary.

Both the Mexicans and our authorities are confident of the ratification of the treaty; they are more sanguine than I have ever seen them.

Mr. Clifford and Mr. Sevier were expected in Querétaro on the 22[d], and the most magnificent quarters that could be found were provided for them, to say nothing of extra quantity of gas, &c. They will no doubt be received there with "all the honors." They are expected to leave here to-day or to-morrow, with an American escort as far as San Juan del Rio, half-way, and then they will be received by a Mexican escort and conveyed with all the pomp and dignity to the presence of the august Peña y Peña and Cabinet. It is a great pity Gen. Pillow has gone home. This would have been a great field for him to figure in. How he could spread himself on his gold-mounted saddle and bridle, and his white-plumed chapeau, all captured by his own hands. I expect the Commissioners regret the loss of his valuable services, as there is no man here of his rank who can fill his place!

The report of Bustamente marching on Querétaro turns out not to be so. This general is with the main body of his forces at Dolores Hidalgo, north of San Luis Potosi. Everything is quiet in the interior, or so say the letters of last evening.

April 26, 1848. City of Mexico.

There are three subjects connected with the army in which I, with them, feel a deep interest, and I hope you will therefore excuse my frequent reference to them. The army, however, is not less interested than the people of our country, generally, for I hold that whatever has a tendency to render the army more efficient, and contribute to its discipline and good organization, particularly at the present time, is of vital importance to the country at large, and possesses a just claim to the consideration of our Government authorities. If they do not give it the proper attention, it is the duty of the people to take the matter in hand and require of their representatives prompt and decisive action.

These three subjects are these: 1st, a refuge for the sick, wounded, and soldiers disabled while in the service of the United States; 2[d], promotion from the ranks for gallantry in the field; and 3[d], a "Retired List" for officers who are incapacitated for active service, by age or injuries, such as wounds or disease incurred whilst in the service of their country.

A retreat for the wounded and disabled rank and file of our army is no less required by common justice than it is dictated by the feelings and sympathies of humanity. The Regular soldier who falls wounded in the service of the United States, or who is taken down and disabled by disease, is discharged from the army by the regulations as being no longer fit for duty, receiving with his discharge, a certificate for a pension, in case he is wounded, either one-third, one-fourth, one-half, or whole pay while in the service, amounting to the enormous sum, at the outside, of eight dollars per month. He is virtually turned out upon a cold and heartless world, helpless and unprovided for, with the loss of some of his limbs, or a slow but fatal disease gnawing at the vitals of life and consuming it by slow degrees. Thus he is left to drag out a miserable existence, suffering for sustenance and the most ordinary necessities of life, "kicked from post to pillar," neither heeded nor cared for, and only because he had the misfortune to fall while supporting the flag of his country.

Do we not all derive a common benefit from his sacrifices, his sufferings, and his exposure? We certainly do. The blood of the soldier makes the glory of the country, and if there were but little blood shed, there would be but little glory, therefore, does not sheer justice urgently and seriously demand that the country should provide for those whose patriotism and devotion have led them to sacrifice their health and means of support? Does not gratitude and humanity demand that our war-worn soldiers should be protected from the pinchings of poverty, and that they should be provided for in the hour of need, and not be forced to wander through the world, helpless and forsaken, soliciting alms at the hands of the passing stranger? Does not the brilliancy of our national pride and the dazzling glory of our national arms reflect our base ingratitude? Can our people hold up our conquering eagle in pride and admiration, challenging the rivalry of, and bidding defiance to the world, while that proud bird looks down weeping, upon the suffering soldier, who has supported it in all its trials and doubtful circumstances?

In reference to this subject, I find the following paragraph in the Annual Report of Gen. Scott, for the year 1845:

> "I venture once more respectfully to invite attention to a *retreat* or *asylum* for the worn out or decayed rank and file of the army. The subject has been twice reported upon

> favorably, with bills, by Committees on Military Affairs in the House of Representatives. See Report No. 74, 2[d] Session, 26th Congress and Report No. 109, 2[d] Session, 28th Congress. *If the want can only be placed fully before Congresss*, it seems impossible to doubt success, as the asylum would impose no burden on the treasury, but be supported from the army itself, in DEDUCTIONS, FINES AND REVERSIONS."

Gen. Scott has never lost sight of this subject, and one of his first acts on entering this city, was to levy a contribution of $90,000 for the purpose of laying a foundation for a home for the crippled and disabled soldier. To this has been added all the fines on hotels, amusements, &c., since the 1st of January last, amounting to some $10,000 to $15,000 per month more. Had this been allowed to remain appropriated to the original object, there would have been but a small appropriation necessary to complete it, but Mr. William L. Marcy has thought proper to apply $100,000 of the amount already sent on by Gen. Scott, to different purposes, and by these means will still longer leave the worn out soldier homeless and friendless.

The following extract in reference to the wants of the army, I find in the Report of the Adjutant General for 1845:

"If a *private soldier* die of *fever*, or other cause, the laws humanely and justly provide for his widow and children; but if a *private of the Regular Army* be even killed in battle, his destitute widow and children can receive nothing from the government."

The spirit of our institutions, "equal laws and equal rights," promptly demand new and just legislation on this subject, and I hope some patriotic gentleman will take the matter in hands and carry it through.

With reference to promotions from the ranks, it is a matter which rests entirely with Mr. President Polk. Congress has already passed a law authorizing the President to grant commissions to non-commissioned officers who have distinguished themselves in the field, and to grant extra pay to privates for distinction in active service. After each of the battles, Gen. Scott called upon his officers to furnish a list of such of the men of their regiments as were entitled to the benefits of the law of Congress. This was complied with cheerfully by the officers. Many as gallant and meritorious fellows as ever the sun shone upon, were recommended for promotion. The lists were sent in to Gen. Scott, and by him forwarded to Washington. There was not an officer in the army but who considered that the new annual Army Register would contain their promotions. But it appears they were entirely mistaken in our honest, upright, and fair-dealing President of the United States, he who talks so much about the *gallant army*, the *brave fellows*, and who, even on some occasions, allows himself scope enough to say *my army*, or *my regiment*, and that I have conducted the war with so much success!

What can be the objection to giving these men their brevet second lieutenancies, according to the act of Congress? Have they not merited and been recommended for it, as strong as it was possible? Or is it because the President desired to hold in reserve a certain amount of executive patronage for the next Presidential campaign? Or is it because he has been insincere in his professions? In many cases the circumstances are peculiarly hard, and the gallant non-commissioned officers outraged. In one of the regiment of the *old line*, there were twelve non-commissioned officers recommended for brevet commissions after the battle of Churubusco. At Molino del Rey, six of them were killed, or mortally wounded. Two of the remaining six fell in the assault upon the Castle of Chapultepec, thus leaving four. Out of these four, one received three wounds, two received two wounds each, and only one escaped unhurt. And this is not the case in one regiment, but a similarity exists in nearly all the regiments. And these non-commissioned officers have not been recommended solely on account of their personal bravery, but also because they are competent in every particular to fill the place. They are men of good association, of character, of education, and gentlemanly deportment, and would do credit to the commissions they would hold.

It is true Mr. Polk has made some appointments, but, pray, who are they, and what are they? Some of them have already been discharged from the army for drunkenness, blackguardism, and sundry other offences coming under the head of "conduct unbecoming an officer and a gentleman." These appointments have not been made because the fortunate recipients of Executive favor had been highly recommended by their commanding officers for good character and gallantry in face of the enemy, but some of them were privates whom their officers say were among the very poorest soldiers in their companies. In some instances, they were so worthless that they were relieved from duty with the company, and sent to do the drudgery around the hospitals, and they are, as individuals, what are sometimes known in the recruiting service as *idle dependents of respectable families*. And these are the men whom Mr. Polk has thought proper to place over the heads of as gallant, noble, and chivalrous a set of non-commissioned officers as any army the world has ever known, many of whom have been in command of companies ever since the battles in the valley, and the command devolved upon them in the heat of battle, when every commissioned officer attached to the company fell under the fire of the enemy. It is not saying too much when we remark that the instances are not rare when the reputations of companies and the character of regiments were saved by the soldier-like and manly conduct of non-commissioned officers? Is it not too hard that these gallant fellows should be over-slaughed by the log-rolling politicians at Washington, in providing for the dregs of the community and the pest of society?

One of the arguments used against West Point by the Democracy of our country, for a long time, was that the institution was of itself aristocratic, and that it prevented promotions from the ranks. Now what are the facts practically? Here are the graduates of the Academy, from company officers to commanders of divisions, recommending promotions from the ranks, and urging them with all the ability they possess. They do not ask that the persons they recommend shall be appointed to other regiments, but they say to the War Department and the President, promote them to our regiments. We will take them by the hand, and we will treat them as brother officers and as gentlemen, and we will pursue our path to fame and distinction side by side with them, only place them in a position where the rules of the service will enable us to do so. Will the Democracy of our country, or the sober thought of the people, second the graduates of West Point in their present effort to reward the meritorious soldier, and demand that the President comply with the law already passed by Congress?[15]

15. By General Order No. 37, Adjutant General's Office, dated July 8, 1848, the following enlisted men were appointed brevet second lieutenants, taking rank from June 28, 1848, and assigned to the following regiments:

The next question is the "*retired list*." This undoubtedly claims our serious consideration in point of even-handed justice and the means of rendering the army more efficient, and at the same time of providing without any additional cost to the treasury of the United States, for the aged and infirm officers worn out in the service of the country. It is a well ascertained fact, that we have many officers on the army list who are incapacitated for service in the field, by age and wounds and disease incurred while in the discharge of their duties. It is impossible, while at the same time it would be inhuman, to order them into the field under these circumstances. Therefore the duties fall upon the other officers of the regiment, taking them away from their proper duties at a time when they are most needed, and therefore rendering the regiments less efficient than they would otherwise be and ought to be.

How, then, is this to be remedied? After many suggestions, and the consideration of many wise persons familiar with the subject,

---

First Regiment of Dragoons—Sergt. David H. Hastings, of the Company of Sappers and Miners.

Second Regiment of Dragoons—Sergt. Samuel H. Starr, of the Company of Sappers and Miners; Sergt. Major Thos. J. McKean, of the 15th Regiment of Infantry.

Regiment of Mounted Riflemen—Sergt. Wm. B. Lane; Sergt. Caleb E. Irwin.

First Regiment of Artillery—Sergt. Thornley S. Everett, of the Company of Sappers and Miners; Sergt. John Dement, of the Regiment of Mounted Riflemen.

Second Regiment of Artillery—Quartermaster Sergt. James M. Robinson; Sergt. Henry Benson.

Third Regiment of Artillery—Sergt. John H. Heck.

Fourth Regiment of Artillery—Sergt. Major Robert W. Howard.

First Regiment of Infantry—Sergt. Henry Wilson, of the 2d Regiment of Artillery; Sergt. Charles N. Underwood, of the Regiment of Mounted Riflemen; Sergt. Walter W. Hudson, of the 15th Regiment of Infantry.

Second Regiment of Infantry—Sergt. George Bruce; Corpl. Robert Bailey; Corpl. James McGill, of the 15th Regiment of Infantry.

Third Regiment of Infantry—Sergt. Henry L. Brown, of the Regiment of Mounted Riflemen; Sergt. Saml. Ross, of the 15th Regiment of Infantry.

Fourth Regiment of Infantry—Sergt. Hiram Dyer, of the Regiment of Mounted Riflemen; Sergt. Fortunatus Lilly, of the 15th Regiment of Infantry.

Fifth Regiment of Infantry—Sergt. Jos. Updegraff; Sergt. Samuel Archer.

Sixth Regiment of Infantry—Sgt. Levi C. Bootes, of the Regiment of Mounted Riflemen; Corpl. John L. Tubbs, of the 12th Regiment of Infantry.

Seventh Regiment of Infantry—Quartermaster Sergt. Wm. S. Bradford; Sergt. Anthony S. Sutton, of the 15th Regiment of Infantry.

Eighth Regiment of Infantry—Sergt. Major Theodore Fink; Sergt. Geo. L. Willard, of the 15th Regiment of Infantry. *Daily Delta*, July 20, 1848.

a retired list is thought to be the most feasible. If economy is the object, it can be accomplished without affecting the design contemplated. The officer of the Regular Army certainly has the same claims to the sympathies of the country as the Volunteer, but strange to say, that while our laws humanely and justly provide for the volunteer officer, and his family, who is killed or wounded in battle, no provision is made for the officer of the Regular Army. And further, does not the principle of justice prompt us, that the officer of the Regular Army who has worn out the prime of his life and the strength of his manhood in the service of his country, should be provided for in his age and infirmity, instead of being called in the field to die a victim to the hardships and labors incident to a campaign, and which his enfeebled state of health is not able to encounter?

As I said above, many of these aged officers are left at home from the mere fact of incapacity, and many regiments left short of the officers necessary to discharge the duties. For instance, there is not a regiment of the old line here commanded by a full colonel, or a brigade commanded by a brigadier general, and many companies left without a single commissioned officer with it. This is prejudicial to the army and to the interests of the country. Therefore, the brigadiers being absent, a colonel has to be assigned to the command of the brigade, and there being, as in many instances, but one field officer with the regiment, the command of the regiment falls on a captain. This captain is compelled to purchase a horse, and his pay is reduced ten dollars per month, while at the same time he has to incur the still greater responsibility of higher command. (A captain receives ten dollars per month for the responsibility of his command of a company, which he loses when he takes command of a regiment, while as a commander of a regiment, his pay is not increased.)

The circumstances of the case require some legislation, both as regards the provision for officers while living, and for their families after their death.

By creating a *retired* list, and placing upon it all officers who are unfit for service, with their pay proper, without the emoluments of their rank, and promoting the officer next in rank to the command, with the pay of his former commission, and allowing him the emoluments of the rank he is filling, would, in a great degree, effect the object, and render the army more efficient.

This would render it necessary to place another lieutenant or more at the bottom of the list, which would not increase the cost of the regiment to the Government of the United States. This is, in substance, the plan recommended some years ago by many officers of the army. Gen. Alexander Macomb thus refers to it in his report of 1840:

> "The effect of the plan as detailed in the first three sections of the 'act recommended,' will be seen by exhibiting the cost of a regiment as it exists, and the cost of a regiment with a retired Colonel on ordinary pay; and it will be seen that there will be an actual saving in money, with the advantage that all the officers would be effective. If the retired Colonel shall have served forty years, he will leave eight rations a day to the public, which eight rations are worth, at 20 cents each, (the regulated price) \$1.60 a day, or \$584 a year; and the additional expense of placing a second Lieutenant at the foot of the regiment will be \$300 a year, making an actual saving of \$284 a year."

Gen. Macomb in his report then goes on to show by a calculation of the number of officers unfit for service, and the number necessary to be put into the regiments, that if his system was adopted, it would leave a net saving to the Government of \$2,322 per annum. This was for the year 1840, but the same principle would produce the same effects now that it would then.

There is no principle of justice or duty that justifies the discrimination between the Volunteer and the Regular, which is the same that exists under the present law, between the officer of the Regular Army and the officer of the Navy. The wife and family of the Volunteer and Naval officer receive one-half of his pay proper if he dies in the service by wounds or disease, while the widow of the Regular, if he is actually *killed in action*, only receives one-half his pay proper for five years, otherwise she is left to shift for herself as best she can. If Republics are not ungrateful, if merit is to meet a meagre reward, I hope that the present Congress will not adjourn without giving this subject their serious and a just contemplation.

Chapter 9

Last Days in Mexico

April 28, 1848. City of Mexico.

The city has been comparatively quiet for the past few days, and what is most singular to relate, we have not had a robbery or murder that I have heard of either in the city or the vicinity, but I suppose it is owing to the extraordinary exertions of our military police.

The all-absorbing topic is "what is the news from Querétaro?" "will we have a peace?" Who can answer the question? The present state of affairs incline us to believe there is a favorable prospect. The Mexican population have settled down on it as a certainty, and those who formerly opposed it, now acquiesce, without much grumbling. The Government at Querétaro, apparently, are making great exertions to consummate their object. They assert positively that they will have a quorum by the 1st or 5th of the next month, and have determined, if there are not enough of members present by that time, they will throw out the representation of the ceded territories, and the State of Yucatan. By doing this, they will have some twelve or fifteen over a quorum, and a majority sufficient to carry any measure.

At the first of the meeting of the Congress, they will confirm the election of Herrera, as President, and the formation of a new ministry will follow, which will facilitate affairs. The present Minister of Relations is a man of considerable ability, but he is most woefully deficient in energy. I think it altogether likely that Señor Luis G. Cuevas will go into a new Cabinet as Minister of Relations. He is a man of as much energy and industry as I know of in the Republic, and may give more stimulus to the actions of the Congress and the Government. Gen. Herrera will not affect much of himself individually, but he carries a great deal of strength with him in his supporters.

The Congress of Mexico I do not think will take a responsible and decided action of the treaty. I think it altogether probable that when they meet they will consider the treaty and the modifications, and debate its provisions to some extent, then they will adopt either one of the two following modes: 1st, adopt the treaty as it was originally made and signed, and then authorize the Government to accept or refuse the amendments and modifications of the Senate of the United States; or, 2d, they will, after debate, authorize the Government to accept or reject the original treaty, modifications and all; in either case, throwing the burden of responsibility upon the Executive and his cabinet of Councillors. One of these modes, I am well informed, will likely be pursued by the Congress, and it seems altogether probable, as it is exactly in keeping with their character. However, whatever is left for the Government to do, I have no doubt will be complied with by them. They are left in a position that they must act, and at the same time are anxious to bring about a peace, if they can do it and survive afterwards. The disturbance in Europe has its effect here in breaking up the monarchies.

Capt. Thomas Glenn, of the 14th Infantry, Capt. James D. Blair, and Lieut. James R. May, of the Voltigeurs, left Toluca this morning at 7 o'clock, and arrived at 2½ o'clock, P.M. They represent the garrison as being perfectly quiet and in good order in every respect, the health of the troops is improving.

The trial of Lieut. Dutton before the Military Commission for murder and robbery, still continues. I will send you the leading features of his case as soon as concluded. The case of Lieut. Hare, which I sent you ten days ago, embraces the general history of the disgraceful affair, and I will compile the balance of the testimony, only giving you at length the defence in each case. The case of Lieut. Hare is reported in all its details.

An escort of 100 picked men and officers left here two days ago under the command of Capt. Larkin Smith, for Vera Cruz, with a large quantity of specie in charge—it was the property of merchants in this city.

Capt. William S. Henry, with a large detachment of recruits, is expected to arrive to-day.

P.S. Since writing the foregoing note, I have received advices from Querétaro to the 26th inst. I have only time, before I am compelled to close my letter, to give you, very briefly, the substance: Seventy members of Congress were present—seventy-three is necessary to constitute a quorum—three will leave here to-morrow. It is feared in Querétaro, if the Government pursues the policy of cutting off the non-represented States of Yucatan, New Mexico, &c., it will produce a schism in the Congress. The Government, writes my friend, is much annoyed at the non-attendance of the Deputies. Almonte is in Querétaro, endeavoring to produce a *pronuniamiento* against the Government, and pledges himself, if he succeeds, to either whip the Yankees, or conclude an *honorable* peace, most likely to do neither. The Government has not yet issued its decree annulling the seats of the non-attending members of Congress. An escort of Mexican cavalry came out on the 24th to receive Mr. Sevier, half-way between here and Querétaro. Mr. Sevier is still here, and it is the general impression in the street that he is standing on points of etiquette which may endanger the object of his mission. If Mr. Sevier wants to go to Querétaro, he should be satisfied to go there under any guard that will insure his safety, it should make no difference whether he is escorted from the lines drawn by the armistice, by American or Mexican cavalry.

April 29, 1848. City of Mexico.

Again, to-day, we had the finest kind of sport in the way of racing over the Peñon Jockey Club Course. The weather was delightful, the course fine, and a large crowd in attendance made the more lively by being ornamented with the bright eyes and laughing faces of the Castilian and Aztec *señoritas*. As usual, the fine band of the 2^{d} Dragoons, on their splendid gray horses, discoursed some beautiful music, while the high-mettled racers were preparing for the contest of speed and bottom. A company of dragoons and an escort of infantry were on the ground to provide against accident while

View of Mexico City from the Convent of San Cosme. *Courtesy Library of Congress*.

the Anglo-Saxons were enjoying themselves, as they will wherever they find a resting-place. Officers of all grades were there, and seemingly delighted and interested in the sports of the day. At the sound of the bugle, the "critters" stripped and saddled, and came to the stand in fine order.

At the tap of the drum away they went altogether, at a rapid pace, until they rounded the second turn, when Big Joe, finding it a little troublesome to accompany the crowd, went it alone in the rear at a gait more to his convenience. Down the back stretch, lick and lick, went the filly and Oliver, both apparently making tall work, for the heat at the third turn the regular stride of the filly seemed to tell, and she led the horse about a length. They rounded the last turn of the quarter stretch, and came home side and side until near the distance stand, when the filly shot ahead, and won the heat by half a length. Big Joe, either for want of regard for his reputation as a racer, or inability to do better, dropped outside the distance stand. Time, 1:55.

Second Heat. At the sound of the bugle, both the competitors toed the chalk-mark in fine condition. The betting, which had before been but very slight, the friends of both nags being suspicious of their abilities, now turned in favor of the filly at four to one, however but few offers and but little taken, as both horses had sweated and cooled off well. They made a bad start, the filly running across the track, and taking the outside. Oliver passed the first turn, hard in hand, some thirty feet ahead. At the second turn the filly came alongside, and they went down the back stretch at a close brush, side by side, and could have been covered by a blanket the whole way. At the third turn, Oliver dropped astern about three lengths, and made no run again until they rounded the turn home, when they came at quarter-horse gait, both the parties with whip and spur, filly winning the heat by a foot. Time, 1:54.

Summary

W. Tyson's ch. f. *Acallia*, 3 y. o., by imp. Leviathan, dam by Stockholder	1 1
D. Lafon's br. g. *Oliver*, by Cripple, dam by Polly Hopkins, b. y. o.	2 2
Capt. George's b. g. *Big Joe*, age and pedigree unknown	dis.

Time, 1:55—1:54.

The next race was an entry of four mustangs, single dash of a mile, entrance one doubloon, the entries to constitute the purse. This was scrape and blow, whip and spur, first one ahead and then the other, and no one could tell whose race it was until they came up the quarter stretch, when two of them yielded up the ghost, and dropped out, the winner taking the heat and money by about four lengths in three minutes.

The sports of the day concluded with an entry of four saddle horses, full weights, single dash of a mile, three doubloons entrance, entries to constitute the purse. This was one of the finest races I ever saw, the whole four going all in a crowd until they rounded the third turn, and three of the party coming home without daylight between them—Mr. Van Austin's bay horse winning the heat in 2:03.

April 30, 1848. City of Mexico.

Our city, that is, Mexico, has been rife with rumors of a revolution at Querétaro for the last two days. It is said to have been headed by Almonte. My letters last evening are to the 27th, P.M., and they do not mention anything of it, but, on the contrary, their whole tone would indicate that the report is a fabrication of some of the verdant minds that would prefer seeing it to anything else.

There was but one deputy wanting to complete the quorum of Congress. There are two on their route from Guanajuato, and six from this State and Puebla, which will complete the number. It was expected that the preliminary meeting, for the reunion of the Congress, would take place on Monday, the 1st of next month.

Mr Sevier was daily expected at Querétaro, and measures had been taken to receive him with their very best, and entertain him according to his rank and position. He will, I learn, start on Tuesday next, 2d of May.

My letters also inform me that every person in Querétaro is sanguine that the peace will be consummated.

Padre Jarauta, I learn by a letter from San Luis Potosi, was in that place on the 20th inst.

The papers from the interior are devoid of interest, in fact, they contain nothing that is worth the trouble of sending.

The stage was attacked to-day, coming from Puebla, by about twenty-five robbers. One of the American guards was killed, and one other out of the three and the driver wounded. Some two or three of the robbers were seen to fall, but they cannot say whether they were killed.

Some persons have come in to-day from Cuernavaca, and represent that there is still some sickness there.

Capt. Henry, with recruits from Orizaba, arrived to-day.

The Marines left to-day, for the coast, and, I suppose, as the saying is, will take water.

Since writing the above, I have seen two persons who have letters from Querétaro, and neither of them place any confidence in the revolution or *pronunciamiento* at Querétaro. Yesterday, Mr. Sevier received an extraordinary despatch from there, and, if it had taken place, I think there would have been some definite intelligence here confirming it.

May 1, 1848. City of Mexico.

This is May day, and it comes to us with countless reminiscences of home, and friends, and country, and it is as impossible for us to divest ourselves of former associations connected with it, as it would be to prevent the annual debut of the harbinger of mirthful Spring, redolent with flowers, and youth and beauty smiling with joy and happiness. The morn was ushered in with a clear unclouded sky, and the sun rose brilliantly, lighting up the gardens of earth, expanding the morning glory, and adding fragrance to the budding rose. The lute-tongued songsters of the forest, ensconced in the green foliage, warble their morning hymns in praise of the God of Nature, and with the flattering prospects of the exchange of the olive branch, we are not behind the balance of Creation, in enjoying the exhilarating scene, and partaking of the pleasures of the day or the season. To you, and to all my old sweet-hearts, married and unmarried, or want to be married, or do not want to be married, Mustang wishes them all a happy and merry May day. He will pay all due homage to Flora, and he hopes they will do the same.

I received the following letter from San Luis Potosi:

> San Luis, April 26, 1848.
>
> Gen. Paredes has been ordered to leave this city, by the government, and in taking his departure, he went in the direction of the city of Aguascalientes. Also Gen. [J.M.] Flores, an agent of Santa Anna, has been ordered to leave this State, on account of his going to Rio Verde, and endeavoring to seduce the troops of Gen. Romero.
>
> Padre Jarauta arrived here about the 19th, from Ciudad del Meir. He presented himself to the *Comandate General*, and afterwards was presented by Lawyer Parada and his brother, as a guest at the Feast of Torres. Through the influence of some of the *Puros*, a benefit was given at the theatre, for the purpose of giving him a reception and public dinner.
>
> The three generals, Parbon, J. M. Ortega, and Francisco Mejia, have been endeavoring to produce an excitement with the public, but without effect. If these three officers were served as Paredes has been, tranquility would be completely restored.

The above is all that is important or interesting in the letter.

May 2, 1848. City of Mexico.

Yesterday I attended the review, at San Angel, of the First Brigade of Gen. Patterson's Division, commanded by Col. Wynkoop, and composed of Light Battery, Lieut. French; New York Volunteers, Lieut. Col. Burnham; 1st Pennsylvania Volunteers, Lieut. Col. Black; Massachusetts Volunteers, Col. Isaac H. Wright; 2d Pennsylvania Volunteers, Col. Geary; South Carolina Volunteers, Maj. Robert G.M. Dunovant.[1] They were reviewed by the general himself in the

1. Educated for a mercantile career, Isaac Wright turned to publishing a Democratic newspaper in Boston and became active in the local militia. Assuming the rank of lieutenant colonel of the Massachusetts Regiment of Volunteers in 1847, he rose to the rank of colonel later that year. In poor health after the war,

presence of Messrs. Sevier and Clifford. Every person was forcibly struck with the discipline and drill of the brigade and their fine soldier-like appearance. The labor and attention paid to their drill and discipline has not been lost, but showed itself most favorably, and I must confess that I was much surprised to see that they had arrived at such a high state of improvement. Woe be to the foe who crosses the path of this brigade. The movements of the Light Battery were splendid. It is the same one that was so cut to pieces in front of Contreras under Capt. John Magruder.

After the drill and review was over, the officers and their guests retired to the quarters of Capt. Joseph Daniels, the quartermaster of the division, where they partook of a fine collation which had been prepared. It was a specimen of true Texan hospitality, and, as one of the commissioners said, if it was a specimen of the living in Mexico, he did not think the army was likely to suffer much. After ample justice had been done to the eatables and drinkables, and several exchanges of compliment and toast, the party, by the invitation of Col. Wynkoop, retired to his quarters, where they again indulged to the utmost of their abilities. Here was really the flow of wit and the feast of soul. Anecdote, song, and sentiment answered each other in a spirit of kindness and conviviality in which none so much as soldiers excel. It seemed as if all the good things of the last year's growth had been bottled up and uncorked on this occasion. The festivities were made the more cheerful and agreeable by the pleasant weather, the beauty of the surrounding scenery, and the recollections of the battle-grounds of Contreras and Churubusco, of which we were in full view. The guests from the city left in the evening in *dem foin spirits*, wishing our friends of San Angel long life, health, and safe return to the land of their homes.

May 2, 1848. City of Mexico.

The *Star* of this morning publishes the following as the list of the officers who came up with Capt. W.S. Henry's train, on Saturday last:

> Capt. Marshal S. Howe, 2^d^ Dragoons, commanding brigade; 1st Lieut. Isaac F. Quinby, 3^d^ Artillery, A.A.A.G.; 2^d^ Lieut.

he began an auction house, studied law, and acted as superintendent of the Springfield armory. Wright occupied a couple of minor political offices prior to his death on December 22, 1886. *Boston Herald*, December 23, 1886; *Boston Daily Advertiser*, December 23, 1886.

Andrew J. Dorn, 3d Dragoons, commanding dragoons; Capt. William Austine, 3d Artillery; Capt. Thomas Shields, 14th Infantry; 1st Lieut. Joseph Stewart, 3d Artillery; 2d Lieuts. Thomas H. Neill, 5th Infantry; John DeRussy, 4th Infantry; Joseph Q. Wilbar, 14th Infantry; Thomas Hart, 14th Infantry.

There is no decision yet in the murder trial now being held in this city. Lieut. Dutton is still on trial. His case is expected to be finished to-day or to-morrow.

The inspections of the different corps of the army have taken place, and I do not think this army ever was in better health than it is at present.

The news from Querétaro continues to be without much interest. It was expected there would be a quorum present yesterday or to-day, and that there would immediately be a preliminary meeting of the Deputies. The letters from Querétaro all speak of there being but a very slight opposition to a ratification of the treaty, though I have not seen anything yet which induces me to change my opinion as to the mode of action by the Congress, that is, that they will throw the responsibility of action on the Government.

The *pronunciamiento* referred to in my last, and which probably has been published in your city, turned out, as I told you it would, a humbug, and now I think it had American origin.

Col. William Preston, who went down in command of the escort which removed the sick, returned day before yesterday, his command all in good health.[2] He lost but six by death on the route, and the balance continued to improve from the time they left here.

2. Graduating from Harvard with a law degree in 1838, William Preston moved to Louisville to begin his practice. When the war broke out, Preston raised $50,000 to arm and equip two regiments of Volunteers from Kentucky. Although he had personally enlisted as a private, he was given the rank of lieutenant colonel in the 4th Kentucky Volunteers. After brief terms in the state legislature and Congress, Preston switched from Whig to Democrat and served as minister to Spain for several years. During the Civil War he served on the staff of his brother-in-law Albert S. Johnston until his death. Appointed a brigadier general in the Confederate army, Preston served with distinction until sent as minister to England from the Confederacy. Being quite wealthy, Preston had "no especial occupation" following the war until his death on September 21, 1887. *New York Herald*, November 22, 1887; *Philadelphia Inquirer*, September 22, 1887.

A party of eight or ten robbers were taken to-day at Rio Frio. They will be hung.

An express extraordinary arrived to-day from Querétaro, to Gen. Mora, informing him of the meeting of the Deputies.

May 4, 1848. At Night. City of Mexico.

My courier has just arrived from Querétaro, having left there yesterday morning. He brings me a very voluminous correspondence, little of which is of interest to you. I enclose you one of the letters and *El Correo Nacional* up to the 3d inst. The Congress has been employed in organizing, the Senate is completed, and fully organized last night. The Chamber of Deputies is not yet organized, but will probably be so to-morrow. I also send you a treaty negotiated between the English authorities and the State of Nicaragua.

Col. Morgan arrived to-day from Vera Cruz with a small train.

Dr. Robert R. Ritchie and one or two other officers arrived to-day from Cuernavaca. I learn from him that the health of the troops is improving there, that the only diseases prevailing are those incident to the army, and are not disposed to be fatal.

The health of the troops in this city is very good at present, but there is a good deal of sickness, I learn, from the surgeons at the posts of Tacubaya, Molino del Rey, and San Angel.

Querétaro, May 2, 1848.

At present there is a sufficient number of Deputies to open the session; but that disorganizing party, that traitorous and foul faction, seeing that it cannot prevent he assembling of Congress, has planned in its Clubs that when the question of the Treaty comes to be voted upon, those attached to their interest shall quit the Chamber, so that a quorum shall not remain. Can they be guilty of such abominable wickedness? Will they show that there are men so depraved, Mexicans so base and so deserving of universal execration? I deplore, as becomes me, the fate of my unfortunate country. I could wish that my blood, my existence, might suffice to extricate her from the misfortunes of which she is the victim, and of the still greater ones which threaten her. But it would prove somewhat less bitter to me if I were exempt from the mission which now weighs upon my debility. It is certain it could not be more unfortunate than it now is. But, patience.

In view of the letter which precedes, by which the scheme of the miserable cowards is plainly exhibited—traitors, who have not resolution to vote either for peace or war, because they dare not express their opinions, in order to be prepared for all emergencies, apart from other plans more reprehensible—I am of opinion that so soon as Congress is ready for the vote on the treaty, the President should order the doors to be closed, or should direct a body of soldiers to guard them and guns should be pointed at those who attempted to leave. Since they are inviolate only as members united, separated and disunited, especially in a manner so vile and fatal to the Republic, they would hereafter be, not like other citizens, but like corrupted members of the body corporate. Prudence, therefore, dictates that the body should not be permitted to dissolve.

The Chamber of Deputies assembled on Sunday. Yesterday, during a session of more than seven hours, it approved the credentials of the members, and was organized. Unfortunately, in order to form a quorum, it became necessary to overlook many elections notoriously null, as those of the Federal District, and this circumstance many tend to diminish the prestige indispensable in that body. To-day, preparations were making in the Senate, and to-morrow the election will take place.

May 7, 1848. City of Mexico.

Within the past few days there has been very little news of interest coming from Querétaro. When I last wrote you, I informed you of the organization of the Senate, and the appointment of the one-third additional, according to the Constitution, necessary to complete the body. I now send you the Constitution of Mexico, and their election laws, in order that your readers may fully comprehend not only the organization, but the action of this most extraordinary body.

Our last advices from Querétaro were to the 5th, and up to that time they were not yet ready to take action on the treaty. Letters inform me that the treaty will probably come before them on the 9th or 10th. I have two letters before me, equally good authority, one of which says there will be a long discussion on the merits of the treaty, while the other says there will not be, so it is hard to conjecture what will be the course pursued, whether the *Moderadoes* will push it through, or whether they will yield to the opponents the desire for debate. Combining all the evidences I have before me, I am inclined to the belief that the discussion will be short, and that the treaty will be ratified, either by the Congress itself, or by the President, authorized by the Congress. As far as they have been able to count noses, the peace party are in a large majority. The Mexican Government look upon the treaty as out of all danger.

A report has been current here for several days, that the Congress did not intend to confirm the election of Herrera for President, but in the meantime appoint some person to discharge the duties. The light I have before me does not lead to any such conclusion, and I do not believe there is any foundation for the supposition.

Among the one-third members of the Senate—named by the Senate itself, the Chamber of Deputies, and the Supreme Court—is the Archbishop of the Church of Mexico. The old gentleman left for Querétaro yesterday, and is there to-night. He is one of the most decided advocates of peace, and will no doubt exercise a powerful influence on the immediate action of Congress.

Messrs. Sevier and Clifford are still here, and I expect they will leave for Querétaro during the present week; they have been expecting to go for the last ten days. I understand it is their determination to use every exertion to march the army out of the country by the Northern route, and thereby avoid the yellow fever. I am in hopes they will succeed, but am apprehensive they will not be able to accomplish their object.

Before I close to-night, I will receive a courier from Querétaro, with dates to the 6th. If he should bring anything of importance or interest, I will forward it.

The trial of five of the persons for the robbery and murder in Calle de la Palma, has been got through with. Lieut. Tilden is now on trial. One of the parties, a man by the name of Hollister, yesterday turned state's evidence, in addition to Armstrong, who has already done so in the trial of those previously arraigned. I forbear giving any opinion on the evidence already brought out, or the guilt of innocence of the parties, until the Court issues its verdict, which will not be done previous to the conclusion of the trial of all the persons charged.

P.S. Eight o'clock at night. The mail starts to-morrow morning for the coast. I have just received my courier from Querétaro—he left yesterday morning. On that morning the Chamber of Deputies adjourned until all the members of the Senate (i.e. the one-third elected by the Supreme Court, the Senate, and the Deputies) shall all be present. The only absent is the one from Morelia. He was on his way and was expected at Querétaro yesterday or to-day. If he should arrive as expected, the body will be ready to proceed with the election of President to-morrow, and the following or the day after, take up the treaty. There is no further news from the interior. I have the papers of San Luis, and letters from Guanajuato, Guadalajara, and Morelia, but they are as dry as I am about this time.

May 9, 1848. City of Mexico.

The Congress at Querétaro has, after some considerable effort, got completely organized. The Message of the President was delivered on the 6th, and replied to by the Congress on the same day. From the length of the document I am not able to send it to-day, but expect to receive it to-morrow, and will send it immediately after receipt. I send you the reply of the President of the Senate, also a letter from my correspondent there.

It is expected that the treaty was laid before the Senate to-day. If it is acted upon immediately, there is a decided majority in its favor, but there is no telling up to the very last hour what these people may do.

An attempt was made at Querétaro by some discontented spirits, who are not enjoying "the loaves and fishes," to produce a revolution, but it proved a most futile effort. Some of the army officers, who have been stricken from the army lists, having been making a similar effort at San Luis Potosi, but without success.

There seems to be but little objection to the treaty of peace throughout the country except by a portion of the army officers who have been thrown on their own resources instead of living on the government.

I am not yet changed in my opinion that the Congress will throw the responsibility of accepting the treaty on the Executive—if so, the better.

Our army is preparing to march, and the Mexican Government is preparing to return to this city, and also to occupy the Palace.

There is a dearth of local news.

May 11, 1848. City of Mexico.

All items of local news at present seem to be absorbed in the intelligence looked for from Querétaro. Even robberies and murders appear to be suspended until the affairs of state are settled by the Mexican Congress.

The intelligence brought from Querétaro is of the highest importance, as shadowing forth the result of peace or war, and the final action of the Mexican Congress on the treaty. The "Diligence" arrived to-night with dates to the 8th, and my courier with the proceedings to the 9th inst.

I enclose to you the Message of the President of the Mexican Republic. The document speaks for itself, and you, after reading it, can judge of the intentions of his Excellency.

The address of La Rosa, Minister of Relations, enclosing to the Chamber the Treaty of Guadalupe, was delivered on the 9th. I expect to receive it to-morrow. It is principally devoted to foreign affairs, and the greater part to the relations with the United States. In the course of his address he refers at length to the situation of the affairs of Mexico and the war. He states that the Government of Mexico has adopted the peace policy and it is their determination to carry out that policy, if possible, and cultivate the friendship of the United States, and that it is for the interest of Mexico to do so. My correspondent writes me that the Minister has taken a very high stand, adopted to an independent course, and evinces every disposition to stick to it, asserting that it is the duty of every patriot to sustain him.

The report of the Minister of War, Gen. Anaya, is also spoken of as a high-toned document.

Gen. Herrera has yielded to the urgent solicitations of his friends and consented to accept the office of President, which he was loath to do for some time, but now says that he is willing to forego his determination to retire to private life, considering that he has been honored by a majority of the votes of the Republic, and devote himself to the service of his country in this most important crisis.

Over two-thirds of the Chambers have avowed themselves in favor of accepting the treaty as modified by the Senate of the United States. My own letters, and a great number of others which I have seen to-night, all speak of the consummation of peace as decidedly certain and beyond doubt.

No discussion has as yet taken place on the treaty, the Chambers having been occupied after organization in receiving the Message of the President, and the expositions of the Ministers.

Don Riva Palacios, a member of the House of Deputies, returned to this city this evening by permission of the House, on account of serious sickness in his family. He says there is no doubt that the treaty will be accepted, and that its acceptance will not be endangered by the withdrawal of any portion of the members.

May 14, 1848. 10 O'clock. City of Mexico.

We have dates from Querétaro to the 11th, which I send you. I received them at a late hour last night, and I am not aware of anything later having arrived in this city.

I did not receive, as I expected, the report of La Rosa, Minister of Relations. It was ordered to be printed in connection with all the documents and correspondence connected with the negotiations of the treaty, among which is a communication from Señor Bernardo Couto, giving an account of his stewardship. From the length of the documents, and the time that will be occupied in printing, I think it hardly possible that we will receive them here before the latter part of the week. As soon as they arrive they will be forwarded to you.

I sent you the message of the President two days ago, also the new Mexican Tariff, to take effect on the exchange of ratifications. I now send you duplicates.

As you will see by the letters from Querétaro, the treaty was referred to the Committee on Foreign Relations on the 9th. It was expected they would report it for the consideration of the Chambers, by yesterday or to-morrow at the farthest. The Committee will, of course, report upon it favorably, as they are all decided supporters of the present government, and in favor of peace. From the letters and all the intelligence received from Querétaro, there appears to be no doubt as to its final passage, unless something in the chapter of accidents should prevent it. Over two-thirds of the Senate and Chamber of Deputies have expressed themselves in favor of ratifying the treaty. Many of the most violent opponents of the present party in power, will support the treaty, not for any love they have for the persons who negotiated, and under whose auspices it will be carried into effect, but because as long as we remain here, they are left perfectly powerless and will remain without any prospect of ascending to power.

There is a good deal of talk about revolutions and *pronunciamientos*, but from all I can learn, the "will is father to the thought," and for the present I have no idea that the action of the government will be interfered with by any internal dissensions. However, I think it altogether likely that a desperate effort will be made to overthrow the government as soon as we leave the country; whether it will be successful, remains to be seen. The government is preparing itself for the struggle. For this purpose they are organizing a "*foreign legion*," and I am told have made some favorable offers to some officers of ability in our army. If they succeed in this plan, "good-bye" to the days of *pronunciamientos*. One thousand American soldiers would secure the government a safe delivery from all the ills they have been subject to, and further, if 3,000 or 4,000 American soldiers are to remain in this country, they would give a tone to affairs here, that would not be disadvantageous to the United States.

Paredes and Father Jarauta are still at Aguas Calicutes, the former has been recognized by the National Guard as an officer of the army, and as such is respected by them. He is still turbulent, and being, by the revolution in France, thwarted in his monarchical schemes, is willing to hoist the flag of dictatorship, or anything else that will place in his hands the reins of government.

Almonte has left the capital and gone to New Leon, where his family resides. No doubt you will soon hear of his endeavoring to set in motion the Republic of the Rio Grande. He is completely defunct in this region.

I stated in my last letter that we all, particularly the Commissioners, would endeavor to march the army out of the country by the North. Upon consideration, I think it would be attended with more difficulty and loss than to go by way of Vera Cruz. We would have to encounter the rainy season in the rich table lands, which, at that season, are almost impassable for an empty stage coach. Then how would it be possible for us to pass it with our large and heavy trains and artillery? Added to this, the troops would be exposed to the rains and all their attending ills, in a march of near three months. Many of our troops would be left sick far in the interior of a foreign land. Small detachments would have to be left scattered all along the route, and the expence and loss of life would be incalculable. These, with many other objections, render the returning of our army by that route next to folly. By going the other way to reach the Gulf, we could stop in the vicinity of Jalapa, if we found the coast too sickly. But I am induced to believe that if we keep our troops out of the City of Vera Cruz, and embark them there, either above or below, we could avoid the *vomito*, as no person has ever been known to take it out of the city, when going from the interior to the coast, although the instances are frequent of persons taking it when coming *from* the coast, after passing through Vera Cruz. Taking, then, all things into consideration, I think we had better *vamos* the *rancho* as quick as possible, by the nearest and most practicable route. From the present appearance of things in these diggins, I think it altogether likely that the greater part of the army will have a Fourth of July spree, not in the Halls of the Montezumas, but in the Crescent City, in the halls of the "white settlements." Won't we make the juleps and white shirts suffer!

The trial of all the persons concerned in the late murder and burglary in this city closed yesterday. The findings of the Court are not yet published; I expect they will be to-morrow or the next day. No doubt some or all of them will be found guilty. The evidence before the Court showed that the private and the two sergeants were seduced into the affair by some of the officers concerned. Sergeant Wragg, on trial, pleaded guilty to the charge of burglary, but not to the charge of murder. I think it very probable he will receive the clemency of the commanding officer, on account of his previous good character and his gallant and meritorious conduct in the battles in Mexico.

To-morrow we expect to have a shooting match and somebody killed. Both the *caballeros* are civilians. I hope they will hallo before they shoot, if they undertake it in the street, and give a fellow a chance to get out of the way.

Give my compliments to that fellow of the *Vicksburg Sentinel*. If he should happen to come to New Orleans, give him a little ice-water, and I don't think it would hurt him to put a little on his head. "I never shoot unless the game is worth the ammunition," particularly against pop-guns. Let him, or that gentleman up the river, call me anything that suits their vivid imagination, unless they say *Whig*—if they call me a Whig, "give them jessie," for that's what I won't stand, any way they can fix it. Their late attacks on me only show how near the same channel the minds of great men run. Many of their sentences are precisely of the same language used by Gen. Pillow in his oral effusions before the Court in this city. Gen. Pillow has not forgotten the value of the Press, nor the Press the value of Gen. Pillow.

Querétaro, May 11, 1848.

The Message of Peña y Peña was not received with much favor, owing to the conviction which pervades it that peace, the dire necessity of the unfortunate, is a measure which will insure honor and prosperity to the nation. This unfavorable impression, however, was dissipated during the session of Tuesday (the 9th), by the reading of Rosa's preliminary remarks upon the Treaty, a composition very skillfully drawn up and devoted exclusively to demonstrating the impossibility of a further prosecution of the war.

The Treaty was referred to the Committee on Foreign Relations, composed of Jiminez, Lares, Solana, Macedo and Lecunza, all decided friends of peace. It is said that they will make their report on Saturday, the 13th. There are two questions in this business: the Treaty and the conduct of the Government respecting it. With regard to the first, it appears certain that two-thirds of each House are in favor of it. Several of the Deputies seem disposed to blame the Government for the manner in which the Treaty was brought about. At all events, this matter will be seized upon as a pretext for those desirous of a revolution, but no one will reflect upon the aggravated evils we suffer.

To-day Otero's project for the immediate organization of the National Guard was read in the Senate. I remarked that it prohibits the Guard from being at the disposal of the commanding generals. The matter was declared to be urgent, and was referred to a Special Committee.

It is now rumored that the report relative to the Treaty will be made to the House by its committee, on Monday, the 15th, or Tuesday, the 16th. The Senate's committee will report a day or two earlier, as the two committees agreed to deliberate in joint session, in order to hasten the business. The number of Congressmen increases daily. There are now in attendance eighty-six Deputies and thirty-seven Senators. The question of peace or war will soon be settled.

Almonte was yesterday in his quarters in Leon, not having been able to enter the Senate. The *Puros* are completely put down; but it is reported they are making preparations to give us any quantity of trouble after the departure of the American troops; but you well know how insignificant they are. You are already aware that Pacheco wishes to be considered the leader of the opposition in the House, but everybody ridicules him.

Gen. Paredes is wending his way towards Zacatecas, and although he is here supposed to entertain revolutionary designs, and has paid a visit to the celebrated Ampudia, I am inclined to believe that he is now a personage of no account whatever.

I will not criticise the President's Message. It was happy in many portions, but I thought there were many things which he should have omitted as unbefitting such a production. However, Congress is at length assembled in quorum, and we breathe freer.

The State of Jalisco has proposed, in the event of Congress not ratifying the Treaty, that the State Legislatures should do so. This will convince the *Puros* of the futility of all their maneuvres.

May 16, 1848. City of Mexico.

One of the most important items received to-night from Querétaro is the election of a Provisional President, which resulted in the choice of Señor Peña y Peña. It may not, perhaps, be amiss for me to explain to you the causes which call for the election of a Provisional President.

According to the Constitution of Mexico, if a vacancy occur in the office of President during the recess of Congress, the Chief Justice, by virtue of his office, becomes the President. But if a vacancy occurs during the session of Congress, and continues for fifteen days, then the Congress must choose a President to fill the office until such time as the regular course supplies them with one, and so in like case if the President-elect is prevented from taking his seat by sickness or other cause. Until the votes of all the States arrive, they cannot be unsealed and counted, and in the present case the vote of one State has not been received at Querétaro, and therefore, although Señor Herrera is the President-elect by a large majority of votes, but for the reason above stated, they cannot be counted, and he consequently cannot be installed, and the Republic is left without a head and front. In this position of national affairs the Constitution provides that after fifteen days of session shall have expired, the Congress must choose a *Provisional* President. This is the present state of affairs, and Peña y Peña is the choice, by receiving the votes of eleven States and Herrera four, the opposition to the Government voting for Herrera.

For the general news from Querétaro, I refer you to the enclosed letters from my correspondent. There seems to be no doubt at present in reference to the final action of the Mexican Government upon the treaty, and we are looking from day to day for the ratification, though, individually, I think it hardly probable that we will receive it before the latter part of this week or the first of next. I have made all necessary arrangements to receive it and forward it by express to Vera Cruz.

From all the lights before us the Mexican Government appear to be able and determined to maintain themselves against all opposition. The prompt and decisive manner in which they put down the late revolution at San Luis Potosi, the order for the arrest of Paredes and Jarauta, the disbanding of the old army and the reorganization of the new on an entirely different principle, and the formation of the foreign legion, all lead us to conclude that they are sincere in their efforts to establish a stable and independent government. The votes cast at the election of the Provisional President show that Herrera will have the support of some of the most belligerent States.

The sentences of the persons lately tried for burglary and murder in this city, has not yet been made public. The proceedings of the Court are still under review by Gen. Butler, the general understanding is, however, that they are sentenced to be hung.

Two sergeants and a private were assassinated in the street a few days ago, by some *leperos*, but I could not learn their names.

I expect in the course of a few days to hear of all the outposts being called in, that they may make preparations for the march to the coast.

Messrs. Sevier and Clifford have not yet started for Querétaro, although they have been expecting to go from day to day. I hardly think it probable that they will go before the ratification of the treaty.

Querétaro, May 14, 1848

It appears that the revolt at San Luis was caused by the troops not having received their pay for three days, although one of the former aides-de-camp of Gen. Paredes appeared as an instigator in it, from having distributed among them some money. He is in prison and from him something may be known as to the particulars.

The Committee, of the Chamber of Deputies, presented at last their report, recommending the adoption of the treaty; it was in secret session, the discussions thereon, to commence next Monday, will also take place with closed doors. I suppose that by Wednesday or Thursday the votes will be given. There are now ninety Deputies present. On the motion of Rodrigeuz de San Miguel, in the Senate, the Minister of War was called on to state the measures which the Government had taken for the security of the District and for the evacuation of the Capital by the enemy. Its situation was represented as being truly deplorable. As Government has done nothing herein, no satisfactory answer could be obtained. We never were in more want than we now are of a Government that will act in all cases energetically. In this respect, we evidently are in great need of a change.

As the constitution requires that eight days after the meeting of the Chamber they should examine the returns in the election of a President of the Republic, the articles thereon were yesterday read by order of the President of the Chamber, and as the number of votes was incomplete by one State not being represented, an extraordinary session was summoned in order to elect a President *ad interim*. Romero proposed this day that two persons should be named with Peña as a Council, but the motion was rejected, consequently they proceeded to the election, and Peña y Peña was named by eleven votes to four for Herrera.

The elections in Morelia have also taken place this day, so that on receiving those votes and Deputies in the course of the week, we may proceed to verify the election of a constitutional President.

Gen. Anaya has asked for and obtained two months' leave to visit Irapuato, on account of his health, until some one is named as his successor.

To-morrow the discussion on the report of the Committee of Foreign Relations will take place. It fully approves the treaty of peace, with the modifications made by the United States Senate. It is to be discussed in private session. This will be the work of five or six days, so that all will be settled this week, as regards the Chamber of Deputies.

Querétaro, May 14th, 1848.

Yesterday, the 13th, the report of the Committee of Foreign Relations, in favor of the ratification of the treaty, was read the first time, and it was decided that the affair should be discussed in secret session, by a majority of forty-four to thirty-six. Although the regulation of the debates establishes nothing in this particular, this agreement has met the views of men of sense, for in fact, political affairs of great importance ought to be discussed with full liberty of speech, and such is not always exercised in open session. At least it cannot be denied that it will prevent our young Deputies from allowing their vanity (*amar propria*) to overcome their reason, on this occasion, when so grave a question is to be treated. The people have given power to their representatives to decide on public affairs without prescribing the mode and the form, and it is to be presumed that the representatives will do their best for the people.

The regulations being well understood, a second reading of the report will be given to-morrow, and then the discussion will take place. Nothing certain can be said as to the result, but something is meant by the threats of certain furious zealots against those whom they call peace-makers; they stick pasquinades against them on the walls, and all that sort of thing, but it will all end in smoke. Those who have nothing to lose, the revolutionary characters, and those that would be the first to run before the enemy, excepting a few honorable exceptions, are for war.

As it is understood that eight days after the assembling of the general Congress, they will proceed to the opening of the returns for the presidential elections, provided that at least three-fourths of the States have voted, which has thus far not been accomplished. This well deserved (*benemerito*) and honorable General (Herrera) will, in all probability, take the reins of government constitutionally, and the provisional government of Peña y Peña will last but a few days afterwards. Having now acted in Morelia, the necessary number of votes are at hand to elect a regular executive, or constitutional President. It has been deemed judicious, for good reasons, not to change the *statu quo* for the remaining few days of the provisional government, and to obviate the necessity of changing the ministry.

A revolt, similar to the ridiculous affair at San Luis, also took place in Morelia, but as in the former place it was instantly quelled.

May 18, 1848. City of Mexico.

During the whole of the day the city has been in a state of extraordinary excitement, on account of the supposed passage of the treaty by the Chamber of Deputies. Shortly the news spread far and wide, and there was scarcely a man in the city who did not believe it. I placed very little confidence in it myself, relying on the extensive arrangements I had made in Querétaro for the earliest intelligence. Some of the newspaper men took the bait, hook and all, and that immortal, extraordinary individual, Don Bugby, of express notoriety, in conjunction with Country McClusky as a bodyguard, who has been held in readiness for some time past, was despatched with orders to "do or die." But "this world is all a fleeting show, for man's illusion given," and no one has a right to complain if he is once in a while sucked in a little.[3] The truth of the whole affair is, that a trap had been set to humbug others, and it worked so admirably that it caught the projectors themselves, and those who were expected to bite at the bait have been too long in the service to be caught with chaff.

I have got an express ready, and as soon as the news arrives, let it be favorable or unfavorable, you shall have it.

I send you, to-night, my correspondence from Querétaro—it will give you a correct account of the proceedings and doings at that place. You will see by it that, as I told you three weeks ago, the treaty will not be definitely acted upon by the Mexican Congress before the 24th or 25th. The vote of Michoacan (Morelia), which had not arrived at the time of the election of the Provisional President, has been cast for Pedraza. As soon as it arrives, which will hardly be before the treaty is ratified, the President will be chosen and Herrera will take his seat.

I send you the sentence of the officers and others, charged with murder and burglary at Calle de la Palma No. 5, in this city. It is shocking to read it, but still we cannot grumble at the stern sentence of justice. The Court who tried them was the ablest Military Court I ever saw organized, embracing not only men of high legal attainments, but of the strictest integrity. Although we all must regret that officers of the American Army have to be executed in the capital of the enemy, which has been subdued by the aid of their prowess and skill, still it is the only way in which we can wipe out the stain they have cast upon the honor of their country. The original sentence has been approved by the Commanding General, and I do not see any chance for their pardon, as they have been tried by their peers.

3. Quote from Thomas Moore.

There is to be a Council of War to-night, at headquarters, for the purpose of consulting on the movements of the army, in retiring from Mexico. There are many conflicting opinions, and the result of their deliberations is looked to with some degree of interest. Some want to go by the way of San Luis and Monterey, while others are in favor of a direct movement for the Gulf, by the Vera Cruz and Orizaba route.

We have a report in town to-day, that Maj. Gen. Patterson's Division is under marching orders for Vera Cruz. I hardly think it is correct, as the movement seems to be premature.

Popocatepetl. A party of officers returned day before yesterday from the heights of this mountain. One of them, we hear, went down some distance into the crater. Several of the officers are very spirited and graphic writers, and have promised me an account of their expedition. They continued their route around Lake Tezcueo [Tezcoco], visiting the ancient pyramids and burial places. Their account may be looked upon as highly interesting.

Gen. Anaya, Minister of War, etc., has asked and obtained leave of absence for several months. He goes to Iraperato, for the recovery of his health.

We have no murders to report to-day. Fires are not known in the ancient city of the Aztecs, and I suppose for the reason that they have not the great improvement of insurance officers, and at the present time a horrible accident maker would starve.

I have the pleasure of announcing to you the annexation, by treaty, this evening, of one of Uncle Sam's sons, Capt. Samuel Head, to one of the fair descendants of the noble tribe of Ancients, her name commences with Ella Señorita Donna ------, and the balance you shall know in my next.

Headquarters, Army of Mexico
Mexico, May 17, 1848.
Orders No. 95

I. Before a Military Commission convened at the National Palace, City of Mexico, by virtue of Orders No. 55, of April 9, 1848, and of which Col. M.V. Thompson, 3[d] Regiment Kentucky Volunteers, is President, were tried:

First—Lieut. Isaac Hare, 2[d] regiment Pennsylvania Volunteers.

Charge 1st—"Murder"—*Specification*—In this, that the said Lieut. Isaac Hare, of the 2[d] Regiment Pennsylvania Volunteers, did, on the 5th day of April, in the year of Christ one thousand eight hundred and forty-eight, in the City of Mexico, commit murder upon Manuel Zorriza, a citizen of Mexico, by shooting him in the head.

Charge 2d—"Burglary"—*Specification*—In this, that the said Lieut. Isaac Hare, of the 2d Regiment Pennsylvania Volunteers, did, on the 5th day of April, in the year of Christ one thousand eight hundred and forty-eight, forcibly, and with a felonious intent, break into and enter a house in the City of Mexico, situate on the street de la Palma and numbered 5.

To all of which the accused pleaded, "Not Guilty."

Sentence—The Commission, after mature deliberation on the evidence adduced, found the accused *guilty* as charged, and sentence him, Lieut. Isaac Hare, of the 2d Regiment Pennsylvania Volunteers, to be hanged by the neck until he is dead, dead, dead, two-thirds of the members of the Court concurring therein.

Second—Lieut. B.F. Hutton, 2d Regiment Pennsylvania Volunteers.

Charge 1st—"Murder"—*Specification*—In this, that Lieut. B.F. Hutton, of the 2d Regiment Pennsylvania Volunteers, did, on the 5th day of April, in the year of Christ one thousand eight hundred and forty-eight, in the City of Mexico, commit murder upon Manuel Zorriza, by shooting him in the head.

Charge 2d—"Burglary"—*Specification*—In this, that said Lieut. B.F. Hutton, of the 2d Regiment Pennsylvania Volunteers, did, on the 5th day of April, in the year of Christ one thousand eight hundred and forty-eight, forcibly, and with a felonious intent, break into and enter a house in the City of Mexico, situated on Calle de la Palma and numbered 5.

To all which the accused pleaded, "Not Guilty."

Sentence—The Commission, having maturely considered the testimony adduced, found the accused *guilty* as charged, and sentence him, Lieut. B.F. Dutton, 2d Regiment Pennsylvania Volunteers, to be hung, at such time as the General-in-Chief may designate, by the neck until he is dead, dead, dead. Two-thirds of the members of the Court concurred in this sentence.

Third—John Laverty.

Charge 1st—"Murder"—*Specification*—In this, that John Laverty, did, on the 5th day of April, in the year of Christ one thousand eight hundred and forty-eight, in the City of Mexico, commit murder upon Manuel Zorriza, by shooting him in the head.

Charge 2d—"Burglary"—*Specification*—In this, that said Laverty did, on the 5th day of April, in the year of Christ one thousand eight hundred and forty-eight, forcibly, and with a felonious intent, break into and enter a house in the City of Mexico, situated on Calle de la Palma and numbered 5.

To all which the accused pleaded, "Not Guilty."

Sentence—The Commission, after having maturely considered the evidence adduced, found the accused *guilty* as charged, and sentence him to be hanged by the neck until he is dead, dead, dead, two-thirds of the members of the Court concurring in the sentence.

Fourth—Lieut. B.P. Tilden, 2d Infantry.

Charge 1st—"Murder"—*Specification*—In this, that Lieut. B.P. Tilden, of the 2d Regiment of Infantry, did, on the 5th day of April, in the year of Christ one thousand eight hundred and forty-eight, in the City of Mexico, with malice afterthought, killed Manuel Zorriza, a peaceable citizen of the said City of Mexico, by shooting him in the head.

Charge 2d—"Burglary"—*Specification*—In this, that the said Lieut. B.P. Tilden, of the 2d Regiment of Infantry, did, on the 5th of April, in the year of Christ one thousand eight hundred and forty-eight, before sunrise or daylight, forcibly and with a felonious intent, break into and enter a house in the City of Mexico, situated on Calle de la Palma, and numbered 5.

To all which the accuse pleaded, "Not Guilty."

Sentence—The Commission have maturely considered the testimony adduced, found the accused *guilty* as charged, and sentenced him, Lieut. B.P. Tilden, 2d Regiment of Infantry, to be hanged by the neck until he is dead, dead, dead. Two-thirds of the Court concurred in this sentence.

Fifth—Sergts. B.F. Wragg and Stewart, and Priv. John Wall, 7th Infantry.

Charge 1st—"Murder"—*Specification*—In this, that the said Sergts. B.F. Wragg and Stewart, and Priv. John Wall, of the 7th Infantry, did on the 5th day of April, in the year of Christ one thousand eight hundred and forty-eight, in the City of Mexico, with malice aforethought, commit murder upon Manuel Zorriza, a peaceable citizen of the said City of Mexico, by shooting him in the head.

Charge 2d—"Burglary"—*Specification*—In this, that the said Sergts. B.F. Wragg and Stewart, and Priv. John Wall, did, on the 5th day of April, in the year of Christ one thousand eight hundred and forty-eight, in the City of Mexico, before daylight, forcibly and with a felonious intent, break into and enter a house in said City of Mexico, situated on Calle de la Palma, and numbered 5.

To all which the prisoners each pleaded, "Not Guilty."

Sentence—The Commission, after mature consideration of the testimony adduced, found the prisoners each and severally *guilty* as charged, and sentence them, Sergts. B.F. Wragg and Stewart, and Priv. John Wall, to be hanged by the neck until they are dead, dead, dead. In this sentence two-thirds of the Court concurred.

II. The Maj. Gen. Commanding approves the proceedings, findings and sentences of the Military Commission in the foregoing cases.

Lieuts. Isaac Hare and B.F. Dutton, 2d Regiment Pennsylvania Volunteers, and B.P. Tilde, 2d Infantry, and John Laverty, will be executed on the 25th inst., between the hours of 8 and 11 o'clock A.M. under the direction of the Military and Civil Governor the City of Mexico.

Upon the recommendations of the Court, the sentences in the cases of Sergts. B.F. Wragg and Stewart, and Priv. John Wall, of the 7th Infantry, are respectively remitted. They will be kept in close confinement until the close of the war, when they will each be dishonorably discharged from the service.

Upon the like recommendations of the Court, no further proceedings will be taken against the prisoners, Jesse Armstrong and J.A. Hollister, who appeared as witnesses for the prosecution. They will be kept in close confinement until the close of the war, and then set at liberty.

III. The Military Commission, of which Col. M.V. Thompson, 3d Regiment Kentucky Volunteers, is President, is hereby dissolved.

By order of Maj. Gen. Butler,
Lorenzo Thomas, Asst. Adjt. General

May 20. 1848. City of Mexico.

We have our dates from Querétaro to the 18th, inclusive—I enclose to you my letters. You will see that the vote has been taken in the Chamber of Deputies on the report of the Committee of Foreign Relations, recommending the adoption of the treaty, and decided in the affirmative by a vote of forty-eight to thirty-six.

The vote had not yet been taken on the treaty direct, but my correspondent writes that we may look for it from one moment to another.

The discussion in the Chamber of Deputies has been animated and pertinacious. The debates have been conducted in secret session. I have made provisions to have them reported but was unable to do so on this account. However, as they will be found interesting, as well as curious, I will send them to you as soon as it is possible to get them.

Among others who have opposed the treaty in the House is Señor Cuevas, brother of the Commissioner. He is said to have made a most violent attack upon it, denouncing in strong terms every thing and person connected with it. Go it, greasers!

The Senate will act on the treaty without much discussion, and I should not be surprised if they adopt it the same day that it comes before them.

Mr. Sevier has been seriously indisposed for several days back, but has recovered. He is now attending to business, or rather waiting the operations of the Mexican Congress, to discharge his duties here and return home. He was attacked with bilious colic.

The State Government at San Luis Potosi is kicking up a devil of a fuss about the late attempt at revolution there—they are threatening to tear the insides out of everyone connected. If they conclude as they have started I don't expect there will be another revolutionary spirit left in the Republic, but unfortunately they always let down on the quarter stretch. Montenegro and Ortiz have *vamosed*. Many of the inferior officers and "pet familiars" have been placed in duress. Montero's wrists have been ornamented with metallic ruffles; he is the king bee of the affair, it is supposed. I informed you sometime since that Ortega and Mejia had gone there, as the agents of Santa Anna, to raise a row, if possible, and it now appears they are suspected of being connected, but the Government is vacillating about arresting them. If these gentlemen should come within the pale of the law, I understand they contemplate pleading "letter-writing," as it is a system of American tactics which is worthy of imitation.

This evening we had a thundering storm, which commenced about 5 o'clock, and has not entirely ceased up to the hour of writing, 10 o'clock. There is one gentleman who expects to get wet up to a most uncomfortable part in getting this letter off to-night. The storm commenced very suddenly, with most unreasonable-sized hail-stones, which made all the dogs, greasers, and white folks take to their dens in double quick time. I just saved myself from the peltings without any time to spare, and coiled up on my bed in comparative comfort and luxury, reading a *Weekly Delta* of the 8th inst., when spang—spang—crash went the whole side of my room, which is entirely glass, for you must know that I live a good ways up in the world. This "moved my boots a little," I assure you, and to-morrow the *Delta* will have to look out for a bill of damages or a law suit. The latter I will avoid, you may depend, as one Mexican can outswear all the Americans in the country, but the way the streets are filled with water, would make all the croakers about Lake Poydras close their mouths forever.

The German population here are much elated at the news received last night from the Fatherland. The ladies have adopted head-ribbons of the old tri-color of their former nationality, and many gentlemen have them tied in the button-holes of their vests, in honor of the late revolutions in the land of their nativity. I should not be surprised if they get up a fandango on the strength of it; if they do, there will be some waltzing in these parts.

I informed you in my last of the negotiation of a treaty in this place, and its final ratification by the parties, and stated that to-night I would send the names of the signers, so here is the official notice from the *Star* of this morning:

> *Practical Annexation.*—MARRIED, in the City of Mexico, on the evening of the 18th inst., by the Rev. G.G. Goss, Chaplain of the Kentucky Brigade, Capt. SAMUEL C. HEAD, late of the Andrew Jackson (Louisiana) Regiment, to Señorita MICAELITA VILLA LOBOS, of this city.
>
> Hurrah for annexation! That's the way to do it. No more arguments on the policy of annexing Mexico, but go to work and annex her daughters—it is the only practicable mode

> just now of annexing the mother. Follow the example of Capt. Head, and the old people will soon follow you. May the union of Capt. Head and Micaelita be blest with many little Heads, who, in their turn, may also be impressed with the idea of practical annexation.[4]

These are the treaties that suit me: Goss in the evening—"through by daylight"—and bitters in the morning. Will the Mexicans claim indemnity for invaded territory? You must recollect that this was my Captain, under whom I mustered as high private on the Rio Grande, in the ever-memorable Andrew Jackson Regiment, and I therefore have a right to rejoice in his successes in this land of infirmities.

A controversy has taken place between the editors of *El Monitor* and the *Star*, in reference to a "*fried greaseress*" said to have been done up at Tacubaya. *El Monitor* calls upon the *Star* for information on the subject, which the man of the *Star* answers partly as follows:

> We always knew that our boys were very partial to the Mexican ladies, but never had an idea that any of them were so far gone as to *take 'em fried*. We cannot say that any Mexican woman has been fried, but we have incontestible proof that *unos Americanos* have been *burnt*!

Although it is a hard matter to raise a sweat out here, still it is a mighty *hot country* in some places.

A train of 140 wagons, escorted by Capt. Sibley's company of Dragoons, under command of Lieut. Thomas J. Wood, came in yesterday in twelve days from Vera Cruz. Lieut. George T. Shackelford, of the 6th, and Lieut. Daniel French, of the 15th, also came up with it.

A current report has been circulating in reference to the movement of Gen. Patterson for the coast on the 22d. I learn this evening that there has been no such order issued from head-quarters, although it is not improbable he will march during the course of the ensuing week.

4. Capt. Head was not the only American soldier to find romance in Mexico. A correspondent of the *Delta*, writing from Vera Cruz on June 11, 1848, remarked, "It is astonishing to perceive the vast number of white children a person sees at this place, while their parents are of a sooty color. I would not be surprised, if our army was to remain in the country for a few years, to see this Republic inhabited by a white population." *Daily Delta*, June 21, 1848.

I was just about closing my letter without a murder, but there is a report of a pistol in the street, and disturbance of some kind. I will go and see what it is.

I was not paid for my trouble in going down stairs, as there was nothing going on expect a greaser killed by some unknown hand. The Mexican police are carrying him out of the street.

May 21, 1848. Sunday. City of Mexico.

This morning, on the arrival of my courier, at 1 or 2 o'clock, from Querétaro, I despatched an express to Vera Cruz, with the important news of the passage of the treaty in the Chamber of Deputies of the Mexican Congress. I now send another extraordinary express, for fear that some accident might occur in the first.

The treaty passed at a quarter past 6 o'clock, on the evening of the 19th, by a vote of fifty-one in favor and thirty-five against.

This vote, beyond doubt, fixes the question of war or peace. The action of the Senate will be with little or no delay, we are momentarily looking for the intelligence. There is no doubt or question about the Senate, they will pass it by a large majority. I enclose you my Querétaro correspondence. Messrs. Sevier and Clifford start for Querétaro to-morrow morning. Gen. Butler is about to order in all the outposts, and prepare for an immediate march.

Gen. Smith starts for Vera Cruz on Wednesday next, to take charge of embarking the army, the most fitting man that can be sent, his military knowledge, and the manner he does business, will be worth to us hundreds of lives.

I expect the army to be marching between the 1st and 5th of June.

The ratification of the treaty by the Senate you will receive by an express. I shall be among the last of the Mohicans.

Get ready to let loose your big guns.

May 25, 1848. City of Mexico.

The officers and others who had been sentenced to be hanged on to-day, have been respited by Gen. Butler, by a special order of the following substance:

> The sentence of death, which has been passed upon persons by Courts of the American Army, whether Americans or Mexicans, is hereby suspended until further orders.

I am not aware what has influenced the commanding officer in suspending the sentence of death passed upon the officers and others for the murder and burglary at No. 5 Calle de la Palma, but really it does seem to many a very strange proceeding, and has surprised the community generally. They were undoubtedly guilty of one of the grossest outrages ever perpetrated upon society, and have, to some extent, stigmatized the corps and the army to which they belonged, which could only have been wiped out by blood, in a manner sanctioned by the laws of the country under which they hold commissions. Their trial was fair and impartial, and I have no hesitation in saying, that the Commission who tried and sentenced them, was the most able I have ever seen convened in the army. There were men upon it of the highest legal attainments, and the body were all men of sound discriminating judgment. The prisoners had able counsel, who labored hard in their defence, and the conclusion of the trial left no doubt as to their guilt. It was even so palpable that, upon its being rumored that they would be pardoned, the officers of the Pennsylvania Regiment, to which they belonged, remonstrated against their receiving any clemency whatever at the hands of the Commanding General, and asked that the law be allowed to take its regular course.

The good citizens of Querétaro are going to give our Commissioners a grand ball.

The exchange of ratifications was to take place to-day.

Gen. Mariano Arista is to be the Governor here when the Mexican Government takes up their quarters here.[5] I expect to see all the Mexican authorities here this week, coming in.

The Commissioners, Messrs. Sevier and Clifford, arrived at Querétaro at 4 o'clock yesterday.

My express has arrived ahead of all others. The Mexican Government express is expected momentarily. If it brings anything additional of moment, I will send another express.

5. Originally an officer in the Spanish army, Mariano Arista switched his allegiance to the Mexican independence movement in 1821. Captured by the French in 1838 at Vera Cruz, shortly after his release he was promoted to command the Mexican army on its northern frontier. Decisively beaten at Palo Alto and Resaca de la Palma in 1846, Arista was relieved of command, although he was soon appointed minister of war. Elected president in 1851, he served less than two years until overthrown by Santa Anna and sent into exile, dying August 7, 1855. Tucker, *Encyclopedia*, 26–27.

May 25, 1848. 12 O'clock at Night. City of Mexico.

I sent you by express at 8 o'clock this evening the news of the ratification of the treaty by the Senate of the Mexican Congress, by a vote of thirty-three against four. Another express is now starting and I now write you a short note more for the purpose of taking all the advantages than anything else, as you will probably receive my former letters far in advance.

Gen. Patterson's Division will march on the 30th inst., and all the troops will follow immediately after.

My former notes contained the letter of my correspondent at Querétaro.

May 26, 1848. 8 O'clock P.M. City of Mexico.

I have this moment received the final ratification of the Treaty of Peace by the Mexican Congress, and hasten to forward it to you. It was put to vote in the Senate on the 25th, at 3 o'clock. The vote stood thirty-three for, and four against it. It was reported by the Chairman of the Committee on Foreign Relations on the 22^{d}, and the debate was continued by several members up to the hour of its being put on its passage. You will see that it did not meet with so much opposition in the Senate as it did in the Chamber of Deputies.

I enclose to you the letters of my Querétaro correspondent.

Gen. Smith left for Vera Cruz on the 24th, to make preparations for embarking the troops.

All the outposts have been ordered in to this city. They will be ready to march in three days after they arrive, which will be in a day or two.

Gen. Patterson's Division, being the first to move, will march in two or three days.

In ten days or less all the American army will be on their march for the coast.

We will be hampered some with our sick, but this cannot be helped, as it would not do to leave those behind who are unable to travel.

Messrs. Sevier and Clifford left here for Querétaro with an American escort on the 23^{d}, at 7 o'clock. The exchange of ratifications will take place in Querétaro. The Commissioners have full power to exchange there or here.

Of course, the citizens of New Orleans will fire a grand salute. Give my compliments to them, and ask them to fire a gun for every regiment in the field, Regular and Volunteer. They will soon be among you. You will then see the boys who "have been baptized in blood and come out steel." They have "conquered a peace" at the point of the bayonet, and for the sake of humanity and justice, let them revel one night in the "Halls of the White Settlements," before you send them down to Yucatan to be eaten up with mosquitoes and sand flies.

It is expected the ratifications will be exchanged to-day, the 26th inst.

The withdrawal of the troops will be in the following order: 1st, Gen. Patterson's Division; 2^{d}, Gen. Marshall's Division; 3^{d}, -------- Division, ten new regiments; 4th, 2^{d} Division of old Regulars, Gen. Stephen W. Kearny; 5th, 1st Division of old Regulars, Gen. Worth.[6]

We have 2,000 sick to take away with us. This will cut short our transportation for the withdrawal.

The heavy batteries (siege) of Lieut. Hagner and Capt. John F. Roland, marched on the 26th inst.

The troops from Pachuca and Cuernavaca are already on their march direct for Peroté.

Querétaro, May 23, 1848.

The following propositions of Señor Solana underwent their first reading in the Chamber of Deputies:

1—The Government cannot alienate, hypothecate, pledge, nor in any manner compromise the indemnity fund allowed by the United States under the treaty of peace.

2—The ministers of the treasury and public credit shall unite for the purpose of proposing a plan whereby the application of said fund shall be regulated, a considerable portion thereof being set apart for the expenses of colonization of the frontier.

6. Stephen W. Kearny left Columbia College for a commission in the War of 1812. He remained in the army and served exclusively on the western frontier, reaching the rank of colonel in 1836. Promoted to brigader general, Kearny led the miniscule Army of the West on an invasion that led to Santa Fé and on into California. He received two wounds in combat in California prior to the Mexican government surrendering that territory to U.S. forces. Appointed governor of Vera Cruz in 1847 and later of Mexico City, he was brevetted major general and died on October 31, 1848 after returning to the States. Tucker, *Encyclopedia*, 336–37.

3—The Government shall be specially prohibited from disposing of said fund, until its whole application shall have been fixed; but it shall be authorized to dispose of a sum not exceeding half a million of dollars, in order to enable it to comply with its most urgent and pressing engagements.

4—With regard to the foregoing proposition, the ministers shall report separately, and with the shortest delay possible, in order that the aforesaid plan may be carried into effect forthwith.

The following propositions of Señor Macias were also read at once:

1—Congress has no power to sell, cede, or in anywise alienate a portion, or the whole, of the territory of one or more of the States.

2—If imperious necessity compels the Republic to make territorial cessions prohibited in the preceding article, it can only be done by and with the express consent and approbation of the State or States ceded, of three-fourths of the members composing each Chamber, and three-fourths of the State Legislatures.

Querétaro, May 25.

To-day the discussion on the report of the Committee (relative to the Treaty) commenced in the Senate, and speeches were delivered by Otero, Robredo, and General Morales, against the treaty.

In the Chamber of Deputies the election of President of the Supreme Court took place, and Peña was chosen by a unanimous vote, except that of San Luis Potosi, which was given to Quintana Roo. Sierra was elected Vice President of the Court by the votes of ten States, four having voted for Morales and one for Navarrete. The Chamber then went into secret session.

The letters received from Querétaro, says the *Monitor* of Mexico, have disgusted us extremely at beholding the attempts of that treacherous faction which was then striving in so base a manner for annexation, and now entertains the design of creating a tumult on the pretext of the Government returning to its capital, while the enemy are yet in the country. They will not succeed, because the Government knows how to take its measures opportunely, to re-organize the National Guard with troops of a respectable and well-known character, and with them it is hoped that matters will be carried on with energy, and that the dissolute and turbulent rabble will be compelled to respect the Government, by being severely chastised, if they disturb the public tranquility. It cannot be doubt that all worthy citizens, who have some stake in the community, will cheerfully enlist in the National Guard, and will sustain the Government, particularly as the commander of that corps is a general selected by the people, in accordance with the requisitions of the Constitution, and one who has already given signal proofs of his worth as of his patriotism.

Querétaro, May 25, 1848.

To-day, a few minutes after 3 o'clock, P.M., the Senate approved the action of the Chamber of Deputies, on the Treaty of Peace with the United States of the North, by a vote of thirty-three ayes, four nays. The matter is now consummated and only awaits the customary exchanges.

The discussion in the Senate was as dignified as luminous. Pedraza, Muñoz Ledo, Ramirez D. Fernando, Rodriguez de San Miguel and Rosa were the advocates of peace. When the nation shall have taken cognizance of their able and eloquent speeches, it will bless, beyond doubt and despite the clamors of factions, such patriots who, discarding the dictates of their feelings, and listening only to the voice of a cool and severe judgment, have determined to save our country—for the adoption of peace is equivalent thereto, less having been yielded to the enemy than he had won by his sword.

If, after the wise conduct of those in power, anarchy raises her horrible head among us, it cannot be considered a consequence of the adoption of the Treaty, although it is so declared according to the extravagant logic of factions. That monster has for many long years fixed his abode among us, and to the disorder and confusion it has caused, the Republic owes its deplorable condition.

Would that we could learn to acquire wisdom from the sad lessons of the past! Would that we could learn to preserve what still remains to us! It is enough to satisfy a nation which, if it conducts itself with judgment and prudence, can yet be happy and respected.

Peace is consummated—let us reap its benefits.

It is now nearly 5 o'clock, P.M., and the American Commissioners have just arrived.

May 30. City of Mexico.

To-day the division of Gen. Patterson left for the coast. Day after to-morrow, the division of Gen. Marshall will leave.

Our Commissioners were at Querétaro on the 28th. My correspondent writes me that there is no news there, and nothing more.

I look for the return of our Commissioners in the course of two or three days.

Gen. Butler will start from here about Monday next, in company with Mr. Sevier.

At the last accounts, Mr. Sevier was sick at Querétaro.

The Yucatan expedition, which was fitting out here, has been knocked in the head by Gen. Butler. It was an awful misfortune to the "go ahead" of the army.

Where are all the harpers and croakers in your city, and the "intelligent officers" and "sagacious editors," who have been continually crying out that there would be no peace? Was not "the wish father to the thought?" Or was it because interest depended upon it? I have something to say on this subject, but am too unwell to-day to write more than a line.

June 3, 1848. Mexico.

[We are sorry to announce to our readers that the sickness of "Mustang" has deprived us and them, for a short time, of the benefit of his enterprise, energy, and judgment, in obtaining and forwarding news. A friend has kindly supplied his place and written us the following interesting letter.]

I regret extremely to announce to you the temporary indisposition of "Mustang." Don't be alarmed, it is not much, and with the kind and devoted attention of the good people of the house in which he lives, the virtues of the *Banos de Jesus*, and his unconquerable spirits, he'll soon be himself again. You would not think he was much sick, anyhow, if you could see him lolling on his luxurious bed, actually enveloped in cologne, but as he says he is, *and no mistake*, I must *gin in* and comply with his request and drop you a few lines to keep you informed of the passing events in this capital of the Aztecs, which we are evacuating as rapidly as possible.

On the 29th, the officers of the 2d Infantry, in a body, with the veteran Riley at their head, called on Gen. Patterson and bid him farewell. The general, with his wonted hospitality, turned out liberally from his store of "creature comforts" (never once thinking of that precious juice which the devouring element destroyed lately in Philadelphia), and made all feel as happy as possible, and beguiled them into the momentary belief that they were not to part from the dark-eyed daughters of this sunny clime. Various toasts and sentiments were drank. One given by an officer of the 2d Infantry, as it conveys a compliment to the worthy general, should go before the public: "The health of Maj. Gen. Patterson—we have served at various times under him with great satisfaction and pleasure, and if war's shrill note is to be again sounded, may it be our fortune to have him for our leader!"

Capt. Lee, that most distinguished Engineer officer, left, with other gallant officers of his corps, on the 28th. Col. Hitchcock, the Inspector General of the Army, with his assistant, Maj. Robert C. Buchanan, of the 4th Infantry, left on the 29th. Col. Hitchcock repairs immediately to New Orleans to make every preparation for mustering the volunteers out of service.

Clothing stores be on the look-out, there's many an "Oliver Oldbuck" who has to "turn over a new leaf;" boot and shoe stores lay low and keep your eyes skinned; hatter shops spread out your ram beavers; fancy stores, who have presents for wives, sweethearts, and children, do not forget to advertise them. Lieut. Hagner, with the ordnance, and Capt. Roland, with his heavy battery of captured guns, left the same day. Lieut. Stewart, with a company of the 3d Artillery, compose the escort. The Mexican Commissioners objected to our taking away the guns, claiming them under the treaty. It reserved to the Mexicans the guns captured in *permanent* works. The guns taken away were captured at Contreras and Churubusco and placed in the Citadel for safe keeping. Because they were there, the Commissioners claimed them. Gen. Butler ordered Col. Hitchcock to make a special report in the case. The report, of course, sustained our claims, and Gen. Butler said he would stand by it, if it renewed the war.

On the 30th, Gen. Patterson moved with his division. On the 1st, Gen. Marshall moved with his division. The ten regiments are formed into a division, commanded by Col. William Trousdale. The 1st Brigade of that division, commanded by Col. Bonham, left on the 3^{d}; the 2^{d} Brigade, under Col. Johnson, will leave on the 4th.

Gen. Kearny's Division will commence their march on the 5th, the 2^{d} Brigade, under Maj. Thompson Morris, marching on that date; the 1st Brigade, under Riley, on the 6th. Gen. Worth, with his division, will march about the 7th, and then the *damned Yankees* will have left. Gen. Butler and staff will move early in the week. "Mustang" will move, if possible, with the 2^{d} Division (Kearny's), if he has to be tied to the tail of a jackass.

The Commissioners arrived this morning. Col. Sevier is convalescent. He will leave early in the week. Col. Morgan has recovered from a severe attack of typhoid fever.

It is the general belief, that the very devil will be to pay in this city when our troops leave it. Old Chaos, it is presumed, will arise in all his majesty. From the bottom of my heart, I pity the well-disposed inhabitants. Rumors were in circulation, that, at the different places which our troops have lately left, many of the women who had shown any attention to our officers, had been most shamefully abused, had their hair cut off, and other shocking outrages offered to their persons. At first it was not credited, but since we have had ocular demonstrations of the fact here, we can believe anything. Three ladies of easy virtue presented themselves at the Bella Union Hotel, with their faces terribly branded "U.S." Can anything be conceived of, more mean, pitiful, and cowardly! This is a foretaste of what others may expect from these semi-barbarians!

Hoping my scrawl may, in a measure, take the place of Mustang's usual epistle, believe me, yours respectfully, W.S.H.

June 6, 1848. City of Mexico.

Severe sickness detains me here longer than I expected, and prevents me from writing you as fully as I desire. But, fortunately, there is but little of interest to communicate.

The troops have all left the city, except Gen. Worth's and the escort to headquarters. These will leave on the 8th and 9th.

The Ministry of Herrera's Administration, I learn, is as follows: Minister of Relations, Mariano Otero; Minister of War, Arista; Minister of Finance, Riva Palacio. Minister of Justice is not yet settled, definitely. Cuevas was nominated as Minister of Relations, but declined. It is thought he will go to the United States, as Minister Plenipotentiary.

The Mexican Government will commence its functions here about the 20th.

There is said to be another *pronunciamiento* at Aguas Calientes, by Paredes and Jarauta. It will end in smoke.

The Governor of the Federal District, José Flores, arrested some of the officers of the former National Guard, and sent them to Querétaro.[7] The reason I believe was, that in the present organization, some of the corps who were not distinguished for gallantry, and were particularly seditious whenever opportunity offered, were not among those designated as a portion of the army, whereupon they wrote the Old Governor a very impertinent and abusive note. Upon the strength of this, the Old Governor had all arrested he could get hold of, and sent them forthwith to Querétaro.

Col. Sevier and headquarters have been detailed here for several days because the Mexicans have not walked up to the chalk mark at the appointed time, to receive the $3,000,000 installment to be paid now.

June 9. City of Mexico.

There is but little news stirring. Col. Fauntleroy and the dragoons left this morning. Gen. Worth's Division and the Headquarters of the Army, together with Col. Sevier, will take their departure on Monday next, the 12th inst. This will complete the evacuation of the capital. All hands would have been gone some days ago, but the Mexicans would not allow us to "walk up to the Captain's office, and settle." They will be here in this city on Saturday, the 10th, and we will settle on the 11th, and *vamos* on the 12th. Voss & Hargous, Santa Anna's old partners, have a finger in the money-changing, somehow or other. They pay one per cent for the specie we have on hand, and then furnish the whole amount

7. In 1842 Captain José Flores went to Alta California to act as military secretary to the governor. After the outbreak of war, Flores and a small force captured the village of Los Angeles. Late in 1846 the Mexican residents elected him governor of California and he began a guerrilla campaign against American soldiers and civilians. Thrown in prison by disillusioned supporters, he was quickly released but Americans had taken advantage of this loss of leadership to gain control of the territory. Flores had little impact on the campaign of 1847, remained in the army, opposed the French, and died in 1866. Tucker, *Encyclopedia*, 237.

of the $3,000,000. These oily-tongued gentlemen, who have been crying out "English Treaty," and who have been the principal contractors to our army, are into somebody, somehow or other. You will recollect that this Mr. Louis S. Hargous is the gentleman who was the contractor for almost everything consumed by our army at Puebla last summer, and who got possession of the letters of a gentleman sent to Mexico on business, having a view to contract with the army, which letters were captured by some of Santa Anna's lancers. This is also the house which lost for us the Shannon Indemnity.[8] A friend of mine suggests that it is not unlikely that Santa Anna has been enjoying a portion of the profits made by the contracts entered into by this firm.

8. Most commony known as the Mexican Indemnity, payments for the annexation of Texas.

Freaner after the War

After his war reporting had come to an end, Freaner followed the army to Vera Cruz. In need of employment, Freaner was soon engaged as an auctioneer by Major Osborn Cross who had been assigned the duty of selling off surplus military equipment as various units embarked for the States. Although there was much interest from natives and speculators from New Orleans, Cross's first sales did not fare well. He hired Freaner to sort jumbled hardware and conduct auctions, turning over proceeds to the quartermaster after retaining a commission. An old friend who had newly arrived in Vera Cruz chanced to pass by one of those auctions:

> How much? how much? going—going—six reals and a medio—no more?—all done? Six—six—a-n-d seven, I have it—all done? A-l-l done? Gone. Seven for the *todos*.

Looking up he saw the auctioneer's hammer come down in the hands of James Freaner. During a brief meeting, Freaner assured his friend that "he had cut loose from all Journals" and planned to make a sizeable percentage in selling Uncle Sam's surplus gear. Writing that Mustang was "a lucky fellow, and quite a pet with government officers of every grade," he explained that "no paper ever had a better agent than the *Delta* had in him." Freaner's old

A Soldier's Return. *Courtesy Library of Congress*.

friend summarized his secret to success: "He would procure letters from different officers, and items of news or gossip, wherever he could find them. Working these into the shape of a correspondence, he would always forward duplicates to the *Delta*, one generally through a Mexican courier, and the other in some other way. Thus one of the letters would be pretty sure to reach its destination."[1]

Major Cross reported that his auctioneer "was indefatigable in his exertions to arrange the property and prepare the same to sell to the best advantage." Although some items brought next to nothing, such as damaged surf boats that sold for five dollars, Cross was satisfied with Freaner's efforts, writing, "What was offered at public sale, and sold by Mr. Freaner, brought, in many instances, a very fair price." Another of Freaner's New Orleans friends commended his work: "Mustang has been harder to work since he has been here, than at any other period during the war. He deserves a great deal of credit for the manner in which he has conducted the sales of public property that was of little or no use to citizens, and the property generally has brought a fair price." Word soon circulated through the country that Freaner had realized as much as $10,000 in commissions on the sale of the army's impedimenta, leading one New England editor to sarcastically comment, "Uncle Sam's pockets are very pickable." Freaner did not do quite as well as the press assumed. During the period of June and July of 1848 his auction sales totaled $66,146, a 5 percent commission leaving him with the still tidy sum of $3,307. He also managed to ship a mustang pony to New Orleans under somewhat mysterious circumstances. When his friend Maginnis wrote for answers, he jokingly noted "There is a Mustang poney (not a brother of yours) now in my charge."[2]

After concluding his auctioneering business, Freaner stopped in New Orleans on August 7 when he rented a room at 222 Tchoupitoulas and shortly thereafter received an appointment as a deputy city constable. He soon decided to make a trip home to

1. 30th Congress, 2nd Session, House Ex. Doc. 1, *Message from the President*, 208–12; *Boston Daily Atlas*, September 11, 1848.

2. 30th Congress, 2nd Session, House Ex. Doc. 1, *Message from the President*, 208–12; *New Orleans Crescent*, August 4, 1848; *Portland Weekly Advertiser*, September 19, 1848; Quartermaster Department Statement of Account, October 30, 1848; Maginnis to Freaner, July 11, 1848, James L. Freaner Letters, Beinecke Library.

see his family, receiving his auctioneering pay in New York on October 30 and arriving in Hagerstown on November 23, 1848. One detail Freaner needed to clear up was the education of his younger sister. He committed her instruction to Reverend Joshua Peterkin at the Landon Seminary in Urbana, Maryland, the school being advertised as "removed from the fascinating temptations incident to city life." In addition to paying for her education, board, and pocket money, Freaner told Peterkin, "I want to be liberal with her in this respect, and am anxious that she shall have the means of procuring every thing that may contribute to her comfort and convenience and gratify her fancy." Although he confessed that he himself could be called "strictly and literally 'a man of the world,'" Freaner insisted that

> she shall be raised with the fear of God before her eyes and that she be taught the importance & necessity of the most firm and implicit reliance upon the Divine Truths, as taught by the Protestant Church, as the only safe & certain protection of virtue, innocence and purity against the evils and misfortunes incident to life, as well as the only means of securing salvation in the world to come.

Having made these suitable arrangements for his sister's worldly education and immortal soul, Freaner headed south.[3]

By February he was back in New Orleans and on the 8th stopped by to visit friends at the office of the *Crescent*, a rival newspaper. The editor noted, "During the time he has been absent at the North, he has improved much; not meaning, however, that much improvement was necessary." There was also an announcement of Freaner's future plans, "Together with all the rest of the world, he is now going to California, where we hope he may realize all his dreams of wealth on the golden banks of the Sacramento." Freaner's hasty departure for the California gold fields may simply have been an attempt to regain his lost fortune. Zachary Taylor and the Whig Party had won the national vote held on November 7, 1848, and the life-long Democrat confessed the following day, "I have bet nearly all the

3. *Cohen's Orleans and Lafayette Directory, 1849*, 69; *Baltimore Sun*, November 27, 1848; Freaner to Peterkin, January 7, 1849, James L. Freaner Letters, Beinecke Library; *Baltimore American and Commercial Advertiser*, August 9, 1847.

money I had on the Presidential Election and every prospect at present of losing it."[4]

When the steamer *Isthmus* left New Orleans bound for the port of Chagres on February 19, Freaner was on board with a new career ahead of him. Instead of reporting for the *Delta*, he would now send reports from California back to a former competitor, the *Times-Picayune*. The latter paper would announce their new arrangement: "We are happy to announce that we have secured the services of Mr. Freaner as a correspondent for this paper. California is to be the scene of extraordinary events, if we are not mistaken, ere the close of the present year." The editor, noting Freaner's "perseverance and energy," continued:

> He acquired a reputation during the Mexican war for spirit, intelligence, and discretion which point him out as one of the best men in the country for a correspondent. His facilities for obtaining information will be second to those of no other man in the Territory, and we anticipate a series of letters from him which will make us thoroughly acquainted with the resources of the country and the events of which it is to be the theatre. We trust Freaner is to play an active and a profitable part in the golden drama, and that he will come back to us richer than Croesus and full of honors.

After reading accolades like these, patrons of the *Times-Picayune* could look forward with anticipation to Freaner's accounts of the western country. For whatever reason, the newly hired correspondent would not send his columns under his famous "Mustang" *nom de plume*, but would simply sign his reports "Freaner."[5]

Chagres was the chief port on the Atlantic coast for travelers and gold seekers who had chosen to cross the Isthmus of Panama rather than journey overland to California or sail around Cape Horn at the tip of South America. Upon his arrival Freaner quickly noted that most natives lived in cane houses with thatched roofs, although eating establishments for visitors offered good meals at reasonable prices. Freaner's party, which consisted of seven men besides himself, had brought over two tons of baggage. Rather than

4. *Baltimore Sun*, August 17, 1848; *New Orleans Crescent*, February 8, 1849; Freaner to McClure, November 8, 1848, James L. Freaner Letters, Beinecke Library.

5. *Pittsburgh Gazette*, January 16, 1849; *Times-Picayune*, February 20, 1849.

consign themselves and their freight to the small steamer *Orus*, the newcomers hired canoes, each poled by three men, to ascend the Chagres River. They left on March 4 and Freaner reported that the banks boasted "cocoa, banana, bamboo, pineapple, and a great variety of blooming shrubbery," all of which sweetened the breezes that wafted over the canoes. The Americans amused themselves by "shooting from our canoe the iguano, (a species of alligator) turtle, pavo, (wild pea-fowl) macaw, parrots of every size and description, and many other birds of beautiful plumage or fine meat, which none of us had ever seen before and do not know the names of."

One highlight of the journey was the sight of monkeys making acrobatic jumps through the trees and hanging by their tails. Although many travelers turned their guns on these frisky animals, Freaner and his companions chose to simply enjoy their antics, the correspondent admitting that "there were none of our party who felt a disposition to kill an animal so much resembling a human being." Freaner also documented hostility between the locals and the monkeys:

> whether it is an honest rivalry as to appearance, or a jealousy and antipathy natural to the two races, I am not able to determine; but certain it is, that as soon as they come in sight of one another the monkey commences chattering and jumping from limb to limb, without pretending to retreat, and the negroes will swear until they work themselves up into a perfect rage.

If one of the travellers should shoot a monkey, the monkey's human rivals would "rejoice over him as much as an Indian would over a fallen foe, and never fail to make a dinner or supper off of him, which they seem to relish with most extraordinary gusto." Undoubtedly writing for his New Orleans readership and revealing his Southern bias, Freaner offered an opinion of the foes that "if either has the advantage of intellect, the odds are decidedly in favor of the monkeys. Undoubtedly the monkeys are the aristocracy of the Isthmus."

After three days on the river, the Americans reached the small town of Gorgona where they had hoped to hire mules for the last seventy-five miles of their journey. What they found were "a few poor broken-down carrion horses" incapable of hauling the two tons of freight. Instead natives were hired to carry the loads over a trail that Freaner thought would someday make a good pack mule road. All along the route he had found the natives to be "harmless, inoffensive, hard-working and honest," but feared that the American propensity to cheat and physically abuse them would turn most into becoming "dishonest, lazy and dissipated." Freaner did predict that the Isthmus of Panama would soon become United States territory. The first reason was that the natives generally enjoyed American society as long as the newcomers behaved themselves. The second reason was that the younger natives demanded to be taught the words and music for "Old Dan Tucker." Freaner reasoned that Uncle Sam "may be induced to yield up soil which he has occupied, but 'Old Dan Tucker,' when he gets fairly located, creates a moral impression which neither time nor circumstances can obliterate."[6]

Freaner's party arrived at the city of Panama on the evening of March 9 and they were not impressed. About one-half of the buildings seemed to be "in the act of tumbling to pieces" and residents appeared "as if they had been laid on the shelf to die off at their leisure." Freaner noted a similarity with inhabitants of Mexico:

> The habits of the people are much like those of all Spanish countries—those who labor work very hard, and the balance are perfect loafers. The small shops and stores are all kept by women, whose husbands are a lazy, worthless, idle class of fellows, who spend all the earnings of their wives at the monte table, or gamble them off in some other way. The principal amusements of the masses are cock-fighting and monte.

Even the local clergy came in for criticism: "Unlike the fat, chubby, full, round-necked and corpulent priests of Mexico or Havana, all I have seen are a lean, lank, half-starved looking set." What was described as "the fashionable circle of Panama" consisted of a few families associated with the American Consulate and some old Spanish families of Castilian descent. Although the native population of the city was estimated to be some 7,000, only about 100 students attended the three established schools. Many natives were illiterate, but a significant portion could read, write, and had

6. *Times-Picayune*, April 2, 1849.

a working knowledge of mathematics. The few police officers had been overwhelmed by this great influx of Americans, so the local military garrison was employed to help maintain security.[7]

This military reinforcement was essential to keep the peace in Panama. New arrivals were first distressed, then angered to discover that the city was a huge bottleneck on the route to California. Quite simply there were not enough ships on the Pacific coast to carry everyone to the gold fields. This lack of space affected everyone. Even Commissioner John B. Weller and Major William H. Emory of the Boundary Commission tasked with surveying the treaty line between the United States and Mexico had to wait for transportation like the lowliest prospector. Desperate men headed north in whatever would float. Freaner saw a number set out rowing a whale boat, while others made ready a large canoe. When a steamer did appear after successfully navigating Cape Horn, tickets for deck passage skyrocketed in price as nineteenth-century scalpers would sell a single ticket for as much as $1,000. When impatient gold seekers sought aid from William Nelson, the American Consul, they often found "his boorishness can only be equalled by his puffed-up self-importance" and his "offensive and insulting deportment." Many emigrants became disgusted and went back to Chagres where they booked passage to Vera Cruz or Corpus Christi in hopes of heading overland or finding space on a ship bound directly for California. After spending his first week in Panama, Freaner advised his readers "to take any other route for California than this" in order to save both time and money.[8]

Despite his frustration, James Freaner continued to prime the emigrant pump. He reported on March 23 that the English steamer *Peru* had arrived at Panama with $350,000 of California bullion. On April 29 he wrote "that a richer deposit of gold than those previously found has been discovered in the vicinity of San Diego." He mused to his readers, "Where will the hidden treasure turn up next?"[9]

Golden rumors from California still persisted, but conditions in Panama continued to deteriorate. When space was occasionally available on a ship, rates for steerage passengers rose along with cabin tickets, although many emigrants who had spent most of their

7. *Times-Picayune*, April 3, 1849.
8. *Times-Picayune*, April 3, 1849; April 24, 1849.
9. *Times-Picayune*, April 24, 1849; May 17, 1849.

money could not afford the higher rates. Tickets were sold and resold after the original purchase, driving prices even higher. For those who could not find passage, disease began to make its appearance, primarily fevers and diarrhea. As the weather turned warmer, the threat of cholera hung over the city. Conflicts arose between the Americans and Panamanians due to overcrowding as thousands of the former waited out being stranded in a foreign land. After some Americans crashed a native ball and started a violent knife fight, the governor ordered more troops sent in to keep order.[10]

While marooned in Panama, Freaner found a way to enrich himself at the expense of his fellow travelers. When the English brig *Two Friends* arrived in port on April 4, he entered into a financial arrangement with the master, Robert Wise. The ship had been chartered for $8,700, but Freaner and a couple of similar-minded speculators offered Wise $35,000. Wise refunded the original passage price and the speculators began selling tickets to San Francisco at the announced rate of $250 for steerage and $350 for cabins. When tickets were offered for sale, one observer noted: "To stimulate bidding among the restive American emigrants, the sharks had their stool pigeons on hand to stimulate the rivalry, and, of course, prices ruled that were unheard of in their exorbitance." The bidding frenzy, mainly by new arrivals who had not yet exhausted their nest eggs, drove prices up to $750.[11]

In typical fashion for the times, the *Two Friends* was overcrowded, carrying 165 passengers—65 more than its authorized complement. One spectator who watched the *Two Friends* sail off dispatched his observations to New Orleans: "The wonder is where such a mass of men can lie, stand, or hang up in the concern. The wonder will be greater, however, if half of the passengers ever see land again, unless it is down

'Full forty thousand fathoms deep,'

among coral caves and shelving rocks. For, cribbed and jammed together, as they were, like cattle in a railroad car, or slaves in a pirate ship, if pestilence and fevers do not make many of them food for sea monsters long ere they reach their destination, they may thank nothing less than providential interference."[12]

10. *Times-Picayune*, May 17, 1849.
11. *Daily Alta California*, December 31, 1886.
12. *New York Evening Post*, November 16, 1849; *Times-Picayune*, May 25, 1849.

Singling Freaner out for criticism, one man, who could not afford the prohibitive prices, called the callous speculator a "wandering Jew" and "Shylock." Master Wise, Freaner, and his silent partners had announced they would list the day of departure in advance. When the *Two Friends*, "jammed by its human freight like cattle in a stock-car," sailed away at midnight against protests by the passengers, friends left behind were convinced that it was "a villainous trick." A deputation sought out Freaner for answers. He had abandoned his hotel room and apparently had gone into hiding with his ill-gotten wealth. As for the *Two Friends*, one ticket holder claimed upon reaching San Francisco

> that the vessel was so crowded that many of the passengers had to sleep on the deck during the whole trip, exposed to all kinds of weather—that the food was of the coarsest kind, and the passengers were compelled to live upon a short allowance of water and provisions during the whole voyage, and that finally provisions became so scarce that many of the passengers abandoned the vessel and travelled to this place by land.

After four months at sea, some seventy of the passengers demanded to be put ashore near San Diego and actually beat the ship to San Francisco by traveling overland. The *Two Friends* did not reach port until October 4, 165 days of pure hell in intolerable conditions. This was more time at sea than steamers consumed running the entire route from New York around Cape Horn and on to San Francisco. There would be lawsuits.[13]

After weeks of waiting, Freaner, his companions, and members of the Boundary Commission obtained tickets on the *Panama*. As the *Panama* steamed off, one man on the dock wrote bitterly: "In the rear, the redoubtable Captain Jim was seen to tread the inviting deck with all the nonchalance of a Spanish don and disport himself at the festive board as would a profligate millionaire." The crowded ship, including two future California senators—William M. Gwin and John B. Weller—and the wife of a third, Jessie Benton Fremont, as well as future mayors and other assorted politicians, reached San Francisco on June 3. As a Southerner, James Freaner did not support the emerging class of

13. *Baltimore Sun*, November 13, 1849; *Daily Alta California*, December 31, 1886; *Weekly Alta California*, October 11, 1849.

politicians, most of whom came from Northern states. He claimed that the legislative assembly at San Francisco was "a humbug of the New York order, conducted by a class of politicians not likely to set the world on fire, and prompted by a few persons having large interests at stake." When Bennet C. Riley, brevet major general and provisional governor of the territory, issued two proclamations that legislators did not support, "some of the members threatened to hang the old hero on the highest tree in California." Personally, Freaner regretted that these politicians "could not have found some Territory nearer home worthy of their patriotism and sacrifice."[14]

Freaner found San Francisco to be a disappointment for three specific reasons: the climate, the exorbitant price of property, and the problem of unloading cargo. He first addressed the weather conditions:

> I have been in every State and Territory of the United States except Minnesota, and I have never felt a climate so disagreeable, and one that renders every person so uncomfortable as that of San Francisco—with the flowing of the tide the wind rises and then, during the balance of the day or night, it blows so violently that we can scarcely walk the street. Our eyes are continually filled with dust, and we, who have been accustomed to a southern clime, are shivering with cold more than half the time.

The wind and cold made it impossible for women to make a respectable appearance on the city streets.

Real estate prices were beyond comprehension. Rooms and offices ranging on average from 120 to 400 square feet rented for $400 to $500 per month, cash. Freaner located a room 20' by 24' that he rented for $18,000 a year, $10,000 cash in advance. The Parker House, a two-story frame building 50' by 75', rented for $95,000 a year. Summing up the real estate market, newcomers could see "there is no want of money, and houses and lots command the gold dust without limit."

The third factor operating against the future of San Francisco was the bay itself. Ships anchored in the bay discharged their cargos onto small launches that carried ithem to the docks. Fees for unloading a

14. *Daily Alta California*, December 31, 1886; *Sacramento Daily Union*, June 4, 1855; *Times-Picayune*, August 4, 1849.

single barrel of goods would cost one dollar, so a launch that carried 200 barrels would rent for $200 with the tides limiting transfer to one trip a day. Some captains found themselves paying out more to unload their cargo than it had cost to ship it from New York. Complicating this situation was the fact the ship crews deserted as fast as they reached port, driving up the wages for an ordinary sailor to $200 per month.

Once he settled into his extravagantly priced room, James Freaner headed out to visit the mines. The southern gold fields were concentrated on various tributaries of the San Joaquin River, which flowed northward through a large valley bearing the same name. Northern gold fields were located on tributaries of the Sacramento River which drained a wide section of northern California. Both rivers eventually emptied into Suison Bay en route to the larger San Francisco Bay.[15]

Although an estimated four-fifths of new arrivals headed up the Sacramento River, Freaner chose to explore the southern mines first. Showing his ignorance of agriculture, he proclaimed the San Joaquin Valley (now one of the most productive regions in the entire country) to be "valueless." Writing on June 30, he reported that although runoff from the mountains still filled streams and rivers, the ground was parched and grass almost non-existent, concluding, "The land is poor, and very little of it would produce an average crop if it were well watered." The only substantial crop was of mosquitoes, "more plentiful than I have ever seen in the swamps of Louisiana, Alabama or Florida." Two redeeming features of the region seemed to be the moderate temperature and cold drinking water from melting snow in the mountains.[16]

Some 20,000 persons were estimated to be working the southern gold fields, "including all ages, sexes, conditions and colors." About 8,000 of this total were emigrants from Mexico and South America who congregated south of Woods Creek to get away from their American competitors. One of the most important points on the San Joaquin River was Stockton where Freaner found "a population of several hundred living in tents, there being but one frame building." Stockton was accessible to vessels year round, leading Freaner to predict "this must inevitably be a place of immense

15. *Times-Picayune*, August 4, 1849.
16. *Times-Picayune*, August 5, 1849.

importance." During this first visit, merchants and traders unloaded $10,000 worth of goods each day.

Freaner's description of the southern gold fields certainly ratcheted up excitement back in the States. He wrote of how the country between the Stanislaus and Mercedes Rivers "had been upturned and ferreted, to the depth of six or eight feet, and still the gold appears as inexhaustible as when the miner first struck a spade into it." He continued: "It would really appear, as if the main body of the glittering metal had not been approached. Up to the present time the only search has been made in the 'dry diggings;' everyone is anticipating a rich harvest as soon as the rivers fall sufficiently to enable them to work the lode." He proclaimed that "volcano after volcano had burst out from the earth, pouring forth over the face of the country layer after layer of pure gold." The precious metal was seemingly everywhere: "Wherever a hole is made in the ground gold is to be found but in some places in greater quantities than others." Freaner claimed that miners on the tributaries of the San Joaquin were extracting "a thousand pounds of gold per day."[17]

With so much gold in circulation, crime became a serious issue. The Mexican War had brought soldiers, teamsters, and army followers to California and the discovery of gold had kept them there. In Freaner's opinion, "they served as a nucleus for all the runaway sailors, robbers, pickpockets and desperate characters who are daily arriving" and "by degrees a series of robberies, outrages on females, murders and riots put the whole community in alarm." Each settlement elected an alcalde, or magistrate, who presided over both civil and criminal cases brought before him. He passed judgment in civil cases, but a jury was empaneled for criminal cases. There was no appeal of a sentence. While attorneys back in the States could quote from Blackstone and Coke, common sense prevailed in the California settlements.[18]

Freaner gave a couple of examples. In one case a man was accused of killing another and the jury found "that the person committing the act was justifiable as he had been attacked, but that he was always ready to quarrel and fight, and dangerous to the peace and good order of the camp, and therefore he must leave the country in thirty days; failing to do which, he should be shot down

17. *Times-Picayune*, August 5, 1849.
18. *Times-Picayune*, September 23, 1849.

by the first person laying eyes on him." Although he refused to confess, another man was convicted of theft. The jury sentenced him "to be stripped naked and tied so that the musquitoes could peg him for an hour, unless he should sooner tell where all the property was secreted." After just fifteen minutes, the perpetrator confessed and agreed to return the stolen property.[19]

An organized party of criminals, known throughout the city of San Francisco as "The Hounds," had gained prominence in the region. Initially pandered to by politicians and local leaders seeking public support, the Hounds soon got out of control and commenced a campaign of violence that became "shocking to humanity and disgraceful even to barbarism," especially against immigrant Chinese, Mexicans, and Chileans. Eventually the citizens rose en masse, arrested the main offenders, confined them aboard the United States sloop *Warren*, tried them by jury, and thus eliminated this threat to peace and progress. The remaining Hounds shifted their base of power to Stockton, but were again confronted by a united citizenry. Two notorious outlaws, "Micky" and "Red the Robber," were hung. Lesser offenders were whipped, had their ears cropped, and were ordered to leave the country, thereby ending the most serious threats to life and property.[20]

By the end of July Freaner was again extolling the riches of California. As miners were able to get into the streams as the water began to fall, they expected to find "an immense yield of the precious metals." Prospectors in the San Joaquin Valley were "continually finding new and valuable deposits of gold." One can only imagine the impact back home that a statement like this would have: "The truth is, the gold is so plenty in many places that in digging down anywhere an ounce or more would be the yield of a day's labor—often five or six ounces, and in some instances fifteen or twenty." Scientific mining—the use of quicksilver (mercury) to extract gold from ore—began to produce spectacular results. Freaner mentioned a pair of mine owners who went over earth that had previously been prospected, this time with the scientific method using pumps, rockers, and quicksilver. The result was that six men produced

19. *Times-Picayune*, August 5, 1849; September 23, 1849.
20. *Times-Picayune*, September 23, 1849; October 6, 1849.

thirty-three ounces of gold in twelve hours on ground that had already been prospected![21]

After two months Freaner had seen San Francisco double in size and population; after another month it had quadrupled. The towns of Benicia, on the straits of Corquinez, and New York of the Pacific, at the head of Suison Bay, became important shipping points to the interior. According to Freaner, "The saw and the hammer of the carpenter have commenced ringing out their music from morning to evening, bringing into existence successively buildings that are to become the centre of a large and thriving trade." Towns sprouted on the Sacramento and San Joaquin Rivers. Investors snapped up old Spanish titles and bought land near mountain passes that might someday bring a railroad to the west coast. Not to be outdone, James Freaner erected a plank house and rented it for $60,000 per year, though a scheme to start a newspaper and serve as assistant editor failed to materialize.[22]

San Francisco Bay resembled a forest of masts on every type of steamer and sailing vessel, from oil-slicked whalers to gleaming clipper ships. Freaner noted the result: "The streets are filled with merchandise, while the beach is fairly covered with goods, arriving and shipping for the coast and rivers. Real estate is cash in hand and sixty days, but still it has continued steadily to advance." The amount of freight arriving at San Francisco can be gleaned from the experience of John Freaner, a younger brother, who had followed a few weeks behind him as a passenger with the loftily-named Baltimore and Frederick Mining and Trading Company. Although the men chose to cross the Isthmus, they shipped around Cape Horn "a steam saw and grist mill, a dredging machine, a pile driver, suction engine, ten carts and wagons, five boats, a house, farming utensils, with provision for two years, together with various articles of merchandise." Another passenger, James S. Graham of Kentucky, had shipped an entire hotel to California.[23]

While thousands of adventurers continued to flood into California, some men returned home loaded with treasure either directly

21. *Times-Picayune*, September 23, 1849.

22. *Times-Picayune*, September 23, 1849; October 6, 1849; *Baltimore Sun*, November 15, 1849; *Planters' Banner*, August 16, 1849.

23. *Times-Picayune*, October 6, 1849; *Baltimore Sun*, April 25, 1849.

from the mines or after furnishing miners their food, equipment, entertainment, or women. Hundreds more left with gloomy news and tales of gold's scarcity. These were the "sick, disappointed and disheartened," who, according to Freaner, were "not fit for the work, either by habits or physical attributes." Gold was abundant and fortunes could be made "in the mines, at the work-bench or in the counting-house," but a man had to commit his labor to a task. In Freaner's words, "This is no country for idlers."[24]

By the end of September there were an estimated 35,000 active miners in California, after accounting for a large percentage of idle and dissipated men. Allowing an average of but $6 per man for 200 days of work a year would mean $42,000,000 in gold dust per year. Freaner calculated that a year's worth of California gold was worth almost three times the annual cotton crop of Georgia. That amazing total would rise exponentially as the 1849 gold rush became a global phenomenon. Fortune seekers continued to arrive from the United States, South America, Central America, Mexico, the Sandwich Islands, and Oregon in addition to more and more native Californians. Critics said that the mines would "give out" and the lofty expectations "would all blow up like a bubble bursting on the water." There was no indication that would happen and inflation continued unchecked. Town lots that had once sold for $100 to $300 in San Francisco before the boom now went for $5,000 to $30,000 and small houses that used to rent for $50 now commanded $500 to $1,000, all paid in advance.[25]

Credit was unheard of for real estate, but some merchants would advance customers funds and keep accounts. James Freaner did acquire the "Accont Buk" of one John McGuire and shared some of the entries with readers of the *Times-Picayune*:

George Williams, the darkey white man	5.00
Manell Sanches groceries	16.00
Red that lives with Dancing bill	30.50
Dancing bill needles, thred shoes stockins	18.00
Inaca that has the woman with the big ring in her ear	53.00
Hamilton fur shoes	5.00
John that speaks English	88.00
Vicente and his two sons 3 oueces in gold dust lent	96.00

24. *Times-Picayune*, October 6, 1849.
25. *Times-Picayune*, November 14, 1849.

The spaniard that took the jacket	10.00
Loreuche the Spaniard that has the cattle	137.00

This was an example of the credit system as it operated during the gold rush. Although primitive, this type of accounting worked in a region where the population was fluid and men were known by nicknames or descriptions rather than proper names. Freaner admitted that "a great many will be ruined in trade, and perhaps lose fortunes which they bring with them," but claimed that the onward progress of California could not be stopped. Gold was their future. Gold would not depreciate in value, nor fluctuate in the marketplace like cotton, sugar, pork, grain, or any other commodity. A never-ending supply of gold would sustain them, a claim backed up by the $1,000,000 in gold dust shipped that fall aboard the steamer *California*. As if to prove his point, Freaner told the bankers at Burgoyne & Company that he had personally seen "a piece of gold, slightly mixed with quartz, weighing upwards of *twenty-five pounds*."[26]

While California had an exploding population and a booming economy, what it needed was a government. Governor Riley called for a constitutional convention to convene at Monterey in September in preparation for obtaining statehood. Representatives from throughout the territory met, approved a constitution, and set elections for November. Politicians from the States had lost their convention fight with locals, who detested being told how to run their own territory by newcomers. Significantly for national politics, the convention excluded slavery from California and banned the influx of free blacks. A host of candidates ran for office and Freaner supported the Democrats, actually being the first speaker at the large mass meeting of that party in San Francisco on October 25. Freaner offered the guarantee that "no portion of our country at any time has been so infested with broken-down politicians, political renegades and political loafers, as this is at the present time. These are persons who desire to live in office, grow and fatten in office, without any other occupation whatever." Of course, he was referring to supporters of the Whig party, not his faithful Democrats.[27]

26. *Times-Picayune*, August 5, 1849; August 12, 1849; November 14, 1849; December 8, 1849.

27. *Weekly Alta California*, November 1, 1849; *Times-Picayune*, November 12, 1849; December 9, 1849

Whaleship *Niantic* after Its Conversion to a Storehouse. *Courtesy Library of Congress*.

One drawback to California's growth had been a lack of quick communication between San Francisco and the interior towns. Shipping goods to Stockton and Sacramento often took as long as ten days, so entrepreneurs began construction on small, shallow-draft steamers that could make those trips in a single day. One of the greatest shipping enterprises involved the whaleship *Niantic*. The firm of Ward, Marsh & Company arranged for the ship to be hauled some 400 yards over the mud flats by the use of water casks as rollers. Once in place, the entire deck was covered by a frame structure and the *Niantic* became "one of the finest and safest store-houses in this country." Freaner was impressed with the firm's ingenuity: "The enterprise has been attended with an immense expenditure of money, and a great deal of anxiety; but they will be handsomely rewarded for their capital and labor, as they have been offered $150,000 for the ship as she lies." Another novel building was the Graham House, which had been shipped around Cape Horn and was then being assembled, which would eventually be 100' wide, 70' deep, and four stories high. While the Graham House was under construction, Freaner had rented one of the choice rooms in the Parker House. Edwin Bell, formerly of Hagerstown, Maryland, recalled his arrival in San Francisco:

> Almost the first person I met was "Jim" Freaner who occupied one of the choice rooms of the house, and that night inflated for me a gum bed which was spread upon the floor of his room, and made me feel at home. From him I learned that a provisional government had been organized and that his brother John was chief deputy of the Sheriff, as well as a member of an industrial company which had been formed in Hagerstown after I left there.[28]

Legal actions over conditions relating to the *Two Friends* had been settled by November. Numerous lawsuits had been levied against Freaner, his partners, the captain, and the ship itself in the ticket speculation. Juries had found them all guilty and the sheriff announced that the ship, along with "her boats, tackle, apparel, furniture, etc.," would be sold on November 10 to satisfy the judgments. The sale was postponed five days so that arrangements could be made to include the sale of 20 tons of coal and 500 feet of lumber from the ship's cargo. Rumor had it that these judgments, along with a passion for playing monte, cost Freaner the small fortune he had swindled out of those desperate men who had embarked on *Two Friends*.[29]

The last mention of James Freaner in the California press for 1849 was a petition by him and several other gentlemen to erect wharves at the ends of several streets. Admitting that these proposals "would in all probability be highly advantageous," the San Francisco town council declined to authorize any obstruction to the free use of public streets. Soon after, he came down with an unspecified "long and severe illness" that curtailed letter writing and public appearances. His first letter to the *Times-Picayune* since the previous December was dated April 20, 1850, in which he "announced his complete restoration to health." Yet just ten days later Freaner admitted to a relapse that prompted a trip farther inland to the Sacramento Valley "for a change of air."[30]

28. *Times-Picayune*, December 9, 1849; Williams, *History of Washington County, Maryland* 1: 282.

29. *Weekly Alta California*, November 8, 1849; November 15, 1849; *New York Evening Post*, December 8, 1849; *Daily Alta California*, December 31, 1886.

30. *Daily Alta California*, January 4, 1850; *Times-Picayune*, June 4, 1850.

Concentrating on politics, Freaner stated bluntly, "Owing to the delay of Congress in admitting California into the Union, and the absence of a district court, land office, mint, &c., &c., we are placed in a most peculiar situation, and one which cannot continue much longer." He then offered a warning:

> I assure you that unless Congress does something for us very soon a movement will be made for independence. In case Congress does not admit us this session the separation of California from the Union is inevitable. A great many prominent men in this country want to make a move at once, and it is my opinion if the question is agitated it will be the cause of a serious strife here between the Northern and Southern men.

Without action from Washington politicians, California was on the verge of collapsing "into a state of anarchy and confusion." The Golden State would finally be admitted to the Union on September 9, 1850.[31]

During his tour of the interior Freaner stopped for a time at Pierson B. Reading's ranch at the head of the Sacramento Valley. Where he had disparaged the agricultural value of the San Joaquin Valley, he now extolled the Sacramento Valley as containing "as fine a soil as man ever looked upon." Writing on June 10, 1850, Freaner claimed that wild oats produced a crop beyond what he had seen cultivated back in the States and the same for grasses that could compete with fields of rye back home. The Sacramento Valley could yield a variety of grains and vegetables "with comparatively little labor" and he listed the "garden truck" on Reading's ranch—"green peas, beans, lettuce, radishes, beets, turnips, cabbage, okra, green corn, tomatoes, &c., and I expect shortly to have to fall back on water-melons and cantelopes." The only drawback to expanding the territory's agricultural development was the continual lure of the gold fields. Again, sounding like a commercial for a Chamber of Commerce campaign, Freaner claimed that the gold region on the Sacramento River tributaries was "unbounded." After a personal inspection of the area, he declared that "fifty thousand laborers could not wash out the placer gold in the next half century." As an example, he told how Reading, employing a small crew of Indians

31. *Times-Picayune*, June 4, 1850.

and whites, washed out $19,000 of glittering gold in a single month. Men would automatically flow toward the latest big discoveries. At the time of his letter, some 15,000 prospectors were waiting for the waters to go down on the Trinity River where miners had struck lodes before the spring floods. All that confined the treasure seekers was the vast expanse of country and the hostility of Indians who inhabited the region.

In Freaner's opinion, the Indians and white intruders were both to blame for the unrest in frontier settlements and at isolated mining camps. Problems developed as the newcomers expanded operations into the Indian country:

> At first they allow the Indians to be familiar in their camps, and thus give them the opportunity of stealing axes, hatchets, knives, tobacco, or other articles of this kind. Sometimes the whites detect them and punish them severely; the Indians retaliate by stealing horses or oxen; the whites pursue them to their villages and fight them, but seldom ever kill any of the Indians, or inflict any more punishment than plundering their villages of their skins, bows and arrows, &c. The Indians finding they got off so easily become more bold, and holding the whole white race responsible for the acts of a few, murder men and steal oxen and mules and all other property, at every opportunity.

Sometimes the whites were the outright aggressors, "compelling the Indians to labor against their will, interfere with the squaws, and even sometimes go so far as to whip the Indians, if they do not do what is required of them." Such outrages naturally led to violence. Retaliation came quickly, the only saving grace being that the Indians were never able to mount a coordinated attack with the potential to kill hundreds of whites.[32]

In mid-November, a former New Orleans resident encountered Freaner at a ranch near Stockton where he was "making ready to go into the Indian wars." Freaner invited the newcomer to drop by his new ranch in the foothills of the Sierra Madre Mountains where he promised to serve up "whiskey with snow in it." After refreshing themselves, Freaner's acquaintance said, "He told me he could give me active employment in the Indian and bear fighting

32. *Times-Picayune*, August 9, 1850.

business, as he claims to have a full supply of both." James Freaner, who had somehow acquired the title of "colonel," soon led a party that responded when Indians descended from the mountains and stole two horses. Assembling a group of eleven mounted men and forty friendly Indians, he followed their trail for two days, discovered their village, and charged into it, killing four and taking six prisoners. Freaner's men found nearly three tons of dried beef, assorted mining tools, and various provisions that had been stolen on previous raids. Not content with this success, Freaner joined the small force under Captain Nathaniel Lyon that had been tasked with punishing the killers of Captain William H. Warner and, hopefully, recovering his remains. Warner had led a topographical exploration of the Sierra Nevada range in an attempt to locate a pass through which a railroad could be constructed. He was killed in an ambush on September 27, 1849, in the Pitt River (now Pit River) watershed. Although Captain Lyon did encounter Indians—one soldier killed and an estimated fifteen Indians shot—his expedition proved a failure.[33]

James Freaner, now occasionally referred to as "The Kit Carson of California," was out with the topographical engineers in 1851 as Lieutenant Robert S. Williamson led a detachment of twenty men northward from Shasta Butte City (now Yreka). Although the "city" was nothing more than forty buildings built from canvas and wood, the surrounding country swarmed with miners and almost 600 men voted in the first election for alcalde. On July 11 Lieutenant Williamson and Freaner left the main body and rode to an elevation for a view: "We saw Mount Pitt, Klamath lake, and Shasta valley; but Rhett lake was hidden by the pine trees on the conical butte. Southward, as far as the eye could reach, the country was densely timbered, and apparently tolerably level, but broken by occasional low ridges. Lassen's butte was distinctly visible." On the following day Williamson and Freaner again rode off together to a summit to view the country. After eleven days exploring the wilds of northern California, Lieutenant Williamson's party encamped two miles from Reading's ranch.[34]

33. *Times-Picayune*, January 2, 1851; *Daily Alta California*, June 29, 1850; July 26, 1851; *Weekly Alta California*, November 1, 1849; *Sacramento Transcript*, August 28, 1850.

34. *California Gazette*, February 14, 1852; 33rd Congress, 2nd Session, House Ex. Doc. 91, *Reports of Explorations and Surveys* 6: 127–29.

A View of San Francisco during the Gold Rush. *Courtesy Library of Congress*.

One object of Williamson's scout was to look for a wagon route east of Mount Shasta that could cut some 200 miles from the pack horse route to Oregon. Freaner had traveled over much of the country while with Captain Lyon and "his knowledge of the country and his remarkable backwoods' instinct" made him the perfect guide. An Oregon newspaper claimed that "if such a route exists it will be found." A California editor spoke of the benefits of such a road: "When we get a clear and good wagon road opened to Oregon, connecting that fertile and beautiful agricultural and lumber country with our rich Sacramento Valley, and extensive, exhaustless mineral resources, we will take a step in progress which will affect with infinite prosperity the future history of the Eureka State."[35]

Since his journey inland to recover his health, Freaner had spent time in Shasta and Siskiyou Counties. During the winter of 1852 he journeyed to Sacramento and encountered numerous hostile Indians, although he suffered no loss in men or stock.

35. *Weekly Oregonian*, August 9, 1851; *Sacramento Daily Union*, July 26, 1851.

These Indians of northern California, outraged by whites who had invaded their homeland, were said to be "more warlike than those of any other section of the State, and they bear the most implacable hatred towards the pale faces." Undeterred by the Indian threat, Freaner proposed that he build a wagon road from the Sacramento Valley to the Oregon border. One newsman enthusiastically backed the project:

> The advantages of the road proposed by Colonel Freaner are apparent to everyone at all conversant with the geography or population of Northern California. The busy and thriving population of Shasta Valley, and the whole of that country embraced within the limits of the county of Siskiyou, where exist, perhaps, the most fertile valleys and richest mines in the State, are entirely cut off from communication with the lower country except by pack mules. From this fact, much valuable trade which properly belongs to the Sacramento Valley, is driven North, and finds an outlet through the Columbia river.

Legislation was introduced into the Assembly that would authorize Freaner to build his proposed road. While the bill moved through committees, David C. Broderick, a political foe, confronted Freaner in a saloon on February 23, 1852, and accused him of corruption. Words were exchanged. Broderick grabbed Freaner's long beard. Freaner used his fists. Broderick seized a bottle to use as a weapon. Freaner picked up either an ink stand or a tumbler (probably the latter since these occurred more frequently in a saloon than ink stands) and threw it into Broderick's face, opening a deep gash in his cheek that disfigured his face forever. Bystanders finally separated the men and restored order in the saloon.[36]

The act authorizing James L. Freaner to construct and collect tolls on a road from the Sacramento Valley to the Oregon line became law on April 24, 1852. The bill had passed the Senate by a vote of nineteen to three and the Assembly by the vote of thirty-eight to five. This bill stated that Freaner had one year to survey and either blaze trees or erect stone markers on a road forty feet in width. The entire length of the roadway was to be completed

36. *California Gazette*, February 14, 1852; *Weekly Alta California*, July 24, 1852; *Sacramento Steamer Union*, April 15, 1852; O'Meara, *Broderick and Gwin*, 31; *Daily Alta California*, February 25, 1852.

within three years, including necessary bridges, ferries, and toll booths. Specific tolls were established for vehicles and animals for each mile traveled on the road and additional tolls for bridges and ferries. Following the completion of his road, Freaner would be responsible for paying the state 5 percent of his net proceeds. The roadway, bridges, and ferries were to be kept constantly in good order. Should the project not be completed within the three-year period, the authorization would be deemed null and void, but if Freaner should meet all of the requirements of the bill he would be free to operate the toll road for the next twenty-five years.[37]

Freaner lost no time setting out to survey his road. By the end of June, he was in Yreka and on July 2 he set out in company with John Brando (a migrant from Maine), "Cayuse" Jackson, a man named Warren, and a Mexican called "Adobe" John. Freaner had been selected as a delegate to represent Siskiyou County at the Democratic State Convention to be held at Benicia on July 20, but he never arrived. No one had heard from the party after it left Yreka, but indications of terrible news arrived within a month of its disappearance. Freaner's favorite mule, Goore Leg, was taken from an Indian and identified in Yreka. This was followed by a statement from a woman of the Shasta tribe who had recently escaped from captivity among the Pitt River Indians. She stated that these Pitt River Indians had "murdered a party of well armed and well mounted white men," which were assumed to be the missing Freaner party. John Freaner led a large posse of miners in a futile search for his brother and everyone assumed the worst. There was little John could do beyond writing home to advise his parents that "there is little of doubt" that James had been murdered. The editor of the *Alta California* admitted, "He sleeps the death of the brave." More than a year later some documents once in Freaner's possession were found along his supposed 1852 route and the Pitt River Indians released another of his mules, more confirmation of Mustang's demise.[38]

37. *Sacramento Steamer Union*, April 15, 1852; *Statutes of California, 1852*, 150–53.

38. 36th Congress, 1st Session, Senate Misc. Doc. 59, *Communication from C.S. Drew*, 4; *Daily Alta California*, September 8, 1852; December 31, 1886; *Daily Placer Times and Transcript*, August 10, 1852; *Baltimore Sun*, October 22, 1852; *Placer Herald*, March 19, 1853.

Details did not emerge until 1855 when Numtariman, a chief of the Cow Creek Indians, asked George Woodman of Cow Creek whether he had heard of the killing of a party of whites on Pitt River. Woodman passed for details and Numtariman gave him the story as he had heard it from the Pitt River Indians. The party of white men had started to cross the river in a canoe with two Indians, swimming their mounts. Halfway across the Indians jumped out and upset the canoe. A large number of Indians then emerged from hiding on both banks and shot scores of arrows into the struggling whites. Within minutes the white men were all dead. The bodies were then supposedly mutilated and burned. Years later someone discovered a pair of pearl sleeve buttons that were identified as having belonged to Freaner, but the most convincing proof of his fate came when a skull was found that contained "a peculiar gold filling in one of the teeth." There was no longer any doubt. James L. Freaner, the famous "Mustang" of the Mexican War, was dead.[39]

39. *Daily Placer Times and Transcript*, November 1, 1855; *Mariposa Gazette*, May 9, 1873; Williams, *History of Washington County, Maryland* 1: 241–42.

Bibliography

Government Documents

U.S., 30th Congress, 1st Session, Senate Ex. Doc. 65, *Message from the President of the United States*

U.S., 30th Congress, 1st Session, Senate Report 136, *Colt's Repeating Firearms*

U.S., 30th Congress, 1st Session, House Ex. Doc. 69, *Treaty with Mexico*

U.S., 30th Congress, 2nd Session, House Ex. Doc. 1, *Message from the President*

U.S., 30th Congress, 2nd Session, House Ex. Doc. 5, *Contingent Expenses*

U.S., 33rd Congress, 2nd Session, House Ex. Doc. 91, *Reports of Explorations and Surveys*

U.S., 36th Congress, 1st Session Senate Misc. Doc., 59, *Communication from C.S. Drew*

U.S., NARA, Record Group 29, 1840 Census, Hagerstown District, Washington County, Maryland

U.S., NARA, Record Group 94, Mexican War Service Records

U.S., NARA, Record Group 94, Orders of General Zachary Taylor, 1845–1847

U.S., NARA, Record Group 94, U.S. Army Register of Enlistments.

Manuscripts

James L. Freaner Letters, Beinecke Library, Yale University

Books And Articles

Adams, George R. *General William S. Harney: Prince of Dragoons*. Lincoln: University of Nebraska Press, 2001.

Anderson, Robert. *An Artillery Officer in the Mexican War, 1846–7*. New York: G.P. Putnam's Sons, 1911.

Annual Reunion and Dinner of the Old Guard Association, Twelfth Regiment, N.G.S.N.Y. New York: Old Guard Association, 1894.

Arnold, Thomas J. *Early Life and Letters of General Thomas J. "Stonewall" Jackson*. New York: Fleming H. Revell, 1916.

Ballentine, George. *Autobiography of an English Soldier in the United States Army*. London: Hurst and Blackett, 1853.

Bauer, K. Jack. *Surfboats and Horse Marines: U.S. Naval Operations in the Mexican War, 1846–1848*. Annapolis MD: Naval Institute Press, 1969.

——— "The Vera Cruz Expedition of 1847." *Military Affairs* 20 (Fall, 1956) 162–69.

Baylies, Francis. *A Narrative of Major General Wool's Campaign in Mexico in the 1846, 1847, and 1848.* Albany, NY: Little, 1851.

Blackwood, Emma J., ed. *To Mexico with Scott: Letters of Captain E. Kirby Smith to His Wife*. Cambridge, MA: Harvard University Press, 1917.

Bullard, F. Lauriston. *Famous War Correspondents*. Boston, MA: Little, Brown and Company, 1914.

Butler, Steven R., ed. *Sketches by a Skirmisher: The Mexican War Writings of Capt. Mayne Reid, Co. B, 2nd Regiment of New York Volunteers*. Richardson, TX: Descendants of Mexican War Veterans, 1998.

Carter, Arthur B. *The Tarnished Cavalier: Major General Earl Van Dorn, C.S.A*. Knoxville: University of Tennessee Press, 1999.

Carter, Ruth C., ed. *For Honor, Glory and Union: The Mexican and Civil War Letters of Brig. Gen. William Haines Lytle*. Lexington: University Press of Kentucky, 1999.

Caruso, A. Brooke. *The Mexican Spy Company: United States Covert Operations in Mexico, 1845–1848*. Jefferson, NC: McFarland, 1991.

Casdorph, Paul D. *Confederate General R.S. Ewell: Robert E. Lee's Hesitant Commander* Lexington: University Press of Kentucky, 2004.

——— *Prince John Magruder: His Life and Campaigns*. New York, NY: John Wiley, 1996.

Chamberlain, Samuel E. *My Confession: Recollections of a Rogue.* New York: Harper and Brothers, 1956.

Claiborne, J.F.H. *Life and Correspondence of John A. Quitman, Major General, U.S.A., and Governor of the State of Mississippi*. New York: Harper and Brothers, 1860. 2 vols.

Clary, David A. *Eagles and Empire: The United States, Mexico, and the Struggle for a Continent*. New York: Bantam, 2009.

Conner, Philip S.P. *The Home Squadron Under Commodore Conner in the War with Mexico*. Philadelphia, PA: 1896.

Copeland, Fayette. *Kendall of the Picayune*. Norman: University of Oklahoma Press, 1943.

Crawford, Ann F. *The Eagle: The Autobiography of Santa Anna*. Austin, TX: Pemberton Press, 1967.

Cress, Lawrence D., ed. *Dispatches From the Mexican War*. Norman: University of Oklahoma Press, 1999.

Croffut, W.A. *Fifty Years in Camp and Field: The Diary of Major General Ethan Allen Hitchcock*. New York: G. P. Putnam's Sons, 1909.

Cullum, George W. *Biographical Register of the Officers and Graduates of the U.S. Military Academy*. New York: D. Van Nostrand, 1868. 2 vols.

Davis, George T.M. *Autobiography of the Late Col. Geo. T.M. Davis, Captain and Aide-de-Camp Scott's Army of Invasion*. New York: Jenkins and McCowan, 1891.

Devlin, John S. *The Marine Corps in Mexico*. Washington, DC: Lemuel Towers, 1852.

Dillon, Lester R., Jr. *American Artillery in the Mexican War, 1846–1847*. Austin, TX: Presidial Press, 1975

Drexler, Robert W. *Guilty of Making Peace: A Biography of Nicholas P. Trist*. Lanham, MD: University Press of America, 1991.

Dugard, Martin. *The Training Ground: Grant, Lee, Sherman, and Davis in the Mexican War, 1846–1848.* New York: Little, Brown, 2008.

Durham, Walter T. "Mexican War Letters to Wynnewood." *Tennessee Historical Quarterly* 33, n. 4 (Winter, 1974) 389–409.

Eisenhower, John S.D. *Agent of Destiny: The Life and Times of General Winfield Scott*. New York: Free Press, 1997.

——— *So Far from God: The U.S. War with Mexico, 1846–1848*. New York: Random House, 1989.

Elderkin, James D. *Biographical Sketches and Anecdotes of a Soldier of Three Wars*. Detroit, MI: James D. Elderkin, 1899.

Foos, Paul. *A Short, Offhand, Killing Affair: Soldiers and Social Conflict During the Mexican-American War*. Chapel Hill: University of North Carolina Press, 2002.

Frazier, Donald S. *The United States and Mexico at War: Nineteenth Century Expansion and Conflict*. New York: Simon and Schuster, 1998.

"Frontier Service of an Old Cavalryman." *Southern Magazine* 15 (July, 1874) 74–86.

Furber, George C. *The Twelve Months Volunteers; or, Journal of a Private, in the Tennessee Regiment of Cavalry, in the Campaign, in Mexico, 1846–7*. Cincinnati, OH: J.A. and U.P. James, 1848.

Gallagher, Gary W., ed. "We Are Our Own Trumpeters: Robert E. Lee Describes Winfield Scott's Campaign to Mexico City." *Virginia Magazine of History and Biography* 95, n. 3 (July, 1987) 363–75.

Geary, Paul M. *Colonel John W. Geary in the Mexican War and California in '49*. Pacifica, CA: Shade Tree Press, 2000.

"A General's Orderly in Mexico." *Colburn's United Service Magazine* (May, 1855) 78–85.

"Gentlemen of the Press," *Harper's New Monthly Magazine* 26, n. 153 (February, 1863) 361–67.

Gordon, George H. "The Battles of Contreras and Churubusco" in *Civil and Mexican Wars, 1861, 1846*. Boston: Military Historical Society of Massachusetts, 1913.

——— "Battles of Molino del Rey and Chapultepec" in *Civil and Mexican Wars, 1861, 1846*. Boston: Military Historical Society of Massachusetts, 1913

Govan, Gilbert E. and Livingood, James W. *A Different Valor: The Story of General Joseph E. Johnston, C.S.A.* Indianapolis, IN: Bobbs-Merrill, 1956.

Grant, Ulysses S. *Personal Memoirs of U.S. Grant*. New York: Charles L. Webster, 1885. 2 vols.

Greenberg, Amy S.*A Wicked War: Polk, Clay, Lincoln and the 1846 U.S. Invasion of Mexico*. New York: Alfred A. Knopf, 2012.

Guardino, Peter. *The Dead March: A History of the Mexican-American War*. Cambridge, MA: Harvard University Press, 2017.

Hadden, James. *A History of Uniontown: The County Seat of Fayette County, Pennsylvania*. Akron, OH: New Werner Company, 1913.

Hartman, George W. *A Private's Own Journal; Giving an Account of the Battles in Mexico, Under Gen'l Scott*. Greencastle, PA: E. Robinson, 1849.

Haynes, Martin A. *Gen. Scott's Guide in Mexico: A Biographical Sketch of Col. Noah E. Smith*. Lake Village, NH: Lake Village Times, 1887.

Heitman, Francis S. *Historical Register and Dictionary of the United States Army*. Washington, DC: Government Printing Office, 1903. 2 vols.

Henderson, Timothy J.A.*A Glorious Defeat: Mexico and Its War with the United States*. New York: Hill and Wang, 2007.

Hinds, Charles F. "Mexican War Journal of Leander M. Cox." *Register of the Kentucky Historical Society* 55, n. 1 (January, 1957) 29–52; n. 3 (July, 1957) 213–36; 56, n. 1 (January, 1958) 47–69.

Hohenberg, John. *Foreign Correspondence: The Great Reporters and Their Times*. Syracuse, NY: Syracuse University Press, 1995.

Hopkins, C.A. Porter. "A Marylander in the Mexican War: Some Letters of J.J. Archer." *Maryland Historical Magazine* 54, n. 4 (December, 1959) 408–22.

Hudson, Frederic. *Journalism in the United States*. New York: Harper and Brothers, 1873.

Hudson, Leonne M., ed. *Company "A" Corps of Engineers, USA, 1846–1848, in the Mexican War*. Kent, OH: Kent State University Press, 2001.

Hughes, Nathaniel Cheairs, Jr. and Johnson, Timothy D., eds. *A Fighter from Way Back: The Mexican War Diary of Lt. Daniel Harvey Hill, 4th Artillery, U.S.A.* Kent, OH: Kent State University Press, 2002.

Hughes, Nathaniel Cheairs, Jr. and Stonesifer, Roy P., Jr. *The Life and Wars of Gideon J. Pillow*. Chapel Hill: University of North Carolina Press, 1993.

Jamieson, Milton. *Journal and Notes of a Campaign in Mexico; Containing a History of Company C, of the Second Regiment of Ohio Volunteers*. Cincinnati, OH: Ben Franklin Printing House, 1849.

Janes, Ann Brown, ed. *Gathering Laurels in Mexico: The Diary of an American Soldier in the Mexican-American War*. Lincoln, MA: Cottage Press, 1990.

Jenkins, John S. *History of the War Between the United States and Mexico, From the Commencement of Hostilities to the Ratification of the Treat of Peace*. Auburn, NY: Derby, Miller and Company, 1849.

Johnson, Timothy D.*A Gallant Little Army: The Mexico City Campaign*. Lawrence: University Press of Kansas, 2007.

Jones, Charles C. *The Life and Services of Commodore Josiah Tattnall*. Savannah, GA: Morning News Steam Printing, 1878.

Kendall, George W. *The War Between the United States and Mexico*. New York: D. Appleton and Company, 1851.

Kenly, John R. *Memoirs of a Maryland Volunteer*. Philadelphia: J.B. Lippincott and Company, 1873.

Knightley, Phillip. *The First Casualty: From the Crimea to Vietnam*. London: Pan Books, 1990.

Law, Robert A., ed. "A Letter from Vera Cruz in 1847." *Southwestern Historical Quarterly* v. 18 (October, 1914) 215–18.

Linder, Jamie S. and Eigelsbach, William B., eds. "To War with Mexico: A Diary of the Mexican-American War." *Journal of East Tennessee History* v. 73 (2001) 74–100.

Livingston-Little, D.E., ed. *The Mexican War Diary of Thomas D. Tennery*. Norman: University of Oklahoma Press, 1970.

Lombard, Albert. *The "High Private," With a Full and Exciting History of the New York Volunteers*. New York: 1848.

Long, A.L. ed. *Memoirs of Robert E. Lee, His Military and Personal History*. Secaucus, NJ: Blue and Grey Press, 1983.

McCaffrey, James M., ed. *Surrounded by Dangers of All Kinds: The Mexican War Letters of Lieutenant Theodore Laidley*. Denton: University of North Texas Press, 1997.

McSherry, Richard. *El Puchero: or, A Mixed Dish from Mexico*. Philadelphia: Lippincott, Grambo and Company, 1850.

——— "A Mexican Campaign Sketch" in *Essays and Lectures*. Baltimore, MD: Kelly, Piet and Company, 1869.

McWhiney, Grady and McWhiney, Sue. *To Mexico with Taylor and Scott, 1845–1847*. Waltham, MA: Blaisdell Publishing Company, 1969.

Maury, Dabney H. *Recollections of a Virginian in the Mexican, Indian, and Civil Wars*. New York: Charles Scribner's Sons, 1894.

May, George S., ed. "An Iowan in the Mexican War." *Iowa Journal of History* 53, no. 2 (April, 1955): 167–74.

May, Robert E. *John A. Quitman: Old South Crusader*. Baton Rouge: Louisiana State University Press, 1985.

"Memories of Mexico." *Harper's New Monthly Magazine* 3, no. 16 (September, 1851): 461–66.

Meyer, Jack A. *South Carolina in the Mexican War: A History of the Palmetto Regiment of Volunteers, 1846–1917*. Columbia: South Carolina Department of Archives and History, 1996.

Miller, Robert R., ed. *The Mexican War Journal of Ralph W. Kirkham.* College Station: Texas A & M University Press, 1991.

——— *Shamrock and Sword: The Saint Patrick's Battalion in the U.S.-Mexican War*. Norman: University of Oklahoma Press, 1989.

Moore, H. Judge. *Scott's Campaign from the Rendezvous on the Island of Lobos to the Taking of the City*. Charleston, SC: J.B. Nixon, 1849.

Moore, John H., ed. "Private Johnson Fights the Mexicans." *South Carolina Historical Magazine* 67, no. 4 (October, 1966) 203–28.

Moseley, Edward H. and Clark, Paul Coe. Historical Dictionary of the United States-Mexican War. Lanham, MD: Scarecrow Press, 1997.

Myers, William S., ed. *Mexican War Diary of General George B. McClellan*. New York: DaCapo Press, 1972.

Ohrt, Wallace. *Defiant Peacemaker: Nicholas Trist in the Mexican War*. College Station: Texas A & M University Press, 1997.

Oswandel, J. Jacob. *Notes of the Mexican War, 1846–47–48*. Philadelphia: J. Jacob Oswandel, 1885.

Peskin, Allan, ed. Volunteers: *The Mexican War Journals of Private Richard Coulter and Sergeant Thomas Barclay, Company E,*

Second Pennsylvania Infantry. Kent, OH: Kent State University Press, 1991.

Pohl, James W. "The Influence of Antoine Henri de Jomini on Winfield Scott's Campaign in the Mexican War." *Southwestern Historical Quarterly* 77 (July, 1973): 85–110.

Ramirez, José F. *Mexico During the War with the United States*. Columbia: University of Missouri Press, 1950.

Reilly, Tom. *War With Mexico!: America's Reporters Cover the Battlefront*. Lawrence: University Press of Kansas, 2010.

Reilly, Tom. "The War Press of New Orleans: 1846–1848." *Journalism History* 13 (Autumn, 1986): 86–95.

Report of the New Hampshire Adjutant General for 1868. Concord, NH: George E. Jenks, 1868.

Roberts, William H. *Mexican War Veterans: A Complete Roster*. Washington, DC: A.S. Witherbee and Company, 1887.

Robertson, J. B. *Reminiscences of a Campaign in Mexico; By a Member of "The Bloody First."* Nashville, TN: John York and Company, 1849.

Robinson, Cecil, ed. *The View from Chapultepec: Mexican Writers on The Mexican-American War.* Tucson: University of Arizona Press, 1989.

Scott, Winfield. *Memoirs of Lieut.-General Scott*. New York: Sheldon and Company, 1864. 2 vols.

"Scott's Battles in Mexico." *Harper's New Monthly Magazine* 11, no. 63 (August, 1855): 311–24.

Sedgwick, Henry D. *Correspondence of John Sedgwick, Major-General*. New York: De Vinne Press, 1902. 2 vols.

Semmes Raphael. *The Campaign of General Scott in the Valley of Mexico*. Cincinnati, OH: Moore and Anderson, 1852.

——— *Service Afloat and Ashore During the Mexican War*. Cincinnati, OH: William H. Moore and Company, 1851.

Sioussat, St. George L. "Mexican War Letters of Col. William Bowen Campbell of Tennessee." *Tennessee Historical Magazine* 1, no. 2 (June, 1915): 129–67.

Smith, George W. and Judah, Charles, eds. *Chronicles of the Gringos, The U.S. Army in the Mexican War, 1846–1848, Accounts of Eyewitnesses and Combatants*. Albuquerque: University of New Mexico Press, 1968.

Smith, Justin H. *The War with Mexico*. New York: Macmillan, 1919. 2 vols.

Sonnichsen, C.L. "Kendall of the Picayune." *Southwest Review* 29, no. 1 (Autumn, 1943): 101–103.

Stevens, Hazard. *The Life of Isaac Ingalls Stevens*. New York: Houghton Mifflin, 1900. 2 vols.

Stevens, Isaac I. *Campaigns of the Rio Grande and of Mexico*. New York: D. Appleton, 1851.

Stevens, Peter F. *The Rogue's March: John Riley and the St. Patrick's Battalion, 1846–48*. Washington, DC: Brassey's, 1999.

Stewart, George R. *John Phoenix, Esq., the Venerable Squibob: A Life of Captain George H. Derby, USA*. New York: Henry Holt, 1937.

Sweeny, Thomas W. "Narrative of Army Service in the Mexican War and on the Plains., 1846–1853." *Journal of the Military Service Institution of the United States* 42 (January, 1908): 127–37.

Traas, Adrian G. *From the Golden Gate to Mexico City: The U.S. Army Topographical Engineers in the Mexican Wear, 1846–1848*. Washington, DC: United States Army, 1993.

Tucker, Spencer C., ed. *The Encyclopedia of the Mexican-American War*. Santa Barbara, CA: ABC-CLIO, 2012. 3 vols.

Wallace, Edward S. *General William Jenkins Worth, Monterey's Forgotten Hero*. Dallas, TX: Southern Methodist University Press, 1953.

——— "The United States Army in Mexico City." *Military Affairs* 13 (Fall, 1949): 158–66.

Warren, Kenneth F. *Encyclopedia of U.S. Campaigns, Elections, and Electoral Behavior*. Thousand Oaks, CA: Sage Publications, 2008. 2 vols.

Waugh, John C. *The Class of 1846*. New York: Warner Books, 1994.

Whiteside, Henry O. "Winfield Scott and the Mexican Occupation: Policy and Practice." *Mid-America* 52 (April, 1970): 102–18.

Wilcox, Cadmus M. *History of the Mexican War*. Washington, DC: Church News Publishing Company, 1892.

Williams, T. Harry, ed. *With Beauregard in Mexico: The Mexican War Reminiscences of P.G.T. Beauregard*. New York: DaCapo Press, 1969.

Williams, Thomas J.C.*A History of Washington County, Maryland*. Hagerstown, MD: J.M. Runk and L.R. Titsworth, 1906, 2 vols.

Winders, Richard Bruce. *Mr. Polk's Army: The American Military Experience in the Mexican War*. College Station: Texas A & M University Press, 2001.

Zeh, Frederick. *An Immigrant Soldier in the Mexican War*. College Station, TX: Texas A & M University Press, 1995.

Newspapers

Atlanta Constitution

Augusta [GA] Chronicle

Baltimore American and Commercial Advertiser

Baltimore Sun

Boston American Traveller
Boston Daily Advertiser
Boston Daily Atlas
Boston Evening Transcript
Boston Herald
Brooklyn Daily Eagle
Buffalo Commercial
California Gazette [Benicia, CA]
Chambersburg [PA] Valley Spirit
Charleston [SC] Courier
Chicago Tribune
Columbian Register [New Haven, CT]
Daily Alta California [San Francisco, CA]
Daily Nashville Patriot
Daily National Intelligencer [Washington, DC]
Daily Placer Times and Transcript [San Francisco, CA]
El Paso Herald Post
Fayetteville [NC] Weekly Observer
Frederick Town Herald [Frederick, MD]
Galveston Weekly News
Hagerstown [MD] Torch Light
Harrisburg [PA] Keystone
Huntsville [AL] Gazette
Lebanon [PA] Daily News
Lexington Leader
Louisville Courier-Journal
Louisville Daily Courier
Mariposa [CA] Gazette
Milwaukee Sentinel
Montgomery Advertiser
Nashville Tennesseean
New Orleans Crescent
New Orleans Daily Delta
New Orleans Times-Picayune
New Orleans Weekly Delta
New York Commercial Advertiser
New York Evening Post
New York Herald
New York Tribune
Newport [RI] Mercury
Niles' National Register [Baltimore, MD]
Philadelphia Inquirer

Philadelphia Public Ledger
Philadelphia Times
Pittsburgh Daily Post
Pittsburgh Gazette
Placer Herald [Auburn, CA]
Planters' Banner [Franklin, LA]
Portland [ME] Weekly Advertiser
Richmond Enquirer
Sacramento Daily Union
Sacramento Steamer Union
Sacramento Transcript
San Francisco Bulletin
St. Louis Republic
The State [Columbia, SC]
Staunton [VA] Spectator
Washington Daily Union
Washington Evening Post
Washington Evening Star
Washington Madisonian
Washington National Whig
Weekly Alta California [San Francisco, CA]
Weekly Mississippian [Jackson, MS]
Weekly National Intelligencer [Washington, DC]
Weekly Oregonian [Portland, OR]
Worcester [MA] Spy

Index

H

T

V